W9-AQS-586

ACCLAIM FOR

WHEN THEY COME FOR US, WE'LL BE GONE

"Superb and likely definitive." — *New Republic*

"Remarkable . . . The author is gifted at weaving this very human and very political tale together." — *Cleveland Plain Dealer*

"The book reads like a thriller, with subplots unfolding on the gritty streets of New York, inside dank Moscow apartments and ominous Soviet Star Chambers, and outside abandoned Russian synagogues, where almost magically thousands of Jews might spontaneously dance the hora — with lurking KGB agents on their tail." — *Los Angeles Times*

"Impressive history." — David Bezmozgis, *Harper's*

"Gripping...thoroughly researched...A brief review can scarcely compass the breadth and richness of Beckerman's narrative or do justice to the unimaginable physical and moral courage and the resourcefulness of the dissidents and refuseniks."
— *Jewish Review of Books*

"Riveting and important . . . Now that [Beckerman] has told the story so well, however, it will surely take its rightful place as one of the greatest dramas in modern Jewish history. . . . an impressive work of reporting."— **Adam Kirsch,** *Tablet*

"Enthralling . . . A must read." — *Russian Life*

"Beckerman's book shines a long-needed spotlight on one of the great human rights struggles of the past century. It is dramatic, revelatory, and deeply inspiring."
— **Ron Rosenbaum, author of** *Explaining Hitler*
  and *The Shakespeare Wars*

"A moving, reliable, and memorable narrative of one of the greatest human rights dramas of our time."
— **Jonathan D. Sarna, Professor of American Jewish History,**
  Brandeis University, and author of *American Judaism: A History*

"Beckerman has written the *Parting the Waters* of the Jewish experience. Some authors spend an entire career trying to write their masterpiece. Gal Beckerman, to breathtaking effect, has done so in his very first book."
— **Samuel G. Freedman, author of** *Jew vs. Jew*

"Colorfully fleshes out personal stories within the headlines . . . A comprehensive, contextually rich study." — *Kirkus Reviews*

"Absorbing and inspiring . . . An outstanding chronicle of a great effort conducted by determined and courageous men and women." — *Booklist*, **starred review**

"Gal Beckerman has written the definitive account of what might be the most successful human rights campaign of our time. This is a wonderful book: The narrative is thrilling and propulsive; the writing is beautiful; and the research absolutely authoritative. The movement to free Soviet Jewry will be studied for years to come as a model of non-violent civil disobedience, and Gal Beckerman's book will be read years from now as the masterwork on the subject."
— **Jeffrey Goldberg**, **National Correspondent**, *The Atlantic,*
    and author of *Prisoners: A Story of Friendship and Terror*

"Masterful and highly readable history."
— *The Forward*

WHEN THEY COME FOR US, WE'LL BE GONE

THE EPIC STRUGGLE TO SAVE SOVIET JEWRY

GAL BECKERMAN

MARINER BOOKS
HOUGHTON MIFFLIN HARCOURT
BOSTON   NEW YORK

First Mariner Books edition 2011

Library of Congress Cataloging-in-Publication Data
Beckerman, Gal.
When they come for us we'll be gone : the epic struggle to save Soviet Jewry /
Gal Beckerman.
p. cm.
Includes bibliographical references and index.
ISBN 978-0-618-57309-7
ISBN 978-0-547-57747-0 (pbk.)
1. Jews—Soviet Union—History—20th century. 2. Jews—Soviet Union—
Social conditions—20th century. 3. Jews—Soviet Union—Persecutions—History—
20th century. 4. Jews—Soviet Union—Politics and government—20th century.
5. Refuseniks. 6. Soviet Union—Emigration and immigration—Government
policy. 7. Soviet Union—Ethnic relations. I. Title.
DS134.85.B43 2010
305.892'404709045—dc22   2010005735

Book design by Brian Moore

Printed in the United States of America

DOC 1 2 3 4 5 6 7 8 9 10

The author is grateful for permission to quote from the following:
    Anna Akhmatova, excerpt from "Epilogue II" from "Requiem," in *Complete Poems of Anna Akhmatova*, translated by Judith Hemschemeyer. Reprinted with the permission of Zephyr Press, www.zephyrpress.org.
    "There's a Fire Burning," from *Songs of Hope for Russian Jews*, music by Moshe Denberg, words by George Weisz. Reprinted by permission of the Archives of Jacob Birnbaum.
    Excerpt from "I'm not asking death for immortality . . ." by Joseph Brodsky, from *An Anthology of Jewish-Russian Literature: Two Centuries of Jewish Identity in Prose and Poetry, 1801–2001*, edited by Maxim D. Shrayer, vol. 2 (Armonk, NY, and London: M. E. Sharpe, 2007), p. 672. Translated from the Russian by Joanna Trzeciak. Translation copyright © by Joanna Trzeciak. Reproduced by permission of the translator, publisher, and editor.
    "Leaving Mother Russia," words and music by Robbie Solomon, © 1978.
    Excerpts from *The Jews of Silence* by Elie Wiesel. Copyright © 1973, 1987 by Elie Wiesel. Reprinted by permission of Georges Borchardt, Inc., on behalf of the author.
    "Babii Yar," translated by George Reavey, copyright © 1960, 1967 by George Reavey, "Bombs for Balalaikas," translated by Stanley Kunitz with Albert Todd, copyright © 1962, 1963, 1965, 1967, 1972 by E. P. Dutton, from *Yevtushenko's Reader* by Yevgeny Yevtushenko, Used by permission of Dutton, a division of Penguin Group (USA) Inc.

FOR MY PARENTS,
Ami and Batia

Contents

And if ever in this country
They decide to erect a monument to me,

I consent to that honor
Under these conditions—that it stand

Neither by the sea, where I was born:
My last tie with the sea is broken,

Nor in the tsar's garden, near the cherished pine stump,
Where an inconsolable shade looks for me.

But here, where I stood for three hundred hours,
And where they never unbolted the doors for me.

ANNA AKHMATOVA, "Requiem"

If we blow into the narrow end of the shofar, we will be heard
far. But if we choose to be Mankind rather than Jewish and
blow into the wider part, we will not be heard at all; for us
America will have been in vain.

CYNTHIA OZICK, *Art and Ardor*

Prologue

LIKE MOST AMERICAN Jews of my generation, I had a twin in the Soviet Union. Maxim Yankelevich. I doubt I'll ever forget that name. I repeated it incessantly in the nervous weeks leading up to my bar mitzvah. Some organization of which I was barely aware had handed down Maxim's information, and my job was to invoke him and what I was told was his "plight" after I read from the Torah—a rite of passage that filled me with such dread I wasn't sure I'd remember my own name, let alone this other boy's. So I compulsively chanted to myself "Maxim Yankelevich." It calmed me down.

The only real information I had about Maxim was on a sheet of mimeographed paper that the rabbi had given me. Maxim's father, Zelman, was a construction engineer. His mother, Elena, was a cosmetician. The family had first applied for permission to leave the Soviet Union in 1980, when Maxim was five. Now it was 1989 and they were still living in Leningrad. His bar mitzvah was supposed to have taken place the year before but hadn't, or couldn't, for reasons unexplained (my imagination, populated by KGB agents in khaki trench coats shooting bullets from their shoes, filled in many of the particulars). By mentioning him, I was told, I was symbolically allowing him to share my bar mitzvah. What I fixated on most was the small photo of

Maxim's father. It was a grainy black-and-white, but one could see the silhouetted outline of a man wearing a cap, scarf, and thick-framed glasses. He looked like a father from another century, a shtetl father, and I pictured him, the construction engineer, carefully laying bricks day after day. Besides the photo there were only a few lines of text and just one sentence to give me a sense of the plight that necessitated my intervention. Maxim had grown up, I was informed, in "an atmosphere of tension and uncertainty."

My rabbi was a sensitive and thoughtful man but he must have matched young boys and girls with thousands of these Soviet twins by the late 1980s and he didn't take the time to explain further. In the days leading up to my Torah reading, while I tried on my new gray suit and red clip-on tie a dozen times in front of the mirror, Maxim Yankelevich took up residence in my overactive brain. I imagined what he looked like: taller than me, blond, without braces, carrying his schoolbooks with an old-fashioned book strap. The fact of his existence though, somewhere far off to the east, thoroughly confused me. These were the last years of the Cold War. I was aware of the "evil empire," if only through the detritus of pop culture, which seemed obsessed with the Soviet-American relationship. For some reason, I was fascinated by the truly awful 1985 film *White Nights*. It starred Mikhail Baryshnikov as a Russian ballet dancer who had defected from the Soviet Union but found himself—through the deus ex machina of a plane crash—trapped once again in the country he had fled. In one scene, the Baryshnikov character lustily dances to the music of the banned raspy-voiced folksinger Vladimir Vysotsky on the stage of the empty Mariinsky Theater while his old girlfriend watches and weeps, knowing that if he had stayed in the Soviet Union he would never have been permitted to express himself with such abandon. Some variety of repression was hidden there behind the constantly invoked iron curtain. Of that, I couldn't help being at least somewhat aware. But still, when I read about Maxim, the notion that he or any other Jew lived in "an atmosphere of tension and uncertainty" was hard to fathom.

On the face of it, the concept shouldn't have been shocking to a grandchild of Holocaust survivors and a son of Israelis. I had grown up with the stories of my maternal grandmother, who had lived hidden in a hole under the Polish earth for a year; with the stories of my paternal grandparents, who had survived the uprising in the Warsaw

Ghetto only to eventually find themselves sleeping next to gas chambers in the death camp Majdanek, where they lost their entire families. Then there was my other grandfather—who, we always joked, had had it easy—who'd spent three years in a Siberian work camp. The fact of Jewish suffering was not a foreign concept to me. Throw in my parents' anxieties for Israel, its very existence constantly threatened, and "tension and uncertainty" should have been well embedded in my psychology by the time I encountered Maxim.

The problem, I think, was that through my eyes then, the history of the world was split into a neat and distinct before and after. As I saw it at thirteen, the horrors of the war had been the terrible price paid for this new era in which Jews had not only physical safety but also a peace of mind that they had never experienced over the two thousand years of Diaspora—Israel, despite my parents' worries, didn't seem to me like it was going anywhere. The little that I knew about Maxim and other Soviet Jews escaped these mental categories of before and after. The fear of death was not hanging over him like it had for my grandparents—that much I knew—but at the same time, he was clearly trapped, denied something as basic and schmaltzy as a bar mitzvah. All I could do was file him away as a historical anomaly, a bit of unfinished postwar Jewish business that I didn't really understand.

My bar mitzvah was on September 1, 1989. I stood in front of the congregation and gave a short speech, trying desperately not to shake. I reminded everyone that it was the fiftieth anniversary of the Nazi invasion of Poland, a significant historical marker for me, the day my grandparents' journey through hell began. But here I was, I said with a flourish, decades after the camps were liberated, having my bar mitzvah in America, a country where I was free to be a Jew.

I did mention Maxim's name. But I didn't give much more thought to the gray space his story occupied. The paradox at the center of the Soviet Jewish experience—a people not allowed to fully assimilate but also not allowed to develop a separate national identity or to leave—was too confounding.

Two months after Maxim and I had our bar mitzvah, the course of history seemed to change in a day. The Berlin Wall fell. Over the next decade, as the Soviet Union crumbled, more than a million Jews fled, joining the approximately three hundred thousand that had trickled out since the end of the 1960s. I don't know if Maxim Yankelevich was among them. I forgot about him for a long time. Only years later, visiting Israel, did I scan the faces of new immigrants and wonder if he had gotten out. It was impossible not to think about Soviet Jews then. They had fundamentally altered Israeli society, from the now ubiquitous line of Russian subtitles on Israeli television to the electoral power the new immigrants wielded as a major conservative voting bloc, not to mention the influx of doctors, physicists, engineers, and musicians. (Israelis joked that if a Soviet Jew didn't get off the airplane with a violin case, he was probably a pianist.) In America too, where hundreds of thousands had arrived and settled, predominantly in New York, their presence was felt, changing the face of large swathes of Brooklyn. The children of these immigrants have already made an impressive impact on American society, becoming influential novelists, entrepreneurs, and computer engineers.

By the time I really started to consider Maxim's story on its own terms, the conversation about Soviet Jews had changed. It was no longer about their plight but about their experiences as a new immigrant group and the various challenges—especially in Israel—of absorption. Maybe because Jews had finally been allowed to emigrate out of the Soviet Union, the fact that they had been denied this right for so long seemed to vanish into historical memory; the mass migration came to be seen simply as a byproduct of the Cold War's end, one of the many walls that fell. That it was the result of a long struggle was somehow forgotten. If people stopped to think of it at all, it was only to invoke the name of Natan Sharansky (once Anatoly Shcharansky), the well-known dissident who sat for nine years in a prison camp and later established a successful second life as a politician in Israel after his release.

Meanwhile, my own interest had shifted. I'd always been obsessed with my grandparents' stories of survival, but by the time I reached adulthood what I understood most about the Holocaust was its fundamental inaccessibility. The admonition to "never forget" was inhibiting enough, but the war's overrepresentation in pop culture had also reduced it to a set of clichéd words and images that overwhelmed my ability to see it clearly. I recorded my grandparents' stories, took in the cascade of Holocaust books and movies, but I also came to accept that this was a door that would always remained closed, even if I stood in front of it forever with my mouth open. Maybe as a reaction, I became absorbed by a much more amorphous period. I wanted to know about the world after. I looked at the quiet drama of my grandparents' lives and realized that there was an unexplored and rich story here. They were simple people who had lost their families, suffered years of physical and psychological torture, and had still managed to have children, love, work hard, think beyond survival. What about the Jewish world as a whole? How to explain what happened to the two largest Jewish communities of the Diaspora, in the United States and in the Soviet Union, in the decades since the war? These millions of Jews couldn't all simply immerse themselves in the building of a Jewish state. How did they cope with their psychic and physical scars?

These were two communities that, each in its own way, were left shattered after the Holocaust. For the nearly three million Jews living in the Soviet Union, the trauma of the war was compounded by a regime that wanted no trace of Jewish communal life, extinguishing even that which was permitted by the Bolsheviks. Stalin, fired up by his own paranoia and fueled by a long-standing popular anti-Semitism, crushed these last remnants. They were discouraged in every way from being Jews—synagogues were shuttered, and Yiddish writers and actors were executed—and trapped in a country that allowed no legal emigration, which might have provided an escape route to Israel. It was obvious to most observers that within a generation or two, the total assimilation, or spiritual genocide, of Soviet Jewry would be complete.

American Jews, the most populous and prosperous Jewish Diaspora community, had easily integrated into American society by the 1950s. The struggle they faced in the decades after the war was more psychological. There was a sense that their efforts to prevent the Holocaust had been insufficient. This stain spread, soaking in and giving a self-conscious character to American Jewish life. It also spoke to a deeper anxiety about assimilation, a weakness that manifested itself in the community's inability to stand up for its own interests. Even as these Jews climbed to the heights of American society they were dogged by a feeling that the literal abandonment of their brethren was a symptom of the figurative abandonment of their own identity.

What happened between then and now? When you look around today, Russian Jewish immigrants are free to live wherever they want, in Jerusalem or Berlin. And though they are facing all the challenges that come with deracination, forced to work out for themselves what it means to be Jewish, they are free to engage in this dialectic, to become Hasidic if they choose or merely read an Isaac Bashevis Singer story. The spiritual genocide never occurred. And American Jews, once afraid it would appear like special pleading if they asked a politician to address a Jewish issue, now wield enormous political power in America. They have formed a lobby whose effectiveness has become the envy of every American minority group.

How then to explain these transformations that took place in the darkness of the war's long shadow? The magnetic force of Israel's existence certainly played a central role. But there had to be more. And here is where I remembered the strange plight of my long-forgotten bar mitzvah twin, Maxim. It occurred to me, before I even knew the complete story, that it was through the effort to save Soviet Jews that these two communities had arrived at the redemption they each sought, physical for one and psychological for the other. What looks to us now like an inevitability—the mass emigration of hundreds of thousands—was actually the culmination of a hard-fought battle; a massive effort to rescue Soviet Jewry from extinction and also a home-grown social movement that shaped the American Jewish community we know today. It's a history that has, strangely, been ignored. Only twenty years have passed since the end of the Cold War, but already the world—even the Jewish community—is losing the memory of this movement. In some ways, it is a victim of its own success. From where we sit today, we can easily forget that for nearly three decades—beginning amid the social and political tumult of the 1960s and culminating with the end of the Cold War—there was a day-to-day struggle whose outcome was not clear to the men and women who made it the center of their lives. And yet, looking back at the twentieth century, we can't understand the eventful postwar Jewish story without examining this struggle in all its human detail, without appreciating how a small number of willful individuals on both sides of the iron curtain took on the superpowers.

This is the story I decided to tell. After years of research and untold hours spent conducting interviews in living rooms from Tel Aviv to Moscow, poring over primary sources in archives, and reading the many memoirs of the combatants, I realized the movement was even more historically significant—and dramatic—than I'd thought at the beginning.

The history of the movement contains two narratives that eventually fuse into one. While Soviet Jews were pushing for unobstructed emigration from inside the Soviet Union, American Jews were pushing for it from the outside. Grassroots efforts developed in other countries, such as England and France, but because of their numbers and the peculiar politics of the Cold War, American Jews were as fundamental to the movement as the Soviet Jews themselves.

Advocating for Soviet Jewry taught American Jews how to lobby. Israel is widely believed to have been the great galvanizing cause for this community, a perception fueled by the fact that Jewish influence would eventually be used to sway policy in the Middle East. But it was the effort to get the American government to pressure the Soviets—when it least wanted to—that first taught American Jews how to flex their political muscle. All the tools in use today, from targeting local congresspeople to asserting influence on the Hill, were first tested on this question. After the Six-Day War and the occupation that followed, Israel became as divisive a factor in American Jewish life as it was a uniting one. But the plight of Soviet Jewry, as soon as it penetrated the consciousness of American Jews, brought together people on both left and right, all impassioned for their own reasons—some were anti-Communist, others saw it as a human rights issue. The cause built slowly and was not without bitter conflict over tactics and directions. But as a result, American Jews discovered the strident voice they had never been comfortable using.

Soviet Jews, during the course of this story, transformed themselves from a community that was disconnected from its roots to a reawakened part of the tribe, some of them taking enormous risks to live as Jews again. Just as on the American side—and as is true of most social movements—the number of people on the frontline was small. Only a few thousand Soviet Jews pushed so hard to emigrate that they risked the consequences of prison and exile. Only a handful of activists were in the core inspiring other Jews to emigrate and helping them when their requests were rejected. But this small group had an outsize influence. And they embodied the feelings of many more Soviet Jews, a silent majority that knew there was something untenable about their life in the Soviet Union, from the quotas of Jews allowed at universities to the almost primordial hatred that came from ethnic Russians and Ukrainians. The refuseniks, as those who applied to emigrate and were refused became known, battled hard against implacable forces and created for themselves an alternative underground society as they waited in limbo. And in resisting, they not only dented the iron curtain, they returned a Jewish face to a community that had been feared lost.

But the movement did more than alter these two Jewish communities. Soviet Jewry became a flashpoint in the Cold War. It went from being an issue that John F. Kennedy ignored to one that Ronald Reagan put on par with arms control. The stories of individual Jews waiting as long as fifteen years to emigrate, often separated from their families, deprived of work, and frequently harassed by the KGB, offered one of the best ideological weapons against Communism. Many factors led to the end of the Cold War, and historians still argue about the relative weight each should carry. By the 1980s, the Soviet Union had serious economic problems, from food shortages to a rapidly declining standard of living, as it struggled with both a quagmire in Afghanistan and an escalating arms race that was bankrupting the empire. Rather than saving socialism, Mikhail Gorbachev's attempt at reform through glasnost and perestroika only sped up the total collapse of the Soviet experiment. But historians neglect another important element: the constant internal pressure the Soviet Union faced from its own dissidents, particularly those Soviet Jews demanding the right to emigrate. They presented a fundamental challenge to a regime that prided itself on having created the perfect society. Soviet leaders worried that even a modest Jewish emigration would be the first crack in the foundation. As the longtime Soviet ambassador Anatoly Dobrynin confessed in his memoirs, "In the closed society of the Soviet Union, the Kremlin was afraid of emigration in general (irrespective of nationality or religion) lest an escape hatch from the happy land of socialism seem to offer a degree of liberalization that might destabilize the domestic situation."

The refuseniks and the activists in the West—often together with those dissidents who demanded democratization—kept the Soviet Union on the moral defensive in the eyes of the world. As a result, human rights moved to the center of international diplomacy, achieving a status that we now take for granted. In the 1970s, for the first time, a country's treatment of its own citizens dictated the United States' trade policy. Human rights have since become a pivotal guide of our relations with other countries, from China to Zimbabwe. But this was not the case before the movement to save Soviet Jewry. The adoption of the Universal Declaration of Human Rights by the United Nations in 1948 was an important milestone, but it took another thirty years for these ethical principles to move out of the realm of rhetoric and become powerful tools. The banner of Soviet Jewry was always pulled taut between two poles. On one end was the tribal instinct of Jews wanting to save imperiled Jews. But there were also these universal principles. From the movement's inception, the biblical injunction to "let my people go" went alongside Article 13 of the Declaration of Human Rights, which states that everyone has the right to leave any country, including his own. This was not, moreover, an inconsequential right. A UN report as early as 1963 identified it as a sort of gateway right, pointing out that a country's allowing its citizens to emigrate is "an indispensable condition for the full enjoyment by all of civil, political, economic, social and cultural rights." The freedom to vote with one's feet is the first step to an open society. By framing their struggle to help Soviet Jews as a moral issue, activists working on both sides of the iron curtain helped spark the human rights revolution and began a dialogue that continues today over how to judge the behavior of the world's countries.

All these triumphs and ramifications are, of course, a matter of hindsight. In this book, the history unfolds just as it progressed in reality, its ending as unknown as it was to the activists committed to the cause and to the Soviet Jews who waited years for exit visas, sure they would never see Israel. I wanted to capture the many internal struggles, the conflicts of personalities, the moments of both lurching progress and sudden hope. This is a narrative that demanded to be told from the perspective of the individuals who formed the movement. Like the other great twentieth-century social struggles, from the fight against apartheid to the push for civil rights in America, it is essentially a story about ordinary people who simply couldn't accept an immoral status quo. Not only does their struggle fill in a missing piece of Cold War and Jewish history, it shows how the risks they took helped shape the contours of our world today.

PART I

AFTER THE THAW
1963–1970

Let time be silent about me.
Let the sharp wind weep easily,
And over my Jewish grave,
Let young life shout persistently.

JOSEPH BRODSKY,
"I'm not asking death for immortality . . ."

AFTER THE THAW
1969–1972

Beneath the Earth
1963–1966

YOSEF MENDELEVICH WAS sixteen when he saw the killing grounds for the first time. It was the fall of 1963. He had heard about the place: just outside of Riga, in the vast woods of tall fir trees and sprawling brush that the locals called Rumbuli. All one had to do was follow the train tracks east, toward Moscow. There, underneath the black soil, in five narrow ditches, lay twenty-five thousand bodies, Jewish bodies, killed by the Nazis and their Latvian collaborators in ten days at the end of 1941. Mendelevich knew this. All the Jews of Riga did. And they knew too about the small group of Jews—Zionists, they were calling themselves—who had searched the year before under the dark shadow of those trees for the exact place of the massacre. In the end, it hadn't been so hard to find. Poking out of the earth were fragments of charred bone, the shriveled brown leather of a child's shoe, a broken Star of David on a necklace.

Mendelevich was a shy, withdrawn boy with pale, pimply skin and thick, horn-rimmed glasses. Most days when he wasn't in school he was alone inside his parents' house in a poor section of Riga. The outside world entered mainly through its brutal noises—the shouts of his Latvian neighbors stumbling home full of vodka; glass breaking; drunken fathers beating their children. Like any sensitive teenage introvert, he found his home, his only comfort, in his imaginings. In Yosef's case, the world he escaped to in his mind was a real place, though a rather fantastical destination for a young Soviet boy. It was a country so far away, so obscured and unknown, it might as well have existed under a different sun. That place was Israel. And he constructed his idea of it with what he had at hand. His aunt Fanya, one of the rare Soviet citizens allowed to immigrate in the late fifties, had once sent a color postcard of a swimming pool at Kfar Giladi, a kibbutz in the northern Galilee. Mendelevich took a magnifying glass to it, counting all the people, scrutinizing the shape and shade of every tree. The sight of so many Jews gathered together wearing swimming trunks seemed unreal. Fanya had also written his family a letter in which she recounted the history of the one-armed Joseph Trumpeldor and his last stand at Tel Chai, not far from Kfar Giladi, where he was killed in 1920 while defending the settlement from local Arabs. He became a legend for his famous dying words: "Never mind, it is good to die for our country." At night, Mendelevich's father would tune their shortwave radio to Kol Israel, the Voice of Israel, and hold the receiver close to his ear, translating the news from Hebrew to Russian. Before the war, his father had studied in a *cheder*, a Jewish religious school, and so he understood the language. But to Mendelevich the sounds were unfamiliar, a mystical, warm tongue from a better place, one he knew little about but felt, even as a teenager, that he was destined to go to.

Mendelevich didn't exactly trust the person who'd first told him about Rumbuli, a boy who sat next to him at the college he attended at night and who seemed to be a bit of a daydreamer. Still, if what the boy whispered to him was true, that young people were gathering on Sundays to clean up Rumbuli and make it a proper memorial ground, then Yosef wanted to go. So the next weekend, he set out with a friend.

What he found there, at the place he began referring to as Little Israel, startled him. Jews, most of them young but some in their sixties, were on their knees, digging their hands into the earth, lifting it up and dumping it clump by clump into homemade crates. Others were filling in the spaces with sand from two enormous mounds. Dozens of people with shovels and pails, rakes, and baskets, working. Some of the men had their shirts off.

In the middle of it all, static amid the activity, stood a huge wooden obelisk, taller than a man, painted pitch-black with a splattering of red at its top. On the obelisk's face, framed and behind glass, hung what looked like a large photograph of an oil painting. In somber browns and grays, it depicted a long line of tearful women, babies clinging to their breasts, followed by ashen-faced, downtrodden men, all marching under a threatening sky—Jews being led to the slaughter.

The scene actually before him was altogether different. The only time Mendelevich had ever witnessed so many Jews in one place was when he'd gone with his father to the synagogue on Peitaves Street in the old town. But those were old men. Here were young people, young Jews, sweating together under the sun. One man in particular caught his eye. He was tanned, strong, straight backed, just what Mendelevich thought an Israeli would look like. In the shock of the moment, he was willing to believe that such a miracle—an Israeli in Riga—might have occurred.

Mendelevich quickly grabbed a crate, got down on his knees, and began moving the earth with his bare hands.

He rarely missed a Sunday after that. He would spend the week looking forward to Little Israel and to the bus rides from Riga. The group of young people grew through 1963 and into 1964, and eventually they took up almost all the seats on the bus leaving the city. And they sang. Mendelevich learned Israeli songs, such as the rousing anthem of the Palmach, the scruffy, pre-state paramilitary force in British Mandate Palestine:

> All around us the storm rages
> But we will not lower our heads
> We are always ready to follow the orders
> We are the Palmach.
>
> From Metulla to the Negev
> From the sea to the desert
> Every fine young man to arms
> Every young man on guard.

Though he understood not a word of the Hebrew, for the first time in his life, Mendelevich felt like part of a group. And when he listened to himself singing along with the whole bus filled with Jewish youth, he also felt, strangely, like a fighter.

Passengers faced with a busload of young Jews singing vociferously in a foreign language would often get off. One day, the driver stopped Mendelevich as he was exiting the bus. "Where do you come from like this?" he asked with a mixture of shock and contempt. Mendelevich didn't answer. He knew that the driver was bewildered and perhaps a little threatened by the loud group. Jews did not generally comport themselves like this, unabashedly strident and unafraid. But on the way to Rumbuli, they did.

It was strange but not entirely unexpected that in the early 1960s the Jews of Riga felt compelled to claw at the earth in search of their recent past. Most people living in the Baltic States were afflicted with a deep nostalgia. Until the summer of 1940, when they lost their independence and were forcibly annexed by the Soviet Union, Estonia, Lithuania, and Latvia had spent over two decades as free, prosperous, and democratic countries. The devastation of the war and then the total subjugation by Moscow's overbearing regime made for a defeated and demoralized population. In the early 1960s, most middle-aged people had a strong memory of and longing for the world they had lost.

For Jews, this tear through history was even more brutal and dramatic. They had seen their entire universe erased, and what they'd lost was a diverse and rich Jewish life.

To judge from population and emigration numbers, the interwar years were good ones for Jews in Latvia. Riga's Jewish population nearly doubled between 1920 and 1935, going from twenty-four thousand to forty-four thousand. Even at the height of the Zionist movement's popularity, few of these Jews opted to go to Palestine—only seventy-five went in 1931. Latvia, which gained its independence and established a parliamentary democracy following World War I, accepted and even to some extent encouraged a Jewish presence. Jews served in the army and in government and formed a wide range of political parties—from religious to socialist Zionist—that were represented in the hundred-seat Saeima, Latvia's parliament. The Jewish bloc won six seats in the first election, in 1920. And among the socialist and communist opposition, it could be said that Jews predominated, many even volunteering to fight in Spain with the International Brigades against Franco.

As far back as 1840, Riga was home to a Jewish secondary school that taught secular studies. In the 1920s, cultural groups named after two of the great Yiddish writers of the day, Sholem Aleichem and I. L. Peretz, multiplied. The state even subsidized some Jewish activities, such as the Jewish Educational Society on Baznicas Street, which ran vocational schools for Jews who wanted to become craftsmen and workers in Latvia or Palestine. Its library was filled with books in dozens of languages, and the society held readings and discussion groups for the local intelligentsia. One such event, on March 30, 1935, was an elaborate ball and lecture to commemorate the eight hundredth birthday of Maimonides.

One of the speakers that evening was Simon Dubnow. With his pointy white goatee and round spectacles, Dubnow was Riga's most famous Jewish intellectual. By the time he moved to Riga, in 1933, escaping Berlin and Hitler, he was already well known for his ten-volume *Die Weltgeschichte des jüdischen Volkes* (World History of the Jewish People), published from 1925 to 1930, the most comprehensive such history ever written. He had settled in the northern Mezaparks district of the city in an apartment lined with his vast collection of books. His years in Riga were spent translating his magnum opus from German to Hebrew and Russian and condensing it into one volume, *History of the Jewish People for Work and Home,* intended primarily for children.

Riga had a society of Jewish physicians and a society of Jewish outergarment tailors; it had Jewish mutual aid groups and sports clubs. A Jewish hospital with internal medicine, neurology, and surgery departments was established in 1924. A professional Jewish theater opened in 1927. And on the radio throughout the 1930s, one could hear the songs of Oscar Strok, the Jewish "King of Tango," who became famous when Peter Leschenko crooned his romantic ballad "Chorne Glaza" (Black Eyes).

Yiddish was in the street; the first newspaper in the language, *Nationale Zeitung,* was published in 1907, and a rich array of others followed: *Yiddishe Stimme, Weg, Das Folk,* and *Frimorgn.* Riga had fourteen synagogues, including the Altneie Schul, built in 1780, and the imposing Gogola Street Synagogue, built in Renaissance style in 1871 and famous throughout Eastern Europe for the vibratos of its cantors.

But it was the number and diversity of Zionist youth groups that provided the strongest proof that Jews felt at home here—young people dressed in uniforms, marching, singing, learning Hebrew, prepar-

ing themselves to be farmers and soldiers in Palestine. Hashomer Ha-
tzair, the oldest and most popular group, was affiliated with the Labor
Zionist movement. Its goal was twofold: to encourage emigration to
Palestine and to defend the interests of the proletariat. At the move-
ment's peak, in 1927, its Riga branch had three thousand members.
At the other end of the political spectrum was a group whose influ-
ence began to eclipse Hashomer Hatzair's as World War II approached:
Betar. The name was both an acronym in Hebrew for the "League of
Joseph Trumpeldor," a tribute to the fallen Zionist hero, and an allu-
sion to the last suicidal battle of the Bar Kochba rebellion against the
Romans in 135 CE. In their brown shirts and shouting military songs,
the members of Betar represented a Zionism of blood and fire.

Betar had sprung from the mind of Vladimir Jabotinsky, a journalist, prolific essayist and translator (he even rendered Edgar Allan Poe's
"The Raven" in Russian and Hebrew) who provided Zionism with its
unaccommodating, proud, and sometimes violent right flank. Born
in Odessa, Jabotinsky, jug-eared and bespectacled in owlish round
glasses, lamented the loss of Judaism's ancient muscle. He was fiercely
opposed to the dominant Labor Zionism; he thought the group was
more concerned with the class struggle than it was with the tough job
of wrenching Palestine from the Arabs and the colonial forces who
controlled it. His political philosophy became known as revisionism,
as he was determined to "revise" what he saw as the Zionists' com-
placent relationship with the British occupiers. He preached Jewish
militarism, a cult of bravery and sacrifice. The world had never lifted
a finger for Jews, went Jabotinsky's teaching—which was passed down
to his followers and formed the basis of their ideology—so Jews had no
choice but to rely on themselves and their strength alone.

Jabotinsky did more than just write and lecture. He put his ideas
into action, organizing Jewish self-defense units throughout Russia
following the devastating pogroms of the 1900s and later establishing a
Jewish Legion to fight alongside the British in World War I. Betar was a
critical part of his vision. It was started in December 1923 by a group of
students in Riga who had heard Jabotinsky deliver a fiery call to arms,
a speech titled "Jews and Militarism." Branches of the group soon proliferated in cities all over Russia and Eastern Europe, and Jabotinsky
eventually claimed the movement as his own. In a 1932 essay, he de-

fined its goals: "[Betar], as we think of it, is a school based on three levels in which the youth will learn how to box, to use a stick, and other self-defense disciplines; the youth will learn the principles of military order; it will learn how to work; it will learn how to cultivate external beauty and ceremony; it will learn to scorn all forms of negligence, or as we call them, poverty or ghetto-life; they will learn to respect older people, women, prayer (even that of a foreigner), democracy—and many other things whose time has passed but are immortal."

Betar and its radical nationalism continued to play a role in Riga long after the world that had cultivated it disappeared. Many of those middle-aged Jews who gathered at Rumbuli in the 1960s had been Betari youth. Ezra Rusinek, the man Mendelevich mistook for an Israeli, had been a member. As a young boy, Rusinek marched in the brown shirt and neckerchief of Betar, saluting by slapping a clenched fist against his chest and belting out "Tel Chai," the name of the settlement Trumpeldor had died defending.

Anti-Semitism, of course, did exist in this prewar world, especially among the members of the local National Socialist Party. And the 1934 coup by the authoritarian Karlis Ulmanis made life more difficult for Jews. Leftist Zionist youth groups like Hashomer Hatzair were outlawed (Betar, whose mission the Fascists at least respected, was left untouched). Businesses were nationalized, which affected many Jewish entrepreneurs. But given the alternatives—Stalin to the east and Hitler to the west—Latvian Jews felt comfortable and settled. After all, it was to Riga that Simon Dubnow had fled when he left Germany in 1933.

Then came August 23, 1939. Molotov and Ribbentrop shook hands, sealing the nonaggression pact between Hitler and Stalin and placing the Baltic States in the Soviet "sphere of influence." By early October, the Soviets were mobilizing thirty thousand troops on Latvian ground. The following summer, Moscow had concocted a border incident that gave it an excuse to bring a hundred thousand troops into Latvia and call for new parliamentary elections from which all but the Working Peoples' Bloc were disqualified. The newly elected Latvian Soviet Socialist Republic then duly asked to be annexed by the USSR. As soon as it was, on August 5, 1940, the Kremlin outlawed all non-Communist groups, which meant the immediate end of Jewish organizational life.

But much worse was to come. By the following summer, Hitler's army occupied most of Latvia. Jews panicked at the German approach, having heard rumors of what was happening in Germany and Poland. Others had memories of being treated well by the Germans after World War I and hoped that the same would be true again. But even if they wanted to, many could not leave in time. Only a small number, about ten thousand, were able to flee farther east into the Soviet Union. The vast majority, about seventy-eight thousand, were stuck.

Their end came quickly. After being corralled behind a double fence of barbed wire in a small section of the old city for four months, the Jews of Riga, by order of Heinrich Himmler and with help from local Latvian volunteers, were liquidated. At four in the morning on November 29, 1941, fifteen thousand Jews were driven outside of the city to Rumbuli, told to undress and lie down, and then shot in the head. A week and a half later, ten thousand more Jews, including eighty-one-year-old Simon Dubnow, the great chronicler of Jewish history, were taken to Rumbuli and murdered.

By the end of the war, there was no Latvian Jewry. A progress report six months after the German invasion, signed by the head of one of the mobile killing units that massacred Jews in the wake of the German army, put the Jewish death toll at 63,238. That included the Jews of Riga. That included the five ditches at Rumbuli. In all, 90 percent of the Jews in Latvia were slaughtered by the Nazis; the rest were scattered through Siberia or starving and lonely in attics and holes waiting for the war to end. The majestic synagogues were burned to the ground. A culture had been totally annihilated; worse, it was as if salt had been spread on the earth so that nothing would ever grow there again.

Yosef Mendelevich was born in 1947 and knew only the world after the war.

His parents were from Dvinsk, in southern Latvia, and they had survived through his father's resourcefulness—he had managed to get a horse and carriage and escape deep into the Soviet Union before the Germans arrived. Like many Latvian Jews, he discovered there was little left of his hometown after the war, so he went to Riga. A committed Communist since the age of sixteen, Mendelevich's father never completely abandoned a sentimental attachment to Jewish tradition. When Yosef was born, his father even found an old mohel to circumcise him, one of the few remaining in Riga. On holidays, father and son would visit the one synagogue left in the city—it was crammed between buildings in the old town, and burning it would have meant destroying the surrounding houses. The Germans had used it as a stable. At home, Mendelevich's mother prepared Jewish meals, matzo balls at Passover and poppy seed–filled *hamentashen* on Purim. Yosef and his sister spent hours peeling potatoes to make latkes for Hanukkah.

But for Mendelevich, the warm world inside did not resemble the world outside. There, he learned early that he was not like everyone else. On the first day of first grade, his teacher asked each child to declare his or her "nationality." Every Soviet citizen was required to carry an internal passport at all times; it gave basic identifying information and, more important, the bearer's *propiska,* the place where he or she was officially registered to live. On the fifth line of the passport was a space for nationality; for most, this was the place to indicate the republic, language, and culture the individual was ethnically connected to: Ukrainian, Georgian, Latvian, Russian. But for 2,267,814 Soviet citizens, the fifth line read *Jewish,* and it indicated only one thing: difference.

In Mendelevich's first-grade class, he was the only one of the forty students who had *Evrei*—Jewish—written on that fifth line. When the teacher asked the children to stand up and state their nationalities, Mendelevich considered lying, but his nose and his name gave him away. "Mendelevich?" the teacher asked. "Jewish," he whispered. The class started to giggle. Among the children, there was a hierarchy of nationalities: the Russians were on top, Ukrainians and Latvians in the middle, the Asiatic peoples of the Far East toward the bottom, and Jews definitely on the lowest rung. The teacher made no attempt to quiet the class. Instead, she looked down at the squirming Mendelevich and asked, "Where does your father work?" He was mortified. It seemed all the other children's fathers were pilots or army officers. His father collected scrap iron. There was no way he could say this out loud. "I don't know," he answered. The laughter bubbled up and exploded as the teacher shook her head. "So big and he doesn't know."

From then on, Mendelevich preferred to stay inside, away from others. He read a lot—many Soviet writers, but also Hans Christian Andersen and the Brothers Grimm. His parents were poor and he was a child eager to please. He tried his best to succeed in school. He made few friends and eventually stopped venturing out into the courtyard to play with the other children.

But when he was ten, in 1957, Soviet reality intruded on him. Mendelevich's father was tried for economic crimes, accused of selling a few grams of lead on the black market. Khrushchev had crusaded against such crimes, and a suspiciously disproportionate number of Jews were tried and sometimes even executed as a result. Mendelevich's father was sentenced to five years and sent to a nearby prison camp, where he was forced to make bricks. Mendelevich's mother took him along when she went to visit her husband, and her son never forgot the barking dogs, the line of soldiers with their guns, and the strange sight of his father in tattered clothes.

His father was released early from his sentence. But a few months after that, his mother died. Mendelevich's alienation seemed complete. By the time he entered adolescence, he was living a double life. In school, he was disciplined. His Russian was so good that he was often asked to read out loud to the class. Once, he was asked to read the part of Maresyev, a pilot, in a famous Soviet novel. Maresyev's plane had been shot down in enemy territory; both of his legs were injured, and he was captured by partisans and interrogated. They asked the pilot who he was. Maresyev's response—"A Russian I am, a Russian"—made the children snicker and Mendelevich blush, but their laughter didn't bother him anymore. His home life, increasingly dominated by thoughts of Israel and revolving around the nightly shortwave broadcasts of Kol Israel, mattered much more.

At sixteen, before he'd even set eyes on Rumbuli, he began finding reflections of his secret desires. He spent the days working as a carpenter's apprentice at a factory, and in the evenings he took classes at School 25. By some fluke, a third of the school's teachers and students were Jews. And unlike at his elementary school, Mendelevich found there was no shame here in being Jewish. On one Jewish holiday, the students even wrote on the blackboard, *No school. Rosh Hashanah.* And to his surprise, he wasn't the only one who dreamed about Israel. Soon he and his new friends were chatting away about what they would do when they got there, what they would take with them, what kind of jobs they might have.

Even more important than his new school was the arrival of an older cousin from Dvinsk who came to stay in his family's home. Small, bookish, and unassuming, Mendel Gordin was studying to be a doctor at the Riga Medical Institute. In 1963, Mendelevich learned that his cousin had a secret. Gordin was part of a small network of Jews that shared illegal books and articles about Israel. It was so dangerous that Gordin kept his extracurricular activities from Mendelevich's father. But Gordin, who was older then Mendelevich by ten years, saw in the teenager a kindred spirit, and although he didn't tell him about his connections in the city, he shared his samizdat with him and talked with him about Israel. The first piece of illegal writing Mendelevich read, typed and loosely bound with a needle and thread, was a collection of Jabotinsky's essays.

That fall, Mendelevich went to Rumbuli for the first time. By then, hundreds of young Jews were arriving every Sunday to work on landscaping the mass graves; delineating them with rocks, planting flowers. The sight of so many young people working together, along with the steady stream of material his cousin was receiving, fed Mendelevich's fantasies about a vast underground Zionist movement operating in Riga. He knew he wanted to be a part of it.

Hardly anything worthy of the name *movement* existed at the time. The revival at Rumbuli and the clandestine distribution of samizdat, though far from spontaneous, were not the work of any formal organization. Riga's Zionist activity was, more than anything else, the result of a handful of connected families longing to reconstitute the lost world of their youth. The orange of Jaffa's citrus groves, the blue of the Mediterranean at Tel Aviv, and the white of Jerusalem stone had first hypnotized them as children and had never left their mind's eyes. In the secrecy of their homes, they played Israeli music on scratchy phonograph records, tried to teach themselves Hebrew, gathered together to listen to Kol Israel, and eagerly read any Jewish material they could find, including Dubnow's history, which they discovered in personal libraries. But a fear of Stalin and the far-reaching tentacles of his secret police made them keep these activities at a barely audible whisper. Even in the Baltics, where the memory of an openly Jewish cultural life was so fresh, almost no one was willing to test the resolve of the dictator, especially in his paranoid later years when he came to see Soviet Jews as a treasonous fifth column. Those few who weren't careful enough or who were just unlucky were arrested and sent to labor camps for long sentences. It happened all the time.

This changed in the 1960s with the ascension of Nikita Khrushchev. For his own political reasons, this crude son of peasant farmers, the unlikely winner of the post-Stalin leadership struggle, began a process of liberalization, an airing-out. The terror that had dominated people's lives for the past few decades began to subside. Khrushchev publicly denounced Stalin and his crimes in his 1956 "secret speech" to the Twentieth Party Congress, an instantly famous address that turned a heat lamp on Soviet society and began the process that became known as the thaw. He tore down the barbed wire of the Gulag, freeing tens of thousands of political prisoners in a mass amnesty. Previously banned books and art were suddenly allowed. People were not jailed arbitrarily as they once were. Jews, who at the moment of Stalin's death were terrified by rumors of his plans to deport them en masse to Siberia, could breathe easy again. In the Baltics, the most enlightened and least Sovietized corner of the empire, the thaw presented Jews with an opportunity.

That handful of Riga families, a few veteran Betar youth, and a couple of men just returning from the Gulag began cautiously, slowly, to open their doors. It helped that in Riga most of the population, including the Communist authorities, were ethnically Latvian. They were resentful of Russian domination, and though most had no great love for the Jews, they largely left them alone. Once the debilitating fear was no longer there, Jews wanted to create a space, however small, for their own national identity. They looked around at the generation born after the war, Mendelevich's peers, and realized that a great tragedy was under way: these young people felt nothing about their heritage but shame. The thaw gave the older Jews a chance to change this, to engage anyone who wanted to learn about Israel or reclaim a sense of Jewish identity. And once this generation saw that they could do something—that by showing a young person a map of Israel, teaching him some Hebrew songs, and exposing him to Jabotinsky's essays, they could alter his sense of himself—the small freedom granted by the thaw became insufficient. It only made them hungry for more.

In this way, Riga became the epicenter of a new type of Soviet Jewish activism. It started in the living rooms of people like Boris and Lydia Slovin. Coming back to her small Latvian town after the war, Lydia found that her home had been destroyed, as had the Jewish high school where her father had been a teacher. Her family moved to Riga, where she went to school and received a law degree in 1952. Like many in these early Zionist groups, Lydia was affected by the news in the fall of 1956 that Israel, in an operation conducted with Britain and France, had conquered the Sinai Peninsula. The anti-Israel rhetoric that followed inspired a few families to go pray in the synagogue for the safety of the Jewish State. One of the first pieces of samizdat distributed by Slovin's small group in the late fifties was Ben-Gurion's speeches on the Sinai campaign. Zionists met with friends for whispered discussions even though they lived in cooperative apartments where all that separated one family from the next was a thin sheet. The artist Yosef Kuzkovsky, who had become a famous painter in the socialist realist style, produced portraits of Lenin and Stalin for official consumption but kept hidden in his house a giant canvas he had been working on for years, *The Last Way—Babi Yar;* it depicted a group of Jews being marched to their deaths under a cloudy sky. It was a photograph of this painting that was later framed and hung on the obelisk memorial at Rumbuli.

Crucial in turning these individual acts into a movement were those former prisoners who had done time in labor camps as punishment for Zionist activity—it hadn't taken much for them to be arrested, usually a letter written to Israel or possession of any type of Zionist paraphernalia. The bonds formed in the prison camps became an important factor in establishing connections between the various centers of Zionist activity. Addresses were exchanged, codes for communication were established. Once they returned to their cities, these ex-inmates were not only the most fearless activists—they had already experienced the state at its worst—they were also hubs of information and material. In Riga, Yosef Schneider was one of the people who filled this role. In 1955, an uncle of Schneider who lived in Israel sent him a package containing a few photographs of Zionist leaders. Displaying a brazenness that would have meant death just a few years before, Schneider took one of the portraits—Chaim Weizmann, the first president of Israel—and put it in the window of his photography studio on the main boulevard of Riga. Even more audacious, the Chaim Weizmann picture replaced a photograph of Lenin that had occupied the spot (there was indeed a vague resemblance between the two bald and goateed leaders). This was clearly asking for trouble. In 1955, Schneider was one of the earliest to apply for a visa to leave the country. He was turned down then and six more times over the next two years. A former officer in the Red Army, he trained a group of Jewish men in marksmanship in an attempt to form a Jewish self-defense group. When the KGB finally came to arrest him, in 1957, it was for taking notes while listening to Kol Israel broadcasts and for allegedly slandering the Soviet Union in letters to his uncle. What they found searching his house didn't help him: along with his rifle, pistol, and bullets were Yiddish newspapers, a map of Israel, and the words to the Israeli national anthem, "Hatikvah," written on a scrap of paper.

In the early 1960s, when Schneider was released, he became an important contact with Moscow, where some of his fellow former inmates were trying to teach Hebrew and disseminate information about Israel. The Moscow activists were vital to the Riga Jews because they had access to an essential resource: the Israeli embassy. The Jewish diplomatic presence in the heart of the Soviet capital had existed since the fall of 1948, when Golda Meir (then Meyerson) made a climactic visit to the Moscow Choral Synagogue. As the first Israeli ambassador to the Soviet Union, she drew tens of thousands of weeping, ecstatic Jews into the street during the High Holy Days. From then on, one of the embassy's main missions became finding a way to keep the light of Jewish culture flickering. The effort primarily involved planting Israelis with Slavic backgrounds in the Moscow embassy and giving them innocuous titles such as "agriculture attaché." Their real job was to travel all over the country and distribute Israeli mementos such as miniature Jewish calendars and Star of David pendants, which were usually handed off in a handshake. They visited synagogues and attended the scarce Jewish cultural events. But while the Israelis certainly boosted morale, there was only so much they could do to help the nascent activists. Any overzealousness could get them kicked out of the country or trigger a diplomatic crisis that Israel couldn't afford, especially given the Soviets' recent alliances with Arab states.

These minimal gestures—as dangerous as they were for the embassy staff—were not enough for the self-proclaimed Zionists who began to coalesce in Riga in the early 1960s. The brand of activism they wanted to pursue fell into the Jabotinsky strain of Zionism. They were not afraid of confrontation. In fact, confrontation seemed the only way to get the Soviet Union to allow them the freedom to express themselves as Jews. As for their more distant hope of living in Israel one day, they knew no one was going to hand them that on a platter. They would have to fight. As early as 1964, the group planned to send an open petition to American Jewry demanding that they do something to help the Soviet Jews. Lydia Slovin was charged with confronting an Israeli official on vacation in Minsk with the idea—the Zionists wanted Israeli consent before they sent off the letter. She was told firmly by the Israeli official to drop it. But listening to albums and looking at postcards of Israel, celebrating Passover and Hanukkah, soon became insufficient for the activists. They were restive. And yet they were afraid to openly discuss the possibility of applying for exit visas. No one was allowed to emigrate from the Soviet Union; people like Schneider had been arrested for even trying. So the Zionists turned to samizdat. Finding material for duplication, copying it using borrowed typewriters and mimeograph machines, and then distributing it demanded organization and provided an opportunity to expand their circle.

There were only a few sources of samizdat. In Riga, private libraries from before the war that contained unpublished works by Dubnow, Jabotinsky, and others provided much of the material. Tourists dropped off articles and pamphlets, sometimes given to them by the Israeli embassy. And the embassy staff members themselves covertly deposited books in places where Jews might find them, on park benches and inside synagogues.

No book caught the imagination of these Zionists like Leon Uris's novel *Exodus*. Published in 1958, *Exodus* was a strange blend of Zionist polemic, Jewish history, and, most important, soap opera. The book had a huge cast and was about six hundred pages long, but it was centered on the character of Ari Ben Canaan, a member of the Aliyah Bet operation that was illegally smuggling Jews into Israel during the British mandate. It opens in Cyprus with Ben Canaan's attempt to pilot a boatload of Jews from detention camps through the Mediterranean to Palestine. It follows him through the war of independence and the trials and tribulations of his father, a Ben-Gurion type of Labor Zionist establishment character, and his uncle, a Menachem Begin look-alike who heads an organization called the Maccabees, which bears a close resemblance to the Irgun, the terror organization that tried to bomb the British out of Palestine. There is, of course, a love story. Kitty Fremont, a newly widowed, non-Jewish American nurse, finds herself enmeshed in the Jewish independence movement and falls in love with Ari Ben Canaan. The book manages to tell the stories of the Holocaust, early Zionism, and the Russian pogroms. It gives the Zionist movement an incredibly romantic glow.

For the handful of Zionists in the Soviet Union, and especially among those in Riga, the book was pure sustenance—many tears fell on the thin typewritten pages. And it served as a remarkable recruiting tool. It's difficult to determine exactly how the book entered these circles, but it's safe to assume that the Israelis had a hand in it since all the copies appeared around the same time. Even though it was written in English, a language not widely spoken in the Soviet Union, the book spread like a virus. In Riga, it found its way to Boris Slovin. Boris hadn't yet met his future wife, Lydia, a blond lawyer; their Zionist cells hadn't crossed. In 1962, Slovin was working at a train station as an electrician. One day a non-Jewish coworker showed him a book he had just been handed by an Israeli diplomat who must have mistaken the Latvian for a Jew. It was *Exodus*. The book was in English, and the coworker thought Slovin might be able to decipher it. Slovin couldn't, but he took it home and passed it on through the Zionist network until Lydia, who knew a bit of English, was brought on as a translator. She wrote a version out longhand, and she was so unsure of her English that if a word she looked up in her Russian-English dictionary had multiple meanings, she simply put all the possibilities in parentheses. Boris received her handwritten translations, typed them out on carbon paper making four copies at a time, and then burned Lydia's originals. He shortened the final version and excised any anti-Soviet sentiment, and he also edited a bit, removing any reference to the affair between Kitty and Ari Ben Canaan, thinking that intermarriage would send the wrong message to Riga's Jewish youth.

Ezra Rusinek, the bare-chested, Israeli-looking man who caught Mendelevich's eye on his first trip to Rumbuli, had managed to get hold of a copy in German. He found a translator and then spent a year meticulously typing out all six hundred pages of the text and making five copies, three of which stayed in Riga and two of which were sent to friends in other cities. So secretive were the separate cells of Riga Zionists that Rusinek was not aware that Slovin was engaged in a similar project. Copies proliferated everywhere. One major source was the prison camps. A group of Jewish inmates inside a Mordvinian camp, Dubrovlag, sneaked in a copy and held nightly readings in which the few political prisoners who spoke some English would read and translate the story. Eventually they transcribed their version into a notebook, which then got passed from one generation of prisoners to the next, converting a few to Zionism along the way. Some who heard it in camps wrote out the story from memory when they were released. By 1964, *Exodus* was a blockbuster in the samizdat circuit. Mendelevich even had a copy, which his cousin had asked him to hide above the cast-iron stove in his room.

But it was more than just the pull of Israel that suddenly inspired Jews to take such risks. It was the push that came with growing knowledge of what had happened during the war. When Adolf Eichmann, a top Nazi official, was captured in Buenos Aires by the Israelis and given a hugely publicized trial in Jerusalem, Jews all over the world confronted the facts of the Holocaust for the first time. Never before had the details been so openly discussed, as survivor after survivor took the stand and faced the glass box where the bored-looking Eichmann sat. David Ben-Gurion had envisioned a trial that would be both cathartic for the Jewish people and useful in making a case for Israel's existence. This is why he balked at the idea of trying Eichmann in an international court. He wanted more than justice; he wanted theater. He wanted the world to appreciate the Jewish tragedy.

When Moscow eventually memorialized the immense suffering of the war, it did so by referring to the trials of "Soviet citizens." No mention was made of the unique fate reserved for the Jews as a people—their loss was subsumed into the twenty million killed in the course of the "Great Patriotic War." But even the Soviets could not ignore the history dredged up by the Eichmann trial, most notably what happened at Babi Yar, the ravine outside Kiev where the Nazis had shot thirty-four thousand people and buried them in a mass grave. On September 19, 1961, the Soviets experienced the first stirrings of this new Holocaust consciousness. That week's issue of *Literaturnaya Gazeta*, the extremely popular and influential cultural and political newspaper started by Pushkin in 1830, contained a poem by up-and-coming young writer Yevgeny Yevtushenko. Its title was "Babi Yar." After making a visit to the ravine and seeing that it had been turned into a garbage dump, Yevtushenko wrote a lament not only for the fact that "No monument stands over Babi Yar," as the poem opens, but also for the history of anti-Semitism in his country. He invokes Dreyfus and Anne Frank; he imagines himself the victim of a pogrom; and he condemns the reflexive anti-Semitism of his compatriots as being un-Russian. As the poem reaches its crescendo, the non-Jewish poet identifies himself completely with Jewish suffering. For Yevtushenko, redemption for the Soviet Union was possible only with the elimination of all anti-Semitism:

> And I myself
> > am one massive, soundless scream
> above the thousand thousand buried here.
> I am
> > each old man
> > > here shot dead.
> I am
> > every child
> > > here shot dead.
> Nothing in me
> > shall ever forget!
> The "Internationale," let it
> > thunder
> when the last antisemite on earth
> is buried forever.

The poem had incredible resonance. *Literaturnaya Gazeta* immediately sold out of the issue containing it. Thousands of students gathered to hear Yevtushenko read "Babi Yar," then stamped their feet and yelled for him to read it again. The strongest proof of the poem's power was the ferocity with which the government tried to squelch it. The papers were filled with denunciations and counter-poems commissioned by the Soviet authorities. They claimed that Yevtushenko's work demeaned the memory of the millions of other Soviet soldiers and civilians who had fallen in World War II. But even Khrushchev's scolding that "this poem does not belong here" could not stop its spreading influence. In April of 1962, Yevtushenko was on the cover of *Time* magazine. That year, Dimitri Shostakovich, the famed Soviet composer who had only recently joined the Communist Party, set the poem to the music that became his Symphony no. 13 in B-flat Minor, opus 113, known simply as "Babi Yar." On the evening of December 18, 1962, the Moscow Philharmonic Orchestra first performed the piece, but only after Shostakovich had been forced to change some of the poem's words.

In Riga, the Soviets reluctantly answered the demand for commemoration by holding an official ceremony in the Bikerniki woods, another place outside town where Nazis had brought prisoners to be executed. A few of the lone Zionists attending hoped to hear mention of the fact that most of these prisoners were Jews. But they heard nothing. The murdered were simply referred to as the victims of Fascism. On that day in October of 1962, the Jews at the ceremony, many of whose families had perished in the war, made a decision to find the place where most of the Jews of Riga had been killed. By the following Sunday, they were at Rumbuli, where the remnants of the mass killing were still evident. Defying the Soviet law that prohibited unauthorized public signs, they took an old board and used a heated nail to inscribe these words: *Here were silenced the voices of 38,000 Jews of Riga on November 29–30 and on December 8–9, 1941.* The makeshift plaque was fastened to a fir tree in an inconspicuous part of the grove. The group of twenty circled the sign as someone recited the Kaddish. It was the first Holocaust memorial service at Rumbuli—and one of the earliest in the entire Soviet Union.

In the spring of 1963, fifty people gathered to hold a twentieth-anniversary commemoration of the Warsaw Ghetto uprising. An impromptu committee of organizers was formed, mostly older men who saw the importance of Rumbuli as a focal point to bring Jews together. A critical person in these early discussions was Mark Blum, a young, charismatic Zionist who had become a leader for the newly active Riga

youth. The older men, including Rusinek, came up with a plan to reno-
vate the place, plant flowers, and make it a proper burial site, but Blum
was the only one who really knew how to engage the young people and
interest them in helping out. It was at that Warsaw Ghetto commemoration that the black obelisk was erected, and the organizers decided
then that they would get as many Jews as possible to come to Rumbuli
each Sunday to landscape the ground.

Rumbuli was the first group effort for these Zionists, people who
had previously relegated their activities to the secrecy of their homes.
Almost immediately, differences in style and tactics emerged. There
were the legitimists, who wanted official sanction for their activities.
And then there were the former Betari youth like Rusinek and the
younger hard-liners like Mark Blum, who believed that confrontation
with the government was the only way forward, a notion the older
Zionists, with their still fresh memories of Stalin, found dangerous.
Clashes had already broken out over the question of whether to participate in the few state-sanctioned Jewish cultural activities. Starting in the early 1960s, partly in response to charges of anti-Semitism,
Moscow allowed the formation of Jewish choral and drama associations in Vilnius and Riga. These groups had to get approval for every
song they sang, and their repertoire subsequently consisted largely of
pro-Communist ballads in Yiddish (with lyrics like "*Lenin, tate, zey
gebentsht, ost verbreided mensch mit mensch*"—Father Lenin be blessed,
you made brothers of us all). But they nonetheless offered rare opportunities for Jewish youth to gather together. That was little comfort
to the self-styled extremists who believed that participating in these
choirs amounted to collaboration with the enemy, helping the Soviet
Union provide visiting dignitaries with supposed proof that Jewish life
was thriving. At performances, Boris Slovin would go up to these visitors and whisper one word in their ears: *Theresienstadt.* (This was the
name of the Nazi concentration camp set up as a model to reassure the
outside world that Jews were being well treated.) Yosef Schneider even
joined one of these choirs in an attempt to break it up.

Rumbuli was initially organized by the more legitimist elements.
They had gone the formal route of trying to get permission to landscape the site and hold public ceremonies there. Letters went back and
forth between the Jewish leaders and the local Latvian Soviet authori-

ties. Though their requests were never officially granted, neither were they explicitly denied. The group felt that this slight opening gave them license to begin their work. Throughout 1963, they managed to wrangle bulldozers and tractors to move earth, as well as large mounds of sand to fill in the ditches—material donated clandestinely by Jewish factory managers and greased with bribes. The local authorities eventually went further, giving a kind of tacit permission by allowing an empty field next to Rumbuli to be used as a parking lot for the hundreds of Jews who started arriving on Sundays. The more extremist activists had a difficult time deciding how to respond, whether to participate in the revitalization of Rumbuli or protest it for being government sanctioned. Conflict emerged more than once, as when Boris Slovin and Mark Blum made a giant Star of David out of willow branches and placed it strategically at the site so that passengers on every train going from Riga to Moscow could see it. This angered the older activists, who tried to avoid needless provocation, and they forced the young men to take it down. By the time the annual commemoration of the massacre took place, in the fall of 1963, five long ditches had been planted with flowers, and about eight hundred people showed up.

While in other cities small groups of Zionists were just beginning to stir with an interest in Jewish heritage, the Riga Jews were now assembling at Rumbuli formally as a community at least twice a year—on the anniversaries of the Warsaw Ghetto uprising and the Rumbuli massacre. And the Sunday gatherings continued, giving hope to the older generation that young Jews might meet this way and marry one another. The ground they stood on covered bones, but Rumbuli was more about revival, about growing a new generation who would view their Jewish identity with pride and not simply as a word entered on the fifth line of their passports.

At first, Mendelevich stayed on the margins of this growing but still quite small group of families who organized the Zionist activities. He went every week to Rumbuli, took part in the ceremonies, and read the Jewish samizdat that his cousin Mendel brought him. But as the months went by, he became more and more active, helping to watch over the Rumbuli tools during the week, organizing some of the other young people. The older activists began to see him as trustworthy.

And Mendelevich was becoming bolder. In 1965, as part of a cultural exchange with Israel, which only became possible in the years after the thaw, an Israeli all-star women's basketball team was allowed to tour the Soviet Union. Eventually it came to Riga. Mendelevich was ecstatic. This was unheard-of, and he wasn't going to miss the chance to finally see Israelis—Israeli women, no less—up close. But the Soviets wanted to make sure the event was no more than symbolic, and they gave out the majority of the tickets to Party members. On the day of the game, Jews swarmed around the stadium where the Israeli women were practicing. When the women's bus left to take them back to the hotel, the young Jews started to sing, and through the window Mendelevich could see one woman crying.

That evening the Israeli team lost by dozens of points, but the Jews were thrilled just to have heard the "Hatikvah" played before the Soviet national anthem. After the game, Mendelevich, along with his sister, Rivka, decided to go to the hotel where the women were staying. This was a dangerous move. During Stalin's time, any person who had contact with foreigners was immediately under suspicion. Also, Mendelevich was painfully shy; even at eighteen, despite his ability to speak in front of audiences, he felt uncomfortable talking to strangers. But he forced himself up the stairs and through the front door of the hotel. Once they were in the lobby, a tanned man came up to the two scared-looking teenagers. Mendelevich sensed immediately that he was Israeli. The man said something in Hebrew that the boy didn't understand. Then he handed him two big envelopes. Mendelevich looked and saw that in each one was a Star of David pendant. He could hardly contain his excitement, and he nearly ran off without thanking the man. From then on, even though his father warned him that it was reckless to draw attention to himself at work, Mendelevich never took the necklace off.

At the Rumbuli memorial ceremony in the winter of 1965, hundreds of people attended, read poetry, and spoke about the history of the place. But Mendelevich felt unsatisfied. After the ceremony, he and his friends went back to his house. He was emotionally wound up and he suddenly felt compelled to say something, to let them know how his soul had been stirred. He talked about the ravages of the war and the responsibility it had bestowed on them to stop assimilating and try to make aliyah—to move to Israel. "Today our fate is in our hands," he said earnestly, his voice near breaking. Then, before he knew what he was saying, he proposed they start a Zionist organization. "Those in favor, raise your hands." Mendelevich looked around the room at his friends, seventeen- and eighteen-year-olds who, like him, had been moved by the ceremony, and all their hands were raised high.

But the next morning, Mendelevich regretted saying it. He was worried he might have gotten ahead of himself. Not only was starting an organization a dangerous proposition—the older groups had managed to avoid KGB arrest because they had stuck to small cells rather than one organization with a hierarchy, which the Communists would view as a direct challenge to their authority—but also it wasn't clear to him exactly what this organization should do. In addition, many of those who had been present the day before were chatty and unserious, and probably would not make for good members of a secret underground. Together, Mendelevich and his sister, Rivka, also a passionate Zionist, conducted a virtual purge—that's how they thought of it, so ingrained was the language of revolution. They ended up with a group of four: Mendelevich, his sister, and two of their friends.

Their activities did not change much. Once a week they met at a house outside the city where one of the members lived, and there they read Jewish samizdat, including a full translation of *Exodus.*

Yosef Schneider soon found out about the small group and introduced them to another group of four young people. They would meet together often, and sometimes in the evenings they'd have competitions to see who knew more Jewish history. Mendelevich, who thought parties frivolous, enjoyed these social gatherings with people who shared his dreams.

Others formed more small groups that linked up. The groups' goal remained innocuous: to prepare themselves for aliyah when the day arrived. They were not interested in provoking or pushing in any way. In the platform Mendelevich wrote up for the federated groups, he stated this clearly: "Out of an emotional love for our people and a responsibility imposed on us we have come to a conclusion that we must unite in order to work toward the self-awareness of Jewish nationality. Our group's central focus is the promotion of Jewish culture."

They each donated a relatively heavy membership fee, even though they were all students. With the pooled money, they bought a used typewriter so they could reproduce copies of a 1912 Jewish encyclopedia they had found in an old library. They spent holidays together. On Hanukkah they invited friends to come light candles. On Simchat Torah, they danced in the narrow street in front of the one Riga synagogue. They became close friends and, sometimes, even lovers. At least two couples in the group ended up getting married. They created an alternative universe for themselves, one in which Mendelevich thrived. But it was also a fundamentally frustrating universe. They felt themselves increasingly in limbo; bodies on Latvian ground whose souls were somewhere else.

In the summer of 1966, they got news they couldn't believe at first. Geula Gill, a popular Israeli folksinger, and Juki Arkin, an Israeli mime who had studied with Marcel Marceau, were coming to tour the Soviet Union, and they'd be stopping for three shows in Riga. As soon as the concert was announced on Kol Israel, Riga's Jews rushed the box office at the municipal stadium. When Mendelevich got there he found a queue of three hundred and fifty people. He had to run off to the university, where he was studying electrical engineering, to take a physics exam, but all he could think about was the Israeli singer coming to town. It was an anomalous event, made possible only because of the brief warming in Soviet-Israeli relations. When the physics test was completed, he ran quickly from the university back to the line. Thousands were now pushing and shoving to keep their places. Mendelevich and a friend tried to maintain order. Each person in line was allowed to buy two tickets. In order to fool the cashier, Mendelevich came back in different guises: he would remove his glasses one time, then return with them on and his hat pulled down low, then he would take off his hat. In this way, he bought tickets for his whole family for multiple shows.

Every city where Gill performed that July seemed to explode in her presence. Jews stood all night to get tickets. The concerts were crammed. The audience sang along raucously to "Hava Nagilah" and "Havenu Shalom Aleichem." In Moscow, Gill had to perform eight encores. By the time she arrived in Riga, the local police already knew that people would mob Gill and her entourage when they left after the show.

Mendelevich stood in the Riga Municipal Sports Stadium shivering with emotion. The small woman onstage was singing in Hebrew. Throughout the performance, dozens of bouquets of flowers traveled over the heads of the crowd toward the stage. Someone yelled for Gill to sing the song of the Palmach, and Mendelevich closed his eyes and joined the audience in the lyrics he had been singing for the last three years on his way to Rumbuli. Arkin, the mime, acted out a scene that the Riga Jews instinctively understood: a man is carrying a flag and walking against a strong wind with much difficulty, and only after many laborious steps does he finally plant the flag in the ground. Vague enough not to be understood by the KGB agents wandering the stadium, it was clearly a reenactment of Israel's struggle.

After the final performance, the audience started leaving the stadium to escort Gill and Arkin to their waiting cars and buses as a way of wishing the Israelis farewell. But blocking all the exits and in full riot gear were groups of policemen who refused to let the audience members past. A big crowd that included Mendelevich surged forward and pushed into the square in front of the stadium. The police tried to block the Jews from approaching Gill's car, where she sat waving goodbye. At one point, shoving people back, a policeman put his hands on the chest of fifteen-year-old Naomi Garber, the daughter of Zionist activists. She was so startled that she slapped the policeman, and he grabbed her by the arm and led her to the police wagon. The sight of Naomi being dragged away inflamed the crowd even more and they began shouting and pressing on the police. Boris Slovin, witnessing the scene, yelled, "Jews, what are you doing? The Fascists are grabbing our girls again."

Within minutes, a riot ensued. The young boys who hung around Mark Blum taunted the police, at one point grabbing a policeman's hat and tossing it between them. They shook the car carrying Garber, trying to stop it from leaving, and they clung to the buses in Gill's motorcade, which was slowly making its way through the square. And the police struck back, swinging at the crowd with batons and yelling curses. When the melee was over, Blum gathered some of his boys and marched to the police station to try to free Garber. When he arrived, he was promptly arrested.

Mendelevich watched the confrontation, stunned and unable to move. The violence was astounding and honest—a physical manifestation of all the frustration they felt, the energy, the tension that could not be resolved. And he was scared. Violent protests against the regime were unprecedented. Fear kept everyone from even complaining, let alone fighting back. What the riot made clear to Mendelevich as he watched the sweating, surging crowd was that the status quo could not stand. Otherwise, this violence would not be the end of the story, but its beginning.

"Failure May Have Become Our Habit"

1963–1964

ADOLF EICHMANN'S TRIAL in Jerusalem shocked American Jews as much as it did the Jews of Riga. Hours and hours of testimony streamed through radios and television sets. Survivor after survivor took the stand, some screaming, some crying. Up until that point, what would become known as the Holocaust had been spoken about rarely if at all, and then only in the neutered terms of a crime against humanity. Now the trial made abundantly clear that this crime had been committed against Jews—as a race, as a people—and that the horrific particulars now unleashed into the world could never again be forgotten. One survivor who testified was Yehiel Dinur, the author of books signed only with the word *Ka-Tzetnik* (Yiddish for "concentration camper") and the number that had been tattooed on his arm. Seconds before fainting to the floor he prophesied, "I believe with perfect faith that, just as in astrology the stars influence our destiny, so does this planet of the ashes, Auschwitz, stand in opposition to our planet earth, and influences it."

Lou Rosenblum was a scientist in Cleveland, Ohio, who worked for the federal agency that would soon become NASA. He was tall and broad-shouldered and wore thick horn-rimmed glasses; a forceful and passionate yet gruff-looking man who loved his work and his young family. And he was one of those American Jews who couldn't tear themselves away from the trial; he followed it closely until the day in May of 1962 when Eichmann was hanged and then cremated, his ashes scattered into the Mediterranean Sea. But for Rosenblum, the survivors' horror stories were more than a lesson in evil. They also pointed to complacency in the face of evil. A series of questions drummed away at him: Why? Why had not one government lifted a finger while European Jews were being gassed and burned? Why did they miss so many good opportunities for rescue? Where had American Jews been during it all? Had they really been too scared to push, to make any noise, to force the problem on FDR or Churchill or someone who could do something to make it stop?

Rosenblum was perhaps more primed to ask these questions than others of his generation. He had recently gathered with a group of other young Jewish men in their early thirties, all professionals, doctors and scientists, who were groping toward a fuller understanding of Jewish history. They called themselves a social action committee but they were really a glorified reading group, meeting in the rec room of their small synagogue, Beth Israel, in a western suburb of Cleveland. Once they began exploring the role of American Jews in World War II, they became profoundly troubled.

They tore through *Perfidy*, an indictment of the Jewish leadership in Palestine during the war, written by Ben Hecht, the legendary playwright and screenwriter. Hecht was a fervent Jabotinskyite, and his book, published in 1961, was considered blasphemous. It centered on the story of Rudolf Kastner, a member of the pre-state Labor party Mapai, who had secretly negotiated with Adolf Eichmann over the fate of Hungarian Jewry. Hecht painted a picture of a Jewish establishment in moral collapse, unable to take a more aggressive, clear-sighted approach to the existential Nazi threat. His overwrought conclusion: "Everyone, Great Britain, the United States, and the leaders of world Jewry—traitors all! Murderers!"

The group followed *Perfidy* with "Bankrupt," a 1943 essay by Hayim Greenberg written half a year after the full scale of the genocide was made known in the West. Published in the pages of the *Yiddisher Kempfer*, the essay described the author's shock at the "epidemic inability to suffer or to feel compassion—that has seized upon the vast majority of American Jews and their institutions; in pathological fear of pain; in terrifying lack of imagination—a horny shell seems to have formed over the soul of American Jewry to protect and defend it against pain and pity."

What the men read sickened them. It stirred a bitter mix of guilt, shame, and anger. Whether American Jews deserved to take on this historical burden—the crisis of conscience that came with knowing they'd done very little while millions of their brethren were led to slaughter—is irrelevant. The point is that by the early 1960s, the seed of this feeling had taken root. And in the American Midwest, it found expression for the first time as an almost desperate need to help another community of European Jews who seemed to be facing, if not physical extinction, spiritual annihilation.

In the nearly twenty years that had passed since the war's end, American Jews had emerged as the most well-off of the three large communities of Jews in the world. While the identity of Soviet Jews was being stifled and Israelis were still engaged in existential battles, American Jews were thriving. The security that Communism had deceptively offered an earlier generation and that Zionism had yet to deliver could be found in the United States. It was both exhilarating and lulling. Even though the sense of ease and comfort could be disturbed—as it was for Lou Rosenblum—by the uncomfortable awareness of the Holocaust, the vast majority of Jews had remained oblivious. They were too busy becoming Americans. Until the emptiness of their Jewish identity itself became a motivating factor for action, this community held tight to America's promise, the chance to forget where they had come from and the cousins they had left behind.

By the early 1960s, American Jews represented something unique and unprecedented in American history: a minority group, only two generations removed from filthy, Lower East Side lives of impoverishment as garment workers and tenement dwellers, who had unequivocally and entirely made it. Multiple studies by local Jewish federations in the 1950s found that an overwhelming 75 to 96 percent of Jews held white-collar jobs. Compared with the American population overall, only 38 percent of whom were middle class, this represented a triumph. Even in New York City, the last enclave of poor Jews, two-thirds of the Jewish residents worked in professional or semiprofessional sectors.

The factories where the grandfathers of Jewish doctors and lawyers had once toiled were now filled with blacks and Puerto Ricans.

With prosperity came social and geographic shifts. For one thing, as the fifties came to a close, the suburbanization of the American Jew was almost complete. Between 1948 and 1958, twelve million Americans left large cities and set down roots in suburbia, and many Jews were among them. In New York City, which had a Jewish population of two million in the late 1950s, geography told the story—the first generation, at the turn of the century, lived in the slums of the Lower East Side; the second generation in the lower-middle-class outskirts of Brooklyn and the Bronx; and the third in the firmly middle-middle-class neighborhoods of Queens, Long Island, and Westchester County. In 1923, only fifty thousand Jews lived in Queens, but by 1957 that number had increased to four hundred and fifty thousand. Similar self-imposed middle-class Jewish ghettos popped up outside other major cities: in Brookline, near Boston; Shaker Heights, near Cleveland; and Highland Park, near Chicago.

These new suburban Jews were comfortable in America. And not just because of affluence or the safe communities they created but because America seemed finally to accept and embrace them. They were normalized. They edged closer to being seen simply as "white people." The American Jewish Committee conducted a poll asking Gentiles if there were "any nationality, religious or racial groups" in the country that posed a threat to America. The results were unpublished but telling. In 1946, 18 percent of those polled named Jews as a threat. In 1954, that number was down to 1 percent. In the first decades after the war, laws against biased housing and hiring practices were established in most states. And even though few Jews worked as senior executives in big corporations or joined exclusive WASP country clubs, no measure of success seemed out of reach. Already in 1945 a Jewish girl from the Bronx, Bess Myerson, had become Miss America, and a Jewish boy from the Bronx, Hank Greenberg, had become a baseball superstar, hitting his famous ninth-inning grand-slam home run to win the American League pennant for his Detroit Tigers.

The Jewish community embraced the boundless optimism and strait-laced uniformity that characterized the postwar boom years in America. No one rocked the boat, certainly no one in this freshly inte-

grated minority group. The darkest part of the collective Jewish conscience—the genocide of European Jewry—was rarely discussed, and
even when it was it never challenged the feel-good ethos of the times.
The Holocaust was Anne Frank. Her diary and the incredibly popular
Broadway play that followed in 1955 (which won both a Pulitzer and
a Tony), along with the movie in 1959, was as close as American society came to examining what had so recently happened to the Jews.
Both the play and the film catered to the collective mood, downplay-
ing Anne's Jewish identity as well as the horror that awaited her once
the curtain fell. "We're not the only people who have had to suffer . . .
sometimes one race . . . sometimes another," Anne tells us (in a line
that was added to the play by the director, Garson Kanin, to avoid any
appearance of "special pleading"). And of course, there is Anne's final
line, so embraced at the time, that "in spite of everything, I still believe
that people are really good at heart." Partly because of the nature of the
diary and partly because it was sanitized to fit audiences' tastes, Anne's
story was never about Jewish suffering or even Jewish survival.

Indeed, the Holocaust as an event with historical and psychological
implications for Jews was almost completely ignored during this period. Nathan Glazer, in his 1957 *American Judaism,* wrote that the Holocaust "had had remarkably slight effects on the inner life of American Jewry." The culture at large did not encourage examining this still
open wound, and the Jewish community followed its lead. What happened during the war was seen as an offense against the free world.

What did animate the American Jewish community during this
postwar period—from the 1950s through the early 1960s—was the issue of civil rights for blacks. The three major Jewish defense organizations, the Anti-Defamation League, the American Jewish Committee,
and the American Jewish Congress, led the crusade for antidiscrimina-
tion laws. The liberalism of the Jewish community was, of course, a
long-established fact, going back at least to the turn of the twentieth
century with the arrival of hundreds of thousands of Eastern European socialists. And famously, not even their growing affluence altered
this political inclination. In 1960, for the first time, Jewish liberalism
proved a major factor in the presidential election. The 82 percent of
the Jewish vote that John F. Kennedy received was instrumental in his
microscopic margin of victory over Richard Nixon (Kennedy, meet-

ing with David Ben-Gurion a few months after he took office, startled Israel's prime minister when he said, "You know, I was elected by the Jews of New York and I would like to do something for the Jewish people").

But the fight for civil rights went above and beyond this seemingly genetic liberalism. There was of course an element of enlightened self-preservation—as late as the fall of 1958, one of the oldest and most prosperous synagogues in Atlanta was bombed by the same Ku Klux Klanners who were terrorizing southern blacks. An America that was safe for all minorities served the Jews' interests. But even this doesn't explain the devotion of those who helped fund breakthrough civil rights protest groups like the Congress of Racial Equality and the Student Nonviolent Coordinating Committee; the commitment of Jewish lawyers who made up more than half the attorneys fighting for civil rights in the South; and the support of rabbis and Jewish students who joined sit-ins and marches in disproportionate numbers. The tragic apogee of this involvement came during the summer of 1964, the Freedom Summer, as it was called. More than half the young northerners who descended on the South to help blacks register to vote in the face of a violently opposed white population were Jews. The disappearance of three of these volunteers—two New York Jews, Michael Schwerner and Andrew Goodman, along with their black colleague James Chaney—caused national alarm. When their brutalized bodies were discovered in a shallow grave outside Philadelphia, Mississippi, it seemed tangible proof that Jews and blacks shared a common American fate.

Jews needed the civil rights movement because it gave them a new raison d'être. By the early sixties, they had found acceptance in American society. The majority of Jews had drifted far away from religion, with synagogues in those newly gilded suburbs resembling community centers more than sources of spirituality or identity—shuls with pools. The nascent Israel, which might have provided a natural glue for the community, was still viewed as an experiment, one that demanded respect but that had yet to inspire widespread love. Civil rights gave Jews purpose.

Even the Holocaust—in its Anne Frank version—was recruited for the black cause. The black experience of intolerance became an extension of the Jewish experience of intolerance, providing a kind of organic justification for the Jewish role in the movement. No one articulated this better than Joachim Prinz, a Conservative rabbi from New Jersey and then president of the American Jewish Congress. From the same podium where minutes later Martin Luther King Jr. delivered his "I have a dream" speech, Prinz addressed the August 28, 1963, March on Washington with these words:

> From our Jewish historic experience of three and a half thousand years we say: Our ancient history began with slavery and the yearning for freedom. During the Middle Ages my people lived for a thousand years in the ghettos of Europe. Our modern history begins with a proclamation of emancipation.
>
> It is for these reasons that it is not merely sympathy and compassion for the black people of America that motivates us. It is above all and beyond all such sympathies and emotions a sense of complete identification and solidarity born of our own painful historic experience.

But despite all this success, something had fallen out of the center of Jewish identity, squeezed out by the American embrace and the single-minded devotion to freedom for blacks. There was increasingly very little Jewish about being a Jew. There was no passion about preserving a separate and unique identity, no care for spiritual or communal continuity. Very few thinkers at the time acknowledged this. Most did not see the hollowness. Those rare conservative Jewish critics who did gave voice to their concerns in the pages of intellectual journals like *Commentary* and *Jewish Frontier.* To them, watching Jewish leaders devote all their organizations' resources and energies to helping blacks while leaving Jewish education underfunded was infuriating. Seeing young Jewish college students clasp hands in the streets and sing "We Shall Overcome" while not knowing a single Jewish prayer seemed to be a disaster waiting to happen. Milton Himmelfarb, a leading sociographer of American Jews and a brilliant phrase turner (it was his observation that "Jews earn like Episcopalians, and vote like Puerto Ricans"), wrote in *Commentary* in 1960 that he was not sure if the American Jewish Congress was "a Jewish organization with a civil-rights program or a civil-rights organization whose members are Jews." About its membership, he lamented that they "have strong proud-to-be-a-Jew feelings, but the feelings are without content and in fact are more attached to civil rights rhetoric than to Jewish religion, education or culture—rhetoric, because in the lives they lead they are not different from the rest of the Jewish middle class."

This was a patently conservative critique arguing that the values of these middle-class American Jews actually worked against their own interests, against Jewish continuity and internal cohesion. In the eyes of the critics, this liberal worldview would tear apart, piece by piece, the foundations that girded traditional society. This creative destruction was everywhere, from the explosion of literary form that was the Beat poets to the introduction of the birth control pill to the quagmire in Vietnam and the ensuing mistrust of all government. But for American Jews, these upheavals came at the same time that they were losing the one element that had always helped to bind Jewish identity in the Diaspora: otherness. With the absence of persecution—the forced apartness of the ghetto no longer an issue—the young Jew coming of age in those years of tumult and transition grew more and more alienated from his own background.

Even the Conservative rabbi Arthur Hertzberg, who believed in the liberalization of American society, who was at the March on Washington, and who would be present with King on Bloody Sunday in March of 1965, came to the conclusion in the summer of 1964 that, as the title of his essay in the *Jewish Frontier* put it, "America Is Galut [Diaspora]": "The Jew cannot settle down in freedom to be himself, 'just like everybody else.' When in his own inner consciousness he begins to approach a real feeling of at-homeness within the larger society, what remains of his Jewish identity is too little and too personalized to sustain a community. It inevitably follows that there is only one possible mode for the survival of a Jewish community in a free society. It can live only by emphasizing what is unique to itself and by convincing its children that that uniqueness is worth having."

When Lou Rosenblum first arrived in Cleveland, Ohio, to work for the National Advisory Committee for Aeronautics (NACA), few Jews lived in his part of town. German Jewish merchants from Bavaria had moved to the midwestern city in 1839 and built the ornate, domed Reform synagogues of Anshe Chesed and Tifereth Israel. Many more Eastern

European Jews followed at the turn of the twentieth century. But they always lived east of the Cuyahoga River, which split the city in two. And the Jews kept moving even farther east as the century progressed, eventually settling in the suburbs of Cleveland and in Shaker Heights. By the early 1960s, this community had firmly established itself. The Jews of Cleveland numbered seventy thousand and had an active federation that included branches of all the major national Jewish organizations; a collection of well-attended synagogues; and even a famous national Jewish leader—Abba Hillel Silver, the Zionist defender and brilliant orator who as chairman of the Jewish Agency had stood before the United Nations in 1947 and argued the case for Israeli independence. Although by 1963 he was aging and sick, Silver still preached every Friday night from the pulpit of Tifereth Israel, as he had since 1917.

All this was in the east, while NACA's lab was in the far west, near the city's airport. This part of the city contained only one small, ailing synagogue; it had been around since 1910 but had suffered during the Depression and never recovered. Its walls were peeling, and the congregation could hardly afford to pay a rabbi's salary.

Rosenblum moved to the city in 1952, hired by the government to work in the fuel research department of the NACA lab. He had grown up on the distinctly Jewish streets of Flatbush, Brooklyn; barely survived the battle of Okinawa in the Pacific; eventually graduated from Brooklyn College; and then went to Ohio University and earned a PhD in organic chemistry. He decided to work for the government because he'd been told that as a Jew, he'd have a hard time finding work with a private corporation (at the time, companies like DuPont still had an unspoken quota system). Also, his wife, Evy—whom he'd met in Brooklyn College at an evening of Palestinian folk dancing—had family in Cleveland.

But the loss of a Jewish community in those western suburbs was palpable. Even though he'd never been religious, Rosenblum missed the social role that a synagogue provided. Driving to the east side of the city for services was almost impossible. It took an hour over roads that were still cobbled. Rosenblum was stuck. Yet many of the almost twelve hundred people working at the NACA lab were Jews, including the lab's director, Abe Silverstein. Rosenblum realized that this was a large enough pool of young Jewish families to feed a new congregation. With the help of his boss, who would become the first temple president, Rosenblum and twenty-five families started Beth Israel in 1954.

The congregation grew throughout the fifties, taking on more and more young families and eventually acquiring the building of the older west side synagogue. Cut off from the established Jewish center of Cleveland, the congregants had to build their community from scratch. If they wanted a day school for the children, they had to create one themselves. They developed a culture of self-sufficiency and volunteerism.

It was out of this congregation that Rosenblum and a few other men formed their study group in 1962. It included people like Herb Caron, a clinical psychologist who worked at the local VA hospital treating veterans. Caron, a logical, academic-minded man, broke down in tears when he first read *Perfidy*. Many of the men had similar reactions. If they had been part of a larger community, perhaps the anger and pain they felt would never have risen to the surface. But in their small, isolated congregation, they encouraged one another and convinced themselves that they needed to do something productive with their outrage.

At the same time, they began examining what could rightly be called the "Passion of Jabotinsky." With more force than any other Zionist leader, Jabotinsky had warned his fellow Jews about what Hitler's rise to power would mean for them. Joseph Schechtman's biography, the second and last volume of which, *Fighter and Prophet*, was published at the end of 1961, describes the tragic, final years of Zionism's most hard-line leader. Jabotinsky traveled widely, desperate to convince anyone who would listen that horrors awaited European Jewry. In an address given in Warsaw in 1937, on the mournful ninth day of the Jewish month of Av, Jabotinsky warned that "the catastrophe is coming closer. I become gray and old in these years, my heart bleeds, that you, dear brothers and sisters, do not see the volcano that will soon begin to spit out its all consuming lava." All that was left to do, Jabotinsky said, was "eliminate the Diaspora or the Diaspora will surely eliminate you." He died of a stroke in the Catskills, in upstate New York, in August of 1940. He was visiting a Betar summer camp as part of this campaign to preach his warning to the Western world.

Jabotinsky's words and, even more, the facts of his life had a strong

effect on the group of middle-aged Jewish men in Cleveland. His ferocity stood in stark contrast to what they were coming to see as the
shameful inaction of the Jewish establishment during the war. Those
venerable leaders, some of whom were still alive and leading, had
been too scared to push hard for fear of undermining their own positions. They were too cautious, too respectable. They fought one another more than they fought the government. They weren't desperate
enough. They never got down on their hands and knees and pleaded.
They never lay down in the streets and refused to move. Jabotinsky's
legacy was the opposite. He fought. And—quite conveniently for his
legend—he died so early in the war that, though proxies carried on
his work, it is impossible for history to judge whether his more vocal efforts might have saved more Jews than the supposedly perfidious
Jewish leadership did.

All this reading stirred the Cleveland men to action. What they
needed was a cause. As it happened, Rosenblum and Caron came
across an article published in the January 1963 issue of *Foreign Affairs*
by Moshe Decter, a man described only as the head of an organization
that neither of them had ever heard of: Jewish Minorities Research.
The article, written in an authoritative and dispassionate tone and
filled with facts, was titled "The Status of the Jews in the Soviet Union."

Fiddler on the Roof opened in the fall of 1964 at the Imperial Theater on
Broadway with the round, robust Zero Mostel sweating and swiveling
his hips in the lead role of Tevye the milkman. Based on the folktales
of Sholem Aleichem, the show was heartily embraced by the emer-
gent Jewish middle class as a kind of origin myth. They loved it. It was
their own story—a family in the old country suffers and struggles with
"Tradition!" but then, as the curtain descends at the end of the show,
their bags are packed and some are off to America. Even though most
American Jews were descended from little shtetls like the play's Anatevka—poor Jewish villages in the Russian Pale of Settlement—this
sweetened musical version of their history was the closest the vast
majority had come to thinking about these roots, let alone imagining
that any Jews might still be living there. Only a contrarian intellectual
warrior like Irving Howe, writing in *Commentary* weeks after the musical's premiere, could wring a cultural critique out of something as

schmaltzy and heartwarming as "Sunrise, Sunset." He saw beneath this light entertainment a "spiritual anemia." He hated the effect Broadway had on Sholem Aleichem's bittersweet tales, twisting "everything into the gross, the sentimental, the mammoth, and the blatant." And Howe had a bigger point about the Jewish community, about the sad reasons why they might love the show so: "American Jews suffer these days from a feeling of guilt because they have lost touch with the past from which they derive, and often they compound this guilt by indulging themselves in an unearned nostalgia."

Howe was frustrated with American Jews' ignorance of their origins, the necessary amnesia that had accompanied speedy assimilation. But *Fiddler* also exposed their ignorance of Soviet Jewry. For most of these Jews sitting comfortably in their red, plush seats at the Imperial, the thought that Jewish life continued long after the mournful closing number, a goodbye to "intimate, obstinate Anatevka," seemed almost unbelievable.

In the late fifties and early sixties, there was only one force struggling to make sure that the Jews behind the iron curtain were not completely forgotten: the Israeli government. It had its reasons, of course. In order for the Jewish State to stay both Jewish and democratic, there needed to be a consistently large Jewish majority. It was clear that American Jews would not be leaving their streets of gold anytime soon. That left the Russian Jews, who, at two to three million, constituted the second-largest Diaspora population in the world. As early as February of 1952, with Stalin still in the Kremlin, David Ben-Gurion read to the Knesset the text of a diplomatic note he had sent to the Soviet leader that made it clear Israel's main goal was "the return of Jews to their historic homeland." Later, in 1960, Golda Meir specifically referred to 9,236 Russian Jews who wanted to be reunited with their families. She was responding to an earlier, characteristically flip comment by Khrushchev that there were no Jews in the Soviet Union who wanted to emigrate.

But there was a problem—namely, the Cold War. Israel was still a fragile new state, and it put supreme value on maintaining its shaky diplomatic relations with the Soviet Union. The Soviets had long courted the Arab countries, and relations with Gamal Abdel Nasser's Egypt had grown increasingly warm following the 1956 Sinai campaign. In May of 1964, Khrushchev even paid a visit to Nasser, celebrating the progress made on the joint Aswan Dam project and awarding the Egyptian leader the title of Hero of the Soviet Union, the Order of Lenin, and the Soviet Golden Star.

So Israel was reluctant to make any hostile moves toward the Arabs while the blue and white Star of David flew precariously over its embassy in Moscow. Instead, the Israelis used their position inside the Soviet Union to offer symbolic support to the few Jews interested in maintaining a connection with Judaism or the Jewish State—slipping miniature Jewish calendars and prayer books into pockets of eager Jews at decrepit synagogues, meeting with the few Zionist activists from places like Riga, and, mostly, collecting information on the condition of the community. These efforts, minor though they were, were directed from Tel Aviv by Shaul Avigur, the éminence grise of Israeli intelligence.

Avigur was typical of the short, stocky, taciturn men who started Israel's secret service. He had immigrated to Palestine from Latvia when he was twelve and made his mark leading Aliyah Bet, the clandestine operation set up with the goal of smuggling as many Jews as possible into Israel during the British mandate period. Once Israeli independence was secure, Avigur shifted his focus to getting Jews out of countries that did not permit emigration. In 1952, this operation was shut down, and he went into brief retirement at his kibbutz, Kinneret, on the shores of the Sea of Galilee. But Avigur was soon called back to duty by the foreign ministry, which wanted him to head up a new, highly secretive office known internally by the code word *Nativ* (the Hebrew word for "path") and to the rest of the world as Lishkat Hakesher, "the Liaison Bureau." It was often referred to as the Lishka, which meant, simply and mysteriously, "the Bureau." Everything about the new endeavor was left vague. Avigur's official title was assistant for special matters to the defense minister. His new office was in the Tel Aviv building that housed the foreign ministry. And, strangely, he reported directly to the prime minister (who at the time was his brother-in-law Moshe Sharett). The office's means were unclear, but its mission was laser focused: make contact with the Jews of the Soviet Union and find a way to get them out.

Avigur felt very comfortable with secret operations, but fomenting change from inside the Soviet Union was recklessly suicidal. So half-way through the decade, he decided on a new strategy: he would start an international movement that would apply external pressure on the Soviets. If Avigur could find a way to inspire intellectuals in Europe and the United States to voice concern for the Jewish minority (at a time when concern for minorities was becoming increasingly fashionable), it just might shame the Russians into letting out a few Jews.

By 1955, Avigur had established an informal committee made up of a handful of Jewish professionals in the Diaspora who, together with Israeli government officials, would direct this part of the Lishka's operations. It was given the name Bar.

Avigur recruited Jewish intellectuals in London and Paris to act as his covert agents. Their assignment was to ignite moral outrage over the issue of Soviet Jewry by appealing to public figures. There was to be no talk of emigration. The focus was on demanding cultural and religious rights. For London, Avigur chose Emanuel Litvinoff, a poet and playwright who had grown up in the city's poor East End and had gained some notoriety for blasting T. S. Eliot's anti-Semitism in a 1952 poem called "To T. S. Eliot." On a visit to the Soviet Union, Litvinoff had been struck by the Jewish condition, and it was an article he wrote about this trip that got him the attention of the Israelis. He used the information the Lishka was able to give him to publish a newsletter, first as a supplement to the *Jewish Observer and Middle East Review* and then, from 1959 on, as an independent journal, *Jews in Eastern Europe*. It was the first publication devoted solely to the problem and it reflected Avigur's instructions. Litvinoff was academic in his presentation, even scientific. In Paris, a young Israeli international law student at the Sorbonne, Meir Rosenhaupt, was tapped. He too quickly got to work, approaching thinkers like Jean-Paul Sartre and François Mauriac for their backing.

But the real prize was New York, the great intellectual and Jewish center of the world in the 1950s. By 1958, the Lishka had a man named Moshe Decter on the payroll there. Decter was on the periphery of the group known as the New York intellectuals, the young Jews, sons of immigrants, who were revolutionizing political writing and literary criticism through journals like *Partisan Review* and *Commentary*. They were all leftists who were sobered by the knowledge of Stalin's crimes and were trying to forge a new anti-Soviet liberal philosophy for America. Decter had grown up as the son of an Orthodox rabbi in a small town outside of Pittsburgh, Pennsylvania, and in the late thirties he began studying for the rabbinate at the Jewish Theological Seminary, the premier training ground for Conservative Judaism. The war cut his schooling short, and he served as an infantryman in North Africa and Italy. Wounded in fighting north of Bologna in the middle of 1945, he was shipped back to America, where he finished his seminary studies and began doctoral work for a degree in social studies at the New School for Social Research in Greenwich Village. The school had become a sanctuary for dozens of European intellectuals who had escaped the war. The refugee scholars, such as Hannah Arendt and Max Wertheimer, and the French thinkers, such as Claude Lévi-Strauss, among many others, created a highly charged intellectual environment. Decter became involved with the Socialist Party and other leftist political movements. And by the mid-1950s, he was close to members of what would become known as the *Commentary* crowd, prominent theorists such as Irving Kristol, Nathan Glazer, and Clement Greenberg. In 1954, he even cowrote a book, *McCarthy and the Communists,* criticizing Joe McCarthy as an ineffective and misguided anti-Communist who had undermined his own cause. Around this time, Decter married Midge Rosenthal, a woman who had been a secretary at *Commentary* and was also ensconced in this world.

Decter was an aggressive, persistent, exacting man who could be impatient and prickly. His black horn-rimmed glasses often slipped to the edge of his nose as he took long drags from his cigarettes. He was committed to ideas and knew how to be ruthless in getting his point across. And nothing made him angrier than Communism and the Soviet Union. He saw himself as a liberal Cold Warrior or, as he put it at the time, a "New Deal anti-Communist." When Decter was recruited in 1958 by Benjamin Eliav, Avigur's right hand in running the Lishka and at that time Israel's consul general to New York, he was told that he would have to suppress his extreme anti-Soviet zeal. The Israelis would provide him with detailed information about Soviet Jewish life but he was warned not to make any of it sound like propaganda. "Make it specific with facts," Eliav told him. "Do not exaggerate, and no using any bombastic expressions."

Decter got to work. In order to avoid accusations that he was an Israeli agent, a roundabout source of funding was established. Decter was set up with an office at the World Jewish Congress, the international organization headquartered on the Upper East Side of Manhattan. The WJC paid twenty-five thousand dollars to the American Jewish Congress, another staple of the Jewish world, and the AJC, in turn, paid Decter. He worked alone in a closet-size room with the sign JEWISH MINORITIES RESEARCH on the door. Nobody knew about Israel's role in the operation. Decter published pamphlets and articles about Soviet Jews that combined information gleaned mostly from agents in Russia and his own knowledge of the Soviet Union—how many synagogues had been shut down, what Jewish education was available, whether Hebrew was being taught, how many books in Yiddish had been published in the past year. But more important, he started drawing on his contacts in the liberal political universe to publicize the issue. Norman Thomas, the standard-bearer of the Socialist Party and its six-time presidential candidate, was a mentor of sorts to Decter. After Decter managed to grab Thomas's interest, a whole range of big names followed. By the end of the fifties, Decter had gotten the theologian Reinhold Niebuhr, Supreme Court justices William Douglas and Thurgood Marshall, and Eleanor Roosevelt to sign a letter to Khrushchev protesting the cultural and religious deprivation of Jews (Eleanor laughed at Decter when he approached her with the idea, correctly predicting that Khrushchev would never respond). Many letters followed in which Decter's hand could be detected by the caliber of the signatories, people such as Saul Bellow and Arthur Miller and Bayard Rustin, the bright lights of the New York intelligentsia—all of whom were unaware that Decter was working for the Israeli government.

By the early sixties, Decter was Israel's most prolific disseminator of information about Soviet Jews. He also used his day job, editor of the leftist magazine *New Leader*, to expose the problem. The cover of the September 14, 1959, issue had the words *Jews in the Soviet Union* over a bloody red map of the empire. The cautiousness of the Israelis can be detected in these pages. The plight of Soviet Jews "is not to be compared with their tragic destiny under the Nazis: Covert discrimination, even the most serious deprivation of guaranteed minority rights, is still a far cry from extermination." Even though Decter was in every way ideologically opposed to the existence of the Soviet Union, there was nothing anti-Communist about his argument. On the contrary, he simply pointed out that the treatment of Jews "clearly conflicts with both Soviet constitutional doctrine and the basic internationalist, egalitarian tenets of Marxism-Leninist ideology." Even though Jewish was a Soviet nationality, "the Soviet government deprives its Jewish citizens of the bulk of even the minimal cultural and spiritual privileges enjoyed by all other Soviet nationalities and religious groups. It provides Jews with neither the means for maintaining a full cultural life nor the opportunity to assimilate completely."

By late 1962, Decter had clearly articulated this paradox as the crux of the problem. For liberal American intellectuals concerned with their own government's inability to apply the nation's founding principles to its most excluded minority, this had a familiar ring. It was then that Decter published the article that Caron and Rosenblum saw in the scholarly journal *Foreign Affairs*, the premier venue for Cold War debates. This was the publication in which George Kennan, in 1947, first discussed the idea of containment. With great precision, Decter presented the case against the Soviet Union's treatment of Jews. He wrote as eloquently as he ever had about what restrictions on Jewish life meant, instantly providing in this well-exposed forum a language for speaking about the problem: "Soviet policy as a whole, then, amounts to spiritual strangulation—the deprivation of Soviet Jewry's natural right to know the Jewish past and to participate in the Jewish present. And without a past and a present, the future is precarious indeed."

In Cleveland, Rosenblum and his friend Herb Caron were electrified by the article. It felt to them like a challenge. They had read about the inaction of American Jews in the 1930s; faced with a similar crisis, would they respond the same way, or would they act differently? Emboldened by thoughts of Jabotinsky and shocked that no one was doing anything about this "spiritual strangulation," they approached the local Jewish federation, the body that effectively oversaw all Jewish affairs in the city. When Rosenblum and Caron learned that there was no program in place to educate the community, they pushed for one and got a meager concession: a subcommittee of the federation's governing body was assigned to deal with Soviet Jewry. It was something, and at least this way, thought Rosenblum, they could widen their reach and inform more than just their small enclave. So in the spring of 1963, Rosenblum and Caron and a handful of others from Beth Israel arrived at the subcommittee's first open meeting. Immediately it became apparent that this had been an empty gesture, a way of placating a noisy bunch of nobodies from the other side of Cleveland. By the close of the meeting, the representative appointed by the federation to handle the issue had declared that as far as he was concerned, Soviet Jews were doing just fine.

Dejected and feeling even more like Jabotinsky—unable to rouse a sleeping establishment—Rosenblum and Caron returned to their congregation determined to set out on their own. Soon, an opportunity arose. The only time Soviet Jews appeared in American newspapers in the early 1960s was around Passover. Up until the spring of 1962, Soviet-run bakeries had made matzo in their ovens and sold it in the government stores. Sometimes people baked the matzo in their own homes and sold it—though this was technically illegal, as it was a form of private enterprise. But just before Passover in 1962, the Soviet authorities announced that from 1917 to 1961, they had unknowingly been violating the Communist principle of total separation of church and state, and therefore the government's baking of matzo would cease. That month, the frail, white-bearded chief rabbi of Moscow, Yehuda Leib Levin, stood before his elderly flock at the city's faded central synagogue on Arkhipova Street and announced that given the government's edict, they would be exempt from the holiday's strict dietary laws. American Jewish religious organizations were shocked by this development and tried unsuccessfully to ship matzo to the USSR. The baking ban elicited a protest in front of the United Nations in New York by religious students from Yeshiva University. Even though the *New York Times* reminded readers of the forgotten fact that, being overwhelmingly nonreligious, "the majority of the Jews in the Soviet capital would not be aware of the presence or absence" of matzo, the paper still published at least a dozen stories about the issue that spring.

As Passover of 1963 approached, the media was again saturated with coverage, starting in mid-March with an Associated Press report that the Soviets had denied the chief rabbi's application to reinstate the baking. Other stories followed, about four men arrested and charged with profiteering for illegally selling matzo and about an Italian performance of *The Diary of Anne Frank* at Moscow's Maly Theater (an unusual event in itself, possible only because of Khrushchev's thaw) in which the audience, almost all Jews, wept openly. They were moved by the play, but as the *Times* reported, they were also distraught because it was Passover and the holiday had been "hampered by Soviet regulations forbidding State bakeries to produce the traditional matzohs."

Herb Caron came to the conclusion that the best way to change the matzo situation was to deprive the Soviets of something *they* wanted. The Cleveland Jewish community obviously didn't have this power. But when President Kennedy announced at a press conference on October 9, 1963, that he was going to permit the sale of $250 million worth of surplus American wheat and flour to the Soviet Union, Caron saw his chance. He would get all the clergy in Cleveland to sign a telegram to Kennedy asking that some of the wheat be earmarked for making matzo. The majority of the city's twenty rabbis quickly signed on, with two notable exceptions: the Zionist leader Rabbi Abba Hillel Silver and Rabbi Arthur J. Lelyveld (Lelyveld's bloodied face would be in the newspapers the following summer after he was attacked with a lead pipe for helping register black voters in Hattiesburg, Mississippi). Both prominent rabbis thought the Jewish community should avoid such brazen interference in Cold War politics. Undeterred, Caron sent out his telegram:

In selling wheat to the Russians, America's traditional concern for reducing human suffering would be made most clear by an official and urgent plea that the wheat not be used as an instrument of discrimination against a minority group. Specifically the Soviet government should make this wheat available as desired use as matzos which are essential for Jewish prayer observance . . . we respectfully submit that American wheat should not become an instrument of the official Soviet policy of persecuting the Jewish minority group.

The telegram was ignored. But Rosenblum and Caron felt emboldened. They didn't need the slow-moving establishment. They would act independently. Moshe Decter in New York inspired their next move. That same October, only a few days after Kennedy's offer of wheat, Decter organized a daylong conference in New York at the Carnegie Cultural Center that drew on all the contacts he had amassed thus far. It was an unprecedented intellectual show of force for Soviet Jewry, and an indication, at least among the enlightened classes, that the issue was indeed gaining traction. James Pike, the idiosyncratic, liberal Episcopalian bishop of California, presided. In attendance were Martin Luther King Jr.; Robert Penn Warren; Walter Reuther, the union leader; and Decter's mentor Norman Thomas. The objective was to draft a statement demanding that the Soviet Union improve the condition of Jews. The process was not entirely smooth. According to the *New York Times,* "some participants held that the original statement was 'too strong,' others contended it was 'too moderate,' and still others that it was 'too long.'" The final list of demands was restrained but, nevertheless, the first of its kind. The signatories that day decided to call themselves the New York Council of 100, and the document was an "Appeal to Conscience," with the following seven demands:

1. To permit Jewish education in the Soviet Union in all its forms
2. To allow Jewish cultural institutions and Jewish artistic life
3. To remove obstacles to Jewish religious life
4. To allow religious and cultural bonds with Jewish communities of the world
5. To permit separated Jewish families to be reunited
6. To eliminate the anti-Jewish character of the official campaign against economic crimes
7. To undertake a vigorous educational campaign against anti-Semitism

Rosenblum and Caron answered this appeal by setting up an organization of their own. Though their motivation was Jewish, they wanted to mirror the universal, humanitarian tone of the New York Council of 100. Caron managed to convince the mayor of Cleveland to be the honorary chairman. Their board too was highly ecumenical, including the monsignor of the local Catholic parish and a prominent black city councilman. The rabbis were almost an afterthought. The name of the group was precisely chosen: since its only goal was to raise awareness about state-sanctioned anti-Semitism, it would be the Cleveland Committee on Soviet Anti-Semitism (CCSA). The first grassroots Soviet Jewry organization was born via press release on October 17, 1963, just a few days after the New York conference.

The new CCSA met twice a month at the City Club with the whole board. They made up a letterhead with Decter's seven points printed on the back. Herb Caron became the executive chairman. His first project was a survey to gauge existing knowledge of the Soviet Jewry question, to get a better idea of what they were working with. He sent out a questionnaire to two thousand rabbis of many different denominations. Over the fall and winter of 1963 and into 1964, they received more than a thousand responses. Caron recorded the answers using IBM punch cards. Most congregations had no awareness of the issue and certainly no response to it. To the question "What role has your congregation taken in informing the community about the deteriorating position of Soviet Jews?" the majority answered "None." To the extent that they had thought about the issue, the rabbis confessed that they were under the impression that the Jewish establishment was taking care of the problem. The response of Murray Stadtmauer, rabbi at the Jewish Center of Bayside Hills in New York, was typical: "It has been my understanding that Jewish organizations have been making representations to Soviet officials at the UN and the Soviet embassy and that only when these fail, will an open, public protest effort be undertaken. Has the time come?"

The group had started to attract outside attention. In November of 1963 Rosenblum put together a pamphlet called "Soviet Terror Against Jews: How Cleveland Initiated an Interfaith Protest" in which he described the problem and asked the reader to sign on to an "Appeal to Conscience of Soviet Leaders." The publication was sent to congregations all over America. The CCSA took out large ads in the Cleveland newspapers and got some immediate notice from the press. People from other cities started writing Rosenblum and Caron, asking to be placed on the group's mailing list. The two were a little shocked by the attention. The CCSA had no office — Herb Caron's house was the mailing address — and no time to answer what were often deeply felt letters, like the one from Lynne Gershman of Springfield, Illinois, who first wrote at the beginning of 1964 in a sloping, elegant cursive on flowery stationery. She offered Caron "a few statistics about us": "my husband, a Sales Representative for the Burroughs Corps., is 31. I am 27, we have three children ages 2.5, 5.5, 7.5, married 9 lovely years, living in Springfield for 7 years, activities include PTA, JWV, Masons, Jr. Chamber of Commerce, etc. How typical can you get?" As to why she was interested in the issue,

> the answer is many faceted and probably the same for many people—after reading reports intermittently in the press, a feeling of sadness I could not shake off, deep gratitude for a wonderful country, loving family, happy children whose future waits secure and free, a belief that the fortunate are the only hope of those who are not, behind it all the awareness of the persecution of Jews through the ages and the fact that it could easily have been our children, our family, in despair. If we don't try to help, who will? My husband feels these things as deeply as I do, as I am sure countless others do.

———

As Soviet Jewry began to penetrate the consciousness of the community in 1963, a number of Jewish American politicians began raising their voices. Most notably were the Senate's two Jewish members and a Jewish Supreme Court justice, the three of whom emerged as a troika of sorts, the unofficial leading voices in government on the issue: Senator Abraham Ribicoff, a Democrat from Connecticut (who had taken Prescott Bush's seat in the 1962 election); Jacob Javits, the liberal Republican from New York; and Arthur Goldberg, who had been appointed secretary of labor but had joined the Supreme Court in 1962, replacing an ailing Felix Frankfurter. All three were the children of Jewish immigrants. All three had also grown up poor: Ribicoff had spent his teenage years working in a zipper and buckle factory; Javits was raised on the Lower East Side. And Goldberg was the son of poor Polish immigrants (from the town of Oświęcim, the original Polish name for Auschwitz); his father worked as a produce peddler in the impoverished West Side of Chicago.

In the fall of 1963, as Lou Rosenblum and Herb Caron were setting up their small group in Cleveland, Goldberg started working with the two senators on getting Kennedy or his then secretary of state, Dean Rusk, to take up the issue. Javits had already warned Congress at the end of September that the time for a protest that was "loud and long" had come; what was needed was a "great surge of indignation—the determined protests not only of Jews but of all free peoples who treasure the rights of the individual." Rusk did meet with the three, but he thought it best that for the sake of Cold War diplomacy, any gripe with the Soviet Union should be expressed by Jewish leaders, not the State Department. Behind the scenes, Averell Harriman, the former ambassador to the Soviet Union who was then serving as assistant secretary of state, received a memo saying that the State Department's "position has been that it is difficult for our government to contribute to direct solution of the problem of minorities in a territory where a foreign government exercises sovereign control." But even more so, "the Department believes that formal U.S. Government representation to the Soviet Government would not be in the best interests of Soviet Jews. These representations could, in fact, antagonize the Soviet Government to the detriment of Soviet Jews."

It was apparent that they would get nowhere with the State Department, so Ribicoff and Goldberg decided to go directly to the president. If Kennedy was going to listen to anyone, it would be these two. Both men had helped the young senator from Massachusetts get elected and had been duly rewarded with high-profile posts (before winning his Senate seat, Ribicoff had been the secretary of the Department of Health, Education, and Welfare). But the president couldn't do any better than Rusk. Only a year had passed since the Cuban missile crisis, and the last thing he wanted was to irritate Khrushchev. He suggested that a delegation of American businessmen headed for the Soviet Union could discreetly broach the subject. But this also seemed weak. Ribicoff and Goldberg asked the president if they had his permission to talk to the new Soviet ambassador, Anatoly Dobrynin, to arrange a visit to Moscow to address Khrushchev. Kennedy said he wouldn't stand in their way.

The subsequent four-hour meeting with Dobrynin on October 29 was even more frustrating. The Soviet ambassador, who had already proven himself during the missile crisis to be a smooth translator of Soviet policy for the American administration, categorically denied that anti-Semitism existed in the Soviet Union. Point by point, he refuted all charges of religious and cultural deprivation, and he said the accusation that economic trials were being used to execute Jews was baseless. "We are proud of our Jewish citizens," Dobrynin told them. "They are treated like everyone else." He would promise the Americans nothing.

A few weeks later, on November 19, Goldberg and Javits met in New York with the members of the powerful Conference of Presidents of Major American Jewish Organizations. The Supreme Court justice and the senator reported on their disappointing meeting with Do-brynin. Goldberg then presented the first tangible proposal: the Jew-ish leaders should organize a conference for the following spring that would gather together various Jewish groups in order to establish a unified plan. This would at least telegraph to the Soviets that the com-munity was serious, and it might even put some pressure on the Amer-ican government. He cautioned, though, that if they moved forward, they should be careful to avoid linking the problems of Soviet Jewry with the U.S.-Soviet relationship in any way. Like the Israelis, Gold-berg wanted the protest to be carried out on a higher plane. As for the "troika," Goldberg promised they would keep pressuring the president to arrange a meeting with Khrushchev. Three days later in Dallas, Ken-nedy was assassinated.

The Conference of Presidents of Major American Jewish Organiza-tions had the power to mobilize but not quite the will. Founded in 1953, the Presidents Conference, as it was colloquially known, was a reaction to complaints from members of the Eisenhower administration who were dealing with a constant stream of Jewish leaders arriving to dis-cuss the issue of Israel, each one making essentially the same points. A deputy of Secretary of State John Foster Dulles suggested that the major organizations, including the three big defense ones—the Ameri-can Jewish Congress, the American Jewish Committee, and the Anti-Defamation League—and the various religious authorities consolidate their forces, at least on the topic of Israel. They formed an umbrella group of twelve. This provisional conference soon became a perma-nent organization with its own executive. It also became the de facto foreign policy arm of the American Jewish community, especially fol-lowing the 1956 Sinai campaign, when Israel's belligerence needed to be explained and defended.

Though the issue resonated with some of the individual members of the Presidents Conference, the condition of Soviet Jews, as much of it as was known, had never provoked anything more than a rhetoric of concern. Goldberg's modest proposal—of directing attention to the problem with a communitywide conference—was anathema. The Jewish establishment was plagued by its own stultifying redundancy. In 1952, Jewish leaders concerned about their own paralysis had commissioned a study, the McIver Report, which came to the conclusion that there were too many organizations doing the same thing and wasting their energies fighting over limited resources. The three defense organizations were all founded early in the century and, despite slight differences in tone and organizational culture, all had essentially the same goal: to fight anti-Semitism at home and abroad. Then there were the organizations that represented each of the three major religious denominations, Reform, Conservative, and Orthodox. These sometimes united under the title of the Synagogue Council of America. On top of these groups were the community's two major umbrella organizations: the Presidents Conference, the official political voice of the community, and the National Jewish Community Relations Advisory Council, which also included representatives of all the other organizations. This group was a coordinating body founded in 1944 to synchronize the activities of Jewish communities at a local level. All this led to a near-constant jockeying for funds and power. There was already some resentment about the Presidents Conference siphoning money and purpose from the individual groups. Any new initiative—even a conference—would necessarily mean more competition.

Adding to this anxiety was the fact that most of the men who made up the leadership of the Jewish establishment did not think it was time to abandon a strategy of quiet diplomacy. Nahum Goldmann was the very embodiment of this view. A dapper elder statesman of the Jewish world, Goldmann was both president of the World Jewish Congress and head of the World Zionist Organization, which effectively made him the most powerful Jewish leader after the Israeli prime minister. He was a Lithuanian Jew who had grown up in Germany and worked in the Jewish division of the foreign ministry until Hitler came to power. Though a lifelong Zionist, he believed in the importance of maintaining a vibrant Jewish community in the Diaspora (part of the reason he founded the World Jewish Congress, an organization devoted to Jewish life outside of Israel).

Goldmann believed foremost in caution, in using a scalpel rather than a sledgehammer. In early 1964, he told an interviewer from the Hebrew University's student publication the *Ass's Mouthpiece*, "It is wrong to generate too much activity on behalf of Russian Jewry, because this could endanger the very existence of three million Jews." He also thought it was simply bad strategy—and bad manners—to put the Russians on the spot. Even though he had been willing to support the efforts of the Lishka and Moshe Decter—Goldmann was one of the few who knew about the secret arrangement—he wanted to avoid a head-on clash with the Soviets at all costs. If he could have it his way, the issue would be settled at a private meeting between him and Khrushchev, not by any sort of public action. He was often heard to say that all he needed was a bottle of vodka and an hour with the Politburo. This thinking quickly gained him the reputation of being a *shtadlan*, the old Yiddish expression for the individual in the shtetl who served as a liaison between the villagers and the local Gentile authorities. It was the *shtadlan* who would privately beg for the revising of anti-Jewish laws. *Shtadlonus* became derogatory shorthand for a leader who never wanted to be too obtrusive, who didn't feel he had the right to make demands. When young Jews like Lou Rosenblum and Herb Caron in Cleveland looked at what leaders like Goldmann had done during World War II and the way they were now turning their backs on Soviet Jewry, they saw *shtadlonus*.

Goldberg, Javits, and Ribicoff were so eager to further the cause of Soviet Jewry that they had dropped this task in the wrong lap. Only a singular figure—someone from outside the walls of the entrenched establishment—would have the independence and the nerve to demand more.

If Goldmann was the consummate insider, a mannered and worldly German Jew with brilliantined hair, elegant double-breasted suits, and sometimes a pipe clenched between his teeth, then Abraham Joshua Heschel was the epitome of the outsider. There was something biblical about him, with his unruly cloud of white hair and his elfin goatee. His lilting Yiddish accent made his constant stream of aphorisms sound poignant rather than pretentious. When Heschel told his rapt listeners that there "should be a grain of prophet in every man," they heard his words and saw his wizened face and believed that Heschel's body must contain a silo's worth.

Heschel was born in Warsaw, a descendant of the great rabbis of Eastern Europe, among them his namesake, the Apter Rebbe, and even—though he was often too modest to admit it—the eighteenth-century founder of Hasidism, the Baal Shem Tov. Heschel, a prodigy in his youth, was trained at a traditional yeshiva and later received his doctorate in philosophy from the University of Berlin. In 1937, Martin Buber, escaping Europe for Palestine, named the thirty-year-old Heschel his successor as director of the Freies Jüdisches Lehrhaus, the innovative Jewish Free University in Frankfurt started by the Jewish philosopher Franz Rosenzweig. But the Nazis soon kicked Heschel out of Germany, and in 1940, after a few wandering years, he was offered a teaching position at the Hebrew Union College in Cincinnati, the main seminary of the Reform movement. It was an invitation that saved his life. But this strain of Judaism turned out to be too starved of ritual for him, too liberal, and in 1946 he found a new home at the Jewish Theological Seminary on the Upper West Side of Manhattan. Here, at the prominent school of Conservative Judaism, where he taught ethics, he began writing the beautifully composed books of Jewish philosophy that gained him a reverent following.

The rabbis at JTS, more concerned with parsing the meaning of Talmudic and Mishnaic passages, never accepted Heschel's eccentricities, his deep love of the spiritual, his desire to make Jewish law come alive. They treated him as an outcast, not even allowing him to teach classes in mysticism, the subject for which he was renowned. He was constantly lamenting to his students that they were being trained simply for synagogue administration. How was it possible, he wondered aloud, for them to complete the entire curriculum without taking a single course on the Jewish conception of God? "Intellectual evasion is the greatest sin of contemporary Jewish teaching," he warned. "Urgent problems are shunned, the difficulties of faith are ignored . . . Jewish thought is sterile. We appeal to Jewish loyalties, we have little to say to the imagination." Through his books *Man Is Not Alone* (1951) and *God in Search of Man* (1955) and in his lectures, he tried to show another way, one that might help Jews confront a post-Holocaust world in which God's love, even among his believers, could not be taken for granted. Rather than waiting for God to seek out the faithful for revelation, Jews were urged to find a state of awareness in which they could more easily be reached by him. Social action was a way to achieve this: through bearing witness, exposing oneself to the sins of the world and then rectifying them. This, Heschel told his students, had to be at the center of Judaism: "A Jew is asked to take a leap of action rather than a leap of thought. He is asked to do more than he understands in order to understand more than he does."

The year 1963 was a big one for Heschel. In January he made his first foray into the civil rights struggle and met Martin Luther King Jr. (a friendship that would provide the most enduring and endearing image of the black-Jewish alliance: the two walking arm in arm to Selma in 1965 with leis around their necks). At the Conference on Religion and Race, a gathering in Chicago of almost a thousand clergy, Heschel made a memorable speech, striking some of the same chords as King. They both quoted Amos: "Let justice roll down like waters, and righteousness like a mighty stream." They both referred to the famed Protestant theologian Reinhold Niebuhr, a personal friend of Heschel's and one of King's intellectual idols. When King told the delegates that "one must not only preach a sermon with his voice. He must preach it with his life," it was a concept that Heschel understood. For Heschel's part, he spoke much as Joachim Prinz would at the March on Washington, seeing the black struggle as an extension of the Jewish one. "The exodus began," he said, "but is far from having been completed. In fact, it was easier for the children of Israel to cross the Red Sea than for a Negro to cross certain university campuses."

For Heschel, however, the problem of Jewish identity was not going to be solved solely by securing black civil rights. He lamented the fact that American Jews seemed to be so alienated from their past, unaware of the tradition from which they descended. And he was also racked with Holocaust guilt. Though he had narrowly escaped death, much of his family hadn't. When a reporter from the Yiddish newspaper the *Day-Morning Journal* asked him where he had been in 1943, Heschel answered, mournfully, that he had just arrived in America, did not speak the language well, and commanded no attention from the Jewish leadership. Still, he said, "This does not mean that I consider myself innocent. I am very guilty. I have no rest."

In that interview, conducted one night in the fall of 1963 in the book-lined living room of Heschel's Riverside Drive apartment, he revealed his bitterness about American Jews' ignorance of Soviet Jewry. "Russian Jews are an abstraction for Americans. They know about Florence, Naples, Miami, [the] Waldorf Astoria, but what do they know about Berdichev, Odessa, Vilna, Warsaw! This exemplifies the indifference."

Out of this anger emerged a sermon. Heschel could not contain his frustration any longer, and on September 4, at a conference at the Jewish Theological Seminary examining the moral responsibilities of the rabbinate, he delivered an impassioned plea for action:

> If we are ready to go to jail in order to destroy the blight of racial bigotry, if we are ready to march off to Washington in order to demonstrate our identification with those who are deprived of equal rights, should we not be ready to go to jail in order to end the martyrdom of our Russian brethren? To arrange sit-ins, protests, days of fasting and prayer, public demonstrations to which every Russian leader will not remain indifferent? The voice of our brother's agony is crying out to us! How can we have peace of mind or live with our conscience?
>
> What is called for is not a silent sigh but a voice of moral compassion and indignation, the sublime and inspired screaming of a prophet uttered by a whole community.
>
> The six million are no more. Now three million face spiritual extinction.
>
> We have been guilty more than once of failure to be concerned, of a failure to cry out, and failure may have become our habit.
>
> The test of the humanity of a human being is the degree to which he is sensitive to other people's suffering.
>
> This is the deepest meaning of our history: The destiny of all Jews is at stake in the destiny of every Jew; the destiny of all men is at stake in the destiny of every man.

Heschel was appealing to the universal and the particular at the same time. Like the Israelis and Decter, who had been trying to graft the cause onto a more general fight for minority rights, Heschel described his reasons as humanitarian and just as important as civil rights for blacks. But he also spoke at another register, a lower, deeper one, calling on Jews as Jews. "We have been guilty," he said, using words that had hardly ever been uttered. The Holocaust was an American Jewish "failure." This was the guilt that was pushing Lou Rosenblum and Herb Caron in Cleveland. Saving Soviet Jewry was not just about man's responsibility to man but also about a Jew's responsibility to Jews.

Heschel's sermon was deeply affecting. It was sent out to two thousand Conservative rabbis, repeated in synagogues all over the country on Rosh Hashanah and Yom Kippur that year, and reprinted in Jewish newsletters and bulletins. He assumed that these stinging, accusatory words would provide the necessary spur for action. Initially, some meetings did take place, including one with the Synagogue Council of America that explored ways of initiating a national campaign. Among the proposals was one similar to Arthur Goldberg's: a massive conference. But as soon as the meeting ended, the plans dissolved. Unbeknownst to Heschel, the concurrent efforts to involve the government—now reeling from the Kennedy assassination—were also going nowhere. The Presidents Conference was paralyzed. On the last day of December 1963, Heschel, impatient and frustrated, wrote a letter to major Jewish leaders in which he issued a threat: if they didn't come up with a plan of action soon, he would publicly call for one himself.

Shame accomplished what reasoning and pleading had not. Not long after Heschel's ultimatum, the national Jewish leadership began preparing for a major conference to be held the spring of 1964 in Washington. The gathering would be as broadly representative as possible, bringing together religious leaders, Jewish *machers*, congresspeople, and civil rights activists: an American Jewish Conference on Soviet Jewry.

Before they even arrived in Washington, Lou Rosenblum and Herb Caron—who had had no trouble getting themselves invited as delegates from Cleveland—were convinced that the conference was going to be just another exercise in Jewish handwringing. They had received a booklet in the mail that included fourteen resolutions that were expected to emerge from the two-day meeting. It was a laundry list of toothless actions—prayer vigils and loosely defined educational activities—not the sustained effort the Cleveland group was hoping would be established. The closest any of them came to that goal was in the fourteenth resolution, which stated vaguely that "immediately upon the adjournment of this Conference, the Presidents of the co-sponsoring national Jewish organizations will meet for the purpose of considering how best to assure that the plans set herein will be systematically implemented."

Rosenblum and Caron decided to agitate. With nothing to lose and few contacts they could draw on, they wrote a letter to the other delegates rallying them to oppose the resolutions: "The question is not whether the coming Conference will denounce Soviet anti-Semitism in sufficiently strong terms. (They will denounce it and this is known to all in advance.) The crucial question is: Will the Conference provide the mechanism for bringing the information to the millions, now uninformed and silent, so that their outcry can be brought to bear." The letter continued, "If we cannot take the step of establishing an 'ad hoc' committee, funded and staffed to coordinate and implement this protest, the Conference may well frustrate the hopes of thousands of persons expecting definitive results. Any plan short of the creation of such an 'ad hoc' group is unthinkable."

The stately but placid vision that greeted them at the Willard Hotel on Sunday, April 5, the conference's opening day, was not promising for men looking for revolution. Every exclamation mark and cocktail seemed scripted. The five hundred delegates, comprising all the major leaders of American Jewry, sat inside the main ballroom flipping through folders of information on the Soviet Jewish plight. The carpet and curtains were a creamy salmon pink; faux-marble columns flanked the doors; a pastoral fresco covered the ceiling. Journalists from every major news organization crammed the back of the hall, with even *Pravda* and *Izvestia* represented. The conference opened with the reading of telegrams of support from prominent Americans, among them Martin Luther King Jr. and George Meany, president of the AFL-CIO.

Conspicuously absent was Nahum Goldmann. He wished the conference well but had serious concerns that it might be counterproductive. Two months before the gathering he had written from Geneva to Lewis Weinstein, the newly appointed chairman of the Presidents Conference, chastising him with a paternalistic slap that only a man in his position could deliver: "Knowing how responsible a man you are, I am sure you will see to it that the conference acts in a responsible way. Demagogic speeches and exaggerated resolutions may do a lot of harm, not only to the demands for which we fight but to the three million Soviet Jews." He went on to warn that "any formal intervention by the USA will probably be rejected by the State Department, and rightly so, and may be very harmful to the very sensitive Soviets. Just imagine if the Soviet Union would hold a conference on the civil rights situation of Negroes and send a formal delegation to Krutchev [sic], asking him to intervene. What would be the reaction in America to such a procedure? And the Russians have the right to react in the same way."

Also absent in any public way were the Israelis. They declined to send a representative to speak at the conference. Outwardly, they were still maintaining a face of passivity. Behind the scenes, however, Israelis were everywhere. The representative of the Lishka in New York was Meir Rosenne (formerly Meir Rosenkampf), the man who had been their contact in Paris, and he was a part of the planning at every level. So was the Israelis' American operative Moshe Decter.

Rosenblum and Caron began lobbying among the delegates. And they found, to their surprise, that people were receptive. Many were still reeling from *Judaism Without Embellishment*, a book that had recently been published in Kiev by the Ukrainian Academy of Sciences. Written by one Trofim Kichko, a Soviet academic, it was anti-Semitism of the crudest sort, filled with caricatures that would have been at home in Julius Streicher's *Der Stürmer*. Lishka agents got hold of a copy and passed it to Decter, who had portions of the book and the captions to the worst cartoons translated. At a press conference at the end of February, Morris Abram, the famed civil rights lawyer (three years earlier, he had gotten Martin Luther King Jr. released from his first jail sentence) and president of the American Jewish Committee, held up the book and proclaimed it a "hodgepodge of misinformation, distortion, malicious gossip and insulting references to Judaism." He read aloud passages to the scribbling reporters: "'No matter what they do—selling matzohs or parts of the Torah, carrying out the rites of burial or circumcision, wedding or divorce, they think above all of money and they despise productive work.'"

The building crescendo of matzo deprivation, the economic trials, and the Kichko book sensitized many delegates. And in rhetoric, the conference strayed from Goldmann's brand of cautiousness. Speaker after speaker railed against the Soviets. But Rosenblum and Caron moved around the room pushing for more. They met with delegates in coffee shops, in the lobby, in their rooms, asking them to think beyond the conference. "What's next?" Rosenblum asked. "When you go back to your community, what are you going to be able to tell the people back there they should be doing? There's no national organization you'll be able to turn to. There's nobody you can turn to for support."

They were convincing. And on the final day of the conference, when the hour came to vote on the resolutions, Rosenblum and Caron shouted from the floor of the ballroom that they had an addition to the list, a fifteenth resolution. Morris Abram, who was acting as chairman, tried to explain from the dais that they could not add resolutions, that the motions were already decided and closed to further discussion. People began yelling in protest. One man shouted, "Is this democratic or not?" There was enough commotion that Abram had to turn around and confer with the other leaders and then with Rosenblum and Caron. When Abram addressed the crowd again, he read out the proposed fifteenth resolution composed by the Cleveland group but asked that it be admitted as an addendum to the already written fourteenth resolution, which he then read in its final version: "'Immediately upon the adjournment of this Conference, the presidents of the co-sponsoring national Jewish organizations will meet for the purpose of considering how best to assure that the plans set out herein will be systematically implemented. *It is our further proposal that the presidents develop the means of continuing this Conference on an ongoing basis, adequately staffed and financed, to coordinate and implement the resolutions of this Conference.*'"

Abram asked for a voice vote on the new addition to the resolution, and a resounding and nearly unanimous "Yes!" came from the delegates. Herb Caron and Lou Rosenblum felt victory flutter in their stomachs. In their minds, they had brought down the establishment.

The next day, they went back to their congregation on the west side of Cleveland, satisfied that they had finally managed to turn the community's attention toward saving Soviet Jewry, that they had succeeded where even Jabotinsky in his time had not. They thought that their work was done. But all that had been achieved so far was talk. Movements, as everyone knew well by 1964, were not built on words. They needed feet marching. And in New York City, five hundred miles from Ohio, where hundreds of thousands of American Jews lived, no one had yet taken to the streets for Soviet Jewry. If the mass movement that Heschel and Lou Rosenblum and the Israeli agents of the Lishka desired was to become reality, it would have to begin there.

———

In early 1964, on one of his first days in the city, Yaakov Birnbaum, a tall Englishman in his late thirties, made his way up the sloping streets of Washington Heights, the hilly immigrant enclave at the northern corner of Manhattan. He glanced up at the tenements and back down at a smudged address on a scrap of paper. From behind the shuttered windows of Cuban fruit and vegetable markets came crackling radio sounds of big-band charanga music, the spicy brass and drums of Tito Puente. It was a Sunday morning and the streets were empty, but Birnbaum could hear Spanish voices pouring out of open apartment windows, parents screaming at children, husbands berating their wives, old women singing. And Birnbaum, though tired from his train ride, stopped to listen. This was America, he thought. The energy, even in this empty, wet street, was brimming.

He felt this every time he arrived in a new place. It offered possibilities, what he called sparks. The idea came from a kabbalistic origin myth: At the moment of Creation, the container that held the eternal light shattered and smashed, throwing sparks all over the world. The job of the holy man was to go looking for these sparks and collect them. For the past two decades, Birnbaum had lived a nomadic existence, never staying in one place for more than a few years. He was still not tired of looking.

Birnbaum, then thirty-seven, wore a thick black Vandyke beard that made him look older. He had grown up in London, the son of a Viennese-born professor of philology who had fled mainland Europe in 1933. Birnbaum spent his youth in the ominous shadow of World War II. Until the age of six, he lived in Hamburg; the city's university had asked his father to develop an institute for Ashkenazi studies, one of the first of its kind. Birnbaum never forgot the day he was assaulted by a group of German boys who jumped into his family's garden and stuffed dirt in his mouth. The family escaped to England, and they received British citizenship just in time to avoid being labeled as refugees and placed in internment camps. Yaakov's father had been recruited to work in the uncommon-languages department of the National Censorship Bureau in Liverpool. Day after day, Solomon Birnbaum, an exacting, academic-minded man, read frantic pleas from Jews all over Europe relating the details of a mass-extermination campaign. Sworn to secrecy by his superiors, Birnbaum's father never openly spoke about what he knew. Instead, he returned home every night, sat down calmly to dinner with his family, and talked about the intricacies and variances of Hebrew script, his academic specialty.

Starting in late 1940 and continuing into 1941, Liverpool suffered a fierce bombing campaign, a blitz not unlike London's; it took the lives of thousands. The tense atmosphere and the hints in newspaper accounts allowed Birnbaum to deduce the extent of the nightmare unfolding just across the North Sea. At the Liverpool high school Yaakov attended, the Gentile students thought he was hysterical for his fevered warnings about Jewish massacres. "Hey, you hear this bloke Birnbaum?" one of the older boys once said. "His people are providing good fertilizer for the Germans."

When the war was over and Jewish refugees, many emaciated and close to madness, began arriving in London, Birnbaum felt that he had found his calling: He joined every effort aimed at resettlement and readjustment. He taught them English, helped them to get social services, searched for lost family members. The work ignited him. It was active, engaged, socially conscious—everything his father's job had not been. Helping one group led to helping another. In the early 1950s, Birnbaum made trips to the slums surrounding Marrakesh, aiding destitute Moroccan Jews who were hoping to immigrate to the newly founded Israel. When he did settle briefly, it was to take a job as the director of the Jewish community council of Manchester, England. But two years spent dealing with a stuffy Jewish bourgeoisie depleted him. He began to wonder why Jewish life had no blood running through it, why these Diaspora Jews were so intent on assimilating into a culture that seemed devoid of any connection to tribe, that stripped away any spiritual identity.

In the early 1960s, he embarked on the journey that would lead him to Washington Heights. He traveled to France and around the United States. He wanted to see models of religious communities more alive than that of the Manchester Jews' he had just left. He explored Buddhism and talked to Trappist monks; he spent time in Kentucky with Thomas Merton, who got a dispensation from his vow of silence so he could speak with Birnbaum. Now nearing forty and without a wife or children, Birnbaum felt that despite all the work he had done with refugees, he had failed to accomplish anything substantial with his life. His father remained distant and disapproving. Birnbaum had managed to learn a little Yiddish on his journey and wrote the old man letters in the language. In response, he received brief thank-you notes along with pages of corrections. To Solomon Birnbaum, a man who prized expertise, his son's failure was that he did not know any one thing well. The more Birnbaum traveled, the more intense his search for an enlightened community became and the more urgently he felt the need to prove something.

His travels eventually took him to Israel in 1963, where he visited kibbutzim, agrarian socialist communes, and tried to see whether he fit into the new society that was flourishing there. But Israel at the time was a rugged place in search of rugged men. With his suit and groomed beard, Birnbaum looked more like an elegant mortician than someone ready to jump on a tractor or fire an M-16. He did contemplate staying, though, and he went about trying to find work, but he quickly realized he wasn't qualified for anything. Jewish rescue wasn't a legitimate job description, and Birnbaum, fiercely independent, refused to be a simple social worker and toil within a bureaucratic machine. Israel was not providing the answer.

And then Birnbaum discovered a few sparks.

He had always been drawn to young people. Even as he grew older, Birnbaum found they understood his drive and his passion much better than adults his age. He tended to get excited, animated, when he talked about ideas, speaking furiously and with great ardor. To adults, this marked him as an eccentric, but young people found nothing off-putting about his vigor. It made him interesting.

Birnbaum found a group of American rabbinical students who shared his search for rejuvenation. Young and idealistic, they were studying at Jerusalem yeshivas for the year, and they longed, like Birnbaum, to make Judaism more dynamic. Students such as Arthur Green, a pimply-faced student from the Jewish Theological Seminary in Manhattan, and Yitz Greenberg, a young rabbi from Brooklyn who was on leave from his professorship at Yeshiva University, had long talks with Birnbaum about how to make Judaism relevant and meaningful in a modern world. Birnbaum felt he had found people who understood him. They encouraged him to come to America. They told him there were young people there craving a more engaged Jewish identity.

He soon arrived on that street corner in Washington Heights. On a wet and crumpled slip of paper in Birnbaum's palm was the address of a librarian from Yeshiva University who had a room to rent. Birnbaum had landed in America in the middle of 1963 and had been living in Rochester, New York. Five months had passed, during which Birnbaum worked with senior citizens at the Rochester Y, but in early 1964 he decided he hadn't come to America to languish in a dreary upstate town. New York City and the friends he had made in Israel were calling to him.

Birnbaum's room was small and crowded with the librarian's musty books. But it would do. Its major asset was that it was on Amsterdam Avenue, only a few minutes from Yeshiva University. Birnbaum had made a conscious decision to settle not far from the institution, an area that was an island of young religious Jews—though an island that had grown smaller in the 1950s with the arrival of Puerto Ricans and Cubans to Washington Heights. Birnbaum didn't know exactly what he wanted to do but he did know it would involve Jewish students, and the best place to find them was Yeshiva University.

He stumbled through his first few weeks, like any new arrival to the city. He sat in his room scouring the *New York Times* and the *Daily News* every day, looking for work and interesting stories. It was winter, and the rain that had greeted him turned into snow. Birnbaum wore his large Russian fur hat as he walked to Yeshiva to continue his discussions with Yitz Greenberg or down through Harlem to reach the large brick edifice that housed the Jewish Theological Seminary, where he met more young rabbinical students.

One day in March, three months after Birnbaum arrived, Greenberg showed him a recent issue of *Foreign Affairs*. In it was the article by

Moshe Decter that had so stirred Lou Rosenblum and Herb Caron, "The Status of the Jews in the Soviet Union."

Decter's article made Birnbaum remember the troubled, distraught faces of the refugees he had seen after the war. Some of them were Russians who had escaped the Soviet Union by pretending to be Polish and claiming displaced-person status. They told Birnbaum of the vast network of prison camps Stalin had established in the east. They spoke of endless detentions and mass executions in faraway forests. But that was nearly twenty years ago. Birnbaum knew the situation had been difficult but hadn't realized it had remained so.

He soon made the acquaintance of a businessman named Morris Brafman, a Viennese Jew who had barely escaped the Nazis and had recently started a small group to raise awareness about the problems facing Soviet Jewry.

Birnbaum found Brafman at his offices on Madison Avenue, where he ran a lingerie business. A sturdy man, passionate and irrepressibly garrulous, prone to speechifying despite his thick German accent, Brafman was a staunch philosophical follower of Jabotinsky. He told Birnbaum about his American League for Russian Jews, a group he and a few other "Jabo" businessmen had started. Birnbaum, so eager he couldn't get the words out fast enough, said he wanted, needed, had to help in whatever way he could.

The following week, Birnbaum and a few Columbia and Yeshiva students went to a meeting of the league; it was held at a Manhattan banquet hall, and Brafman had invited a few local politicians. Speakers who had recently visited the Soviet Union described the tattered and torn prayer shawls they'd seen on the old men at the synagogue; they reported that the authorities had refused to give more land for Jewish burial grounds. Brafman stood up to speak and bellowed: "Do you realize what they are doing? They want to erase them! They want to destroy them!" The hall was filled with many of Brafman's fellow businessmen, and they all nodded vigorously in agreement.

Despite Brafman's bluster, Birnbaum felt roused. And he could see the students were moved as well. When the meeting was over, they walked outside in a daze. The feeling that had been slowly building, that this cause had great potential power, was now confirmed. Not only could it save three million Jews in the Soviet Union; it also could revitalize the millions of Jews in America. This could galvanize them, get them emotionally involved. He already knew that young American Jews could be moved to action for the cause of freedom. They had turned up by the thousands at the March on Washington the previous year. And preparations were being made for the Freedom Summer of 1964, when hundreds of young Jews would infiltrate the segregationist counties in the South and help black sharecroppers register to vote. What if he could convince these young activists to direct this same energy toward their own people? It was in many ways Abraham Joshua Heschel's vision, and Birnbaum was just the man to carry it out. Walking together through the streets of Manhattan, past closed butcher shops and kosher markets, Birnbaum asked the students what they thought about a youth movement for Soviet Jewry.

When Yaakov Birnbaum heard about the Washington conference, he was furious. He had read an article in the *Jewish Exponent* that quoted Morris Abram speaking shortly after the gathering: "If Soviet authorities invite us to a discussion of the status of Soviet Jewry . . . we will be prepared to form a delegation to go to the USSR and meet with Soviet officials of the highest level." He was shocked that a Jew like Abram, so committed to using direct action in support of blacks in America, could sit back and do nothing tangible for Soviet Jews other than wait for a phone call from Khrushchev. To Birnbaum, the conference was just another example of what he had seen in Manchester. The dynamism had been drained out of American Jewry.

In the weeks following the Brafman meeting, he realized that he was ready to throw himself completely into this cause—to focus his restless spirit. Birnbaum had always looked to his grandfather Nathan Birnbaum as a model. A nineteenth-century Viennese intellectual, Nathan Birnbaum had coined the term *Zionism*. He was an eclectic man, a passionate assimilationist who became one of the original proponents of Jewish nationalism (in the late 1880s, he published the first Zionist journal, *Selbst-Emanzipation*) and then turned toward Yiddish, translating shtetl writers such as Sholem Aleichem and I. L. Peretz. By the end of his life, the once freethinking secularist who had refused on principle to eat in kosher restaurants founded his own neo-Hasidic group, the Olim, or Ascenders, and searched for a spiritual expression of Judaism. He embraced each one of these dramatic shifts with a prophetic spirit, and he was a constant reminder to Birnbaum to pursue a dynamic, engaged life.

Birnbaum tried to combine his grandfather's passion with his father's meticulousness. To the students who started coming to his cluttered room in increasing numbers, this conviction translated at times to a comical self-righteousness. They would jokingly call him Messiah behind his back and giggle at the speech impediment that caused his every *r* to become a *w*. But Birnbaum's impassioned tirades mesmerized the students and gave the cause more urgency.

In mid-April, with the help of his Columbia students, Birnbaum got permission to hold an organizing meeting in that university's Philosophy Lounge. He scheduled it for Monday, April 27, and he went to work typing up an announcement. He called the group the College Students' Struggle for Soviet Jewry. The leaflet he designed radiated his ambition for the new endeavor.

> The time has come for a mass grass-roots movement—spearheaded by the student youth. A ferment is indeed at work at this time. Groups of students all over New York are spontaneously coming together and hundreds of signatures have been collected.
>
> There is a time to be passive and a time to act. We believe most emphatically that this is *not* the time for quietism. We believe that a bold, well-planned campaign, to include some very active measures, can create a climate of opinion, a moral power, which will become a force to be reckoned with.

His roommate, the librarian, had access to an old mimeograph machine and ran off a few hundred copies. Students distributed the fliers at Yeshiva, City University, Columbia, the Jewish Theological Seminary, and New York University.

On Monday night, the oak-paneled Philosophy Lounge was packed with students. Tables were pushed aside to make room, and many people had to stand in the back against the massive bookshelves that lined the walls. Birnbaum hadn't expected so many students. He tried to count how many there were and gave up after a hundred and fifty. He could feel his heart beating fast.

Morris Brafman gave the opening address, pumping his arms and decrying the "spiritual and cultural strangulation of our brethren." Birnbaum walked around the room nodding and handing out typewritten fact sheets that detailed the problem in more specific terms, from the number of synagogues closed to the lack of prayer books. When Brafman achieved his final flourish, telling the students to "fight with all you've got," Birnbaum asked for suggestions from the audience about what they wished to do next. Immediately, a hand shot up. A Columbia freshman stepped forward and offered to sing a chant he had thought up. Birnbaum said he should come to the front of the room. The boy cleared his throat dramatically and the students laughed. "'History shall not repeat,'" he sang. "'History shall not repeat.'" The room grew quiet. There was no need to specify which history he meant. The trial of Adolf Eichmann in Jerusalem three years earlier was still fresh in their minds. The news from the Soviet Union, especially coming from the fired-up Brafman, sounded ominous to them. Maybe it heralded the start of another extermination campaign. Suddenly the meeting was heavy with significance and emotion. It was more than Birnbaum could have hoped for.

Another student suggested they hold a rally as soon as possible. Birnbaum told them that the soonest they could demonstrate would be Friday—which, to his great satisfaction, was May Day. He got a thrill out of subverting Soviet symbols. For the group's name, he eventually dropped the word *College* and went with Student Struggle for Soviet Jewry, a conscious wink at the Marxist concept of class struggle. Even if the students didn't catch the irony, he found it hilarious. But May 1, he told them, was only four days away.

Birnbaum set up an office in his bedroom, pushing aside the stacks of books and manila folders stuffed with newspaper clippings. The students sometimes wondered how he had managed to amass so much paper in the short time he had lived there. His roommate, frustrated at the incessant phone calls from students, offered to hook up a separate line in the bathroom.

Several students came forward to help with the organizing. One of these was Glenn Richter. A native of the outer boroughs and a student at Queens College, Richter had a reedy frame and always wore a green trench coat and a peddler's cap. At nineteen, he was also an amateur comic in search of an audience. Sometimes he talked in a Donald Duck voice. When he did speak normally, every sentence contained a pun or wacky rhyme. "That's Glenn Richter, as in the Richter scale," he cracked. Before he'd started spending most of his time at the barely functioning typewriter in Birnbaum's room, Richter had worked at the New York office of the Student Nonviolent Coordinating Committee, the most youthful of the civil rights groups spearheading the voter registration campaign in Mississippi. But the mood at SNCC had started to shift slightly over the past ten months, since King's speech in Washington. Richter used to sit in the office at lunch with a yarmulke on his head, and he'd get approving looks from the SNCC workers, many of whom had friends who were nursing bruises from the increasingly violent white retaliation in the South. But more exclusionary forces within SNCC, led by its aggressive and rising star Stokely Carmichael, were beginning to take over, making young Jews feel unwanted by the civil rights movement that had so seduced them. Richter welcomed a cause where he could unabashedly be a Jew and work hard for, as he saw it, the redemption of his own people.

Days of organizing out of Birnbaum's bedroom ensued. Richter manned the typewriter. Students contacted professors at all the major universities. Birnbaum followed up with phone calls and letters. Congressman Leonard Farbstein of Manhattan, seeing a possible photo op for his upcoming campaign posters, agreed to march. By Friday afternoon, Birnbaum's and the students' fingers were dyed blue from the ink of the mimeograph machines.

The Soviet mission to the United Nations, the protest target, was an imposing white building on a residential block of Sixty-seventh Street on the Upper East Side. At nine in the morning on May 1, Birnbaum paced the street nervously. He rubbed his beard. He took off his white straw hat and put it on again. No one was there yet, but Birnbaum tried to convince himself that at least a handful of his own student friends would show, at least the few who were absolutely committed. In an hour, they started trickling in, young adults dressed as if they were on their way to synagogue. Birnbaum had told them to look sharp. The boys wore black suits and thin dark ties, and the girls wore long dresses and pumps, not high heels. Birnbaum had tried to think of everything.

By ten there were a thousand people, mostly students, but some parents as well. They picked up the hand-lettered signs that Birnbaum had been churning out all week: I AM MY BROTHER'S KEEPER and LET THEM PRAY, simple black paint on white poster board. Congressman Farbstein, in glasses and a porkpie hat, put on a sandwich-board sign and insisted on standing at the head of the line.

Just like the early civil rights protesters in the South, the students marched two by two. Birnbaum stood to the side, speechless for a few minutes, and watched what seemed like a great mass of young people organizing themselves. He couldn't believe this was happening. Birnbaum picked up a sign and started marching. The kids were singing the hymn "Ani Ma'amin," the Hebrew phrase meaning "I believe" sung over and over again.

The demonstration lasted four hours and was covered by all the major newspapers and news agencies, from the AP to the *New York Daily News.* The big three TV networks were also there. It was described as an unprecedented gathering for a cause hardly anybody outside the Jewish community had been aware of, and it was depicted as subdued and respectful. The *New York Times'* reporter Irving Spiegel, who wrote a page-two story, remained for the entire four hours. He told Birnbaum he had stayed so long because it was refreshing to see such an orderly protest in contrast to the water cannons and German shepherds that had begun to mark the civil rights marches. Birnbaum was glad; he wanted the protest to be "responsible." The article on the march in the *National Jewish Post and Opinion* reported that the students "made it a point not to protest against the convictions of Jews for economic crimes, feeling that anti-Jewish motives would be harder to prove. They also avoided urging mass immigration, attacking the Russian people, or indulging in name-calling."

Days after the May 1 protest, Birnbaum, electrified by the sense that his vision was being fulfilled but scared that the students, who were now entering finals, might lose interest, sent an excited memo to his small flock. "Our great demonstration attracted over 1000 college students from all over the city," he wrote. "We think that the strength of feeling here expressed will catch on spontaneously all over America and beyond, as well as among Christian students and civil righters. According to experienced observers, our movement has very great potential. Out of this student ferment there is emerging a wave of constructive, dynamic yet responsible action."

A few days after the American Jewish Conference on Soviet Jewry adjourned, presidents of the twenty-four organizations that had sponsored the conference paid a visit to Secretary of State Dean Rusk at the White House. They delivered the list of demands generated by the meeting, measures needed to restore Jewish life in the USSR. The most provocative was the last point, which called on the Soviets "to make possible on humanitarian grounds Soviet Jews who are members of families separated as a result of the holocaust to be reunited with their relatives abroad." In order to soften a point that might seem like Cold War meddling, the leaders also read a statement to Rusk affirming that "our action is not to be considered in any sense as an exacerbation of political conflict between East and West. This is not a political issue." What they were asking, essentially, was for the government to become aware of the problem.

Halfway through the White House meeting with Rusk, there was a knock on the door from Myer Feldman, recently appointed assistant special counsel to President Johnson and the administration's Jewish liaison. Feldman said the president wanted to meet with a delegation of the group in a half hour. Six delegates from among the most prominent organizations were quickly chosen. Johnson entered, and in his usual jocular and domineering Texan manner, he put his arm around Morris Abram's shoulder and showed what looked like sincere concern as he talked knowledgeably for fifteen minutes about Soviet Jewry. Half a year had passed since Kennedy's assassination, and Johnson was still trying to prove himself to a Jewish community that had played such a pivotal role in securing Kennedy's slim margin of victory in 1960. Only a month before, Johnson had received a Presidents Conference delegation at the White House and told them, "You have lost a good friend. But you have found a better one in me."

Johnson promised to meet with the Soviet ambassador Dobrynin and raise the matter. And the next day, April 17, when the Jewish leaders opened the evening papers, they found that Johnson had held his first encounter with the envoy. It wasn't clear what the two discussed, but the Jewish leaders felt a Johnsonian wink in his statement to the press that he had "some specific things on his mind" as he entered the talks.

And yet, the Jewish establishment was floundering. In a closed meeting at the end of April to finalize the logistics of the new American Jewish Conference on Soviet Jewry, the sponsoring presidents decided there would be no staff, office space, or specific budget. Instead, the twenty-four organizations would rotate the home of the conference, a different one taking over every six months. The American Jewish Committee had the first round and agreed to loan out one of their young staffers, a Soviet specialist named Jerry Goodman. But that was it. The conference would have an itinerant existence and no real funds. The Israelis at the Lishka had wanted more. But the American Jewish world just didn't sense the urgency.

In the middle of June, Birnbaum, emboldened by the early success of Student Struggle, decided to test the seriousness of the conference. He was hoping to send informational kits to all the major Jewish summer camps, and he needed money. The group was subsisting on Birnbaum's small savings and the three-dollar membership fee collected from each student. This meant he had total independence, much like Rosenblum and Caron. No one could dictate what the group should or shouldn't say—an important prerequisite for its goal, which was to draw as much attention to the cause as possible. But Birnbaum didn't write off the establishment completely. He needed resources. So together with the group of students he now called his executive committee, he decided to crash a steering committee meeting of the new American Jewish Conference that was taking place at the Delmonico Hotel in Midtown Manhattan.

As soon as he entered, he was confronted by George Maislen, the president of the United Synagogues of America (an association of Conservative Jewish synagogues) who had been elected the first chairman of the steering committee. Birnbaum made his case, asking for money to fund the summer-camp information kits. Maislen later described the interaction in a memo: "We asked Mr. Birnbaum whether his group would accept the discipline of the American Jewish Conference on Soviet Jewry and he informed us that under no circumstances would they recognize any form of discipline and only required money from us."

Birnbaum stormed out, offended that his proposal to cooperate was misread as his begging for a few dollars. To the eyes of the Jewish establishment, this group of religious teenagers and their bizarre leader, an overexcited Englishman, seemed uncontrollable. Maislen, who also wrote in his memo of how he had quelled a recent independent Soviet Jewry protest by a group of rabbis from Philadelphia, telling them it was "not in our best interest," described Birnbaum as a kind of outlaw and a nuisance. With annoyance, he wrote that the "Birnbaum group," as he referred to the students, was clearly getting funding from some outside force, an "agency" that he wouldn't name but that anyone involved with Soviet Jewry understood meant the Lishka.

Only a month after the May 1 protest, Birnbaum made it into the papers again with a weeklong interfaith fast in front of the Soviet mission. A Catholic priest, a Protestant minister, and a rabbi each fasted for a day. Images of the group linking arms and singing Hebrew freedom songs appeared in all the major dailies. Eventually, Abram and the other Jewish leaders began paying more attention to the man behind the protests. It was difficult to believe that in such a short time, this newcomer, this total unknown, had managed to organize such a wide array of events.

On the morning of October 16, Birnbaum realized he had a problem. His bedroom was full of placards that read KHRUSHCHEV, LET MY PEOPLE LIVE, which the group members were planning to use in two days at a rally near Seward Park in the Lower East Side. But that morning, Birnbaum and the rest of the world learned that after eleven years, Khrushchev had been ousted. Birnbaum gathered his volunteers in his room. "Listen," he told them. "We cross off *Khrushchev* and we replace it with *Moscow.*"

This was an important rally, the culmination of a half a year of work, and Birnbaum wanted it to be perfect. As he saw it, he had finally infiltrated the White House. Myer Feldman, the president's liaison to the Jewish community, was coming with a message from Johnson himself. And Birnbaum's correspondence with Senator Jacob Javits was paying off. Birnbaum had written to Javits in July with a harsh critique of the conference. "Who is leading whom?" Birnbaum wrote. "This is leadership in a vacuum, quite lacking in a grass roots basis. Most notable is its remoteness from the future of American Jewry sitting on the campus right now—more than 300,000 of them who [don't] have the vaguest notion of who they are or what they are doing or supposed to be doing."

Not only did Javits show up to speak on October 18, he also brought the non-Jewish senator Kenneth Keating. The rally drew more than two thousand people to a long program with speeches by many of the rabbis and university professors who had been supporting the students' work since May. Birnbaum wanted to give everyone a chance to speak. Only ten months had passed since the rainy day in January when he'd arrived in Washington Heights. He had managed to build an organization from scratch, a dynamic one with dozens of passionate students. But he wanted to grow beyond the solid core of religious and socially conscious New Yorkers who had kept it going so far. The summer kits and the news coverage had provided national exposure. The fact that two of the Jewish establishment's most prized commodities, Javits and Feldman, were attending the rally suggested that his activist approach had captured a spirit that had eluded the movement thus far.

The moment was almost religious. Here were Jewish politicians, professors, and students unabashedly singing Hebrew songs in public in support of unseen Jews on the other side of the world. For him, it was both a cry of conscience and an inkling of the Jewish reawakening it might bring about. Birnbaum's ultimate hope was that this surge of enthusiasm would be met by Soviet Jews themselves, that they too might begin protesting their fate. The world didn't know, after all, exactly what it was these Jews wanted. But for Birnbaum, it didn't really matter. He looked out at the chanting, applauding, exuberant crowd. A lifetime of searching for sparks and here he was, suddenly feeling the warmth rising off hundreds of individual flames.

3

A Circumcision at the Dacha
1966–1969

THE SIX MEN met on the evening before the Day of the Great October Socialist Revolution. Factories and offices were closed in preparation for this forty-ninth anniversary of the 1917 Communist takeover—a blizzard of red flags, rolling tanks, and speeches piped over loudspeakers declaiming the glory of the Bolsheviks. The men could get away without attracting attention. For a gathering spot, they had chosen Pushkin, a small town just south of Leningrad; they met in a park near the Tsarskoye Selo Lyceum, the nineteenth-century boarding school that had once educated the ruling elite of czarist Russia, including the young Alexander Pushkin. Fall had stripped the trees bare, and when they finally sat down at a lone wooden picnic table—three friends on one side, a group of three others facing them—it was cold and they shivered, pressing their shoulders together.

Anyone who saw the six middle-aged men in caps and scarves with their shoulders hunched together would have thought they'd chosen an unusual site to meet on such a miserable, gray day but nothing worth reporting to the local KGB bureau. And yet, what the men were discussing was the height of sedition. They were making a verbal pact to form an underground Zionist organization—primarily for the long-term goal of aliyah, but more immediately to increase Jewish self-awareness in their city.

This was not so different from what other small groups of Jews were working toward in most major cities in the mid-1960s. But there was one important—and dangerous—distinction. Instead of meeting at someone's house and sharing samizdat, they were starting an organization. They would collect dues and, most risky of all, write up a constitution for their group. This instantly made their activities illegal and gave the authorities grounds for prosecuting them. Other than State- and Party-mandated groups, such as the Komsomol, independent organizations were illegal in the Soviet Union. The six men debated briefly about whether to take this step. In other cities, such as Riga and Moscow, Jews had purposely avoided formalizing their activities. The Leningrad group, however, decided that there was much to gain from acting together. They would be more efficient; everyone would know what everyone else was doing. And they were seduced, like Mendelevich in Riga with his small group of friends, by the Leninist model of ideologically committed cells, each working independently but in a coordinated way toward the same radical objective.

That this risky leap was taking place in Leningrad made it even more significant. The men sitting around the picnic table were—unlike the Jews of the Baltics—pure products of the Communist experiment, now almost fifty years old. In Yosef Mendelevich's home in Riga, the memory of Jewish communal life persisted, a Passover Seder was not an oddity, and the sound of Yiddish was still heard, if only between those four walls—the Soviet occupation of Latvia was, after all, only two decades old. But Jews in the heart of the Soviet Union—living in a state that denigrated religious identity as a principle and among a people who had always been suspicious of them—had experienced a complete and total disconnect, one that had placed them at a three-generation remove from any positive sense of Jewishness.

Leading the group that sat on one side of the table was Gilya Butman, small and loud, a mischievous jokester with eyes that squinted to thin slits when he smiled. Next to him was his childhood friend Syoma Dreizner, a man with the massive shoulders and the stoic quiet of a longshoreman. They had grown up in thoroughly assimilated Leningrad Jewish families, becoming aware of their Jewish identity only when they were taunted in elementary school (a problem Dreizner always solved with his fists). Their parents explained that there was no shame in being called a Jew. They should take pride in defending themselves. But this is where the conversation usually ended. From elementary school onward, Butman and Dreizner were constantly reminded of their Jewishness, though it meant almost nothing to them. Even the ancient names that appeared on their birth certificates, Hillel and Solomon, respectively, were unknown to them until they were older.

It took Butman many years to turn against the system and become a Zionist. First, he had to experience anti-Semitism, the whispering kind that existed in Soviet society, of unspoken quotas, constant insinuations, and *zhid* (kike) spoken just loud enough for the intended target to hear. When he applied to universities, he was rejected, first by the Institute of Foreign Languages and then by the city's journalism school—both times because of the fifth line on his passport. When he finally got to the head of the registration line at the journalism school, the tired-looking admissions secretary looked at his unmistakably Jewish face and said, "I advise you not to apply. You won't pass." When he tried to enter the air force in 1953, enrolling in a fighter-pilot program that the Komsomol was desperately recruiting for, he came under strange questioning by the credentials committee. He was asked for his nationality and his patronymic, which was Izraylevich. An older man, the only one in civilian clothes and surely from state security, asked Butman if he had any relatives abroad. Butman wasn't sure, but he answered no. "Do you know why I am asking you in particular about this?" the man queried Butman. "The Jewish people are dispersed throughout the world. Many have relatives in various countries. Intelligence agencies of imperialist powers utilize this and we must take it into consideration." Butman never made it into a fighter jet.

These incidents scarred Butman, each one turning his thoughts more and more dissident. He eventually went to law school, worked as a criminal investigator in a far-off northern Soviet republic, spent some time unemployed and hungry, got a job as a proofreader in a publishing house, and, in 1957, found some stability as a detective in the Leningrad Criminal Investigation Department, where he was given a pistol and a locker to keep it in. And all this time, the feeling of alienation that overtook him every time he saw *Jew* underlined on his application forms continued to grow. Every limitation made him despise the state more. He realized that he was surrounding himself

only with Jews, that he had no more Russian friends, that he no longer sought their approval the way he had as a boy. Instead, he and his
friend Dreizner found themselves talking about Israel, trying to gather
as much information as they could. During the 1956 Sinai campaign,
Butman would go to the public library and stare at issues of the London *Times*. He couldn't read English but he would gaze jealously at the
photos of bearded Israeli paratroopers smiling widely.

The men's curiosity grew. It eventually drove them to visit the city's
Central Synagogue on Lermentovsky Prospect one night. It was Simchat Torah, the holiday celebrating the end of the Torah reading cycle.
It was a joyous day on which religious Jews were commanded to dance
and sing and drink. Starting in the mid-1950s, outside the major remaining synagogues of the Soviet Union—the Grand Choral Synagogue in Moscow, the Great Synagogue in Leningrad, and of course
the narrow street in front of the Riga synagogue—Jews had begun
an annual tradition of gathering on this night. Someone, usually an
older person, one of those Stalin-era Zionists, a former Gulag prisoner,
would lead a dancing of the hora. Songs in Hebrew and Yiddish would
be sung. Young people would come, more as a way to meet other young
Jews than out of any religious conviction. They came because it was a
good time, because they might find a future husband or wife. Most had
never set foot near the synagogue before. On the Simchat Torah when
Butman and Dreizner went to the synagogue, they found small clusters
of people gathered in front of the ornate but faded concrete Moorish-
style façade. In the center of one group was a woman who seemed to
be talking about an uncle who was sending her letters from Israel. Butman was intrigued. He approached her, but she quickly became quiet
and started to walk away. Butman followed her. He walked behind her
block after block, aware that the woman was frightened of him. When
he finally managed to stop her, she signaled to him not to say too much
in the street and handed him her address and phone number.

They eventually found a mentor in this woman, Leah Lurie, and an
entry into the small and elderly circle of Zionists in the city. Over the
next few years, Butman and Dreizner listened to Israeli music and read
samizdat together, practicing Hebrew with the help of a text the Israelis had put into underground circulation, *Elef Millim* (A Thousand
Words). They loved the other world they found in the little apartments

of these aging Zionists, many of them former Gulag inmates. They managed to keep it all secret until 1960, when they were questioned by the KGB in connection with the arrest of Natan Tsirulnikov, a World War II veteran and engineer who had been caught with multiple copies of two innocuous little magazines produced by the Israeli embassy, *Vestnik Israilya* (*Israel Herald*) and *Ariel,* covering mostly arts and literature. The Israelis had kept the writing completely clean of politics. But this mattered little to the KGB. Butman and Dreizner were swept up in the investigation and subjected to three days of questioning. Butman lost his job with the police. But he seemed to care less now about all the turbulence Zionism was bringing to his life. He became a refrigerator repairman, work that gave him an excuse to visit the houses of other Jews. He discussed Israel with those who would listen, offered to teach them Hebrew (he had managed to secure a samizdat copy of *Elef Millim*), and sometimes even invited them over to listen to radio broadcasts. He had no real hope of leaving the Soviet Union. No one was even talking about emigrating in 1960. But he knew that he had ceased to be a normal Soviet citizen.

This kind of radical break wasn't unique to Butman. Sitting across the table from him in that park in Pushkin was Arkady Shpilberg, who led the other cell. A true bon vivant, he had a strong jaw, thick dark hair, and a barrel chest, the kind of man who spent his summers snorkeling in the Black Sea, always accompanied by a beautiful girl. But he too was restless. He wanted to do more than just feel different; he wanted to understand what his difference meant. In the summer of 1965, while standing in line to buy a plane ticket for a vacation in the Crimea, he overheard someone say the Hebrew word *Palmach.* Shpilberg struck up a conversation with the man, a Jew from Riga, who went on to tell him about what was taking place there. That man gave him the name of Mark Blum, the militant activist organizing the gatherings at Rumbuli.

Later that year, Shpilberg visited Riga. He found Blum and discovered, for the first time, a truly unabashed Jew—open, free, and unafraid. Blum taught him how to dance the hora and gave him a few Israeli albums. He promised to send more material to Shpilberg and his friends in Leningrad. And he helped with another problem. Shpilberg had not been circumcised. This was not uncommon for Jewish men in the Soviet Union. Mohels, the traditional circumcisers, were scarce and were allowed to function only under very tight supervision. Many parents didn't want to bring undue attention to their children. Like calling a child Grisha instead of Hillel, not circumcising an infant boy was a way to avoid future problems. But Shpilberg wanted to have the procedure done. Blum said he would try to find him a mohel; there was more likely to be one in Riga than in Leningrad.

In the spring, Blum fulfilled the first part of his promise: a young woman, Margarita, arrived at Shpilberg's home with a copy of Dubnow's history. This was invaluable to the group. Shpilberg began an affair with Margarita that would lead to a marriage proposal within a few months. In the summer of that same year, 1966, Shpilberg went to Riga to see about the other part of the promise, the mohel. With no legal permit to stay in the city, he set up a tent in its forested outskirts. Blum introduced him to the old man. But a few days after Shpilberg's arrival, Geula Gill came to town, and in the riot that followed Mark Blum was arrested and detained.

The mohel, who was not legally registered to practice his trade and who had used his knife on an adult only once, was nervous about circumcising Shpilberg. He wanted to find a place far outside the city. Luckily, a friend knew of a dacha in the countryside that was not being used. She gave the mohel the keys, and, together with a medical student who carried a small black suitcase filled with anesthetic, they left for the country. Shpilberg wasn't sure what the medical student did wrong, but after a dozen shots, Shpilberg could still feel when the mohel began to cut. He just closed his eyes and squared his large jaw and let the tears fall. When it was done, and Shpilberg sat there with his pants off and a white bandage wrapped around the wound, there was a knock on the dacha door. The husband of the woman who had given the mohel the key was doing his army reserve service nearby and, after drinking with his friends, had decided to stop by the dacha. When he saw Shpilberg with his pants down, he yelled at the men to get out. The mohel and the medical student, both afraid of getting caught for illegal activity, hurried out, holding up Shpilberg between them. They took the train back to the city, and only then was he bandaged properly.

For the next month, Shpilberg lived in the tent and went to Riga every day to have his bandages changed by the mohel. He saw Margarita and told her what he had done. She gave him a Star of David pendant made out of scrap metal. He asked that she no longer call him Arkady. From then on he wanted to be known by a new, Hebrew name: Aron.

One can imagine that these Leningrad Jews had to take such extreme measures because they were up against a conquering ideology that had worked hard to erase their Jewishness. But in truth, the Soviets never knew exactly what to do with their Jews. The Marxist ideal *was* to create one single, socialist society that would eliminate all national, religious, and even ethnic attachments. But in practice, the Soviet Union's attitude about nationalities, and Jews in particular, was schizophrenic. On the one hand, from the Bolshevik Revolution onward, Jews were viewed as a people who would soon assimilate into nonexistence and were therefore denied any real opportunity to flourish as a separate culture. On the other hand, the Soviet state never stopped reminding Jews that no matter how assimilated they became, they were still somehow foreign. It was a paradox that the Soviet leaders perpetuated. By mandating a separate nationality in the internal passport, which needed to be displayed every time one applied for a job, registered at a university, or enlisted in the army, they ensured Jews had a feeling of otherness. If the Soviets had simply eliminated the fifth line of the internal passport, they could have assimilated hundreds of thousands of Jews who had no other reason than that line to think of themselves as Jews. Stalin clearly believed, as he stated in his 1913 essay "Marxism and the National Question," that Jews did not constitute a unique people, but he also set up the ill-fated Jewish autonomous region in the far eastern Birobidzhan as a Soviet promised land for his Jews, and in 1932 he enshrined the internal passport law, making Jews as separate from Russians as Ukrainians were from Latvians. It seemed the desire to integrate Jews was weaker than the totalitarian state's need to control its populations—and to do this, the Soviet bureaucracy needed to keep tabs on everyone.

The paradox of Soviet Jewish life wasn't always so clearly etched. Large numbers of Jews had enthusiastically taken part in the Bolshevik Revolution with hopes that the new egalitarian social order might make their lives easier. It was a generation marred by memories of the violent czarist-era pogroms at the turn of the century. Men like Lev Davidovich Bronshtein (later known as Leon Trotsky) thought the only way to prevent explosions like the 1903 Kishinev massacre—in which dozens of Jews were killed by mobs that were driven by the belief that Jews were ritually murdering Christian children for their blood in order to use it in making matzo—was to abandon Jewish identity for international proletarian struggle. Liberation from provincial religious identity, Marxism preached, would open people's eyes to the only meaningful human distinction: that between workers and owners. And once the Soviet Union became a reality, a space did open up for secular Jewish culture. Stalin initially encouraged national expression. In fact, there was an effort to create a culture that was, in Stalin's words, "socialist in content, national in form." The new Jewish section of the Communist Party, the Evsektsii, cracked down hard on Zionism, Judaism, and Hebrew, all perceived as remnants of the Old World. But Yiddish was allowed, and by the 1930s, there was a flourishing of Yiddish theater and newspapers. One of the greatest Jewish actors of his time, Solomon Mikhoels, the heart of the Moscow Yiddish Theater, could be seen onstage as King Lear. Famous Jewish poets such as Itzik Fefer were allowed to write and publish in Yiddish, producing work such as the poem "So What If I've Been Circumcised": "So what if I've been circumcised / With rituals, as among the Jews? / Field winds have tanned my middle-sized / Pale, dreaming feet to darker hues." During the war, Stalin formed the Jewish Anti-Fascist Committee and made Mikhoels its head; together with Fefer, Mikhoels embarked on a celebrated tour of the United States, urging political and financial support for the Soviet Union.

But before Jews—or any Soviet citizen, for that matter—could become too comfortable in this Communist paradise, everything changed, brutally and swiftly. In the late 1930s, Stalin undertook a bloody purge that would end the lives of hundreds of thousands of his imagined enemies—most of the Party leadership; the military; the intelligentsia; and the kulaks, small landowners. The Jewish Bolsheviks, like all the other revolutionaries, were taught a cruel lesson during those years, and many wound up dead or in the Gulag. But it was the period after the war and just before Stalin's death, in 1953, that was darkest for Soviet Jewry in particular. In January of 1948, a few months before the birth of Israel, Mikhoels was murdered by the KGB, his death made to look like a car accident. The same year, the Jewish Anti-

Fascist Committee was dissolved. Hundreds of Yiddish actors, writers, and journalists were sentenced to long prison terms. By 1950, Stalin had established a full-scale campaign against what he called "rootless cosmopolitanism." Nothing captured Russian anxiety about Jews more perfectly. They were perceived as an unnatural presence. Russia was not their motherland, and they were trying to influence, pollute, somehow outsmart everyone else. Newspapers were filled with accounts of Jews as traitors and subversives; accused currency speculators and embezzlers were publicly tried and executed. On the night of August 12, 1952, fifteen people connected with the Jewish Anti-Fascist Committee, including the poet Itzik Fefer and four other Yiddish writers, were tried for various trumped-up crimes; thirteen of them were shot in the basement of Lubyanka Prison.

This frenzy of anti-Semitism came to a head in the first months of 1953 when Stalin, increasingly paranoid, arrested a group of Jewish doctors and accused them of plotting to poison members of the Soviet political and military leadership. The initial arrest included thirty-seven physicians but the numbers soon grew. Other "doctors' plots" proliferated. And though it has never been conclusively verified, there is evidence that Stalin was using these plots to justify a wide-scale deportation of the entire Jewish population to Siberia. Rumors of long lists of deportees spread through Jewish households in Moscow and Leningrad. Then, miraculously, Stalin died, and the plotters were released. Jews, however, had already suffered months of newspaper articles and public pronouncements portraying them as sinister elements, poisoning the water supply and killing babies.

Stalin was long dead by the 1960s, but he cast a dark and menacing shadow for decades to come. Whenever Jews began to feel safe, normal, he was the terrible reminder that things could always change. He was the potential of brutality, the coiled threat of physical harm, that lay in the backs of Jewish minds when they looked at that fifth line of their passports. The twenty- and thirty-year-olds growing up during the thaw had been impressionable children in the dark days of the Doctors' Plot. They had watched their mothers taunted and called *poisoner* on the subways, heard the hushed talk of deportation lists, remembered their doctor fathers abandoned by all their fearful patients in one day.

In the terror of his last years, Stalin *had* succeeded in crushing Jewish identity. A Jew in Leningrad or Moscow in 1964 thought of himself as a Jew simply because an anti-Semite said he was or because the state made him declare it every time he had to show his passport. But it did not mean much else to him. Jewish boys were not circumcised. Bar mitzvahs were nonexistent. There was no legal way to teach Hebrew. Other than a few old men who went to the remaining synagogues, and even then more out of habit than love, Jewish life had been completely gutted.

By the time the generations raised in the 1960s came of age, little of Jewish substance remained — maybe a Yiddish lullaby, a pair of silver candlesticks, a grandparent who still fasted on Yom Kippur. Jewishness was a negative identity, a reminder of avenues that were closed. Being Jewish meant that there were certain universities one couldn't hope to attend, certain jobs that were for all practical purposes forbidden. Being Jewish was a natural disadvantage, a handicap, like being born deaf or missing a limb, and it meant you would just have to work harder to overcome it. The Jew of this generation growing up in a big Soviet city had a different culture: Russian. The books he loved were Russian and the only language he knew was Pushkin's. And yet, that he was different was as inescapable as the nose on his face. The dichotomy was difficult to live with. What turned men like Butman and Shpilberg into Jewish nationalists was the realization that they no longer wanted to try.

When the two small groups in Leningrad decided to join and become cells of a larger entity, they immediately faced the problem of any merger: reconciling their various visions. The ultimate goal was never in question. They had settled on that in Pushkin. But the question of how to get there was very much up for debate. To start, would it be an open struggle or a clandestine one? Would they challenge the regime loudly and directly or focus on quietly planting seeds and cultivating in Jewish young people the desire to leave?

Butman was eager to do something big. And already in the first few weeks of 1967, not long after the organization was formed, he called a meeting of all eight members (both groups had been missing a member on the day they'd met in Pushkin). He wanted to write the Kremlin a letter. In it, he would describe what it meant to be forcibly assimilated, how he thought the Soviet Union's treatment of Jews was a violation of the United Nations' 1948 Universal Declaration of Human Rights. He proposed a very public statement to be signed by all eight members and presented at a press conference. Soviet citizens wrote to the government to ask for help all the time, a tradition that went back to the czars. But the letters were a form of begging—asking for an exemption from military service or for a pension to be paid in advance. What Butman proposed was a letter of protest, something altogether new and dangerous. He managed to convince his own group, but Shpilberg and his group were opposed. The authorities would quickly crack down, and the organization would be squashed before it even got on its feet.

The lack of unanimity killed the idea, but the tension remained. Butman and Dreizner's group wanted to make noise, while Shpilberg and his friends opted for the slow build, the raising of awareness, the recruiting of soldiers. Before long, though, another question arose, this one potentially more divisive: whether the group should align itself with the growing, but still fairly isolated, dissident movement.

The thaw had opened up a small place in Soviet society for all thinking people—not just Zionists—to start imagining an alternative reality without fearing arrest and death. The liberalization loosened the restraints on culture, allowing books like Alexander Solzhenitsyn's account of life in Stalin's Gulag, *One Day in the Life of Ivan Denisovich,* to appear in the literary journal *Novy Mir* in November 1962—unimaginable a decade before. And in the late 1950s, Khrushchev had given mass amnesty to millions of people in prison and in Siberian exile. Their detached gazes and beaten bodies were living proof of the regime's inhuman core. Its unintended consequence was that, especially in big cities like Moscow, a desire for further openness, for further reform, arose among a young intelligentsia. Already in the summer of 1958, students were meeting at Mayakovsky Square in Moscow for open-air poetry readings that included increasingly subversive work. In September of 1965, a year before Butman's and Shpilberg's groups came together, Andrei Sinyavsky (who wrote under a Jewish pseudonym, Abram Tertz) and Yuli Daniel (who actually was Jewish) were arrested for publishing essays and satirical novels and stories that were perceived as critical of the Soviet Union. Protests were organized on their behalf, and more dissidents were arrested in the following months. When their trial was held, in February of 1966, the government used the writers' published work as evidence that they were guilty of "anti-Soviet agitation and propaganda." Both were sentenced to years in prison camps. This outraged the members of the new dissident movement. Petitions and letters of protest reflected a new willingness to confront the regime head-on. But the arrests signaled that Khrushchev's thaw had reached its limit.

In Leningrad, the new Zionist organization debated the advantages and disadvantages of joining forces with the wider dissident movement. Both the Zionists and the dissidents thought the entire Soviet regime hopelessly corrupt and wanted it reformed. And the groups used similar tactics—Butman's letter-writing idea was straight from the dissidents' toolbox. But in the end, the Zionists decided that it was best to keep their distance. Their reasoning—worked out over long walks through the forest—had its roots in Jabotinsky. He was emphatic about not mixing the Zionist cause with any other humanist agenda. In Jabotinsky's essays, which Jews in Riga and Leningrad devoured in samizdat, Jews were advised not to waste their energy trying to improve the state of the world, which at the time meant joining the Communist or Socialist movements. They needed to focus on fighting for a Jewish state. To the Zionists of the 1960s, this made a lot of sense. They had seen what happened to the Jews who played a part in the Bolshevik Revolution. They were done with efforts to remake Russia. They wanted out of Russia. And by distancing themselves from any overtly anti-Soviet activity, they believed that the government might not see them as a threat to its existence—the way it perceived the dissidents—and therefore might eventually let them leave.

Mostly the new organization continued the work that its members had been carrying out for years, only now in a more coordinated manner. They met with small groups of young Jews, taught Hebrew from smudged mimeographed copies of *Elef Millim,* and listened to miniature vinyl albums of Israeli music passed to them surreptitiously by Israeli embassy workers. But throughout the winter of 1967, they were devising a plan to consolidate all this activity and make it more effective. They would start an *ulpan,* the Hebrew word meaning "gathering." They would run small educational seminars that would teach Jewish history and Hebrew and, at the same time, instill in Jewish youth a hunger for Israel. There would be no more than ten people in a class, and the hope was that the graduates would serve as the leaders and teachers of future classes. The *ulpan* would start in September, as the school year did, and meet weekly in different apartments, changing locations so that the KGB wouldn't catch on to what were, in effect, illegal gatherings. That winter, Shpilberg brought some small groups outside Leningrad and began teaching; come fall, the *ulpanim* would start in earnest.

As their work progressed, the need for teaching material increased. As if in response, one day in March of 1967, a stranger from Riga handed Shpilberg a note. He said he was an activist who had gotten Shpilberg's contact information from Mark Blum, who was then sitting in jail for his role in the Geula Gill riots. Shpilberg read the note and then convened a meeting of all eight members of the Zionist organization; they gathered in giant Komsomol Square, in the center of Leningrad (the group met only in public). He told them what the note said: if they could find a safe way to receive a suitcase full of Jewish samizdat, Riga would pass one along to them.

As it turned out, the abundance of samizdat came from Boris Slovin, one of the activists in Riga. Slovin had become friendly with a Jew who was the night watchman at a school that trained Soviet border patrol agents, and the watchman had access to a photocopy machine, an Era Duplicator. This rare piece of technology allowed Slovin—who up until then had been producing his samizdat painstakingly with typewriters and carbon paper—to increase his production by incredible leaps. Without any discussion, Slovin would hand the night watchman the material and then later receive hundreds of copies back. Soon he had a fortunate problem: how to get rid of suitcases full of photocopied books.

The Leningrad group wasn't sure if they trusted the message about the available samizdat. They decided to take the man up on the offer, but they sent someone to Riga who had no connection to the organization and who would be able to claim innocence if this was all a KGB provocation. Slovin, in Riga, also tried to protect himself; he spent the afternoon with the messenger and gave him a decoy suitcase containing a blanket, sausage, and wine—for a picnic—in case he happened to be an agent. Only as the messenger's train began chugging away did Slovin grab the fake suitcase and deliver the real one. Back in Leningrad, Butman devised an elaborate scheme to pass the heavy bag—filled with a hundred and fifty books—from hand to hand, going from the station and through a series of courtyards until it reached its destination, the apartment of one of Butman's unsuspecting friends.

As absurd as these precautions seem, they were necessary. The suitcase was full of illegal items: dozens of copies of Slovin's translation of *Exodus,* a few exemplars of Jabotinsky's feuilletons, and some collections of poetry, most by Chaim Nachman Bialik. Once the samizdat was secured, the group fell to arguing about how to distribute it. Shpilberg wanted to disseminate it as soon as possible. Butman was still attached to his idea of a grand gesture, a letter to the authorities, and he worried that getting arrested for samizdat wouldn't have quite the same publicity impact.

But in May of 1967, events far from Leningrad suddenly put an end to the bickering. Israel was in trouble. The news traveled fast over the staticky airwaves. Butman sat, as he had every evening for the last few years, with his radio tuned to Kol Israel. When the strains of the "Hatikvah," Israel's plaintive national anthem, suddenly filled the crackling air, he pressed his ear close to the speaker. On May 18, the Egyptian president Gamal Abdel Nasser had ordered the UN buffer force out of Sinai, and the United Nations complied. He then sent his troops and tanks into the peninsula up to the Israeli border. On May 23, he closed the Straits of Tiran to Israeli ships. War seemed imminent. Israelis fled, convinced a massacre would follow. The sense of panic for Butman and his friends was compounded by the difficulty of getting solid information about what was really happening. Soviet radio said one thing and Kol Israel another. But all eight members of the Zionist organization knew that if there was ever a time to release pro-Israel material to young Jews in Leningrad, this was it. In one day, with their hearts beating frantically in their chests, they ran around Leningrad and dropped all the books off at Jewish homes, like letter bombs slipped into mailboxes.

———

The war that consumed the Middle East in June 1967, pitting Israel against four Arab enemies, led to a Jewish victory that felt delivered by God, miraculous in its magnitude. The Jewish State quadrupled its area in less than a week and took hold of the old city of Jerusalem. And the implications—for Israel's place in the world, for Jewish identity, for how Jews in the Diaspora were perceived—reverberated far and wide. It wasn't just the small band of committed Zionists in the Soviet Union who suddenly felt emboldened, their lonely cause now validated. The Six-Day War's impact was felt in the most unlikely of places, such as the military factory on the outskirts of Kiev where Boris Kochubievsky worked as a radio engineer.

On one of the war's last days, Kochubievsky, a thirty-year-old loner with a long gaunt face dominated by round, watery black eyes that rarely blinked, was sitting in a factorywide meeting listening to a lecture delivered by a local army officer. These types of propaganda meetings were taking place all over the Soviet Union in the first weeks of June. After predicting a humiliating defeat for the "imperialistic" Israelis, the Soviets now had to explain how their Arab client states had been so badly beaten, how Israel had managed to destroy almost the entire Egyptian air force—consisting of Soviet-made planes—in a single morning. The solution was to portray the Israelis as demonic aggressors. On June 15 *Izvestia* described how Israeli "invaders are killing prisoners of war and defenseless peasants, driving the inhabitants from their homes and publicly executing men, women and children," crimes, the article claimed, that were "similar to those the Nazis perpetrated on the occupied countries during World War II." In early July, Brezhnev, addressing the graduates of a military academy, called Israelis "the worst of bandits" and said they "want to copy the crimes of the Hitler invaders."

The officer speaking at the Kiev military factory made similar allusions. As Kochubievsky listened to him denounce the Jewish State, something in him snapped. He stood and asked to speak. He wanted the record of the meeting to reflect that he was utterly opposed to what was being said. And then he went further. He asked how he was supposed to take these allegations against Israel. How could he continue to work in a factory that made arms to supply the enemies of the Jews when he himself, whether he wanted to be or not, was a Jew? How could he continue to be complicit? The realizations came to him as he spoke. He felt guilty but also angry. The state had put him in the terrible position of having to help kill his own people. The room fell silent. He directly addressed the other Jews present, who made up almost half the engineers in the factory. What were they to do with this irreconcilable difference? When the factory manager tried to quiet him, other people yelled that he should be allowed to finish. He went on to defend Israel—it had the right to attack preemptively against an enemy that was clearly preparing for war—offering an interpretation diametrically opposed to the Soviet one. When he was finished, he sat down.

In that instant, Kochubievsky's life changed. He knew little about what it meant to be a Jew, and even less about Israel—which he imagined to be a vast desert filled with camels. But his restive existence had suddenly found an objective: he would go there. In the span of that one factory meeting, he had felt the paradox viscerally, and now he wanted to solve it.

At that moment, Kochubievsky also became a marked man. A union meeting was called to put pressure on him to resign. He began desperately looking for relatives in Israel so that he could apply for an exit visa through family reunification—the only basis for emigration that the Soviets would even consider. Within a year of his factory speech, he had managed to get an invitation from a distant cousin, but his life only became more difficult. KGB informers seemed to be everywhere. People he hadn't seen in years and who shouldn't have known his address suddenly appeared at his door holding bottles of cognac. Kochubievsky felt that the authorities were looking for a way to trap him, trying to find some pretext for putting him away other than his political opposition.

Eventually his application for an exit visa was refused. He decided to take his new public stance to the next level, and he wrote a short essay, "Why I Am a Zionist," which was circulated in samizdat. "We are convinced that there is no more room for Jewish patience," he wrote, echoing the sentiment of the American Jewish activists. "Silence is equivalent to death. It was that kind of patience that created Hitler and the likes of him. If we remain silent today, tomorrow will be too late."

The endgame came in the fall of 1968, and in the most appropriate of places. For the past several years, on September 29, Kiev's Jews had gathered in very small numbers by the Babi Yar ravine, where the 1941 massacre of the Jews had occurred. By the mid-1960s, after the wide attention given to Yevgeny Yevtushenko's poem, it had become a well-known site, though it still had no memorial. But that first September after the Six-Day War, more Jews gathered than ever had before. And in 1968 there was such a crowd that the local authorities had to organize an official commemoration. But true to form, the government speaker described only "victims of fascism," never mentioning that the overwhelming majority of those victims were Jews. Kochubievsky was at Babi Yar that September in 1968. Once he had taken the step of embracing his Jewish identity, he felt guilty about having ignored it for so long. And he had another reason for being at the commemoration. His father, a soldier in the Red Army, had died during the war, under mysterious circumstances. There were a few secondhand stories about his death, one that placed him in a hospital a hundred kilometers south of Kiev, both of his legs missing. But another story, the most compelling one for Kochubievsky, was that upon invading the city, the Nazis had shot all the Jewish soldiers in the Red Army, right there at Babi Yar.

After the official ceremony came to a close, the Jews milled around the edge of the ravine, in itself an act of bravery since everyone could see the KGB agents hovering nearby. Someone Kochubievsky knew came over to him and described a conversation he had just overheard in which a Ukrainian man lamented that the Nazis had not killed more Jews at Babi Yar. Kochubievsky, already annoyed by the official ceremony, became incensed. He pointed down the steep edge of the rocky ravine and said that "here lies part of the Jewish people." This was a massacre of Jews, he insisted. The crowd around him grew larger and his speech became more intense. The outburst at the factory had been impromptu, but this speech was not. Kochubievsky had found his voice. Look what they did to us here, he told the silent gathering. "In this country, I belong to no one. I want to go somewhere where I belong." He told them not to be afraid, that they should try to emigrate, that it was entirely legal, that his desire to go to Israel was in line with the minority rights outlined in the state constitution. When he finished talking, the Jews quickly dispersed. He was alone again.

The KGB eventually came knocking, throwing his apartment into disarray in a search meant to intimidate. He began to feel it was only a matter of time before he was arrested. He needed to take hold of his fate. He was growing impatient for the inevitable moment of his arrest to come. And while his indignation about the search was still fresh, he sat down and wrote an impassioned, audacious letter to Leonid Brezhnev, a furious confession that opened with words Kochubievsky would have been reluctant to utter just two years before:

> I am a Jew. I want to live in the Jewish state. That is my right, just as it is the right of a Ukrainian to live in the Ukraine, the right of a Russian to live in Russia, the right of a Georgian to live in Georgia.
>
> I want to live in Israel. That is my dream, that is the goal not only of my life but also of the lives of hundreds of generations that preceded me, of my ancestors who were expelled from their land.
>
> I want my children to study in the Hebrew language. I want to read Jewish papers, I want to attend a Jewish theater. What's wrong with that? What is my crime . . . ?
>
> . . .
>
> I am not asking for mercy. Listen to the voice of reason: Let me out!
>
> As long as I live, as long as I am capable of feeling, I will do all I can to leave for Israel. And if you find it possible to sentence me for it, all the same, if I live till my release, I will be prepared to go to the homeland of my ancestors, even if it means going on foot.

Less than a week after he posted the letter to the Kremlin, on December 4, Kochubievsky was summoned to the local KGB bureau. It wasn't his first visit. In the weeks since the Babi Yar incident, he had been questioned many times and asked, sometimes politely, other times more firmly, to desist from his provocations. But this time, there was no conversation. Almost as soon as he arrived, Kochubievsky was put into a black Volga and driven to Kiev's local mental institution.

The Six-Day War affected Jews all over the Soviet Union. Very few went to the lengths that Kochubievsky did or suffered his fate. But, to varying degrees, the war instilled in thousands a new and unfamiliar sense of pride. They felt a subversive joy in the fact that their own people, derided and ridiculed as they often were in Soviet society, had triumphed over this vainglorious power and its allies. Some of them felt for the first time that there was value in belonging to the Jewish people, that it didn't have to be only a line in a passport that weighed one down. The victory upended Soviet propaganda, which had painted Zionism as sinister and Jewish defeat as imminent. In a matter of a month, the weak colony in a hostile desert became a muscular and powerful nation.

The war also changed the political relationship between Israel and the Soviet Union. On the morning of June 10, the day of Kochubievsky's factory speech in Kiev, a note addressed to the Israeli ambassador was delivered to Israel's embassy in Moscow: "The Soviet government declares that in light of Israel's continued aggression against the Arab states and its flagrant violation of the decisions of the Security Council, the government of the USSR has taken the decision to break off diplomatic relations between the Soviet Union and Israel."

With that, nineteen years of shaky but consistent diplomatic relations (broken off only once, after the 1953 Doctors' Plot) came to an end. A day later, the Israeli flag was lowered and the delegation flew home. The Dutch embassy took over responsibility for Israeli interests — it was to this embassy that Kochubievsky had gone to submit his documents in Moscow.

In the months before the war, there had been a small increase in exit visas — a jump from the 891 who left in 1964 to 1,406 in the first half of 1967. This had mostly to do with an incident in December of 1966, when Premier Aleksei Kosygin, the most liberal of the troika then running the Soviet Union following Khrushchev's ouster, was asked at a press conference in Paris by a correspondent from UPI if he could possibly give Jewish families separated by the war "any hope of meeting, as was done for many Greek and Armenian families." After shaking off his annoyance at the question and insisting that there was no problem of anti-Semitism in the Soviet Union, the premier made the following unprecedented statement: "We, on our side, shall do all possible if some families want to meet or even if some among them would like to leave us, to open the road for them, and this does not raise here, actually, any problem of principles and will not raise any." After his comments were reprinted — strangely, they appeared in *Izvestia,* one of the state-run newspapers — hundreds of Soviet Jews bombarded the Office of Visas and Registration (OVIR). Many carried copies of the article in their hands. But this brief increase in visas—most still went to elderly or sick people the state didn't want anyway—ended as soon as the war began. In the remainder of 1967, after the Israeli delegation left, only 116 Jews were allowed to leave.

And yet, at the same time, the burst of energy provided by the victory increased the hopefulness of those few active Zionists and made more Jews curious about their Jewishness and Israel.

On November 17 of that year, Yuri Andropov, who had only recently been appointed head of the KGB by the Central Committee of the Communist Party, wrote a memo to the Soviet leadership describing the alarming trend of young Jews massing before the synagogues on Simchat Torah. The gatherings had been taking place for years, but this Simchat Torah, just months after the Six-Day War, was particularly joyous. In what remains one of the best contemporary descriptions of the scene at the Moscow Choral Synagogue that October, Andropov wrote, "The autumn Jewish religious holidays have attracted a large number of citizens of Jewish nationality who, for the most part, are not believers or regular congregants. They come to the synagogue as a sort of club where they can meet with relatives, acquaintances and conclude various deals (speculative, marital, change of apartments, etc.)."

He noted that "these holidays are celebrated by young people of college age" and that on Simchat Torah, "several thousand individuals of Jewish nationality attended including students of several faculties of Moscow State University, the Moscow Auto Transport Institute, the V.I. Lenin Moscow State Pedagogical Institute, the Moscow State Pedagogical Institute of Foreign Languages, the Moscow Institute of Transport Engineers and other Higher educational institutions in the capital." The popularity of the synagogue gatherings could be "partially explained," he said, by pointing to

the intensifications of Zionist propaganda on the part of foreign centers and the Voice of Israel radio station, which calls on Jews "not to forget Judaism, and to struggle against assimilation, for the purity of Jewry." Infected with Zionist ideas, nationalistically inclined individuals from among Soviet citizens try to take advantage of religious gatherings at the synagogue to stir up nationalistic sentiments. They talk about the need for Jewish solidarity, express their sympathies for the state of Israel, and try to stir up nationalistic feeling among the youth.

Based on observations compiled by informers, Andropov's memo goes on to describe, in some detail, what took place on that Simchat Torah:

> Individual instigators organized a performance of Jewish songs and dances near the synagogue. Nationalistic calls were heard, such as: "Long live Dayan!," "We'll go to Israel, machine gun in hand!," "Long live the Jewish student body!," "Long live the Jews!" . . . Ia. I. Bogomol'nikov, a scientific worker who was present at the gathering, declared in a closed circle of young people: "If in the Soviet Union the situation were different, i.e. if there were more Jews than Russians, then we would, in fact, crush the goyim." Then he went on: "What would the Soviet Union do if there were no Jews? Think of the losses Soviet science, technology and culture would suffer."

Andropov ended with the caveat that "such provocative actions of individuals are not supported by the fundamental mass of those in attendance, but neither are they met with any active resistance." His official recommendation was that the activities of those "instigators" should continue to be "monitored and documented" by the KGB, and that the Komsomol organizations at the universities should "intensify educational work among students who are exposed to Zionist influence."

But that "Zionist influence" only expanded following the Six-Day War. In Leningrad, *ulpanim* began functioning regularly in the fall of 1967. The first one took place in a rented dacha in a distant suburb of Leningrad with no more than a dozen students. In order to justify the group's presence, leaders drafted a note explaining that these were ill children who needed fresh country air. Half the day was devoted to studying—Hebrew and Jewish history—and the other half to skiing. Everyone took the lessons very seriously, and exams were even given at the end. But the dacha was not winterized, so the students spent much of their time just sitting around the large ovens trying to stay warm. They read samizdat together, three or four people peering over the shoulders of a single person holding up the mimeographed pages.

Butman and Dreizner held another *ulpan* a month later, also in a large, freezing dacha on the outskirts of Leningrad. Butman was happy to see that the university students, even if they weren't exactly picking up Hebrew, were enjoying one another's company. They sat close together to stay warm. They ate all their meals as a group, sang songs, and looked at the slides of Israeli postcards on the wall of the dacha. One of Butman's objectives was to create a community, and this was beginning to happen.

After that first fall, a more regular *ulpan* began with a schedule that paralleled the school year's. Starting in September, the group would meet in various apartments in Leningrad. Students quickly transformed into teachers: those who knew fifty words in Hebrew were soon teaching those who knew only five. Already by the end of 1967 there was another group of four added to the original two cells of the Zionist organization. These were all young men from Kishinev who were studying at the Polytechnic Institute in Leningrad. The original organization had decided to stop meeting as a group—it was too risky—so they created a central coordinating committee with one representative from each cell. This way, contact among the groups would be minimal.

An active but less structured group of Zionists had existed in Moscow since the late 1950s. But it was Yasha Kazakov, a twenty-year-old university student, who captured the post–Six-Day War spirit when on June 13, 1967, he publicly renounced his Soviet citizenship. This was unprecedented. A few months before the war, Kazakov, a stocky bulldog of a man, had barreled his way past policemen into the Israeli embassy. Once inside, he told a member of the embassy staff that he had no family in Israel but desperately wanted to leave the Soviet Union. The Israeli staff member signed a document inviting him to emigrate, a *vyzov*, but said that it was up to Kazakov to figure out how he was going to get out. The officials at the Moscow OVIR laughed at Kazakov when he presented them with the invitation. He had no chance. Once the war started and it became clear that the Israeli delegation was going to be kicked out, he grew desperate and wrote his letter to the Kremlin declaring that he was no longer a citizen of the Soviet Union.

Like Kochubievsky in Kiev, Kazakov shocked and confused the regime by taking such a public stand. He was called many times to the Moscow KGB headquarters and asked to repudiate his statement. The authorities threatened to draft him into military service. But when almost a year later, in May of 1968, Kazakov saw no change in his situation, he wrote another letter, this time addressed to the Supreme Soviet: "I, Yakov Iosifovich Kazakov, a Jew, born in 1947, residing at No. 6 Third Institutskaya St., apt 42, Moscow 2R-389, renounce Soviet citizenship, and, from the moment that I first announced my renunciation of USSR citizenship, that is, June 13, 1967, I have not considered myself a citizen of the USSR."

"I am a Jew," he wrote, anticipating Kochubievsky's letter to Brezhnev later that year. "I was born a Jew and I want to live out my life as a Jew. With all my respect for the Russian people, I do not consider my people in any way inferior to the Russian or to any other people and I do not want to be assimilated by any other people." His words were harsh and combative:

> I do not wish to be a citizen of a country that arms and supports the remaining fascists and the Arab chauvinists who desire to wipe Israel off the face of the earth and to add another two and half million killed to the six million who have perished. I do not want to be a collaborator of yours in the destruction of the State of Israel because, even though this has not been done officially, I consider myself to be a citizen of the State of Israel (the more so as I possess an invitation for permanent residence in the State of Israel). On the basis of the above, I renounce Soviet citizenship, and I demand to be freed from the humiliation of being considered a citizen of the Union of Soviet Socialist Republics.

Kazakov was gambling that his bombast would force the Soviets to resolve his case one way or another. They'd send him to jail or they'd allow him to leave for Israel, and either option, he figured, was better than his interminable state of limbo. But first he needed publicity. He tried desperately to get his letter to the West, stuffing copies in the mailboxes at the British embassy and stopping tourists to ask in broken English if they could take his statement out of the country. Eventually a copy did make it out. And on December 19, 1968, the *Washington Post* ran an article headlined "Jew Living in Moscow Hits Regime" that included excerpts from it. Within a week, a friend told him she had heard his name mentioned on a Voice of America broadcast. Kazakov told his mother that this was it, the regime would now be forced to do something. He was headed to either Israel or Siberia. He hoped that his lack of connections to other Zionists, compounded by the amount of attention he had managed to generate, would make it easier for the country to just get rid of him. But this had been Kochubievsky's calculation as well, and he was now sitting in a Kiev mental hospital.

Two weeks later, Kazakov received a phone call asking him to appear at the Office of Visas and Registration with all his documents. When he got there, an official told him he was being given an exit visa and had two weeks to leave the country. He couldn't believe his luck. The OVIR official leaned in close and told him he'd better not engage in any anti-Soviet activity during his remaining days.

A few months later, Yasha Kazakov was starting his basic training in the Israeli army.

Meanwhile, Boris Kochubievsky thought he was going crazy. Even though the doctors didn't try to medicate him, he couldn't escape the contorted faces of men in straitjackets, the screams from the electroshock rooms, the monologues of the murderer who lived in his dormitory and described in detail how he had killed his whole family. But by the end of January 1969, Kochubievsky's story was making its way to the West, and the authorities had no choice but to transfer him to a prison cell and formally charge him under Article 187-1 of the Ukrainian Criminal Code. According to the official indictment, he was accused of "systematically disseminating by word of mouth slanderous fabrications, defaming state and social systems of the USSR, the slander being expressed in his disseminating fabrications alleging that the Soviet Union oppresses and keeps down Jews."

The trial began on May 13. In an ironic twist, it was held in the same courtroom in Kiev where Mendel Beilis had stood in 1913 in an infamously anti-Semitic blood libel case, accused of ritually murdering a young Russian boy—not a connection the Soviets should have been eager to make. As had been true for the recent trials of dissidents Daniel and Sinyavsky, the courtroom was filled with people handpicked by the local KGB. Kochubievsky was not allowed much of a defense. The prosecution's argument focused on what Kochubievsky had said at Babi Yar and at the OVIR offices. For more than three days, various Communist Party members with only tenuous connections to Kochubievsky were brought in as witnesses against him. Kochubievsky did not buckle. He pleaded not guilty to all the charges, and in fact he figured that now, with nothing to lose, he might as well be as audacious as possible. At one point he told the court that he did not begrudge the Ukrainian people their Communism. He sincerely wished them five hundred more glorious years of Communist rule. He, however, wanted out. (In response, the prosecutor said that Kochubievsky's real problem was not his desire to go to Israel but what he called his "mania of superiority.")

In his final statement, on the last day of the three-day trial, Kochubievsky sparred with one of the judges. He tried to talk about Yevtushenko's poem "Babi Yar," how it had expressed the sentiments for which he was being tried. The judge cut him off. "Accused, you have been given the chance to make a final statement in your defense, not to make excursions into history and literature." Kochubievsky stared straight at the judge and answered, "I ask that it be placed on record that I have been admonished for mentioning Yevtushenko's poem 'Babi Yar' . . . Very well, I omit this part of my final statement. All my statements at Babi Yar fully coincided with the sense and the spirit of this poem." Kochubievsky relentlessly attacked the court's procedure, pointing out inaccuracies and insufficient evidence. But his exhaustion was clear, and in the end he offered not much more than this exasperated rhetorical question: "You, citizen judges, have said that we have class justice. But does the wish to emigrate to Israel turn a person into a hostile element?"

After Kochubievsky was finished speaking, the court sentenced him to three years in a labor camp. Within a month, he was in the Urals, head shaved, in a prison uniform, and eating soup with rotten fish out of a wooden bowl. The Soviet Union had produced yet another political prisoner whose only stated crime was Zionism.

———

Between the Six-Day War in June of 1967 and early 1969 when, almost simultaneously, Kazakov was allowed to leave for Israel and Kochubievsky was sent to the Ural Mountains, an intellectual revolution took place inside the Soviet Union. In the summer of 1968, Soviet tanks rolled into Czechoslovakia to put an end to the Prague Spring—Alexander Dubček's experiment in economic and social liberalization, what

he called "socialism with a human face." It was an unabashed and mili-
tantly extreme reaction, and the Czech people greeted the Soviet army
with jeers and curses. And it exposed the true character of the post-
Khrushchev Soviet leadership: strong enough that it felt no compunc-
tion about using an iron fist to destroy any form of opposition, yet at
the same time deeply insecure about any popular discontent.

The August invasion disturbed the young city-dwelling generation
who had grown up during the thaw. It offered conclusive proof that
whatever part of Soviet society had opened up in the early sixties was
closing again. And for the growing dissident movement, drawn mainly
from the Muscovite intelligentsia, it reinforced the need for opposition while making clear how hard the struggle would be. There could
be no more illusions about how the state would react if it felt threatened. Since the Daniel-Sinyavsky trial in early 1966, a loosely organized
movement had taken shape, circulating samizdat literature and publicly protesting every heavy-handed government action. Some of the
more prominent protesters were on trial by 1967, including Vladimir
Bukovsky and Alexander Ginzburg, mostly for the crimes of holding
what were called "disorderly demonstrations" or engaging in "malicious hooliganism." But trials of dissident leaders only begat more protests. Soon a highly competent group of activists had organized themselves in Moscow and begun refining a powerful tool of dissidence:
recording, documenting, and bearing witness to the regime's injustice.
When they could, they also publicly protested. Each December 5, Soviet Constitution Day, starting in 1965 after the arrest of Daniel and
Sinyavsky, at least a hundred people would gather silently at Pushkin
Square at six in the evening to bow their heads. Often they were out-
numbered by the masses of KGB officers scribbling down names and
descriptions in notebooks.

And young writers and college students were no longer the only
ones trying to loosen Soviet society. A highly esteemed member of the
Soviet Academy of Sciences, Andrei Sakharov, had entered the fray. His
groundbreaking first essay, "Progress, Coexistence, and Intellectual
Freedom," was passed from hand to hand in that hopeful spring of
1968. A highly gifted physicist and the inventor of the Soviet hydro-
gen bomb, he had every luxury the Soviet Union could offer—special
housing, bodyguards, and consumer goods unavailable to most other
citizens. This made him an unusual recruit for the democracy move-

ment—his character and prestige alone were an enormous threat to the regime. Sakharov's political evolution came in slow steps. He began moving into the political realm after becoming a critic of nuclear atmospheric testing in the early sixties. By 1966, he had signed his name to a letter to Brezhnev demanding Stalin not be rehabilitated and was meeting with underground intellectuals like the brothers Roy and Zhores Medvedev (Roy would write the massive samizdat indictment of Stalin titled "Let History Judge"). By the time Sakharov wrote his essay, he had developed a fully formed concept for the direction Russia should take. His idea was "convergence," which he described as "the rapprochement of the socialist and capitalist systems." This had to take place "accompanied by democratization, demilitarization, and social and technological progress." Sakharov believed it was "the only alternative to the ruin of mankind." He pointed out many of the ills of Soviet society, including one that no Russian had dared discuss so publicly: "In the highest bureaucratic elite of our government, the spirit of anti-Semitism was never fully dispelled after the nineteen-thirties."

The popularity of Sakharov's essay and its appearance in the West made it hard for the Soviet leadership to ignore. Following the Czech invasion in August 1968, he lost his job and was stripped of all his privileges. So began Sakharov's new career as the moral sun around which the dissident movement revolved.

The democracy activists were emboldened. In response to Czechoslovakia, a group of eight staged a daring protest in Red Square, sitting down and unfurling a banner that read FOR YOUR FREEDOM AND OURS. In less than a minute, they were set upon by a group of police and KGB agents wielding clubs and shouting, "They're all Jews. Beat up the anti-Soviets!" One man's teeth were knocked out, another man was hit repeatedly in the head—within a month almost all the protesters were sentenced to years in labor camps or internal exile. One was injured so badly that he was not put on trial but placed in a mental institution—the new destination of choice for political "deviants."

The only one of the protesters who managed to escape prosecution was Natalya Gorbanevskaya, who arrived at the demonstration wheeling her three-month-old son in a stroller. She was the editor of the *Chronicle of Current Events,* known simply as the *Chronicle* (or *Khronika,* in Russian), a kind of human rights bulletin and one of the dissidents' most successful endeavors. Little noticed at first, by the end of 1968 *Khronika* had become a source of information for thousands—documenting various abuses and trials taking place all over the Soviet Union—and a high-profile target of the KGB. It had a straightforward, dispassionate, almost legalistically accurate style and managed to appear regularly every two months (produced, of course, on typewriters and handed from person to person with no identifying address on its masthead). In its sixth issue, dated February 29, 1969, *Khronika* also began keeping track of the Zionist movement, starting with the story of Boris Kochubievsky. All through the rest of 1969, it relayed the details of his trial, including transcripts that had been sneaked out by *Khronika*'s contact person in Kiev. From then on, the journal reported on Jewish activities and repression in the major cities, bringing the two movements together—at least for the moment.

By the beginning of 1969, reality had begun to sink in for Soviet Jews. Pulled by Israel's victory in the Six-Day War and pushed by the Czech invasion, they finally realized that the Soviet Union was not going to change for them. They needed to leave. As a result, the movement—still mostly small clusters of Zionist groups operating in the major cities—became bolder and more desperate.

As the contradictory treatment of Kazakov and Kochubievsky showed, the Soviet leadership had not come up with a coherent policy for dealing with troublesome Jews. Unlike the democracy movement, which the regime ruthlessly suppressed, Zionism seemed to provoke some debate about the best tack to take. On the one hand, officials felt a need to crush even vaguely anti-Soviet sentiments, as they had with Kochubievsky. Jews declaring that they wanted out of the socialist paradise seemed no less subversive than dissidents crying for reforms, and the solution—prosecuting and jailing them—was the same. On the other hand, the Soviets wondered, what if they were dealing with small pockets of troublemakers? If they let just a few of these people, like Kazakov, go, then perhaps the rest of the Jewish population would calm down. Andropov's November 1968 memo about the seditious young people singing and dancing in front of the synagogue on Simchat Torah suggested this was the prevailing thought: a few agitators were to blame for Zionism.

Andropov extended this line of reasoning in another memo on June

10, 1968, exactly one year after the Soviet Union severed its relations with Israel. Emigration had completely shut down since the war, and he was now proposing that it be renewed but limited to no more than fifteen hundred people. The reasons were clear. Andropov (along with Andrei Gromyko) wrote that the decision to stop emigration had been "perceived as a manifestation of anti-Semitism on the part of the Soviet authorities in response to the events that had arisen in the Middle East." So the two proposed that "in order to contain the slanderous assertions of Western propaganda concerning discrimination against Jews in the Soviet Union, it would seem expedient, along with other measures, to renew in the coming year departures of Soviet citizens for permanent residence in Israel." But this was not just about looking good in the eyes of the world. Letting out some Jews would also "permit the elimination of nationalistically inclined individuals and religious fanatics who exert harmful influence on their surroundings."

By the end of 1968, Riga's oldest and most seasoned activists were being asked to show up at OVIR to begin the process of receiving their exit visas. It was hard for many people to understand at first. The noisiest and most extreme Zionists were being allowed to leave, just like that: Mark Blum, who had been on trial and spent a year in jail for his role in the Geula Gill riot; Yosef Schneider, the one-time Gulag prisoner; Boris and Lydia Slovin, who just that year had been investigated by the KGB. Almost the entire old guard of the Baltic movement—those who had inspired Rumbuli, held hundreds of meetings in their apartments, taught Hebrew, and distributed samizdat—were gone by January of 1969.

But if the Soviet leadership thought they would be able to kill the movement by decapitating it, they had made a terrible miscalculation. The Slovins were invited to the Riga OVIR offices, and when they showed up early, they saw from a distance that almost two hundred Jewish acquaintances and strangers were waiting outside. These were not activists. They were just people who had somehow gotten word that the Slovins might get visas for Israel, and they wanted to see what would happen. The crowd was so thick that the OVIR officials and the Slovins could hardly make it to the door. When Boris and Lydia finally emerged with their papers, people began murmuring that they too were going to apply. Boris Slovin heard one man say, "Look, if they let Slovin leave, then for sure they'll let us too."

Rather than dampening people's Zionist impulse, seeing others off at the airport only increased the yearning. And the Soviets, inadvertently, had taught those activists who remained an important lesson. Clearly, the more noise one made, the better one's chance of getting out. The lesson of Kochubievsky—that noise could also land you in prison—was not forgotten. But it was evident to people like Mendelevich in Riga and Shpilberg in Leningrad that now was the time to at least apply for a visa, a step that many had previously thought futile and possibly even dangerous.

Without realizing it, the authorities had also solved a technical problem for the activists. OVIR demanded that any application be accompanied by a formal invitation from a family member in Israel, preserving the illusion that all emigration was for the purpose of family reunification. Letting the Israelis know to whom they should send an invitation was always a difficult business, but now every departing Jew brought out coded lists with dozens of names. And once in Israel, these former activists became important contact people and advocates for those left behind.

In Leningrad, even as people held invitations in their hands, actually applying still seemed like a frightening step. As long as the Zionists operated underground, they could feel part of normal society. They could still work or study and raise families in relative quiet. But once they declared their desire to leave, they crossed a psychological rubicon and jeopardized their fragile existence. Moreover, in spite of the thaw, any encounter with the authorities still inspired deep fear. Grisha Vertlib, the first of the Leningrad group to go to OVIR and present his invitation, in early 1969, called his close friends beforehand and asked that his family be taken care of should he fail to return. It was not unusual for a man to assume he wouldn't emerge safely from a government office.

Still, one by one, throughout the next year, most of the members of the Leningrad organization did apply to leave. They quickly became familiar with the formal process of requesting an exit visa, a set of steps that seemed designed to deter even the most ardent Zionist. After having received an invitation and contacting OVIR, an applicant had to gain a special recommendation, called a *kharikteristika,* from his place of work. This involved informing his supervisor of his desire to emigrate. In a few cases, the boss was annoyed but signed off on a standard recommendation. But it was more common for a factory- or office- or unionwide meeting to be held to debate the request. The applicant would be in attendance, and every effort would be made to persuade him of the insanity of going to Israel. And then, once this *kharikteris-tika* was obtained, the applicant was usually fired from his job or expelled from his school. As if this weren't burden enough, anyone seeking to emigrate also had to obtain permission from any dependents, such as elderly parents or in-laws. Often this added a further indignity, as poor older relatives, afraid of being abandoned, sometimes denied their children permission.

In a very short time, committed Zionists learned this story line well. Every person who went through the process made it easier for the next. They all knew what to expect. Bosses became less surprised when their Jewish employees asked them for *kharikteristikas;* local Communist Party secretaries less frantic when they received phone calls from factory managers asking what to do with a Jew who wanted to leave. And eventually, OVIR offices were transformed from places of fear into Jewish clubs where applicants stood in line for hours with their documents, sharing information and complaining to one another about how long they had been waiting.

But those who started applying in 1969—after seeing the brief exodus of the older activists—were not getting permission. In fact, they were uniformly being refused. As Andropov's directive made clear, the leadership did not want to fling open the gates. They were taking a gamble that letting out a small number of Zionists would solve the problem. Refusal usually came in the form of a phone call from OVIR a few months after a person had filed an application: The state does not presently find it convenient to grant your request.

Yosef Mendelevich received his invitation by sending a postcard to a woman from Riga who had recently left for Israel. "Dear uncle," he wrote her. "Have you forgotten us? Send the documents as soon as possible." Two months later, in November of 1968, he received an invitation from a Yaakov Mendelevich (a made-up relative) in Bat Yam inviting him and his family to Israel. He held on to the invitation for a month, waiting for the right moment to approach OVIR and begin the process. Then, in late December, Mark Blum, mentor to Mendelevich and many of Riga's Zionist youth, got permission to leave. He spent his last evening in Riga with Mendelevich, and before leaving, Blum promised him that they would see each other soon, in Israel. The next morning Mendelevich woke up early and made his way to OVIR.

He had a fairly easy time getting his *kharikteristika.* The manager at the factory where he worked, more curious than angry, asked only that Mendelevich tell him everything he knew about Israel. He happily obliged. In February of 1969, he received a letter telling him that he and his family had been refused, that OVIR had decided that he did not need to emigrate. Mendelevich went to the Interior Ministry to talk to someone about the decision and found a man who handled applications. He smiled at the pale, bespectacled twenty-one-year-old. You're young, the ministry worker told him, and you'll probably be drafted if you go there and then you'll have to fight against the Arabs who are now our allies. Now why would we want to supply manpower to our allies' enemy?

The refusal hit Mendelevich hard. He couldn't bring himself to work or study. He could no longer pretend that anything mattered to him more than being in Israel. Even though he was still very young, he was becoming a forceful presence in the small community. At the most recent Rumbuli memorial ceremony, in the fall of 1968, he had been asked to be a kind of master of ceremonies, reciting poems and giving a lecture he had memorized on the history of Riga's Jews written by a local historian. He was moved by the moment, by the sacredness of the place and the silence in the forest broken only by his booming voice telling the story of the massacre of his people. He had to hold back tears. And when the ceremony was finished, he quickly walked off on his own. His friends thought he was being pretentious, but he just couldn't bring himself to talk. As he walked under the fir trees, he made a vow: he would begin following Jewish law, eat kosher as much as possible, not work on the Sabbath, keep the fast days. His performance at the ceremony had made him a recognizable leader to the Zionist Jews of Riga, but it had also made him decide to pursue his own spiritual route. This decision isolated him even more, not just from the Latvians and Russians around him but also from his fellow Jews.

After OVIR's refusal in February, Mendelevich dropped out of school. He decided to devote himself fully to the struggle. But as soon as he quit the university, he lost his exemption from military service and was immediately drafted. Nothing could have been worse for

Mendelevich than to join the Red Army. He showed up at the recruitment office with his stepmother, who told the officer in charge that she was pretty sure something was wrong with Mendelevich. He had stopped studying and had fallen into a deep depression. The officer sent him for a psychiatric analysis, and sensing that this was his chance to get out of service, Mendelevich mumbled his way through the interview, blurting non sequiturs and generally trying to appear crazy. The psychiatrist decided that he should be admitted to the local psychiatric hospital for observation.

For a few weeks, Mendelevich lived in the hospital. He brought with him a copy of the *Iliad* and a book on learning English, both of which were taken away when he refused to engage in the menial tasks required of patients, such as licking envelopes, which Mendelevich found demeaning. The food was terrible. He avoided the other patients, who all seemed to be sedated. His father came to visit him and brought along a radio, and the two listened to Kol Israel. For a few minutes, he could imagine that he was somewhere else. In his isolation, Mendelevich began talking with God. He decided that if he somehow managed to cheat the regime and get out of military service and the hospital, he would deepen his religious commitment. He would begin to study Torah as best he could, and he would pray. He didn't quite know who would teach him Torah, but he was willing to make this bargain with God. If God helped him, then Mendelevich would devote his life to being a devout Jew.

After a month, the doctors at the hospital issued their verdict: though his antisocial behavior made him ineligible for the army, Mendelevich posed no threat and could be released. The next day, he went to the synagogue in Riga's old quarter, where his father had taken him as a boy, and he began to pray.

Many Jews had been inspired to try to leave after the Six-Day War, and now most were stuck, unable to return to life as it was before or to look forward to a life somewhere else. Seemingly out of options, many finally took to writing impassioned letters to the Soviet authorities or Western leaders or both, demanding that the Soviet Union abide by international law and allow free emigration. The idea was not new—Lydia and Boris Slovin, Butman, and others had all considered it at one time or another—but letter writing had always seemed dangerous. Until Yasha Kazakov. His letter had gotten him out. With *Khronika*, the dissidents offered an example of the power of a movement that was engaged in a totally open struggle.

One of the first letters written by a group of Jews was dated February 15, 1969, and came from a few academics in Vilnius, Lithuania; it was addressed to the Lithuanian Communist Party. It detailed examples of state-sponsored anti-Semitism and demanded that these be controlled. It did not insist on emigration, only the resolution of that paradox: "We are not wanted here, we are completely oppressed, forcibly denationalized, and even publicly insulted in the press while at the same time we are forcibly kept here. As the Lithuanian proverb goes, 'He beats and he screams at the same time.'" But the signers decided it was best to leave their names off the letter, writing that "we know well how people who had at one time or another protested against flourishing anti-Semitism in the Soviet Union were summarily dealt with. The Party has taught us to be watchful, and we have to be watchful now as we write to the Central Committee of the Lithuanian Communist Party. What painful irony."

But very soon, people were signing their names to individual letters renouncing their Soviet citizenship. One of these was Mendel Gordin, Mendelevich's cousin, now graduated from Riga's medical school and a rising young researcher at the Central Bacteriological Institute. His request for an exit visa in February was quickly denied a month later. So on June 1, he sent a letter to Nikolai Podgorny, one of the three men running the Soviet Union. "I categorically declare that it is my will to live only in my own motherland, and I regard Israel as such," he wrote. "Taking this into account, I hereby give up my Soviet citizenship and enclose herewith my passport." Few things could be more dangerous in the Soviet Union than not having an internal passport. It was grounds for immediate arrest and prosecution.

Many such individual petitions followed in the first half of 1969, others from Riga and a few from Moscow, all making similar points. But the authorities saw these as nothing more than small nuisances. Then in August, a letter arrived from an unlikely place, written with such overwhelming poetry that it was impossible to ignore.

The ancient Georgian Jewish community is thought to have arrived in the region following the Assyrian destruction of the northern kingdom of Israel in 770 BCE, which would make them one of the ten lost tribes. Some date their arrival a little later, to the Babylonian exile in 586 BCE. No historian thinks they came later than the Roman destruction of the Second Temple in the first century CE. They had lived in Georgia for centuries by then and developed their own unique Judeo-Georgian language, Gruzinic, along with separate literature and liturgical traditions. They managed to isolate themselves and their culture in enclaves of tightly bound traditional communities. The czars respected their skills as small traders and artisans—with a firm monopoly on the production and sale of Georgian wine—and exempted them from having to live within the Pale of Settlement, the western region of the Russian Empire where most Jews were confined from the time of Catherine the Great until 1917.

Not even the Bolshevik Revolution changed their lives. They managed to keep their synagogues open. In the late 1960s, no more than fifty or sixty synagogues remained in the whole of the Soviet Union, but half of them were in Georgia. And this even though Georgian Jews actually made up a very small percentage of Soviet Jewry. According to the 1959 census, only around fifty thousand of the roughly two and half million Jews in the empire were Georgian Jews. But they held on to their tradition fiercely. In the town of Kutaisi, the Jews famously lay down in the road that led to the synagogue in order to block the local Communist Party's attempt to turn their house of worship into a Komsomol club. These communities continued to keep kosher and, remarkably, circumcised all their male children. There was even some prosperity under the Soviet regime. Flower and fruit sellers had enough money to fly to Leningrad and Moscow each morning to sell their fresh goods in the city streets.

And yet, they wanted to go to Israel. The kind of Judaism practiced by the Georgians was messianic. It preached the ingathering of the exiles, even after more than twenty centuries of Diaspora. They felt that one of the holiest expressions in Judaism was the sentence spoken at the end of the Passover Seder and the Day of Atonement: "Next year in Jerusalem." And so it wasn't surprising that Andropov's directive to allow very limited emigration permitted the departure of the forty-nine Georgian Jewish families who had previously applied. They left in late 1968 and early 1969; these families, along with Riga's Jewish activists, represented the majority of the fifteen hundred exit visas the regime decided to distribute.

As they had in Riga and Leningrad, these Jewish departures inspired hope in others. And as had happened there too, the next applications were followed by mass refusals. Hundreds of families who had believed something miraculous was taking place were left disillusioned and despondent. Some wrote individual letters, and a few made contact with Zionist activists in Moscow. But it was a letter written by eighteen families on August 6, 1969, and addressed to the UN Human Rights Commission, with a copy sent to the prime minister of Israel, Golda Meir, that had the greatest impact. It was a petition in almost biblically poetic form. The Georgian Jews took a long historical view on the state of the Jewish people in exile:

> Showered with insults, covered with the mud of slander, despised and persecuted, they earned their daily bread with blood and sweat, and reared their children. Their hands were calloused, their souls were drenched in blood. But the important thing is that the nation was not destroyed—and what a nation.
>
> The Jews gave the world religion and revolutionaries, philosophers and scholars, wealthy men and wise men, geniuses with the hearts of children, and children with the eyes of old people. There is no field of knowledge, no branch of literature and art, to which Jews have not contributed their share. There is no country which gave Jews shelter which has not been repaid by their labor. And what did the Jews get in return?
>
> When life was bearable for all, the Jews waited fearfully for other times. And when life became bad for all, the Jews knew that their last hour had come, and then they had to run from that country.
>
> And whoever got away began from the beginning again.
>
> And whoever could not run away was destroyed.

The letter went on to catalog the long history of persecution of European Jewry and then declared that now "the Prophecy has come true; Israel has risen from the ashes; we have not forgotten Jerusalem, and it needs our hands. There are eighteen of us who signed this letter. But he errs who thinks there are only eighteen of us."

Their plea was a desperate one: "We will wait months and years, we will wait all our lives, if necessary, but we will not renounce our faith or our hopes."

Coming from uneducated peddlers and artisans in what many considered a primitive and backward place, this letter was extraordinary. Once in the hands of the activists, it was reproduced in samizdat form and delivered to the Dutch embassy for transmission to the Israelis.

The movement matured in 1969, and not just because of the letters and increasing openness of the struggle. Coordination and communication among the different centers of activity also increased. Some level of contact had existed since 1967, but it was mostly the result of fortuitous personal connections. Ruth Alexandrovich, a young woman from Riga, knew David Khavkin, a respected activist and former Gulag prisoner from Moscow. He in turn knew some Jews in Novosibirsk, in Siberia, who had access to a photocopy machine and were able to print hundreds of copies of *Elef Millim*. In this way, the books were distributed all across the empire—from Novosibirsk to Khavkin to Alexandrovich and eventually to Leningrad, where Ruth knew Aron Shpilberg and his friends in the Zionist organization.

But this was all too tenuous and haphazard. There had to be a better way to coordinate their efforts. In the summer of 1969, with the letters beginning to get some press in the West, a few Moscow activists—Khavkin among them—decided to call a meeting of representatives from the various cities. Even though such a mass gathering posed many risks, they had the perfect excuse for being in the same city at the same time. Sasha Blank, an elderly Zionist from Leningrad known to many of the activists, was leaving for Israel, and they would all be attending his farewell party the first week of August. There were ten representatives in all, two from every city. Syoma Dreizner was one of the two from the Leningrad organization. In addition to those from Riga and Moscow, there were Jews from Tbilisi, Kiev, Kharkov, and Minsk. With the exception of Leningrad, none of the cities had anything resembling a structured group. The only city that came close was Riga, where a samizdat committee had recently been set up to help facilitate distribution. But for the most part and with good reason, none of the others had any authority to make decisions. And this was the first point of contention as the activists sat beneath a tree in a park in the middle of Moscow. Dreizner thought that there should be a Soviet-wide organization, with a clear hierarchy, a charter, and dues, just as had been established in Leningrad. Everyone else objected. It would be reckless. It would hand the authorities the perfect premise for staging arrests: illegal organization.

They decided instead to remain a loose federation, meeting periodically, exchanging information, working on samizdat projects together, and encouraging open letters and petitions. Nothing more than that. They would call themselves the All-Union Coordinating Committee, referred to as the VKK, its acronym in Russian. After two days of meetings, most of them outdoors, and a goodbye party at the airport for Sasha Blank, the various representatives went back to their respective cities.

The second VKK gathering was in Riga three months later. Aron Shpilberg had recently moved there to be with his wife, and he, along with Boris Maftser, a tall, handsome student who had emerged as a charismatic leader among the younger activists, represented the city. They decided to put out a samizdat magazine. For three days they met in a dacha and worked out the details. It would be a journal intended to educate and interest Soviet Jews. Production would take place in Riga. A three-man editorial board with representatives from Riga, Leningrad, and Moscow would collect the material and meet in January to put together the final product. Maftser had a recommendation for the editorial board, a thoughtful young man who had the respect of people in the movement: Yosef Mendelevich.

This was exactly the kind of task Mendelevich was looking for. After being refused an exit visa and quitting school, he needed an outlet for his increasing nervous energy. He started work on what they'd decided to call *Iton* (the Hebrew word for "newspaper"), writing a few articles himself and collecting materials from others. At the same time he was developing another idea, collecting a list of all anti-Semitic incidents in the Soviet Union, a Jewish version of *Khronika*. He discussed it with Maftser, who was eager to make it a national project for the VKK and who also gave it the name Operation Pushkin, *Pushkin* being the code word for the Soviet Union in their frequent chats.

As their activities became more aggressive, the activists in Riga became more careful. They decided to divide into two groups, one that would be engaged in the open, public struggle, and another that would continue at a clandestine level. They needed to isolate those who were doing the work of preparing samizdat from those signing their names to petitions and making themselves known to the KGB. Group Aleph would be open, and Group Bet secret.

It was probably naive to think that the two groups could remain distinct from each other or that discipline could somehow be maintained over individuals who worked mostly independently. Mendelevich, being an editor of *Iton,* was told to remain in the clandestine group. His role was too important for him to be exposed. Mendelevich acquiesced but he was jealous of his friends who had gone public with their opposition. A major initiative of the VKK was to increase the number of signed open letters and petitions. In the fall of 1969, a number of collective letters, all written in Moscow with a similar style and making identical demands, were released in city after city. First came the letter from a group of twenty-five Jewish Muscovites, and shortly after a similar petition from twenty-two Riga activists addressed to U Thant, the secretary-general of the United Nations. Both the Moscow letter and the Riga letter made direct reference to Article 13 of the Universal Declaration of Human Rights: "Everyone has the right to leave any country, including his own, and to return to his country."

Mendelevich heard the Riga letter read on Kol Israel. Then he heard the names of those who had signed it, and he started shaking. These were his friends. People who had worked with him in Rumbuli, whom he'd known for years, with whom he'd produced samizdat and celebrated Jewish holidays. They were declaring their desire in the most public way possible. He wanted to be among them. It seemed pointless to remove himself from the open struggle for the sake of a job he felt anyone could do. He wanted to hear his own name read over the radio by an Israeli. Even though he knew it would make his journey more complicated and dangerous, the sound of it, pronounced in that guttural Middle Eastern voice, would make him feel that much closer to home.

The Overall Orchestra

1965–1969

THE REB SHLOMO CARLEBACH had a few days to spare. It was the Sabbath before Purim in the spring of 1965, and the Jewish folksinger had just performed in Frankfurt. His next show wasn't for another four days, in Lyon, and he didn't like sitting still. So he decided to travel to Prague. His entourage tried to dissuade him, worried about the difficulty of entering a Communist bloc country, assuring him that without a visa he would be turned away. But Carlebach, in his typical style, said that God, in his all-embracing, all-knowing power, would guide him to his destination if that was where he was truly meant to go.

Already a recognizable Jewish celebrity—with his large smile, black beard, long hair, and rotund, energetic body—Carlebach would become known as the singing, dancing hippie rabbi, the Jewish answer to the culture of the 1960s. Almost every story of his eventful life had the flavor of the Hasidic tales he endlessly recounted, filled with mystical revelations, unexplained coincidences, and ecstatic crying. Like Abraham Joshua Heschel and Yaakov Birnbaum, Carlebach drew sustenance from the pure Hasidic tradition, which saw joy as the most direct form of religious observance. But more than either of them, he was this joy manifest. Carlebach onstage was a dynamo of energy and charisma, singing folk songs and prayers set to simple melodies that he'd composed; he performed with fervor to the point of collapse. He spoke in the language of the growing hippie movement (everyone was a holy brother or holy sister), but he combined it with a distinctly Old World *Yiddishkeit* from his childhood days studying in a Polish yeshiva. At performances, he would tell his young, excited audiences: "You know, *chevra* [friends], if everyone in the whole world would hold hands and love each other, I swear *mamesh* [truly] those hands would go straight up to heaven."

Carlebach's family, a famous German Jewish rabbinical dynasty, arrived in New York in 1939, just barely escaping the Nazis. Shlomo was fourteen. His father started a synagogue on the Upper West Side of Manhattan that became known as the Carlebach Shul, and Shlomo began his rabbinical studies. But it was an attraction to the Hasidic tradition that set him on his path. He began frequenting the headquarters of the Lubavitch rabbi, sometimes walking all the way from the Upper West Side to Crown Heights, Brooklyn, the seat of the Lubavitchers, just so he could spend the Sabbath there. One day in 1949, Shlomo and a friend were summoned into the study of the elderly Lubavitcher rebbe, Joseph Isaac Schneerson, and told to begin an outreach program for college students. Shlomo had been composing for piano, but he switched to guitar. Soon he was performing Jewish music and telling his Hasidic tales on campuses all over the country, and by the mid-1950s he had developed a following. In 1959, he produced an album that sounded like no other Jewish music that had come before it. Arranged by Harry Belafonte, *Haneshama Lach* (Songs of My Soul) was thoroughly American in its folksiness, but also distinctly Jewish. He performed at all the most popular folk venues—the Village Gate and Town Hall in New York—and was considered a kind of novelty act, a rabbi with a guitar who sang about love. His popularity among the folk crowd, many of whom (like Bob Dylan) had a suppressed Jewishness, climaxed in his appearance at the Berkeley Folk Festival in 1966. It was on this visit to San Francisco, observing the growing throngs of hippies crowding Haight-Ashbury, that he came up with the idea for a House of Love and Prayer, a kind of Jewish halfway house/ashram/yeshiva. He stayed in the Bay Area to start it up. This planted him firmly in the counterculture—unlike other Hasidic rabbis, his hair was long, he hugged women, and he saw his job as helping drug-addicted hippies—but he also became an unlikely bridge between Jewish tradition and the new American Jewish youth.

The story of how he came to write the anthem of the Soviet Jewry movement is infused with that same spirit of Jewish awakening. On the flight from Frankfurt to Prague in 1965, Carlebach decided to open his mail. In the stack was a letter from Yaakov Birnbaum. Shlomo had already appeared at a few small Student Struggle for Soviet Jewry protests, events consisting mostly of a handful of yeshiva boys loudly singing along to his guitar. Birnbaum had an idea. He wondered if Shlomo would consider writing a melody to accompany the ancient Jewish motto "Am Yisrael Chai" (the people of Israel live). As Carlebach was reading he noticed the man next to him peering over his shoulder. Realizing that the stationery read *Student Struggle for Soviet Jewry,* he quickly crumpled up the paper and went to the bathroom to flush it down the toilet.

Once Carlebach arrived in Prague, he charmed an emigration officer into giving him a visa by explaining that he was related to Yehuda Loew, the famous sixteenth-century chief rabbi of Prague. Every little boy in the city, Jewish or non-Jewish, knew Loew as the creator of the myth of the magical Golem of Prague. Carlebach even managed to convince the head of Prague's main synagogue, an annoyed Communist bureaucrat, to let him perform on Purim. That evening, a few dozen young Jews accompanied him to a small concert hall, arguing with him all the way about the superiority of the Communist system. The concert did not go well at first. Around midnight, after a few hours of singing, Carlebach felt he hadn't reached them. He got up on a table and said to them, "*Chevra,* I have to tell you, tonight is Purim night. Tonight we are not afraid of Haman, we are not afraid of anyone in the world. I am telling you there is only one thing in the world: *Uvnei yerushalayim, ir ha kodesh*" (rebuild Jerusalem, the holy city).

With that he began dancing wildly, his black hair sticking to his sweaty round face. And the young people began dancing too, and soon they began crying. Before he knew it, it was after four in the morning, and many of them had come up to him and put their heads on his shoulder to weep.

At dawn, he found himself with some of the group back in his hotel room, and he wrapped his phylacteries around the arm and forehead of each boy, one after the other. When he was alone again, he felt so moved by the transformation he had witnessed that he grabbed his guitar and began working on the task Birnbaum had assigned him, a new "Am Yisrael Chai." He decided that one more phrase was needed, and he remembered the story of Joseph from the Bible. When Joseph's brothers discovered him in Egypt, where he was a prosperous adviser to the pharaoh, the first thing Joseph said to them was *"Od aveinu chai?"* (Is our father alive?) Shlomo added the affirmative answer to this—Our father *is* alive—as a refrain, and within minutes he had composed the song and sung it into his tape recorder. His version had the rhythm of an assertive battle cry, of a military chant; each word was belted out slow and strong and then repeated again and again. *The people of Israel live.* He left Prague that night, and within a few weeks he was in New York again, playing "Am Yisrael Chai" for the first time to a rapturous audience; their fists pounded the air with so much enthusiasm, it seemed to Shlomo that they themselves had pulled the song out of him.

By 1965, Carlebach had become the centerpiece of an increasing number of Student Struggle for Soviet Jewry rallies and his "Am Yisrael Chai" its quintessential anthem, distilling perfectly all the emotions that were motivating the young, mostly yarmulke-wearing ranks of Yaakov Birnbaum's growing army. The group still worked mostly out of Birnbaum's apartment in New York and survived off the dollar bills collected from the small membership dues and from selling SSSJ buttons at rallies. Birnbaum himself was obsessively driven; he was draining his savings and subsisting mostly on cans of Heinz beans, and his apartment was a jumble of stencils and cardboard, leaflets and books on Russian Jewry. Birnbaum's strategy had been to provide a steady drumbeat, to keep poking again and again at both the Soviets and the American Jewish establishment, trying to force them to take more serious action. And the students had responded. In the year and a half following the first protest, in May of 1964, they had organized more than thirty increasingly elaborate public demonstrations.

His pace was frantic. In the first issue of *S.O.S. Russian Jewry,* a mimeographed newsletter put out two months after the group's inaugural protest, he wrote, "Ever since the days of its inception, the SSSJ has been a dynamic movement. For a number of us, a 20-hour day has been the norm; the necessity of action compels us not to stop. . . . What we must now do is work, and work must be done by all, whether in the cities or at camps: work at our headquarters, lecture, talk, argue, persuade, write, organize, everything—everything to ultimately educate the American public to the shocking situation of Russian Jewry."

It was during this prolific period that the American movement's distinctive character came into focus, and it was largely shaped by Birnbaum.

He wanted it to be Jewish. The cause would be helped, he thought, if the act of protesting looked and felt like religious devotion. He linked demonstrations to Jewish holidays, beginning with the Jericho March around Passover 1965 in which he loaded Jewish symbol upon Jewish symbol. On Sunday morning, April 4, on the block of Sixty-seventh Street just west of the Soviet mission to the United Nations, a couple of thousand young people carrying hand-stenciled signs with slogans like WHY ARE MATZOS SUBVERSIVE? and HISTORY SHALL NOT REPEAT (each one seen and approved by Birnbaum) were arranged into two distinct columns. Between the columns marched seven men carrying Torah scrolls, and behind them seven rabbis, all wrapped in fringed blue and white prayer shawls and carrying shofars. Two rabbis read out Hebrew psalms as the procession walked by, and when the seven rabbis reached the edge of the police barrier that had been set up, at the closest point to the mission, the shofars were blown seven times, the high-pitched wails bouncing off the red-brick townhouses of the Upper East Side. Standing directly behind the rabbis and their shofars on that brisk spring day was Birnbaum, supervising from his commanding height, dressed in a dark suit and fedora.

The shofars, the choosing of a date near Passover for the protest, the Torahs, the singing of Isaiah's prophecies, the prayer shawls, even the biblically significant number seven—Birnbaum had used it all to turn the protest into a religious pageant. Following the blowing of the shofars—meant to echo the trumpets that brought down Jericho—the crowd marched to Dag Hammarskjold Plaza, across the street from the United Nations, where Shlomo Carlebach, his shirt open and his jewelry jangling, mounted the stage and led the crowd for the first time in "Am Yisrael Chai."

All of Birnbaum's demonstrations received extensive press, with most news organizations reporting on the activities as profound acts of religious witnessing, in much the same way that the voter registration battles down south and the civil rights march from Selma to Montgomery were depicted. On April 4, the eleven o'clock news on WNBC reported, "The sound of ceremonial rams' horns echoed against the walls of the Soviet mission on Manhattan's East Sixty-seventh Street as two thousand Jews conducted Operation Jericho to protest Soviet anti-Semitism. However the walls of the mission did not come tumbling down." In December of 1965, the Menorah March was reported by ABC News this way: "A group that uses as its motto 'I am my brother's keeper' marched in protest today against the treatment of Jews in the Soviet Union. The Student Struggle for Soviet Jewry used the ancient holiday of Hanukkah to stage their protest march. They carried a ten-foot menorah, the traditional symbol of the Jewish Maccabees, who fought for their religious freedom against the Syrians in the year 165 B.C."

Yossi Klein was only in sixth grade when he came upon Glenn Richter, dressed in his usual outfit of green trench coat and peddler cap, standing on a street corner in Klein's neighborhood of Borough Park. Richter was handing out leaflets and making puns to anyone who would listen ("I *am* my brother's keeper! Or is it my kipper's brother?"). Klein was the sensitive son of a Holocaust survivor, and he had posters of Jabotinsky and Bob Dylan on his bedroom wall. He listened intently to Richter's spiel, and soon this engaging jokester dubbed him the Borough Park Elementary School Chairman of SSSJ and promptly loaded his arms with boxes of leaflets. Some had images of Soviet anti-Semitic cartoons, others had facts and figures about synagogue closures and economic crimes. On top of the leaflets Richter placed a box of buttons and stickers. "Don't call us," he told Klein. "We'll call you."

For a boy like Klein, although he was much younger than most of the SSSJ student activists, the chance to participate, to be engaged, at a time when everyone seemed to be marching for one cause or another was elevating. Birnbaum and Richter made it a point to treat the students, even those in sixth grade, like adults, giving them responsibilities and a sense of their own integral importance to no less lofty a goal than saving three million of their brethren. Klein soon found himself in his first SSSJ rally, the Menorah March of 1965. A procession of a thousand students snaked across Central Park from the West Side of Manhattan to the East on the freezing night of December 19. Led by a team of four strong young men lifting a two-hundred-pound lead-pipe menorah, the marchers each carried a flashlight covered in red cellophane and sang the Hebrew words of Isaiah's prophecy: "Nation shall not lift up sword against nation and shall study war no more." Later that night, Klein excitedly watched the coverage of the rally on the evening news and was thrilled to see his own face, tucked between earmuffs and a visor, in the long line of protesters.

The Holocaust continued to be a motivating factor, one that only grew in significance as the genocide slowly began to take its place at the center of American Jewish identity. In the early and mid-1960s, and especially following the Eichmann trial, talk of what had happened during the war became more widespread and normalized. New history books began the work of detailing the final solution, and even popular culture took the first steps toward depicting the Holocaust. In December of 1965, the same month as the Menorah March, *Hadassah* magazine ran a feature on SSSJ in which it described the Holocaust as the motivating factor behind the group's activism: "The Soviet Jewry protest campaign has captured the imagination of youth to whom the Nazi disaster represents not simply an historical fact but a pressing reminder of the need for Jewish brotherly concern. Fate prevented these students from being alive in the 1930s and early 1940s and they are determined that this horror, in any of its manifestations, not be repeated in their generation. As such, the effort to save Soviet Jewry represents a new focal point for Jewish identification — in addition to traditional religious and Zionist organizations."

Yeshiva students were not the only ones at the Student Struggle rallies. Young secular Jews looking for a cause and a stronger sense of Jewish identity were attracted to them as well. This was 1965, the tipping point of the civil rights movement. Images of protest were everywhere. The Selma-to-Montgomery march was also made up of two neat columns of well-dressed young people singing religious hymns and asking for liberation. For most Jewish students, ending segregation was a much more immediate and urgent cause than Soviet Jewry. But Birnbaum knew that appropriating for his protests the same language and the same set of gestures as the civil rights movement used made his cause seem equally worthy of sacrifice.

Even as he encouraged a Jewish character, Birnbaum consciously piggybacked on the general spirit of the times. Though painfully less evocative than "We Shall Overcome," the opus of protest songs Birnbaum commissioned and collected during this period were nevertheless his movement's own. "There's a Fire Burning" was a typical example:

> There's a fire burning brightly in the sky
> And the roar of thunder crashing from on high,
> I see a nation there awakening
> Iron yokes will soon be breaking,
> And a nation long oppressed shall arise—
> A nation long oppressed shall arise.
>
> A trumpet rings through the night,
> The dawn appears—we see the light,
> We wake the world, we make them see
> That our people must be free.
>
> Freedom's train is racing swiftly through the land
> swiftly through the land
> And the tide of love is
> pounding on the sand,
> I can hear the whole world crying
> For a nation that's been dying,
> It will soon hold out its helping hand,
> It will soon hold out its helping hand.

What was most striking about the fervor of those students who trudged through Central Park in the cold night following a gargantuan menorah is how little they knew about the actual "plight of the Soviet Jew," as they referred to their cause. Soviet Jews themselves were still unseen and unheard. So the passion and activity of these young American Jews was largely self-motivated and self-directed. The reaction to all their activity from the other side of the iron curtain was silence. Before 1967, before there was a Kochubievsky and a Kazakov and the letter of the Georgian Jews, there was no image in the minds of these students to correspond with the people they were defending. The problem was understood as a theoretical one and expressed mostly in cold facts and figures: How many synagogues had been closed down? What proportion of economic crimes had been blamed on Jews? Was matzo readily available? When was the last book in Yiddish published?

When Moshe Decter, the man working secretly for the Israeli Lishka, spoke to a group of SSSJ students on November 1, 1964, at the West Side Jewish Community Center, the extent of this disconnect was palpable. After spending most of the four-hour session recounting Russian Jewish history going back to czarist times, he opened the floor to questions. "When did you make your most recent trip to the Soviet Union?" one student asked. Decter was sitting next to Yaakov Birnbaum; both men wore beatnik goatees. Decter lit a cigarette, adjusted his black horn-rimmed glasses, and answered, "I've never been there."

Another student wanted to know if there was any evidence the Soviet Jews actually cared about being Jews, whether they were fearful or just apathetic. He preempted Decter's prepared answer about the large yearly Simchat Torah celebrations. "Beyond the Simchat Torah?" Decter asked. "Well, that is a fact. I wouldn't snipe at that fact," he barked harshly. "It happens every year. There are people perhaps better informed than I on this particular facet who can perhaps tell you of the large numbers—I don't know what numbers there are and I doubt if even the better informed people know what numbers there are, but large numbers—of young people who, with self-sacrifice, endangering their freedom and maybe even their lives, are engaged in the study of the traditional Jewish texts, secretly."

But this fuzziness about what Soviet Jews themselves desired did not stop Decter from presenting the students with an exalted vision of their own responsibility. "What can we do?" he asked them.

Well, we can do the kind of thing that we're doing. You are providing a stimulus to Jewish public opinion. Only when Jewish public opinion in this country becomes totally aroused, and acts on this question daily in every conceivable way, dramatic and undramatic . . . and there are hundreds of things that can be dreamed up to do, responsibly and based on factuality and dignity and self-respect, to demand, to insist, to appeal, in two different directions, one to the Soviet government and one to our own government. Our hope, I think we can rest assured, is that we will do no harm. Our hope is that the Soviets may be sufficiently sensitive that they may succumb to the pressure of world opinion and the insistence of our own government, if we can ever achieve that, that they modify their policies sufficiently.

Resentment and disappointment with the Jewish establishment added fuel to the self-generated motivation of Birnbaum and his students. For Lou Rosenblum, Herb Caron, and the professional middle-aged men who made up the Cleveland Committee on Soviet Anti-Semitism, it shaped their identity. The group who found inspiration in the Cassandra-like wartime prophecies of Jabotinsky expected the slowness of American Jewish organizations. But that didn't alleviate their feeling that an unconscionable neglect was taking place. "We don't have much hope at this time that the existing Jewish community organizations will do the job that is required," Rosenblum wrote in a May 1965 letter. "At the national level, the American Jewish Conference on Soviet Jewry is a paper organization . . . The whole operation reflects compromise and indecision; in a word, it is a farce." This feeling came through month after month in the publication Rosenblum and Caron started, *Spotlight,* a simple compilation of as much Soviet Jewry news as they could get their hands on. In the November 1965 issue, Rosenblum editorialized: "From its inception in April 1964, to the present, the Conference has given the appearance of action without the effect of action. Possibly this shadow organization may serve to salve the conscience of our Jewish leaders. In truth, however, the American Jewish Conference on Soviet Jewry has a been a sorry response to the impending religious and cultural genocide of three million Jews."

After Rosenblum and Caron returned from the Washington conference in 1964, the Cleveland group decided that it would have to fill the void. Rosenblum, the NASA scientist, soon eclipsed Herb Caron as the leader of the organization, which had changed its name in early 1965 to the more permanent Cleveland *Council* on Soviet Anti-Semitism. And with the change, a new seriousness and productivity came to characterize the activists. Rosenblum was a meticulous and organized man who immediately grasped that the struggle would be a long-term one.

Where Caron was emotional and impassioned, Rosenblum was more concerned with the logistics of building an organization. In a May 1965 letter to Louis Nemzer, a Sovietologist at Ohio State University, Rosenblum set out his goals: the CCSA was "operating under the premise that vital to a solution of this problem is 1) the U.S. government on record as condemning Soviet anti-Semitic practices and 2) the U.S. government prepared to exact concessions, at an appropriate time, from Soviet leaders involving cessation of their anti-Jewish policies."

The second step, Rosenblum knew, could not be achieved without the first, without increasing—as Moshe Decter implored the students to do—public awareness. It would take more than a hundred or even a thousand voices of protest. He needed to excite the whole community if he wanted to create any real pressure. But unlike Birnbaum, who had the advantage of New York City's huge Jewish population, the UN Soviet mission, and national media, Rosenblum did not have the resources of public protest at his disposal.

He decided to focus on two fronts: create educational materials and build a network of like-minded individuals in other cities. The objectives would feed off each other. The materials started pouring out first. He developed a kind of Soviet Jewry handbook, forty pages in length, that provided lists of possible activities that any community could undertake (prayers to incorporate into services, tools for teachers, and so on). He commissioned an artistically inclined member of Beth Israel to create a dramatic logo that could be used for buttons and seals. As it turned out, that drawing, a collection of sad-looking Russian Jews in peddler caps and babushkas drawn in Communist red, was compelling enough that Rosenblum sold sheets of seals for fifty cents each. Yaakov Birnbaum bought them by the box.

In 1966, Rosenblum coordinated the filming of a short movie. Up until that point, the only available film relating to Soviet Jewry was a twenty-nine-minute piece narrated by the gangstery actor Edward G. Robinson (born Emanuel Goldenberg of Romania), who played the role of a prosecutor putting the Soviet Union on trial for its treatment of Jews. Rosenblum set out to make a more streamlined film. It took a few months, but he convinced the local Jewish federation to fund the cost of the camera rentals and got Abraham Joshua Heschel to narrate from behind his desk at the Jewish Theological Seminary. The finished film jumped between Heschel's rumpled-looking face and scenes of a fake Russian family, who were portrayed by Rosenblum's young daughter Miriam and members of Beth Israel.

All these materials were featured in *Spotlight*, which acted as a key resource for far-flung communities that wanted to be involved. Through it, Rosenblum made contact with other activists, who saw in him an adviser and guide. He even received a letter from a Jewish community in South Africa ordering half a dozen copies of the film. Rosenblum set up distribution points where he could send a few hundred copies of *Spotlight* at a time—three hundred to Los Angeles, a hundred to Houston. Then when he traveled to these cities for work—as he increasingly did once he was promoted to section head and then branch chief of his lab—he arranged to meet new contacts. By the mid-1960s, he had a mailing list of twelve hundred people, half of whom came from outside Cleveland.

Rosenblum and his CCSA were serving a different function than Birnbaum with his singing students in New York were. They were developing the rudimentary infrastructure of an alternative national organization made up entirely of volunteers. Even though Rosenblum worked full-time at NASA and had a family with young children, he committed himself obsessively. Evenings he would come home, kiss his wife, Evy, wave to the kids, and then descend to the basement to type answers to the hundreds of letters he received weekly. From 1966 on he was so busy with the Soviet Jewry work that he hired a full-time office manager to help him.

Rosenblum's and Birnbaum's anger at the Jewish establishment was often overwrought. But it wasn't entirely misplaced. The organization that had been launched with much fanfare at the April 1964 conference in Washington was useless. Supplied with neither budget nor staff, it spent its first two years in a dysfunctional rotation system that passed responsibility to a different Jewish organization every six months. This left no time for any one person to take the initiative. Eventually, the National Jewish Community Relations Council, the umbrella group that coordinated the activities of hundreds of centers of Jewish life all over the country, adopted the orphaned entity.

When representatives of the composite organizations met in April

of 1966 to mark two years of the American Jewish Conference's existence, the language was lofty. Gathered at Congress Hall, the site of the
birth of the Bill of Rights, the Jewish leaders read out a Declaration
of Rights for Soviet Jewry that was then voted on and adopted. "We,
the representatives of American Jewry, are met today in a Hall hallowed by history, echoing with the voices of men who made the age-
old dream of liberty the law of these United State of America . . . The
year was 1791. Nearly two centuries later countless millions throughout
the world still wait. Among them are three million of our fellow-Jews
in the USSR."

Lou Rosenblum once again crashed the proceedings and tried to
push through yet another resolution providing permanent resources
to the organization. As in 1964, he found wide support among the delegates. But there was still no will among the leadership to move beyond
rhetoric. Disappointed, Lou wrote in the next issue of *Spotlight* that
the "event was merely a reshaping of previous pronouncements and no
means were provided for carrying out the suggested actions."

In spite of Rosenblum's disenchantment, the establishment was not
completely silent or irrelevant. It was impossible to ignore the growing clamor among American Jews to get at least some information on
Soviet Jewry, if not a response to the problem. And in fact, when it
did act, the Jewish leadership could harness incredible manpower and
resources. The first two public events organized by the American Jewish Conference on Soviet Jewry dwarfed Birnbaum's student demonstrations. A rally in Madison Square Garden in June 1965 drew nearly
twenty thousand people. In Washington, the Eternal Light Vigil in
Lafayette Park, across from the White House, brought ten thousand
people from more than one hundred communities. The "Matzoh of
Oppression" program of Passover 1966 was very popular. In two hundred and fifty thousand distributed booklets, the AJCSJ instructed
American Jews to include an extra matzo in their Seders to represent
the oppression of Soviet Jews.

The establishment also had the clout. The Madison Square Garden
rally drew the likes of Mayor Robert Wagner—who declared the day,
June 3, Conference on Soviet Jewry Day in New York City—as well as
the civil rights leader A. Philip Randolph and Senators Jacob Javits and
Robert Kennedy; there was even a message of solidarity from President

Johnson. But, like the general atmosphere of the rally, the president's tone was absent much passion: "In a spirit of peace and reason, we express our earnest hope that the Soviet leadership will ameliorate the situation of its Jewish minority. Doing so would go a long way toward removing a moral and emotional barrier between us and contribute to a relaxation of tensions."

For the establishment, there was still a very strong kinship between the struggle for civil rights and the support of Soviet Jewry. Morris Abram, then the U.S. representative to the UN Commission on Human Rights, told the Madison Square Garden rally, "We shall protest; we shall march; we shall overcome." At one Philadelphia rally in March of 1965, a banner read SELMA OR MOSCOW: HUMAN LIBERTY IS INDIVISIBLE. END SOVIET ANTI-SEMITISM.

Jewish leaders maintained close connections to those older, now mainstream civil rights leaders—even while younger and more militant activists were taking over. Bayard Rustin, who organized the March on Washington, a moderating force and a genuine believer in the black-Jewish coalition, frequently participated at Soviet Jewry demonstrations. At the Eternal Light Vigil in front of the White House—an event that was almost postponed because some Jewish leaders thought it was too provocative—Rustin used one of Dr. King's favorite lines, "Injustice anywhere is a threat to justice everywhere," and said that he would therefore not be silent "about what happens to my brothers and sisters who happen to be Jews in the USSR." King himself frequently spoke on the issue, a result partly of his close friendship with Heschel. In December of 1966, from his home in Atlanta, King addressed thirty-two Soviet Jewry protests simultaneously by phone hookup. He told them that "the sincere and genuine concern felt by so many people around the world for this problem should impel the Soviet government not only to effect a solution, but to do it with all deliberate speed." The last line was an echo of the *Brown v. Board of Education* decision.

Maintaining this analogy, civil rights for both blacks and Soviet Jews, appealed to the establishment because it had a way of neutering the struggle. If the goal of the civil rights movement was to pressure the U.S. government to change its laws, than that of the Soviet Jewry movement was to pressure the Soviet Union. This avoided the conclusion that Lou Rosenblum and Yaakov Birnbaum had come to—that the real pressure had to be directed at the American government, that only an American president had the carrots and the sticks to make a Kosygin or a Brezhnev change his policies. It was this fundamental tactical difference that began to divide the activists and the establishment. For all the rhetorical flourish of Morris Abram wanting to "overcome," these Jewish leaders were reluctant to put the onus for change on the U.S. government. They did not want to be confrontational. It was easier to complain to the deaf and distant Soviet Union.

These limited objectives put the Jewish establishment in lockstep with an administration that was unwilling to open up another front in the Cold War, especially given the escalation in Vietnam. In one memo, Walt Rostow, a close adviser to Johnson, noted that leaders of the Jewish community had met on August 4, 1966, with Dean Rusk, the secretary of state, and been told that "the current Vietnam situation was a limiting factor on how much influence he or the President might have with Soviet leaders on the Jewish problem." Speaking at the Madison Square Garden rally, Dr. Max Nussbaum, the head of the American Zionist Council, emphasized, as many others had before him, that "it is not the purpose of the American Jewish community to add to East-West difficulties and to make the 'cold' war hotter." At the same time, Rosenblum and Birnbaum had decided that this was precisely what they should be doing.

Then there was Nahum Goldmann, an aging but still influential voice in the Jewish community, who refused to condemn the Soviet Union. When he heard about the Madison Square Garden rally, he quickly released a statement disassociating himself from some of the more emotional rhetoric of the speakers. "To compare in any way the policy of the Soviet government with the Nazis is not only a hideous distortion, but highly unfair to Soviet Russia, which has saved hundred of thousands of Jews when they escaped from the Nazis at the beginning of the Second World War," he huffed.

Goldmann had heard that some of the younger people at the rally, Birnbaum's students, were carrying placards that read LET MY PEOPLE GO. The implication was too provocative for him. It would offend the Soviets and would be seen as an affront to their sovereignty. It was also, he felt, naive to assume that it was what the Soviet Jews themselves desired. This was increasingly the official line of the Jewish establishment, whose members insisted in all their pronouncements that family reunification was their concern, not wide-scale emigration. In his famous December 1966 statement that had stimulated demands for visas, Kosygin had promised his government would try to accommodate these requests. But as the slogan—a powerful allusion to the biblical story of Exodus—made clear, there were many who were starting to think that simply allowing people to study Talmud or eat matzo was not enough. They were beginning to feel—even before they heard from Soviet Jews themselves—that there was only one solution to this problem.

Interestingly, Rosenblum and Birnbaum weren't the only ones frustrated by what they saw as the *shtadlonus* of the American Jewish community. The Israelis also were growing increasingly impatient. Still working secretly through Lishkat Hakesher, the almost completely unknown office in Tel Aviv run by Shaul Avigur, Israel used its emissaries in London, Paris, and New York to push its agenda. In the United States, Meir Rosenne had been working since 1961 as the consul-general in New York and had at his side the indefatigable and ornery intellectual Moshe Decter. The message the two were trying to impart was that the Jewish establishment needed to do more. In his typically eviscerating tone, Decter wrote in April of 1965 to the Central Conference of American Rabbis, the coordinating body of Reform Judaism, berating it for its passivity, or what he described as a "wait-and-see ostrich policy while Soviet Jewry continues to be spiritually atomized and pulverized." He continued, "Doesn't your conscience, and perhaps even some slight vision of history's judgment, intrude ever so slightly on your ill-informed and unwarranted complacence?"

The two most active groups, Rosenblum's in Cleveland and Birnbaum's in New York, were perfect foils for prodding the establishment toward deeper involvement. Through Rosenne and Decter, Israel gave subtle and sometimes not-so-subtle direction, helped the groups find funding, and provided information. Starting in 1965, the Lishka had a forceful leader running its operations out of Washington, Nehemiah Levanon. A brusque, barrel-chested Israeli, Levanon had been with the Nativ operation practically since its inception, and with Avigur now aging and increasingly detached, he was taking on more responsibility.

Levanon was born in Estonia and had grown up in the Zionist socialist youth movements of the Baltics, immigrating to Israel in 1938 and starting a kibbutz in the upper Galilee, Kfar Blum, where he happily worked as a farm manager until 1952. That's when the head of the Mossad, Isser Harel, personally recruited him and sent him to Moscow with the first group of Nativ secret agents—his cover at the Israeli embassy was agricultural attaché—where he traveled the country trying to connect with Jews. So began his career with the Lishka. In 1955, he helped set up Bar, the secret campaign to foment an international movement, and ten years later he was directing most of its activities—including overseeing Decter and Rosenne in New York—from his perch in the American capital. In 1965, not long after his move to Washington, Levanon flew to Cleveland to meet with Rosenblum at his suburban home, but he didn't reveal to him then or subsequently the nature of the Lishka. Rosenblum was under the impression that the hearty Israeli sitting in his living room and drinking coffee was simply an expert on Soviet Jews, perhaps a case officer at the Soviet desk of the Foreign Office, one privy to a lot of information. He would never have guessed that Levanon answered directly to the prime minister of Israel.

In a letter to Rosenblum in November of 1965, Decter made cryptic reference to his bosses and expressed what must have been Levanon's opinion of the midwestern agitators' usefulness: "Let me again for the nth time—and I shall never tire of repeating it—tell you how deeply impressed and moved I am (and this goes also for some of our mutual Jewish friends from abroad) with the devotion, intelligence and energy that you and your colleagues in Cleveland have demonstrated for so long against such frustrating odds. I believe, and please convey this to Herb and the others, that when some day the history of the rescue of Russian Jewry will be written, the Cleveland group will occupy an honorable place in it. What higher aspiration can there be for us who are members of so history-conscious and so historic-laden a people?"

Decter was a mysterious figure to Rosenblum and Birnbaum. They had a vague sense that he was connected to the Israelis but had no real understanding of the source of his authority, why he was able to sit in on the most important establishment meetings, why his letters sounded more like directives than the musings of a one-man operation. His letters in fact strongly reflect the balancing act the Israelis were performing. While they were committed to working through the establishment, sensing that only these respected Jewish leaders could attract real attention to the issue, they also saw the passion of the grassroots groups and wanted desperately to harness it for their own purposes. In Decter's correspondence with the CCSA he disparaged the establishment over and over again in solidarity with a frustrated Rosenblum, describing the "nearly Byzantine bureaucratic and organizational red tape" that had begun to "dominate [the] thinking and actions" of the current head of the American Jewish Conference on Soviet Jewry, or painting Hillel, the national campus association for Jewish students, as a "top-heavy, tired and moribund organization of empty rabbis." The letters were filled with a growing anger: "But after all these years and all the alleged brains at their disposal and with the enormous budgets at their command, they can still ask, like simpletons, what is there for us to do."

At the same time, though, Decter tried to moderate the ardor that was coming out of Cleveland, telling them to simplify and be more realistic, to exercise "circumspection and caution," and discounting the idea that the establishment could be written off. In a revealing letter to Herb Caron on December 16, 1965, Decter wrote,

> As you well know, these past six years have provided me with enough bitterness and frustration in dealing with Jewish lay and professional "leaders" to last a lifetime; were it not for this cause, I would continue to be, as I was when I began, the alienated, aloof American Jewish intellectual which all my friends are. . . . Yet despite my long-range detachment, at least from the leadership high and low, the bedrock fact with which I must live in this work—*and that goes for anyone else in this work*—is that we must work with and through the Jewish community, which unfortunately but inescapably means *coexistence* with the leadership. As Weizmann is reputed to have said, "such are my Jews; I have no better ones."

He ends the letter with a PS that is the clearest articulation of the role he envisioned for the Cleveland group: "I continue to regard the existence and activity of the CCSA not only as invaluable in themselves but also as goads to the Establishment. Thus, I am fully aware of the tricky and delicate task involved in being a goad which at the same time does not entirely alienate the goadee—but this is what I believe your path must be."

Decter traveled the country in 1965 and 1966 trying to motivate other communities to follow the Cleveland model, with only moderate success, and he had some hesitation about how well he could control a whole legion of Rosenblums or Birnbaums. At the same time, he worried his activities might alienate the establishment. In a letter to a Rabbi Shimon Paskow in Northridge, California, Decter advised that "it is time for you to create an ad hoc committee in your community along the lines of the Cleveland group." But he ended his letter on an ominous note, indicative of how hamstrung Decter and the Israelis behind him were in their manipulation of the American Jewish community. "I ask you with the utmost seriousness to destroy this letter, for despite everything and regardless of even the most optimistic of eventualities, I must willy-nilly continue to cooperate with the Establishment, to seek ends which only the official power structure can achieve. As you see, each instrument has its tone and its own function in the overall orchestra."

One of Meir Rosenne's duties as an Israeli agent of the Lishka was to brief and debrief the few people who visited the Soviet Union. In the fall of 1965, Rosenne sat down at the Israeli consulate in Manhattan with a thin, sallow-looking man who had sunken eyes and wisps of thin hair plastered against his wide forehead. Rosenne was to give him advice for his upcoming trip to Russia. Since the publication in 1960 of the English translation of his minimalist Holocaust memoir *Night,* Elie Wiesel had fashioned himself into a *maggid,* a kind of Hasidic storytelling preacher that was common in his childhood shtetl of Sighet, Romania. And though the point of his preaching was to "give testimony for the dead," he was now on a mission that would make him, as he put it in his typically self-aggrandizing and slightly overblown style, "a messenger of the living." The jovial Rosenne, faced with the seriousness of the thirty-eight-year-old writer, told him to beware of beautiful Russian women who might suddenly show up naked in his hotel room or train compartment. They could be KGB agents. Wiesel did not laugh.

Night began life as an eight-hundred-page Yiddish account of Wiesel's family's war story, starting in 1941 when he was thirteen and ending with his lonely liberation by American soldiers from Buchenwald, where he had watched his father slowly die. The book was clearly influenced by the existentialist writers then popular in France, where Wiesel lived following the war, working as a journalist for the Israeli newspaper *Yediot Aharonot*. Championed by his friend the French writer François Mauriac, who once said about Wiesel that "he has the look of Lazarus about him," he cut down his text to 121 pages, transforming a long, anguished screed into a novel with the cool, spare detachment of Camus. The book was extremely popular; its power lay in its simplicity, the horror distilled to a fine, sharpened point. In America, where Wiesel moved in order to become UN correspondent for *Yediot,* Wiesel's book found as much success as it had in France. He was soon churning out books at a rapid rate, adding *L'Aube* and *Le Jour* to form a trilogy with *La Nuit,* and gaining many accolades for writing about the Holocaust at a time when very few were (a reviewer in *Commentary* declared *Night* "almost unbearably painful, and certainly beyond criticism"). The awards began arriving in the mid-1960s. By 1965, Wiesel had become more than just another memoirist: he represented the Holocaust. Just as the genocide was beginning to become an accepted topic of thought for Americans, Wiesel's mournful face, which he presented at an endless stream of readings and moralizing lectures, became the image of the quintessential survivor, righteous in his insistence that we never forget.

In September of 1965, during the High Holy Days, Wiesel began his personal fact-finding mission to the Soviet Union, traveling to Moscow, Leningrad, Kiev, and Tbilisi. As he would write in his popular account of the trip, *The Jews of Silence,* he had been skeptical for many years about the true state of Soviet Jewry.

> I refused to believe it. Like many people, I was alive to the reports of Jewish suffering in Russia. I read all the books and articles and heard testimony given at public meetings or behind closed doors. Yet I was unwilling, or unable, to believe it. I had too many questions, too many doubts and misgivings — not about the fact of Jewish suffering in the Soviet Union but about its scope . . . If synagogues are being

closed in Russia, I reasoned, Jews will simply go on praying in the ones that remain open. Are families prevented from reuniting? A new regime will soon come to power and the policy will change. Does the press conduct a campaign of anti-Semitism? Does it portray Jews as black marketers, swindlers, drunkards? Does it disparage the state of Israel and malign the Zionist movement? This, too, will pass. . . . The essential thing is that they be permitted to live, that their existence itself not be endangered, that there be no pogroms. And in Russia there are no pogroms; no one will dispute that. There are no detention camps. The situation, in other words, is not so unbearable.

Wiesel's few weeks in the Soviet Union changed his mind. He was bewildered and agitated in equal measure by the Jews he met. Some of these encounters were as mystical as Shlomo Carlebach's account of the spontaneous weeping of the young Jews of Prague. On Wiesel's first day in Moscow, a man came up to him, tightly wrapped in a coat and wearing a hat pulled down so far that his face was obscured. In a voice "choked and fearful" he whispered to the writer in Yiddish, "Do you know what is happening to us?" and then quickly scurried away. In Wiesel's telling, the whole trip had this quality, a cross between a Hasidic tale and the work of Kafka. The Jews he discovered were fearful to the point of paralysis. "Time after time, people with whom I had been talking slipped away without saying good-by or left me in the middle of a sentence." The book the trip produced was an examination of this fear, an attempt to penetrate it. "Why do they behave like a community of terrorized captives, on the brink of some awful abyss?"

Wiesel didn't really know what to make of these furtive Jews because, counterbalanced with this mysterious secretiveness, there was also great exuberance. Present at the annual Simchat Torah celebrations in front of the Great Choral Synagogue in Moscow, Wiesel was filled with awe. "Where did they all come from?" Wiesel wondered.

Who sent them here? How did they know it was to be tonight on Arkhipova Street near the Great Synagogue? Who told them that tens of thousands of boys and girls would gather here to sing and dance and rejoice in the joy of the Torah? They who barely know each other and know even less of Judaism—how did they know that? I spent hours among them, dazed and excited, agitated by an ancient dream. I forgot the depression that had been building up over the past weeks. I forgot everything except the present and the future. I have seldom felt so proud, so happy, so optimistic. The purest light is born in darkness. Here there is darkness; here there will be light. There must be—it has already begun to burn.

It was the highlight of his visit, but a confusing one. He stood amid the swirling dancing and singing, and in his book he described a moment that exemplified the incongruousness of all this light suddenly emerging out of darkness. He observed a young woman, "dark-haired and vivacious," standing in the middle of a circle and leading a chorus. "Who are we?" she shouted. "Jews!" the group answered. "What are we?" "Jews!" "What shall we remain?" "Jews!" Wiesel was moved by such a pure expression of passionate identification—this when he could hardly get random Soviet Jews he met on the street to admit they were, indeed, Jewish. Later on, he found the young woman. He peppered her with questions, but it was clear that she knew nothing about Judaism and even regurgitated some of the state propaganda (Israel, she said, was "aggressive, racist, and capitalist"). When he asked her finally why she wanted so much to be a Jew, she answered, "I'll tell you why I'm a Jew. Because I like to sing."

Wiesel captured in his book this desire for identity mixed with a profound state of ignorance and fear. *The Jews of Silence,* published in the fall of 1966 and based on his *Yediot Aharonot* dispatches, offered an impressionistic account of what it meant to be a Jew in the Soviet Union, the first work to fully illustrate their strange state of limbo. It was an overdramatic report and one filtered through the prism of Wiesel's own ego ("I went to Russia drawn by the silence of its Jews. I brought back their cry"), but it began the process of chiseling a distinct form out of the rough slab that until then had been known simply as Soviet Jewry.

The Jews of Silence was received as a potent illumination of a previously obscure problem. Reviewing the book for the *New York Times,* the Yiddish writer Isaac Bashevis Singer deemed it a little too "emotional" for his taste but nevertheless felt that Wiesel captured a certain truth. "His account is as full of contradictions as is the life of the

Jews in Soviet Russia," Singer wrote. A critic for the *Los Angeles Times* concluded that "if this is not the violent suppression, the genocide of Hitler's Germany, it is certainly, in terms of its ends, no less an affront to humanity."

But what most American Jews took away from the book, even more than a picture of a psychologically tortured population, was the sense that Wiesel was pointing an accusatory finger at them. In his closing pages, he makes his indictment explicit:

> One may question whether we have any way of knowing that the Jews of Russia really want us to do anything for them. How do we know that our shouts and protests will not bring them harm? These are very serious questions, and I put them to the Russian Jews themselves. Their answer was always the same: "Cry out, cry out until you have no more strength to cry. You must enlist public opinion, you must turn to those with influence, you must involve your governments—the hour is late" . . . I promised I would do it, but I wept before them as I promised. I wept because I knew that nothing would help. Our Jews have other problems on their minds. When you tell them what is expected of them in Russia, they shrug their shoulders. It is exaggerated; or, we can do nothing about it; or, we must not do too much lest we be accused of interfering in the cold war. The Jewish brain has killed the Jewish heart. This is why I wept. . . . I believe with all my soul that despite the suffering, despite the hardship and the fear, the Jews of Russia will withstand the pressure and emerge victorious. But whether or not we shall ever be worthy of their trust, whether or not we shall overcome the pressures we have ourselves created, I cannot say. I returned from the Soviet Union disheartened and depressed. But what torments me most is not the Jews of silence I met in Russia, but the silence of the Jews I live among today.

If one event acted as an air-raid siren piercing this silence and complacency, it was at 7:45 in the morning on June 5, 1967, the moment when bombs dropped from Israeli jets destroyed nearly the entire Egyptian air force in just a few hours. Within six days the war in the Middle East would be over. The result would be a new map for Israel but also a new sense of Jewish identity. The war pushed Boris Kochubievsky to boldness, cut off as he was in the Ukraine from the larger Jewish world and receiving his news only from a small shortwave radio he kept tucked under his desk at the factory. For American Jews, part of a self-aware and organized community, the sense of collective pride and redemption was equally overwhelming. Or as Lucy Dawidowicz, the Jewish historian, put it a few months after the events in June, "American Jews, so frequently accused of indifference and passivity, turned into a passionate, turbulent, clamorous multitude, affirming in unprecedented fashion that they were part of the Jewish people and that Israel's survival was their survival."

The lead-up to the war that May had been as emotionally distressing as its outcome was exhilarating. As Nasser's pronouncements and actions became increasingly more bellicose, there was a deep sense of foreboding that he, together with Syria and Jordan, would make good on his word to bring about another holocaust. In New York, Jews rushed to the Israeli consulate to offer their help. Before war broke out and travel to Israel was banned by the government, tens of thousands of young people, half of them in New York, applied to take over civilian jobs in Israel that had been left vacant by mobilized soldiers. The Jewish Agency, the Israeli body charged with immigration, could not handle the influx of requests. By most estimates, between the day Nasser closed the Straits and the end of the war, the Israeli Emergency Fund of the United Jewish Appeal collected over a hundred million dollars, with money coming in faster than the office could tabulate it. Several banks even loaned their employees to the United Jewish Appeal to help it keep up with the receipts. There were stories of people who cashed in securities and insurance policies so they could give larger contributions.

Arthur Hertzberg, the New Jersey rabbi and history professor, wrote about the phenomenon for *Commentary* in August 1967, two months after the war's end: "Many Jews would never have believed that grave danger to Israel could dominate their thoughts and emotions to the exclusion of all else; many were surprised by the depth of their anger at those of their friends who carried on as usual, untouched by fear for Israeli survival and the instinctive involvement they themselves felt. This outpouring of feeling and commitment appears to contradict all the predictions about the evaporating Jewishness of the American Jews."

That summer of 1967, while the counterculture and its colorful and suddenly robust protest against Vietnam burst into the mainstream and the civil rights movement devolved into violent riots that spread through the inner cities of Newark and Detroit, a certain kind of young American Jew was feeling a different stirring. The war had given these young people a renewed sense of Jewish identity, a connection, and even a new sort of moral compass by which to guide their political views. One college student's letter to the editor of the *Village Voice* captured this strange new identification:

> I think it must have been this way for many of my generation, that the Israeli-Arab collision was a moment of truth. For the first time in my grown-up life, I really understood what an enemy was. For the first time, I knew what it was to be us against the killers.... I will never kid myself that we are only the things we choose to be. Roots count.... I was walking along the street listening to a transistor radio when I first heard that the Israelis, the Jews, had reached the Wailing Wall and with guns slung over their shoulders were praying there. No one was watching me, but I wept anyway. Sometimes even the tear-glands know more than the mind.

These feelings were echoed many times over. The American Zionist Youth Foundation asked 510 of the volunteers who signed up to go to Israel to fill out a questionnaire about their motivations. The answers show consistent bewilderment at the unexpected awakening of this sense of pride and duty. A man described as a twenty-one-year-old part-time college student with four years of Hebrew school who did not belong to a synagogue and was not affiliated with any Jewish organization wrote, "When I was driving to work I heard on the radio what had happened. I went to my office and could not work. Chills went through me and I knew that I must go and fight for my people. I am not very religious, but I knew that I had to try and help. I got my passport but I could not get a visa because of the State Department. Since I would have given up my life for Israel, I would like to spend my next vacation there. I bought Israeli bonds with my vacation money this year." A twenty-two-year-old college senior wrote, "I called the Israel Embassy to see if I could enlist to fight. I have never in 22 years felt a strong Jewish attraction. As a matter of fact, at times I even rejected my heritage. For the first time in my life I was forced to resolve this problem within myself. I still have doubts as to what the 'Zionist' movement stands for, but I felt obliged not just to sit back and see the State of Israel wiped off the map."

On the streets of Borough Park, Brooklyn, where the young Student Struggle activist Yossi Klein was finishing eighth grade, the excitement was no less palpable. Transistor radios blared the latest news all day long from every corner. And the victory was celebrated with the open waving of Israeli flags and public singing of "Hatikvah." Yossi wanted to emulate the rugged, vigorous Israelis, the new Jews who had, in the most dramatic manner, controlled the direction of history rather than been dragged along by its flow. Wearing blue-tinted granny glasses that he'd bought in a psychedelic shop on a street bordering his Ortho-dox neighborhood, Yossi watched the images of hippies dancing in the parks of San Francisco on his television that summer. And the happi-ness and exuberance they expressed seemed to be attached and akin to his own.

By the time of the Six-Day War, the civil rights movement had turned into a race revolution. The focus on black power and its attendant violence not only alienated the moderates like King and Rustin but also brought an end to the black-Jewish coalition. The tension had always been there. Younger militants in the movement resented and mistrusted the liberal Jews, who wanted to advise on strategy and di-rection. The definitive rupture occurred in the summer of 1966, when SNCC, the student wing of the movement, decided to exclude whites from leadership positions. There was growing frustration with the slow pace of change and a sense that white liberals were imposing too much moderation and compromise. Self-determination was the goal, not a few nice laws passed by Congress. They rejected the slow and painstaking path of building coalitions and acquiring political power that many of the Jewish activists, such as Allard Lowenstein, had been advocating. Jews as a group came to be perceived as obstacles, no dif-ferent than any other whites.

The other divisive element was the start of the northern campaign in 1965. As interest turned to the deep poverty of the inner cities of

Chicago, Detroit, and New York, it was clear that there might be a clash of interests between the blacks and the poor Jews who still shared those communities. The South was distant and the victories there obvious (the right to vote, the right to ride buses), but many Jews felt that they would be the casualties of any move by blacks to take power and privilege in the North. School busing, for example, made Jewish families worry about the impact of an influx of poor blacks on their children's education. Already in 1964, a *New York Times* article had found that almost half of Jewish New Yorkers felt the civil rights movement should "slow down." And from the black perspective, Jews were the nearest white symbols in their communities—the grocer setting the price on food, the landlord collecting money and refusing to fix a leak, the teacher disciplining their children, the social worker taking those children away. The fact that these Jews were socioeconomically only a few steps removed from poverty themselves was irrelevant. In the dozens of riots that spread across the country between 1964 and 1968, they were the symbols of a racist economic system.

The members of the Jewish community were turning inward, both because they were being ejected from the civil rights movement and because their own identity was shifting. They were becoming much more assertive and proud, in the spirit of the Six-Day War. Black power was another catalyst. While some Jews were reacting against the new militancy, others were emulating it. A new interpretation of the Holocaust emerged, one informed by all these different social forces but also by the extreme feeling of embattlement in those weeks before the war, when extermination stopped feeling like an abstract concept. It was a more tribal understanding of the genocide's meaning than the universalist and humanistic one that had been flowering since the fifties. The Holocaust now became a Jewish story and its lesson was that Jews had to be vigilant. The ax was always inches away from the neck.

Even progressive Jews began looking at their fellow travelers in the New Left differently, seeing a fundamental incompatibility between this new imperative to prioritize their communal concerns and the liberal demand that they fight for the wretched of the earth. After the war, Israel was viewed by this New Left as just another oppressive colonialist state keeping down a minority people. A real split ensued, causing liberal Jews to choose sides in a way they had never felt compelled to before. The argument that conservatives had been making since the beginning of the decade began to have wider appeal. Emil Fackenheim, the Jewish theologian, wrote in 1960 that "the liberal Jew of today is in a dilemma," because he will have to confront the "possibility that he might in the end have to choose between his Judaism and his liberalism; that, as critics on both right and left have charged, liberal Judaism is a contradiction in terms." In 1967, Fackenheim upgraded this idea to a 614th commandment (to add to the 613 of the Torah): "the authentic Jew of today is forbidden to hand Hitler yet another, posthumous victory." Survival and commitment to Jewish continuity, Fackenheim was saying, trumped all other considerations. The world was still treacherous, and Jews needed to stop thinking about everyone else's rights and start defending their own.

In New York City, these currents crossed explosively in the fall of 1968, contributing to the break in the black-Jewish coalition and giving birth to a new type of militant Jewish power. It happened, predictably, in Brooklyn.

The neighborhood of Ocean Hill–Brownsville had undergone a dramatic demographic shift in the course of one generation. What was once a heavily Jewish area was now mainly black and Puerto Rican. The community had many black power activists who were eager to get rid of New York's centralized education system and exercise more control over their children's schooling. In the fall of 1967, Mayor John Lindsay decided to give in to these demands and create three experimental school districts that would be run by local community boards. Ocean Hill–Brownsville would be one of them.

The battle lines had already been drawn. In 1967, two-thirds of New York's teachers, supervisors, and principals were Jewish. To the disgruntled, it seemed like they had a monopoly. The main teachers union, the United Federation of Teachers, was almost exclusively Jewish. It was even run by a Jew, Albert Shanker. But the teachers were not rich by any means — most couldn't survive on the $10,000-a-year salary and had to take second jobs. And they had a strong liberal ethos. Shanker himself had raised money for the 1964 Freedom Summer and had joined King in the march from Selma to Montgomery. Jewish organizations and teachers were largely supportive of the community control program when it was inaugurated in 1967.

The problems began when the school board named as superintendent Rhody McCoy, a pipe-smoking black nationalist who used to frequent Malcolm X's militant Mosque Number Seven in Harlem. McCoy held a particular grudge against Jewish liberals. Influenced by Harold Cruse's 1967 book *The Crisis of the Negro Intellectual*, McCoy thought Jews had usurped control of the civil rights movement from black intellectuals and thereby stunted the growth of the black community. He came to Ocean Hill–Brownsville with a clear mission: to build a completely self-sustaining black environment. But his resentment at the Jewish educators soon overshadowed any good he might have done. One activist teacher, Les Campbell, started what he called the African-American Student Organization, an angry, aggressive student group that encouraged its members to taunt and harass the Jewish teachers. In February, the revolutionary atmosphere caused the popular Jewish principal of Junior High School 271 to transfer out of the district, taking with him thirty teachers. When Martin Luther King Jr. was killed in April 1968, the district became a raging bonfire of hate and aggression. A school assembly was held at JHS 271 in which Campbell ordered the white teachers to leave the auditorium and then explained to the students that violence was justified.

At the end of the first school year, May 1968, McCoy tried to forcibly transfer a handful of Jewish teachers and administrators that he felt were antagonistic to the experiment, and the conflict came to a head. Three hundred and fifty other teachers in the district threatened to strike at the end of the summer if their colleagues were not reinstated. Shanker, the head of the union, raised the stakes by saying he would put all fifty-seven thousand teachers in New York City on strike, effectively shutting down the system.

Three successive strikes ensued, keeping the schools closed for almost two months. A local dispute between the union and community board soon turned into a citywide debate over the extent of black anti-Semitism. In mid-September, in the middle of the second strike, a few teachers brought Shanker fliers they had found distributed throughout the schools. THE IDEA BEHIND THIS PROGRAM IS BEAUTIFUL, BUT WHEN THE MONEY CHANGERS HEARD ABOUT IT, THEY TOOK OVER, AS IS THEIR CUSTOM IN THE BLACK COMMUNITY, the fliers declared. Shanker printed five hundred thousand copies of the flier in order to bolster his argument. Soon all of New York was talking about the recriminations and hate volleying between the two sides; Black Panthers in berets paraded down Herkimer Street holding shotguns, and the threat of riots hung like a noose over the whole city.

By the time the strike ended, on November 17, 1968, with the Board of Education suspending community control and installing its own superintendent in a clear victory for Shanker and the union (though Shanker still had to serve fifteen days in prison), irreparable damage had been done. The black community felt betrayed by Jews who hadn't supported their struggle for self-determination; Jews felt betrayed by blacks who had misdirected their rage; and the poor Jews who still lived in communities close to Ocean Hill–Brownsville felt abandoned by rich Jewish liberals who lived on the Upper East Side and continued to host fancy fundraisers for the Black Panthers.

One month after the strike ended, on the evening of December 26, something happened that destroyed any future chance of reconciliation. Les Campbell, the militant teacher in the dashiki, was invited to speak on a WBAI radio show. On the air, Campbell began reading a poem he said had been composed by a fifteen-year-old student of his. Titled "Anti-Semitism" and "dedicated" to Shanker, the poem's opening words would be repeated many times in the closing days of 1968: "Hey, Jew boy with that yarmulke on your head / You pale-faced Jew boy—I wish you were dead / I can see you Jew boy,—no you can't hide / I gotta scoop on you—yeh, you gonna die. I'm sick of your stuff. Every time I turn 'round—you pushin' my head into the Ground. I'm sick of hearing about your suffering in Germany."

The Jewish community was incensed. Shanker and the union filed a complaint with the Federal Communications Commission to fine the radio station. Efforts were made to kick Campbell out of the school system. Most disturbing, though, was how differently blacks and Jews read the incident. Where one community heard a legitimate expression of anger, the other heard blatant and disgusting anti-Semitism. The two groups had once shared a common language, marching together the way Heschel and King had only a few years earlier, but now they could barely shake hands.

Black militants weren't the only ones goose-stepping up and down the streets of Ocean Hill–Brownsville in 1968. Dressed in a distorted mirror image of the Black Panthers, Jews wearing blue berets, army fatigues, and dark sunglasses wielded baseball bats and threw clenched fists into the air. They called themselves the Jewish Defense League—a collection of mostly young, tough-looking local men, the children of those poor Jews who still lived on the urban frontier of Brooklyn. This was a new demographic that had lost trust in the Jewish establishment across the East River. Where once they had accepted their leaders without question, now they felt abandoned and threatened by the changing face of the city around them. This schism was represented in a July 1969 Harris poll that showed that twice as many Manhattan Jews as Brooklyn Jews were sympathetic to the black cause. Meir Kahane, a charismatic and restless rabbi from Brooklyn, had tapped into this newly alienated population—a group that felt a paradoxical mixture of powerlessness and resentment combined with a newfound post-Six-Day War explosion of pride—and he gave it its most primitively tribal and violent expression yet.

In May of 1968, following the firing of the Jewish teachers, Kahane began imagining the formation of a Jewish militia. Then thirty-seven and cobbling a living as a columnist for the Orthodox newspaper the *Jewish Press* while also working as a rabbi at various Queens congregations, Kahane thought poor and old Jews in the outer boroughs were suffering from black street crime. They needed defending. His model, his hero, was Jabotinsky. A fervent revisionist himself, Kahane knew the stories of Jabotinsky's efforts to build a Jewish army during World War I, and the work of his disciples to bring attention to the Holocaust during World War II. In the tense atmosphere that was building in Ocean Hill–Brownsville, Kahane decided one Saturday morning to broach the subject with two friends, both of whom, like Kahane, had come out of the Betar youth movement. A few days later, he took out a small ad in the *Jewish Press* looking for more Jews who were concerned with upholding "Jewish Pride."

What drove Kahane was the same disgust with the exigencies of the New Left that former liberals were beginning to express in the pages of *Commentary* (what was beginning to be called neoconservatism). Except in Kahane's case, this anger was not a backlash. It had always been a part of his political thinking. As early as 1962, with the decade's cultural revolution not yet at full throttle, Kahane wrote with reactionary anxiety in one of his *Jewish Press* columns about the loss of Jewish souls: "The age we live in is not one of faith. It is an age of reason, of doctrinal skepticism, of pragmatism, of agnosticism. It is an age of science that questions all. It is an age of Marxism that preaches materialism, not spirit. It is an age of cynicism and fraud. . . . It is an age that threatens the values we hold dear. Torah and its pillar—faith—face a life and death struggle with this new age and its flashing rapiers, doubt and materialism. Day by day the struggle continues. In every hamlet, in the soul of every Jew, the battle rages."

On June 18, 1968, Kahane held the first meeting of what was initially called the Jewish Defense Corps (one person had suggested the group be called Protocols of the Elders of Zion, ironically appropriating the name of the notorious and fake czarist document that "proved" Jewish world domination). This was the army with which he would fight the battle. Gathering the group at the West Side Jewish Center, where his cousin was rabbi, Kahane addressed an audience made up mostly of professional middle-aged men. Wearing gray slacks and a white shirt open at the neck, clean-shaven and with dark eyebrows and thick black hair, Kahane went on a tirade about the Jewish establishment, how it had abandoned Jews and slavishly supported black civil rights. He denounced Mayor John Lindsay for caving in to black militants. He painted a picture of the Panthers as the successors of Nazis, with a second holocaust in the works. Kahane had just returned from a visit to Israel, which was still flush with victory. He saw Jerusalem and the newly acquired territories and failed to understand how Jewish youth in America could be so disconnected. They fight for blacks, for the Vietnamese, for Cubans—for lettuce!—but not for themselves, Kahane told the group.

Kahane wasted no time getting the league on its feet. The morning after the inaugural meeting, he set up an office at 156 Fifth Avenue in Manhattan, which he rented for two hundred dollars a month. He installed his doting mother, Sonia, as the first secretary. That very same day he took the train to Washington, D.C., and in his first act as head of the Jewish Defense League, he testified as one of two rabbis before the House Un-American Activities Committee. The subject: the plight of Soviet Jewry. Kahane introduced himself as the "founder of a group called the Jewish Defense League, which is currently being organized to defend Jewish people against anti-Semitism and to defend this country against various extremist groups, such as the Communists and the Black nationalists, functioning at the present time." The next morning, Kahane's name made its first appearance in the *New York Times*. "Jews in the Soviet Union are afraid to speak out," he told the committee. "It is our responsibility to protest openly, to cry out and await public opinion."

But Soviet Jewry was only a peripheral concern of his at the time, more a function of his broad anti-Communism. Kahane saw the JDL's role as primarily a local street defender. He would counter every instance of black anti-Semitism and use any means necessary, to borrow Malcolm X's rhetoric (as Kahane frequently did), to retaliate. In those early days, Kahane was more bluster than action. His following was fairly small and the threat of violence more a posture. The first real JDL activity was on August 5 and consisted of Kahane and fifteen young followers from Brooklyn gathering at noon at Washington Square Park, the de facto campus center of New York University. He demanded that the director of the school's new Martin Luther King Jr. Afro-American Student Center be removed because he'd written an article that accused Jewish educators of "mentally poisoning" black pupils. In an intimation of Kahane's media savvy, the signs the group carried read NO NAZIS AT NYU and BLACK IS BEAUTIFUL; NAZISM IS UGLY. It was a noisy but otherwise uneventful affair.

The community control struggle, which gave the group its declared raison d'être, offered Kahane many opportunities to make his presence felt. Jewish teachers began to rely on the young thugs that he was cultivating, his *chayas* ("animals" in Hebrew), as he called them, to escort them in and out of schools. Kahane would stand outside community board meetings yelling at the black picketers on the other side of the street. And even after the crisis ended, when Les Campbell read the infamous "Jew boy" poem on WBAI in December, Kahane organized pickets of the station and filed charges in a Brooklyn court demanding Campbell be banned from teaching. Kahane's idea was to make up for his small numbers by being pervasive, giving the impression that the group was everywhere. In January 1969, the Metropolitan Museum of Art presented an exhibition called "Harlem on My Mind," about the history of the black neighborhood, and Kahane got word that an introduction in the show's catalog contained anti-Semitic remarks. One of the writers, a black woman, said that the black community's "contempt for the Jews makes us feel more completely American in sharing a national prejudice." For days, the same group of twenty high school students marched with Kahane up and down the steps of the Met until the catalog was pulled.

All this time, through the end of 1968 and the beginning of 1969, he looked for any opportunity to provoke conflict and generate publicity. The young men who were attracted to him rode in trucks around black Brooklyn neighborhoods swinging chains out their windows and yelling through megaphones about the *schvartzes* (the Yiddish word for "black," which when spit out of hateful mouths meant "nigger"). Kahane, though never gifted at speaking one-on-one—he had a slight stutter that became more pronounced when he was nervous—orated at more and more synagogues, becoming more and more belligerent and developing a unique charisma when he was in front of crowds.

It was only in the spring of 1969, however, that the group really began to command attention, thanks to the provocative actions of James Forman, a black radical and one-time member of SNCC who had become disenchanted with its gradualist approach (he once said that "if we can't sit at the table of democracy, we'll knock the fuckin' legs off!"). That May, he interrupted services at Riverside Church in Manhattan to demand five hundred million dollars in reparations for slavery. He then announced that his next stop would be Temple Emanu-El, the Fifth Avenue synagogue started by wealthy German Jews in the nineteenth century and in 1969 an institution of Reform Judaism. Upon hearing Forman's demand, the temple's rabbi offered to give him some time to address the congregation after the services. Kahane had other ideas. He used the press to fan the rivalry between himself and Forman, telling one journalist, "Most Jews came here in galleys long after the Blacks were freed. Blacks deserve nothing from us and that is what they will get."

On Friday evening, May 9, when Forman was to present his grievances, Kahane stood guard at the synagogue with forty of his toughest-looking kids, telling each of the reporters who gathered there that if Forman should show up, he personally would break both his legs. The *chayas* were all dressed in combat fatigues and berets and carried assorted weapons, from iron pipes to nunchucks. As it happened, Forman never arrived. But Jewish leaders were horrified by the appearance of these Jewish gang members. The head of the Anti-Defamation League immediately issued a statement saying, "The Jewish Defense League is a self-appointed group of vigilantes whose protection the

Jewish community does not need or want." The head of Reform Judaism in America, quoted in the *New York Times*, went a step further: "Jews, carrying baseball bats and chains, standing in phalanxes, like goon squads, in front of synagogues are no less offensive and, in essence, no different from whites wearing robes and hoods, led by self-styled ministers of the gospel, standing in front of burning crosses."

Kahane knew that he had stabbed the Jewish establishment where it hurt most: their respectability. And now he wanted to turn the knife a bit. On June 24, more than a month after the Temple Emanu-El incident, Kahane placed an advertisement in the *Times* that contained a photo of six of his *chayas* standing with their bats in front of the synagogue doors beneath the words *Is This Any Way for a Nice Jewish Boy to Behave?* It was targeted at the Jewish leadership, at the "rich and respectable Jews," as Kahane referred to them. He wanted to humiliate them, and he wanted to gain publicity by presenting to the world another image of the American Jew, a mixture of militaristic Israeli and lawless Black Panther. Enough of the "nice Irving"—Kahane's term for the obsequious Jew. "Maybe there are times when there is no other way to get across to the extremist that the Jew is not quite the patsy some think he is" was Kahane's answer in the ad. "Maybe some people and organizations are too nice. Maybe in times of crisis, Jewish boys should not be that nice. Maybe—just maybe—nice people build their own road to Auschwitz."

The Jewish establishment got his message—as did everyone else. The prospect of Jews joining the ranks of bomb-wielding youths, committing violence as a way of upsetting the social order—riots were then burning through American cities—was horrifying, and not just to Jewish leaders. The *New York Times*, in an editorial that took up the question of whether this was appropriate behavior for Jewish boys, said, "No—not Jewish boys, nor Christian boys, nor white boys, nor black boys, nor any other kind of boys." Referring to Kahane's hysterical exclamations in the ad—"We are speaking of Jewish survival! We are speaking of the American Dream!"—the *Times'* editors had their own exclamation for what this vision of Jewish vigilantism would herald: "It's more like an American nightmare."

For Jewish leaders, this "American nightmare" making headlines almost every week seemed to have emerged from nowhere. Like Shlomo

Carlebach, who combined a distinct tradition—Hasidism—with early 1960s counterculture, Kahane blended the political philosophy of revisionism with the extreme identity politics of the late 1960s. Kahane was born in Brooklyn in 1932, the son of revisionists. In 1940, at the age of eight, he had seen Vladimir Jabotinsky drink a cup of tea in his parents' Flatbush, Brooklyn, living room, hours after delivering a speech calling for a Jewish army to fight alongside the allies in the war.

Martin David Kahane's father had become deeply involved with the revisionist freedom fighters (or terrorists, depending on how one perceived them) struggling to free Palestine from its British protectors and predominantly Arab inhabitants. During the war, he was one of the main American operatives of the Irgun, the right-wing pre-state Jewish militia, raising money to buy rifles and bullets that he would then smuggle to Palestine. Even as a boy, Kahane echoed the passions of his father, a popular rabbi at a local synagogue on West First Street. In addition to dinner guests from the Jewish underground, the war in Europe was a constant presence, and at the age of seven, Kahane drew a comic strip, *The Adventures of Bagelman,* in which a bagel in a cape saves Jews from Nazi Germany.

His penchant for flamboyance showed early, with his first arrest at fifteen. Kahane had joined Betar. Upon hearing that Ernest Bevin, the British foreign minister, was coming to speak at the United Nations, he and his friends gathered at the docks to pelt Bevin's boat with eggs and tomatoes. The police caught the boys, and a photo of Kahane with a cop's arm around his neck appeared in the *New York Daily News* the next day.

All the paradoxes that would define the adult later were present in the young man. While he was always ambitious, Kahane had a hard time carrying out the simple tasks of daily life. He was a daydreamer and a narcissist, deeply convinced of his own chosenness. Even his parents loaded him with a kind of messianic weight. Interviewed just as the JDL was gaining notice, Charles Kahane said of his son that "maybe destiny sent him to bring redemption to his tortured people throughout the world." He had striking features—bushy eyebrows, a thick wavy pile of black hair, and a long, brooding face—and other students seemed to be attracted to him.

After five years at the Brooklyn Talmudical Academy, he tried attending a secular school, Abraham Lincoln High School, but quickly returned to his religious world. Betar played an important role in his youth and he was often dressed in the blue pants and brown shirts of the Betari (the same uniform the young Riga Jews had worn back in the twenties). And his father even encouraged him to help the group load crates with weapons that were being smuggled from the docks of Hoboken, New Jersey, to Israel. As he would in later years with his young JDL followers, Kahane often rode through Brooklyn in a sound truck, Hebrew songs and the speeches of Jabotinsky blaring into the night. Even as a teenager, he saw himself as a future leader, the eventual prime minister of Israel.

In the fifties, while continuing his Betar activities (the FBI opened a file on him in 1955), he earned a number of degrees, first graduating with his bachelor's from Brooklyn College and then receiving, in the same year, a law degree from New York Law School (though he never managed to pass the bar exam), a master's in international affairs from NYU, and his rabbinical ordination from Yeshiva Mirrer in Brooklyn. It was at the yeshiva where he changed his name from Martin to Meir.

In 1958, he took a job at a Conservative congregation in Howard Beach, a working-class section of Queens, more to support his new family—he had gotten married to a local girl, Libby Blum, in 1956—than out of any real desire. His idealism immediately made itself known and he set out to move the members of the synagogue toward Orthodoxy. He loudly critiqued the bourgeois Judaism of the suburbs, where Jews attended synagogue only on the High Holy Days and ignored most of the commandments. The teenagers in the congregation listened, and he discovered here his effect on young people, many of whom eventually announced to their parents that they had decided to keep kosher and not use electricity on the Sabbath. In 1960 he tried to put up a *mehitza,* the traditional dividing wall between men and women, and the congregation finally ousted him.

Thus began nearly a decade of floundering and the start of a strange double life, full of secrets and dealings with the government. He was lost, convinced of his own greatness but unable to convince others. His first job after leaving the rabbinate, and the one that he would maintain for the rest of his life, was as a writer for the *Jewish Press,* an influential Orthodox weekly with a circulation of a hundred and thirty thousand. Kahane started as a sportswriter, working out of the paper's rundown Coney Island office, covering the Yankees during the 1961 World Series. Then, restless and disconnected from the political life he wanted to pursue, he went to Israel, telling people before he left that the next time they heard from him he would be a member of the Israeli cabinet. After a few frustrating months during which he struggled through his stutter to speak Hebrew, he returned to the United States. Needing money to supplement his *Jewish Press* income, he took a paper route in his neighborhood in Queens. Now over thirty and with children at home to feed, he was ashamed at how little he had accomplished despite his big dreams.

When he was asked in 1963 to join one of his old neighborhood Betar buddies, Joseph Churba, in a moneymaking political scheme, Kahane jumped at the opportunity. The idea was to start a research and intelligence-gathering business in Washington, D.C., where they could offer their services to government agencies. Churba, a shady figure, had already forged ties with the CIA and the Mossad. Soon, Kahane was developing a new persona and new contacts. He began using the name Michael King and splitting his week between Washington and Queens. The enterprise was called the Institute for Research in Foreign Affairs, and the two received a few ghostwriting jobs, once putting together a position paper on Cyprus for Senator Javits.

Kahane effectively had two lives. He rented an apartment on the Upper East Side, on Eighty-fifth Street, which he kept secret from his family. During this period, he resembled a con man more than a respected rabbi. He would often meet people at parties and introduce himself as a foreign correspondent who worked for a wire service in Africa. He told more than a few people that he was Presbyterian. And there were women. In June of 1966, Kahane, using his Michael King pseudonym, met a twenty-two-year-old model in a Second Avenue bar. Gloria Jean D'Argenio, who sometimes used the name Estelle Donna Evans, had come to the city seeking fame. Captivated by her beauty (olive skin and long black hair), Kahane fell in love. And without revealing the fact that he was a rabbi or that he had a wife and four children living in Queens, he proposed; they set a wedding date of August 1, 1966 — his thirty-fourth birthday. Two days before the wedding, he dropped off a letter at her apartment demanding an end to the affair. Evans, distraught, walked around the city that night with her roommate, and at four thirty in the morning climbed up the beams of the Queensboro Bridge and jumped into the East River, three hundred and fifty feet below, his letter stuffed into a purse slung over her shoulder. Incredibly, she survived the fall. A photo of her broken body being pulled out of the water made the front page of the *New York Daily News* the next morning. She died later that day, and Kahane—according to the 1971 *New York Times* article that exposed the story—was heartbroken. "In the year after she died," the article revealed, "he would sometimes place roses on her grave."

But women were not the only secret part of Kahane's life during this period. He also worked for the FBI. In 1963, the agency asked him and Churba to infiltrate the John Birch Society, the extreme right-wing anti-Communist group that also happened to be virulently anti-Semitic. They took on the job, traveling periodically throughout the West, where most of the members lived, and providing names to the government. This lasted until 1965, when they began working covertly in a different capacity: they started another front group, Consultant Research Associates, whose goal was to promote the Vietnam War among American Jews, something Kahane was already doing in his *Jewish Press* columns. Through this group they set up what they called the July Fourth Movement, which was an attempt, funded by the government, to counter antiwar activism on college campuses.

The rising tide of anti-Vietnam sentiment among Jews and college students was too powerful to counter, though they did try, publishing a book in 1967 titled *The Jewish Stake in Vietnam,* based partly on Kahane's columns. The listed coauthors were Churba, Meir Kahane, and Michael King. In the introduction, Kahane delineated the source of his virulent anti-Communism: "All Americans have a stake in this grim war, but Jews have a very special interest in the successful outcome of this struggle. For whenever the Communist machine achieves power, not only are political, social, and economic rights swept away, but spiritual persecution is inevitable and mercilessly practiced. Because of this, it is vital that Jews realize the danger to their very survival as free human beings should Communism ever achieve victory." And the dedication of the book? "To the enslaved Jews of Russia, with the fervent prayer for redemption."

Not long after the book was published, Kahane left Churba's company, dropped the King persona, and took a job as a rabbi back in Queens. He hadn't yet found a true outlet for his unbridled ambition or a large enough audience for his gospel of Jewish pride and purity. But within the year, he would start the JDL, and with young disaffected Jewish men as his shock troops, he would quickly have all he wanted, as well as one more new identity: the militant Rabbi Meir Kahane.

In mid-1969, Kahane and his Jewish Defense League were on a collision course with the Soviet Jewry movement. But before he could grab the movement and mold it into his image, it was already beginning to change. After the Six-Day War, the Jews of Silence stopped being so silent. The letters that came out, first from Kazakov and then from Kochubievsky, were covered in the major American newspapers. When Kochubievsky's plea was reprinted in the *New York Times* and his arrest and ultimate sentencing were later reported in detail, the protest stopped being abstract. Here was a real man, inspired by the Six-Day War, who was answering back, saying that he did want to leave and providing the student activists of SSSJ with a human face. That face was soon plastered on posters and made into buttons that demanded FREE KOCHUBIEVSKY! He was their first political prisoner. Yaakov Birnbaum felt vindicated. The publication of Kazakov's letter in the West had earned him a quick exit visa. Kochubievsky's story didn't emerge in time, and he was arrested and imprisoned for three years. More noise, not less, was what the Soviet Jews needed.

By 1969, more and more letters from Soviet Jews were reaching the West. Letters from Riga. Letters from Leningrad. A few from Moscow. All pleading to get out. The fear of speaking that Elie Wiesel had described seemed to be dissipating—at least to some degree. The Israelis had lost their outpost in Moscow after the Six-Day War, but they had still been wary of picking a fight with a superpower that could easily send more arms to Egypt and Syria. Yet in 1969, the news of the heart-wrenching letter from the eighteen Georgian Jewish families made it impossible for the head of the Jewish State not to comment. Golda Meir read their letter on television, and then, in a major address opening the seventh Knesset at the end of November, she announced a shift in policy. The days of "quiet talks and quiet diplomacy" were over. Not only was Israel declaring itself opposed to the Soviet Union's treatment of Jews, it was demanding that the Soviets "allow every Jew who wants to leave the country to come here to us."

To the grassroots groups in America, even this new, public engagement on Israel's part did not go far enough. Lou Rosenblum, for one, continued to be frustrated. His web of contacts was growing wider and wider. He had a student in Los Angeles who had started an organization at UCLA. There were two small groups in San Francisco, one just starting up in Washington, and a handful of other isolated activists. And here he was, still working a full-time job at NASA, playing the role of linchpin and drawing on the help of volunteers to do it.

Rosenblum's tenuous connection to the Israeli Lishka—the nature of which was still a mystery to him—had by late 1967 almost completely snapped. The disenchantment had begun after a strange meeting with Nehemiah Levanon in September of that year. The Israeli representative of the secret office had flown to Cleveland to deliver a directive. He arrived on a Sunday morning while Rosenblum was still teaching Hebrew school at his synagogue. Levanon, a man used to being treated deferentially, was made to wait. When they finally sat down to talk, he was curt and gruff, thoroughly annoyed. He had just acquired ten thousand dollars for the cause, he told Rosenblum, and he wanted to start an academic committee for Soviet Jewry, an association of hundreds of college professors who would sign petitions and place ads. Levanon wanted Rosenblum to take a prominent role in organizing the committee. Rosenblum, sure this would be a waste of money, refused. Four years of grassroots activism had taught him that Jewish academics were not the best way to publicize the problem. He could think of at least a dozen better ways to use the funds, he said. Levanon got upset and insistent. Few people ever turned him down. In Israel, Zionist authority was not questioned, and Levanon, who took orders from the prime minister only, was being rejected by this little scientist. He left angry. And Rosenblum was confused. He began wondering about Levanon's identity—who was this man to demand such unquestioned authority? And he wondered too about the Israeli's judgment. With so much pressing work to do, why propose such an uninspired and futile organization as an academic committee? Why these overly cautious steps?

A few months after the meeting with Levanon, Rosenblum turned his attention to the third biennial meeting of the American Jewish Conference on Soviet Jewry, to be held in April of 1968. He once again prepared to show up and agitate for a national organization with teeth. This time he had real numbers. He figured it would take half a million dollars a year. This would fund a newsletter and a full-time staff, including people to develop community groups and do public relations. He had calculated that this amount constituted only about 0.5 percent of what was collected annually by the American Jewish Welfare Fund Appeal. Just as he was getting ready to present all this information, he received a letter that made him realize the full extent of the anger that was building in the grass roots. Hillel Levine was a student at the Jewish Theological Seminary who was studying under Abraham Joshua Heschel, and he had just returned from a clandestine trip to the Soviet Union—Wiesel himself had asked Levine to go. He wrote to Rosenblum about a sit-in he had just staged at one of the planning meetings for the conference: He'd burst in with six students, declared that the seven of them were the Emergency Committee for Soviet Jewry, and demanded, as he wrote in his letter, that "should they not provide for a budget for the AJCSJ, we will picket and expose them to the press." The students' anger, Levine wrote, was treated as "youthful rebellion" and they were kicked out.

Rosenblum wanted to send a message to Jewish organizations that unless they acted, they would have an insurrection on their hands. He wrote to his closest collaborators around the country, including Yaakov Birnbaum. He specifically included Meir Rosenne and Moshe Decter, the two Israeli agents, because he wanted Jewish leaders to get word of his maneuverings. He invited them all to his hotel room on the second evening of the biennial conference for a discussion about the future of the Soviet Jewry movement. He called it his "shot across the bow." He would present them with an idea he had been considering for some time now: the creation of an independent Soviet Jewry organization, a federation of groups from different cities that worked together to fulfill the task the establishment was shirking.

That meeting in April during the biennial was largely a chance to vent among like-minded friends. They talked about how little they felt was being accomplished and how pathetic it was to attend one more biennial without any serious change to the organization, and they imagined how they might do things differently. The meeting closed inconclusively. A month later, on May 11, Rosenblum called his friends together for a smaller, closed gathering with only the grass roots. He'd fleshed out his earlier idea. He even brought an organizational flow-chart to show how it could all work—how all the Soviet Jewry groups could maintain their independence but also pool their resources. This time, the meeting ended with Rosenblum offering to chair a "committee of correspondence"—he loved the allusion to the Revolutionary War—so they could stay in touch and keep developing the idea. When the time was right, they decided, they would make it happen, start another organization to rival and outdo anything the establishment could ever dream of.

On a cold New York morning in December 1969, a year and a half after Kahane first formed the JDL, he received an Israeli visitor in his Fifth Avenue office. Geula Cohen was a woman with a reputation in Israel as a right-wing fighter, an extremist with big hair who strode into the Knesset wearing tall black boots and a large Jewish star around her neck. In the 1940s, she had been a member of the Stern Gang, the most violent of the militias operating in Palestine before Israel's independence. Responsible for bombings and assassinations of British diplomats, the Stern Gang, or Lehi, as it was also known, was considered by both the embryonic Jewish government and the United Nations to be a terrorist organization. Cohen had initially been involved with Menachem Begin's Irgun—the bombers of the King David Hotel in 1946, an attack that killed ninety-one people—but left the group because she thought it was too moderate. By the late 1960s, this revisionist fringe had long since dismantled its militias and become the long-suffering opposition in parliament, centered around Begin's Herut Party, which Cohen had also joined.

The revisionists were vehemently opposed to almost every Labor government policy. Among these was its approach to Soviet Jewry, Cohen's pet cause. The strategy of working through back channels and using quiet diplomacy disgusted her, and Golda Meir's decision to come out following the Georgian Jews' letter felt to her like too little too late. Of the few Soviet Jews who had arrived in Israel by 1969, most were of the militant Riga variety, like Lydia and Boris Slovin, and they too were frustrated by the government's silence. This catapulted them into the arms of Herut and the right. Geula Cohen's trip to New York at the end of 1969 was funded by a group of older Jabotinskyites and Holocaust survivors. They wanted to know what more could be done. Cohen was aware of the stir Kahane was causing among American Jews and she asked for a meeting with him. In the cluttered, dirty office the JDL called home, Geula Cohen had one question for Kahane: "Why are you wasting time fighting the *schvartzes?*"

She proposed that he turn his attention to Soviet Jewry. They began discussing the possibilities of a terror campaign against the Soviet presence in New York, with Cohen offering to provide clandestine training. Together with Yitzhak Shamir, the short and rambunctious former chief of operations at the Mossad and one-time leader of the Stern Gang, she offered to supply resources if he would turn his publicity-generating powers to Soviet Jewry. The idea immediately appealed to Kahane. He had built up a group of committed followers, gained a small degree of fame, and upset the Jewish establishment. But what next? He had been wondering how best to use this accumulated capital. Any consideration he'd had of the plight of Soviet Jews in the past had simply been an offshoot of his general anti-Communism. When he announced the day after his meeting with Cohen that Soviet Jewry would now be his central concern, it took the group by surprise. But by then, whatever the Reb said, they did.

In the months after the Jewish Boys ad in June of 1969, Kahane had continued to increase both his following and his notoriety. That summer, he had opened a paramilitary training camp in the Catskills. Camp JEDEL was located not far from Grossinger's, the famed resort that was once the heart of the Borscht Belt. The fifty campers who attended the nine-week program woke at five in the morning and then spent their days learning karate from two black belts, shooting pistols and automatic weapons on a firing range, and being indoctrinated by courses like History of Anti-Semitism. His tougher and older boys, the elite *chayas* unit, made pipe bombs and threw them into the bottom of a pool that Kahane had drained for that purpose. So sensational was the notion of the camp that the *New York Times* ran an article headlined "Jewish Militants Step Up Activity."

In the city, the JDL still acted like a gang, provoking so many fights with the Black Panthers that September that the FBI contemplated using the JDL in its attempt to undermine the black militants. Street fights between the *chayas* and local black youths took place regularly. The toughness of these characters was attracting more and more notice. Young Yossi Klein, a dedicated Student Struggle member who spent his afternoons selling FREE KOCHUBIEVSKY buttons at high schools and giving speeches to local synagogues, could not resist the draw of the JDL. On Halloween of that year, he rode along on a JDL patrol, scouring the streets of Borough Park for black gangs that might be causing trouble. Yossi clutched a baseball bat in his small, cold hands, terrified that if the situation called for it he wouldn't be strong enough to bring it down on a sinister head. Even though he was still mostly enthralled by Yaakov Birnbaum's more spiritual and nonviolent approach, he, like other young newly empowered Jewish boys growing up in Brooklyn and Queens, felt a definite pull in the direction of Kahane.

It wasn't just blacks on the receiving end of this new Jewish rage. Kahane expanded his constituency by striking out aggressively at anyone who committed an offense against Jews. On August 29, the left-wing Palestinian militia PFLP hijacked TWA flight 840 from Rome (mistakenly thinking that Yitzhak Rabin, the Israeli ambassador to the United States, was on board), and the JDL went on a rampage. They broke into the PLO's offices on the Upper East Side of Manhattan, wrecking the place and stealing files that they later handed over to Israeli authorities. In September, Kahane led a threatening protest of five hundred supporters on a tour of the UN missions of five Arab countries.

Not a week went by without another Jewish group denouncing him. In October of 1969, Theodore Bikel, the actor who was then on Broadway playing Tevye in *Fiddler on the Roof,* wrote a letter to the editor of the *New York Times* that summed up the fearful backlash Kahane was provoking: "During the long history of the Jewish people we have faced anti-Semites, anti-Zionists, Jew-baiters and Jew-haters. We have fought them and we survived. But we did so on our terms; we never allowed ourselves to become like our enemies, unintelligent and unreasoning hate-mongers."

Nothing, however, prepared the Jewish world for what Kahane would do in the last days of 1969, just three weeks after talking with

Geula Cohen. First, he held a one-hundred-hour vigil on the block next to the Soviet mission to the United Nations on Sixty-seventh Street, where groups like Student Struggle had been protesting for years. Then, on the afternoon of December 29, Kahane launched a three-pronged attack. Between 12:30 and 1:00, he and three teenagers broke into the Rockefeller Center office of TASS, the Soviet wire service; two other groups stormed the offices of Aeroflot, the Russian airline, and Intourist, the tourist service; and, most dramatic of all, a group of JDL members ran out onto the tarmac at JFK Airport to vandalize and then handcuff themselves to a giant Ilyushin Il-62 passenger plane that had just arrived from Moscow.

They were all quickly arrested, but not before grabbing major publicity. At the TASS office, Kahane's group had ordered the two journalists present to shut up, then pulled out cans of red spray paint and wrote the words *Am Yisrael Chai* in large, dripping Hebrew letters on the walls. Avraham Herkowitz, a twenty-five-year-old from Brooklyn leading the Intourist takeover, told all the Soviet officials that they could leave if they wanted, and then he slammed a drawer on the hand of one who was reaching for a pair of scissors. At the airport, two teenagers (one of them fourteen) handcuffed themselves to the nose wheel. As stewardesses stared out the window, the other league members, all dressed in army coats and wearing sunglasses, ran alongside the plane, pulled out spray-paint cans, and scrawled on both sides of the fuselage the same words, this time in English letters: *Am Yisrael Chai.*

The words of Carlebach's popular song had become graffiti. Like the decade itself, which had seen a desire for integration and unity devolve into separatism and rage in a matter of just a few years, the phrase *Am Yisrael Chai* had morphed from a joyful expression of the Jewish people's enduring survival to an angry assertion that threatened violence should anyone choose to question its truth.

Out of jail the same day, Kahane rallied his troops for another protest, December 30 at the Soviet mission. But this time he wanted to do something unprecedented. Demonstrators had always been corralled between Lexington and Third Avenue, a half a block away from the narrow Upper East Side stretch of Sixty-seventh Street that contained the mission. The Soviets could easily ignore them. Kahane wanted to get in their faces, and he was willing to cause a riot to achieve his goal.

Gathered in the cold and the light rain of the New York winter evening, dressed in heavy coats and black hats, Kahane and a hundred of his flock—both the young, tough *chayas* and the older men, many of them Holocaust survivors and ancient Jabotinskyites—stood pressed against the barrier maintained by riot police. Directly across the street from the mission was the Orthodox Park East Synagogue, whose rabbi was sympathetic to the cause of Soviet Jewry, though presumably not to Kahane's rough tactics. Kahane told the riot police commanding officer that he wanted to go and pray in front of the synagogue. "Come on, Rabbi, you don't really want to pray," the police captain told him. Kahane then gave a speech about exercising his freedom of religion. A voice came over a megaphone asking the protesters to move back, and Kahane decided instead to push up against the barrier and the handful of police. The crowd surged, and a short scuffle ensued, the teenagers pushing toward the mission. The police started grabbing and arresting them, and within half an hour they had taken twenty-seven into custody, including Kahane.

For the second time in twenty-four hours, he was in jail. And he loved it. Kahane knew the cause would benefit. This was action with a clear goal. He knew how to get attention. The problem was finding the right focus. Sitting that night in an Upper East Side holding pen with his young followers sleeping on wooden benches next to him, he felt gleeful at his success.

The following day, the last of the tumultuous decade, Kahane sent out a menacing press release, an indication of where the movement was headed: "Our attacks upon the institutions of Soviet tyranny in America represent the first step in our campaign to bring the issue of oppressed Soviet Jews and other religious groups to the attention of an apathetic public and indifferent news media. . . . We have pleaded, implored, and tried in the traditional methods of diplomacy. They have failed to open the gates. There is little remaining for us to do but to heed the requests of the Russian Jews themselves who have commanded us to shake the world."

5

"Escape, Daughter of Zion Dwelling in Babylon"
1969–1970

WHEN YOSEF MENDELEVICH met Eduard Kuznetsov for the first time, at a Hanukkah party in December of 1969, he thought Kuznetsov seemed like a Solzhenitsyn character come to life—one of the wise, rough men of the Gulag in *The First Circle*, or perhaps Ivan Denisovich himself. Kuznetsov fit every romantic stereotype of the political prisoner. He stood very straight, as if he were marching out of a forest carrying logs on his shoulders. His blue eyes were cool and hard; tattoos in green ink lined his muscular arms; and the words that came out of his mouth always stung with a kind of bitter wit, cynical yet brilliant. There was something unmistakably Russian about him, and not just his looks—which, with his blond hair and sharp jaw, were very Russian indeed; it was more his dark humor, the way he brandished his intellect. He couldn't have been more thoroughly out of place anywhere than at a Hanukkah party in Riga with earnest young yarmulke-wearing Jews singing songs in Hebrew. But after choosing to throw in his lot with the Jewish people, Kuznetsov was now experiencing his new tribe, watching them warily on this winter's night in a city on the edge of the empire as they held hands and prayed excitedly in a foreign language over the flames of the menorah.

Kuznetsov's decision to embrace his Jewish heritage had come less from the heart than from certain strategic considerations. In the late sixties, he was living on the extreme margins of Soviet society. His Jewish father had died during the war before he was old enough to know him. It was his Russian mother who had raised him and given him her own last name, making sure that the fifth line in his internal passport said *Russian*. He had never identified as a Jew, and his struggle, from a young age, was more about artistic freedom. As an impetuous and gifted student of philosophy at Moscow University in the late 1950s, he tested the temperature of the thaw by starting some of the first underground journals, *Syntax* and *Boomerang*, unauthorized collections of poetry and prose, including his own. Kuznetsov was part of the first real manifestation of the dissident movement, the open-air readings at Mayakovsky Square. What had started as students gathering under Mayakovsky's statue to honor the revered poet soon turned into weekly happenings at which various literary works, even the poems of forbidden masters like Pasternak, Mandelstam, and Tsvetaeva, were read. The meetings were a magnet for agitated young intellectuals, and students often milled around afterward openly discussing politics and their frustrations with the regime. The authorities managed to shut the meetings down in 1958, but they started up again in late 1960, and Kuznetsov was one of the main organizers. The content of the poems and speeches became increasingly radical, and the readings' suppression more extreme. KGB agents hovered around the square writing down students' names in their notebooks. Soon many of them were thrown out of school. In October of 1961, Kuznetsov, by then also the editor of *Phoenix-61*, the riskiest samizdat poetry compilation so far, was arrested at four in the morning and quickly tried and convicted for "anti-Soviet agitation and propaganda." At the age of twenty-two, he was sentenced to seven years in Vladimir Prison, located a hundred miles east of Moscow.

Those seven years were a harsh education for Kuznetsov. He read and talked with the other inmates about the nature of Communism. He saw great brutality and hunger in the camps. Men would tattoo anti-Soviet slogans on their faces and then be summarily shot by sadistic guards. Most talked only about how to escape the Soviet Union. A popular tattoo showed a cartoon man standing on the border between Russia and Turkey, one foot in the free world. Kuznetsov had vivid daydreams of living alone in a hut far from civilization with time to think and write. Like the rest of the inmates, he began to despair that there was any hope of changing the system. And like them, he began to see nationalism as the best solution. The Ukrainians saw the possibility of a better existence in a free Ukraine; the Tatars in the dream of getting back their Crimea. And for the first time in his life, Kuznetsov considered that his Jewish heritage might be his salvation. He saw this evolution in other Jewish prisoners as well. By the time he was released, in 1968, he was twenty-nine and a Zionist, not out of any great love for Israel but because Israel represented the possibility of freedom. Two months before leaving Vladimir Prison, he put in an application to the prison governor to change his nationality to Jewish. The request was refused.

There was no such thing as a completely freed political prisoner in the Soviet Union. Former convicts were not permitted to live within a hundred-kilometer radius of any major city. They had to report weekly to a KGB bureau and accept that their every move would be monitored. Kuznetsov felt especially burdened by this new life. After being isolated for so long, he wanted to reengage with the world. But he lived in a village called Strunino, outside Moscow, and needed written permission even to go see his mother in the city on Sundays. He had not been broken in the camps, he had never agreed to cooperate with the KGB, and that made him all the more threatening to the secret police. He was sure that he'd be arrested again. They'd find a reason. Kuznetsov was exhausted and lonely.

During this period, he made secret visits to Moscow and reacquainted himself with the dissident community. He was astounded at how much more open and combative it had become. He met many of the most active dissidents, at least those who weren't already in prison camps, including a middle-aged pediatrician with whom he became especially close, Elena Bonner. He searched out Zionists and got in touch with David Khavkin, the godfather of the scattered Moscow movement. Khavkin gave him a copy of *Exodus*, which Kuznetsov thought was awful as literature but which in one read introduced him to much of Jewish history. It was Khavkin who suggested that if Kuznetsov really wanted to leave, and leave as a Zionist for Israel, he might try moving to Riga.

Kuznetsov was not allowed to relocate unless he had a legitimate reason to do so; the easiest option was for him to marry a woman from Riga (his wife had left him while he was in prison). He asked a friend, a former campmate who had connections to the Zionist underground in Leningrad, if he knew anyone who might be interested. By chance, the first woman the friend suggested was Mendelevich's sister, Eva. In her midtwenties and deeply involved in the movement, she would make a good match for Kuznetsov. But Mendelevich's father refused. Eduard Kuznetsov was simply not Jewish enough.

Another suggestion was a woman who was quickly becoming one of Riga's most well-known activists. Sylva Zalmanson had signed her name to the first collective protest letter from Riga's Jews and had an exuberant, almost bubbly, personality. Girlishly small and curly-haired, she was extremely principled and emotionally connected to the cause. Even before she signed the protest letter, she was already engaging in risky activities. Early in 1969, she and Aron Shpilberg, whom she knew through his wife, Margarita, went looking for a suitcase filled with Jewish samizdat that had been buried in a forest outside Riga. Shpilberg had been shown the spot, between three trees, where an activist had buried it before leaving for Israel. Sylva and Shpilberg spent an entire afternoon poking into the black earth with a long wire trying to find it, but they couldn't. They went back again and eventually dug it out. The suitcase was covered in dirt, and they rode with it in a public streetcar to a beach, where they rinsed it off. Then Sylva took a train to Leningrad and delivered the materials to Syoma Dreizner's apartment without any zigzagging through courtyards. The Leningrad activists were astonished at her boldness.

When she was introduced to Kuznetsov, in the late fall of 1969, Sylva was twenty-five and working at a moped factory. Their first meeting was at a party in Leningrad for a departing Jew. At first she was put off by his toughness, but when she saw him smile a few times, she began to fall in love, romanticizing his prison experience. She had read Solzhenitsyn and loved the way life seemed purer in prison, the way men idealized women, talked about them like Petrarchs rhapsodizing about their Lauras. Within a few weeks Sylva and Kuznetsov were married and living in Sylva's father's house.

By the time Yosef Mendelevich was introduced to him at the Hanukkah party, Eduard Kuznetsov (whom everyone called Edik) had already gotten a job as a researcher in a psychiatric institute in Riga. He was amassing statistical data for a few university students who were writing doctoral dissertations about suicide. The newly married couple had begun the process of requesting an exit visa using an invitation from a real uncle of Sylva's who lived in Israel.

Kuznetsov was impressed with the community he found in Riga. They were disciplined and fully committed and they had significant numbers; three thousand people attended the Rumbuli ceremony in the fall of 1969. They were also productive: Mendelevich and a whole network of activists were busy developing the first issue of *Iton,* the samizdat journal of the Zionist movement.

But for all their activities, there was pervasive despair. Most had been refused exit visas and saw no point in reapplying. Sylva and Edik soon realized how hard it was just to get a *kharikteristika,* a simple character reference. The Riga psychiatric institute staff told Kuznetsov that their giving him one would ruin their reputation. Sylva was told she could lose her job. Even though the Riga KGB gave him more breathing space than the Moscow KGB had, Kuznetsov found that his circumstances had not changed much. He was still stuck in the Soviet Union without any prospect of leaving.

The situation was no different in Leningrad. By the end of 1969, the Zionist organization had become an institution; it had thirty-eight members who were represented by a central committee of five men. They were running a number of different *ulpanim* simultaneously and, pyramid-like, were churning out Jews knowledgeable enough to become teachers of future *ulpanim.* Though they too had all been denied exit visas, the authorities let their extensive activities continue unimpeded. The activists began to believe that as long as they stuck with teaching Hebrew and Jewish history to small groups of young people, they would never be bothered.

However, Hillel Butman, the impractical dreamer, still had visions of one overwhelming action that would bring world attention to their problem. The *ulpanim* were important, but the organization, he felt, was in a Catch-22. Success for them meant increasing their numbers, but that could only happen if they made themselves more visible and actively recruited Jews. And such moves would surely be suppressed, perhaps even lead to the end of the organization itself. The only thing that made sense to Butman, a man prone to dramatic gestures, was to find a single action that would somehow reconfigure their whole relationship with the state. It was around this time that Butman received a call from Mark Dymshits.

Like Kuznetsov had been, Dymshits was a stranger to the movement. Forty-three in 1969, and a former major in the Soviet air force, Dymshits was both older and more thoroughly Russian than any of the other activists. Also like Kuznetsov's, his path to Zionism was a circuitous one, born more out of frustration with the regime than out of any self-realization. His father was killed in the German assault on Leningrad and he was evacuated with his elementary school to the Ural Mountains and separated from his mother. The army became his new family, and piloting airplanes his overwhelming passion. He attended a military prep school in the Caucasus and then trained as a fighter pilot. Only in 1949, when he received his first post—on a base in far eastern Siberia, near the Mongolian border—did he begin to understand what his Jewishness meant. This was the most undesirable place the air force could send a pilot, and all four Jews in his graduating class were stationed there. Twice in Dymshits's next decade of service, on vodka-laden nights, his superior officers drunkenly confessed that the slow pace of his advancement was the result of his nationality and nothing else.

In 1960, the Red Army reduced its numbers, and Dymshits's position was cut. By then, he was married, to a non-Jewish woman, and had two small daughters, so he needed extra work to supplement his pension. Even more than the work, he needed to keep flying. Dymshits loved being a pilot. Nothing made him as happy as manning a plane and cutting through sky and clouds. In a cockpit, he felt in control, powerful, free. Leaving the air force was like kicking a strong addiction, and he was in withdrawal. At first, he was able to fly small passenger planes in Uzbekistan for the national airline, but it kept him far away from his family, in Leningrad. He tried repeatedly to get transferred but was refused each time. Eventually he had to move back and consider another career. For a while, he worked in a factory that manufactured planes, and he took classes in electrical engineering in the evenings. Every few months he would go to the airport to ask about work as a pilot but the answer was always the same.

Then came the Six-Day War, and it awakened something in him. Dymshits couldn't stop thinking about the Spanish Civil War and how the Soviet Union had sent volunteer troops and arms to help a small, beleaguered popular front fight the Fascist forces backed by Mussolini. If Soviet radio was to be believed, Israel was on the verge of destruction. They would be the weak underdogs in this fight (a distortion that other Jews, like Mendelevich, listening to Kol Israel knew was not exactly true). Why wasn't any help sent to them? Dymshits suddenly felt willing to drop everything to go serve in the Israeli air force. The anti-Israel mood that followed the war heightened this feeling. The burden of having been discriminated against weighed even more heavily on him. And, being a military man, a man who thought in terms of objectives and the strategies needed to achieve them, he began planning his escape. He knew these thoughts were reckless, but he couldn't stop them. They were as intense as his desire to fly again. First came fantasy. He thought of building a hot-air balloon and guiding it over the border. Then he remembered an old plane graveyard in Uzbekistan. What if he could steal one of the old fighter jets and fix it up? Soon, he found himself tiptoeing around a dark but most promising thought: what if he hijacked a plane?

One afternoon in 1969 he went to Smolny Airport, a small airstrip about twenty kilometers outside Leningrad that handled local flights not served by the larger international Leningrad airport. He told a man working there that he was in the process of applying for a job and wondered if he might be able to look around. He walked into one of the AN-2s, the kind of small twelve-seater planes he used to fly in Uzbekistan, and even tested the doors of the cockpit and the outside hatches to see how they locked. With two or three people, he was sure he could hijack one of these planes. He started discussing the idea with the few Jews he knew and they looked at him as if he were suggesting a flight to the moon. The talk was so bizarre that no one even informed on him to the KGB.

Discouraged and alone, Dymshits realized that he had let himself get carried away. His own desperation to leave, to fly, had made him act carelessly. And so he decided to take a more sensible route: he would focus on learning more about Israel and Jews. He began going to the Oriental Languages section of the Lenin Library. And this is where one of Butman's neighbors spotted him: a middle-aged man with thick, slicked-back black hair and bushy dark eyebrows sitting perfectly straight and staring at the page of a notebook covered in scribbled, malformed Hebrew that he had copied out of a dictionary. Butman's neighbor walked over to Dymshits and told him that if he really wanted to learn Hebrew he should call this man. And he wrote down Hillel Butman's phone number in Dymshits's notebook.

Informers were everywhere, so Butman approached Dymshits, as he did all new friends, with caution. But despite the fact that the former military man still carried his Communist Party membership card in his pocket, Butman instinctively trusted him. He immediately sent Dymshits to an ongoing *ulpan*. On their third meeting, in early December of 1969, Dymshits and Butman walked the streets outside Butman's apartment and talked about OVIR. Butman told Dymshits how often he dreamed of going to Israel. "You don't have to fantasize," Dymshits responded. "You can simply fly away."

Dymshits laid out for a dumbstruck Butman the hijacking plan that he had abandoned: They'd buy up all the tickets for one of the flights of a small AN-2 plane going from Leningrad to Yerevan, Armenia. Then in midair they would demand that the pilot fly to Turkey, just a short distance farther south. If the pilot refused, Dymshits said that he himself would simply take the controls.

Butman's first reaction was revulsion mixed with fear. He thought of his wife and daughter and the danger his merely having this conversation could cause them. But he couldn't bring himself to categorically reject the idea. He told Dymshits that he would think about it.

He did, that whole night. What if this was his only opportunity to leave? It was just the type of action he had been thinking about for years. A successful, dramatic escape could capture the sympathy of people everywhere and maybe even push the Kremlin to change the emigration policy. Butman imagined a planeload of Jews—men, women, and children—stepping out onto a tarmac in Sweden, a modern exodus. Once there they would hold a giant press conference where they would declare emphatically that they had suffered enough.

The plan would have to be different than the one Dymshits had suggested. They would need a large plane, the biggest possible, a whole plane full of desperate Jews. Yerevan was out of the question because there was no large group of Jews there. They would have to leave from Leningrad. And since Finland had an extradition treaty with the Soviet Union, the best nearest landing option was Sweden. By morning, Butman seemed to have forgotten his reservations. The hijacking became real to him.

He decided to keep it a secret, telling only Dreizner, his closest childhood friend, who then took Dymshits drinking in order to check him out and concluded that the pilot was sincere, not a KGB provocateur. Still, Dreizner told Butman he could not take part in the hijacking. One of the possible outcomes, which they discussed openly, was that the plane would be shot down. He had a pregnant wife at home and was his widowed mother's only son. He couldn't leave them. But he would help.

Throughout the rest of December, though they didn't give Dymshits a definite answer, Butman and Dreizner met with him almost every day. They began to work out more details. They would take hold of either a TU-124 or a TU-135 plane, both of which carried up to sixty passengers, as it flew from Leningrad to Murmansk, right along the Soviet-Finnish border. Once they had commandeered the plane, it would take about ten minutes to cross the border; not enough time, Dymshits thought, for Soviet fighter pilots to deploy. They would ask the pilots to fly to Sweden, and if they refused, Dymshits would fly it, dipping low enough to evade the radar but staying high enough to be safe. If ground control in Leningrad radioed, they would disguise their voices by placing cheesecloth over the receiver and say that two people had forced the plane to fly to Helsinki. The authorities would assume that the passengers were hostages, not accomplices, and would think twice before downing the plane. They decided to avoid flying over a large body of water like the Baltic, fearing that if they were shot down, their reasons for the hijacking would be lost forever.

Dymshits was eager to proceed but Butman felt he had to inform his fellow activists before going any further. In the Zionist organization they had built, each cell acted independently. Butman could have gone ahead with the approval of only his own group, but the hijacking was so serious and potentially destructive that he wanted everyone's opinion. He called a special meeting to be held at his father's apartment, which had been vacated for the occasion. Before the gathering he told each of the five committee members what was to be discussed. They were all as shocked as Butman had been upon first hearing the plan, and only Anatoly Goldfeld, the youngest member in the committee, who was representing the group of university students from Kishinev, gave his immediate support.

They met on January 3, making their way to the apartment through a thick blanket of snow, and gathered around a table. More than four years had passed since they'd first sat huddled together in the rain in Pushkin and formed their Zionist organization. But now, the mood was different. Butman had introduced a terrifying new possibility and he was bombarded with questions. They wanted to know, among other things, the chances of success. Butman gave them Dymshits's estimate, 80 to 90 percent, but this only held, of course, if the KGB didn't discover the plot. The point though, he reiterated, was not the mission's success. Their own personal escape would be secondary. There was a bigger goal to keep in mind: opening the gates for *all* Soviet Jews. They were going to draw the world's attention whether they succeeded or failed. It was exactly what Butman had been telling the group they needed for years.

The strongest opposition came from David Chernoglaz, the treasurer of the organization, an agronomist who had taken control of the cell once dominated by Aron Shpilberg after he left for Riga. Chernoglaz argued that the hijacking would give the KGB a perfect opportunity to paint Jews as terrorists. The group would hand them an ideal excuse to shut the organization down completely. Chernoglaz was angry. This was not the type of action they should pursue. It should be undertaken, if at all, by another, more secretive group. They should not mix their minor offenses, like teaching Hebrew and Jewish history, activities the KGB had never bothered them about, with something that threatened to destroy everything and put them in jail for decades. Chernoglaz also didn't quite trust Butman's motives. Over the past year, Butman's authority had started to wane. Unlike most of the others in the organization, he had yet to take the risk of applying for an exit visa, and this made him suspect in the eyes of some. To

Chernoglaz, the hijacking was Butman's way of regaining some power. Butman had always looked at the *ulpanim* as second in importance to finding a way out, and now, if given the chance, he would bring them all down with him.

Butman called for a vote on the operation. Chernoglaz refused to even take part. Two others, Dreizner and Vladik Mogilever, after reiterating that they would not be able to join the hijacking, formally abstained. Only Goldfeld joined Butman in voting for the plan. The only thing the group members could agree on was that they'd provide Butman with one hundred rubles from the organization's coffers, drawn from membership dues, so that he and Dymshits could fly the route and research the idea's feasibility. Chernoglaz handed over the money. On their way home, Dreizner and Butman each added twenty-five rubles to the pot.

Butman was shaken by the committee's response and decided not to mention the idea again until it was more concrete. He gave Dymshits half the hundred and fifty rubles and told him they could move forward. Dymshits was thrilled. They would draw up a detailed plan. Dymshits would be responsible for the operational details, and Butman would recruit passengers. The committee had not given Butman its approval, but he decided that under the cover of researching the plan, he would begin to put it into action.

Between January and March of 1970, Butman began collecting names for his operation. This was a delicate matter. The wider the circle got, the more chances that someone's girlfriend or mother or brother would tell the KGB. For this reason he didn't provide many details to those he talked to. Butman also purposely downplayed the plan's danger. He didn't want people to buckle under the psychological stress of involving themselves in what could well be a suicide mission. A few trusted potential participants were given a broad outline of what would occur. Everyone else was told only this: There is a possibility of escaping to Israel illegally. It is highly risky and must be kept a secret. Are you interested? If the answer was yes, the person was added to the list.

The names began to accumulate. Butman wrote out the list on a small strip of paper, then rolled the paper up and placed it in a tube. He tied a long piece of string to the tube and pushed it through the ventilator grate in his bathroom so that it dropped down into the air shaft but could be fished out when he wanted to add a name. He could not afford to compromise any of his people.

Throughout these first months of 1970, Dymshits worked closely with Butman and another member of the organization, Misha Korenblit, a young oral surgeon who was Butman's most steadfast supporter. Korenblit even traveled to Kishinev in early February to collect more passengers. Dymshits flew to Moscow, sitting in a cockpit with pilots he knew from his days in Uzbekistan. He took note of how the space was laid out, the number of crew members and where they sat. Once in the capital he went out to dinner with the pilots and even asked what kinds of weapons they normally carried. The pistols, they told him, were usually kept in the navigator's case. The plan began to take shape. The hijackers would have to deal with the five crew members who normally flew the large plane, and they would need to surprise them before they could reach for their weapons. In order to find out if the two doors leading to the cockpit were normally locked, Butman decided to take a plane trip to Riga. He had been planning to go anyway, to see if he could add some of the city's activists to his growing list.

On February 19, Butman got on the flight to Riga; he sat in the first row, a bottle of wine in his lap. As the plane began descending, Butman got up, took two steps, and pulled the handle of the first door, which opened. He walked another four steps, counting in his head how much time it took, and tried the cockpit door. It opened. Butman found himself facing the backs of four crew members' heads. He could see the shimmering lights of Riga at night through the cockpit window. As he closed the door behind him, one of the crew members jumped up and grabbed him. Butman quickly handed him the bottle of wine, proclaiming with a wide grin that it was a gift from the passengers.

Butman knew only two people in Riga: Aron Shpilberg, from his days in Leningrad, and Sylva Zalmanson. Butman thought Shpilberg, the hothead who was circumcised in the dacha, would second-guess every aspect of the operation. Sylva, however, was a good candidate, and she knew all the young Zionists in Riga. He called her up and said he was in town and had something urgent to tell her. She had some news of her own. She had just gotten married.

They sat at a café, gossiping about their mutual acquaintances. Sylva told Butman about Kuznetsov. Though he kept it to himself, Butman was concerned about the suddenness of their marriage. He wondered if Kuznetsov might be taking advantage of her to get an exit visa. Only when they left the café and began walking through the darkened streets did Butman reveal his own surprising news. Sylva didn't know how to respond but she immediately told Butman he should discuss it with her new husband. He would know whether this was a plan worth pursuing. But she wanted to prepare him.

That night, Butman paid a visit to their apartment. Sylva had not yet spoken to Kuznetsov about the hijacking. She wanted the men to meet each other first. Like most of the local activists, Butman was impressed with Kuznetsov's intelligence and straightforwardness. As soon as Butman left, Sylva sat her husband down and told him everything she knew. Kuznetsov's first reaction was that he couldn't believe Butman had discussed such a serious and sensitive subject with a woman. He also wanted more details.

The next day, with snow covering the ground and a strong sun reflecting off the blinding whiteness, Kuznetsov and Butman, eyes squinting, visited Rumbuli. As with any stranger, Butman remained vague about the details of the illegal escape. But Kuznetsov was a veteran dissident and he knew when a man was hiding something. Butman seemed nervous and fidgety, constantly glancing over his shoulder for men in leather coats. Kuznetsov demanded to know more. And as soon as Butman began expounding, Kuznetsov was filled with dread. If there was already a list of fifty people, as Butman claimed, it was too late. Kuznetsov knew from his own experiences and all the stories he had been told in the camps that secrets did not exist in the Soviet Union. The KGB had too many ears. Kuznetsov eventually recorded in his diary what he told Butman that day. "Just you listen to me," he said as they sat on the edge of a wet wooden bench.

You'll have to give me the opportunity of having a chat with every one of those taking part now—right at the beginning—before it's too late . . . We must take each one by his collar, drag him off into a corner, knock his vanity out of him, give him a good shake-up and make sure he knows just how much the fate of a dozen people is going to depend on his being able to keep his mouth shut. You have to understand, it's not the intentional treachery that scares me, although this cannot be discounted either . . . No, if on the night before our projected escape, someone should let his imagination get the better of him, and start bragging about his escapades of the morrow; if his girlfriend were to wound his vanity in some way or other, he may take offense, "Come now, who do you think you are? Never mind, just you wait until tomorrow!" And this could be just enough to put a spoke in the wheel! You know what this country's like? You've got to talk to each of them until his eyes pop out of his head — and then, and only then, can you be sure of him.

Butman swore that he could vouch for his people, a notion Kuznetsov found laughable. If there are two people involved in an operation, he said, you can be sure that one of them is an informer. But despite his reservations, Kuznetsov committed to the plan in principle. He was curious mostly about Dymshits, the pilot. Butman charged him with looking for a few others to take part, and Kuznetsov mentioned two of his friends from the camps who were feeling hounded by the KGB and might be willing to try an escape. Butman left that night and promised he would call soon.

Within a week, Sylva and Kuznetsov decided they would ask Mendelevich to join. Kuznetsov respected his patience, his ability to rise above daily frustrations. And he knew he could be trusted.

Mendelevich was busily working on what was already the second issue of *Iton* — Sylva had been helping him type up copies and had become a good friend. His second exit visa request had just been denied and he had been fired from his job. Without work or school, Mendelevich made the movement his life. When he arrived at the Zalmanson house to see Kuznetsov, the veteran political prisoner turned up the volume on the radio. He leaned in close to Mendelevich. "Would you be willing to try to escape from the Soviet Union even if it meant risking your life?" Immediately, without asking any questions, Mendelevich said yes. Kuznetsov laughed. He hadn't expected such a quick answer and he told Mendelevich to take some time to think about it, that the danger involved was great. "I've been thinking about it my whole life," Mendelevich said. "A few more days won't change anything."

In Leningrad, Butman, Dymshits, and Korenblit, the young oral surgeon sympathetic to the plot, continued to plan. They even had a code name: Operation Wedding. A group of fifty Jews traveling together would arouse suspicion, so they used the pretext of a wedding. Korenblit volunteered to be the groom, and his friend Polina Yudborovskaya, another *ulpan* student, agreed to be the bride. Dymshits decided that the hijacking should take place on May 2, the day after May Day, which was one of the most important holidays on the Soviet calendar. He hoped to take advantage of the fact that most officials would be nursing hangovers. They would board the last flight to Murmansk, leaving a little bit after four in the afternoon.

The group discussed how much violence they felt comfortable using in order to gain control of the plane. They knew that if someone was killed, the whole plan would backfire. Not only the authorities but the rest of the world would think of them as terrorists. They considered taking a pistol and hand grenades but quickly decided against such powerful weapons. Butman looked into using cotton soaked with nitrous oxide or throwing tobacco in the pilot's eyes—he had seen both done in the movies—but they finally settled on taking a weapon that would merely frighten the crew: a starter's pistol, loud but harmless, and Dymshits's old handmade revolver filled with blanks.

On March 29, in Leningrad, Kuznetsov sat on the floor of Butman's neighbor's apartment—a safe space, since the woman was not involved in the movement—and made final preparations with Dymshits and Korenblit. They decided that Butman would contact everyone on his list at the end of April and arrange a dress rehearsal of sorts. He wouldn't give anyone more than forty-eight hours to prepare so as to limit behavior that might draw suspicion. When they were done with their planning, Kuznetsov and Dymshits went off to the airport to look at the flight schedule. It was their first chance to talk alone. Dymshits was just the sort of person Kuznetsov liked to work with. He was serious and simple. He didn't overintellectualize things, but he was also not naive. The opposite, it seemed, of Butman. When they parted, as Kuznetsov headed back to Riga, the two exchanged information so they could keep in touch independently.

With a date set, a full list of passengers, and the details worked out, the plan was moving forward. But Butman had gotten ahead of himself. He was acting as if he had permission from the larger organization when he did not. Anytime he was asked about the "wedding" by anyone in the group, he would say it was not safe for him to speak openly about it. But the committee members had told him to investigate the *possibility* of hijacking a plane, not to prepare to do it. And yet it was increasingly clear that that was precisely what was happening. David Chernoglaz, the strongest opponent of the plan, became deeply worried. In Chernoglaz's eyes, Butman was dragging them all toward destruction. He began looking for ways to stop him.

The organization had never formally drawn up a charter or a list of bylaws. Chernoglaz realized that having one would be the best way to rein in Butman. He called a conference, asking that two representatives from each of the five cells take part. On April 4, all of them, including Butman, gathered at the apartment of one of Korenblit's friends, a woman who worked for Aeroflot and would never be suspected of housing an illegal meeting. If there were any suspicious knocks on the door, the secretary of the conference would lock himself in the bathroom and destroy all their papers. The others would claim they were there to toast the birth of Dreizner's new son.

The charter was quickly adopted. The bylaws, however, took longer. They debated who should be considered a Jew, whether a member of the organization needed to give up Communist Party membership, and, most critical, how decisions would be made. Without mentioning the hijacking plot, Chernoglaz introduced a rule that took away some of the independence of the individual cells, saying that a decision made by the committee was binding on every one of the groups. Just as they were wrapping up, the doorbell rang. They all froze. It rang again, long and insistent. Goldfeld, the secretary, quickly grabbed everyone's notes and ran into the bathroom. But when Butman opened the door, there was no one there. Two members went downstairs and saw a car with an antenna parked across the street.

When they settled back down, hearts still racing, Chernoglaz, clearly agitated, stood up and said, "Our organization now stands on the edge of destruction. If we don't take measures today, our organization won't survive much longer. This is because of the activity of a member of the committee, Hillel Butman. He is now preparing for a deed that could result in the arrest of members of the organization, searches, cessation of all of the organization's activities."

Not everyone present was aware of the hijacking plan. Those who knew looked around uncomfortably, not sure how much they could reveal. Those who didn't wanted to be filled in. With euphemisms, they discussed the "wedding" but never described it specifically, using their eyes more than their mouths. One member then exclaimed, "If Butman doesn't stop, I'll go to the KGB."

Then someone knocked hard on the door. Again Goldfeld gathered the papers and went into the bathroom. Butman opened the door to find his wife, Eva, doubled over and so out of breath that she could hardly speak. She said Dreizner had called her at home from a public phone—he had left the conference early to take care of his ailing wife. Dreizner had said only that he had been "poisoned by canned food" and told Eva to go to this address to warn them all. Butman knew what this meant: he had been trailed by a KGB agent.

The meeting broke up quickly without any further decision about the hijacking, but Butman realized what the new bylaws meant. If he wanted to continue, he would have to do so on his own, without the organization. The committee would never unanimously approve it.

A few days later, Butman was returning from a walk with Korenblit, who, though his staunchest ally, had been rattled by the conference. They were confronted by the rest of the committee, who'd been waiting in the dark outside Butman's apartment. They had all been meeting at Dreizner's and decided it was time to force the issue. Butman, Korenblit, and the rest of them started walking together, and the committee members—including Dreizner, who had turned on his closest friend—reiterated how detrimental they thought the hijacking would be to the organization. Butman kept trying to defend the plan, but as it got later his friends' opposition became more vehement, and he started to consider, for the first time, that maybe he was wrong.

It was after midnight, and they stood in a circle in an abandoned schoolyard. Butman suddenly felt the weight of responsibility. If his friends were right, he was going to put Zionists all over the country at risk. How could he carry that burden? There was, however, his pride. This was his operation, he had coordinated it himself, and many people had put their trust and hope in him. How could he call it off now? He would look like a coward.

Then one member presented a kind of face-saving compromise: ask Israel. If the Russian activists were Zionism's far-flung soldiers, then why not defer to the leaders? They would find a way to share details of the plan with Israeli officials. Whatever the Jewish State then commanded, they would do. Butman worried that this would throw off the timing of the hijacking. But he said he would consider it and they all shook hands. Only Chernoglaz remained angry. By this point he and Butman had stopped talking altogether. Everyone else was relieved. They walked away, leaving Butman standing alone in the dark.

Butman slept miserably that night. He had nightmares about a horrific plane crash, with flames leaping and charred bodies strewn about; he even saw the small form of his little daughter, Lilya. He woke up with tears in his eyes.

The next day, he agreed to the compromise. It didn't take long for them to find a liaison. On Passover, a few weeks later, the group contacted two bearded Scandinavian Israeli tourists—long-haired men in jeans—who were traveling through Leningrad. The two had just immigrated to Israel and were using their Swedish and Norwegian passports to get in and out of the Soviet Union. Butman met one of the Norwegians, Rami Aronson, and brought him to a Seder at Vladik Mogilever's house, where everyone watched dumbfounded at the ease with which the young man led the ritual dinner. The next day, April 23, they gave Aronson the details to pass on, making sure he emphasized that they were not out for personal salvation. The hijacking was for the good of the movement.

Sasha Blank, the veteran activist who had immigrated the year before, would call with Israel's official response. Butman's mother-in-law had been diagnosed with cancer, and Blank, a doctor, had been calling regularly on the twenty-fifth of every month to give him advice. They settled on a code: If Blank told Butman that his colleagues suggested his mother-in-law take the medicine, it meant they were being given permission to carry out the operation; if he said she shouldn't take it, it meant the Israelis were against it. They also took the opportunity to probe what Israeli officials thought of a large demonstration or a press conference. Blank would refer to these as medicines two and three.

The next regular telephone appointment was May 25. Until then, planning was called off. But they all knew, even Butman, that the Israelis would never approve. What official would support an operation that seemed indistinguishable from the Popular Front for the Liberation of Palestine's recent hijacking of an El Al plane? In the middle of the Cold War, with America now a close ally, Israel could never sanction such a provocation. It could easily lead to war. Contacting the Israelis was a formality, a way to step back from the brink. Operation Wedding was dead.

––––––––

Mark Dymshits's wife had left him. As soon as he began explaining the plan and how she and their two daughters, eighteen and fifteen years old, could join him, she told him he was crazy and kicked him out. On top of this, he had recently quit his job. He was living alone in a rented apartment, staring at maps of the Soviet Union's western frontier and waiting. He was now a bullet, and May 2 was the target. When Butman told him about the compromise, Dymshits was annoyed and frustrated. Why had he let himself sacrifice so much for such unserious people? How could he ever have trusted such a joker as Butman, Butman and his fifty passengers? Once he calmed down and stopped frantically pacing, he called Kuznetsov.

The mini-cell of Sylva, Mendelevich, and Kuznetsov had also been busily preparing. They took care to recruit the most reliable people they knew. Sylva asked two of her brothers: the younger one, Israel, a twenty-one-year-old student at the Riga Polytechnic Institute living at home, and her older brother Vulf, a lieutenant in the Red Army. Mendel Bodnya, a worker at a local bread factory, wanted to join his mother living in Israel. Mendelevich also asked Aryeh Khnokh, his half-sister Meri's fiancé. Khnokh had only recently moved to Riga from Dvinsk, where he had helped organize an officially sanctioned Jewish choir and had signed his name to the early petitions. Aryeh and Meri had a wedding planned for late May. Mendel Gordin, Mendelevich's older cousin who was one of the first to renounce his Soviet citizenship, had already been fired from his job for refusing to work on Jewish holidays and was now working as a lab technician at a clinic that treated sexually transmitted diseases. He was also on the list of potential passengers. But he told Mendelevich he wasn't interested. He had already chosen his form of struggle: petitions and letters. A few other people who were tapped declined as well. One man was in the middle of his doctoral dissertation and couldn't imagine leaving his books behind.

Dymshits arrived in Riga in late April to meet with Kuznetsov. Together they decided not to wait for Israel's response. The Leningrad problems could be a blessing in disguise — now they could move ahead independently and on a much smaller scale. And they wouldn't be constrained by committees or bylaws.

While Dymshits was at the Zalmanson house discussing the new details, Mendelevich showed up and asked who the quiet, dour-looking man sitting in the living room was. "This is our driver," Kuznetsov said jokingly, not wanting to mention the word *pilot* while they were indoors. He asked Mendelevich to keep Dymshits busy for the afternoon and Mendelevich decided to give him a Jewish tour of the city. But as soon as they got near the Riga synagogue in the old quarter, Dymshits got spooked. This was the closest he had ever come to a Jewish place of worship. After Mendelevich forced a yarmulke on his head, the pilot stepped into the cavernous building, saw the old, swaying men wrapped in tallithim, and jumped right back out into daylight. Mendelevich scrapped the rest of the tour — Rumbuli and the location of the former Jewish ghetto — and instead they made their way to a forest on the outskirts of the city to discuss the new plans in secret.

They would steal a small plane, an AN-2, the kind of twelve-seater Dymshits knew well, and they would work with only a limited group of trusted friends. Dymshits believed that the AN-2s at Leningrad's Smolny Airport were left unguarded at night and that they could easily sneak into one and fly off. Sylva and Kuznetsov volunteered to visit Smolny in a few weeks to see if this was really possible.

The Riga group was eager to move forward, so Kuznetsov and Dymshits met with Butman in Leningrad on May 1, a day before the original operation would have taken place, to find out what would happen if the Israelis said no, as seemed likely. Not being members of the organization, they reminded Butman that they were not compelled to abide by its decision. He agreed but asked only that if they continued with the hijacking that "Jewish ears should not stick out from it." He didn't want his Zionist organization implicated. Butman asked that Kuznetsov's two non-Jewish friends be included in the new plot and requested that Kuznetsov and Dymshits avoid making any ideological statements at the press conference in Sweden, should the hijackers succeed. Finally, Butman wanted advance warning. He was uncomfortable throughout the conversation. He had lost control over the operation. Dymshits and Kuznetsov now seemed to be on the same team, and he was just another obstacle for them to overcome.

Kuznetsov had always thought the Leningrad organization was sloppy in their planning — talking about the hijacking indoors and letting too many people in on it. As it turned out, by the beginning of May, the KGB had a pretty good idea that something was in the works. On April 30, Yuri Andropov, the head of the KGB, had sent a memo to the Central Committee identifying Butman, Dreizner, and Chernoglaz as leaders, outlining the organization's objectives, and even introducing the word *ulpan*. At the end of the note, he added, "Unconfirmed sources report that at the meeting of the committee on 26 April of this year an action was proposed, the nature of which is being kept in strictest confidence and for the implementation of which Jewish nationalists living in Riga are being enlisted." He remarked, accurately, that "the majority of the members of the committee spoke out against the action, fearing that it could pose a threat to their organization and to its members. Thus, they considered it necessary to receive sanction from Israel's ruling circles."

Andropov knew about not only the organization's existence but also its divisions. And, even more important, he had information that pointed to Riga as the new center of the plot.

It was a strange kind of bliss. Mendelevich couldn't really articulate it, but he knew that escape was God's plan for him. This didn't necessarily make him optimistic about his prospects. On the contrary, nobody was more sure that the group would fail, that it would end in death or arrest. But in his mind, this only added to the righteousness of the act. After putting in his second request for an exit visa early in 1970, he was actually worried for a moment that it would be granted and he would be prevented from participating. It was a holy undertaking, and like Dymshits, though for vastly different reasons, he needed it to be realized. Even when he perceived it as a suicide mission, he remembered and felt almost encouraged by an image he had once seen in a newspaper: a Buddhist monk sitting cross-legged at an intersection in downtown Saigon in 1963, flames engulfing his body and licking the top of his head as he waited patiently, not moving a muscle, to die.

He did, however, worry about his little half-sister Meri. She was eighteen, planning to marry Aryeh Khnokh at the end of the month, and though Mendelevich was more than willing to sacrifice his own life, he did not want to be responsible for jeopardizing hers. Khnokh had enthusiastically accepted the offer to be part of the hijacking. There was no way to convince him now that he should relinquish his spot. But Mendelevich did try to talk him out of taking Meri. He listed all the reasons why he was sure they would not succeed. Then Khnokh revealed that Meri was pregnant, and he wouldn't be able to live with himself if he got out and left a wife and child here. Better that they tie their fates together. Mendelevich suggested that once he was in Israel, Khnokh could petition for Meri and the child to be let out so they could join him. But this was all speculation. No one knew what would happen. At the end of the conversation, perhaps only to relieve Mendelevich's anxiety, Khnokh agreed to leave Meri behind.

On May 23, Khnokh and Meri were married. Mendelevich, clean-shaven and dressed in a white polo shirt, posed for photos with his new brother-in-law and his sister. Meri had a large Star of David around her neck and a bouquet of flowers in her arms. Mendelevich was pre-occupied but happy, even singing during the reception, something he was generally embarrassed to do.

Conspicuously absent at the wedding were Sylva Zalmanson and Kuznetsov. They had gone to Leningrad with Dymshits to take a night-time tour of Smolny Airport. The next day, they returned to Riga with bad news. Smolny was guarded by both dogs and watchmen, and the AN-2s were chained together every night. It would not be as easy as they had thought. Mendelevich was crushed.

Two days later in Leningrad, Butman received the phone call he was waiting for. As for the first medicine, all the best experts in Israel had been consulted, he was told, and the answer was "categorically" no. The tone of Blank's voice was unambiguous. As predicted, the Israelis would not give their blessing. Blank also said no to the second medicine (the protest), and advised proceeding with great caution on the third (a press conference). That was it. Butman accepted his fate, was almost relieved, and began making plans for a three-week vacation with his family in Siversky, a resort town not far from Leningrad.

As May dragged on into June, Kuznetsov held together the Riga group. He told them they could carry out the hijacking, and they believed him. But after the trip to Smolny with Dymshits, the way forward was no longer clear.

Just as he was about to call it off for good, or at least to wait a year, as he had suggested to Dymshits earlier that month, he received a phone call. It was the evening of June 1 and Dymshits was on the line, his voice frantic. He told Kuznetsov to come to Leningrad as soon as he could. When Kuznetsov arrived, a week later, Dymshits could hardly contain himself. He had found another way, almost by accident. He had started looking for work again and had gone, as he had many times in the past, to Smolny to see if there were any openings for pilots. And there he noticed something strange. On the schedule, a flight that hadn't been there before was listed, Smolny–Priozersk–Sortavala, flight 179, tracing a course that ran parallel and extremely close to the Finnish border. It was an old route that had been canceled, but now it seemed to be running again. An idea had entered his head, fully formed. They would board the Smolny flight; hijack the plane when it landed at Priozersk, a small town on the shore of Lake Ladoga; leave the two-man crew tied up on the landing strip; and then fly the plane over the Finnish border and on to Sweden. Dymshits had quickly bought a ticket and flew the route. Priozersk was as desolate as he imagined, just a battered runway in the middle of a forest. It was a perfect plan.

When Kuznetsov arrived, they flew the route together and began filling in details. Dymshits did not want to waste any time. The longer they waited, the more chance something could go wrong. The route could be canceled again or the secrecy of the operation could be compromised. They would carry out the hijacking the following week, on Monday, June 15.

Mendelevich was ecstatic to hear about the new plan. He began working on a kind of last testament for the group to sign and leave behind—a statement, in case they were killed, that would make their objectives clear, that would ensure their deaths would not have been in vain. Kuznetsov had included two of his non-Jewish camp buddies, Yuri Federov and Alexander Murzhenko, in the hijacking, and so Mendelevich insisted on some kind of declaration of the group's Zionist dreams and motives. His sacrifice would seem worthless otherwise.

On June 10, standing in a shady circle underneath a tree in Shmerli Cemetery, almost all the Riga participants met as a group for the first time. Sixteen people would take part in the hijacking: Kuznetsov; Sylva; her two brothers Israel and Vulf; Mendelevich; Aryeh Khnokh and—he insisted, now that he was her husband—his pregnant wife,

Meri; Dymshits and his wife (they had reconciled) and their two daughters; Boris Penson, a local painter; Mendel Bodnya, who hoped to be reunited with his mother; Anatoly Altman, a recent arrival in Riga from Odessa, a free-spirited Buddhist; and the two non-Jews, Federov and Murzhenko.

Kuznetsov explained how the hijacking would work. Twelve of them would be passengers that morning on the first flight out of Smolny. They would fly to Priozersk. When the pilot stepped outside to open the plane's hatch, Kuznetsov and Altman would jump on him, subdue him, and tie him up. At the same moment, Mendelevich and the Zalmanson brothers, both big men, would grab the copilot in his seat before he could reach for the revolver in his briefcase. Waiting for the plane in the forest surrounding the Priozersk landing strip would be the four other participants—Mendelevich demanded that his sister be in this second group. The four would run up to the crew members with their sleeping bags. The pilot and copilot would be placed in the sleeping bags and left in the forest with a bottle of vodka to keep them company until they were found. Dymshits would then take off and, as in the original Operation Wedding plan, fly low enough to evade radar detection; they'd pray that there was enough fuel to get them all the way to Sweden, a four-hour trip.

When Kuznetsov finished, they were all speechless. It seemed so easy, just within reach. Even Mendelevich convinced himself for a brief moment that it really was possible they would make it to Israel. But then he remembered the testament he had written, the last will of these people smiling at him on this summer day, and he pulled out of his pocket a folded piece of paper and began to read. He started with an epigraph from Zechariah: "Flee from the Northern land . . . Escape, daughter of Zion dwelling in Babylon." The testament clearly defined the group as part of a greater struggle: "We are part of those tens of thousands of Jews who, for many years now, have proclaimed to the appropriate authorities of the Soviet regime their desire for repatriation to Israel. But unfailingly, with monstrous hypocrisy, distorting human, international, and even Soviet laws, the authorities deny us the right to leave. We are impudently told that we shall rot here, that we will never set eyes on our fatherland." Mendelevich wrote that "the fate which awaits us here is at best spiritual assimilation." He demanded that American Jewry awake from its slumber and accused the United Nations and Secretary-General U Thant in particular of being "indifferent to the fate of a whole people," asking him, "Are you simply afraid of infringing upon the interests of a great power? But, if so, who needs you? What right have you to speak in the name of the peoples of the world? We demand that you take steps to put an end to the violations of elementary human liberties which have been going on for many years, to lighten the plight of the three million Jews of the Soviet Union."

Mendelevich added a postscript, which constituted the living-will part of the testament: "P.S. We appeal to all of you with the request that, if our attempt fails, our relatives and close ones be taken care of and protected from paying the price for our action. It should be stressed that our actions represent no danger to outsiders. When the plane takes off, we will be the only ones on board."

The group decided that the women—Sylva, Meri, and Dymshits's wife and daughters—would keep their signatures off the testament. That way they could claim ignorance. Sylva resisted. She wanted to be treated like everyone else. But Kuznetsov prevailed on her not to add her name. She had to think of her elderly father, who would suffer greatly if Sylva was forced to serve a lengthy sentence. In silence all the others signed, each man writing both his name and his city, and then Mendelevich folded up the paper and put it back in his pocket. He would leave it with a friend who in the event of their deaths would transmit their collective suicide note to the West.

As soon as they set out for Leningrad, a day before the zero hour, they felt they were being watched. Nobody saw anything in particular. It was just a feeling and a series of strange coincidences.

On the morning of June 14, Mendelevich went to pick up the Zalmanson brothers. Sylva had left the night before with Kuznetsov. The three Zalmanson children had already stuffed a goodbye note for their father inside the casing of his old shortwave radio. As for Mendelevich, he felt like he was doing everything for the last time: the last bite of bread and cheese, the last look at his father's face at the breakfast table. In the taxi on the way to the airport, he noticed a man riding in the car just ahead of them, a man in a blue suit. When the taxi stopped at a railroad crossing to wait for a passing train, the blue-suited man got out and went into the crossing guard's booth, only coming out once the train had passed. The Zalmansons told Mendelevich he was being paranoid. But as Mendelevich settled into his airplane seat, he noticed that the same blue-suited man was sitting right in front of him.

The group of four who took the train from Leningrad to Priozersk to spend the night in the forest waiting for the plane to arrive also began to feel people were shadowing them. Aryeh Khnokh overheard a man standing in the space between the two train cars saying to another man, "The leaders stayed in Leningrad." Khnokh went back to his compartment and told Boris Penson what he had heard. They could not turn around. They couldn't contact the other group. They could only keep moving. Khnokh shredded an address book that had the names and phone numbers of activists (he and Meri had burned other incriminating documents the night before). He threw the pieces out the window. Then he and Boris took out the two rubber clubs they were carrying and threw them out the window, along with Dymshits's old pistol and a pair of brass knuckles that Israel Zalmanson had made. Sylva suggested they try to lose the KGB men by jumping off quickly and switching trains. They did this. But they had to continue in the same direction. When the next train came they got on and kept moving toward Priozersk.

The small town was already dark when they arrived. Dymshits had drawn a map showing them how to get from the train station to the landing strip, but after an hour of wandering in the blackness, they decided they would pitch a tent in a nearby forest, build a fire, eat something, and try to get some sleep. They would have better luck in the morning. While they were warming themselves by the fire, they suddenly heard people approaching. A young couple walked up to them and asked if anyone had a light for a cigarette. When they said they didn't, the couple walked off. The group decided to take turns sleeping so that two people could stand guard. But it was not easy to fall asleep; everyone was buzzing with nervous energy. The incident on the train and the strange people in the forest had convinced them they would be caught.

In Leningrad, the rest of the group was also anxious that night. Kuznetsov, who was quite familiar with the ways of the KGB, had packed his bags for prison rather than for the West. They would be caught. The only question was when. Dymshits, however, was very confident. And the others contemplated all the possibilities, wondering whether the next day they would be dead, arrested, or in Sweden. Mendelevich and a few of the others camped close to the airport. In the evening, a black Volga parked nearby. Two men emerged, glared at them, went off to urinate, and then drove away. The group had drawn straws to see who would get the few sleeping bags, and Mendelevich had lost. So he lay on the ground, covered by Vulf Zalmanson's coat, looking up at the night sky through a thicket of trees. Eventually, he managed to fall asleep.

At four in the morning, in the forest of Priozersk, another man walked up to the campfire where Sylva Zalmanson was sitting staring at the flames, unable to sleep. He also asked for a light, then bent down to use an ember from the fire. But when he straightened up, he let out a scream, almost like a howl, and the forest was suddenly jolted by people and dogs scrambling toward them. Sylva's breath caught in her throat before she was able to yell. They jumped on her and quickly slipped on handcuffs. Aryeh Khnokh stood up and saw one of the men pull out a gun and shoot at him. He was immediately blinded, his eyes burning. Tear gas filled the air. Boris Penson was the only one sleeping and he was woken up when one of the policemen leaped on top of him in his sleeping bag, pulled him up by the arms, and dragged him away.

Near the Smolny airport, unaware of what had happened to the others in Priozersk, the group woke at dawn to a clear, sun-drenched morning. Vulf Zalmanson went to pick up Dymshits and Kuznetsov and some of the others at the Smolny train station. Anatoly Altman, who had spent the previous day wandering around Leningrad in a daze, marveling at the sights of the imperial city, helped Mendelevich prepare the backpacks the men would carry. Each contained a rubber-coated club. Mendelevich's pack also had rope to tie up the crew, a hunting knife, and a small ax.

When the whole group had arrived, they started trickling into the airport's waiting lounge, trying to appear as if they didn't know one another. The Zalmansons had told Mendelevich to change his appearance a little, just to look less conspicuous. He had been wearing a long brown raincoat and a beret that he used to cover his head in place of a yarmulke. He took off the coat, but not the beret. The waiting lounge was filled with people. There were old people and children, but Mendelevich noticed a disproportionate number of young men, many of whom seemed fidgety and expectant. There was nothing to do now. He just sat down, breathed slowly, and forced himself to remember that he was carrying out God's will.

At 8:35, a voice came over the loudspeaker announcing flight 179 to Priozersk and Sortavala. They were boarding ten minutes earlier than expected. The runway and the AN-2 were within sight through a pair of glass doors. And suddenly they realized that Dymshits was not at the gate. He was the most critical piece. Without him, there could be no hijacking. Mendelevich left his place in line and convinced a policeman to let him exit the building. Outside, not far from the airport, he found Dymshits with his wife and daughters sitting on a blanket, serenely eating their breakfast. Dymshits had thought he had time, not aware that the flight had been called early. They ran together back into the airport and got in line, Dymshits and his family just behind Mendelevich.

The doors opened and they began walking onto the tarmac. Another group of passengers whose flight had also just been called walked next to them in a parallel line. When they were just a few feet from the plane, a man in the line of other passengers yelled, "It's starting!" And just like in Priozersk, policemen emerged from everywhere, clubs in hand and German shepherds at their sides. Someone pounced on Mendelevich and he could feel his glasses crack against his face when his head hit the ground. Looking sideways through the broken lens, he saw almost all the members of the group lying facedown, their hands bound with rope. Only Dymshits was on his knees, his face covered in blood. He had been shot with some kind of irritant to paralyze him. His wife and daughters lay pale and shaking next to him. Mendelevich closed his eyes. *It's over,* he thought with some relief. His old life—with all the compromises and terrible longing—was over.

———

The authorities finally had the opportunity they had been looking for, a chance to prove to the world that these so-called Zionists, increasingly gaining sympathy in the West, were nothing but hooligans.

In March of that year, the Soviets had launched what could only be called a public relations offensive to counter the angry petitions and letters of Jews who had been refused exit visas and whose statements were being widely publicized in the West. In accordance with what the Central Committee called its Plan for Basic Organizational and Propaganda Measures Connected with the Situation in the Middle East and the Intensifying Struggle with Zionism, it authorized a large, televised press conference that would condemn Zionism's attempt "to act as a vanguard of imperialism." The pièce de résistance was a collection of prominent Soviet Jews who would denounce Zionism and proclaim their love for the Soviet Union.

On March 4, under glaringly bright lights, forty Soviet Jews sat on a stage at the House of Friendship in Moscow. Many had never even publicly identified themselves as Jews—like the redheaded prima ballerina Maya Plisetskaya, known to Soviet citizens for her famous interpretation of the Dying Swan in Tchaikovsky's *Swan Lake*. Facing an audience of a few hundred journalists, Leonid I. Zamyatin, head of the Foreign Ministry's press department and a non-Jew, began by reading a letter signed by fifty-two leading Jewish figures, many of whom were seated behind him: "'Every day brings new reports about the crimes of the Israeli military, reviving memories of the barbarity of Hitlerites. This aggression has become a component of the imperialist, neocolonialist plot directed against the people and progressive regimes of the Middle East and closely intertwining the interests of oil monopolies and international Zionist operations . . . Zionism has always expressed the chauvinistic views and racist ravings of the Jewish bourgeoisie. It has now reached the apogee in preaching national intolerance and hatred. Zionists supply imperialism with cannon fodder in the struggle against the Arab people.'"

At the question-and-answer session, some of the participants, such as Arkady Raikin, a well-known comedian and a Jewish boy from Riga, looked uncomfortable and remained silent, while others strongly defended the Soviet line. Veniamin E. Dymshits, the highest-ranking Jewish official in the Soviet Union, a deputy of the Supreme Soviet, waved around a copy of the Soviet constitution and insisted that no country in the world treated Jews better than the Soviet Union did, not even America. Another panelist, Ilya A. Yegudin, a Ukrainian collective-farm chairman, said: "I have had Leonid Ilyich Brezhnev, the General Secretary of the Communist Party of the Soviet Union, in my Jewish home, at my table. In what other country could that happen?"

Butman watched the spectacle on his television in Leningrad. Mendelevich watched it in Riga. They were both shocked and saddened at the lengths the authorities would go to to denounce Israel. But neither knew that this was just the opening act. The main anti-Zionist show was still to come.

The KGB had discovered the hijacking plot slowly, starting with Operation Wedding in Leningrad and then tracing it to Riga. The hijacking was a gift—a blatantly illegal act that the West could never condone. That December, representatives of seventy-seven Western countries were planning to draw up the Hague Convention for the Suppression of Unlawful Seizure of Aircraft. Knowing that this was in the works, the Soviets saw an opportunity to put more than just the hijackers on trial. The whole Zionist movement could be condemned as dangerous and seditious.

The KGB came for Butman at the Siversky dacha where he had been vacationing with his family, reading books to his daughter Lilya and following the World Cup on television; Israel had managed to qualify for the finals in Mexico City. As the KGB was arresting the hijackers on the Smolny tarmac, another group of agents in leather jackets carried out an intensive search of the dacha and eventually drove Butman away in a black Volga, taking him back to Leningrad. Dreizner was at work when they came for him. So was Chernoglaz. By the evening of June 15, all the members of the Leningrad organization's central committee, eight men, were sitting in prison cells in the Big House, the nickname for Leningrad's KGB headquarters, even though their participation in the hijacking plot had ended almost two months earlier.

That same day, the KGB searched the houses of most of the other major activists in Riga, Leningrad, and Moscow. By November, five more people had been arrested in Leningrad, six in Kishinev. In August, they had come for Aron Shpilberg, as well as Boris Maftser, Ruth Alexandrovich, and a fourth man in Riga, Misha Shepshalovich, who had been helping to produce samizdat. Altogether, thirty-four would stand trial—and the Soviet Union would present to the world what it said was the true face of Zionism.

The cells in the Big House were each ten feet by six feet, with a metal cot, a sink, and a toilet. Mendelevich could reach up and touch the ceiling of his. Most of the activists had cellmates, who were presumably informers. Kuznetsov, familiar with prison, was able to tell immediately which ones were spying on him. He began keeping a diary, scribbling on the small strips of paper the guards were obligated to provide him so he could prepare for his trial. To obscure what he was doing, Kuznetsov started each sentence he wrote with the words *Gorky says* and then put quotation marks around what followed, making it look like he was simply recording something the great Soviet writer had penned. He knew the guards would never read carefully enough to discover the truth.

Sylva Zalmanson hardly ate anything but bread those first few weeks. Butman asked for toilet paper because he knew that the guards would bring him cut-up newspaper that he could piece together and read. They tried to communicate by tapping on the thick walls of their cells. And they all saw, at one point or another, the cell where Lenin had been imprisoned in 1896, now preserved as a historic monument. Kuznetsov wrote in his diary in his usual sardonic style, "It's kept unoccupied, a relic not to be profaned. If you look at our block from the yard down below, it's the fifth window from the right on the fifth floor that immediately catches your eye. In contrast to the gloomy regularity of the rusty shields on all the other windows, its freshly scrubbed panes flash in the light of day . . . On the dawn of the Revolution—or, as a friend of mine put it, of the 'Dissolution'—they were going to destroy all the churches and prisons, they said. As far as the churches are concerned, they seem to have done the job fairly thoroughly, but something must have gone terribly wrong when they started demolishing the prisons."

The interrogations started immediately, right after the June arrest, and lasted up until the trial in December. Almost forty investigators worked on the case, moving from one room to another, trying to piece together the story of the Zionist movement and the hijacking. They used tactics that, to Kuznetsov at least, were "banal": other prisoners who were obviously informers; recording devices sticking out of walls. And then there were the psychological ploys. As Kuznetsov described it, they toyed "with the intimate details of your life, promising to mitigate your sentence and threatening to execute you."

They told Sylva that Kuznetsov had already broken and had confessed to everything. They made Kuznetsov believe that Federov, his iron-willed former campmate, had supplied them with all the details. Mendelevich's interrogators asked him to name the friend he thought was least likely to talk. He said, "Israel Zalmanson," and they laughed, saying that he had cracked long ago. They chipped away at the Jews' resolve, working slowly but steadily, using one piece of information to gain another. On Sylva and most of the others, it worked. Some even started talking, though nobody in the hijacking group widened the circle of the accused. Kuznetsov wouldn't open his mouth. Mendelevich kept quiet as well.

The investigation took its toll, and as the months went by the group grew emotionally exhausted. Mendelevich had to keep convincing himself that his friends had not really confessed—otherwise he felt his faith would collapse. Even Kuznetsov, who maintained the strongest exterior, began posing existential questions in his secret diary. "Why ever did I agree to take part in such a plot if I knew how impossible it was to fight the powers-that-be?" he wrote. "Could I really have thought I would win? My logic and my experience told me, no—a miracle was needed. And if suicide is often a cri de coeur, then so was my participation a sort of suicide, the cry of the persecuted for salvation. This is it. Whatever I said, I could never give a satisfactory explanation for what I did. Has not the whole of my life been a constant search for escape? Perhaps I never really grew up."

The trial finally began on December 15. Dymshits's wife and daughters and the now very pregnant Meri Khnokh had been released in what was called a "humanitarian gesture." The twelve remaining people would be tried together (Vulf Zalmanson, being an army officer, would be given a separate military trial). Since there was no formal anti-hijacking law in the Soviet Union, they would be charged under two different articles, both carrying a punishment of no less than eight years and possibly death by firing squad: Article 64, for treason and "betrayal of the fatherland," because of "flight abroad or refusal to return from flight abroad," and Article 93, for stealing state property. All but four of the defendants—the two non-Jews, Penson, and Bodnya—were also being tried under Articles 70 and 72, "agitation or propaganda carried on for the purpose of subverting or weakening Soviet authority, or of committing particular, especially dangerous crimes against the state."

Room 48 at the Leningrad City Court could hold about two hundred people, and at 9:00 A.M. on Tuesday, December 15, it was filled with party bureaucrats and KGB officials. TASS, the Soviet wire service, and *Pravda* were the only news organizations given permission to cover the trial. The front row on the left side of the courtroom facing the panel of judges was reserved for family—there sat the father of Sylva, Israel, and Vulf Zalmanson, looking anxious and tired; Mendelevich's father; Dymshits's wife; and Elena Bonner, who had told the court that she was Kuznetsov's aunt. After being led into the room, the defendants looked at one another for the first time in six months and saw skinnier, older versions of the people they had known. Sylva's hair now had some gray in it. They weren't allowed to talk to one another but they smiled at their families. They could feel the unsympathetic stares of the crowd.

Each of them had been given a defense lawyer but there wasn't much these men could say. They could not be seen to slander the state, so all they could do was seek leniency.

In preparation for the trial, the defendants had been allowed to read the transcripts of the interrogations. Mendelevich was worried that his friends would be as weak in court as they were in the interrogation rooms. But his fears were soothed as soon as Dymshits, the first witness, took the stand. Mendelevich couldn't believe what he was hearing. The pilot who had been scared to step into a synagogue only half a year before was now angrily denouncing Soviet anti-Semitism and recounting how his difficulty finding a job had pushed him to plotting a means of escape. Next was Sylva and then Mendelevich himself. He tried to be unapologetic, to manifest as much bravery as he could in that imposing, marble-floored room. He made it clear that he wanted nothing from the Soviet Union except to be allowed to go to his homeland. To this, the state prosecutor declared, "The Russian people have reserved Birobidzhan for you, so go there." Mendelevich looked at him and said, "Permit me to decide for myself which state and not which province is my homeland."

Over the next four days, each one of the group took the stand. Butman was brought in to testify as well. Each was asked, almost contemptuously, what kind of state secrets he was planning to pass along after arriving in Israel. They all answered similarly—they had tried to emigrate legally and were refused; this had been an act of desperation. Kuznetsov's lawyer asked him point-blank, "Did you commit this crime out of political motives?" Kuznetsov answered, "No. I was guided by considerations of a spiritual and moral nature." His lawyer continued, "Did you intend to bring harm to the USSR?" "No," Kuznetsov responded. "Were you not disturbed by how this would be taken by the enemies of the Soviet Union?" The seasoned political prisoner smiled and answered, "It's not my fault that the Soviet Union has enemies."

By Friday, the last day of questioning, it was clear that none of the defendants was going to recant—other than Bodnya, who wept and said that he had only wanted to see his mother and thanked the Soviet Union "for having opened [his] eyes" to his crime. Except for Federov (one of the non-Jews), they all pleaded guilty, arguing only that they were not being charged correctly: they hadn't intended to keep the airplane, and the crime they were being tried for had never been carried out.

The prosecution's closing speech echoed the argument used earlier that year in the televised press conference. How could the defendants claim they were being discriminated against in the Soviet Union given the percentage of Jewish students in higher education, the number of Jews who had won Heroes of the Soviet Union medals? The prosecutor focused on the criminal nature of the act and, by extension, the "intrigues of international Zionism." Interestingly, though Mendelevich's "suicide note" penned on the eve of their departure was referred to in court as a virulently anti-Soviet document, it was never admitted as evidence. If it had been, it would have revealed that in their last minutes, these supposed terrorists had explicitly said that they wished to do no harm, that they wanted only to avoid "spiritual assimilation."

After recessing for the weekend, the prosecution made its sentencing recommendation to the judge: death by firing squad for Dymshits and Kuznetsov, fifteen years for Mendelevich, ten years for Sylva, and ten to fifteen years for everyone else (except for Bodnya, whose tears got him five). The defense lawyers then tried to make their case, pointing out the absurdity of such harsh sentences for a crime that hadn't been committed. Sylva's lawyer said, "We have been speaking about 'death,' yet the pilot is safe and sound; we have been speaking about the theft of a plane but it is standing at the airport. We have been speaking about what might have been."

Kuznetsov was so angry that night, so desperate for quiet to contemplate his fate, that he beat up his cellmate, who wouldn't stop chattering about a letter he had received from his girlfriend. In the ensuing silence, Kuznetsov lay on his cot contemplating one thought: "Does it really make any difference when you die?" He was sure, entirely sure, that the judge would follow the prosecutor's recommendation, and he was concerned only about whether he would be able to face death as bravely as he'd always imagined he would.

The defendants gave their final statements the following day. Normally, this was when the accused asked for clemency. Sylva had been rehearsing all night in her cell. She remembered how much she had wanted to be an actress when she was a little girl. When she stood up, cleared her throat, and began to project loudly, the courtroom went silent. If the authorities thought they might soften up the others by letting this vulnerable-looking woman speak early on, they were wrong. "We shall never abandon the dream of being united with our people in our ancient homeland," she said. "Some of us did not believe in the success of the escape or believed in it very slightly. Already at the Finland Station [in Leningrad] we noticed that we were being followed, but we could no longer go back . . . go back to our past, to the senseless waiting, to life with our luggage packed. Our dream of living in Israel was incomparably stronger than fear of the suffering we might be made to endure."

She continued, "I wanted to live over there with my family, work there. I would not have bothered about politics—all my interest in politics has been confined to the simple wish to leave. Even now I do not doubt for a minute that some time I *will* live in Israel . . . This dream, illuminated by two thousand years of hope, will never leave me. Next year in Jerusalem!" Sylva was almost shaking now, but she took a deep breath and finished by quoting Psalm 137, which had been echoing in her head since the start of the trial: "And now I repeat, 'If I forget thee, O Jerusalem, may my right hand wither . . .'" And then she said the words in Hebrew, *"Im eshkachech Yerushalayim."* The judge interrupted her, yelling that she should use a language familiar to the court. Sylva said simply, "I have finished."

The final statements all aspired to the drama of Sylva's, but none quite captured the pathos of the situation the way she had in that moment. Most of them asked the court to spare the lives of Dymshits and

Kuznetsov and to give Sylva a lesser sentence. Anatoly Altman beamed his Buddhist smile and said, "Today on the day my fate is being decided, I feel wonderful and very sad: it is my hope that peace will come to Israel." Mendelevich stated that his only crime was being "indiscriminate in the means of achieving my dream."

At six in the evening the following day, Christmas Eve in the West, the defendants stood up to hear the verdict and sentencing. The Communist Party members in the courtroom had brought congratulatory bouquets of red and orange flowers for the judge. The state had decided to accept the prosecutor's recommendation in full: Dymshits and Kuznetsov would be executed. The audience burst into wild applause, passing their flowers to the judge. Sylva began weeping loudly. Dymshits stared straight ahead, not a muscle moving in his face. Kuznetsov whispered to himself, "Haven't these Bolsheviks drunk enough blood? Haven't they had their fill? That's okay. They'll soon choke on that blood." The family members, fighting to be heard above the others in the audience, stood on their wooden chairs, reaching out and shouting, tears in their voices: "Be brave," "You will be free," "Children, we will wait for you," and, most reassuring, "They know about you in the West."

They began escorting Kuznetsov out and Sylva ran up to him and pressed her wet cheek to his. Mendelevich pushed the approaching guards out of the way so the pair could embrace, but they pulled Sylva, wailing and moaning, off her husband. Kuznetsov, Dymshits, and Mendelevich quickly hugged, and then they too were taken out. Mendelevich looked back at his father, who was arguing furiously with members of the audience. He was worried the old man might have a heart attack. They should sing something defiant, Mendelevich thought as he was led out of the courtroom—"Hatikvah" or the "Song of the Palmach," something a fighter would sing. But they were all too stunned, the grip of the guards was suddenly too tight, everything was moving too fast, and the weight of history as it pressed down on them made it impossible for anything more than cries to rise out of their throats.

PART II

THEIR OWN DÉTENTE

1970–1980

We cannot gear our foreign policy to the
transformation of other societies.

RICHARD M. NIXON

6

Outrageous Things
1970–1972

IT STARTED WITH Molotov cocktails. As the sixties curdled into the seventies, the teenage boys of Meir Kahane's Jewish Defense League, like many other disaffected and angry young men of the time, found the flash and heat of violence irresistible. Dressing up in their bar mitzvah suits to lob balloons filled with chicken blood at the ballerinas of the touring Bolshoi didn't cut it anymore. They began building crude pipe bombs and exploding them at the bottom of a drained pool at Kahane's summer camp in the Catskills. These were the kind of bombs they placed in the doorways of the Aeroflot and Intourist offices in Manhattan in the fall of 1970, causing a minor diplomatic crisis between the superpowers. The informers and the undercover police officers that swelled the ranks of the JDL were warning their superiors that something bigger and more dangerous was in the works. One officer from the NYPD's intelligence unit who had infiltrated the group gained access to its cache of weapons, which were hidden in closets all over Brooklyn. The JDL had enough shotguns and rifles to arm a small militia.

The narcissistic, theatrical, publicity-hungry rabbi seemed barely able to control the resentful young men, many from dysfunctional backgrounds, who swam around him like parasitic fish. His office on

Fifth Avenue was a reflection of the chaos—a jumble of mismatched desks and tables, all piled high with unopened bills, placards, old newspapers, and rolls of duct tape. Over Kahane's desk was scrawled *Office of the Reb,* next to a photo of the bespectacled and jug-eared Jabotinsky. But out of the emotions he had unleashed—most of his followers were studies in Jewish inferiority complex—Kahane had built an organization that claimed seven thousand members. Where so many others had floundered, he had found a simple and direct response to the problem of Soviet Jewry: Never Again. The two-word slogan perfectly captured the allure Kahane held for American Jews: it simultaneously stirred the memory of their historic helplessness and unblinkingly asserted a newfound strength.

His simple doctrine of confrontation resonated at a moment when the shifting politics of the Cold War were presenting a new challenge for Soviet Jewry activists. Early in his first term, Richard Nixon had hewed largely to his Cold Warrior reputation, carrying out controversial bombing campaigns in Cambodia and Laos and dragging out arms limitations talks with the Soviets in the hope of giving the United States time to reach the Russians' number of offensive missiles. But with the country convulsing with violent antiwar rallies and a difficult reelection campaign ahead of him, the president began to see the wisdom in a new approach. His national security adviser, Henry Kissinger, wanted to alter the relationship between the superpowers by weaving what he called "an intersecting web of interests"—increased trade, strategic arms limitation talks (SALT, as they were known), cultural and scientific exchanges. A scaled-down Cold War would allow the Soviets to shift resources away from defense and toward their growing economic problems. Nixon would have the leverage he needed to end the war in Vietnam and stabilize the United States after a decade of political and cultural revolution. But the warming trend, which became known as détente, presented a problem for Soviet Jewry activists. The belligerent anti-Communism of the last decade had at least provided a context for their cause. Détente, based purely on realpolitik, threatened to pave over the problems of Soviet Jews with a new amicability that would be blind to such moral questions as the right to emigrate.

Kahane, however, saw an opportunity. Nixon and Brezhnev clearly wanted something—namely, calm—and he could take that something away. As he told the *New York Times* in a long profile (testament in itself to his growing celebrity): "The most important thing to the Soviet Union at this moment is détente with the West. So what we are basically trying to do is give the Russians a hard enough time on something they want badly—and then trade with them: 'Look, you want your détente, take your détente. Build your bridges. Pay us off. Give us 8,000 Jews, 10,000 Jews, 12,000 Jews. . . .' How does the U.S. come into this? The U.S. wants exactly the same thing right now—a détente. What we want the president and the Soviets to know is it doesn't take much to plunge the world into a terrible, terrible crisis." How exactly did he intend to get his message to Russian and American leaders? By doing, as he put it, "outrageous things."

News of the hijacking made many young people take another look at the JDL. Such a suicidal act seemed to demand the kind of response that only Kahane could provide. One such young person was Yossi Klein, the blond-haired, baby-faced boy from Borough Park, now a senior at the Brooklyn Talmudical Academy. He had remained throughout his teenage years an avid follower of Yaakov Birnbaum and his Student Struggle. And he still regarded Birnbaum as a sort of messianic figure, an eccentric convinced he could achieve with righteous indignation what Kahane was now accomplishing with bombs. But after letters dramatically pleading for action started to emerge from the Soviet Union, Klein began to feel like Birnbaum's responsible resistance was insufficient. When he asked his mentor about Kahane, Klein heard only bitterness. "I know Meir," Birnbaum told him, laughing disdainfully. "He came to a few of our rallies in the beginning, made a speech or two, very passionate and all the rest of it. But no substance, you see. He's ruining *years* of our work with wild acts of self-aggrandizement. Meir is a violent soul, he dreams of chasms of blood."

On the evening of December 27, two days after the death sentences of Dymshits and Kuznetsov were announced, Kahane held an emergency rally at Hunter College, a block away from the Soviet mission. Klein, agitated by the news, showed up ready to join the Jewish Defense League. On his shirt he had carefully fastened a button that read UP AGAINST THE WALL, MOTHER RUSSIA. When he found his friends, they awkwardly greeted each other with the black power salute. Hundreds packed the college's auditorium, most of them young men, and

Kahane whipped them into a frenzy. His public speaking had improved over the past two years. He could control his stutter, and he declaimed with simple, strong sentences. "Never again will Jews watch silently while other Jews die. Never again!" he yelled. "We must break every law to save three million Soviet Jews. The time has come for us to bury our respectability before it buries us," he continued, echoing Jabotinsky. The *New York Daily News* described the ecstatic reaction: "Pandemonium erupted in the hall. It turned into a sea of clenched fists and waving placards and Israeli flags as chants broke out again and again: 'Never Again!' 'Freedom Now' and 'Am Yisrael Hai!'" By the end of his speech, fist slamming against the lectern, Kahane made a threat he knew the papers would have to print: "Listen, Brezhnev, and listen well: If Dymshits and Kuznetsov die, Russian diplomats will die in New York. Two Russians for every Jew!" The crowd repeated after him, and Klein along with them, "Two Russians for every Jew! Two Russians for every Jew!"

When the rally was over, a mob of almost twenty-five hundred people rushed down the block toward the Soviet mission. Klein was running too. When they arrived at the barricades, Kahane shoved his way to the front and charged into a line of riot police. The cops swung their clubs around haphazardly as young demonstrators pushed closer to the mission's white façade and threw stones at the windows. Eventually a bottle of red paint smashed through the building's glass doors. The last thing Klein saw before hurrying home was someone stumbling down the street with a bloodied head. By the time the fracas was over, eleven people had been arrested, including Kahane, who happily spent the night in jail.

The whole world seemed to respond to the verdict in Leningrad; the death sentences only further emphasized the reckless courage of the initial act. Italian longshoremen in Genoa went on a twenty-four-hour strike. The president of Switzerland made an impassioned plea. Protests took place in every major city, including one in Rome that interrupted the pope's weekly address from the balcony of St. Peter's Basilica. Schoolchildren in Stockholm marched with torches through the streets. The Knesset met on a Friday night for only the second time in its history, and air-raid sirens blasted through the cities of Israel. Nobel Prize winners and congresspeople sent telegrams and sponsored resolutions. The *Washington Post* titled its lead editorial on the sentencing "Murder." Even Nahum Goldmann, the infamously cautious Jewish leader, frantically called his contacts in the Kremlin, only to learn that they were all at their dachas for the New Year's holiday.

Most unexpected, and most troubling for the Soviets, was the criticism coming from the Communist parties in the West. Salvador Allende, the Socialist leader of Chile, demanded leniency as a "highly humanitarian gesture." Complicating matters was another death sentence making headlines that week. In Spain on December 28, six Basque separatists were sentenced to hang for the murder of a Spanish policeman. Protest greeted this verdict as well. The Fascist regime was being criticized for its lack of transparency in the trial, and Francisco Franco was being pressured to commute the penalty. It would have been sheer hypocrisy for Communists not to condemn on the left what they were so vigorously denouncing on the right.

New York, as always, was the center of the action. In addition to Kahane's well-publicized theatrics, other demonstrations were occurring. Yaakov Birnbaum led solemn Student Struggle protests opposite the UN building, the students carrying oversize black-and-white photos of the condemned—Zalmanson, Khnokh, Mendelevich. Mayor John Lindsay declared a Day of Concern and held a rally of two thousand people at the base of the giant neoclassical columns of New York's supreme court. The patrician mayor with the WASPy good looks addressed the crowd in impassioned tones: "We meet this afternoon as Jew and Gentile, black and white, young and old, not to plead our own interests, but to speak out for thousands of Soviet Jews who cannot speak for themselves."

It was clear that more was at stake than just the fate of the two condemned men. Soviet Jewry itself now became the central issue. And the problem, as it was framed, was Jews' right to emigrate—not simply the preservation of their culture and religion. A *New York Times* editorial following the verdict powerfully accentuated this sudden shift in focus. "This was one of the most important political trials held in the Soviet Union since World War II," the *Times* declared. "The real defendants in the court were not the handful of accused, but the tens of thousands of Soviet Jews who have courageously demanded the right to emigrate to Israel."

On December 30, Richard Nixon felt compelled to meet with a

troika of Jewish leaders at the White House. Though he and Kissinger had hoped to avoid any move that might alienate their new partners in détente, they had to at least make a symbolic gesture, something to quell the surge of anger coming at them from all directions. Nixon appeared appropriately dismayed and angry, but in the end, after a forty-minute discussion, he promised nothing. Still, such a high-level meeting was unprecedented. Never before had an American president invited anyone from the Jewish community into the Oval Office to discuss Soviet Jewry. The embattled leaders of the Jewish establishment took it as a small victory.

———————

At ten in the evening on December 31, Eduard Kuznetsov sat in his prison cell and toasted the new year with a mug of warm water. A few minutes later, as he smoked the day's final cigarette, the door opened and four uniformed guards stepped inside. They ordered him to stand up, put his hands behind his back, and start walking down the dark hallway. The looks on the guards' faces convinced Kuznetsov that he was being taken out to be shot. A few weeks later he wrote in his secret prison diary, "I cannot remember my heart beating. I cannot remember what thoughts were in my head—it was someone else this was happening to. It wasn't I who slowly stepped down that corridor with my hands behind my back, it wasn't I who painstakingly avoided stepping on the heels of the guard in front of me or bumping into the guards on either side or treading on the feet of the guards behind me." Terrified, he was led into the office of the prison's warden, who stood there in his epaulettes with a smile on his face. "A humanitarian gesture has been made on your behalf," he announced. "The sentence of death passed against you has been commuted to fifteen years on special regime. May I wish you a Happy New Year." "Tears of humiliation and hatred" started running down Kuznetsov's cheeks. He was confused. Was he being deceived again? Someone had once told him that in the moments before execution, prisoners were usually lied to in order to prevent resistance. When the warden handed him a telegram from Sakharov and Elena Bonner congratulating him on the good news, he wondered if it had been forged. The terror took weeks to subside.

Never before in Soviet history had an appeal been heard and decided so quickly. It usually took at least two months. Earlier that day, hardly a week after the trial's end, with Sakharov present in the courtroom and a dozen freezing activists waiting in the snow outside, the supreme court of the Russian Republic had commuted Kuznetsov's and Dymshits's death sentences to fifteen years. A few of the other hijackers also got reduced time, including Mendelevich, who now had to serve just twelve years. The court's official reason, reported by TASS, was that "the hijacking attempt was averted in time and that under Soviet law, the death penalty is an exceptional measure of punishment."

It was a major setback in the Soviets' ideological fight against Zionism. With the world watching, they were forced to admit they had gone too far. The international outcry had become unbearable, and on December 30, Generalissimo Franco had commuted the death sentences of the six Basque separatists; if the Soviets had insisted on carrying out their execution, their brutality would have stood in stark contrast to the clemency of the Fascists. As the *New York Times* put it in an editorial, "It is encouraging that the Kremlin has acknowledged the need for paying attention, in some cases at least, to the sensibilities of the civilized world."

In an attempt to divert attention from the Soviets' "Jewish problem," the trials of the twenty other Zionist activists arrested in the wake of the hijacking were postponed for weeks, and then months. Only in May did nine leaders of the Leningrad Zionist organization, the originators of the hijacking plot, finally take the stand. This time, the trial was kept as quiet as possible. Though officially public, it was closed to journalists. The KGB had succeeded in coercing a few of the defendants to cooperate. Some offered "confessions" that implicated the others. In the end, all were convicted on conspiracy charges, the main evidence being their attempt to contact Israel and get permission to carry out the first, larger hijacking plot. According to TASS, Hillel Butman, who along with his friends had pushed the hardest for dramatic action, was guilty of having "maintained illegal ties with the Government and Zionist circles in Israel." There was little evidence to link these Jews to the hijacking that was actually attempted. Their benign activities were largely portrayed as the acts of subversive malcontents. Still, the sentencing was harsh. Butman got ten years, the others only slightly less.

Later that May came the trial of the four Riga Jews, including Aron Shpilberg, the Leningrad-born activist who had moved to Latvia after his midlife circumcision, and Ruth Alexandrovich, whose case had been followed closely by Soviet Jewry activists in the West. The charges against them had nothing to do with the hijacking. Their crime was disseminating samizdat. Here too the trial turned ugly. At least one of the Riga activists, Boris Maftser, had been broken during the months of intense interrogation, and in an attempt to win leniency he now accused the others. In the end Shpilberg got four years and Alexandrovich and Maftser each received one—guilty, in TASS's phrasing, of "fabricating and circulating slanderous materials for subversive purposes and attempting to draw acquaintances and colleagues into activities hostile to the state." The last of the trials took place in Kishinev a month later and involved nine young students engaged in "Zionist activities." The case rested mostly on their having disassembled and transported an Era Duplicator copy machine from Kishinev to Leningrad, though they had never managed to make it work. All the defendants were found guilty. David Chernoglaz, the member of the Leningrad Zionist organization who had been against the hijacking, was also put on trial with this group. He received five years in prison.

Many of those already sentenced, like Kuznetsov, Dymshits, and Sylva Zalmanson, were kept at the Big House that entire spring so they could be used as witnesses in the other trials. But by early July, all those convicted—more than thirty activists—had begun their long journey east to be deposited at various labor camps in Mordvinia and the Ural Mountains. A whole generation of Zionist activists, the first to form a truly organized opposition, was about to be swallowed up by the Soviets' well-oiled penitentiary machine.

The fact that Kuznetsov and Dymshits had escaped death seemed concrete proof that the loud tactics so long decried by the Jewish establishment actually worked. It put to rest the question of *whether* to pressure. The battle now was over *how much*. The Israelis, in particular, were paying close attention. Nehemiah Levanon, who until 1970 had been the Washington representative of Lishkat Hakesher, had just succeeded Shaul Avigur as the head of the secret organization. Now working out of the Tel Aviv office, he still had the same vision. He wanted the American Jewish establishment to create a national organization, one with teeth, that would be focused solely on the Soviet Jewry issue. This had become an even more urgent objective if only because Levanon saw that his control of the movement's direction was being threatened—and not just by Kahane and his high-profile shenanigans. After he'd spent much of the sixties helping Moshe Decter encourage grassroots activists to prod the establishment into action, Levanon now saw that a real alternative organization was being formed, one that might fulfill Levanon's goal of a serious national effort but that would be outside his authority, dictating its own strategy without Israel's guidance or foreign policy in mind.

The threat, of course, came from Cleveland. In April 1970 Lou Rosenblum, still at his job at NASA, had finally created what he called the Union of Councils for Soviet Jews. It was a binding together of a half a dozen energetic local groups from cities such as San Francisco, Los Angeles, and Washington, D.C. Even though he feared his work at NASA would suffer, Rosenblum, with almost ten years of experience, was the expert on Soviet Jewry, and so he reluctantly became the group's first chairman. In his first memo to the six councils, he made it clear that the Union of Councils would embrace its role as "'loyal opposition' to spur the national Jewish organizations to greater activity," but he also made sure to emphasize: "We shall avoid guiding our policy or actions by the political exigencies of either the government of Israel or the United States."

Very soon, the Union of Councils was going where no one had gone before. Rosenblum began looking for what he called "people-to-people" opportunities, ways that American Jews could communicate with Soviet Jews, thereby humanizing the cause. It was a critical next step. If Yaakov Birnbaum provided the basic religious and civic tropes that informed every Soviet Jewry protest, then Lou Rosenblum's major contribution was increasing the points of contact between Soviet and American Jews, producing an essential intimacy between the two communities that fueled the movement.

Rosenblum had a list of seventy-five names and addresses of Soviet Jews who had gone public by signing petitions. He decided to get as many people as he could to send Passover cards to them. This modest plan became more elaborate when he managed to convince the head of the American Greeting Cards Company, who was Jewish, to mass-produce the cards at a discounted price. The Union of Councils sold packages that each contained five cards, five envelopes, and the names and addresses of five of the dissident families. The message on the cards was simple. In Russian, Yiddish, and English, it read: "Happy Passover. From the Jews of the USA to the Jews of the USSR—We have not forgotten you."

During that first spring of the Union of Councils' existence, it sold sixty thousand packages, mostly through the local councils and other groups—Student Struggle in New York ordered them by the box. And the initial correspondence often elicited further contact, with photographs sent back and forth, and letters in broken English telling the individual stories of jobs lost and bureaucratic headaches, and even giving coded messages about KGB interrogations. So successful was the program that Rosh Hashanah and Hanukkah cards were made up, and they also sold by the tens of thousands. The income for the local councils was significant. The production cost of a package of five cards was twenty cents, and each packet was being sold for a dollar. So this brought in money to secure the independence of the new Union of Councils, providing funds for activities and helping to pay the telephone bills at Rosenblum's home office.

The first calls to the Soviet Union soon followed. Rosenblum had developed a crucial contact in Israel, Ann Shenkar, an American woman who had married a wealthy Israeli and lived in a suburb of Tel Aviv. She had taken it upon herself to become familiar with the community of Soviet Jews, most of them from Riga, who had emigrated in 1969. They were increasingly unhappy with the Israeli government's measured tone when it came to the Soviet Union. (Abba Eban, Israel's foreign minister, was annoyed by the outspoken new arrivals and had once publicly asked them to shut up, saying, "Recent immigrants are not the best people to carry this message forward because we don't want them to be the last.") Shenkar fed off this frustration, starting an activist group that, among other things, compiled lists of names, addresses, and phone numbers of their Soviet Jewish brethren, along with notes on who spoke English or French or German. This fit well with Rosenblum's commitment to independence, because by going through

Shenkar, he avoided Levanon and the Lishka, who would surely have tried to control the calls. Rosenblum was soon dialing Moscow numbers from Cleveland and sending off contact lists to all the councils so they could make their own calls. Transatlantic connections to the Soviet Union went through two operators, one in New York and one in Moscow. But at the time, with the KGB largely unaware of the proliferating conversations—which in 1970 were mostly innocuous greetings and expressions of solidarity—the Moscow operators let the calls go through.

The effectiveness of people-to-people contact was clear. One conversation with a Jew in the Soviet Union who described the hardship of his life made an abstract issue exceedingly real. Heard over a crackling wire, an Old World Russian accent—which might remind an American Jew of his grandfather—did more for the cause than any policy paper or rally. Understanding this was Lou Rosenblum's genius.

At the end of 1970, still in the first year of his Union of Councils, Rosenblum invited a Soviet Jew who had managed to emigrate to Israel to come visit the United States. Lyuba Bershadskaya, a large, gold-toothed Muscovite woman who had lived a particularly difficult life, toured America in the winter of 1970. In synagogue after synagogue she told her story in her broken English: Stalin had sent her to the Siberian Gulag for ten years for the crime of having worked at the American embassy during World War II. It was there, in conversation with other imprisoned Zionists, that she discovered her Jewish identity, and from the moment of her release, in 1956, she tried to get out.

Rosenblum managed to recruit a writer to meet with Bershadskaya and dramatize her story for an American audience. Cynthia Ozick, a young novelist living in New Rochelle, whose first novel, *Trust,* had been published four years earlier, was then working on a book of short stories and raising her young daughter. She had reservations at first about taking the job, fears shared by other American Jews. Her father still had relatives in the Soviet Union, and she had grown up being told not to bring too much attention to them as it could only hurt them. As she wrote to Rosenblum: "All my life, from babyhood on, I've been trained (I'm sure that word isn't too strong) to be cautious. . . . The huge SHAH of my father's fear concerning his family in Russia descends on me like a cloud." In spite of this, she agreed to meet with

Bershadskaya. "I'll be glad to do it; though trembling. Because there is nothing about Jews in Russia that doesn't make me tremble, from this old old old training in fear."

The resulting six-thousand-word account of Bershadskaya's life appeared in the *New York Times Magazine* in March 1971. Ozick insisted on publishing it under a pseudonym, Trudie Vocse. Three months after the Leningrad verdict, the article presented the character and voice of a Jew who had struggled against the regime. Ozick found a way to channel Bershadskaya and let her longing speak for itself. "The Six-Day War changed everything," she wrote in the Russian woman's voice. "Suddenly, you saw young men and women openly wearing the Star of David around their necks. People began coming to OVIR flaunting their Stars of David. And once I saw a man walking all around a huge square in Moscow, holding the hand of a little girl about 6 years old. Her dress was pinned all over with big Stars of David. He walked around and around the square, not going anywhere, just for everyone to see what was on the little girl's dress. A policeman chased him away finally. . . . We had stopped being afraid. We began fighting openly, we began to give our names and addresses. The silent time was over for us."

The Israelis were not happy with the way things were playing out in America. The grassroots activists, along with Kahane, seemed to be grabbing hold of the movement. The Israelis needed to reassert control. As Nehemiah Levanon saw it, it was the Lishka that had first given the issue life in the United States. Why should it cede power to people like Rosenblum—useful as he had been—when he now refused to listen to the Israelis or follow their orders? Protesting in a way that seemed too anti-Soviet or struck the wrong tone could jeopardize the whole movement. This wasn't a game for amateurs. After the victory of the Six-Day War, Israelis were filled with an almost biblical conviction that they had single-handedly ensured Jewish continuity, giving them the last word on all things Jewish. Unfortunately, the man Levanon chose to carry out the delicate mission of checking the grass roots while still harnessing their power turned out to be an uncompromising bully. Yoram Dinstein was an Israeli lawyer in his early thirties who had just received his doctorate from NYU. Rather than gently persuading activists like Rosenblum to do what he wanted, he almost immediately declared war on them.

Lou Rosenblum had never had a good feeling about Dinstein. On a car ride to the Cleveland airport in March 1970—they had both just attended a regional Soviet Jewry conference—Dinstein had threatened him. "You people are doing everything you can to destroy the Soviet Jewry movement," he said as the car neared the airport. "What are you talking about?" Rosenblum asked him. "I hear that you're starting a new organization. It's no secret. But if you go ahead with this, I'll see to it that you are destroyed—all of you." Rosenblum, amazed that Dinstein would menace him so publicly, simply said, "Yoram, shut up!" And they drove the rest of the way in silence.

Then Dinstein targeted Zev Yaroslavsky, a young Los Angeles college student whose group, California Students for Soviet Jewry, was part of the initial Union of Councils. Yaroslavsky was splitting his time between grassroots activism and a job at the Los Angeles Jewish Federation, the establishment's local arm. About two months after Dinstein and Rosenblum's strange car ride, Dinstein called Yaroslavsky. As Yaroslavsky recounted in a letter to Rosenblum the next day: "He went on to inform me that if I did not find some way to eliminate the CSSJ's name from the stationery, I could no longer be working for the Federation. He said that this was a 'declaration of war' on my part, and that I could not expect to be working for the Federation after a period of two or three weeks."

By the end of the month, Yaroslavsky had lost his job, and Rosenblum wrote to his fellow activists that Yaroslavsky was "the first martyr on our side to fall in this new Jewish holy war. . . . There is little that such stupidity can do other than polarize the situation to a greater extent. We are, in our respective communities, the de facto leaders in matters of Soviet Jewry. The initiative has been and will remain ours."

Rosenblum was incensed. But he was also worried. Dinstein's aggressiveness suggested that the Lishka really did intend to destroy his nascent grassroots group. In the beginning of May, Rosenblum decided to send a letter to Yitzhak Rabin, then the Israeli ambassador to the United States. In his note, he described what he called the "tiresome bullying tactics" of Dinstein, listing the many instances when he had carried out "an overzealous discharge of his instructions." And Rosenblum presented a threat of his own. The Lishka's actions in America made Israel susceptible to charges of illegal foreign intervention, a potential diplomatic disaster if its full scale was discovered. Rosenblum wanted to hint to Rabin that the Lishka was leaving obvious tracks, that Dinstein's heavy-handedness was making the Israeli government's manipulation of the American Jewish community that much more transparent. "Dr. Dinstein's behavior is calculated to exacerbate the issue of Israeli control of American Jewish organizations," Rosenblum wrote. "Certainly, in view of the above, there will be interest in observing the role played by the Israeli government representative."

Rabin did not answer beyond confirming that Rosenblum's letter had been received. But that summer, Nehemiah Levanon, not known for conciliatory gestures, invited Rosenblum to Washington for a talk. Feeling like he had the upper hand, Rosenblum brought three demands. He wanted lists of those who had applied for exit visas; telephone numbers so he could make calls; and names of recent Russian immigrants to Israel who could tour the United States, as Bershadskaya had. Levanon begrudgingly offered to send over a list with several hundred names. But he said telephone calls were out of the question, that they put Jews in danger. And as for activists who could speak to American audiences, he thought this could be arranged as long as it was done in a low-key manner, without television cameras or journalists—the emigrants often said bombastic, imprudent things about the Soviet Union (and about their reception in Israel) and he didn't want these broadcast. The differences in approach couldn't have been more stark. It was the last time Rosenblum and Levanon would ever meet.

The Leningrad trials altered the landscape. There now seemed to be a potentially massive base of support for the movement, and Levanon felt the time had come for an international conference, one that would make the plight of Soviet Jews a global issue. Internationalizing the movement would also deny the Soviets the chance to treat the issue as just another front in the Cold War, subject to the state of relations between the superpowers. Levi Eshkol, prime minister of Israel until early 1969, never liked the idea. But his successor, Golda Meir, eventually, cautiously, told Levanon to go forward.

In spite of early skepticism about it, the Brussels conference, as it came to be known, took on a life of its own. The conference was planned for February 24 through 27, 1971, and the timing of the recent death sentence and commutation in Leningrad gave it an urgent feel. There would be almost eight hundred delegates from thirty-eight countries meeting at the stately Palais des Congrès in the Belgian capital, including representatives of Jewish French youth groups and British parliamentarians, American writers and film directors, Argentinean community organizers, and two of the lodestars of the Israeli political establishment: right-wing leader Menachem Begin and the ailing eighty-five-year-old David Ben-Gurion, who was to give the closing speech.

The Soviets inadvertently helped publicize the conference by responding to it with a barrage of anti-Zionist propaganda filled with blatant threats not heard since Stalin's time. *Pravda* warned that anyone expressing Zionist beliefs would "automatically become an agent of international Zionism and hence an enemy of the Soviet people." This was followed by a two-part "research" article arguing that Jews were behind the Prague Spring—the sole backers of the liberal Dubček regime. Belgium was soon under attack for hosting the event, and the Soviets even threatened to cut diplomatic ties. A few Soviet Jewish personalities, those the activists referred to as "court Jews," were sent to Brussels to talk to any journalist who would listen. Among them was David Dragunsky, a sixty-year-old three-star general of the Soviet army, who announced that the conference organizers had personally insulted him by planning this festival of Soviet slander to fall exactly on Red Army Day. A week before the conference, only a handful of press passes had been issued. But by February 23, after all the Soviet commotion, 255 journalists had been accredited. There would be one reporter for every four delegates.

The conference officially opened the following day. And it seemed to progress according to plan—a showy event full of grandiloquent speeches. The American delegation, two hundred and fifty strong, was particularly large and eclectic. It included Albert Shanker, the head of the New York teachers union, recently embroiled in the Ocean Hill–Brownsville dispute; film director Otto Preminger; and screenwriter Paddy Chayefsky. Elie Wiesel, of course, was there, as was Gershom Scholem, the Jewish philosopher who'd helped popularize the study of kabbalah. The first day was filled with more ceremony than substance and included a performance of Russian Jewish folk songs. Levanon planned a more substantive program—to discuss a series of nonbinding recommendations—for the following day.

But just as the last speaker was about to address the room that morning, a scuffle broke out. Morris Brafman, the Holocaust survivor and charismatic Jabotinskyite with the Manhattan lingerie business, jumped on the stage, grabbed the microphone, and began yelling, "Meir Kahane has been arrested! I demand to know who ordered Meir Kahane's arrest!"

The day before, Kahane had been standing in a suit and tie in a Manhattan courtroom listening to the verdict in his first Soviet Jewry–related trial. He was found guilty of "obstructing government administration" and disorderly conduct for storming through the police barricade blocking off the Soviet mission during the December 1969 rally. The judge released him to await sentencing, at which point he raced to the airport to catch a plane for Brussels. It didn't matter that he hadn't actually been invited. As he saw it, he was saving the conference from irrelevance. Kahane entered the Palais des Congrès carrying a list of ten demands that he intended to present to the delegates. These were not recommendations but strict guidelines for getting the Soviets to buckle on emigration. He knew that his hero Menachem Begin would be present, and so would a handful of revisionists, including a group of French Betar youth; he thought he had nothing to lose by disrupting the proceedings. As he later wrote, "If I could speak and outline my ideas, I knew that a large number of the delegates would agree."

As soon as he walked into the lobby, he was surrounded. Kahane asked to send a note to the head of the American delegation demanding permission to address the floor. When the inevitable response was issued, Kahane turned to a few journalists and denounced the meeting as undemocratic. He said he would be holding a press conference in his hotel room later that afternoon to lay out his ten-point plan. That might have been the extent of the interruption. But when he stepped out of the building Kahane was grabbed by three plainclothes Belgian policemen and taken to a local station for questioning. He was told that he was a security risk, held there all day, and then driven to the airport and directed to leave the country.

To the dismay of Levanon and the Israelis, the conference ground to a halt. All anyone could talk about was Kahane and whether he should have been allowed to speak. This only heightened the feeling that little would be accomplished. At one point, Paddy Chayefsky took to the stage and said, "I have listened to your moans but I have not heard

your ideas for action." He later told journalists he thought the conference was as tame as "a Wednesday night Hadassah meeting." When the
official recommendations were finally presented, the next day, they validated his assessment. The conference leadership proposed either quiet
diplomacy—calling for direct contacts with Kremlin officials—or in-
offensive forms of action, like establishing a world conference of Jewish youth for Soviet Jewry and designing a symbol for the movement.

There was one moment of grace at the closing ceremony, when
the stooped eighty-five-year-old Israeli patriarch David Ben-Gurion
slowly made his way to the stage as people stood and cheered. His
white hair billowing above him like a halo, he spoke for only a couple
of minutes, uniting the delegates for a few brief moments, and then
returned to his hotel room where he had been lying sick with a cold for
three days. The mood quickly became gloomy again. Herb Caron, the
early Cleveland activist, wrote that the conference could be summed
up in two words: "lost opportunity." Even the *New York Times* had to
note the "sense of frustration" that "hung over the proceedings," and
the fact that the conference's resolution "disappointed a large number of delegates, particularly younger ones, who had hoped for more
militancy." Menachem Begin, encountering a distraught Nehemiah
Levanon brooding in the hallway outside the conference hall, tried to
reassure him that history would not record the Kahane incident, only
the progress that had been made in the cause of Soviet Jewry.

In the short term, however, Kahane had won again. When he landed
in New York, he laid out his ten-point plan—a series of harsh measures meant to isolate the Russians—for the reporters gathered at JFK.
Among other things, he demanded "an immediate end to all Western
talks with the USSR, including disarmament, space, cultural and trade
talks" and called for "legal harassment of Soviet officials, including
picketing of private residences and mass telephone calls to embassies,
consulates, etc." Almost every article about Brussels included this list
of demands. And his detention, whether ordered by the Israelis or not,
gave him the chance to present himself as a martyr. He later wrote:

> I went to Brussels because I feared the conference would content
> itself with platitudes. It did. I went to Brussels because I sensed that
> concrete programs would not even be on the agenda. They were not.

I went to Brussels because, if playwrights and producers and authors and architects who have had little or no share in the struggle for Soviet Jewry were allowed hallowed entry, representatives of an organization that has literally spilled its blood on barricades and gone to prison for our oppressed brethren had a moral and natural right to speak. . . . Brussels, where dissent was stifled, where fearful men kept out Jewish militancy, where a Jew was seized by the Belgian police and expelled by force with the knowledge and approval of Jews. This was the story of Brussels. And more it was the story of the Jewish Establishment and why JDL came into being.

It was Kahane's moment and he grabbed it. In the weeks leading up to and following the Brussels conference, he brought unprecedented attention to Soviet Jewry. His methods were, as always, surprisingly simple but ferociously provocative. After the New Year's Eve commutation of the death sentences in Leningrad—which Kahane considered a personal victory—he launched his campaign of harassment. Soviet diplomats everywhere would be targeted—spat on, followed, cursed at, and generally driven crazy by his young followers. "The life of each Russian will be made miserable," Kahane told reporters in the first days of 1971. Yossi Klein, the former Student Struggle member turned JDLer, was one of the harassers. He would skip school and stand near the Soviet mission, which he and his new friends now referred to as simply "the mission." When a black limousine with telltale DPL (diplomat) license plates turned the corner onto Sixty-seventh Street, they would surround the car, spit at the windows, and flash their middle fingers. If a Russian man in a fur hat was spotted walking down the street, Yossi would start following him. "Hey, Igor! Got one of those hats for me?" Moving in closer, the gang would hiss and call out, "*Roosky khoy!*," a popular Russian curse that meant "Russian prick." One of their favorite pranks was posting the mission's phone number in public bathrooms below the words *For a good time, call Sonya.*

Amazingly, within days the actions of this small group of teens provoked a full-blown diplomatic crisis. On January 5, 1971, Anatoly Dobrynin, the Soviet ambassador, delivered a terse note to the State Department protesting the lack of security for Russians in America and threatening that if the situation did not improve,

Americans in Russia could expect similar treatment. Sure enough, by the end of the week, American diplomats were being manhandled in the streets of Moscow. Three young people surrounded an embassy worker and his wife outside a theater, grabbing the man by his lapels and asking how he would like to be beaten. A series of Soviet citizens' delegations visited the U.S. embassy in Moscow bearing petitions protesting the "Zionist hooligans." And as payback for the protests over the Leningrad trials, the Soviets staged demonstrations to denounce the trial of Angela Davis, a Black Panther and a Communist being tried in a California courtroom for the murder of a judge that past summer. Feebly mimicking the activity in the wake of the Leningrad arrests, *Izvestia* published a letter by a group of Soviet intellectuals addressed to Nixon and demanding that the president spare Davis's life.

Then on January 8, another pipe bomb exploded—this time at the Soviet cultural building in Washington, D.C. No one was hurt, but it was powerful enough to shatter all the windows and hurl an iron gate two hundred and fifty feet. "We do not condemn the act—nor did we do it," Kahane told the press the next day. "The applause for the bombing in Washington comes from imprisoned Soviet Jewry. The commuting of the death sentence was but a skirmish in a war of liberation. We call upon the people of the world to join that war."

The FBI went into panic mode. The elderly and increasingly paranoid J. Edgar Hoover, then nearing the end of his thirty-fifth year as director, personally reviewed every one of Kahane's utterances. Most of the daily reports on the rabbi were provided by the many young informers in the JDL, one of whom was described as "a 'hippie' type individual . . . sloppy in appearance and discourteous in manner." Much of the material given was absurd, and yet it was treated with the utmost urgency. A typical memo received by Hoover on January 15, 1971, from the bureau's New York City field office contained this ominous piece of information: "Kahane has seriously discussed capturing a Soviet city. His intent is to secure germs of a virulent disease from a hospital or bacteriologist, grow a sufficient amount of these germs, and then smuggle them to a Soviet city. He will then threaten to contaminate the city unless the Soviets allow Jews to emigrate to Israel. Source advised that the problem of securing the germs and growing them is relatively simple for any bacteriologist. However the details of getting them into the Soviet Union have not been worked out."

No statement by Kahane was too trivial to investigate. When he told a group of his followers in January that they should target Leonard Bernstein in retaliation for his hosting of a Black Panther fundraiser (immortalized by Tom Wolfe in his book *Radical Chic*), the news quickly made its way to Hoover himself. Apparently, Kahane had said he was planning to go to the New York composer's Park Avenue duplex and "take over the entire building, sit in it, and see how much pressure Bernstein can take."

In one week, Kahane's antics managed to shatter the general goodwill that had recently come to characterize Soviet-American relations. The *New York Times,* in its Week in Review section, described the two countries as entering a "nasty phase" and foresaw no less than the end of détente. "It is impossible to predict how far the present unpleasantness will go or what its full impact on Soviet-American relations will be," the *Times* article concluded. "But already it is putting a damper on the plans of Americans thinking of visiting the Soviet Union as tourists or businessmen. And the possibility exists that Moscow could choose to use the tension on this issue as a means or an excuse to end or postpone the Soviet-American SALT negotiations looking towards strategic arms limitations."

At the beginning of 1971, détente was an explicit goal of both the United States and the Soviet Union. And Kahane was turning out to be its biggest enemy. The FBI and the Justice Department were instructed by the White House to find a way, any way, to silence him. Kahane's FBI files—where he is referred to at one point as a "Yiddish Frantz Fanon"—are filled with requests from Kissinger and the State Department to prioritize the prosecution of Kahane. The attorney general issued an order for a wiretap of the JDL offices and Kahane's home. One telegrammed message from the Los Angeles FBI office to Hoover pointed out that Kahane had told his followers they could get tax deductions for their JDL contributions; the agent wondered if this minor breach of federal tax law could be a potential avenue for indictment.

Kahane basked in the attention and cared only that his name and his cause appeared day after day on page one of every national paper in America as well as on the smudged copies of *Pravda* and *Izvestia* pinned to bulletin boards on the streets of Moscow. When Charles Yost, the American ambassador to the United Nations, met with him in private to demand that he call off the harassment campaign, Kahane took it as a sign his plan was working. He played with the press, at one point announcing an "indefinite moratorium." He had been convinced by "people in government and major Jewish groups" to put a leash on his young troops for a "reasonable period of time." But this too was a stunt. Two weeks later, in early February, Yossi Klein and his friends were hanging out in front of the mission with signs that had the word *pig* written in Russian. And worse—bricks were thrown through the windows of Aeroflot and Intourist. So successful was the harassment campaign that Kahane moved on to targeting American companies engaged in trade with the Soviet Union, setting up a hot line run out of an office above a porn theater in Times Square that would supply the names of a thousand guilty firms.

In March of 1971, Kahane pulled off his most dramatic move yet. In almost all of his speeches, he asked why the older generation of American Jews hadn't done anything to stop the Holocaust. Even the slogan Never Again was a rebuke. One of the ways he dramatized the point was by speculating what would have happened if Jews in the 1940s had sat down in the streets of Washington and refused to move until the concentration camps had been bombed. Kahane decided to use most of the JDL's budget for just such a demonstration. He rented a fleet of buses, and on the morning of March 21, a group of more than a thousand young people, mostly from the outer boroughs of New York, headed to the capital.

Yossi Klein and his sister Chani were among the protesters; they left in a chartered bus that took them from Borough Park straight to the Ellipse in front of the White House. The weather was good, a day of sun and wind, and the mood was exuberant. About thirteen hundred people showed up, far fewer than the thousands predicted by Kahane, but it didn't seem to matter. They began marching toward the Soviet embassy, and at the intersection nearest the building, Kahane turned on his megaphone: "I'm asking you to do today what Jews didn't do while the gas chambers were burning. Sit down in the streets of Washington." And they sat. Kahane had assured DC police that this would be a nonviolent protest. The cops would tap the protesters on the shoulder and they would calmly stand up and be arrested. There was not much confrontation. In fact, it felt to Yossi more like a party. One of his friends had brought along his guitar and was playing Grateful Dead songs. When Yossi's turn came to be arrested, he asked the officer how he could get a copy of his mug shot. He was escorted onto a waiting bus with barred windows. There his friends were all banging on the roof and singing together, "One, two, three, four, open up the iron door! Five, six, seven, eight, let my people emigrate!" They all spent a few hours in jail, paid their ten-dollar fines, and were back home in Brooklyn by evening. The protest was a success, though there was some discrepancy in reported arrests—Kahane claimed twelve hundred and newspaper accounts said eight hundred. Either way, it was the largest mass arrest in the capital in American history, at least until the May Day protests a few weeks later, when ten thousand people were arrested in their attempt to shut down the federal government over the Vietnam War.

For Kahane, the Washington demonstration was more than just a publicity stunt. It was proof of a new wave of Jewish youth. Here were Jews who were not afraid to do something risky for their own people and go to jail for a Jewish cause. It was the fulfillment of Kahane's Jabotinskyite dream. He later wrote about the day: "What marked March 21, 1971, as so different was that instead of being arrested for Vietnam, Angola, Chicanos, Blacks, Indians, or Eskimos, for the first time, huge numbers of young Jews were beginning to look at themselves not with self-hate or disinterest but with pride and self-respect. From a period of time when young Jews looked at themselves and asked, 'Who am I?' and answered either: 'I don't know,' or, worse, 'I don't care,' we had moved to thousands of young Jews marching off to jail after looking at themselves in the mirror and saying 'I am a Jew and I am beautiful. I am a Jew and Jewish is beautiful. I am a Jew and I give a Jewish damn.'"

If Kahane had stuck with nonviolent civil disobedience, he might have continued for a long time as the de facto leader of Soviet Jewry in America. Certainly no one else was providing Jews with their own brand of identity politics or matching his flair for publicity. But he truly believed that violence had its place as well.

On April 22, a group of tough Jewish teenagers from Queens placed

bombs on the nineteenth and twentieth floors of the building containing Amtorg, the corporation dealing with Soviet-American trade. The
first blast, which came a little after five thirty in the evening, was so
powerful it collapsed the ceiling, blew out doors and windows, ripped
through part of the concrete stairwell, destroyed some office chairs,
and lit the carpet on fire. Miraculously, no one was injured. Kahane sat
calmly in his office at JDL headquarters. After news of the first explosion was announced, he raised two fingers in a V-for-victory sign. He
knew there was another bomb.

The police were able to take apart the second device in time. It
was the largest JDL bomb yet (packed dynamite as opposed to a pipe
bomb), and the government was not willing to wait and see what
would happen next. On May 12, ten NYPD officers and agents of the
Alcohol, Tobacco, and Firearms Division of the Treasury Department
raided the two Midtown JDL offices. After arresting twelve JDL members, they tracked Kahane down and took him into custody. He was
charged with violating the Federal Gun Control Act of 1968 by illegally
purchasing firearms and setting off explosives without obtaining a federal permit or paying the necessary taxes.

Kahane insisted that whatever remained in the JDL coffers be used
to bail out the young JDL members first. Sitting in the federal house
of detention that night, he was truly worried for the first time. Kahane
had been arrested before, but only for small infractions. This was bigger. He needed a good lawyer, and he made a call that evening to Barry
Slotnick, a defense attorney famous for taking on high-profile criminal
cases. That night, Slotnick happened to be having dinner with one of
his most infamous clients: Joe Colombo. The boss of the notorious
Colombo crime family, this barrel-chested, greasy-haired gangster had
spent his early years as a hit man. In 1970, beset by legal problems, he
had come up with an ingenious cover, consistent with the spirit of the
times. He started the Italian-American Civil Liberties League, a group
whose purpose was to defend the reputation of Italian Americans
against a legal system that was allegedly biased. The league picketed the
FBI, claiming that it unfairly targeted Italian Americans. Colombo had
even held a recent league fundraiser at Madison Square Garden featuring Frank Sinatra and Sammy Davis Jr. Over dinner, Barry Slotnick
told Colombo about his new client Kahane. The mob boss, impressed

with the rabbi's willingness to stay in jail and aware that a radical rabbi might make for a good ally, decided to put up the twenty-five-thousand-dollar bail himself.

The next day, on the courthouse steps, Kahane proclaimed his allegiance to Colombo. Standing next to him in a brown trench coat, Colombo told the press that Kahane was "a man of God and his cause is just." The rabbi, he said, was "fighting for his people in Russia and we're fighting for our people here." Asked how he could justify the coalition, Kahane replied, "It's a human brotherhood. People of other faiths and backgrounds have come to help. It's the kind of thing which, had it been blacks helping Jews, it would have drawn raves. The Italians are no worse than the blacks."

It was a bizarre partnership and one that alienated many of Kahane's followers. It was hard to understand why he would taint the purity of his mission. For the next two months, Kahane could be seen eating with Colombo at his favorite deli on the Lower East Side, and JDL members joined the Italian pride pickets in front of the FBI. Kahane and Colombo even participated in a golf tournament together on Long Island. Kahane's reasons for embracing the Mafia seemed weak. He never denied that it was a marriage of convenience, but he mistakenly thought there was no need for further justification. Yossi Klein was disappointed. A few months earlier, Kahane's former double life as Michael King had been exposed on the front page of the *New York Times*, including information about his affair with Estelle Donna Evans and his role in her suicide. This had bothered Yossi, but he had accepted the JDL line that the article was just a smear, proof that those respectable Jewish Irvings were simply threatened by Kahane's growing power. Now he began to wonder whether Kahane was nothing more than a talented self-promoter.

At the end of June, two months after the joining of the Jewish and Italian leagues, Colombo was shot in the head at an Italian-American Unity Day rally in Columbus Circle; it left him brain-dead and paralyzed. Kahane was soon back in court facing federal indictments. But the case that might have put him away for a few years—as Nixon and Mayor Lindsay had both hoped—ended up giving him his final triumph. After a few weeks in court, the government was forced to settle. Part of the evidence against Kahane was based on illegal wiretaps, and therefore—like the rest of the material collected on radical left-ist groups through the bureau's infamous COINTELPRO program—it was inadmissible in court. Ten of the thirteen defendants would get off free. Kahane and two others pleaded guilty, but their firearms charges were dropped once they revealed the location of the stockpile.

All that remained was the matter of the pipe bombs set off at the Catskills camp. Kahane commanded the courtroom on the day of his sentencing. He defended his tactics, claiming that everything he had done was for the good of the Jewish people. The judge, though, wanted him and his two teenage codefendants to know that their ends did not justify their means: "While these three defendants may believe them-selves to be in a superior moral position, so far as the law is concerned, when they use guns and bombs illegally they are not readily distin-guishable from the Weathermen or Black Panthers on the left or the Ku Klux Klan on the right. Those groups too use terror to encourage a way of life that their members, in good faith no doubt, think needs to be encouraged and protected." The judge—Jack Weinstein—went further, lecturing Kahane on his own turf. "In this country, at this time, it is not permissible to substitute the bomb for the book as the sym-bol of Jewish manhood." The sentence, however, was surprisingly light. Kahane had to pay a five-thousand-dollar fine. There was also a five-year jail term, but it would be suspended as long as Kahane abided by the judge's specific conditions: he could have nothing to do with guns, bombs, dynamite, gunpowder, fuses, Molotov cocktails, clubs, or other weapons.

Kahane emerged from the courthouse with a large smile on his face. His young JDL followers had already crowded the steps and were danc-ing the hora and singing. They lifted him onto their shoulders and bounced him around triumphantly. With a wide-collared white shirt open at the neck, and his supporters pumping their fists into the air around him, he looked carefree and energized. "I want you to know that I can't talk about guns. But I want you all to have this," Kahane said, making his hand into a pistol and shooting imaginary bullets into the air. He was defiant, already determined to violate the terms of his probation even as the judge sat in his chambers. "Our campaign motto will be 'Every Jew a .22,'" he shouted to the cheering crowd. "I didn't ask for mercy. I cannot compromise my principles with expediency. Some time or other, there is no other way than violence. I am not against the use of violence if necessary."

Kahane's days in America were numbered. A handful of other cases against him were still pending, and despite his loud rhetoric, he knew that if he wanted to stay out of jail and in the public eye, he'd have to leave the country. He had always planned on moving to Israel. The dream of his life, after all, was to one day become the prime minister of the Jewish State. He couldn't do that from a basement office in Brooklyn. With pressure mounting, now was as good a time as any. On a humid September morning, a caravan of cars accompanied Kahane to JFK Airport. He gave a brief press conference, announcing that he was moving his family to Jerusalem, where he would establish a world headquarters for the JDL, and that he would split his time between the United States and Israel. His plane taxied to the runway, and JDL boys ran with it along the airline terminal's balcony, which was festooned with the flags of the world; the boys cheered and sang and ripped off any flag that had a hammer and sickle or an Islamic crescent. Kahane's departure, however, did not guarantee his silence. Just a week later, when he received word that Sylva Zalmanson, still in a prison camp, was ill, suffering from tuberculosis and ulcers, he told a reporter in Israel, "If anything happens to Sylva Zalmanson or another Jew, Soviet diplomats throughout the world will be open targets for every Jewish militant. Two Soviets for every Jew!"

But without a full-time leader, the JDL in New York devolved into a gang of angry and undisciplined young men and their girlfriends, aimless and still primed for violence. At the same time, the administration was even more determined to put an end to their activities. An internal FBI review of Kahane's book *Never Again* called his ideas "un-American, nationalistic, and extremely dangerous." George Bush, the new U.S. ambassador to the United Nations, was particularly eager to subdue Kahane's followers. At the end of October, four shots were fired from the roof of nearby Hunter College into an eleventh-floor window of the Soviet mission. The room that was hit was in a diplomat's residence where four children were sleeping. Amazingly, the children weren't injured, but it raised the anger of the Soviets to an unprecedented level. An overweight, mustachioed eighteen-year-old JDL member, Isaac Jaroslawicz, was taken into custody. He seemed an unlikely assassin. On the weekends, he performed magic tricks at birthday parties in Borough Park under the name Izzini. A friend of Yossi Klein's told him that Jaroslawicz was not the gunman, just the fall guy for a new, more violent cell within the JDL. He was released within a few weeks.

The reaction at the United Nations was fierce. There were "chaotic floor debates of rare bitterness," according to one paper, at one point leading to a "virtual breakdown in the [General] Assembly's proceedings." The Soviet ambassador even engaged the Israeli ambassador Yosef Tekoah in a yelling match about the superiority of Communism to Zionism. "It was the Soviet Union, not Zionism or the Jewish people, who had concluded a treaty with Hitler and von Ribbentrop!" Tekoah screamed back, his voice shaking with emotion. Eventually the Arab ambassadors got involved also, with the representative of Saudi Arabia blaming Mayor Lindsay for the attack because he'd failed to provide enough security for delegates in the city. "Who is responsible?" he asked and then responded to his own question: "The politicians—the mayor, who goes to synagogues and acts like a rabbi to obtain Jewish votes."

George Bush was tired of constantly apologizing to the Soviets. Kahane was back in New York protesting outside the United Nations when Bush spotted him one day. He called Kahane a "madman," and told him, "You have damaged your country's cause, the cause of Soviet Jews and the name of American Jewry." Kahane moved closer and tried to strike a conciliatory pose. "Well, I came here for a dialogue," he told Bush. "I don't want to see you," the ambassador shot back. There was real pressure from the government to stop the JDL from undermining détente. A confidential memo from the State Department to the FBI around this time warned "that further incidents of [JDL] violence would have a damaging impact on our overall relations with the USSR." A month after the shooting, in late November, Bush convened a high-level meeting in his apartment at the Waldorf Astoria with officials from the Justice Department, the Secret Service, and the FBI to try to figure out how to deal with the problem of the JDL. But the JDL would soon implode without any outside help.

Sol Hurok, the last of the New York impresarios, stepped out of his car and into his Midtown office at nine thirty on the morning of Janu-

ary 26, 1972. Practically a New York institution, Hurok had been putting up money for European artists to tour America ever since World
War I, when his concerts had filled the New York Hippodrome on
Sundays. He'd discovered Marian Anderson in 1935 and represented
Arthur Rubinstein throughout most of his career. With his gold- or
silver-headed cane (depending on the occasion), horn-rimmed glasses,
and black slouch hat, Hurok could be seen and heard at the back of
concert halls most nights. Over the years his Sol Hurok Presents had
become particularly well known for its Soviet acts. Even during chilly
periods in the Cold War, Hurok, born Solomon Isaievich in a town
not far from Kharkov, found a way to get Soviet performers into the
United States. From the Kirov to the Igor Moiseyev Ballet Company,
Hurok knew them all and took delight in the company of testy ballerinas and musicians. The pinnacle of his career came in 1959 when he
finally brought over the Bolshoi Ballet (something he would do three
more times over the next decade) and rented a three-room suite for
the prima ballerina Galina Ulanova, filling its refrigerator with caviar
and champagne.

For Kahane, there was no greater domestic enemy than Hurok.
Speaking at a press conference at the Overseas Press Club in February
of 1970, just as he was gaining attention, Kahane described Hurok as
a modern-day Shylock, a man "whose appetite for profits leads him
to abandon his obligations as a human and his loyalties as a Jew." In
the past year, hardly a single Soviet performer had mounted a stage
without some JDL-organized incident. That winter, to Hurok's great
disappointment, the Kremlin canceled a planned tour by the Bolshoi.

But Hurok was in a good mood that January morning, swathed in
a large brown fur coat with a Russian fur hat on his head, his cane
tapping the ground in front of him. The night before, Vladimir Ashkenazy, the famous young pianist, had performed at Carnegie Hall. The
son of a Jewish father who had defected to England in the early 1960s,
Ashkenazy had protested on behalf of Soviet Jews and had elicited a
JDL promise not to disrupt the evening with bottles of ammonia or
scurrying mice.

A few minutes after Hurok arrived at his office on the twentieth
floor, two young men walked into the office's reception area, one of
them carrying a suitcase. They asked about tickets to a performance

by a dance group from Kiev, sat down, placed the suitcase on the floor, got up, and left. A few seconds later, a small incendiary bomb in the suitcase went off, igniting a purplish flare and setting a nearby couch on fire. The heat of the blast was so strong that all the typewriters in the reception area melted, and the nails holding up framed photos of Russian performers bent in two. The area quickly filled with thick black smoke. The fourteen people in the office, including Hurok, a few secretaries, and some maintenance workers, began running in a panic toward the back rooms, but this only trapped them. Soon black plumes engulfed the entire floor. One of the men ran to Hurok's office, grabbed a chair, and smashed the window that looked out on the Avenue of the Americas. He started screaming for help into the cold morning air. Hurok lay on the floor, still in his furs. In the next room, three secretaries huddled together on the ground trying to escape the smoke. They too tried to break a window but weren't strong enough to shatter it. Crying and frightened, they all passed out within minutes. Afterward, lying in a bed in Roosevelt Hospital, one of the secretaries, Myra Armstrong, described the panic: "We were scared stiff. Smoke was coming in the ventilators. Virginia said, 'It's all right; somebody will come for us.' Iris was real frightened. I can't remember what she said, but she was absolutely still after a while."

Iris was Iris Kones, a twenty-seven-year-old Jewish secretary from Long Island. After the firefighters arrived and put out the flames with water cannons, she was discovered lying dead on the office floor. Thirteen people required hospitalization, including Hurok. He was carried out on a chair with his fur hat still on his head, his brown coat spread across him and pulled up over his nose, only his horn-rimmed glasses showing.

The attack on Hurok's office was one of two that took place simultaneously that morning (the other, at Columbia Artists Management, injured no one). In phone calls an hour later to a few news services the words *Never again!* were yelled. Kahane, in Jerusalem, claimed he had nothing to do with the attack. And maybe he didn't. But he had inveighed against Hurok for years, painting him as an enemy of the Jewish people. And it was Kahane who promoted a culture of violence in the JDL. It had only been a matter of time before something like this happened. Reached by phone in Israel, he sounded sincerely shocked that a Jewish woman had died. "I think the people who did this are insane," he said. "What else can I say?"

The news that an innocent woman had been killed and that Kahane was responsible—however indirectly—shook many people in the Jewish community, some of whom had looked at JDL members as mischief-makers but not murderers. A *New York Times* editorial grouped the Hurok bombing with other recent JDL actions and wrote that "these firebombings fit a terrible pattern of mad violence that has shown no regard for innocent life, a violence wholly alien to every decent impulse." The FBI and the city's police began a massive operation to find the bombers. Even Yossi Klein, at home in Borough Park and only peripherally connected to the more violent elements in the group, received a visit from two FBI agents.

For days after the bombing, the papers were full of stories that painted the JDL and Kahane as responsible for the death of Iris Kones. As if this publicity weren't bad enough, Yevgeny Yevtushenko happened to be in New York during the bombing and announced that he was going to write a poem about it. The Russian poet, whose "Babi Yar" had brought international attention to the issue of Soviet anti-Semitism, was about to depart on a cross-country tour. The Soviet leadership had continued to indulge his occasional dissent because he generally toed the line. When he'd heard about the explosion, Yevtushenko saw an opportunity to please the KGB minders who were accompanying him on his trip. He asked to see Hurok's office so he could observe the damage firsthand. That afternoon, the blond-haired, high-cheekboned Yevtushenko walked solemnly through the soot-covered rooms. At one point he stopped to clear the ash off a black-and-white photo of Feodor Chaliapin, a Russian singer and the first performer Hurok had brought to America, nearly fifty years before. It was after this twenty-minute visit that Yevtushenko told the press, through his translator, that a poem about the incident was slowly writing itself in his mind.

The following night, Yevtushenko was slated to give a reading at Felt Forum in Madison Square Garden. It was sold out, with five thousand people in attendance. Eugene McCarthy, once again a candidate for the Democratic presidential nomination, was present to read his own poetry; Allen Ginsberg and James Dickey were there, and both read translations of Yevtushenko's work. The Russian himself appeared on the stage in blue jeans and a turtleneck and stood framed by a white spotlight. He told the audience that before he read from his published work, he wanted to recite a poem he had written the night before, dedicated to Iris Kones. He said it was a poem protesting those who were trying to prevent cultural exchange. He unfolded a page that had been stuffed into his pocket and read the title, "Bombs for Balalaikas":

> Poor Iris,
>> victim of the age,
> you've fallen,
>> fragile,
>> dark-eyed
> Jewish girl suffocated by smoke,
> as though in a Nazi gas chamber.
> It's hard to vent out poisoned air.
> …
> Damn you, servants of hell
> who seek coexistence between peoples
> by building bridges of cadavers.

The poem, which was published in *Izvestia* days later, went on to describe the Hurok offices as having the "stench of Auschwitz." It was at this moment, when a Soviet poet effectively used Kahane's own Holocaust rhetoric against him, that the rabbi lost all credibility—and along with it, the power to dictate the direction of the Soviet Jewry movement in America.

The JDL became increasingly irrelevant and dysfunctional. Kahane took fewer trips to the United States, choosing to focus instead on his other obsession: ejecting the Palestinian Arab population from greater Israel. Within a year of the bombing, he had resigned his position as head of the American branch of the Jewish Defense League. The young people he had left behind still managed to make news occasionally with their exploits. Before dropping out of the JDL altogether, Yossi Klein took part in an especially elaborate protest: in April of 1973 he flew to Moscow with seven other young militants and tried to chain himself to an OVIR office. The protest ended uneventfully when, after briefly arresting them, the KGB simply encouraged Yossi and his friends to rejoin their tour group.

Violence eventually undermined the JDL's mission, but the attention Soviet Jewry received in 1971 undeniably made a difference. The Soviets began to approve exit visas at a faster pace. Whereas a little over a thousand Jews had gotten out in 1970, new records were now being broken every month. Fifty left in January 1971, 130 in February, 1,000 in March, 1,300 in April. And the numbers continued to climb so that by the end of the year, an unprecedented 13,000 Jews had emigrated—more than in the previous ten years combined.

On the first working day of 1972, an Aeroflot cargo plane left the Soviet Union heading for Israel; it carried eight tons of luggage and personal effects, as well as a coffin with a Jewish body bound for Israeli soil. Two hundred and ten exit visas were granted that day, breaking a record. That month, January 1972, also saw the biggest single group of Jews, three hundred and fifty, that had ever arrived in Israel on one plane. Most of them were from Georgia—poor, rural Jews who arrived in the Mediterranean nation wrapped in heavy coats and fur hats. And the West began to take notice. "Russ Let 25 Jews a Day Go to Israel" read a March 1971 headline in the *Los Angeles Times,* a wave of emigration "unprecedented in the 53-year history of the Soviet Union." The paper reported that its sources "could recall no instance since the Bolshevik Revolution of 1917 when the government permitted such a sizeable number of Russian citizens to leave the country through normal emigration channels." Something remarkable was taking place. The Soviet government seemed to be bending to the pressure and doing the unthinkable.

7

Birth of the Refusenik
1970–1972

A FEW HOURS after Eduard Kuznetsov and Yosef Mendelevich were wrestled to the ground on the Smolny tarmac, the KGB carried out searches four hundred miles away in three Moscow apartments. Vladimir Slepak was home with his wife, Masha, and two sons when the doorbell rang. His bushy beard, streaked with gray and parted at his chin, kinky hair, and thick body, usually encased in a wool sweater, gave Slepak the appearance of a fairy-tale wolf. Six agents—one in military uniform and five in gray suits—announced that they would be conducting a search in connection with the arrests made that morning. Slepak stepped aside as the men entered and began rifling through drawers, throwing books off shelves, and piling in one corner all journals and scraps of paper.

The invasion of the small apartment lasted eighteen hours. Eighteen-year-old Sanya, the elder of the Slepak sons, watched with fascination and fear as these men—who insisted on accompanying him everywhere, even to the bathroom—ransacked his father's library. In the evening, two friends stopped by unannounced, a frequent occurrence at the Slepaks', and the agents detained them as well, fearing they might alert Western journalists. At two in the morning, the apartment now littered with paper and crowded with people, the unexpected sound of heavy snoring was heard from the living room. Volodya, as everyone called Vladimir, had fallen asleep in an armchair. In the early-morning hours, the agents woke him and asked him to sign a detailed inventory. They were confiscating four bags of material—tape recorders and cassettes, letters, and a typewriter. Slepak refused to sign. There was nothing anti-Soviet here, he told them. The agents made off with their booty anyway.

As the KGB men left, one of them was overheard saying that "sometimes they jump out the window or hang themselves in the toilet by their tie" but he'd never seen someone fall asleep during a search. But this was how Slepak greeted most things, with geniality, a sense of humor, and ease. His life as a dissident had, in fact, only just begun. A few days earlier, a bureaucratic voice had informed him over the phone that his application for an exit visa to Israel had been denied. The reason: "Secrecy."

It was a word uttered by OVIR officials hundreds of times a week in 1970 and 1971 to men and woman like Slepak—educated engineers who had worked most of their lives in research institutes and factories. Their supposed past access to state secrets, often insignificant or nonexistent, rendered them ineligible for emigration. After people had finally completed the arduous application process, these refusals were cruelly arbitrary. Secrecy was just one of a dozen excuses—they ranged from the bluntly evasive "departure inexpedient" to the maddeningly nonsensical "the reason itself is a state secret." Memos penned by Yuri Andropov, the head of the KGB, confirm that the decision to refuse or allow an exit visa was based on little more than whim or political vendetta. In one note, Andropov described the case of a translator identified as A. M. Smelianskaia who, he wrote, "sent a letter to the address of her relative in Israel in which she transcribed the song 'Erets-Israel.'" Because the song "glorifies Israel and contains appeals to Jews to unite and struggle against 'their enemies,'" Andropov wrote, the KGB "has decided to carry out preventive measures, calling them to account for their actions, and afterwards refusing them permission to leave the Soviet Union." In another memo, a screenwriter, Efim Sevela, was deemed suspicious because of his "nationalist convictions and his low moral and professional qualities" but was given permission anyway in order to get him out of the country.

By allowing a handful of isolated, bothersome activists to leave in 1969, the Soviets had hoped to decapitate the growing Zionist movement. But they succeeded only in convincing others to apply—and to make noise when they were refused. A deluge of requests followed the first departures. In the wake of the Leningrad trial, an unprecedented number were allowed to leave—thirty-two thousand in 1972 alone. But a pattern was emerging. The Jews who were being granted exit visas were overwhelmingly from the periphery—either geographically, from the ancient communities of the Caucasus, or in terms of age or health. They were Jews the Soviet Union was happy to do without.

Those who were refused en masse were the cosmopolitan Jews of Moscow and other large urban centers—a highly skilled, highly educated, highly assimilated cohort. Over half a million Jews lived in Moscow alone (this was the population, coincidentally, of the entire state of Israel when it gained independence). For them, this new wave of emigration meant frustration. These doctors and scientists and engineers were not only being refused, they were suddenly thrust into a life of interminable waiting. As the refusals multiplied and the refused discovered one another, a new underclass was born, a community of people now living outside the norms of Soviet society: they were the *otkazniki* or, as it was translated into English, refuseniks.

The frontlines of the battle quickly shifted to the massive gray landscape of the Soviet capital, covered in communal apartment complexes and concrete public squares. The fighters were no longer the young, combative Jews of Riga with Yiddish-speaking parents. They were the grandchildren of Jews who had abandoned the tiny shtetls in the Pale of Settlement and sought opportunity in the city following the Bolshevik Revolution. And like the children of Jewish factory workers in New York, the descendants of the shtetl families were now professionals and academics. Soviet anti-Semitism, official and unofficial, had bred in them an intense work ethic, a realization that to succeed they would have to excel, they would have to make themselves indispensable.

Moscow's Jews had learned to live with unofficial quotas and daily slights. They knew which professions were prohibited, which universities would not take them, what kinds of conversations to avoid, and how to cover their ears when someone on the subway began preaching about the innate greediness of the *zhid*. These were survival tactics, and they worked. So well, in fact, that in this city of hundreds of thousands of Jews, it took time for a Zionist or Jewish emigration movement to emerge as it had in other parts of the empire. In the Baltics, the memory of Jewish life had never been erased, and in the Caucasus, Jews had been allowed to live a traditional existence for hundreds of years. But in Moscow and Leningrad, decades had passed without any sense of Jewish identity, and nothing but one crumbling synagogue on Arkhipova Street full of old people was left as a reminder of what once was.

For these Jews, becoming a refusenik—a de facto dissident—meant more than just opposing the regime. It was a personal transformation, an awakening. It required taking a hammer to the solid status quo of family and society in order to forge a whole new persona, and this always involved a private drama.

Solomon Slepak, Volodya's father, was a gruff, die-hard Bolshevik who'd named his only son after Lenin. He had made his way up the Party hierarchy early in his adventure-filled life. After leaving the small Belorussian town of his birth, Dubrovno, when he was only thirteen, Solomon Slepak joined the throngs headed for America. It was there that he first became radicalized, a true believer in Communism. When he had had enough of his life as a window washer in the squalid Lower East Side, he decided to answer the call of the revolution that was then taking place at home. He made his way back to the Russian mainland via the far eastern city of Vladivostok, where he fought off the White counterrevolutionaries occupying the city and amassed a ten-thousand-man partisan army. His return to the new Soviet Union was triumphant, earning him a respected place in the Party and plum jobs as a propagandist and an agent-ambassador for the Comintern, the body charged with fomenting Communist revolution all over the world. Solomon and his wife were on one of his missions, this one to China, when Volodya was born, in 1927.

To come of age in Moscow in the late thirties as a child of the Bolshevik aristocracy was to experience a disorienting combination of privilege and unrelenting terror. Volodya witnessed tearful children in his class whose fathers had disappeared the night before; he saw his own father frantically ink out the face of Trotsky in history books on the Russian civil war; and one day he was told to never again utter the name of his favorite uncle, his mother's brother, who had been swept up in a purge and then lost to the Gulag. Volodya even woke up one night to find his father frozen with fear in the living room; he'd thought he'd heard someone pounding on the door, coming to take him away. Somehow, that knock on the door never came for Solomon Slepak. He managed to escape the extreme bloodletting of 1937 and 1938 that Stalin inflicted on almost all the Bolshevik leaders of his generation. Through it all, Solomon dutifully carried out his job, delivering a daily digest of the foreign press for Stalin and the Politburo. It took the Nazi invasion of Russia to break this rhythm. The family was forced to separate, with the children fleeing Moscow on their own, traveling until Volodya and his older sister, Rosa, reached a town in the Urals where they waited out the war.

Once life returned to normal and the family settled together in the capital again, Volodya began to focus on his career. He decided to study radio electronics at the Aviation Institute. With a father as well known as Solomon Slepak, Volodya felt his path was clear. If anyone had a question about the impeccable Communist bona fides of the Slepak family, that person had only to see where they lived. Their apartment, first granted to them in 1940, was on the eighth floor of a stately slate gray building on Gorky Street, the wide boulevard that radiated out from Red Square and was home to the Soviet Union's most extravagant hotels and shops, a street memorialized by Pushkin. Every year, a military parade rolled beneath the Slepaks' balcony displaying the empire's tanks and rocket launchers. After the war, the city installed an equestrian statue of Prince Yury Dolgoruky, the founder of Moscow, in Sovetskaya Square across the boulevard. The extended arm of the Middle Ages warrior seemed to point directly at the entrance to Volodya's building.

Volodya graduated with a master's degree in 1950, an unfortunate time for a Jew born in China to be looking for work. Stalin was railing against "cosmopolitanism." If there was any check on his boundless possibility, it was from this, the dictator's whim. Every potential employer looked at him suspiciously and he was finally forced to take a job as a television repairman in a small shop. Very little came out of this work besides a chance meeting with the woman who later became his wife. Maria Rashkovsky, or Masha, as she was known, walked into the shop one day wearing glasses and a knitted sweater. She had grown up in Moscow but, unlike Volodya, had some awareness of her Jewish roots. As a girl, she would watch her grandmother light Sabbath candles and cook food for the Jewish holidays. When she met Volodya, she was studying to become a doctor at a medical school in Ryazan, on the outskirts of the capital. After less then a dozen dates, he proposed to her. A day after their wedding, she left to do a summer internship two hundred miles away. When it was over, she transferred to a Moscow medical school and moved into the family apartment on Gorky Street.

It was Stalin's last act of paranoid anti-Semitism that prompted the initial rift between Volodya and his father. In the fall of 1952, the aging leader had arrested a number of Jewish doctors for allegedly plotting to poison the Kremlin leadership. Masha was in her last year of medical school, and she knew a few of the accused personally. The charges, she told Volodya, had to be false. She told Solomon about this and he responded with an old Russian proverb: "Whenever you cut down trees, chips will fly in all directions." The authorities were engaged in a class struggle, rooting out capitalist enemies. "Isn't it better to arrest and prosecute a hundred innocent people and catch one spy than to let the spy go free?" the old Bolshevik asked.

Volodya found this logic revolting, the twisted reasoning of a man who needed to justify the cause he had devoted his life to. And there, in the small living room of their Gorky Street apartment—the same one that would be searched eighteen years later—Volodya Slepak replied that he could "never accept such a philosophy." The more they talked, the angrier his father's defense of Stalin made him. Volodya accused Solomon of having blood on his hands, of supporting a corrupt system, of joining a political party that demanded total faith but gave nothing in return.

He was shocked by his own vehemence and the sudden realization that the world he had inherited from his father was not one that he could ever embrace. The crisis of the Doctors' Plot passed when, in March of 1953, Stalin died. Volodya saw his father cry for the first time. A new period in Soviet history was beginning.

Throughout the 1950s and early 1960s, life became more comfortable for Volodya and Masha Slepak. They advanced in their careers and raised a family. Masha decided to give up her dream of becoming a surgeon and settled for radiology, which allowed more flexible hours. Their first son, Alexander, was born in 1952, and their second son, Leonid, in 1959. Solomon Slepak moved out of the Gorky Street apartment in 1960 after his wife died, and he married a Russian woman. Volodya's career was solidifying. He started working as a senior radio engineer at the Scientific Institute for TV Research, and then in 1962 he was asked to lead his own laboratory, one that would work exclusively on a project to design better display screens for the Soviet air defense system. Even though the job would not give him access to any highly sensitive secrets—the technology he was working on was well known in the West—the project fell under Ministry of Defense supervision, and Slepak was vetted by the government. He received first-form security clearance, the second-highest level possible—a classification that would ensure his exit-visa refusal many years later. The thaw touched the Slepaks, as it did all Soviet citizens, and they felt the slackening of fear and government control. They read, with special interest, a copy of Khrushchev's 1956 speech repudiating Stalin. Even Solomon Slepak was pleased that the cult of the Party was finally winning out over the cult of Stalin's personality.

During the sixties, Volodya and Masha Slepak's social circle widened to include a number of other Jewish families, all professionals like themselves, engineers and doctors. Many of these new friends Slepak met at his institute, a place that would eventually serve as a kind of petri dish of Jewish nationalist feeling because of its unusually high percentage of Jewish scientists. The friends raised their children together and on weekends would leave the city center for the forested outskirts of Moscow. There they camped, cooked, went fishing, and enjoyed being in nature, free from the stifling grayness of the city. They were able to talk more openly, discuss politics and the ways Soviet society was changing or not changing. Raised by their parents to fear that "walls have ears," they felt the forest was their freedom. The radio was a key piece of this. Outside the city, it was easier to bypass the jamming technology that kept out foreign stations. The friends would sit around a campfire listening to the shortwave broadcasts from the Voice of America, European stations in Germany, and Kol Israel, the Voice of Israel. Hearing news from the outside made the Slepaks wonder what it was like to be a Jew in America or Israel, if all that they had become accustomed to—the subtle anti-Semitism, the quotas, the pervasive undercurrent of aggression—was normal. So addictive were these broadcasts that in 1963 Slepak started listening to his shortwave inside their apartment, using a metal beam in the wall to block the jamming. Late at night when Sanya and Leonid were asleep, Volodya and his wife would huddle around the radio, the volume turned down low.

Among their friends were David Drabkin and his wife, Naomi. Drabkin was a stubborn man who had become a fierce Zionist, one of the few who was trying to organize the Moscow Jews. His wife was from Riga and through her he became acquainted with the Latvian Zionists. In the forest around the fire, he argued with his friends, trying to persuade them to take a more aggressive stance. The Slepaks often listened just out of curiosity. But Drabkin's talk was attractive. His reasoning had an elegant simplicity. What was Russia to them anyway? How had it treated its Jews? What belonged to them here? For Drabkin, Israel was the obvious answer. Only Israel was theirs. Volodya and Masha listened, took it all in, and slowly—without being fully aware of the transformation at first—the frustration that had caused Slepak to lash out at his father turned into a positive desire, an objective. One day Masha even said impulsively that she could imagine them living in Israel. But these still seemed just escape fantasies, words that made them laugh seconds after they were uttered. When Simchat Torah arrived each year and it was time for the annual celebration in front of the Moscow synagogue, Volodya Slepak decided it was too dangerous to join.

The Six-Day War had an energizing effect on this small group of friends. That summer they were vacationing at Lake Tzesarka, near Vilnius, the capital of Lithuania. The war was over but they stayed glued to broadcasts from Kol Israel, curious to pick up any information about the victory. This was the summer that Drabkin finally decided he was going to find a way out. Slepak was still not convinced. After the vacation, which took them all through Latvia and Estonia, he returned to his life in Moscow, the work in the institute, the apartment on Gorky. The next summer, 1968, vacationing this time along the Dnieper River, south of Kiev, they followed news of the demise of the Soviet invasion of Czechoslovakia and the brief, seemingly crazy protest by eight people in Red Square. But still, that Simchat Torah, Slepak wouldn't go to the synagogue.

That fall, David Drabkin told his friends that he had requested an invitation from Israel, the first step to obtaining an exit visa. The small group of Riga activists had just gotten permission, among them Mark Blum, who had organized the cleanup of Rumbuli. When Blum came to Moscow to collect his exit visa, he met with Drabkin and his friends and asked if anyone else wanted an invitation sent. The meeting took place in Drabkin's dark apartment on a winter evening at the end of December. Volodya and Masha had to make a quick decision. They went off to confer. They knew that their comfortable life was at stake. They might lose everything. But Masha said it was an opportunity they simply could not pass up. Volodya reluctantly agreed.

The invitation finally arrived in March of 1969, two sheets of paper fastened together. It referred to a "relative" of the Slepaks who requested that the family be reunited. Volodya and Masha didn't know quite how to feel about those flimsy pages. They held them between their fingers with both dread and exhilaration. They would now begin the process, one that was familiar to all applicants. But first, Slepak realized, they would need another invitation—their names had been misspelled and all their details confused. He looked for someone else to take his information to Israel. The KGB, however, now aware of his intentions, wasted no time. Before Slepak had a chance to tell his bosses about his decision to emigrate, the KGB informed them. He was fired on the spot. This was a shock. Even though he knew the consequences of applying, he was unprepared for how swiftly it would all happen, how suddenly he would be spit out by a society that had once made him feel so comfortable. Losing his job placed him in an impossible situation with regard to his application. He needed to include a character reference, a *kharikteristika,* from a workplace. No job, no *kharikteristika.* On top of that, it could take months to find someone to bring his request for a new invitation to Israel. Volodya and Masha both tried to be strong for the other, to maintain a pose of confidence, but inside there were moments when they both felt like they were in free fall, as if the ground had opened up beneath them and they were not sure how long it would take before they landed somewhere solid again.

Around this time, Volodya decided to tell his father about his plans. Solomon Slepak was not pleased to hear that his son was leaving the paradise he himself had fought to build. He felt betrayed by his son, by his whole weak and undisciplined generation. Before slamming the door on his way out of the Gorky Street apartment, Solomon yelled that he would do whatever he could, work every connection he still had, to prevent his son from gaining an exit visa.

Volodya and Masha Slepak were quickly pushed to the margins. It was becoming difficult to obtain even the basic necessities—and they hadn't even formally applied to leave. In August, they finally sent another request for an invitation. While they waited, now with much less to lose, they decided to participate in the Simchat Torah festivities. If the world they knew was going to turn its back—all those former friends and coworkers who now refused to speak to them—then they would retreat deeper into this second society of Jews. Soon they were dancing to the unusual sound of Hebrew music blaring out of two speakers set up in front of the synagogue. They found themselves twirling for hours, becoming drunk on the idea that this might all end well.

They received the second invitation in January 1970, this one with their names spelled correctly. Slepak began the long application process that, as one of the refused wrote at the time, served "to isolate the applicant, put stumbling blocks in his way, and train a spotlight on him." First, they had to submit *kharikteristikas* signed by their supervisors—luckily Slepak had managed to find part-time work—and then by various members of the Party apparatus, such as the local secretary and the head of the trade union committee. Then an additional certificate was needed from the office in charge of their specific housing complex, attesting to their legal status as residents of Moscow. Finally, and hardest for the Slepaks, they needed to obtain letters from any former spouses or living parents stating whether they approved of the departure and whether there were any outstanding financial obligations.

By the end of this process, dozens, if not hundreds, of friends, coworkers, neighbors, and acquaintances had been made aware that the good citizen they thought they knew was challenging their way of life. Often the required documents were simply impossible to obtain. A signature could be withheld out of fear or malice. All it took was one disgruntled ex-wife or terrified boss or, in Slepak's case, resentful father. Solomon told his son he considered him an "enemy of the people" and he would never grant permission. Volodya had to include a notarized affidavit attesting that his father refused to participate in the process. His employer agreed to sign his *kharikteristika* on the condition that he then resign from his job. Everyone, from the Slepaks' most peripheral friends to their neighbors to the local KGB office, knew they had applied for an exit visa. The family felt watched, scrutinized, in a way they had never been before. These consequences were enough to prevent thousands from applying. For those who did, the process transformed their relationship to society from one of complacency to one of hostility.

In April of 1970, four months after they received the second invitation, having gathered all the necessary documents, they visited OVIR and submitted their applications. It was a relief to think that the anxiety, the interminable limbo, that had suffused the past year might soon be over. But now a new wait began. Every time the phone rang, they rushed to see if it was OVIR. One month, and then two. Finally, in early June, Volodya called OVIR, and the impersonal voice on the other end of the line read the decision. Application denied. The Slepaks could try again in five years.

A community of the refused began to coalesce. But unlike the Leningrad Zionists, the Moscow activists never created a formal organization with membership fees and a hierarchical structure—they knew that would be a death wish. Natural leaders such as Volodya Slepak did, of course, emerge, but there was no detectable structure.

Moscow itself provided a good setting for the movement, if only because it was saturated with foreign journalists. Most major Western news outlets, including the big American and European papers and wire services, had bureaus in the city. Reporters such as Hedrick Smith from the *New York Times* and Robert Toth from the *Los Angeles Times* were usually walled off from the reality in the Soviet Union, watched over by minders and forced to work with little more than Kremlin press releases. The story of Soviet Jewry was a huge opportunity for them, combining great human drama with accessible characters. Some saw their coverage as a moral imperative—Christopher Wren, a *New*

York Times reporter, told colleagues they should treat the refuseniks' struggle like the civil rights movement. Many of these journalists became openly friendly and sympathetic, inviting Jewish activists to their homes for meals and introducing them to their families. These associations did not go unnoticed: in 1970 alone, three American correspondents in Moscow had their visas revoked, and in early 1971, Anthony Astrachan, the *Washington Post* correspondent in Moscow, was ordered to leave. But for the refuseniks, such contact was critical. It saved them from the more severe retribution they would have otherwise suffered at the hands of the KGB.

Also unique to Moscow, and beneficial to the refuseniks in many ways, was the presence of the members of the dissident movement (the democrats, as they were sometimes known). The Moscow Jewish activists were for the most part secular humanists who sympathized with opponents of the regime. Many of them came from the democratic movement and saw their struggle for freedom as part of a wider push to liberalize the Soviet Union. On the other side, some of the most important democracy activists had Jewish parents. The emergence of a robust Zionist movement was a kind of challenge to them, forcing many to confront issues of identity. Were they Russians first, or Jews? Anti-Semitism was just as present in their lives. But for most of them, Israel was not the solution. They wanted to try to create a more tolerant society at home.

Larisa Bogoraz embodied this tension. She was at the nexus of much dissident activity; she had been married to the poet Yuli Daniel and then to Anatoly Marchenko, the nearly illiterate former prisoner whose memoirs—a devastating account of the Gulag as it persisted after Stalin—she helped write. She was also a Jew and struggled with her conscious decision to distance herself from the Zionists. She explored the question in a samizdat essay: "Who am I now? Who do I feel myself to be? Unfortunately, I do not feel like a Jew. I understand that I have an unquestionable genetic tie with Jewry. I also assume that this is reflected in my mentality, in my mode of thinking, and in my behavior. But this common quality is little help to me in feeling my Jewish identity as a similarity of external features . . . such as community of language, culture, history, tradition; perhaps, even, of impressions, unconsciously absorbed by the senses: what the eye sees, the ear hears, the skin feels. By all these characteristics, I am Russian."

This deeply felt Russianness was a part of Volodya Slepak and most of the other refuseniks as well. And it created both tension and kinship. The dissident movement paid close attention to the persecution of Jewish activists. In 1969, the widely circulated dissident newsletter *Chronicle of Current Events,* or *Khronika,* described the arrest and trial of Boris Kochubievsky. From then on, at least one page was always reserved for news of the Jewish emigration movement.

A key link between the two movements was Andrei Sakharov and his Jewish wife and fellow activist, Elena Bonner. In the early 1970s, Sakharov was still considered untouchable. His criticism of the Soviet system was well known and his samizdat essays widely read, but his standing as an esteemed physicist made it hard for the regime to prosecute him openly. This special status turned him into an important anchor for the movement. His apartment was a gathering place for anyone who had problems with the authorities, including the growing community of Jewish activists. As the number of exit visa applications — and rejections — mounted in the early 1970s, Jews looked to Sakharov for help. The KGB noticed. In a memo from April 1971, KGB chief Yuri Andropov described the situation: "As a result of enemy propaganda, the name of Sakharov is gaining even greater popularity inside the country as an 'uncompromising fighter' against injustice. His apartment has become a place of pilgrimage for various kinds of 'victims' of 'arbitrary actions' by Soviet authorities. Some citizens come from remote regions of the country to Moscow specifically to meet with him." Referring to Jews, he added, "Many people who have been denied permission to leave the country ask Sakharov to help them obtain exit visas. . . . He advises people to make 'noise' each time an exit visa is denied, to publish relevant material in samizdat, and to resort to the services of the bourgeois press and Western radio stations."

In the fall of 1970, Sakharov joined with Valery Chalidze, a man with a sterling reputation in the dissident community, to form the Moscow Committee for Human Rights. Chalidze, who was married to the granddaughter of Maxim Litvinov, the prewar Jewish foreign minister of the Soviet Union, was a physicist turned legal expert. His ingenious strategy for challenging the regime was to remind it of its own laws. The way he saw it, the Soviet constitution granted all the rights the democrats were seeking. All the dissidents had to do was shame the state into abiding by its own governing document. The Committee for

Human Rights was a small group set up to investigate and expose human and civil rights violations. It survived its initial months by claiming it wasn't an organization but simply "a creative association acting in accordance with the laws of the land." The KGB nevertheless began watching it closely. And so did ordinary citizens, who turned to the group as they might a legal aid society. Among the issues Chalidze took up was emigration. For him, it was not a matter of allowing Jews to go to Israel but of the Soviet Union respecting the United Nations' Universal Declaration of Human Rights, which allowed for freedom of movement. Sakharov himself often said that he saw freedom of movement as the most fundamental human right—if a citizen could freely leave his country, he could never be a slave. And there were also tactical reasons to fight for this right, as Chalidze made clear in his book *To Defend These Rights:* "Any mass restrictions of rights affecting Jews attracts the attention of 'world public opinion' since historically any form of restriction on the rights of Jews is a critical question for our civilization."

In 1971, the year that the Committee for Human Rights did its most groundbreaking work, Chalidze took up the specific cases of a number of Jews. People like Jonah Kolchinsky, a nineteen-year-old from Kharkov who had been called up for military service after he announced his intention to emigrate to Israel. Chalidze went so far as to ask the minister of defense to have Kolchinsky demobilized. When it became known that Yosef Mendelevich, then in a prison camp in Mordvinia, was not being allowed to wear a yarmulke, Chalidze wrote to the minister of internal affairs asking that a prisoner's right of religion be respected in the camps.

The democrats had developed a good model. The idea of writing protest letters and petitions came directly from them. They were the first to realize that a letter passed to the West and read aloud over the BBC or the Voice of America was a sort of insurance policy. The Jewish activists took this method and expanded it, and in June of 1970, seventy-five refuseniks—including, for the first time, Vladimir and Masha Slepak—signed a letter addressed to U Thant. The message to the secretary-general was dramatic: "We sign this open appeal to you fully aware of the fact that if the Rights of Man are not implemented, humanity has no future." By February of 1971, there was a petition with two hundred names, and this time the emphasis was on the legal basis for their demand: "The right of Jews to emigrate to Israel is based on recognized international judicial norms and must not be hindered in the Soviet Union."

Also in 1970 there emerged a Moscow samizdat journal for the emigration movement that resembled *Khronika,* the democrats' successful endeavor. It wasn't the first. Yosef Mendelevich had managed to put together two issues of his journal *Iton* before he was arrested. But when all the Riga activists were locked up, *Iton* died. In Moscow, activist Victor Fedoseyev began assembling *Iskhod,* or *Exodus,* his own samizdat journal with a distinctly Moscow sensibility. *Iton* had tried to stimulate Jewish consciousness with articles about Israel and Jewish history; *Iskhod* was a documentary account of the movement itself. Like *Khronika,* it printed court transcripts and protest letters. In its third issue, released in the fall of 1970, there was an account of the June 15 search of Volodya Slepak's apartment. The fourth issue was devoted to the Leningrad trial and contained a reconstructed transcript of the proceedings. The shift in tone from *Iton* to *Iskhod* mirrored the change in the movement's character when its center moved to Moscow. The opening page of every issue contained the same two quotes. First, from the book of Psalms, were the words uttered by Sylva Zalmanson at the Leningrad trial: "If I forget thee, O Jerusalem, may my right hand wither." Next to this religious exhortation were the words of Article 13 of the United Nations' Universal Declaration of Human Rights: "Everyone has the right to leave any country, including his own."

Iskhod was interesting for another reason. Victor Fedoseyev, its organizer, was not a Jew. Only in Moscow, with its cross-pollination of democrats and Zionists, would such a thing have been possible. Fedoseyev had become immersed in the world of refuseniks after marrying a Jewish woman whose mother was trying to emigrate. Soon he was penning collective petitions and letters (though never signing his non-Jewish name to them). *Iskhod* was his lasting contribution to the Moscow activists, his attempt to organize their activities. Emulating what the democrats were doing with *Khronika* and the human rights committee, Fedoseyev understood that the movement needed to pinpoint cases of abuse and catalog them minutely. In all, only four issues were produced, the first appearing in April 1970 and the last in February

1971, when Fedoseyev and his wife were given exit visas. Shortly after arriving in Israel, he explained in an interview the role that *Iskhod* had played: "The movement continues to exist as it is reflected—when it is reported. It withers and dies in silence . . . The KGB began to let people out, not because no one angered them, but because Jews shouted about their rights. To be silent—to fail to report everything—is to play the KGB's game. Not to reflect all the facts is to permit the movement to decline—to betray Jewish history."

On the morning of February 24, 1971, a group of two dozen refuseniks marched right into the reception room of the Presidium of the Soviet Union, an imposing gray building with an interior of plush red carpet, and a giant hammer-and-sickle flag hanging on the wall. They were demanding, unbelievably, to see a member of one of the most powerful government bodies in the empire. For decades, these Jews had been made to fear the state and given every reason to avoid drawing attention to themselves. Yet now they wanted to present a petition signed by thirty-two Jews asking for a clarification of the Soviet Union's emigration policy. When the receptionist denied them an audience, they sat down on the floor.

The refuseniks were fast eclipsing the democrats in their activism. The only real precedent for this type of sit-in (a distant echo of the American university takeovers of the late 1960s) was the infamously suppressed Red Square demonstration against the Soviet invasion of Czechoslovakia in the summer of 1968—and that had ended seconds after it started, with all the protesters dragged away. But with the Twenty-fourth Communist Party Congress approaching, and the World Jewish Conference on Soviet Jewry taking place at that very moment in Brussels, the Soviets wanted to avoid yet more bad press. So after a full nine hours of waiting, after the cleaners had started vacuuming the red carpets, the protesters were greeted by the administrator of the Presidium; he took their petition and promised an answer the following week.

That they were taken seriously, that no one was arrested, that a Soviet official spoke to them was extraordinary. News of the breakthrough spread among the refuseniks, who realized that there might be an even more effective form of protest than letter writing. When the group returned to the Presidium on March 1, the same official committed himself to investigating each of their complaints and taking another look at their applications. They were not naive. The Soviets might simply be play-acting for the sake of the Western media. But these Jews knew that once a precedent was set, it was hard to undo.

Two weeks after the first sit-in, more than a hundred and fifty refuseniks, mostly Baltic Jews who had seen their friends and family get permission to leave while they were denied, crammed into the Presidium reception room. Mark Azbel, a renowned and charismatic physicist—a quirky, colorful man who usually wore a Hawaiian shirt and who had started to think about applying himself—joined the group of Moscow Jews who witnessed the scene. He later described this protest as having "changed the face of Soviet history—something so impossible that you would not have even dared to dream of it."

It started early in the day on March 10 when fifty-seven Jews from Riga walked into the reception room and presented a petition addressed to the Soviet president, Nikolai Podgorny, and the premier, Aleksei Kosygin. They would not leave, their spokesman announced, until they and their families received permission to emigrate. With that, they began a siege of the building. They were joined by a contingent of sixty-nine Lithuanian Jews and another twenty Muscovites. They sang songs, and one older man read loudly from a samizdat copy of Leon Uris's *Exodus*. That afternoon, Western reporters arrived and interviewed the refuseniks until KGB agents chased them away. Then, at five, when the lights were shut off, all 146 Jews began a hunger strike.

By seven that evening, the authorities had a problem, and with the Western press at a safe distance, more than four hundred and fifty policemen in riot gear and equipped with helmets and clubs rushed into the building and surrounded the group. The lieutenant general of the Moscow police, backed by this threat of extreme force, got them to acquiesce. They would leave. But they returned the following day, only to be greeted by the minister of the interior, surrounded by police officers: "Zionism is Fascism!" he yelled at them. "No one can try to prevent the Soviets from building Communism and go unpunished. You should not forget what we did with the Tatars!" Mark Azbel recorded what happened next: "The people from Riga, with their reinforcements, remained silent and obdurate. And with international attention focused upon these demonstrations, the authorities felt themselves prevented from using force. In the end, they had to back down. They finally offered to reconsider the entire list, as a unit, and only then did the refuseniks leave. The majority of them got out of the country within two weeks."

A few days later, Volodya Slepak stood with a group of almost a hundred Moscow refuseniks at the Presidium and presented a petition signed by 213 people. This time, they wanted more than a reexamination of their own cases. They asked that those Jews being held in connection with the Leningrad hijacking be either released or given retrials immediately (the second Leningrad trial and the trials in Riga and Kishinev had yet to take place). They were told that this issue was under the jurisdiction of the prosecutor general, Roman Rudenko, renowned as the chief Soviet prosecutor at the Nuremberg trials. A smaller group of about fifty refuseniks, including Slepak, walked over to Rudenko's office on Pushkinskaya Street. There they waited, ignored, until a group of thirty policemen in riot gear stormed the reception room. They grabbed Slepak by the arm, lifted him up from where he was sitting on the ground, and escorted him and the rest of the group onto a bus parked outside.

The KGB liked to give fifteen-day detentions. It was a convenient weapon in their war against the dissidents, obviating the need for formal charges. Two weeks in a bare cell without decent food was uncomfortable enough to act as a deterrent for most people. Slepak was brought into a small interrogation room and questioned for twenty minutes. They wanted the names of leaders and any connections to the democrats. Slepak said nothing. He simply repeated his demands and then added that, if he was not released immediately, he would begin a hunger strike. The others said the same.

That night for the first time in his life, Volodya Slepak slept in a jail cell. It had two iron beds with no mattresses, a table and bench bolted to the floor. A small tin drum in the corner served as a toilet. His cellmate was Victor Polsky, a physicist and one of Volodya's closest friends. He was part of the group of Jews Slepak had met during his years working at the Scientific Institute for TV Research; his family was one of the ones the Slepaks camped with in the summers. Polsky had also lost his job. Redheaded and blue-eyed, he had an unusually forceful presence (his nickname was Commander), and from the moment he became a refusenik he was determined to sign every petition, be part of every protest. Old friends, he and Slepak tried to make the best of their situation.

The next morning, ten of the refuseniks, the men of the group, were brought in front of a judge, a severe-looking woman in a dark jacket and skirt, and told that "because of your noncompliance with the demands of the representatives of the authorities, you are hereby sentenced to fifteen days of administrative imprisonment." Placed back in their cells, they decided they would begin their hunger strike and drink only water. Slepak and Polsky bided their time, playing chess on a board they had made out of scraps of paper and using morsels of torn-up bread for pieces. Days passed in boredom and eventually most of the refuseniks gave up the strike. By the thirteenth day, only Slepak and one other man were still fasting. When the guards made it clear that they would start force-feeding him, Slepak relented. The other man was Mikhail Zand; he was in his midforties, a professor of Oriental studies renowned for his work on Persian and Tajik literature. His ambition to go to Israel dated back to 1948 when he naively wrote to Stalin asking that Soviet Jews be given permission to fight in Israel's War of Independence. The only thing that saved him from a labor camp was that he'd used a pseudonym to sign the letter. In March of 1971, he wasn't so lucky. A day before the end of his detention, the last man still fasting, Zand was strapped down and force-fed bouillon through his nose. When he finally agreed to eat, he was served a meal of grits and pork and beef, which injured his liver and gallbladder. He left the prison in an ambulance and was driven straight to a hospital.

Slepak was able to come home and joke with Masha about losing his large paunch. But there was also acute fear. The life they had chosen was going to get more difficult. There would be extreme deprivation, and perhaps even physical pain. Slepak entered this new existence with a clear conscience, but not without trepidation.

The activists' new militancy, which bordered on recklessness, was wholly unexpected by both the Soviet authorities and, to some extent, the Jews themselves. At one point during the spring of 1971 an anonymous letter was sent to the minister of the interior that sounded as if it had been composed by Meir Kahane. It warned the minister to take action against threats and physical violence aimed at Jews. "We demand that effective measures be taken to stop such provocations no matter what their source is," the letter read. "Otherwise we will be compelled to defend our lives and human dignity ourselves. If the ministry you head cannot manage this problem, we will have to study the question of finding appropriate self-defense: The times of Czarist pogroms and assassinations, when our fathers would perish without defending themselves, are over." Sit-ins and hunger strikes continued throughout the summer, usually followed by the fifteen-day detentions. A familiar routine was established, a dance of demonstration and detention that only served to further radicalize the movement.

This willingness to engage in extreme and risky (and publicity-generating) protest was enhanced by another unanticipated and paradoxical development: a new crop of refuseniks hailing from the scientific establishment. This gave the Moscow movement even more legitimacy and respectability.

Jews made up a large percentage of the Soviet Union's scientific elite. At the beginning of the 1970s, one-fifth (18 percent) of all educated Jews fit in the category of scientific worker—compared with one-tenth of all educated Russians. For the generation that came of age during the last years of Stalin's reign, science provided an escape from the constraints of ideology. One could excel at science without being forced to make the moral compromises required in literature or history. Chemistry, physics, mathematics—all had laws over which Communism had no jurisdiction. When the regime tried to control these fields, it simply damaged itself. So Jews naturally gravitated to these meritocratic disciplines, where advancement wasn't simply a function of one's adherence to Party doctrine. The sciences often ignored the quotas sometimes placed on other fields. The authorities would generally not deny employment to an exceptional mind willing to work in the service of the state, regardless of that person's ethnicity.

Mark Azbel, the physicist who witnessed the protest at the Presidium, later wrote about how science was key to his "moral survival" in the Soviet Union. His physics theories were "independent of every external factor" and helped him cope with the daily self-deceptions needed to get along. Science meant more than a free conscience. At the highest level, scientists were given much privilege—big apartments, country homes, trips abroad, the right to shop at special stores that contained consumer goods from the West. To remain competitive in the arms race, the Soviets needed the scientists, so they did everything to keep them happy. Azbel wrote that physicists constituted "a privileged caste, an aristocracy. There were fewer controls on our freedom than on those of any other members of Soviet civilian society. . . . Relatively speaking we were free people."

So it came as the greatest shock when members of this caste began asking to leave. They had far more to lose than the average Soviet engineer. And since most scientists had worked for the government at some point in their lives, they were almost certain to be refused. Still, they persisted. In the last months of 1971, the news quickly circulated in the Moscow scientific community that fifty-eight-year-old Alexander Lerner, one of the most esteemed scientists in the country, had applied to leave.

Alexander Lerner was a small man with a large belly, a balding pate, and heavy jowls. He was internationally known in his field of cybernetics—a science founded in the 1940s that examined communication and control in both machines and living things—and had spent the previous summer working at a research institute in Naples, Italy. This was Lerner's world until the spring of 1971, honored and privileged—he had a large apartment in Moscow, a spacious dacha in the country, and, incredibly, two cars.

Lerner was born and grew up in Vinnytsya, a large town in the Ukraine not far from the shtetls where his parents had lived before the revolution. As a boy, he fiddled with radios for hours until he could hear the Gypsy music played on the Polish station, and he was fascinated by American movies, especially films with Douglas Fairbanks. In 1932, at the age of eighteen, he was urged by his mother to go to Moscow for his education. Arriving with little more than the address of a childhood friend and a suitcase with three shirts and two changes of underwear, he joined the throngs of young men from the provinces coming to the city to work in the factories and on the many building projects. The next few years of his life were a constant struggle to find a place to live as he moved through a dismal series of closets and kitchens and small rooms teeming with bedbugs.

But he soon made his mark. His first invention was conceived while he was working at a textile mill: it was a simple device that signaled when a thread tore on a loom. He spent the three-thousand-ruble reward to secure a stable living situation. He was initially refused entrance to Moscow's prestigious Power Engineering Institute because his father, the owner of a small drugstore before the revolution, was part of the "bourgeois," but he eventually found his way in. At the age of twenty-one, he was profiled in the magazine *Soviet Student* as a model Soviet youth, a man who had pulled himself up by his bootstraps. Soon he married Judith Perelman, a girl from back home. He started graduate work at the Power Engineering Institute and was even given a small apartment. By the time he was an assistant professor, at the age of twenty-seven, he had already collaborated on a book and published several articles in international science journals.

The German attack on the Soviet Union in June of 1941 tore Lerner's life apart. His two young daughters were staying with his parents in the Ukraine over the summer. There was no way for Lerner and his wife to get to them before the Nazis arrived with their mobile killing units. Lerner was mobilized and sent all over the empire, first to a factory in Novosibirsk and then in 1943 back to Moscow to supervise a laboratory at the Iron and Steel Ministry. As soon as the Red Army liberated Vinnytsya, he rushed to find his family, only to discover that his two daughters and most of his relatives had been shot not long after the Germans entered their town. There was nothing to do but go back to the city and start a new life, build a new family.

Lerner and his wife went on to have two more children, and he continued to pursue his scientific interests. After the war, science remained one of the few fields open to Jews. The Cold War technology race trumped anti-Semitism. Lerner's field, automation, was especially valued, and this largely insulated him. For example, in the late forties, the government banned cybernetics, labeling it a "bourgeois pseudo-science," but Lerner simply began referring to his work as "the theory of optimal control." He was left alone.

Only Stalin's last delusional campaign against "rootless cosmopolitans" (that is, Jews) was able to puncture this safe existence. The purging of Jews from the sciences, fields where their contributions were critical, was testament to Stalin's madness. It didn't take much to be charged with "cosmopolitanism." Having one's name mentioned in a foreign publication was enough. For Lerner, it was guilt by association. He had an aunt who had emigrated from Vinnytsya to Mexico in the late twenties. Lerner was fired in an effort to "purify personnel" and contain the threat of foreign influence. He was blasphemed in newspapers as a suspicious character and reduced to knocking on doors all over Moscow looking for work; his friends and colleagues were afraid even to admit they knew him.

Then Stalin died, and Lerner's troubles evaporated. Those who had maligned him now embraced him. He began working again at the Iron and Steel Ministry and in 1956 was made laboratory chief at the Automation Institute. But the anti-Semitic campaign scarred Lerner, as it did many Jews of his generation. It made him aware as never before of the fundamental insecurity of his position in Soviet society, no matter how many awards he won.

Lerner's evolution began slowly. On the one hand, he was gaining more and more notoriety in the Soviet Union and abroad. He earned the degree of doctor of science, the highest level awarded, and was allowed to take trips to Paris, Beijing, and many other places, occasionally guest lecturing for a month at a time. His fiftieth birthday was spent in Florence. His book on cybernetics became a seminal text on the subject. On the other hand, as the sixties progressed, he felt more alienated, more attuned to the hypocrisy and the compromises he felt he had to make in order to maintain his privileges. And he worried for his children's future. He was in his fifties and had accomplished much in his life, but what about Vladimir and Sonia, his son and daughter? Their Jewishness was already impeding their progress. His daughter, despite having exemplary grades, was denied entrance into the university, and his son was the only student not allowed to go on a class trip to London.

Lerner had very little awareness of his Jewishness beyond the memory of his grandfather's teaching him the traditional Passover phrase "Next year in Jerusalem!" But he found himself increasingly drawn to the idea of immigrating to Israel, especially after the Six-Day War. He'd begun following the exploits of the dissidents, admiring the Red Square protesters in 1968 and reading Solzhenitsyn's *Gulag Archipelago* in samizdat. Then the Riga Jews began emigrating in 1969, and finally a few Moscow Jews were let out in early 1971. Lerner agonized about what to do but he knew this might be his chance to give his children the gift of a better life. He also knew what this would cost him. As he later wrote in his memoirs: "Anyone who took the first step toward getting permission to leave was breaking away from Soviet society, condemning himself to isolation and persecution until he managed to leave or perished in the attempt."

On an evening in May 1971, he gathered his family together, drew the shades, disconnected the phone, and then told them in a whisper that he had decided to apply for an exit visa. His wife was worried, but his children embraced the idea. In that instant, after a lifetime of accumulated compromises, Lerner felt his conscience finally clear. He described the moment this way: "When we had made our decision, we were able to breath more easily. We had no illusion about the fight that lay ahead and how hard it would be to achieve our goal, but we were filled with the joy of certainty. Away with uncertainty, doubt, misgivings! We had chosen, so let the storm rage. I suppose a defendant in court feels something similar when a terrifying period of interrogations, cross-examinations, and hearings is over. The sentence is finally pronounced, and everything falls into place. It may even be worse than he had hoped, but at any rate, it's definite. In our case we had pronounced our own sentence."

Lerner found someone to deliver his request for an invitation to Israel and then waited anxiously all summer for a response. It didn't come until September, but the KGB, which controlled the post office, intercepted the invitation and informed Lerner's bosses at the Institute of Control Problems of the Academy of Sciences. It was not a mistake, Lerner told them, not the Zionist provocation they had assumed, but a request he himself had made. His bosses couldn't believe it. They cajoled and threatened, afraid that his actions would jeopardize the entire institute (Stalin's purges had ingrained in Soviet citizens the fear of guilt by association). The reputation of the institute would be tarnished in the eyes of the Academy of Sciences and in the district and central committees of the Party. They would lose funding. One colleague at the institute was recruited to dissuade Lerner, and he told him pointedly, "Stop to think what you're giving up by following this risky path. You're guaranteed comfort till the end of your life as a prominent Soviet scientist. You have a fine apartment, a splendid country house, you get high pay and extra income. And what are you exchanging it for? A poor, backward Asian country surrounded by enemies who have dedicated themselves to destroying it. You'll be going to a land of religious fanaticism with never a hope of economic, political or social progress. You'll be dooming yourself to degradation, both as a man and a scientist."

The degradation came sooner than expected. The following week, he began one of his cybernetics lectures—he was also teaching at the Physico-Technological Institute—and was interrupted in the first few minutes by a school administrator who asked him to go. He would no longer be teaching this course. Lerner demanded official justification of his dismissal, and his loyal students refused to leave their seats. When the administrator threatened to expel them if they didn't exit the room within three minutes, they silently filed out. Lerner's years of teaching were over. A few days later, an order was posted at his institute announcing that his laboratory was being dismantled "in view of the fact that its research was not topical."

Out of work and exposed, he finally submitted his application. Almost immediately, he became a sort of father figure for the other activists, much like Sakharov was for the dissident movement. His spacious apartment served as a meeting place for both Soviet refuseniks and dignitaries from abroad. In December of 1971, just weeks after submitting his application and losing his job, Lerner had a visit from a U.S. congressman, James Scheuer, a representative from the Bronx. Lerner prepared for the day meticulously and invited a few other prominent activists. Volodya Slepak was there, along with his friend Victor Polsky. Lerner's wife had baked some pies. It was the first chance they had had to communicate with so prominent an American official. Scheuer soon arrived with his entourage. The refuseniks found the congressman friendly; he offered to help in whatever way he could. But not long after the meeting began, the doorbell rang and two police officers entered, claiming they were looking for a dangerous criminal disguised as a foreigner. They demanded to see Scheuer's papers. As the congressman described it in a phone call from Lerner's apartment later that evening, "I tried to identify myself by showing my New York driver's license, Diners' Club card, American Express card and finally my Congressional ID card but nothing helped. They evidently had orders to take me down to the station." Lerner demanded an explanation but got none. Scheuer was escorted to the local police headquarters; after about ten minutes he was released, and he eventually made his way back to Lerner's apartment.

Meanwhile, Lerner received one of the calls he often got from American Jews, this time from the Chicago branch of the women's group Hadassah. He told them what had just happened in his living room, and within half an hour, the news was all over American radio. Lerner never knew exactly what had led to the confusion. The KGB must have been given a faulty tip. In any event, the story of Scheuer's brief detention made all the U.S. papers the following day, and most of the articles mentioned Lerner. From then on, a visit to the professor's apartment became an almost obligatory part of any American lawmaker's junket in Moscow.

Shortly after Lerner submitted his exit visa application, an even more prominent scientist declared his intention to emigrate. In March 1972, Benjamin Levich, a fifty-five-year-old corresponding member of the Academy of Sciences and the internationally known founder of the study of physiochemical hydrodynamics, submitted his request for an exit visa. Unsurprisingly, it was quickly denied by OVIR. This made him the highest-ranking Jew on the growing list of refuseniks—an Academy of Sciences member, like Sakharov.

Lerner and Levich opened up possibilities. They showed other, less prominent scientists that it was possible to make this dramatic move if they wished, that life continued even in refusal. It was a powerful example for people to see that these men, already past middle age, were willing to discard the social capital they had accrued over a lifetime. Neither of them was ideologically Zionist, but their desire to leave a country that made Jewishness a liability soon transformed into a wish to live in Israel. With these new refuseniks, the Soviet authorities had a complex public relations problem. The Kremlin's propagandists had always portrayed the Zionists as a group of mostly young and misguided hooligans, troublemakers, and hijackers. The distinguished, gray-haired Levich and Lerner put the lie to this characterization.

In the spring of 1972, Volodya Slepak had been a refusenik for two years. His leadership role in the community had certainly singled him out for extra abuse, but most refuseniks could tell stories similar to his. Slepak was now completely estranged from his father. He assumed the old man was secretly using his Party connections to prevent Volodya's emigration. Volodya and Masha had both lost their jobs; they earned about two hundred rubles a month from tutoring the children of other refuseniks in physics and mathematics. The struggle to maintain some form of steady occupation had become epic. His last boss had fired him after he'd signed the character reference for his visa application. Volodya then bounced from one job to another until September of the following year when he finally just accepted his status as unemployed. Masha, despite her having much-needed medical skills, was rejected by every hospital.

They found they could make ends meet with their tutoring. But there was one problem: it was illegal to be unemployed in the Soviet Union. Anyone not working was liable to be arrested for parasitism, especially a refusenik who had lost his job. In February of 1972, Volodya was charged and sent to work as a porter at Moscow Concrete Factory 23. He managed to appeal this assignment but continued to be dogged by the authorities, who demanded he take some kind of menial job. Eventually the former radio engineer found work as an elevator operator.

So absurd did the refuseniks find their new lives that it inspired a unique brand of gallows humor, a new kind of Jewish joke to help ease the pain. A typical one revolved around the Jew Rabinovich (the Soviet Jewish everyman): Rabinovich is filling out a job application when the Soviet official looks at him skeptically. "You say here you don't have any relatives abroad, but we know you have a brother in Israel," the official tells him. "Oh, but you're wrong," Rabinovich says. "He's not the one who's abroad. I am."

In the first months of 1972, despite the miserable situation of individual refuseniks, the movement's members were finding reasons to be hopeful. The number of people receiving exit visas was rising; some were even from Moscow, and it looked like the total might surpass the level of 1971 (thirteen thousand). Contact with the West had proliferated, and prominent refuseniks like Slepak and Lerner sometimes received a dozen phone calls a day from American Jews in Ohio, New York, Los Angeles, and Washington. They were developing clear lines of communications, passing on information about the status of various refuseniks and becoming more sophisticated about what was happening on their behalf in the wider world.

The announcement that Richard Nixon would visit Moscow at the end of May was greeted with great expectation by the refuseniks. They assumed that Jewish emigration, the problem they represented, would be dealt with at length. The presence of an American president in the Russian capital for the first time in history would surely compel the Soviets to eliminate any possible points of friction between the two superpowers. Leaders like Slepak and Lerner were so sure they would be able to meet with the visiting Americans and air their grievances that a month before Nixon's trip they issued a group letter providing their addresses: "In order to facilitate contacts with the president or members of his delegation, we, Jews, signing this letter, scientists and specialists living in Moscow and long unsuccessful in obtaining permission to emigrate to Israel, have formed an information committee for the occasion of the president's visit. We are ready to apprise him objectively concerning the situation of the Jews mentioned above so that the representation to the president on this question may be based on facts and correct data."

Hundreds of refuseniks signed letters requesting that Nixon meet with them—a group of ninety-three from Riga; fifty friends appealing on behalf of the defendants in the Leningrad and Riga trials. So many petitions were produced that one group of refuseniks in Moscow organized what they called a "White Book of Exodus," which assembled all the various material generated by Nixon's historic trip. There was an optimistic feeling that their cause would soon be catapulted to international attention. In one of many letters to Mrs. Nixon, the wife of Lassal Kaminsky and the sister-in-law of David Chernoglaz—two of the Leningrad activists recently sentenced to long terms in labor camps—begged her to grant them an audience. "We would be very grateful to you if you would consider seeing us and personally speaking with us," they wrote, naively and hopefully.

The Soviet authorities, who in preparation for the visit had meticulously water-blasted the sidewalks, repainted government buildings, and locked up the prostitutes, had other ideas. A dozen young activists, including Alexander Lerner's twenty-eight-year-old son, were sent cards informing them that they were being drafted into the army, effective immediately. All the phones in refusenik apartments were disconnected. Radio stations from the West, the Voice of America and Radio Liberty, were all jammed.

Then, a day before Nixon's plane touched down, police officers arrived at the Slepaks' apartment and took Volodya to a holding pen a few miles outside of Moscow. There he was joined by a handful of other refuseniks. Other activists were stopped on the street and arbitrarily arrested for made-up crimes, such as harassing a woman or blocking traffic. Non-Jewish dissidents all over Moscow had the same experience, all detained as a preventive measure. Alexander Lerner was in the hospital at the time; he suffered from chronic cholecystitis and needed an operation to remove his gallbladder. To his surprise, he was placed in a special ward usually reserved for Party leaders; his doctor at first advised that he wait a few days before undergoing the procedure, but then Lerner was told that he would be operated on immediately. The KGB, Lerner later discovered, had pressured the surgeon to rush the operation so that Lerner would be recovering when Nixon arrived and therefore unable to receive visitors.

As the American president and his national security adviser, Henry Kissinger, made the diplomatic rounds, toasting Brezhnev over numerous glasses of vodka and praising a new age of peace and cooperation, Slepak and his friends sat in cells. During the ten days that the group was sequestered, the wives and mothers—including Masha Slepak, who was worried about her husband and her son, both of whom had been taken without explanation—petitioned the Soviet prosecutor general. They received no response. It wasn't until days after Nixon's departure that Volodya returned to the Gorky Street apartment.

The detentions may have prevented the refuseniks from participating in Nixon's visit, but they had an unanticipated benefit: they helped expose the superficial nature of détente. "Soviets Said to Seize Jews as Nixon Visit Approaches" read a front page of the *New York Times*. While the American president and the First Lady toured an elementary school and watched a display of traditional Russian folk dancing, men who wanted nothing more than permission to emigrate were locked up with criminals and drunks. The Soviets clearly believed that granting an unprecedented number of exit visas, in itself a concession of sorts, would be enough to quiet the growing criticism in the West. In 1972, thirty-one thousand Soviet Jews were allowed to leave, more than twice the amount allowed in 1971. But this ignored the equal number that had applied and been refused. If the warming in relations between the two Cold War enemies was to continue, there was no way to avoid the fundamental contradiction of a diplomacy that talked peace but ignored basic human rights. Many people other than the refuseniks were starting to wonder: Was détente reserved for national security, arms control, and the showy "scientific and cultural exchanges," or was it also about how human beings lived in these two countries and the universal rights they deserved? Henry Kissinger had his answer to this question. But so too did the growing number of Soviet Jewry activists in America.

8

Linkage
1972–1975

SENATOR HENRY JACKSON had been called many things in his life. Scoop was the most common and the most affectionate, a childhood nickname. Those who were suspicious that his demands for increased defense spending had less to do with his convictions and more to do with the giant defense contractor in his home state of Washington dubbed him the Senator from Boeing. But in the summer of 1972, congresspeople began referring to him behind his back by another mocking sobriquet: Churchill. Jackson was seeing appeasement everywhere and railing against it loudly. America, he warned again and again, was surrendering to the Soviets. Opposing Nixon and Kissinger's détente became Jackson's mission. Through it he seemed to find his voice — self-righteous and stubborn though it often was.

The son of Norwegian immigrants who had settled in the Pacific Northwest, Jackson first ran for Congress in 1941 and then moved to the Senate in 1953. His politics had not changed much since then — a combination of New Deal social democratic principles and the idea, forged by Roosevelt and Truman, that America need not be afraid to use its strength to enforce its values. Partly because of these unmovable convictions, he gained a reputation as a man of principle. But as the 1960s progressed, he was increasingly out of step with his own party. He was a Cold Warrior at a time of national self-doubt. His run for the Democratic nomination for president in 1972 was disastrous. When most candidates were outdoing one another in their opposition to the Vietnam War, and Nixon was touting a record of cooperation with the Soviets and the Chinese, Jackson tried to convince Democrats to confront Communism, build a strong nuclear program, and believe in the inherent greatness of America (imploring, "This society is not a guilty, imperialistic and oppressive society. This is not a sick society"). The Democrats chose George McGovern, darling of the antiwar left, leaving Jackson behind in the early primaries.

The election further defined Jackson as an outsider, a maverick in his own party. He found himself largely alone in opposition to détente; the policy seemed to have triumphed. On June 1, 1972, half an hour after returning from his historic Moscow summit, Nixon made an appearance before both houses of Congress to announce the dawn of "a new relationship between the two most powerful nations on earth." An arms limitations treaty would soon be signed. A comprehensive trade deal was also forthcoming, one that would give the Soviets most-favored-nation trading status, lowering tariffs placed on Russian goods such as caviar and, more important, granting them credit to buy badly needed American technology and grain. The Soviets had long sought this lucrative concession, and the president had finally acquiesced. As he told Congress, "When the two largest economies in the world start trading with each other on a much larger scale, living standards in both nations will rise, and the stakes which both have in peace will be increased."

Jackson found détente offensive. To make peace and to work toward a secure world while leaving a powerful undemocratic empire in place seemed to him both a perversion and a strategic mistake. The Soviet Union, as he saw it, was still a totalitarian state with erratic and ideologically driven ambitions. Détente for them was simply a stalling tactic, he thought, a way to buy time for their long-term plan of hegemony. He believed that Nixon and Kissinger misunderstood Americans, that American citizens would be able to stomach a fight if the moral illegitimacy of the Soviets was made clear. He was of the opinion—not shared by Kissinger—that the Soviet Union was on its last legs, that its increasingly vulnerable economic state presented an opportunity. The United States' objective should not be a stalemate but the collapse of the Soviet Union. Jackson was also deeply motivated by the need to defend human rights. For him, the greatest sin of détente was that it let America turn a blind eye to the internal character of the Soviet Union while making an illusory peace. It was a frustration shared by the activists struggling to help Soviet Jews. They too were feeling overwhelmed by Nixon's well-produced spectacle of Cold War friendship, which made their objection, no matter how righteous, seem churlish.

Then, like a gift straight from the Politburo, came ukase 572. The news appeared on the front page of the *New York Times* just two and half months after Nixon's visit: "Jewish sources reported tonight that Soviet authorities are instituting a new system of heavy exit fees ranging from $5,000 to $25,000 for educated Jews who want to emigrate to Israel. The sources said they learned of the new measure, replacing the old general fee of about $1,000, while some Jews were applying for exit visas with a branch of the Interior Ministry today. No official confirmation was possible." It looked bad; it seemed to be no less than the ransoming of Soviet Jewry. As Benjamin Levich, the eminent chemist turned refusenik, told the *Times,* the new Soviet decree would make scientists "the slaves of the 20th century." The article contained only one government response: "The fees were necessary repayment to the government for the cost of state-financed education."

More details soon emerged. The new fees were tied to the level of education of the aspiring emigrant, with a steep sliding scale depending on the amount of schooling: 4,500 rubles ($5,400) for a graduate of a teachers' institute; 9,500 rubles ($10,800) for an applied arts degree; 11,000 rubles ($13,200) for a university degree; up to 22,000 rubles ($25,400) for the Soviet equivalent of a PhD. With a teacher making about 100 rubles a month, an engineer or doctor making 130 rubles, and a scientist earning 250 rubles, this was beyond the reach of almost any Soviet citizen. The required $600 fee for renunciation of Soviet citizenship and the $530 fee for an exit permit were already heavy burdens.

The Soviets had once again miscalculated. The imposition of the exit fees was proof that the Kremlin was panicking, frightened by a potential brain drain. Brezhnev's move might have been meant to intimidate, but it had the opposite effect. It immediately provided the refuseniks a new banner. The rest of the world responded angrily as well. George McGovern, not exactly known for harsh condemnations of the Kremlin, said the Soviet Union was "holding these people hostages of the state." Kahane, predictably, raised his voice from his now permanent home in Jerusalem and warned that the Soviets had one month to abandon the exit fees or the JDL would kidnap Soviet diplomats and hold them for ransom. And in one of the strangest protests thus far, six demonstrators led by the borough presidents of Manhattan and the Bronx occupied minuscule Belmont Island in the East River, renamed it the Soviet Jewry Freedom Island, and unfurled a banner with that name that could be seen from the United Nations building across Turtle Bay. After two and a half hours and much publicity, they got back in their dinghy and motored home. Then came the inevitable Holocaust analogies: An editorial cartoon in the *Los Angeles Times* showed a caricature of two almost identical prisoners; the first held out an arm tattooed with a number from a concentration camp and was captioned "Germany, 1936," and the second had the same tattooed arm and was captioned "Russia, 1972." The difference was that the number on the second arm had a dollar sign in front of it.

In this new "diploma tax," Jackson saw a convergence of all he was opposed to: it was a violation of human rights and a reminder of a brutal Communist system that had to be defeated, not coddled. Jackson had always been a strong defender of Israel and the Jews, a stance he traced back to the stacks of emaciated bodies he'd witnessed as a young congressman visiting the newly liberated Buchenwald concentration camp. He wanted to take the opportunity to do something. But what? How to use this Soviet misstep to his advantage? The day the news of the tax broke, he called his legislative aide Richard Perle into his office and told him to prepare a strong response.

Perle, a thirty-year-old, dark-eyed, aggressive chain smoker in a sweater vest, shared Jackson's worldview completely and wasn't afraid to throw his elbows around in the service of his boss. In many ways, it was a fortuitous match for both men. Jackson provided the moral grounding, the mentoring, and his young protégé could aggressively pursue Jackson's policies while keeping the senator's hands clean. Perle's path toward Jackson began early, at Hollywood High School, where he dated the daughter of Albert Wohlstetter, the renowned nuclear strategist. The precocious Perle—he wore ties even as a teen-

ager—was exposed to Wohlstetter's conservative critique of containment and the doctrine of mutual assured destruction. Wohlstetter
thought that America should ratchet up the arms race as opposed to
simply being satisfied with a world-threatening stalemate, because it
was a race that the Soviets could never win. Perle was persuaded.

Years later, in 1969—after Perle had attended the London School of
Economics and become known as a pipe-smoking Cold Warrior in a
sea of pacifists—Wohlstetter invited him to come to Washington. He
advised Perle to abandon his PhD and join the staff of a new ad hoc
group, the Committee to Maintain a Prudent Defense Policy, which
was chaired by former secretary of state Dean Acheson and composed
of Democratic Cold Warriors (soon to be called neoconservatives)
intent on getting congressional approval for a new missile defense
system. Perle spent the summer with two other Wohlstetter protégés—one was Paul Wolfowitz, a graduate student at the University of
Chicago—writing position papers, briefing senators, and serving as
liaisons to the press. The campaign was successful, and the twenty-
seven-year-old Perle emerged as an intelligent and tenacious striver.
Before he could leave Washington and return to academia, he was offered a job working for Scoop Jackson.

In no time, Perle became an indispensable part of Jackson's close-
knit foreign policy team, known in Washington as the Bunker because
of the cramped, windowless office where its members worked. Running the shop was Dorothy Fosdick, a chief adviser to Jackson for decades and a character in her own right. At five foot one and with a
fiery streak, Fosdick was called Bubbe (Yiddish for "grandmother")
by the other staffers. She was a longtime Cold Warrior who was, im-
probably, the daughter of a famously pacifist preacher of Manhattan's
Riverside Church, Harry Emerson Fosdick. In the 1940s, she was the
first woman to hold a senior position in the State Department, helping
to administer the Marshall Plan. She later worked on setting up the
United Nations; while advising Adlai Stevenson on his 1952 presidential campaign, she became his lover. From 1954 on, she was Jackson's
chief foreign policy adviser, and the two, like Jackson and Perle, shared
an absolutely identical political perspective.

Perle and the Bunker didn't have much trouble coming up with a
response to the diploma tax. The outlines of a good, aggressive idea
were already circulating. Kissinger's détente was based on the concept

of linkage, a game of self-interested tit for tat in which the superpowers helped each other in those areas where their geopolitical goals overlapped. The Soviets wanted credit to buy American goods. The United States wanted to de-escalate in Vietnam. On this foundation, Kissinger wove his web. But what if linkage could be used in another way, to force the Soviets to change their behavior? It was obvious during that summer of 1972 that the Kremlin was hungry for trade. Why not make the granting of most-favored-nation status and credit contingent on the elimination of the diploma tax and an increase in emigration? Congress had often used its power of the purse to influence foreign policy—that was one of its few real tools—but such a move would be a bold challenge to the president's agenda. It would demand that the Soviet Union alter its internal domestic policies if it wanted anything from the United States. The Cold War had never been fought this way.

Such a daring proposition needed a powerful base of support. This was Perle's greatest challenge. When he looked out at the American Jewish community, he saw a small but noisy grassroots Soviet Jewry movement. These people would make good foot soldiers in any legislative campaign. But he needed more. The entire Jewish establishment would have to be involved. And here there was reason for hope. In the past year, whether because of the headline-grabbing moves of Kahane, the surge of protests on the streets of New York, the widening network of local Soviet Jewry councils united by Lou Rosenblum, or the increased prodding from the Israelis, the Jewish establishment had finally decided to get serious. In the spring of 1971, the coalition of national groups that made up the flimsy ad hoc American Jewish Conference on Soviet Jewry reconstituted itself into an independent umbrella organization that finally had a budget and a staff. In August 1971, the newly named National Conference on Soviet Jewry started operating with $250,000 and an enthusiastic executive director, Jerry Goodman, who had been working intermittently on Soviet Jewry issues for almost a decade. To be its first chairman, the National Conference chose Richard Maass, an affable and respected foreign policy expert who was conciliatory toward the grassroots activists. Shortly before Maass became chairman, Yaakov Birnbaum invited him to a two-day seminar at Yeshiva University. Maass went and listened to angry students rail

A ceremony at the Rumbuli memorial in April 1963 marking the twentieth anniversary of the Warsaw Ghetto uprising. On the black obelisk is a reproduction of Yosef Kuzkovsky's painting *The Last Way—Babi Yar*.

Beit Hatfutsot Photo Archive, Tel Aviv

More than any other group, Student Struggle for Soviet Jewry captured the spirit of the 1960s with its protests. Here, in June 1964, a weeklong interfaith fast takes place in front of the Soviet mission in Manhattan. Yaakov Birnbaum is third from right, with beard and white hat.

Jacob Birnbaum Archives

Starting in 1971, a rally and march known as Solidarity Sunday was held every spring, bringing huge crowds into the streets of Manhattan. They massed at Dag Hammarskjold Plaza in front of the United Nations after walking down Fifth Avenue. This photo was taken on April 15, 1975, at the fourth annual Solidarity Sunday.

Meir Kahane's Soviet Jewry exploits were regularly covered by the New York tabloids. Here he stands outside the Manhattan Criminal Court on January 21, 1971, at the height of his anti-Soviet harassment campaign.

Lou Rosenblum (seated, second from right) traveled to the Soviet Union in May 1974 with three other Union of Councils activists. To his right is Sasha Lunts, and standing behind them is Anatoly Shcharansky. Most of the rest of the group were part of the Hong Wei Bing protest strike force, including Leonid Tsypin (standing, with blond beard and glasses), who would later denounce Shcharansky. *Courtesy of Louis Rosenblum*

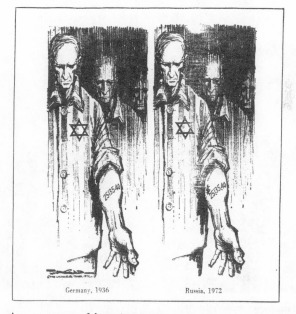

Germany, 1936   Russia, 1972

As soon as news of the emigration tax reached the West, Holocaust analogies came quickly to mind, as in Paul Conrad's political cartoon in the September 24, 1972, *Los Angeles Times.*

After their release from prison in 1979, Eduard Kuznetsov (in black-rimmed glasses) and Mark Dymshits (seated, at left) visited New York City. Senator Henry Jackson, embraced by the Jewish community for his amendment, sits between them.

Beit Hatfutsot Photo Archive

An iconic photo of the most famous refusenik activists, taken in 1976. Front row, left to right: Vitaly Rubin, Anatoly Shcharansky, Ida Nudel, and Alexander Lerner. Second row: Vladimir Slepak, Lev Ovsishcher, Alexander Druk, Yosef Beilin, and Dina Beilin. *Beit Hatfutsot Photo Archive*

The movement inspired some striking poster art, including this 1969 design by Israeli artist Dan Reisinger.

Beit Hatfutsot Photo Archive

Anatoly Shcharansky's trial turned him into the face of Soviet Jewry and a symbol for all that was untenable about détente. © *Time, Inc.*

Simchat Torah, the holiday celebrating the end of the Torah-reading cycle, became a joyous annual occasion for Soviet Jews. In Moscow, thousands would cram narrow Arkhipova Street in front of the city's main synagogue, as here in 1981, and dance late into the night.

Photo © Bill Aron

Ronald Reagan championed the cause of Soviet Jewry from his first days in office. In May 1981, he invited Avital Shcharansky and Yosef Mendelevich, only recently released from prison, to the White House. *Beit Hatfutsot Photo Archive*

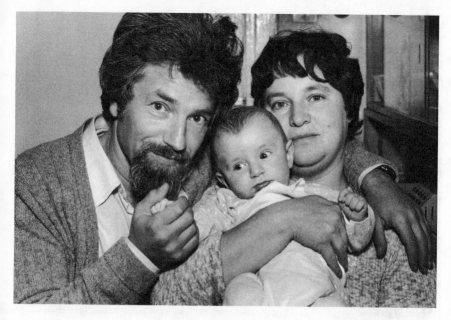

Yuli Kosharovsky, here with his wife and baby in 1981, kept alive a network of Hebrew teaching all over the Soviet Union, even during the darkest days of the early 1980s.
Photo © Bill Aron

The gatherings in the Ovrazhki forest outside Moscow created a small island of vibrant Jewish life. Popular song contests were held, including this one in 1978. Leonid Volvovsky, who was later imprisoned for his activities, is at the microphone.
Yona Schwarzman / Beit Hatfutsot Photo Archive

One of the first signs that Mikhail Gorbachev's liberalization was affecting the refuseniks was this protest in March 1987. Instead of being suppressed, the small group of Leningrad Jews was invited to speak with the authorities. Third from the left, in the white Russian hat, is Misha Beizer. To his left are Aba and Ida Taratuta.

Beit Hatfutsot Photo Archive

On Freedom Sunday, December 6, 1987, a quarter of a million people gathered in Washington to protest Gorbachev's first visit to the United States. Vice President George Bush addressed the demonstration, demanding, "Mr. Gorbachev, let these people go!"

AP Images / Ira Schwarz

against the paralysis of the establishment. But rather than respond defensively, he promised greater engagement.

Another change was the emergence of a federation of New York–based Jewish organizations. Run by Malcolm Hoenlein, a former Student Struggle activist from Philadelphia, the group borrowed heavily from Birnbaum's protest style—the large rallies, the religious tropes, the focus on individual refuseniks and prisoners. The Greater New York Conference on Soviet Jewry became an important bridge between the energy and irreverence of the activists and the resources and breadth of the establishment.

These new groups, however, had yet to make an impact. Jewish leaders had been trying since the start of Nixon's presidency to get him to agree to a meeting, incessantly bugging Leonard Garment, Nixon's liaison to the Jewish community. Only after the Leningrad hijacking did Nixon pay some attention to the problem. One chairman of the American Conference on Soviet Jewry wrote the State Department in 1970 demanding it take a harder line on the repression of refuseniks, and he received this response, which summarized the government's view, virtually unchanged since the early 1960s: "You will understand, of course, that we must choose the forum and the occasion thoughtfully so that our efforts cannot be dismissed as merely 'cold war propaganda.'"

The frustration and restlessness could be felt in the weeks following Nixon's 1972 summit. In a letter to Max Fisher, a rich Republican supporter with deep ties to the administration, the National Conference chairman Richard Maass wrote, "Since the president's trip to Moscow, there seems to be a stiffening of Soviet response to the activities of those Jews who are trying to obtain exit permits, including additional arrests, firings and anti-Semitic propaganda, while at the same time the rate of emigration continues at a high level." Maass went on to say that "many Jews here look at the negative factors as evidence that the President 'did nothing' for Soviet Jews while in Moscow and at the same time tend to ignore the favorable implications of increased emigration." He closed his letter reiterating his "strong feeling" that a meeting with the president was necessary.

Perle decided to capitalize on this frustration. On September 26, a month after the announcement of the diploma tax, the members of the National Conference held an emergency summit at the B'nai B'rith building in Washington. Something more than the usual statement of concern (followed by letters, demonstrations, and petitions) was in order. Most of the participants had spent the past few weeks staving off the appalled anger of their communities and executives boards. During this time, Perle had been working with sympathetic legislative aides to hammer out the details of an amendment to whatever trade bill would emerge from the Soviet-American trade negotiations, an amendment that would link benefits to behavior. The Jewish community was never going to be more receptive than at this moment. They needed a forceful response, and Jackson had one to offer. Perle arranged for the senator to address the gathering.

Jackson arrived with a copy of his proposed bill and immediately energized the room. He asked for more than their support; he asked to be their leader, a surrogate father, capable of harnessing their political power in ways they had never experienced. "The time has come to place our highest human values ahead of the trade dollar," he told them. "You know what you can do? I'll give you some marching orders. Get behind my amendment. And let's stand firm." There was a powerful logic to his idea, a moral clarity that was difficult to dispute—even if it was rooted in political ambition as much as in principle. Why should the Soviets get what they wanted without first making a real sacrifice? Jackson hit all the right notes, even invoking the Holocaust, and he received a standing ovation when he finished his twenty-minute speech. There was an undercurrent of shame motivating these local and national leaders. Here was a non-Jewish lawmaker proposing to go further and push harder for Jews than they themselves had been willing to do. After Jackson's speech, Perle stayed behind to try to influence the debate.

A few months earlier, Richard Maass had sent a memo to Jerry Goodman, the National Conference's executive director, saying that they should avoid upsetting détente, and specifically the planned trade agreement. "I am mindful that we do not seek to limit expanding trade—especially if President Nixon in Moscow favors large scale expansion," Maass had written. Yet Jackson was proposing to do just that. But rather than give in to their usual cautiousness, after a debate that lasted until three in the morning, the National Conference finally

decided unanimously to support the principle of the senator's amendment. The demand from the community was just too great to ignore,
and they would look out of touch if Jackson went ahead without them.
But the members were not naive about the consequences. It would be
a direct affront to the Nixon administration. This quickly became clear
after Richard Maass announced that the National Conference was going to back Jackson's initiative. Maass expressed anger and disappointment in the administration in a way that at least one newspaper, the
Los Angeles Times, characterized as "unusually strong for leaders of
what is sometimes called the 'Jewish Establishment.'"

Two days after the vote, following a meeting with some Jewish leaders in New York, Nixon made his dismissal of Jackson's proposal very
clear. The president's spokesman said that Nixon "does not intend to
politicize this issue." And furthermore, "the Soviet Union is well aware
of the United States' view on this matter. Nothing will be served by extensive public debate or extensive public confrontation on this issue in
the next six weeks." Six weeks, of course, was the time remaining before
the presidential election.

Jackson tried to gather as many Senate cosponsors for the bill as possible before the Ninety-second Congress adjourned. The victory would
be largely symbolic, since there was no time for a vote. But in some
ways this made the task easier. Senators needed only to agree to the
amendment in principle. The support of the Jewish establishment
helped immensely. Most states had at least a small Jewish population
bombarding senators' offices with phone calls and letters. Backing the
bill would cost the senators very little, but opposing it would mean
risking the ire of these possibly influential Jews. On top of this, no
politician wanted to be accused of appeasing the Soviets.

Jackson was quickly adding names to his list of cosponsors, and by
Saturday, September 30, he had reached thirty-two. Then he achieved
two major victories. First, he managed to get the support of Senators
Jacob Javits and Hubert Humphrey, both of whom had been working
on more moderate versions of Jackson's proposal. Javits, the Republican, thought the bill was "unnecessarily irritating" to the Nixon administration. But the National Conference's support of Jackson just a
few days before had won both men over. And once they capitulated, a

few influential liberals, such as Edward Kennedy and Edmund Muskie, joined as well.

Even more significant progress was made that Saturday afternoon in the Rose Garden of the White House. Jackson was attending the signing of the SALT agreement, whose passage he'd almost prevented. Nixon did not feel seriously threatened by Jackson's latest ploy. He didn't think the senator could pull it off. But with only a month until the election, the president knew that a public conversation about the Soviet Union and its emigration policies could cost him a few Jewish and anti-Communist votes. A confidential White House memo had just been leaked describing how disastrous Nixon's Moscow visit had been for the refuseniks—"they expressed the opinion that the United States seemed more interested in selling corn than in protesting human rights and individual freedom" was how the feelings of the Jewish activists were summed up. On an awkward forty-five-minute walk through the garden with Nixon, Jackson proposed a deal. If Nixon would release those Republican senators who wanted to support the amendment, Jackson would not push for a vote in the weeks before the election, in effect promising not to make Soviet Jewry into a political liability. The two shook hands, and within days, eight Nixon loyalists added their names to Jackson's list.

Amazingly, when Jackson stood up in the Senate on October 4 to introduce his bill, he had the commitment of seventy-two senators. Even though he was still dealing in symbolism rather than actual legislation, he knew he was well on his way. It would not be easy for these senators to retract in January the support they had promised in October. Jackson laid out his plan. No "non-market economy country," by which he meant no Communist state, could get most-favored-nation (MFN) status or any credits, credit guarantees, or investment guarantees. Only by removing all restrictions on emigration and eliminating any but the most nominal exit fees for leaving the country could this condition be waived. If a waiver was granted, the president would have to report semiannually to Congress on whether the country was keeping its word. In a press conference following the introduction of the bill, Jackson said that the Soviet diploma tax had been the impetus but that assuring basic human rights was the main motive. Nothing in the proposed bill referred specifically to Jews; Jackson simply pointed to Article 13 of the Universal Declaration of Human Rights—the first time since the declaration's ratification in 1948 that it would serve as the foundation of a proposed law. If he was motivated by his own presidential ambition, Jackson hid it well. He seemed to be acting out of pure principle. Yitzhak Rabin, Israel's ambassador to America, once recorded in his diary that the senator had told him, "Just imagine. If Norway had instituted a law similar to the one now in force in the Soviet Union for Jews, my father would not have been able to emigrate to the United States, and I would not be an American citizen now."

On October 18, two weeks after the bill's introduction, Nixon signed a trade agreement with the Soviets that eventually became the Trade Reform Act; Jackson would attach his amendment to this. The Soviets committed to paying back $722 million of the $11 billion they still owed America for the war materiel given to them to fight the Nazis, and in exchange, Nixon promised to provide the Soviets MFN status and authorize the Export-Import Bank of the United States to extend credit for purchases of American goods. As it was described in the papers the next day, a gallon of vodka was five dollars but with MFN status it would cost only a dollar fifty. After announcing the deal, William Rogers, the secretary of state, faced the inevitable question during his press conference: "Mr. Secretary, two-thirds of the Senate have put themselves on record as opposing ending discrimination against Russia unless they end discrimination against certain persons wishing to leave. How are you handling that problem?" Rogers answered, "I have had several meetings with the Jewish leaders in the country and I think there is a general feeling that the conduct of the Administration, what we are doing in the field of quiet diplomacy, holds the greatest promise of success and, after all, that is what we are all interested in, so I have nothing further to say on that today."

A little after eight that same evening, the Ninety-second Congress adjourned. A few weeks later, Nixon beat McGovern in a landslide, earning 37 percent of the Jewish vote, almost double that of 1968. The president saw this as a mandate to continue along the path he had laid out in his first term. Jackson was determined to stand in his way.

When the new session began, so did the real battle for the bill. Richard Perle worked on it every day. But he wasn't alone. Sprinkled among some of the key legislators were young, motivated Jewish aides like himself, people personally invested in issues like Israel and Soviet Jewry who were now in a position to do something about it. Senator Abraham Ribicoff's foreign affairs expert Morris Amitay spoke fluent Hebrew, had family living in Tiberius on the Sea of Galilee, and was constantly pushing Ribicoff, the only Jewish Democrat in the Senate, to support arms deals for the Jewish State. Perle was already motivated by his Cold Warrior outlook, and Amitay made him see the tribal reasons for supporting a bill that would help fellow Jews. Interviewed at the time for a book about Jewish political power and assuming he was speaking off the record, Amitay revealed how the background of these high-placed staffers made a difference:

> There are now a lot of guys at the working level up here who happen to be Jewish, who are willing to make a little bit of extra effort and to look at certain issues in terms of their Jewishness, and this is what has made this thing go very effectively in the last couple of years. These are all guys who are in a position to make the decisions in these areas for the senators. You don't need that many to get something done in the Senate. All you need is a certain commitment to get something done, if guys are willing to put time into that instead of a million other things they have to do, if they're willing to make a couple of calls, if they're willing to become involved, you can get an awful lot done just at the staff level.

From the beginning, Perle and Amitay had worked together closely. Once the battle moved to the House, they gained a third partner: Mark Talisman, legislative aide to Charles Vanik, a congressman from Cleveland whose district auspiciously included Lou Rosenblum's neighborhood. With many Soviet-bloc refugees among his constituents, Vanik championed the bill early on, introducing a version in the House in October 1972 before the end of the congressional session and giving his name to what would be known as the Jackson-Vanik amendment.

While the administration seemed to be ignoring Jackson's challenge, assuming it was simply posturing from an ambitious senator, the staffers were busy working out a plan for pushing the bill through the lower house of Congress. They decided to individually pressure every single House member. It might not take too much to convince them. It wasn't only the Jewish community that supported the bill; labor had signed on as well. George Meany, the head of the AFL-CIO, was even more opposed to détente than Jackson, especially when it came to trade. The labor movement would not stand for a trade deal that would turn the Soviets into competitors. Following the election, Meany got in touch with Jackson and pledged the backing of the unions. It would take an extremely secure—or foolish—politician to oppose a bill backed by both Jews and labor.

Still, the job of convincing individual House members was a big one. By Mark Talisman's count, sixty would support the bill because of the Jews in their districts, and sixty more would join because they were anti-Communists. But that left many others who needed special handling. Talisman spent ten days in January calling all 435 representatives' offices, sometimes speaking with members dozens of times before they added their names to the growing list of cosponsors. He tried to tailor his pitch and dispense with the generic "Dear Colleague" letter. Different approaches worked for different members. Some were moved by Holocaust guilt. Others were upset that Nixon had not consulted with Congress before signing the trade pact. The Jewish community helped make Perle's and Talisman's jobs easier. The grassroots force of the Union of Councils combined with the authoritativeness of the National Conference added effective pressure. Both groups directed their members to flood their respective House representatives with phone calls and letters. Perle met frequently with Lou Rosenblum. Yaakov Birnbaum often called him late at night. Jerry Goodman at the National Conference had to fight accusations by older Jewish leaders that his office had become merely an arm of Jackson's office.

At the local level, activists tried to humanize the issue for local representatives. They presented the stories of individual Jews. In many cases they got congresspeople on the phone with refuseniks. Conversations like this one—organized by the Minnesota Action Committee for Soviet Jewry—between Congressman Albert Quie of Minnesota and Boris Einbinder, a young Moscow activist, were very common:

CONGRESSMAN ALBERT QUIE: Hello, Professor Einbinder.
BORIS EINBINDER: Yes, it is me.
AQ: Hello, hello.
BE: Hello, yes.

AQ: Yes, this is Congressman Quie from Minnesota. How are you?
BE: All right. Pardon me, I don't know who you are.
AQ: Q-U-I-E . . . I am a member of Congress in the United States.
BE: Yes, I see. Have we spoken before?
AQ: I have not spoken to you before, but I have talked to friends of yours, and am interested in you and wondering how you were and how's your health?

Einbinder explained how he had just been detained in prison for fifteen days for participating in a demonstration. Congressman Quie listened raptly and after the conversation promised the small Minneapolis Soviet Jewry group that he would do whatever he could to support the amendment.

Through this kind of informal and concerted lobbying, the Washington group—as the collection of Jewish staffers led by Perle was soon known—signed up many of the cosponsors, including Wilbur Mills, the powerful chairman of the Ways and Means Committee. Grassroots Jewish power had never been mobilized so strategically before. Morris Amitay talked at the time about how the Washington group deployed their secret weapon:

> If we get a senator from an industrial state, a state with a sizeable Jewish population, and he doesn't come out [for the Jackson Amendment], we don't let him get away with it. That's when we call for outside help. . . . What you have in this country is a fantastic, untapped reservoir of Jews who are in influential positions who were never asked to help. And now it's just a matter of finding them and asking them to help. There are so many Jewish organizations, so many Jewish people sitting out in small towns in Iowa and in Oregon, and there are rabbis with congregations, who are just dying to get a call saying, "We need help with somebody. Can you help?" They understand the issue immediately—you're dealing with very sophisticated people.

With Mills onboard, the bill seemed unstoppable, and suddenly both the White House and the Soviets were taking notice. Nixon had allowed Republican senators to support it because he didn't think the amendment would amount to anything. Talisman's clandestine vote collecting had masked how much progress was being made. When Mills made the announcement that he and 259 House members were supporting the amendment, the White House was truly surprised. Within a few weeks, another thirty more would join.

Henry Kissinger now woke up to the threat. The Jewish secretary of state—the highest post a Jew had ever achieved in government—was now in the seemingly uncomfortable position of standing up to a bill that the Jewish community had rallied behind in force. But Kissinger, an enigmatic man in many ways whose ideological allegiances were sometimes as hard to pin down as his gravelly, German-accented voice was to understand, was not one to feel the tribal pull. If anything was consistent about his worldview, it was a cold pragmatism that put stability above all else and eschewed the emotional forces that were driving American Jews. Though he took pains not to delve into it too deeply—in public at least—his identity as a refugee who had barely escaped the Holocaust had a lot to do with his adoption of realpolitik. Most Jews of his generation had drawn one lesson from the war—that they would never again abandon their brethren. Out of the upheaval that had intruded on his young life, Kissinger had drawn a different lesson, one that would guide him as he entered this battle and make him impervious to the appeals of his fellow Jews.

Kissinger had grown up in the small Bavarian town of Fürth, the son of a teacher, a comfortable middle-class upbringing as part of a segregated but not yet despised Jewish minority. He was ten when the Nazis came to power. Within five years, in 1938, his family had fled to America, where he began his rise, which took him from the German-Jewish enclave of Washington Heights to City College, the U.S. Army, Harvard, and eventually to the White House. When still at an impressionable age, though, he had observed firsthand the fickleness of democratic institutions, how easily Weimar Germany had crumbled and how no one stood up against the ensuing chaos. It was this experience above all that had seared his consciousness and made him forever wary of democracy's ability to sustain itself on its own. Experienced hands needed to guide foreign policy and keep it from being dictated by passion. The role of a diplomat—like his great hero Metternich—was to maintain a balance of power in the world, keeping at bay the forces that threatened peace and stability. This also meant being realistic: human rights and ethical considerations could be compromised when dealing with other states. He observed with dismay and annoyance the zeal of those intent on making a giant cause out of Soviet Jewry and obstructing détente. It's not that he didn't care about Soviet Jews—he thought that behind-the-scenes dealmaking could ease their problems—only that he thought that they distracted from a more significant calculation: how to make the Soviet-American relationship less adversarial, more consistent and predictable. For this goal, which he saw as his mission in government, he was going to find himself opposed to most American Jews, who were guided by different imperatives.

When Kissinger, that paragon of Jewish accomplishment, began pressing congresspeople to turn against Jackson, he was effectively trying to persuade mostly non-Jewish lawmakers to ignore the demands of their Jewish constituents.

On March 1, Nixon met with the Israeli prime minister, Golda Meir, and Rabin. The president tried to convince her that the administration's tactic of "quiet diplomacy" was more effective than the proposed amendment would be and asked her to lean on the Jewish community to stop supporting the bill. "The problem is that the members of Congress say they are guided by the Jewish organizations here. The future of détente with the Soviet Union is liable to be foiled by the Congress. Personally I can get better results for you," Nixon told her. Kissinger, who was standing nearby, tried to drive home the point: "Don't let the Jewish leadership here put pressure on the Congress." Golda Meir replied: "You must understand my situation. I cannot tell Jews in the United States not to concern themselves with their brethren in the Soviet Union!" Kissinger's pressure tactics were useless. Israel had decided early on to stay out of the fight publicly; it did not want to be caught between two branches of the American government or to be accused of stirring up Cold War tension. It was hard for Kissinger to believe, but the only ones with the power to stop this snowball were the formerly docile leaders of the Jewish community.

The Kremlin was also getting the picture. Nixon made sure of this by sending treasury secretary George Shultz to Moscow in early March to give Brezhnev a lesson on the American political system, specifically about how easily the legislature could upset the objectives of the executive branch. In a Politburo meeting on March 20, the effects of this tutorial were clear. Not only did Brezhnev understand the political dynamic in the United States, he also acknowledged the power of the activists. With a June summit in Washington fast approaching—a follow-up to Nixon's 1972 trip to Moscow—he showed his irritation. "When you read the materials, and I read everything, then you see that, all the same, the official visit to the U.S. has been seriously impeded by the issue of Zionism," Brezhnev told the Politburo. "In the last few months, hysteria has been whipped up around the so-called education tax on individuals emigrating abroad. I have thought a lot about what to do." He then got angry at Yuri Andropov, head of the KGB, for not following the order Brezhnev had given him at the last Politburo session to "stop collecting the taxes, that is, without repealing the law, let out a group of 500 Jews who have no relation to either secret work or to party organizations. Even if some middle-aged people fall into the group, say from Birobidzhan, let them out. They will talk about it and everyone will know."

Andropov apologized and pointed out that a few people had indeed left without being charged. But Brezhnev just got more worked up. He started rattling off statistics about how many educated Jews had emigrated and how many thousands of rubles they had paid to get out. "This is why the Zionists are yelling," he said. "Jackson relies on this, and Kissinger comes to Dobrynin and says, 'We understand that this is an internal matter and we can't interfere. We also have laws.' At the same time he says: 'Help us out somehow. Nixon can push through the [trade] legislation. He's working with the senators.'" Then Brezhnev asked whether all this headache was worth the money collected so far from the education tax: "Why do we need that million?"

"There's no need to repeal the law," he reiterated. "We agreed not to change the law. But at this particular time, when the Zionists have incited a campaign around the Jackson Amendment and around the bill granting us [most favored nation] status, we need to let them out."

Strangely, Brezhnev then went even further, wondering in a bizarre ramble why more couldn't be done to appease the "Zionists." But his ideas betrayed how little he understood about the Soviet Jewish condition: "Why not give them some little theater with 500 seats for a Jewish variety show that will work under our censorship with a repertoire under our supervision. Let Auntie Sonya sing Jewish wedding songs there. I'm not proposing this, I'm just talking. And what if we open a school? I see it like this: we could open one school in Moscow and call it Jewish. The program would be the same as in other schools. But the national language, Yiddish, would be taught there."

He chided himself for this "impudent thought," but it was clear he wanted his colleagues to think more creatively about the "Jewish question." Aleksei Kosygin, the premier, agreed with him. "Of course, we need to think, because we are creating the Jewish problem for ourselves." Brezhnev concurred. "Zionism," he said, "is making us stupid."

The same day, foreign reporters and an American television crew were invited to film Jews being called to Moscow's OVIR office and told that their fees had been waived. American newspapers reported that over the course of two days, March 19 and March 20, forty-four Soviet Jews were given permission to leave without having to pay the tax. "Soviet Waives Its Exit Tax for Five Leaving for Israel," the *New York Times* reported on its front page. Writing in, of all places, the Israeli newspaper *Yediot Aharonot* on the day following the Politburo meeting, the journalist and not-so-secret KGB agent Victor Louis, Andropov's messenger for disseminating information in the Western media, reported that the tax would no longer be enforced. Just as Brezhnev had ordered, it would remain on the books but for all intents and purposes would be ignored. "It seems that the Soviet citizens who have decided to emigrate from the Soviet Union have won a victory in the six month war against the education tax."

Jackson considered himself vindicated. The Soviets would abandon their policies if the price was right. But this new development caused the American Jewish leadership to reassess their support of Jackson. What was the ultimate goal of this campaign? Was Jackson merely trying to eliminate the diploma tax or did he have a more extreme objective in mind? For those who had simply wanted to see the debilitating tax done away with, the Kremlin's move was enough. But Jackson and Perle made it clear that they had no intention of backing down on the amendment. On March 22, 1973, Jackson told the New York Press Club: "Now, I have heard it said that the Soviets are going to keep the ransom tax on the statute books but they won't apply it in practice. I say that we are going to put the Jackson amendment on the statute books but in the hope that it won't apply to the Soviet Union because they will be in compliance with the free emigration provision."

The extent to which Jackson was getting ahead of some of his Jewish supporters was apparent in a memo written by a clearly agitated Bert Gold, the executive director of the American Jewish Committee. He described what had happened on a recent visit to Jackson's office. He ran into Perle, whom he depicted as "a brash, opinionated, frequently arrogant young man." Gold made the mistake of wondering out loud if Brezhnev's willingness to drop the tax might preclude the need for the Jackson amendment.

> No sooner did I even finish the first question when he fell upon me like 16 tons of bricks, suggesting that the very asking of the question suggested a selling-out, a back-tracking, etc., etc. I calmly (for a while, calmly, anyway) suggested that if guys like us can't discuss such things and try to evaluate what the effect might be, then we are not helping our joint cause. But it didn't work. He kept asserting that whatever the rumors, whatever the *facts,* the amendment is going to be adopted, etc. When I then said that it just might happen that the Jackson amendment *might* achieve its ends even without having actually to be adopted — *if* it should turn out to be true that the Soviets were willing to change their practices — he got absolutely hysterical, and raised his voice with declamations that stopped everybody from working and they all listened to the rest of the conversation.

"What the hell have you done in the last couple of days to get support for the amendment?" Perle shouted then. Gold wrote: "I stood up and said I simply won't take that kind of crap, I had nothing to explain to him, our record was too clear to need any justification. At which point, Perle's superior, Dorothy Fosdick, rose from her chair, and screamed at me: 'Now you just get out of here! Get out! Nobody is going to insult Dick Perle or any member of my staff.' After a minute or so of hesitation, I left, of course. Her parting words were that she'd report me to Scoop."

Jackson's staff wanted the Jewish community behind them, but they didn't want to deal with people like Gold who argued that "flexibility and moderation" might be a better strategy. Now that the initial impetus for the bill—the diploma tax—seemed to be no longer an issue, doubts from certain leaders would grow. And the brashness that everyone had come to associate with Perle would flash often and brightly.

Henry Kissinger thought he had all the proof he needed to convince the senators to back off: two letters from the Soviet ambassador Anatoly Dobrynin definitively affirming that the diploma tax would be suspended. On April 18, Nixon invited Jackson, Ribicoff, Javits, and three other, more accommodating senators to meet with him at the White House. The president opened harshly, practically berating Jackson. His amendment would not only obliterate future Soviet-American trade but also jeopardize Brezhnev's upcoming trip to Washington. Kissinger dramatically pulled out Dobrynin's two communications and read them to the assembled senators. Jackson listened carefully and then told Nixon, "Mr. President, if you believe that, you're being hoodwinked." Ribicoff added that "there's nothing new in this. We have known about the suspensions for several weeks. But that in no way diminishes the need for passage of the Jackson amendment." The meeting ended. This was the senators' final word. As Jackson put it in a one-sentence press release following the meeting, "I am standing firm on my amendment, period."

With the senators unmovable, Nixon and Kissinger resorted to plan B: strip Jackson of his Jewish support. If the two men had really understood the popularity of the amendment, they would have realized the futility of this tactic. But they didn't. Nixon imagined threats could work, yelling that "a storm will hit American Jews if they are intransigent." Instead of employing scare tactics, Henry Kissinger preferred a combination of flattery and pressure. And there were two prominent Jewish leaders in particular who were ripe for influencing: Max Fisher and Jacob Stein.

A retired multimillionaire who had devoted his life to Jewish philanthropy and the Republican Party, Fisher was a strange kind of Jew, anti-intellectual and plainspoken. The son of a storeowner, he had grown up in the decidedly un-Jewish Salem, Ohio, and went on to Ohio State University on a football scholarship. When he graduated, he joined his father's new venture, a small oil-reclaiming business in Detroit. In a few years, he turned it into one of the biggest gas station chains in the Midwest; it was worth $40 million when he sold it, in 1959, and he invested most of that money in lucrative real estate. Fisher's affinity for the GOP led to his becoming the financial chairman for Michigan governor George Romney's presidential run in 1968. When Nixon beat Romney in the primaries, Fisher joined the national campaign and was responsible — as the new administration saw it — for lifting the Jewish Republican vote from Barry Goldwater's dismal 10 percent to Nixon's 17 and then 37 percent. Fisher had a tendency to imply that he was speaking for the whole community, and he became a sort of unofficial Jewish adviser to the president, given incredible access. His sidekick was Jacob Stein, a millionaire who had made his money developing shopping malls in Long Island and had recently become the head of the Presidents Conference, the powerful umbrella organization charged with preserving a united voice on Israel. He was less doctrinaire than Fisher but still had deep ties to the Nixon administration that he didn't want to jeopardize.

Kissinger assumed that Fisher and Stein were his way into the Jewish community, so the day following the meeting with the senators, April 19, he invited them and a dozen other Jewish leaders to the White House to meet with the president. It was a historic event — an American president had finally chosen to make time for Soviet Jewry. The great lesson — one the activists hoped the establishment was learning — was that this had come about only as a result of Jewish opposition. Kissinger again passed around the Dobrynin letters. "You're now back to August 1972," Kissinger said, referring to the month the diploma tax was instituted. The effect on them was entirely different than the effect on the senators. It was disorienting. They were being openly courted by the president. Nixon acknowledged the weakness of his position, saying that if Jackson's bill were voted on that day, "I know the amendment would go through like that," and he snapped his fingers. He then pleaded with them not to help Jackson destroy détente. His policies were important; they would bring peace and ultimately help the Soviet Jews. "You gentlemen have more faith in your senators than you do in me," Nixon excoriated them. "And that is a mistake. You'll save more Jews my way. Protest all you want. The Kremlin won't listen." Fisher and

Stein were certainly receptive. Others were less so, but they had a hard time challenging Nixon, especially when he repeated his commitment to helping Soviet Jews and waved the Soviet memos around, tangible proof that the Russians had indeed conceded. After seventy minutes the meeting was over and the participants left the White House, with some now converted. One approached William Safire, the president's speechwriter, on his way out and, referring to Nixon, whispered, "This may be the only thing I trust him about."

Following the meeting, the leaders gathered in Max Fisher's office to put together a press release. Fisher managed to control the deliberations, which in the end produced a vague three-paragraph statement praising the president's support of Soviet Jewry and, strangely, neglecting to mention anything about Jackson or his amendment. It was a glaring omission, and it suggested that the community was abandoning the senator. As the *New York Times* reported the next day, it was apparent that a "struggle for the support of the Jewish community was under way between Mr. Nixon and Senator Henry M. Jackson." The paper added that the "overwhelming Congressional backing" for the amendment "could fade away if the Jewish leaders begin withdrawing their support."

Richard Perle went crazy when he read the statement. He knew how popular the amendment had become among the grass roots. And so he used all his resources, drawing on his contacts in the Union of Councils and Student Struggle, pleading with them to voice their disapproval of the diminishing support for Jackson. Suddenly, Fisher and Stein had an insurrection on their hands. Richard Maass and Jerry Goodman, the heads of the National Conference, could hardly contain the anger. Constituent members of the National Conference independently restated their support for Jackson and the amendment. The biggest defection came when Richard Perle called Malcolm Hoenlein, the head of the large New York Soviet Jewry umbrella group. Hoenlein felt he had to reflect the desires of his constituency, and even though he was nominally under the authority of the National Conference, he issued a statement in the name of the seventy-four local organizations that he represented reaffirming their backing of the Jackson amendment. This was the entire Jewish community of New York. Two million people. And it could not be ignored. Neither could Lou Rosenblum's Union of Councils, two dozen groups spread all over the country, or Student Struggle, both of which immediately emphasized their unwavering support for Jackson.

Rosenblum made sure Soviet Jewish activists in Moscow would have a say in the debate. After all, he figured, it was their fate being discussed. Over a crackling line, he spoke with Kyrill Henkin, a refusenik whose command of English had made him a spokesman of sorts. Rosenblum explained that Jewish leaders had turned their backs on the community's wishes: "They had their own interests at heart or they sought to advance their own position. You understand?" It wasn't clear if Henkin understood exactly what his American friend wanted. But when Rosenblum called back, Henkin was ready with an emotional statement signed by a hundred refuseniks, including Volodya Slepak, and aimed, as he put it, at "the leaders of Jewish organizations of the United States": "Remember—the history of our people has known many terrible mistakes. Do not give in to soothing deceit. Remember—your smallest hesitation may cause irreparable tragic results. Remember—your firmness and steadfastness are our only hope. Now, as never before, our fate depends on you. Can you retreat at such a moment?"

The conflict came to a head on April 30 during a meeting of the Presidents Conference (there was a tacit agreement that any big policy decisions would be approved by the umbrella group). Stein and Fisher made their last stand. Stein, chairman of the Presidents Conference, argued that opposing the president so openly would undermine the link to the White House. It would exacerbate the Cold War and alienate Nixon, who perhaps was the only one capable of achieving any real progress through quiet diplomacy. A few people supported his position. But the past week had turned most of the participants combative and angry, and soon a statement was produced that articulated the position of American Jews: though they had "appreciation" for the "initiatives of President Nixon," the Jackson amendment had "contributed" to the "effort to alleviate the plight of Soviet Jewry and we continue our support for this legislation."

Defeated, Stein and Fisher, along with Maass, met with Kissinger the next night and informed him of the community's decision. There was nothing they could do. The issue had become too emotional for Jews.

Kissinger was to travel the next day to Moscow for talks with Brezhnev, and they gave him a list of eight hundred refuseniks to discuss with the Soviet leader. Kissinger said he would see what he could do. Resigned, he told them, "Look, you go your way and I'll take my road and we'll meet in the fall," when the bill would presumably be brought up for a vote in the House.

By now, Jackson had spent a year fighting for his amendment. It had taken on larger significance for him as a stand against a misguided American foreign policy. Morality, he believed, had been sucked out of decision making. He was placing so much importance on emigration because it was a gateway right; the bigger issue was that human rights should guide American policy. As he explained that summer in a commencement address at Yeshiva University, where ten years earlier Yaakov Birnbaum had called on religious students to rally for the little-known cause of Soviet Jewry: "Of all the human rights contained in the Universal Declaration of the United Nations none is more fundamental than that in Article 13—the right to free emigration. And as we assess the developing détente there is no more basic measure than its impact on the free movement of people. The importance of free emigration stems from the fact that whatever other liberties may be denied—speech, press, religion, employment—any and all of these can be restored by emigration to the free countries of the West. Of human rights, emigration is first among equals."

The forcefulness Jackson projected also had to do with a changing political landscape. At the end of April, Nixon's attorney general and his two closest aides, H. R. Haldeman and John Ehrlichman, had resigned over their connection to a break-in at the headquarters of the Democratic National Committee (at the Watergate hotel). And the day before Jackson's speech at Yeshiva, John Dean, the former White House counsel (recently fired by the president), had admitted talking with Nixon at least thirty-five times about how to cover up the crime. Jackson saw weakness and he attacked, ripping détente apart piece by piece. "Now, the White House prefers to use 'quiet diplomacy,' and with that they dismiss the tough bargain that the Jackson amendment calls for," the senator told the Yeshiva audience. "Well, we have seen that sort of 'quiet diplomacy' before. . . . It got us a new wave of repression and trials following the Moscow summit. It got us the infamous education ransom. It brought about the appearance of détente and the reality of an even lower Soviet tolerance of individual liberty."

Jackson and his allies were now on the offensive. The Soviets didn't really know what to do anymore. They had abandoned the diploma tax, so they assumed the problem would go away. If they went any further—actually putting in place an emigration process or letting more Jews go—it would mean acknowledging that they were altering their system in response to American pressure. Brezhnev made it very clear that the Soviets were unwilling to do this. On the eve of his visit to Washington in mid-June, uncharacteristically, he let foreign journalists ask him questions at a Kremlin press briefing. Most of the time was spent on the Jackson amendment. Brezhnev laughed off the questions nonchalantly: "We do not have in the Soviet Union any law forbidding a Soviet citizen from leaving the Soviet Union and going to another country if that departure is justified. Now I'm sure that any nation has a law whereby it is forbidden for certain categories of people connected with national security from leaving their country. Now I don't want to assert this—I'm not all that sure—but I'm told that there is such a law in Israel, too. And I'm sure the United States has rules to that effect."

A few days later Brezhnev was in the capital meeting with members of the Senate foreign relations committee and rattling off emigration figures from a little red book he kept in his pocket. He made claims that were maddeningly false; for example, he said that 97 percent of visa requests were approved. The supporters of the Jackson amendment never got close enough to grill him. His visit didn't elicit the kind of large protests the Soviet Jewry activists had hoped for. The summit had been announced only three weeks earlier, and the National Conference, even with its tentacles in every Jewish community, couldn't manage to get more than twelve thousand people to the Washington Mall. Israel had granted a State Department request that Meir Kahane's passport be suspended so he couldn't fly to Washington and lie down in the street.

The Jewish leaders who did come across to Brezhnev on that visit were the ones who had lost all credibility on this issue with the Jewish community: Fisher and Stein. On Monday night, June 18, the two were invited to a White House state dinner for the Soviet premier. Fisher, a Republican loyalist, could hardly refuse the president's invitation. Only a few weeks earlier, at the height of the Watergate scandal, he had written Nixon a short note pledging his support: "Mr. President: With all your problems, let me say that anything I can do to [be] helpful to you, I am available to the fullest extent of my time and ability." As for Stein, he sincerely thought this might be an opportunity for some quiet diplomacy and was undeterred by the Jews who had set up pickets outside his home and yelled shrilly that he was stabbing his fellow Jews in the back by dining with a modern Hitler. When Nixon and Brezhnev walked down the receiving line in the Blue Room, the president stopped in front of Fisher and Stein and pointed out to Brezhnev that these were Jewish leaders.

During the reception, the two cornered Gromyko, the Soviet foreign minister, and suggested that maybe the Jewish issues could be settled quietly, between them, and without bullhorns and bombs. Gromyko passed the message on to Dobrynin, and a few weeks later, Fisher and Stein and their wives found themselves having lunch with Anatoly Dobrynin beneath a crystal chandelier at the Soviet embassy. "I do not know why right now the Jewish community is pushing for Jackson-Vanik," Dobrynin told them. "I do not understand it. The levels of emigration are going up. I, myself, have a lot of Jewish friends in the Soviet Union. I play chess with them when I go home." Dobrynin's wife, exasperated that Fisher and Stein kept bringing the conversation back to the business of liberalizing emigration, chimed in at one point, saying, "Why don't we put all our Jews on a TWA plane and send them to the United States?" "Could you do that?" Fisher answered excitedly. "We would be happy to pay their way."

By the fall of 1973, the Jackson-Vanik amendment looked unstoppable. But then fate gave Kissinger one more chance to make his case to American Jews. Egypt and Syria's attack on Israel on October 6, Yom Kippur, the holiest day of the Jewish year, destroyed the confidence Israel had gained since the Six-Day War. Israel eventually prevailed, but only after a few incredibly tense days—Golda Meir even prepared cyanide pills for herself in case Israel had to capitulate—and only with massive American help. Five hundred and sixty-five cargo flights brought twenty-two thousand tons of materiel to counter the Soviet tanks, guns, and fighter jets that were arriving by the hour in Cairo and Damascus. Kissinger tried to use Israel's sudden dependence to his advantage. At a moment of high anxiety, with Israel circling Egypt's Third Army in a precarious checkmate, the secretary of state warned Jewish leaders that persisting with the Jackson amendment was dangerous, that it would antagonize the Soviets at a moment when their cooperation was needed to arrive at an armistice agreement. He wanted them to drop it. Not surprisingly, people like Max Fisher and Jacob Stein were receptive and tried to argue Kissinger's case. Jackson fought back hard. "The administration is always using you," he told them during a particularly tense meeting at his office. "The only way to get Soviet Jews out of the Soviet Union is to stand firm on the Jackson-Vanik amendment."

That's exactly what the Jewish community did. Even Stein and Fisher knew that they were basically a constituency of two. The only other force in Jewish life offering any opposition to the amendment was the American Jewish Congress, whose president, Arthur Hertzberg, had recently been cornered by a group of angry students. Passing the amendment in full, Hertzberg warned, "will result in the closing of the doors of Russia." A few weeks after the Yom Kippur War's end, the situation in Israel eased considerably, and American Jews were again ready to focus on the Soviet Union. Nixon was weak and preoccupied, consumed by his mounting troubles—in late November, the press revealed that the White House tapes the president had handed over contained a mysterious, unexplained eighteen-and-a-half-minute gap of buzzing white noise. Kissinger was distracted too, running the country's foreign policy on his own and shuttling constantly from Moscow to Cairo to Tel Aviv. On December 4, after requesting numerous times that the vote be delayed, Nixon finally accepted the inevitable, that the trade bill would go forward—though he warned that he would deem it "unacceptable" if it arrived with the Jackson amendment attached.

In the weeks leading up to the vote, the amendment took on renewed moral urgency. In a powerful letter of support from Moscow, Andrei Sakharov—who along with Solzhenitsyn had been facing increasing harassment by the KGB—wrote that the bill represented "a defense of international law, without which there can be no mutual trust." To abandon it in the face of Soviet opposition would be tantamount "to total capitulation of democratic principles in the face of blackmail, deceit and violence. The consequences of such a capitulation for international confidence, détente and the entire future of mankind are difficult to predict." Sakharov's letter made it nearly impossible to vote against Jackson-Vanik. Who wanted to debate the great dissident's invocation of American principle? Liberals, who up until then had been silent partners to Jackson, suddenly spoke up loudly. Arthur Schlesinger wrote in the *Wall Street Journal* that one must "always trust the man on the firing line." I. F. Stone reached the same conclusion in the pages of the *New York Review of Books*. So did Anthony Lewis in the *New York Times*. Sakharov's words further bound together Soviet Jewry and the human rights movement. He knew that Jews would be the biggest beneficiaries of liberalized emigration, but he did not harp on that fact. He folded their fight into a greater struggle for openness. This made it easier for a wider circle of people to support Soviet Jewry and gave the activists a larger stage from which to shout.

Finally, on December 11, a year and a half after the introduction of the Soviet diploma tax that inspired it, the Jackson-Vanik amendment came to a vote in the House. It passed overwhelmingly, 319 to 80. Then the entire trade bill, with the amendment intact, passed, 272 to 140. For American Jews, this was a victory, not just over the Nixon administration but also over their own accommodationist elements. It seemed the Jewish community was finally ready to take action. Having the leadership of a respected senator helped, but in the end they themselves had decided to take a great risk. Kissinger's argument that they would have to choose between Israel and Soviet Jews was also shown to be a ploy—on the same day the Jackson-Vanik amendment passed, the House approved $2.2 billion in aid to Israel.

Henry Jackson now had a choice. If he brought his amendment to a vote in the Senate, it would surely pass. But the Soviets would most likely balk at the demands and reject the trade bill altogether. The other option was to make a deal. Even though he was ideologically opposed to the concept of détente, he was practical. He wanted his amendment to lead to actual changes. With that in mind, Jackson decided to come up with some concrete conditions, a settlement agreement on his terms. The amendment would be made law, but if the Soviets met these requirements, they would gain an automatic waiver. As long as the president could prove to Congress through regular reports that the Russians were abiding by the conditions, they could keep their trade benefits. Jackson and Perle realized that this way they could use their leverage to actually increase Soviet Jewish emigration—which was, after all, the goal.

Kissinger was finally facing up to the inevitability of the amendment. He railed against the bill every chance he got, denouncing it as "counterproductive" to both détente and emigration and never missing an opportunity to tell Jewish and Israeli leaders that they were jeopardizing Middle East peace. But in fact he had resigned himself to its passage. Because of Watergate, all the work of détente that he and Nixon had delicately constructed over the past two years was crumbling. By early 1974, the Russians were less willing to keep cooperating. If Kissinger hoped to maintain any sort of relationship with them, he needed to demonstrate that he could deliver the trading terms they wanted. So he was open to the idea of compromise.

To start with, Jackson and Perle aimed high. In addition to ending all harassment of applicants, the Soviets had to grant a minimum of one hundred thousand visas a year. On March 6, in a meeting at the State Department, Jackson presented Kissinger with his terms. Like a bargainer in a bazaar, though, he told the secretary that first he wanted to know what the Soviets were willing to offer. As it turned out, Kissinger was scheduled to be in Moscow later that month. He was doubtful they would accept the notion of a deal, but he agreed to feel them out. A week later, Perle had a list of five principles the Soviets needed to agree to if negotiations were to continue.

To Kissinger's great surprise, Brezhnev and Gromyko were willing to talk. At some point during the twenty hours of conversation at the Kremlin, they said they could commit to keeping emigration at 1973 levels (about thirty-five thousand a year). This wasn't any great concession, but it did signify progress. No longer were the Soviet leaders protesting in public and private that they would never stand for meddling in their internal affairs ("Would you agree to making United States trade with the USSR dependent on the solution of the racial problem in the United States?" an angry Soviet official had once asked). It seemed that they understood that Jackson and the Jewish community had the power to deny them what they wanted. Brezhnev would finally have to appease the "Zionists" by doing more than just organizing a Jewish variety show for them.

Kissinger returned from his trip. And at a party at the Israeli embassy a few days later, just before he was to leave on his honeymoon with Nancy Maginnes Kissinger, his new wife, he pulled Jackson aside and told him what had happened. Jackson didn't think it was much of an offer and neither did his Senate cosponsors Javits and Ribicoff. When they all met again with Kissinger at the end of April, they told him he would have to do better. The dynamic of the next few months was established. Kissinger became the go-between, eliciting offers from the Kremlin, bringing them back to Jackson, and then returning with counteroffers. Much would rest on whether Kissinger was dealing in good faith.

The negotiations were overshadowed by Nixon's slow demise. In May, transcripts of the president's White House tapes were released. Nixon apparently used the expression *Jew boy* with some regularity. Meanwhile, the secretary of state was shuttling around the world, occupied with the aftermath of the Yom Kippur War. But he was also negotiating with Gromyko and bringing the information back to Jackson. The Soviets had increased their offer to forty-five thousand visas a year and promised to issue a statement saying that harassment was "inconsistent with Soviet law." But just as Kissinger was making progress, Nixon emerged with a scathing critique of Jackson, which he delivered at Annapolis during the graduation ceremony of the U.S. Naval Academy. "Eloquent appeals are now being made for the United States, through its foreign policy, to transform the internal as well as the international behavior of other countries, especially the Soviet Union." But, he said, "our primary concern must be to help influence the international conduct of nations in the world arena. We would not welcome the intervention of other countries in our domestic affairs, and we cannot expect them to be cooperative when we seek to intervene in theirs."

Nixon and Kissinger took another trip to Moscow that summer, a strange summit, given the inevitability of impeachment. The Soviets had a hard time taking Nixon or his promises seriously, and Congress debated whether to prevent him from making any commitments.

Jackson and the Jewish leaders were frustrated by the slow pace. In fact, to listen to Brezhnev as he raised one of many glasses of vodka on Nixon's first night in Moscow, it was unclear whether there was any compromise in the works at all. Expressing his desire for further trade relations, Brezhnev said, "Experience shows that progress along this path requires effort—sometimes quite a bit of it. The relaxation of tensions in Soviet-American relations, as in international relations generally, comes up against rather active resistance." Smiling in the direction of Nixon, Brezhnev added, "There is no need for me to dwell on this subject since our American guests know better and in more detail than we about those who oppose international détente, who favor whipping up the arms race and returning to the methods and mores of the cold war." These were the words of a man on the defensive reassuring another man on the defensive. But they highlighted the extent to which Jackson and his ideas had become an insurmountable obstacle for both of them.

On Friday morning, August 9, at Andrews Air Force Base, Nixon lifted both his arms above his head, hunched his shoulders, and made a V-for-victory sign with both hands before being whisked away from Washington forever. Only then did Jackson's amendment begin to pick up steam. Gerald Ford, the new president, had been a longtime member of Congress and was close to the legislative body; three days after being sworn in, he promised a "good marriage" with the branch of government that had become so antagonistic to Nixon. From the start, he was much more amenable to compromising with Jackson. Back in May when he was still vice president, Ford had met with Jewish leaders, and he'd left them with a positive impression. Jerry Goodman wrote in a memo that "he expressed wonderment that two reasonable people like Henry Kissinger and Henry Jackson could not somehow work out the situation. . . . It was suggested that he, Mr. Ford, might try his hand at getting the two Henrys together."

The Soviets knew that Ford was a different type of political animal. They were suddenly motivated to make deeper sacrifices in order to salvage the trade bill. On August 14, Ford met with Dobrynin and told the Soviet ambassador that he was sympathetic to the emigration argument and that no trade bill would pass until the Soviets accepted

some form of the Jackson amendment. The next day, Jackson, Ribicoff, and Javits had breakfast with Ford at the White House. (It was the
first time that a president had gotten directly involved in the negotiations—Nixon had always left this job to Kissinger.) They all reiterated
the formula. The amendment would pass as it was. The strict trade
restrictions would be left in. The onus would now be on the Soviets.
If they stuck to the promises they had made—an immediate increase
in emigration to the agreed-upon number and an end to all harassment—then a waiver would be granted. It would be the president's job
to ensure that they were keeping up their end of the bargain. If they
didn't—if the Soviets fell short by even one person—then Ford would
be forbidden to use his waiver. Jackson was giddy after the meeting,
telling the press corps that "the President's direct intervention in this
matter, which is a new development, has given it new momentum, new
movement . . ." Asked whether he would demand something in writing from the Soviets, Jackson said: "That is up to the President, he is
the one who will have to guarantee, and what arrangements he makes
with the Russians, that will be a matter for him. But he has assured us
that whatever is worked out that he will see that guarantees are there,
period. And we will rely on his integrity for those assurances, and we
have faith in that integrity."

All through late August and early September, Perle worked on writing the waiver language into the bill and formulating the letters that
would constitute the heart of the deal. On the evening of September 6, Kissinger, Jackson, and Dobrynin agreed the letters would be
exchanged two weeks from then, when Gromyko visited Washington.
And they agreed on a number: sixty thousand exit visas—a compromise between the forty-five thousand offered by the Soviets and the
seventy-five to a hundred thousand proposed by Jackson. Perle had
worried that if the number was too low, the Soviets could let Jews who
lived outside the major cities emigrate—like those Jews from Georgia—and still avoid giving exit visas to the scientists and doctors of
Moscow and Leningrad. With a number as high as sixty thousand,
Perle was satisfied there would be a real change.

On September 20, Ford held back-to-back meetings with Jackson
and Gromyko. Leaving the Oval Office after his appointment, the senator ran into the Soviet foreign minister in the waiting area. Jackson,

who knew he was viewed by the Kremlin as a villain, wanted to ease the tension with a bit of humor. He put his fingers up to his head to make the horns of a devil. Gromyko, a grim man who years before had earned the Washington moniker Comrade Nyet, looked puzzled. His translator tried to explain while Jackson stood there awkwardly, but Gromyko remained bewildered. Their exchanges with the president went more smoothly, and by the end of the day, the details were agreed upon by all.

It still took another month before it could be voted on by the Senate. The nature of the deal—involving a convoluted exchange of letters in which Kissinger vouched for the Soviet promises on behalf of the executive branch, and Jackson laid out Congress's conditions—lent itself to confusion and misinterpretation. At one point Kissinger refused to sign. He and Jackson even stopped speaking. Only the Jewish community's pressure—now they were pushing the senator who had for so long been dragging them along—forced Jackson back to the negotiating table.

Finally, on October 18, Jackson, Javits, and Vanik met with Kissinger and Ford at the White House, and the secretary and the senator signed the letters. Two years had passed since Nixon had sent Congress his trade bill. Jackson had managed to obstruct a piece of legislation that he considered too advantageous to the Soviets and add an amendment that forced the Russians to change their policies if they wanted to benefit from détente. It was Jackson's moment of triumph.

Ford and Jackson decided to make the letters public. The night before the signing, Perle and Amitay had mimeographed copies, and now they ran around the briefing room, their fingers still stained with the purple ink, distributing them to journalists. "We have reached what I think is an historic understanding in the area of human rights. I think it is a monumental accomplishment considering that so many said it could never be accomplished," Jackson happily told the reporters to the repeated flash of cameras. "Let me just say that what we started out with two years ago we have accomplished," Jackson continued. "I am not going to comment on what the Russians have done. I can only say that there has been a complete turnaround here on the basic points that are contained in the two letters." There was no moderating his sense of victory, and the normally staid senator got far ahead of himself and any Soviet promise when he said "I anticipate that it should go beyond sixty thousand based on the number of applications, which we know exceed one hundred and thirty thousand."

Jackson and Perle were not the only ones basking in their success. The Jewish community could hardly believe what it had accomplished. Haskel Lookstein, the rabbi of an influential and affluent Upper East Side synagogue, captured the mood of elation and accomplishment in a letter to the executive director of the National Conference: "I doubt whether we have seen anything in our own lives which had greater historical importance than the agreement concluded on Friday. Perhaps the Six-Day War ranks with it, but I am not sure it ranks above it."

The victory would be hollow. The Kremlin was not about to have its emigration policy dictated by the Jews of the United States. Perhaps under the impression that the arrangement would remain secret, they were humiliated by Jackson's very public gloating. When Kissinger spent three days in Moscow in late October, he received earfuls of hurt pride and anger at every meeting. "The Soviets felt deeply wounded by the implication that they had knuckled under to the American demands affecting their internal affairs," Kissinger told the press. To make sure the full extent of the Soviets' dissatisfaction was clear, Gromyko handed Kissinger a letter before he left, a document that basically negated any deal over the amendment. The promises Jackson claimed had been made, wrote Gromyko, "create[d] a distorted picture of our position as well as of what we told the American side in this matter . . ." He then went on to reject the assurances previously given regarding the departure of "Soviet citizens": "Some figures are even being quoted as to the supposed number of such citizens, and there is talk of an anticipated increase in that number as compared with previous years. . . . We resolutely decline such an interpretation."

Kissinger kept the Gromyko letter a secret. He showed it to Ford and his top aides but not to anyone in Congress. Asked later about this concealment, he said he had simply forgotten about it. But he had every reason to withhold the letter since passage of the trade bill depended entirely on his ability to convince Congress that the Russians had promised to change their ways. Two years later, in a 1976 speech to the National Conference, Jackson referred to Kissinger's action as "among the shabbiest deceits ever perpetrated by a Secretary of State on the Congress of the United States." It was a "deplorable breach of good faith." Jackson never overcame the feeling that if he had known about the strong Soviet opposition, he might have altered something in his amendment, made a strategic change of some sort to preserve its effectiveness.

But it wasn't until December 13, the morning of the Senate vote, that Jackson became aware of the Soviets' position. TASS printed Gromyko's letter, the first time since the Cuban missile crisis that the Kremlin had made diplomatic records public. Not only did the full text appear but an adjoining article said that "leading circles in the USSR" (a euphemism for Brezhnev) found the conditions set forth in the exchange of letters totally unacceptable. At that moment, with the trade bill and the amendment only hours away from passing, neither Jackson nor Kissinger wanted to make any rash moves. Jackson told the press, "We should keep our cool." He hoped that the Gromyko letter had been released for domestic consumption only, in order to save face.

Predictably, the amendment and the new waiver provision passed by an overwhelming 88 to 0. Then the entire Trade Reform Act, the Jackson amendment included, passed by a vote of 77 to 4. A conference committee reconciled the House and Senate versions, and the final version was adopted on December 18, two days before Congress was to adjourn, and sent to Ford's desk. Equally predictably, the Soviets came out against the new law and what it demanded of them. Following the Gromyko letter, the Soviet press went on the attack; *Pravda* blamed the "advocates of tension" in Congress for trying to "undermine the very foundation of détente." It ran a political cartoon in which a fat capitalist wrote the words *interference in internal affairs* on a large ball and chain that was attached to a truck labeled *international trade*.

The Kremlin was angrier than anyone in Congress suspected. And not only because of Jackson's grandstanding in the wake of his victory; another piece of legislation was about to rob the Kremlin of what it most coveted. The Stevenson amendment had been conceived by Adlai E. Stevenson III, an Illinois congressman, great-grandson of the one-time vice president and son of the two-time Democratic presidential nominee. It set a $300 million limit on the amount of credit that could be issued to the Soviets, and of that, there was a ceiling of $40 million for projects involving exploration for gas and oil. As Kissinger would later say, this amount was "peanuts in Soviet terms." They had already received half a billion from the Export-Import Bank of the United States since 1972. The bill stipulated that these restrictions could be waived only if it was deemed in the "national interest." It was shot down in the House, but Stevenson had managed to sneak his amendment into the Senate's version of the Export-Import Bank bill—legislation that renewed the life of the institution charged with issuing credit to foreign countries—and it looked like it might actually pass.

The Soviets badly needed American technology. Eventually, they might have been convinced to swallow their pride and accept the demands of the Jackson amendment to boost their economy. But with the Stevenson amendment in place, even if Brezhnev stood by his "assurances" on emigration, he would not be able to get any more than a measly $300 million in credits. This would not buy them much. And now it seemed that every policy decision of the Soviet Union would become a matter of debate in the U.S. Congress. As Kissinger succinctly put it in a letter to the head of the National Conference, "When the Soviet Union looked at the totality of what it had to gain from the trading relationship we were able to offer, as against what it considered intrusions in its domestic affairs, it drew the balance sheet of which we have the result today."

Once the trade bill came before Ford, he had no choice but to sign it into law. Trying to appease the Soviets, he added, "I will, of course, abide by the terms of the act, but I must express my reservations about the wisdom of legislative language that can only be seen as objectionable and discriminatory by other sovereign states." A few days later in a letter to Kissinger, the Soviet Union's government declared it was pulling out of the 1972 trade agreement. Too much had changed since Nixon's first trip to Moscow. The Soviets saw little reason to comply with Congress's demands. Kissinger gave a press conference in which he made clear exactly what the Soviet repudiation would mean: "The 1972 Trade Agreement cannot be brought into force at this time and the President will therefore not take the steps required for this purpose by the Trade Act. The President does not plan at this time to exercise the waiver authority."

The drama that had lasted for more than two years was finally over. It was hard at first to see what had been gained. The Soviets would not be getting MFN status or credits. The White House's power over foreign policy had been seriously eroded. And though Jackson's law was on the books, he had lost any real leverage with the Soviets. They had told him he could keep his carrot.

But though it didn't feel like a clear, concrete win, a giant shift had nevertheless taken place. Jackson and his allies had effectively manipulated détente for their own purposes. With the amendment in place, the Soviets could not improve their trade relationship with the United States until they dealt with their Jewish problem. The two issues were now linked. For the first time, the direction of the Cold War and of American foreign policy hinged as much on ethical and human rights questions as it did on the arms race.

Even though American Jews had reacted to the Soviet rejection with "shock and consternation," as one Jewish leader put it in a letter to Ford, the process of the past two years had thoroughly transformed them. They had learned that they could change laws. Gone were the days of simply following policy. If the community cared deeply enough about an issue to exert its power, it could make the policy. A *New York Times Magazine* article published days after passage of the trade bill captured the magnitude of what had taken place: "For the rest of the decade at least, the state of U.S.-Soviet relations will be linked to the Russian Politburo's willingness to risk an open-door policy on emigration, particularly toward the dissident Soviet-Jewish minority. This is a linkage that Kissinger, the two U.S. Presidents he has served, and the entire ruling hierarchy of the Soviet Union had hoped mightily to avoid." Though exaggerating the amendment's instantaneous effects, the article noted, "What is extraordinary is that the moral position of an ethnic minority representing 3 per cent of the American population could eventually force another country to reverse its internal police policies—especially when the other country is the Soviet Union."

They had been led, often forcefully, by a non-Jewish senator, but the Jewish community had finally injected themselves into the middle of the Cold War—an intrusion that would have been unthinkable a generation earlier. The implications of the amendment—the amount of real, immediate pressure it would exert—were impossible to determine. But whichever direction a future American president or Soviet premier might take, there was now no way to erase Jewish emigration from the agenda. American Jews had managed to direct foreign policy so that every administration would have to deal with their concerns. They had exercised power as never before. The result was unambiguous: after the Jackson-Vanik amendment, if the superpowers hoped to draw close to each other ever again, they first had to resolve the problem of Soviet Jewry.

9

Politiki and Kulturniki

1975–1977

LIKE MOST REFUSENIKS, Anatoly Shcharansky could no longer disentangle the political and personal forces that shaped his life. He had become a dissident because he could not accept being disrespected as a Jew and as a human being. He was also hopelessly in love, and the woman who filled most of his waking thoughts lived outside the closed borders of the Soviet Union. Emigration became his desperate cause; if he couldn't get an exit visa, he would never see her again. Many other refuseniks had similarly mixed motives—the political bled into the personal and vice versa. They gathered together on dark Moscow winter afternoons in small, dry apartments, more as friends than as the secret society the KGB imagined. Around folding tables, interiors illuminated by brass lamps inherited from long-dead grandparents, they drank tea or sometimes vodka and ate pickles and mushrooms. They listened to a record of one of the sad Russian bards, Vysotsky or Okudzhava, or watched someone's child, a Sashenka, play with wooden blocks on a fake Persian rug. They discussed the letter received from a sister in Haifa; the cough of a sick daughter—a new Israeli—heard over the phone; or the state of friends in America or England, devoted supporters who had come to seem like separated family members. And Shcharansky talked to whoever would listen about his Natasha.

Known to everyone as Tolya, Shcharansky was just twenty-seven, part of a new generation that had no memories of life under Stalin. His age made him conspicuous among the Jewish activist leaders, especially in June of 1975, when he joined other refusenik representatives for a meeting with a delegation of fourteen U.S. senators visiting Moscow. Led by their respected elder Alexander Lerner, the Soviet Jews were a bedraggled contingent, the exhausted collective face of what had become over the past three years a successful resistance movement. Shcharansky had a prematurely balding head, but despite that, his ruddy cheeks, thick lips, and extreme shortness made him look like a cherub sitting unassumingly alongside these graying, middle-aged engineers, physicists, and chemists. His English was heavily accented and tinged with a slight lisp, but it was better by far than anyone else's in the room. It was this linguistic skill, along with his irrepressible charisma and energy, that had earned him his place and made him indispensable to the group, a one-man public relations bureau.

The meeting that summer day in Senator Jacob Javits's suite at the Hotel Rossiya represented both a pinnacle and a nadir for the refuseniks. For the first time, they had the ear of some of the most powerful men in the world — Hubert Humphrey and Hugh Scott, the Senate's majority and minority leaders, led the U.S. delegation. The refuseniks expressed their hopes for the Jackson-Vanik amendment. But they also described a degradation in their situation since the bill's adoption. Emigration figures were dismal, down from thirty-five thousand in 1973 to twenty-one thousand in 1974, with the precipitous decline continuing in the first six months of 1975. They handed over a report proving that the harassment and pressure on exit visa applicants and refuseniks had only increased.

There were handshakes and expressions of sympathy, but the united front presented by the Soviet Jews to the senators that day was a lie. A serious divide had opened up between the refuseniks in Moscow. There were now two distinct factions, and they were so resentful of each other that the two groups had initially refused to sit in the same room. Much of what constituted this feud was petty, a matter of two different social circles — two bands of friends — that had fermented in refusal independently and resented the other's successes. But this bitterness and jealousy was heightened by a deep ideological argument.

Ever since Soviet Jews had begun organizing themselves, two competing visions of their activism had shared an uneasy coexistence. The contours of the conflict had not changed much since the first Zionist activists in Riga and Leningrad had argued about whether to write protest letters or quietly teach Hebrew. Should the movement have a purely political character—aligning when it could with human rights and democracy activists—or should it be a uniquely Jewish struggle, motivated by Zionism and concerned primarily with reunifying Jews with their culture, history, and homeland? What had changed was the amount of attention the movement was receiving from the West. It was maturing and gaining notoriety, worthy of visits from senators and the inspiration for an important piece of legislation.

In an earlier era, the ideological combat between these two groups of refuseniks, dubbed the *politiki* and the *kulturniki*, would have been seen as inconsequential squabbling. Now, however, the direction of an international movement depended on the outcome of this argument. Many people were watching. Between these two poles, a clear objective had to emerge: What did the Soviet Jews want?

Shcharansky's side in this argument had been determined long before he became a refusenik. He was with the *politiki*. Though he was friendly with all the leaders and knew they shared a common experience—the alienation from Soviet society, the unique euphoria of being part of a Manichaean struggle, the paranoia of being watched—the instincts and principles that guided the *politiki* fit perfectly with his own. Above all else, he believed that asserting his rights as a human being only reinforced what he was claiming for himself as a Jew.

The politics had come first. Shcharansky had grown up in the Ukraine, a studious boy and chess prodigy—by fourteen, champion of the Donbas region—who had a penchant for subversive writers like Bulgakov and Dostoyevsky. He had arrived in Moscow in 1966 with the coveted gold medal, an award given to the highest-performing students. It allowed him to study at a prestigious mathematics institute and then to move on to graduate work in cybernetics, the field developed by Alexander Lerner; his dissertation examined how computers might be programmed to play chess. Affected by Sakharov's samizdat essays, the Six-Day War, and the Leningrad trials, in 1973 he saw no other solution but to emigrate. He was quickly made to endure the myriad indignities familiar to most refuseniks, including an open hearing organized by the Komsomol at which the chairman asked those assembled, "Does anyone have a question for Shcharansky, who has betrayed us all?" After Shcharansky applied for an exit visa, he began making contacts in the refusenik community. He started visiting Alexander Lerner's apartment. He attended one of the underground Hebrew classes and spent his Saturday mornings hanging out in front of the synagogue. But his real introduction to the activist life came when he met Sasha Lunts.

Lunts was a mathematician, tall, slim, and confident in his own ideas—a natural leader. He was a member of the *kulturniki*, which was made up mostly of unemployed refuseniks who had fallen from great heights and were looking for a way to channel their energy and intelligence while they waited for exit visas. They very quickly found themselves engaged in two activities—both led by Alexander Voronel, another formerly high-ranking scientist and their unofficial leader—that bonded them as friends and that influenced their thinking about the movement. Starting in 1972, the year they all became refuseniks, they began meeting every Sunday afternoon at Voronel's apartment for a scientific seminar. A blackboard was brought in, tea was served, and then they were treated to a two-hour lecture, usually by a physicist, mathematician, or computer engineer. This was a different kind of activism for the refuseniks. It was nonpolitical and concerned more with building their cultural infrastructure and combating boredom. Week after week, they gathered to discuss one another's fields and work on problems together, sometimes even producing papers that were then smuggled to the West and published in respected scientific journals. The seminars were so successful, growing from a core of eight or nine people to about twenty, that the model was duplicated by other refuseniks. Alexander Lerner even started a weekly talk about the problems of constructing an artificial heart.

Another initiative of the *kulturniki* begun in the fall of 1972 was a new samizdat journal, *Jews in the USSR*. This too was meant to fill a void. So much attention was being paid to political action, so much publicity given to those who were being denied exit, that hardly anyone was engaged with the more essential question of what it meant to be a Jew in the Soviet Union—why they should seek to leave; why they should go to Israel. Voronel, like most Muscovite intellectuals, was alienated from his own Jewish identity. He envisioned the samizdat journal as "a form of getting to know ourselves, as self-instruction and self-education." Each issue, carefully assembled by the group, explored the question of Soviet Jewish identity from as many different angles as possible: through scientific articles, personal essays, fiction, and poetry. The pieces ranged widely, from an examination of the origin of Yiddish to an article titled "Who Are the Marranos?"—the objective being to provide an education about the breadth of Jewish history and tradition. In his first editorial letter, Voronel even solicited writing from "those who are critical or even sharply negative to the role of Jews in the history of Russia." The back pages contained a recurring feature, a column titled "Who Am I?" in which writers dissected the meaning of their own conflicted Jewish identities.

As they worked together on these projects and others—including a two-week hunger strike in Lunts's apartment in 1973 and a failed attempt at an international scientific symposium in 1974—they bonded, first as friends and then as activists. They agreed to always stay within legal limits, to request that the Soviet authorities grant them the same rights as any other national minority in the empire: a bit of autonomy to express their culture. They had also come to the conclusion that emigration could not be their sole focus. Equal energy had to be spent on resuscitating Jewish consciousness in the Soviet Union. The seminars and the journal were attempts to create a sanctuary where they could remain intellectually engaged and use their time in refusal to explore their own Jewishness and perhaps encourage others to do the same. They were prioritizing self-analysis and the rebuilding of a small (and mostly cerebral) Jewish society.

Sasha Lunts was at the center of all this activity, but he was growing restless. He craved political action beyond editing journals and holding seminars. His break from his friends soon took a very militant form. In 1973, he joined a group of young men who were organizing regular public demonstrations. They jokingly called themselves the Hong Wei Bing, after the student Red Guards that terrorized the population during China's Cultural Revolution. They became a strike force, with an elder mentor in Lunts, who made sure their exploits were well covered by Western journalists. Protesting in the Soviet Union was, of course, practically impossible. A successful demonstration lasted no more than a minute and involved protesters unfurling a banner or lifting a sign in a prominent public place for a few seconds before being dragged away by police. So the Hong Wei Bing very quickly began living like fugitives, rotating in and out of jail as they served the standard fifteen-day detentions given for disturbing the peace. This could not have been more contradictory to the aims of Voronel's group. The Hong Wei Bing were purposefully confrontational and political.

Tolya Shcharansky, not even a refusenik yet, became one of these demonstrators. Lunts offered him purity of purpose. No respect for Soviet laws that the authorities themselves refused to uphold. No wasting energy on those hundreds of thousands of sleeping Jews who failed to see the reality of their situation. They would demonstrate relentlessly until their right to emigrate was granted. Along with a mentor and a cause, Shcharansky gained a group of friends, his fellow frontline soldiers in the Hong Wei Bing. It was not unlike the solidarity felt by the angry young Brooklyn boys in Kahane's JDL. Between the danger and passion of Lunts and the reasonable argumentation of Alexander Lerner—in whose apartment the young mathematician had become a frequent guest—Shcharansky had tapped into the political argument the refuseniks had been building for several years. He was seduced by its clear-cut morality, even apart from his desire to emigrate. And then, one freezing fall day in 1973, the personal intruded.

Shcharansky had never before seen the strikingly tall and beautiful young woman who approached him in front of the synagogue. Natalia Stieglitz, or Natasha, as she was known, was soft-spoken and painfully shy and had the innocent face of a little girl. Her brother, Misha, had recently been arrested at a demonstration and she had come to the synagogue to find someone who could help her figure out where he was. It was October, the waning days of the Yom Kippur War. The street in front of the giant white columns was filled with people chattering, gossiping, and trying to learn what was actually happening in the Sinai Desert—the Soviet newspapers were not exactly forthcoming on this matter. Someone thought Shcharansky might have information about Misha and had given Natasha his name. Shcharansky tried to comfort her, explaining how the fifteen-day detentions worked and suggesting that Misha might even be given an exit visa following his release, as was sometimes the case. She brightened, and he began talking to her about Hebrew, whether she was taking any classes, what her level was. He bragged that he knew a thousand words already. Despite their being physically mismatched—he gnomish and she a beauty—Natasha was immediately taken with Tolya, with his wit and confidence. She lied about her knowledge of Hebrew so she could join the weekly classes he was taking with Misha Chlenov, an ethnographer who spoke more than six languages and who, together with a few other underground teachers, was training a whole generation of refuseniks (once a week, a few of the groups would gather for a Hebrew-only evening). Within a month, the two were a couple, deeply in love. Natasha had moved into Tolya's small apartment.

Soon after Shcharansky met Natasha, his exit visa was denied, and he became a true refusenik, throwing himself more deeply into his activism. Natasha sometimes joined him, and once they were arrested together for protesting in front of the Lebanese embassy. By the spring of 1974 they were talking about marriage. She herself applied for an exit visa and began waiting. They were anxious to have the wedding. If she got permission and left for Israel, Shcharansky's case would be strengthened—he would need to be reunited with his wife. But when they approached the registry office that spring to apply for a marriage license, they were told that their request would take months to process. They decided to sidestep the bureaucracy altogether and have a traditional Jewish wedding. But here too they had difficulties. The elderly guardians of the synagogue were wary of the young troublemakers and feared the consequences of holding an event that would draw many refuseniks and attract the attention of the KGB.

When Nixon made his second visit to Moscow that summer, Shcharansky was one of the refuseniks detained. He was driven two hours outside the city and dumped in a prison cell. No sooner was he gone than Natasha got the call from OVIR. She had been given an exit visa that was valid for just one week. Her first thought was to turn it down, but there was an unspoken rule among refuseniks that no one ever declined an exit visa—every opportunity should be taken. Natasha found an elderly scholar at the synagogue who was willing to marry them, and Shcharansky was released from prison just a day and a half before Natasha's visa expired. The wedding was quickly planned, a chuppah was hastily assembled, and their apartment soon filled with guests, some of whom were dirty and unshaven, having just been released from detention. The next morning, they took a taxi to the airport. Shcharansky had never seriously doubted his resolve, his decision to fight for emigration, until that moment. As he prepared to say goodbye to the woman he loved—they had met only nine months before and been married for just a few hours—he wondered if perhaps entering this struggle, which would now separate them, had been a mistake, if they should have just been content to have each other. He told her he would join her soon—in six months, he said—but they both knew this was impossible. "See you in Jerusalem," Shcharansky whispered to her before she boarded the plane. And then she was gone.

What had started as a desire to live in Israel was now a desire to be with Natasha. In the many letters he sent through tourists, his longing for her was overwhelming. In a telegram in December 1974, six months after she left and when he'd gone a few days without news from her, he wrote: "I'm writing to you from a telegraph office. Two curious characters in hats are circling around me like sharks before an attack. And although I'm not deprived of their company for a minute, I am alone now as never before. I haven't received anything from you; I am gradually losing not only the details, but the whole picture of your life; this is terrible and sad. I am counting very heavily on our conversation tomorrow."

With Natasha gone, Shcharansky immersed himself in work. He moved in with Sasha Lunts, sleeping on his couch, and joined his frenetic life of constant meetings with Western reporters and tourists. He continued protesting with the Hong Wei Bing. At the end of February 1975, two months after the passage of Jackson-Vanik, he and eight others marched to the Supreme Soviet carrying signs—his said VISAS FOR ISRAEL INSTEAD OF PRISON—and within thirty seconds they were set upon by men in civilian clothes who twisted their arms behind their backs and dragged them away. The group was detained for eight hours in a drunk tank at Moscow's central police station, familiar territory for the demonstrators. But when they were finally released, they discovered that two of the protesters, Mark Nashpits, a twenty-seven-year-old dentist, and Boris Tsitlionok, an electrician, were going to be charged with criminal offenses. At the trial the following month, the two were sentenced to five years of internal exile for violating Article 190 of the Russian Republic's Criminal Code, disturbing the public order. The harsh response took the Hong Wei Bing by surprise. They had never suffered anything worse than fifteen-day detentions or fines. Now that the trade agreement was off the table, the authorities no longer needed to maintain their light touch.

Just as Shcharansky's activities were becoming more risky, he began taking on more responsibility in the *politiki* circles. The departure of Alex Goldfarb, a young microbiologist who had acted as a translator and default spokesman for the refuseniks, opened up a space for someone with polished English and enough energy to escort the constant stream of Western visitors. Now out of work, without his wife, intelligent and driven, Shcharansky relished the opportunity, and soon his days were spent organizing press conferences and talking up journalists.

There were no rules for climbing the ranks in the decentralized world of the refuseniks. This added to the tension that often coursed through the community, but it also meant that if one had the nerve to take on a particular task, one could very quickly amass power and responsibility. Dina Beilin had done just this. An engineer who was refused an exit visa in 1972, Beilin gave herself one of the most important jobs: maintaining a written record of each refusenik's name, address, profession, and the reason given for refusal. With characteristic thoroughness, she went to great lengths to make sure the list was comprehensive. She organized regular stakeouts of the street in front of the synagogue and OVIR offices; anyone exiting with a dejected look on his face was a possible addition. Activists in other cities sent their names to Moscow, and Beilin appended her register constantly, typing out the names and details on an old typewriter. Individuals were added or stricken as circumstances changed.

The gregarious Volodya Slepak already had a well-defined role as the central contact for tourists who were looking to connect with Soviet Jewish activists. His apartment was easy to find, just a few steps from the Kremlin. All one had to do was walk down Gorky Street, look on the right for the equestrian statue of Yury Dolgoruky, and follow the direction of his outstretched arm. Once a visitor was inside, the Slepaks' was a place of warmth and chaos. Masha served hundreds of cups of tea every day for the constant stream of guests, and the Slepaks' shaggy sheepdog, Akhbar (Hebrew for "mouse"), stuck his nose into every corner. By 1975, the KGB had effectively cut off all telephone communication between the refuseniks and the West—Andropov boasted in a memo that "in 1973–74, more than 100 telephone lines were exposed and disconnected in the cities of the USSR, thereby inflicting a noticeable blow on foreign Zionist organizations." The refuseniks had found other ways to communicate, using public phones or abandoned lines in newly vacated apartments, but face-to-face contact was increasingly the only way to pass information. Much of this traffic went through the Slepaks' apartment, where Volodya would tell tourists—most briefed by the Lishka or Soviet Jewry groups in America—important news or needs.

Of all the information relayed to the West, nothing was more critical than the lists of names of refuseniks. Slepak came up with the most ingenious way of smuggling them out: he photographed the list of names and then pushed the rolled-up negatives through holes drilled into the smallest of the ubiquitous *matryushka* nesting dolls; conspiring tourists could transport these home without raising suspicion. The refuseniks saw the lists as their insurance policy. If their names were known in America or Israel, they were provided with a measure of protection. The Lishka used the lists to deliver financial help to unemployed refuseniks, a complex process that kept Dina Beilin and the other *politiki* busy. Typically, a check was sent through a Soviet bank and could be redeemed only as coupons for use in special Moscow shops known as Beryozki. These stores were intended mostly for Westerners and the families of the nomenklatura and were the only places where one could buy quality consumer goods. A refusenik would use the coupon to buy a pair of jeans or a radio, and then he would sell it on the black market; this would give him enough money to survive for a month or two. Occasionally, a family was in need of quick funds—a man whose ex-wife wouldn't let him emigrate unless he made all his alimony payments at once, or a mother who could not afford the plane fare to visit her son in a Mordvinian prison camp. The problem would be communicated to Western activists or the Israelis, and soon a friendly tourist would arrive with a "gift" of an expensive camera. Beilin and other leaders regularly appropriated the money and assets of those given permission to emigrate—there was a cap on how much one could take out of the Soviet Union—and then distribute them among the needy refuseniks. The emigrants would be reimbursed once they were in Israel.

The *politiki* divided up the many responsibilities of caring for a community. For example, the families of imprisoned refuseniks went to Ida Nudel. A tiny, bespectacled woman who had the solitary intensity and self-denial of a nun, Nudel was an economist who'd been refused an exit visa in 1971 because, as the official at OVIR put it, "You don't possess any specific secrets, but you might have overheard something." Nudel became the prisoners' families' self-appointed guardian angel. In her early forties, unmarried, and without children, she fanatically devoted herself to those who became known in the West as prisoners of Zion. One of her first contacts was Yosef Mendelevich's father. He visited Nudel in Moscow, and together they sat down and made a list of all those who, like his son, had been sent to prison camps in 1971. Nudel tracked down their places of detention, relatives, medical problems, and birthdays (this last detail so she could send them yearly postcards, often with pictures of their hometowns). Then she began the tortuous process of establishing contact with them and trying to improve their conditions. It was guilt as much as compassion that motivated her, she often said. These people had sacrificed their freedom so that others could find a way out.

Once Sasha Lunts joined the *politiki,* he took on his own projects. In addition to organizing the Hong Wei Bing, he began to compile empirical evidence of Soviet misdeeds. It was his way of helping the Jackson-Vanik proponents in America make their case. His first report detailed the convoluted exit visa application process and illustrated the arbitrary nature of refusal—helpful material for Jackson and Perle. He smuggled it out of the Soviet Union through a contact at the U.S. embassy, and it ended up in Congress. When the amendment was later in trouble, Lunts sent activists out to the farthest reaches of the Soviet Union to gather more information. He himself went to Derbent and Baku, followed by a bevy of KGB agents. The trips were often dangerous. A young man who went to Kishinev was physically assaulted and then detained for almost a month. But the resulting report offered a panoramic view of the Jewish problem and showed the depth of support for Jackson-Vanik, even in the distant Uzbek city of Samarqand. Lunts handed it over to the delegation of senators who visited in the summer of 1975.

The freedom of individual refuseniks to act as they saw fit in the name of the movement was generally useful, but it could backfire. One wrong move by a single person could jeopardize everyone. This is just what happened in the middle of 1975, and Sasha Lunts was the one responsible. The summer before, Lunts had come up with an unusual idea: What if he engaged with the KGB directly? Imagining that the combination of constant Hong Wei Bing demonstrations and the progress of the Jackson-Vanik amendment had sufficiently irritated the authorities, he thought he could sell them some calm and silence. The refuseniks would stop making noise if certain conditions were met. He wanted an exact time frame for approval of exit visas and a promise to release any imprisoned activists. It was, of course, a risky proposition. The KGB were experts at psychological manipulation. Once they knew there was something you wanted, they could turn you into an informer before you even realized it. But Lunts felt he could outsmart them. He asked the advice of Slepak, Lerner, and Alexander Voronel—the other leaders—and they agreed that it was dangerous but perhaps worth trying. So Lunts simply walked into KGB headquarters one day that summer and asked to speak to someone in charge of Jewish issues. He ended up having four meetings, but he grew more hopeless after each one. They were not taking him seriously. He met smalltime KGB agents who tried to play mind games with him, never anyone higher up the chain of command. So as suddenly as he'd begun the talks, he called them off.

Lunts thought this would be the end of his experiment. But a few days after he stopped the discussions, KGB agents started spreading rumors about him among the *kulturniki,* those who had once been his closest friends. They managed to convince various people in Voronel's circle that Lunts was actually an informer. In early 1975 KGB agents called in one of these activists, Pasha Abramovich, and gave him the distinct impression that Lunts was working with them, telling him that he would do well to follow in Lunts's footsteps and freely give them information. The accusations began to spread. Lunts was hoarding money intended for refusenik activities; he was a spy; he was going to put the entire movement at risk. The refuseniks were constantly and justifiably paranoid about KGB infiltration. Such stories threatened to turn Lunts into a pariah and ruin his reputation. He eventually called a meeting at Lerner's apartment to clear things up. After waiting a few hours, he realized that only his *politiki* friends were going to show up.

By June of 1975, the suspicions and resentments had been brewing for months, aggravating the underlying ideological differences. The *kulturniki* thought the *politiki* members were reckless and self-destructive, the aggressive Hong Wei Bings being a prime example. They also felt the *politiki* held an unfair monopoly on Western resources. The *politiki*, for their part, were comfortable with their preeminent position in the movement and saw the *kulturniki*'s preoccupation with cultural rebirth as a waste of time and resources.

Any supporters in the West unaware of just how acrimonious it was getting between the two groups soon found out when the delegation of fourteen senators led by Humphrey and Scott came to visit. The *kulturniki*, sure that their concerns would be overshadowed and ignored, refused to attend. Only when Senator Jacob Javits intervened and offered an adjoining room in his suite so that two separate meetings could take place did they relent and eventually even agree to join the *politiki*. But by that point, anyone familiar with the refuseniks could see to what degree the animosity had built up. Robert Toth, the *Los Angeles Times* correspondent, had been aware of the growing rift and now took advantage of the incident to write an article headlined "Split Among Activist Soviet Jews Breaks into Open Over Talks with U.S. Senators." One of the embittered activists quoted accused the opposing group: "For us, the central problem was the concentration of power—money, information, contacts with Jewish organizations abroad—in very few hands . . . No one else could get in." What should have been a moment of great publicity for the refuseniks turned into an embarrassing episode that made them look like bickering children and threatened their support in the West. It also gave the KGB a new wedge to exploit.

If there was a positive side to the *Los Angeles Times* article, it was the reconciliation it eventually forced on both groups. The divisiveness, they realized, could only benefit the Soviet authorities. For the sake of the movement, they had to maintain at least the illusion of solidarity.

And they did, coming together to meet with an American Jewish activist from Philadelphia that summer to show they were making peace. But the two groups never managed to repair the breach entirely and in fact became even more invested in their divergent approaches to the movement. They kept their resentments to themselves now, but the feeling on each side that the other was taking the wrong tack never went away.

In this complex web of Soviet Jewry activism, Shcharansky played the role of translator, and not just in the literal sense. He explained the movement's objectives to the West better than anyone who had come before him, leading journalists to the most emotional, compelling, lede-worthy parts of the story. Increasingly, he also became a bridge between those fighting for emigration and those engaged in the greater democracy movement; this was partly because of his new job as an assistant to Andrei Sakharov, a man he had long admired.

By 1975, the esteemed physicist had been forced to give up any illusion that his status as a member of the Academy of Sciences protected him. Already the authorities had waged a nasty campaign against him in the press, and earlier that year he had fought to get permission for his wife, Elena Bonner, to go to Italy to receive medical treatment for a serious eye condition that was causing her to go blind. Her two children, his stepchildren, had continually been refused permission to go to the United States, where they had been invited to study and teach at MIT. Dozens of visitors arrived every day at his apartment to seek advice. Sakharov would sit calm and pensive in his chair, his shoulders stooped, looking out from behind his large glasses, quietly answering questions and carefully choosing the letters and statements to which he would affix his respected name. He was only fifty-four but had the air of a sage. Dealing with all the Western journalists required a good translator, and Shcharansky had been recommended as reliable and available. In March of 1975, the young refusenik began working for Sakharov, and it wasn't long before he found himself sucked into the dissident world that revolved around the physicist and his wife.

Shcharansky never found it jarring to jump between the democrats and the refuseniks. In fact, it was just the opposite. He saw no contradiction in committing fully to both causes; he believed they reinforced each other. The principles of human rights that Sakharov tirelessly espoused provided more justification for the refuseniks' argument. Shcharansky wasn't alone in this thinking—it was a logic that Eduard Kuznetsov had understood when he joined the Riga Zionists and that Muscovite refuseniks such as Slepak, people who were longtime friends of the democrats, instinctively accepted. But no one championed this idea like Shcharansky. The fight between the *politiki* and *kulturniki* had become so intense partly because—following the failure of Jackson-Vanik to improve the Soviet Jewish condition—the movement was now at a crossroads. Would it turn inward or outward? Shcharansky's answer was clear. Jews needed to put political pressure on the Soviet Union, and that pressure needed to be framed in the universal language of human rights. And in the summer of 1975, as he was becoming even more convinced of this strategy, an unexpected development in the international arena suddenly made it seem like the only way forward.

One August day in 1975, Soviet citizens opened up their copies of *Pravda* to find a thirty-thousand-word reprint of a treaty that their government had just signed: the Conference on Security and Cooperation in Europe. Anyone with the stamina or curiosity to actually read the document surely must have thought it a hoax. There, in black and white, the Soviet Union was reaffirming all the human rights contained in the 1948 UN declaration, a document the USSR had never ratified. This new agreement, signed by thirty-three European countries plus the United States and Canada, specifically called for the free flow of people and information across borders, upholding what it referred to as the "fundamental freedoms" of thought, culture, religion, and belief. Even more incredible, each signatory was obligated to participate in regular reviews—checkups, essentially—to determine whether these provisions were being upheld.

Why would Brezhnev sign such a document? Only a few months before, he had refused to exchange sixty thousand Jews a year for the economic aid the Soviets needed. This time, the terms must have been better. And on the face of it, they were. Since the end of World War II, Soviet leaders had been trying to convince Europe and the United States to validate the new postwar contours of their empire, including the Baltic States, and their dominance in Eastern Europe. In 1954, they proposed the idea of a conference that would take up this question. After the squashing of the 1956 insurrection in Hungary and then the Prague Spring twelve years later, Europe was not eager to reward Soviet rapaciousness. But in 1973, with the spirit of détente in full flower, the European powers agreed to the process, which culminated in an elaborate signing ceremony in the Finnish capital of Helsinki in August 1975. The Soviets had gotten exactly what they wanted: the document referred to the "inviolability of borders" and respect for "territorial integrity." To the many detractors of the Helsinki Final Act, as it became known, it looked like the West was formally validating the Brezhnev doctrine, the Soviet leader's post–Prague Spring declaration that he would enter and secure any Communist satellite state whose government was being undermined by capitalist forces.

The Helsinki Accords consisted of three interlocking sets of agreements that came to be known as baskets. The first two dealt with arms and trade, the most important elements for the Soviets. In return, the Europeans, with American acquiescence, insisted on a third basket filled with human rights provisions. This was the quid pro quo.

Hardly anyone thought it was a fair deal. On the eve of President Ford's trip to Helsinki, the lead editorial in the *Wall Street Journal* cried, "Jerry, Don't Go!" As a *New York Times* piece put it, "The Kremlin seems to have decided that it can afford to make such concessions abroad without risking any real liberalization at home." The human rights sections were composed "in a flurry of final compromises and it remains to be seen what effect they will have." Brezhnev, speaking at a press conference after the signing, made it clear that the Soviets were simply going to abide by certain parts of Helsinki and ignore the rest. "No one should try to dictate to other peoples ... the manner in which they ought to manage their internal affairs," he defiantly proclaimed.

Where Americans and Europeans saw another Cold War defeat, Andrei Sakharov perceived a unique opportunity. In a leaked copy of his essay "My Country and the World," which would be published the following month in the United States, he lamented that the West had yielded "one concession after another to its partner in détente" without asking for anything substantial in return. Jackson-Vanik had failed because of "divisiveness, disorganization, and lack of affirmation" in the

West. The Soviet insistence on separating foreign and internal policy, Sakharov thought, was a dangerous diversionary tactic and had to be fought. Helsinki was a good first step. A country that abuses its own citizens *is* a threat to world peace. If the Soviets refused to accept this reality, it was the West's responsibility, through weighty levers like the Final Act, to force a change in their behavior.

In the months following the signing, Soviet citizens began referring to the new treaty in appeals to their government. But they were ignored. When inmates at a Mordvinian labor camp went on a hunger strike that summer and pointed to what Helsinki said about prisoner treatment, no one paid any attention. In fact, in the remaining months of 1975, the authorities seemed to harden their policies. Just a few weeks after the signing, Georgi Arbatov, the Soviets' chief expert on America, wrote a long article in *Izvestia* accusing the rest of the world of exploiting Helsinki as "an instrument for interfering in the internal affairs of the socialist countries." The third basket "appears to be the only point of interest" for the United States, Arbatov fumed in an op-ed. But the West, he angrily declared, should be under no illusions that the Soviet Union "owed" them anything.

In early October, Sakharov was awarded the Nobel Peace Prize, providing an incredible boost to the demoralized democracy movement and validating his views on Helsinki. The award's citation read: "In a convincing fashion, Sakharov has emphasized that the inviolable rights of man can serve as the only sure foundation for a genuine and long-lasting system of international cooperation." For the Soviets, this was another ideological attack from the West. Sakharov was cursed daily in the Moscow newspapers, a "Judas" whose Nobel Prize was his "30 pieces of silver." He wasn't even allowed to travel to Oslo—the Soviets refused to assure his safe return—and Elena Bonner, then in Italy receiving her long-denied cataract treatment, accepted on his behalf.

The promise of Helsinki remained out of reach for Soviet Jews. In the six months after the document was signed, not one prominent refusenik was given an exit visa, and in all of 1975 fewer than twelve thousand Jews left the Soviet Union, a third of the peak number in 1973. In February of 1976, a headline in the *New York Times* admitted, "So Far, the Helsinki Accords Have Not Opened Soviet Doors." Still, Shcharansky, now working closely with Sakharov, saw possibility in

Helsinki. In September of 1975, Shcharansky had recorded a Rosh Ha-shanah greeting to American Jews that was smuggled out and played at many synagogues. In it, his preoccupation with Helsinki was evident, as was his frustration: "Every time the Soviet Union undertakes new international obligations, such as the Helsinki Accords now, the authorities do their best to frighten all the people who can make use of them . . ." This certainly seemed to be the case. To mark the six-month anniversary of Helsinki, the Communist Party's Central Committee ran a four-thousand-word article in *Pravda* leaving no doubt as to how they would deal with anyone who dared criticize the regime's human rights record: "Our law proceeds from the fact that just as slander smearing the good name of one person is punishable, so is slander towards the entire society—social defamation—punishable."

Then, in March of 1976, Shcharansky came up with a way to make Helsinki work for both the democrats and refuseniks. His first sounding board was a dissident he had been tutoring in English, Yuri Orlov. Orlov was a small man with a large cloud of bushy red hair (which earned him the nickname Angela Davis); his troubles with the authorities began in 1956 when as a young physicist he wrote a letter in support of Khrushchev's infamous denunciatory secret speech. The letter was deemed overzealous. In 1976, Orlov had only recently returned to Moscow after spending sixteen years of self-imposed exile twelve hundred miles away, in Yerevan, Armenia, where he had become an expert on particle acceleration and had been elected a corresponding member of the Armenian Academy of Sciences. Not long after he returned, Orlov wrote another letter, this time to Brezhnev in support of Sakharov. He was promptly fired from his new job as a senior scientist at the Institute of Terrestrial Magnetism and Dissemination of Radio Waves and became a full-time dissident. He even started a branch of Amnesty International in his apartment.

Orlov's interest in human rights made him a natural partner for Shcharansky, who was eager to share his idea. It was simple: encourage citizens in the West to bypass their governments and form grass-roots committees to monitor how well their own countries and those in the Communist bloc were complying with the Helsinki Final Act. If this took off, Shcharansky thought, such a monitoring group could be formed in the Soviet Union with less fear of suppression. Orlov took a long time to think about it. A few weeks later, he came back with an even bolder proposition. He hesitated to give the job of monitoring their own societies to people in the West, since he doubted they cared enough about human rights to follow through—at the time, Europeans seemed most interested in nuclear disarmament. If the dissidents wanted to see Helsinki taken seriously, they should monitor it themselves. "We should stop wasting time convincing people to talk and start instead to collect and share facts about human rights abuses," Orlov told Shcharansky.

As they both knew, any nongovernmental group was de facto illegal in the Soviet Union, never mind one whose objective was to embarrass the authorities in the eyes of the world. But even if it only survived as a publicity stunt, the idea of a committee that would monitor implementation was compelling. Orlov chose an official-sounding name, the Public Group of Assistance to Implementation of the Helsinki Agreement in the USSR, and began making his case to others. By May, he had recruited eleven highly regarded dissidents. Sakharov, the obvious choice to lead the group, said he preferred to stay on the sidelines. But Elena Bonner joined, as did Sakharov's private secretary, Alexander Ginzburg, the long-bearded dissident and former prisoner then busy administering the Prisoners' Aid Fund started by Solzhenitsyn before his exile (subsidized from the sale of *The Gulag Archipelago*). Shcharansky enthusiastically became the group's Jewish representative. Along with him was Vitaly Rubin, a gaunt, good-humored scholar of Confucian philosophy. When Rubin unexpectedly received an exit visa a month later—he had become a cause célèbre in the international Sinology community—he was replaced by Shcharansky's good friend Volodya Slepak.

On the morning of May 12, 1976, Orlov was close to finalizing a formal declaration of purpose when he got a summons to appear at KGB headquarters. He sensed a preemptive strike in the works. Sakharov called an AP reporter to his apartment and hastily put together a press conference to announce the group's formation. The group, Orlov explained, would function as a sort of fact-finding team. Soviet citizens could bring written complaints to them, and they would also compile their own reports on "direct violations of the articles." Copies of their research would be sent to all the signatories of the Final Act. The press conference had begun at ten thirty at night and it went on past midnight. Orlov was sure the KGB would be looking for him in the morning. So he returned home, got in bed, turned out the lights, and then climbed out his window and went into hiding. He wanted the new group to exist for at least a few days before the inevitable occurred.

Orlov's and Shcharansky's pessimism about the group's viability was warranted, given all that had transpired. But Moscow Helsinki Watch, as it became popularly known, turned out to be an enormous success. On the surface, there was nothing radical about the group's mission. Over the past decade, the airing of human rights violations had been the main focus of the democracy activists, and the *Chronicle of Current Events* had been their primary instrument. Since the early 1970s, Valery Chalidze had advocated using international treaties and Soviet law to hold the regime accountable. What made Moscow Helsinki Watch different was not its philosophy but its application. The principles laid out in the Helsinki Final Act and adopted by the Soviets provided cohesion to the human rights argument. Dissidents could refer again and again to this one document. They could quote from it. They could own it.

From the moment the news of the group's founding was broadcast on international shortwave stations, people from all over the Soviet Union began tracking down members of the committee, sometimes traveling great distances to get to them. Orlov called them *khodoki,* an old Russian word meaning "walkers." On May 18, the group presented its first report, an examination of the legal case against a Crimean Tatar who was being tried for his nationalist activities. The next report came just a few weeks later and looked at the KGB's disconnection of phone lines and confiscation of mail to refuseniks and dissidents, activities in direct violation of Helsinki.

A steady stream of reports followed, about two a month, covering a wide range of Final Act infringements. The tone was always dispassionate, with hard facts and little rhetoric. For example, one report about living conditions of political prisoners examined their extremely low calorie intake (fourteen hundred a day, compared to the World Health Organization's mandated three thousand) and came to this conclusion: "The Group's information on the Soviet penal system ... indicated that the Soviet administration has committed gross violations of Article VII, Section 1(a) of the Final Act. ... The Group believes it is necessary to form an international commission to study these alleged violations, beginning with torture by hunger and torture by confinement in punishment cells ... The Group is prepared to turn over all relevant documents to such a commission."

Orlov originally wanted each report to be no longer than a page and a half. And the first one was. But a certain inclination toward long-windedness took over, and the second was twice as long. The third report, the summary of the conditions of political prisoners, was twenty-eight single-spaced pages, including footnotes and a table breaking down the nutritional components of one day's worth of meals. The task of reproducing all these pages at least forty-five times (one for each of the thirty-five signatory countries, nine for reporters, and one for their own archives) fell to Ludmilla Alexeyeva, a longtime dissident who had worked for the *Chronicle of Current Events*. She coordinated with an underground samizdat press that employed ten full-time typists. Copies of the first few reports were sent directly to the Moscow embassies of the signatory countries with return receipts requested. Only the receipt from Brezhnev's office was returned. After six lost reports, they began using journalists and diplomats to transmit their work to the West. And their targets became more precise: specific countries and organizations that would publicize their findings.

Through his work on the committee, Shcharansky became a central, indispensable figure. By 1976, he had formed deep friendships with Western journalists—some of them were even willing to use the U.S. embassy's diplomatic pouches to ferry books and other materials. The most fruitful of these contacts was Robert Toth, a *Los Angeles Times* reporter. Toth gave Shcharansky an education in dealing with Western journalists; he explained the demands his editors placed on him for stories beyond the dissidents'. So rather than becoming frustrated each time Toth ignored some twist in the tale of a particular refusenik, Shcharansky gave him other leads, helping him cover, in particular, the Soviet space program, a personal interest of Toth's. For a journalist working in the Soviet Union, living in a walled-off compound and fed only the official line, this was a chance to find out what was really happening. Shcharansky led Toth to important stories and acted as his translator, so Toth found ways to thank him.

Shcharansky's celebrity in the West received a boost on June 14, 1976, when the documentary film *A Calculated Risk* was shown on television in Britain. Two months earlier, a British production company called Granada had managed to sneak out footage of Shcharansky in his leather jacket slunk down in the front seat of a car and talking into a clunky microphone. He was giving a reporter a refusenik tour of Moscow, including a quick stop outside KGB headquarters. There were shots of Shcharansky with Slepak, his big beard spilling over his turtleneck, chatting together in the back seat. The two came across as charismatic and eccentric, a Don Quixote and Sancho Panza team, though with a slightly more disheveled air. In the last shot of the film, their faces are weary as they walk off into the cold mist of a Moscow winter morning. The film was seen by hundreds of thousands of people. Shcharansky had acted as a guide for countless Western tourists, and now he was the warm, open face of the refusenik movement for a much larger audience.

Baptists, Russian Nationalists, Crimean Tatars, Zionists, and Pentecostals, among many other Soviet citizens, bombarded Moscow Helsinki Watch throughout the summer and into the fall of 1976. Strangely, the authorities showed restraint. Although followed constantly and frequently harassed by KGB agents, the Helsinki Watch monitors were largely left alone to collect information for their reports. And so the work continued and even grew more ambitious. In October, Ludmilla Alexeyeva went to Lithuania to look into the story of seven boys who had been expelled from their school in Vilnius for attending Mass and becoming friendly with Viktoras Petkus, a Catholic dissident who had just completed sixteen years in labor camps. Shcharansky and Slepak drove four hundred miles south of Moscow to investigate the strange story of an undiscovered rural community of a hundred and thirty Jewish families who lived and farmed together as a kolkhoz, or collective farm. Ethnically Russian, the community had mysteriously converted to Judaism generations before and were long settled in a forest in the region of Voronezh, faithfully practicing Jewish tradition (and even traveling six hundred and fifty miles to the Caucasus to have their sons circumcised). They had been left to themselves, hidden and peaceful, until the 1960s when their collective, Ilynka, was absorbed by three other Russian villages. The story of the community and of how the chairman of their new, consolidated collective farm was preventing their emigration to Israel made up the ninth Moscow Helsinki Watch report.

It wasn't long before the refuseniks learned the power of this approach. On the morning of October 17, after a night of dancing the hora in front of the Moscow synagogue for the annual Simchat Torah festivities, a handful of refuseniks decided to stage another demonstration inside the Supreme Soviet waiting room. As usual, their demands were ignored. When the office closed for the day, at five thirty in the evening, uniformed policemen arrived, loaded them onto three buses, and then dropped them off in a forest fifteen miles outside of Moscow. Undeterred, the protesters returned the following day. The police once again took them away in buses, but this time they left them farther out, forty miles from the city. When the buses stopped, it was dark and the refuseniks were afraid to get off, imagining an ambush. The policemen, many of whom were wearing the red arm badges of the volunteer militia, started kicking and punching them, forcing them out of the buses and even throwing some of them into the water-filled ditches that lined the road. For the next half hour, they were chased through the forest and beaten by the police. David Shipler of the *New York Times* interviewed the group that night after they'd walked a few miles to a nearby town, taken a train back to Moscow, and gathered in Slepak's apartment. Slepak, who had been with the group, described how his fingers were smashed as he tried to hold on to the bus. "Then I was kicked on the back and the head," he said. They all remembered one plainclothes leader of the police crew, who they thought might be KGB, warning his men not to beat the Jews in the face. Nevertheless, Shipler observed many bruises and at least one broken nose.

Never had the government responded with such raw violence. Slepak, Shcharansky, and Boris Chernobilsky, another prominent refusenik, demanded an audience with a government authority; incredibly, they were invited to meet with the minister of internal affairs, Nikolai Shchelokov. He denied any involvement with the physical assault, telling them he had only heard about it on the BBC and was as astounded as they were. "I would never permit beating," he told them. "If it were my affair, I would arrest the organizers." After half an hour the three left the ministry empty-handed—Shchelokov said he would review the case but refused to put anything in writing. They were met by a group of waiting protesters, now numbering more than forty. The refuseniks had pinned yellow cloth Stars of David to their jackets. They started marching. The group walked down Gorky Street to the sounds of jeering crowds and then back to the Supreme Soviet building, where they resumed their protest. That evening they were again put on buses and dumped at the edge of the city. More sit-ins followed during the next two days, culminating in the arrest of thirty protesters, all of whom were given fifteen-day detentions for hooliganism.

The authorities' heavy-handed response was widely reported. Jimmy Carter, the Georgia governor then in the last days of his campaign as Democratic candidate for president, felt compelled to send Slepak a cablegram through the American embassy: "I have read with great concern about the treatment that you and some of your colleagues suffered recently. As you know, I have spoken out on this matter as governor and during this campaign and have referred to your case by name. I want you to know of my deep personal interest in the treatment you and your colleagues receive."

During the following weeks of detention, it became clear that two of the refuseniks arrested that day, Chernobilsky and Joseph Ash, a young doctor, were not going to be released but put on trial for "malicious hooliganism," a charge that carried a penalty of up to five years' imprisonment. Dina Beilin, the keeper of the refusenik lists, quickly organized a defense committee on the model of Moscow Helsinki Watch. All the major refusenik activists, both *politiki* and *kulturniki,* took part. Beilin then put on a mock trial in Alexander Lerner's apartment. She invited Sophia Kalistratova, who was one of the most revered defense attorneys in Moscow and was sympathetic and often helpful to the dissidents, to make the case for the two men. All the material gathered that day, including details of the beatings, pointed to an abuse of Soviet law and the Helsinki Accords. The information was written up in a report and passed to the West through the committee's channels—Ludmilla Alexeyeva added a letter in support of the cause. Within days, on November 15, and to the utter disbelief of the refuseniks, Chernobilsky and Ash were released without trial on the grounds that they were both family men with no prior records. "It's unprecedented—I don't remember any precedent in our movement," Shcharansky excitedly told David Shipler.

This was the power of Helsinki. By the end of 1976, local Helsinki Watch groups were founded in the Ukraine and Lithuania. In January, Georgia Helsinki Watch began operating. Each of these offshoots engendered the same cooperation among varied dissident groups as the original in Moscow had. In these remote cities, collaboration was even more critical, as many of the refusenik activists were vulnerable and working in total isolation. In Lithuania, for example, members were mostly persecuted Catholics, but Eitan Finkelshtein, an active refusenik, played a central role.

For all its success—the committee produced eighteen reports from May 1976 to February 1977—Yuri Orlov and his fellow members knew it was only a matter of time before the government made its move. In the first weeks of 1977, this foreboding grew. Shcharansky experienced the pressure in a very physical way. The number of KGB agents assigned to him had increased, and he often had as many as half a dozen men in suits trailing him as he ran around Moscow. When he hopped in a taxi, they usually followed in their cars. Sometimes he would get stuck riding with them in elevators. Shcharansky, typically, tried to joke about the situation, insisting that his tails split the cab fare on those occasions when they actually jumped in along with him. But it was becoming clear that the refuseniks had finally struck a nerve. The scene of a small man in a leather coat followed by a swarm of black suits might have been comical, but it was also a sign that the regime was reaching a point of desperation and was trying to zero in on the source of its troubles.

Not all the refuseniks in Moscow supported Shcharansky's involvement with the democrats. While most of the *politiki* hitched themselves to Helsinki and the rhetoric of human rights, the *kulturniki* continued to reject direct confrontation with the authorities. The circle that surrounded Alexander Voronel and helped him start his journal *Jews in the USSR* and the weekly scientific seminars had only become more entrenched in their thinking. Even though the two sides of the movement had reconciled and were civil toward each other, they continued along separate tracks.

At the beginning of 1975, Jackson-Vanik had failed to live up to its promise of ensuring sixty thousand exit visas a year and a release of Zionist political prisoners. The two groups again diverged in their approaches. The *politiki* began searching for other levers to pull, like Helsinki. The *kulturniki* turned inward. Not only had Jackson-Vanik failed to deliver, but the number of Jews leaving for Israel was decreasing every year. And the problem was not just stricter emigration. Fewer

Jews were applying. According to the *kulturniki*, this was because the great mass of Soviet Jewry had no knowledge about Israel or their own Judaism. They were not being sensitized. If the *kulturniki* didn't do something soon, it wouldn't matter whether the Soviet Union allowed them to leave. No one would go.

This had been Alexander Voronel's preoccupation. After Voronel received an exit visa in 1974, Vladimir Prestin, a member of his group, took over many of his responsibilities and pushed the *kulturniki* even further in this direction. A lanky, athletic man with a dark goatee, Prestin had grown up sharing a room with his grandfather Felix Shapiro, author of the only state-commissioned Hebrew-Russian dictionary, which had been published in the 1950s. His earliest memories were of falling asleep in a tiny apartment filled with books in Hebrew and Yiddish. The letters of the Hebrew alphabet were ingrained in his mind from a young age; his scholarly grandfather gave private lessons to KGB operatives who needed Hebrew so they could spy on the Israeli consulate. Prestin didn't become an activist immediately after his refusal, in 1971. He started giving classes in rudimentary Hebrew, a language he himself was just learning. Using a manuscript of a beginners' Hebrew textbook he'd discovered among his grandfather's papers, he set up shop in his minuscule apartment. Ida Nudel was one of his first students.

It wasn't until the end of 1974 that he decided he needed to do more. He was motivated by a trend that was beginning to trouble refuseniks and roil their community of supporters in the United States and Israel: an increasing percentage of Jews who left the Soviet Union did not end up in the Jewish State. In Vienna, their first stop in the Western world, many abandoned their Israeli visas and presented themselves instead as refugees bound for America or European countries. In 1975, the magnitude of this trend registered for the first time. Nearly 37 percent of emigrating Soviet Jews took this option, double the amount of the previous year. Confronted with this declining interest and in some cases clear disdain for Israel, some refuseniks felt personally betrayed.

Mark Azbel, the physicist and *kulturniki*, later described his own reaction: "When people who expressed these strong patriotic sentiments turned out to have America or England or Western Europe as their destination, we were not only disillusioned; we were humiliated.

The very possibility of anyone leaving the Soviet Union was due to the heroic efforts of Jews who dreamed of Israel, who sacrificed their liberty, and in some cases their lives, to build the road to freedom. In our opinion, those who rejected Israel cast shame and mockery upon the memory of those people."

For Prestin, the solution to the dropout situation, as it was called (or *neshira*, in Hebrew), was to reject the path of the *politiki*. Refuseniks had a responsibility to do more than just help themselves and the prisoners. They had to be more expansive in their thinking, addressing the two million Soviet Jews who had absolutely no connection to their identity. The motivation was practical as well as ideological. If the movement continued to overlook this problem, one of two things would happen: either there would be fewer and fewer demands for exit visas and the Soviets could justify shutting down emigration altogether, or a majority of departing Jews would head to America, allowing the Soviets to argue that Jews were not interested in family reunification but in capitalism.

In 1975, Prestin found a kindred spirit in Dr. Benjamin Fain, a physicist who was based at the Institute for Chemical Physics in a town just outside Moscow and who was a regular attendee of the weekly scientific seminars. Together, Prestin and Fain decided a few innovations were in order. First they introduced a new samizdat journal, *Tarbut* (the Hebrew word for "culture"), which would be more accessible than *Jews in the USSR* and include explanations of Jewish holidays, recipes, and calendars with important religious dates. Aware that they were trying to reshuffle the movement's priorities at a time when attention was focused on the protests and press conferences of people like Slepak and Shcharansky, they needed a forum where they could make their case to the world. In March of 1976, they came up with the idea for an international Jewish symposium. Planning for the event, which would take place at the end of the year, consumed them. Throughout the summer and fall, with help from a few sympathetic Western supporters, they invited experts from around the world and the Soviet Union—even the Soviet minister of culture—to submit papers in two areas, the "present situation of Jewish culture" and "future prospects." The symposium would have a completely nonpolitical tone. Fain's invitation made this clear; there was no mention of the word *emigration*. The focus was on "preserving and reviving Soviet Jewry," and they hoped that on this basis they might be given a small space to maneuver.

They even tried to involve the *politiki,* going to the most respected name among them, Alexander Lerner. The éminence grise of the refuseniks agreed, but only if he could present a paper—eventually titled "Emigration or Culture: Which Is More Important?"—that opposed the emphasis on Jewish culture. Lerner conceded the *kulturniki*'s point that "we cannot wash our hands" of those Soviet Jews who were rapidly assimilating. But, he argued, making Jewish culture the focus of the movement would give the Soviets a chance to offer a superficial solution to their Jewish problem, quieting criticism with a few token concessions, and might even lull activists in the West into thinking that everything was all right: "A misapplied orientation in regard to priorities of aims and objectives could result in the Soviet Union receiving from the West a series of important privileges (preferential credits, technology, the status of most favored nation, etc.) in exchange for ephemeral steps in the direction of liberalization in the attitude of authorities towards dissemination of Jewish culture in the USSR, while the problems of freedom and free emigration for those who have linked their fate with that of their people will remain unsolved."

Fain and Prestin included Lerner's paper, but they couldn't have disagreed with it more. It was not enough, in their minds, to focus on emigration. The state had to be forced to open up a space for Jewish life. Otherwise it would be impossible to cultivate the emigrants of the future.

As the symposium approached, it became clear that the authorities were intent on crushing it. The apartments of all the organizers were raided and any material related to the meeting was confiscated. Fain stood by, nearly in tears, as his research and books were dumped into a bag. The invited foreign guests were all denied entry visas, told there were no available hotel rooms in Moscow. Activists traveling to Moscow from other Soviet cities, such as Riga and Leningrad, were taken off trains or detained in KGB offices. As a sarcastic *New York Times* editorial put it, "It seemed at times as though all the non-nuclear forces of the Kremlin had been mobilized to halt this fearsome threat against Soviet power."

On the morning of December 21, the day of the symposium, Fain stepped out into the snowy street with his wife; he was trying to remember his opening statement, the text of which had been confiscated from his apartment the day before. Two men, one in a police uniform and one in a suit, came up to him, grabbed his arm, and escorted him to a black Volga, leaving his wife standing on the sidewalk. The same thing happened to dozens of other organizers and speakers. They were either picked up on the street and detained or placed under house arrest for the week. Some form of the gathering did, however, take place that day. The wife of Grigory Rosenshtein, one of the detained refusenik speakers, led a handful of people, including Sakharov and Elena Bonner, to her apartment, the designated secret meeting spot for the symposium. Of the forty speakers slated to present their work, only two were present. Seven papers were read, two of which were by the absent Rosenshtein, one about the history of Jews in Europe and one about Jewish mysticism. Periodic loud knocks on the door punctuated the proceedings, and more than a dozen policemen stood downstairs in front of the building, but the refuseniks continued until the end of the day, content with their small triumph.

Fain, Prestin, and the others were soon released and suffered little personal retribution (Fain was even given an exit visa six months later, in June of 1977). But the destruction of the Jewish symposium itself taught the *kulturniki* and the wider refusenik movement an important lesson. The Soviets were not going to allow any sliver of unsanctioned Jewish cultural expression. They saw little distinction between the Hebrew teacher toiling away in his apartment and the hunger striker sitting down in the middle of Red Square. Both were manifestations of Jewish nationality and both presented a threat to Communist ideology. But despite the symposium's failings, the *kulturniki* had made their point: the problem of how to inspire more Soviet Jews to choose emigration—and emigration to Israel in particular—was not going away. With the number of dropouts increasing by the month, the concerns of this group no longer seemed so irrelevant.

The image of Vladimir Slepak moving in slow motion on Soviet primetime television on January 22, 1977, ushered in a new phase in the life of the movement. Hundreds of thousands of Soviet citizens were shown an hour-long documentary titled *Traders of Souls*, which told a conspiratorial tale of lies and deceptions. In the process, the state did the unthinkable, providing the faces, names, and even addresses of four leading refuseniks for members of the public to do with as they pleased. When the camera zoomed in on the bearded Slepak hugging a visiting Israeli athlete at an international competition in Moscow, the voice-over intoned, "How can it be that Zionist cadres were allowed to form inside the Soviet Union?"

The film was a classic example of Soviet propaganda. The refuseniks saw it as a terrifying sign that the authorities had very few remaining boundaries. A response of sorts to the British film featuring Shcharansky, *Traders of Souls* tried to make two arguments. First, it presented the Jews who had immigrated to Israel as having been lured into a trap. Using crude techniques like staged scenes and cartoons, it showed the miserable existence of Jews who had left and were now clamoring to get back to the Soviet Union. The film even presented what it called "Zionist abuses of the Helsinki Accords," referring to emigrants who had left their parents behind when they went to Israel. "This is separation of families, not reunification of families," the narrator insisted. Even more perilous was the depiction of Jewish activists as Western agents out to undermine Soviet society. Slepak and Shcharansky were mentioned by name, as was Yosef Begun, a Hebrew teacher close to the *kulturniki*. A still shot of a check made out to Begun, one of many that was often sent to refuseniks in need, appeared on the screen. The refuseniks' addresses were then displayed while the narrator warned, "These people are all soldiers of Zionism within the Soviet Union and it is here that they carry out their subversive activities."

It seemed Brezhnev had had enough. In the first few weeks of 1977, all the dissident forces in the Soviet Union, from democrat to refusenik, began to feel the vise tightening. At the beginning of January, three weeks before *Traders of Souls* aired, most of the apartments of the Moscow Helsinki Watch members were searched. When he heard the knock on his door, Yuri Orlov quickly tried to dump important documents into the oven and down the toilet. The KGB agents who finally broke down his door found him sitting calmly in a room filled with smoke and the smell of incinerated paper. At Ludmilla Alexeyeva's, linen bags filled with Helsinki Watch reports and other samizdat were carted off. After a bomb exploded in a Moscow subway station on January 8, killing seven and seriously injuring thirty-three, the official press insinuated that the dissidents were responsible.

Shcharansky's apartment wasn't searched with the others in early

January, but the film and the media articles supporting its message (like one in *Ogonyok* headlined "The Espionage Octopus of Zionism") was proof that the government was on the offensive. So was the increased number of KGB agents that surrounded Shcharansky, which, he joked, had transformed them from a "tail" to a "box." Tolya told his friend the reporter Robert Toth, "There is always anti-Semitism among people in this country and as a Jew you learn to sense it. But now it is at a very much higher level than normal. Everyone in buses and subway are discussing these films and articles. It smells of pogrom." The refuseniks tried to fight back in the immediate aftermath of the film. Shcharansky filed a formal legal complaint in the local people's court, arguing that the film "distributed information that did not correspond with reality and that constituted an insult to my civil honor and national dignity." He demanded a retraction of the "slanderous information" and insisted that it be presented "in the same way the information was distributed." All through the first half of February, those refuseniks featured in the film tried to sue the state television company, to no avail.

It was hard for Shcharansky to focus on the film, because while this was happening, the leaders of Moscow Helsinki Watch were disappearing one by one. On February 3, Alexander Ginzburg was arrested as he stood at a phone booth outside his apartment. In charge of Solzhenitsyn's prisoners' fund, he handled and distributed tens of thousands of rubles. Now he was being accused of currency speculation. The same day, the KGB came looking for Orlov. He tried to hide, first in a village two hundred kilometers south of Moscow and then in Ludmilla Alexeyeva's apartment, but he was finally arrested on the morning of February 8.

A day later, Shcharansky visited Alexeyeva. He was concerned about what would happen to the Helsinki monitors now that their leader was imprisoned. His experience with the bickering refuseniks had taught him that a strong personality like Orlov's could sometimes hold an otherwise fractious group together. Alexeyeva gave him something to eat and the two talked for the first time about their own paths to dissidence. Shcharansky explained why he had embraced his Jewish identity. "I would like to be tall, curly-haired, and broad-shouldered. But, instead, I'm short, bald, and pudgy. So I have to be the best of what I have. Same with being Jewish. I had to make the best of it." When he met Sakharov and the other dissidents, he told her, he discovered that he could "be proud not only of being a Jew, but also of being human." Ludmilla Alexeyeva was forced into exile in the West at the end of February.

Shcharansky saw the Helsinki group destroyed in just a few weeks. The bonds that he had formed with others in the group during a period he called the happiest in his life were shattered. He felt increasingly targeted. The number of KGB agents following him was growing, and though he tried to fight it, the sensation that he might be next never left him. He just hoped that he could approach the moment as resolutely as possible, without fear or weakness.

That moment finally arrived on March 5, when he opened *Izvestia* and saw a stunning denunciation of him by a fellow refusenik, Sanya Lipavsky. A kindly, soft-spoken, gray-haired doctor with a mysterious past in Uzbekistan, Lipavsky was well known in the activist inner circle. A former neurosurgeon, he had access to medicines and could sign prescriptions, which proved very useful. He checked Alexander Lerner's blood pressure almost every day. Lipavsky also had a car, a black Volga, which was unusual for the average Soviet citizen, even a doctor. But the refuseniks never questioned his identity. In the hectic early months of 1977, Shcharansky was looking for a new apartment and Lipavsky, ever helpful, said that he had just found one for himself and would be happy to share it. Shcharansky moved in that February, but within days, Lipavsky disappeared. Only after his betrayal did people like Dina Beilin look back and see the subtle signs that should have tipped them off—a moment when he was caught in a lie, his strange omnipresence, his reluctance to talk about his past. The refuseniks had always assumed their circle was teeming with informers, but they knew they would lose their sanity if they started letting themselves be led by every suspicion.

Lipavsky's story was more tragic than the refuseniks could have known. His relationship with the KGB began in the early 1960s when he sold his soul to save his father's life. They were living in Tashkent at the time, and both Lipavsky's father and father-in-law were accused of stealing huge quantities of expensive fabric from a textile factory where they worked as engineers. The men turned on each other, and the father-in-law produced evidence that would have resulted in a death sentence (the penalty for "economic crimes") for Lipavsky's father. Lipavsky eventually found his way to the local KGB office and offered to make a deal: he would become an informer if his father was spared. The KGB agreed, and blame was pinned on the father-in-law instead, who was later executed (Lipavsky's wife left him soon after). His father received a ten-year sentence. It took a decade for the KGB to extract its full payment from Lipavsky. They asked him to infiltrate the refuseniks, which he did with charm and obsequiousness. And that wasn't all. In 1975, the KGB had Lipavsky present himself as a walk-in to CIA agents operating in Moscow and offer to provide information on Soviet technology based on what he said were his contacts in the scientific community. It was unusual for the CIA to employ such walk-ins, given that they were mostly undercover KGB agents. Aware of the risk, the Americans decided to string him along and see what would come of it. After nine uneventful months, they let him go.

Of course, Shcharansky and the other refuseniks knew none of this when they saw Lipavsky's denunciation in *Izvestia*. "It was not easy for me to write this letter, but after thinking long and hard, I arrived at the conclusion that I must do this," he wrote. "Perhaps [it] will open the eyes of those who are still deluded, who are still deceived by Western propaganda that shouts from the rooftops about the persecution of 'dissidents' in the USSR and which balloons the so-called question of human rights." What followed was the accusation that refusenik leaders, including Alexander Lerner and the already emigrated Vitaly Rubin, were in collusion with the CIA. Shcharansky was fingered as the bridge between the Jewish and democracy movements, one of those "adventurers and money grubbers posing as champions of 'human rights.'" Lipavsky claimed that refuseniks regularly passed on secret information to the CIA and received instructions from operatives working in the embassy and disguised as American journalists. There could hardly be a bigger trespass in Cold War Soviet society.

A tense quiet followed. Shcharansky wasn't sure what to think. An arrest seemed imminent. The number of agents following him was now absurd. At all times, he carried a bag that held warm clothes for prison and a book. His friends treated him like he had a terminal illness, saying their goodbyes but assuring him he would be okay. Vitaly Rubin, now in Israel, spoke with Shcharansky on March 13, a week after the article. He recorded the conversation in his diary: "Today I talked to Tolya and Alexander Yakovlevich [Lerner]. They said there is no news. Tolya is still being followed by eight people. They are in a good mood—what good souls. I told Tolya about Natasha and how she and Misha [her brother] will soon leave for the U.S. and that powerful forces are starting a campaign on their behalf in the U.S. When I told Tolya that I thought that with every day the odds of their arrest decreased, he replied, 'I think so, too. It's almost a pity—we are so well prepared.' 'I see you haven't lost your sense of humor,' I said. 'Of course not. We laugh all the time,' he replied. That's what we call Jewish laughter."

Two days later, on March 15, Shcharansky, who had been staying with the Slepaks since the *Izvestia* article, got word that Mikhail Stern had been released early. A refusenik from the Ukraine, Stern had been falsely charged with bribery two years earlier and sentenced to eight years in prison. Two journalists, one from the *Financial Times* and one from the *Baltimore Sun,* delivered the news to the Gorky Street apartment, and the group toasted over cognac. Slepak was by now used to the two black Volgas on the street outside his apartment and the gaggle of KGB agents in the stairwell. They had arrived shortly after Shcharansky moved in. But suddenly he noticed something unusual. Peeking out his window, he saw that the Volgas had apparently left. Shcharansky offered to run downstairs and check it out. He wanted to use the pay phone anyway so that he could tell a few other correspondents about Stern's release. He stepped out of the apartment with the two journalists and Slepak. When they arrived at the elevator, two agents suddenly appeared out of nowhere and jumped into it, leaving Slepak to take the stairs. Shcharansky, who had come to know his tails well, could tell that something was not right. "They're nervous," he told the crammed reporters on the elevator. "Something's about to happen."

As soon as Shcharansky walked outside, and before Slepak could reach the bottom of the stairs, half a dozen KGB agents grabbed Shcharansky by the arms and pulled him into an idling car. The anxious wait was over.

10

The Shaming
1977–1978

As harassments and arrests plagued the Moscow dissident community in the first weeks of 1977, Andrei Sakharov received an unexpected visitor at his apartment. Martin Garbus, an American lawyer and at that time the assistant director of the ACLU, introduced himself as someone with close ties to the incoming Carter administration. He had two hours before his return flight to the United States and he wanted to take a message back with him from Sakharov to the new president, who had been inaugurated just the day before. While Elena Bonner was in the kitchen preparing an omelet for Garbus, Sakharov wrote a quick draft of a letter that included the names of sixteen political prisoners. He also mentioned the recent Moscow subway bombing, which he increasingly felt had been a KGB ploy to ensnare the entire dissident movement (Sakharov compared it to the burning of the Reichstag in 1933). Letter in hand and omelet eaten, Garbus rushed off. Sakharov was sure that his message—if it even made it out of the country—would just be filed away in a drawer of one of the new president's men.

A week later, to Sakharov's surprise, his appeal appeared on the front page of the *New York Times*. "It's very important to defend those who suffer because of their nonviolent struggle, for openness, for justice, for destroyed rights of other people. Our and your duty is to fight for them," the physicist had written Carter. "I think that a great deal depends on this struggle ..." That his letter was presented to such a wide readership at a time when Orlov and Ginzburg (and soon Shcharansky) were all under arrest was promising. But what happened next was unprecedented. Carter wrote back. In the middle of February, Sakharov was summoned to the U.S. embassy, escorted inside by Soviet policemen, and handed a letter dated February 5. "I received your letter of Jan. 21, and I want to express my appreciation to you for bringing your thoughts to my personal attention. Human rights is a central concern of my Administration.... We shall use our good offices to seek the release of prisoners of conscience, and we will continue our efforts to shape a world responsive to human aspirations in which nations of differing cultures and histories can live side by side in peace and justice. I am always glad to hear from you, and I wish you well."

Throughout his decade of opposition, Sakharov had never received a communication from an American president. Holding up the letter for a photographer in his apartment, he smiled triumphantly. Just two years before, Ford had refused to meet with Alexander Solzhenitsyn, the exiled dissident and Nobel laureate, fearing it would be "inconsistent with détente." Now, Carter was sending an open letter to the Soviet Union's public enemy number one. Sakharov wrote back immediately. "I said in a congratulatory cablegram after your election what deep admiration your attitude evokes in us ... Today, having received your letter, the exceptional character of which I recognize, I can only repeat this once again."

The letter to Sakharov was just one of the ways Carter was trying to make good on his oft-repeated campaign promise to put human rights at the center of his foreign policy. The issue had been a winning one for the toothy Georgia governor in his long-shot presidential bid. People had become disenchanted with Henry Kissinger's realpolitik approach, the guiding principle of American foreign policy since 1969. As Carter put it to the national convention of B'nai B'rith two months before the election, Ford, like Kissinger, had "rationalized that there is little room for morality in foreign affairs and that we must put self-interest above principle." It was a criticism that resonated on both ends of the political spectrum. Liberals had been railing since the early 1970s about the government's support of right-wing dictatorships like Augusto Pinochet's Chile. And on the right, the idealistic anti-Communism of Henry Jackson had been taken up by a large faction of the Republican Party, including Ronald Reagan, the governor of California, who had nearly clinched the Republican nomination. Throughout the election, Ford insisted on pursuing Kissinger's model of détente, focusing on disarmament and increased trade relations and viewing human rights as a secondary, domestic matter not to be confused with foreign affairs. As his loss indicated, there was no longer a real constituency for this compartmentalized way of thinking.

In his first few weeks in office, Carter, through tone and substance, began making good on his vow to abandon Kissingerian diplomacy. At his inauguration, he released a taped address to the "citizens of the world," pledging "to shape a world order that is more responsive to human aspirations." On January 26, Carter's State Department publicly berated Czechoslovakia for violating the Helsinki Final Act: A group of three hundred leading Czech intellectuals, including the playwright Václav Havel, had signed a document called Charter 77, which established a watch group similar to Yuri Orlov's in Moscow; many of the charter's signers were interrogated and detained. This was the first time the State Department had singled out a particular country for violating the Helsinki Accords. As one anonymous analyst told a reporter, "I doubt that under Kissinger we would have bothered drafting a statement." The very next day there was yet another declaration from the State Department, this time about Sakharov. "Any attempt by the Soviet authorities to intimidate Mr. Sakharov will not silence legitimate criticism in the Soviet Union and will conflict with accepted international standards of human rights."

One could write off these early moves as the naive idealism of a new administration not yet schooled in the harsh realities of power politics. Carter was under the impression that he could slap the Soviets on human rights with one hand while cordially signing arms reduction pacts with the other. It remained to be seen in those early days of 1977 whether this was in fact possible. Undeniable, though, were the societal forces that propelled Carter and his ideas to victory. Helsinki was a promising document, and not just for Soviet dissidents and refuseniks like Shcharansky. Americans saw it as an effective tool. And

American Jews in particular understood that it might be their next best chance—now that Jackson-Vanik had been rendered impotent—to press the case for Soviet Jewry. With an administration that was suddenly a potential ally as opposed to a perpetual obstacle, human rights was the tool that might finally pry open the Soviet Union.

Carter's election put real power behind the principles of human rights for the first time in American history. But it was Congress that had begun laying the groundwork as soon as the Helsinki Final Act was signed—struggling, like the Moscow activists, to monitor the Soviets' adherence to their new promises. Leading this effort was a very eccentric sixty-five-year-old congresswoman who had been deeply affected by a trip she'd taken to the Soviet Union in the summer of 1975. Millicent Fenwick had the wit and patrician grace of a Katharine Hepburn character. Six feet tall and a pipe smoker, she was from New Jersey's affluent horse country and made an immediate impression when she was elected to the House in 1974—so much so that Garry Trudeau based a character in his *Doonesbury* comic strip on her, the aristocratic do-gooder Lacey Davenport. Fenwick grew up in a fifty-room mansion in Bernardsville, the daughter of a wealthy financier with a record of public service. Her mother had drowned in the torpedoing of the *Lusitania;* she had been on her way to Paris to set up a hospital for war victims. Fenwick was a striking beauty and spent her early life as a model and then as a writer and an editor for *Vogue.* By the time she arrived in Moscow, in the summer of 1975, she had settled into her new role as a legislator, projecting a certain noblesse oblige attitude about the poor and the oppressed.

A week after the signing of the Helsinki Accords, Fenwick, together with eighteen other congresspeople, landed in the Soviet capital. The trip was organized as a standard press junket—Moscow, Leningrad, a trip to the Black Sea coast, and a final stop at Brezhnev's dinner table. Fenwick and another congressperson had been charged with the nearly impossible task of reporting on the human rights and emigration situation. One night a group of refusenik leaders paid a visit to their hotel. Among them was Lilia Roitburd. Her husband, Lev, had tried to attend the June 1975 meeting with U.S. senators but was arrested in Odessa as he was boarding a plane. He was now awaiting trial. Lilia looked exhausted. She showed Fenwick a recent picture of herself from before the arrest, and the congresswoman could not believe that this was the same woman, so small and damaged did she appear compared with the person in the photo. The brief interaction nearly brought her to tears. "To know the pain of those people is very different from the abstract figures and the abstract stories we hear in the United States," she told Christopher Wren, a reporter covering the visit.

It was Wren who took Fenwick even deeper into the world of the dissidents. He brought her along the following day to see Yuri Orlov and Valentin Turchin, the two men who had set up an embattled chapter of Amnesty International in their apartment. That encounter became the most memorable part of her trip. Fenwick sneaked away from the rest of her group and, smoking her pipe, drove with Wren in his white Volga to an apartment in southwest Moscow. She was deeply impressed with the dissidents she met. They drank tea and talked about Helsinki's human rights provisions and how best to force the Soviets to comply with them. This was still a very new development, and Fenwick's enthusiasm about the "spirit of Helsinki" seemed slightly premature. But it made Orlov think, perhaps for the first time, about monitoring the Helsinki Accords, and it planted a seed that would later become the Moscow Helsinki Watch.

As for Fenwick, she returned to Washington determined to establish a congressional body that would enforce Helsinki. Within a month, she had drafted a bill that would create the U.S. Commission on Security and Cooperation in Europe, known simply as the Helsinki Commission. The accords themselves demanded regular checks on implementation. This was her way of taking them seriously. She wanted the commission to act as a clearinghouse for information about the state of human rights in the Soviet Union and Eastern Europe. In order to avoid the tension between the executive and legislative branches that had crippled the Jackson-Vanik amendment, she conceived of a commission that would include not only Democrats and Republicans but also representatives from the State, Defense, and Commerce departments. Fenwick mandated that the president deliver a semiannual report to the commission addressing how well countries were complying with Helsinki. She teamed up with Clifford Case, a fellow New Jersey Republican, who introduced the same bill in the Senate. Both houses' deep resentment of Kissinger made the bill an easy sell. As Case put it, the commission would once again allow Congress "to play an important role in the all-important area of human rights, which all too often appears to be of secondary concern to the executive branch."

Kissinger took the creation of the commission as a personal offense. He protested loudly, telling Fenwick, whom he jokingly called his "tormentor," that her proposed commission's blending of executive and legislative branches would set a "dangerous precedent." However, there was little that Kissinger could do. Ford was fighting to get elected, and many of his fellow Republicans backed the bill. There was growing support from various Eastern European ethnic groups, some in crucial swing states. Both the National Conference on Soviet Jewry and the Union of Councils for Soviet Jews, seasoned by their experience with the Jackson-Vanik amendment, threw their considerable lobbying weight behind Fenwick's bill.

By the spring of 1976, momentum was building, though Fenwick had been forced to hand over more power to a senior Democratic congressman who sat on the Foreign Relations Committee, Dante Fascell. He refashioned the composition of the commission to give Democrats a majority presence. Fascell was a short Italian American World War II veteran representing Dade County, Florida, and his support guaranteed the bill's passage; it also ensured that he would be chairman of the new body. On May 5, the Fenwick-Case bill passed in the Senate, and on May 17 it finally arrived back in the House.

Fenwick's role had been overshadowed, but she was the one who best articulated the significance of the new commission. She reminded everyone that earlier that week, from Andrei Sakharov's apartment in Moscow, Yuri Orlov had announced the establishment of a Helsinki monitoring group. "They and we are hoping that these international accords will not be just another empty piece of paper," she said. Fenwick talked about the idealistic strain in American history, the "respect for the dignity of the individual," and argued that "this ought to be the basis of our international relations. These ought to be the things of which we speak to the world: a concern for our fellow human beings, knowing that we are all one family, regardless of distance and descent or any other kind of barrier; concern for their right to freedom of religion, for their right to travel and be unified with their families. This is what this bill is about."

Only Fenwick and Case were at the White House when Ford signed the commission into life. The administration had no interest in trumpeting the passage of a bill they had opposed and that, according to a memo from Kissinger's deputy Brent Scowcroft, represented "another Congressional intrusion into Executive Branch functions." A few weeks after the signing, Kissinger told his staff, "The President signed the bill only because I had not been told what was happening. I would have fought it to the death. It never would have passed if I had known more about it." And that wasn't the end of it. Throughout the summer, Kissinger tried to find ways to kill the new initiative, fearing that its activities would undermine the effectiveness of his quiet diplomacy.

The young and energetic staffers who were hired to run the commission only added to Kissinger's worries. Spencer Oliver, a lawyer and Democratic Party activist, was named as director. He brought on people like Alfred Friendly, just back from a tour as Moscow bureau chief for *Newsweek* and personally familiar with many of the dissidents and refuseniks, and Meg Donovan, a longtime staff member for the National Conference on Soviet Jewry and an expert on the emigration issue. They set to work gathering information, including the reports produced by Orlov's Moscow Helsinki Watch and by the other monitoring groups that popped up all over Eastern Europe in the final months of 1976. Dante Fascell exchanged letters with Orlov, telling him, "We look forward very much to receiving more of [your] reports in the months to come."

In November of 1976, the commission decided to embark on an ambitious three-week fact-finding trip to all the signatory countries of the Helsinki Accords. They quickly found themselves thwarted by both Kissinger and the Soviets. Kissinger forbade the executive members to go any farther east than Brussels. Soon after the secretary of state made this decision, the Soviet Union and the Eastern bloc countries, with the exception of Romania, refused to grant the commission members entry visas. So extreme was the animosity between the secretary of state and the commission that it was rumored Kissinger had encouraged the Soviet ambassador Anatoly Dobrynin to stonewall the visit on the Communist side.

The Helsinki Commission went on their trip anyway, sticking to Western Europe. And by the time they returned, everything had changed. Carter had won the election, and almost overnight, the antagonistic relationship between the nascent commission and the administration was transformed. Carter's language of human rights was their language. Carter's inaugural address, which in content and tone made the president's humanitarian priorities clear, came partly from a set of bullet points composed by Dante Fascell. Fascell's proposed language, typed in all caps, found its way into the speech: "THE PROMISES MADE IN HELSINKI *MUST* BE KEPT — ESPECIALLY THOSE THAT PROMISE TO RECOGNIZE BASIC HUMAN RIGHTS AND TO PROVIDE FOR GREATER MOVEMENT OF PEOPLE, INFORMATION AND IDEAS AMONG NATIONS."

To those involved in the Soviet Jewry movement, the commission immediately proved its worth. By 1976, Soviet Jewry had become nearly synonymous with human rights. The refuseniks had become poster children for the failure of Kissinger's détente, with their individual stories of families torn apart or kept in jobless limbo for years. Now that the situation had flipped and government forces were massing behind an approach that would put humanitarian concerns first, the movement stood to benefit. In fact, the Helsinki Commission's opening hearing, in November of 1976, presented the results of its first, extensive research project: a look at the emigration policies of the Soviet Union. Unable to examine the problem firsthand, the commission sent eight Russian-speaking staffers to absorption centers in Israel to talk with recent arrivals. In this way, they were able to paint a surprisingly complete picture of the barriers to emigration, covering all the cases that the refuseniks had been trying to publicize in the West for years — from the man whose son was drafted to prevent him from leaving to the family that lost their apartment as a result of their application. The report's findings were read on Capitol Hill as an example of the type of abuses the new commission hoped to highlight. Western activists were learning what the refuseniks had already discovered: an emphasis on human rights could greatly amplify their cause.

The tension between the grass roots and the establishment that characterized the movement in the West for most of the 1960s was largely neutralized by the mid-1970s. To be sure, there were still differences in tone and strategy, but in many ways, a convergence had taken place. In the wake of the Jackson-Vanik amendment fight, the grass roots had become more organized, and the establishment was now freely borrowing from its toolbox. In addition to shifting their focus to lobbying efforts in Washington, the organizations that made up the National Conference on Soviet Jewry were more willing to hit the streets. Malcolm Hoenlein, the former Student Struggle member and now head of the New York body coordinating all establishment Soviet Jewry activities in the city, organized demonstrations every spring that were basically larger versions of Yaakov Birnbaum's 1960s rallies. Starting in 1971, an annual Solidarity Sunday drew anywhere from one hundred thousand to two hundred thousand people in parade demonstrations that ended in Dag Hammarskjold Plaza outside the UN after a procession down Fifth Avenue. At the 1975 event, 353 chartered buses brought marchers from all over the tri-state area, with the single largest delegation a caravan of nine buses from suburban Merrick, Long Island. Local politicians and presidential candidates showed up yearly to pay their respects. The scenes of massive, singing crowds waving homemade signs and blown-up photos of the "prisoners of Zion" were covered widely in the press, a regular reminder of Soviet Jewry's centrality for American Jews. At that 1975 rally, a gigantic banner hung over the crowd: THEIR FIGHT IS OUR FIGHT.

The Jewish establishment had learned the power of loud, clamoring public pressure, and the grass roots had internalized the need to focus. Although they refused to be "responsible"—a constant plea from Jewish leaders—in their denunciations of Soviet leaders, the activists were also employing more conventional forms of protest. The Union of Councils, started by Lou Rosenblum as a ragtag collection of local groups, had proved incredibly durable. Rosenblum himself had decided to retire from Soviet Jewry activism to focus on work and family, but the organization he had started as an end run around the establishment now had affiliates across the country, from Los Angeles to Chicago to Des Moines to Omaha. Rosenblum's use of these chapters to apply local political pressure during the Jackson-Vanik campaign had turned the Union of Councils into a true alternative national Soviet Jewry organization.

In the mid-1970s, Irene Manekofsky, a forceful, matriarchal figure running the Washington chapter of the Union of Councils, had as many high-level contacts on the Hill as any of the Jewish establishment leaders, and she frequently hosted fancy fundraisers for the city's most influential personalities (at least one was written up in the society pages of the *Washington Post*—fish-wrapped broccoli and cheese soufflés were served). Activists at these local councils matched the work of the National Conference or the Lishka, recruiting Jewish tourists who were going to the Soviet Union and then briefing them on whom to visit, how to escape the KGB's attention, what telephones to avoid using, where bugs might be hidden, and what to bring the refuseniks (pantyhose and jeans). When the tourists returned, they were debriefed, and the Union of Councils, just like the Israelis, amassed a growing body of information detailing the situations of specific individuals.

What distinguished these activists from the salaried men and women working at the offices of Jewish organizations in New York City was the sense of personal connection—they imagined themselves working *for* the refuseniks. If the National Conference dealt with Soviet Jewry on a larger, more abstract scale, an issue to be packaged and sold to the government and the American public, members of the Union of Councils thought in terms of people. They were helping their friends, the ones whose voices they could now recognize over the phone, whose children's names they now knew by heart.

Each of the councils revolved around a small number of passionate volunteers, many of them housewives with the time and energy to devote to the cause. Lynn Singer was the perfect example. A fiery self-admitted loudmouth and *yiddishe* mama, she lived with her husband, Murray, a piano teacher, and her two kids in the suburbs of East Meadow, Long Island. Within months of becoming involved, she was organizing massive rallies and making herself known as a lovable irritant to the local politicians. She eventually became head of the Long Island affiliate of the Union of Councils and called Moscow and Leningrad almost every day and at all hours. The refuseniks became her friends, and helping them was an integral part of her life. Most Soviet Jews who came through New York eventually spent a night on her couch, including Sylva Zalmanson, who was released early from prison and received an exit visa in 1974.

For some American Jews, activism was triggered by a life-altering trip to the other side of the iron curtain. Two young couples from Philadelphia, Connie and Joe Smukler and Stuart and Enid Wurtman, single-handedly brought the issue of Soviet Jewry to their city after they spent a few days in the Soviet Union meeting face to face with refuseniks. They devoted weekend after weekend to speaking in living rooms and in front of congregations; they identified with them. Most American Jews had Russian Jewish roots, and it seemed that only a simple twist of fate—what if their own grandparents had not left half a century before?—had saved them from the same miserable circumstances. It was like seeing an image of themselves in an alternate reality. Another couple from Philadelphia described the sensation in their 1977 debriefing report: "Their dress, their speech, their physical appearance, their values, their temperaments, are so familiar to us, and we are so comfortable with them, that it is hard to believe we are sitting in a Moscow apartment under KGB surveillance, rather than in suburban Philadelphia."

In the early 1970s, the Union of Councils made an important discovery in Michael Sherbourne, a sober, professional London high-school teacher who taught metalwork and engineering. A self-taught Russian speaker, Sherbourne became a popular contact for the refuseniks. He took down and quickly translated their statements and then passed them on. And unlike the Lishka, which filtered what it received, and American journalists in the Soviet Union, who had to worry about pleasing their editors back home, Sherbourne had only one concern: to get the refuseniks' messages and news out exactly as they wished.

Michael Sherbourne had come to the movement by chance in 1968 after he attended a talk by a recently emigrated Soviet Jew. Soon his wife was reheating his dinner again and again as he made as many as six phone calls a night to Russia—some of the Russian operators even recognized his voice—and the work took over his life. It was Sherbourne who coined the term *refusenik,* looking for an English equivalent for the Russian word *otkaznik.* He passed on all the information he got directly to the Israeli embassy in London, but he had no qualms about also sharing it with the grass roots. His first contacts were in England, where he became close with a formidable women's Soviet Jewry group called the Thirty-fives, named for the age they'd been in 1971 when they'd staged their first protest around the cause of Raiza Palatnik, also thirty-five, an arrested refusenik from Odessa. Soon Sherbourne was passing on information to the United States as well. In December of 1972, a few years into his phone calling, he began feeling that the Israelis were either distorting or withholding certain information from the Lishka-sanctioned newsletters, so Sherbourne started his own bulletin, recording every bit of news he collected. He spoke with everyone as regularly as he could, from Volodya Slepak, Alexander Lerner, and Dina Beilin to those involved with *kulturniki* activities. And in 1974, he got on the line with Anatoly Shcharansky, the first of what would be almost four hundred phone conversations with him over the next three years. Sherbourne and Shcharansky developed a deep bond, sometimes talking for more than forty-five minutes—a rich English benefactor subsidized all of Sherbourne's calls—and Sherbourne eventually acted as a go-between as well for the statements Shcharansky passed along from Andrei Sakharov and other dissidents. Sherbourne saw himself as a vessel, a way for messages to emerge from the Soviet Union. For Soviet Jewry activists who wanted to know everything about their refusenik friends—from their position on a piece of legislation to whether someone's sick baby was feeling better—Sherbourne's calls provided the kind of sustenance that gave the Western side of the movement energy and will.

But just as American Jews were beginning to cohere, tensions between grassroots groups and the establishment once again flared. A new conflict, which first presented itself in 1976, pitted these two forces against each other over an issue that touched the most sensitive place of both Israeli and American Jewish identity: the dropouts. The term itself was a Zionist concoction, meant to stigmatize those Soviet Jews who got out of the Soviet Union and then abandoned their Israeli exit visas and opted instead to go to a Western country, most often the United States. What had started as a small trend quickly ballooned out of control. In March of 1976, 50 percent of Soviet Jewish emigrants dropped out. The alarm bells were sounding for the Israeli government, and especially the Lishka. Unlike American Jews, Israelis had always seen the refusenik movement as having one overriding purpose: to bring more Jews to Israel. Soviet Jews were the great demographic hope. They would help to maintain the population of a Jewish state that was perpetually worried about the higher birth rates of its Arab citizens and its occupied Palestinian population. Soviet Jews, as every premier since Ben-Gurion had understood, were the secret weapon. When the dropout trend became visible, the Israelis immediately began arguing with American Jewish leaders about all the reasons why drastic measures needed to be taken to stop it. They argued that the Soviets would cease issuing visas altogether; that one visa used by a Jew headed for the West and assured assimilation was one visa lost to someone who sincerely wished to live in Israel. But the real source of their opposition was that the dropouts undermined the very reason for Israel's effort. Why should the Jewish State continue to pour resources into fighting for emigration if those Jews who left did not end up in Israel? What was the point?

The question of who exactly was dropping out preoccupied even the most informed Soviet Jewry activists throughout 1975 and 1976. The trend was shocking because it involved a population of Soviet Jews who were practically unknown in the West. These weren't the brave Zionist refuseniks, the Zalmansons of Riga or the Slepaks of Moscow, people who had an almost desperate desire to live in Israel. These were the silent majority, Jews who were not pulled toward Israel so much as pushed out of the Soviet Union. After the initial waves of Jews from the Caucasus and the Baltics, the next Jews who applied to leave were the minuscule groups of Zionists in the urban centers of Moscow and Leningrad, Kiev, Odessa, and Minsk. Those who were given permission became the next wave, while those who weren't became refuseniks. The émigrés inspired a larger group of Jews who were beginning to suffer the effects of Soviet anti-Semitism. These were the highly assimilated Jews, people who often identified more with Russian culture than Jewish culture and were extremely well educated. But once they started seeing their children rejected from university programs for which they were more than qualified and heard how more and more factories and labs would not hire Jews to do certain jobs, they realized they had no future in the Soviet Union. Restricting education was a particularly huge blow to a group that valued it so highly. Throughout the 1970s, Jewish enrollment in Moscow institutions of higher education decreased by half. Many who were interviewed once they'd left the Soviet Union said they could have lived with having *Jew* written in their passports; they could even have stood being called *dirty zhid* every once in a while. But what they simply couldn't tolerate was a ceiling on their children's educational opportunities. And since they were motivated primarily by economic and educational factors, they felt that America was the place to go.

These Soviet Jews had never spared a thought for Israel, and after

1973, there was even less to draw them there. If the Six-Day War in 1967 had inspired a generation of born-again Zionists, the Yom Kippur War in 1973 had the opposite effect. Even though Israel won the war decisively, the Arab states' surprise attack made Jews question the aura of invincibility engendered by the 1967 victory. Suddenly, everyone remembered that Israel was still an embattled and insecure country surrounded by enemies. Its economy also suffered in the mid-1970s, and horror stories quickly made the rounds in Moscow of former university professors cleaning toilets for a living. The Jewish Agency, the Israeli-backed organization in charge of immigration, often took the view that these new arrivals should feel grateful for any help they got, and so the government provided very little to cushion their landing. Hebrew seemed an impossibly foreign language for most of them. On top all this, a large proportion of Soviet Jews in the big cities had married non-Jews. They knew that Israel was a *Jewish* state, and they were afraid they'd be ostracized if they went there. The Soviets preyed on all these fears and anxieties, making sure that disenchanted letters sent from Israel to Russian relatives were frequently printed in the newspapers. They assumed this would cause Soviet Jews to stay in the Soviet Union. But all it did was redirect them to America.

Logistically, this was easy enough. Those who had received permission to leave the Soviet Union made their way via overnight train to Austria. Their destination was the Schoenau Castle, south of Vienna, built as a hunting lodge for Hapsburg royals and now used by the Jewish Agency as a transit center. The agency controlled the processing of all Soviet Jews until 1973, when a terrorist incident caused the Austrians to alter the arrangement. In the fall of that year, Palestinian militants boarded a train filled with Soviet Jews bound for Vienna and took a handful hostage. They demanded that the transit center be dismantled and that all flights to Israel from the Schwechat airport be terminated. Bruno Kreisky, the Socialist chancellor of Austria, and a Jew, agreed to the demands of the fedayeen. But after the hostages were returned, he quietly continued to allow the castle to be used as a transit point, on the condition that it be supervised by the Austrians. Kreisky insisted that he would ensure freedom of choice for those Jews who did not want to go to Israel. In 1973 there was a 3.6 percent dropout rate, but in 1974, after the Austrians took over the transit center, the rate was 18.7

percent, and in 1975 it was 36.9 percent. By the mid-1970s, hundreds of Soviet Jews arrived at the transit center every month. New arrivals were still met by representatives of the Jewish Agency and the Lishka, and those who decided to continue to Israel usually boarded an El Al flight for Tel Aviv within a day. For those who declared their intention to apply for a visa to America, a different procedure was in place.

Two American Jewish institutions, both founded at the turn of the century to deal with Eastern European emigrants and refugees, were on hand and happy to be given a new raison d'être: one group was the American Jewish Joint Distribution Committee, which housed and financially supported the refugees until they received American visas, and the other was the Hebrew Immigrant Aid Society (HIAS), which dealt with the process of securing those visas. When new arrivals insisted on going to America, they were transferred to agents of the Joint and HIAS. Representatives of the Jewish Agency tried to convince the émigrés to rethink their decision, but it was usually in vain. As one 1975 report written by a rabbi observing the procedure described it, "The Israelis admit that these sessions, which are held at the HIAS office, often become emotional. They share with many of their countrymen the conviction that every Jew should live in Israel, and feel this most deeply in regard to the Russians whom they have helped rescue and who are putting down fresh roots." But, the rabbi noted, "the plain fact is that these talks almost never succeed. Decisions reached over a period of years are unlikely to be reversed in a brief interview. Besides, misconceptions [about the difference between living conditions in America and Israel] rarely fall easily—people believe what they want to believe. Finally, many of the noshrim [Hebrew for "dropouts"] present reasons that the Jewish Agency cannot challenge. What do you tell a person who doesn't want to serve in the army?"

The dropouts were then flown to Rome, where they were either put up in hotels or given subsidies to settle temporarily in one of two suburbs of the Italian capital, Ostia or Ladispoli, while their American visas were being processed. This usually happened quickly. When it came to Cold War refugees, the United States had a very liberal immigration policy. The anti-Soviet sentiment in America combined with the stories of anti-Semitism made the U.S. government more than willing to admit these refuseniks. In 1976, Congress raised the quota on annual refugee admission from twenty thousand per country to a hundred and twenty thousand total. And if visas were limited, American Jewish organizations found loopholes that simply required the refugee to be financially sponsored. Once these escapees of Communism got to America, there were abundant funds for resettlement, medical care, English classes, and job training. The local Jewish federations embraced their Soviet Jewish brethren, and the U.S. government also contributed to the pot, adding thirteen million dollars between 1973 and 1976 to support the new immigrants. Compared with Israel's difficult economic situation and limited work options, America's opportunities looked to these Soviet Jews like a much smarter choice.

The Israelis were panicking. As the headline of a column in the Tel Aviv daily *Maariv* put it, "We Are Losing the Soviet Aliyah." And that was written in early 1975. As the dropout rate surpassed 50 percent the following year and continued to rise, Nehemiah Levanon, the head of the Lishka, began pursuing a radical plan. He would try to eliminate all aid to Jews who dropped out in Vienna. The offices of the Joint and HIAS had to be shut down.

Levanon began lobbying. One of the most receptive to his plan was Max Fisher, the Detroit philanthropist who had opposed passage of the Jackson-Vanik amendment. Fisher was chairman of the Jewish Agency's board of governors, the body in charge of determining the agency's policy, and he called a meeting in July 1976 to discuss the issue. Yitzhak Rabin, Israel's prime minister, was present. "We succeeded in opening Russian gates on the assumption that the Jews are leaving for Israel and Israel only," Rabin said. "Had we departed from that, we would never have obtained Soviet consent to Jewish emigration." Others were even harsher in their assessment. Arieh Dulzin, the Mexican-born chairman of the Jewish Agency, said that their "first duty is not to save Jews, we must save only those who will go to Israel."

The meeting resulted in Rabin's appointment of a committee of eight Jewish professionals (half of them American, half Israeli); two months later they produced a concrete proposal. All aid to dropouts would end on February 1, 1977. They assumed they could sell the plan to American Jews by explaining that they were preserving the freedom of choice, simply shifting the moment of choice earlier—from Vienna to the Soviet Union. If Jews wanted to emigrate to America they could always apply for exit visas to America. As soon as it became clear that Israel was actually serious about their plan, Carl Glick, the head of HIAS, wrote a confidential letter to his counterpart at the Joint saying that he and his organization could not accept the proposal. There were many problems, as he saw it. First, even if HIAS and the Joint left Vienna, there were several other refugee aid organizations—such as the International Rescue Committee, the Tolstoy Foundation, and even a group run by Hasidic Jews from the Satmar sect, Rav Tov—that would happily step in to help the dropouts. After all, the Austrian chancellor Kreisky had made it clear that his priority was ensuring freedom of choice. But the bigger problem was that the Israeli proposal rested on a false assumption: that Jews who wanted to go to America could easily get exit visas to emigrate there. This was simply not true. With the exception of a handful of visas for family reunification, the Soviets categorically refused to allow legal emigration to the United States. If the Israelis blocked the path now available to the dropouts, Glick argued, those Soviet Jews who were determined to go to America would be forced to stay in the Soviet Union.

Before the Committee of Eight, as they were known, could respond to these very real concerns, news of the proposal leaked and triggered an incredible backlash. Irving Howe spoke to *Time* in 1976 and expressed the shock of many American Jews: "We didn't campaign to 'let our people go' only to Israel. The central moral and humanitarian issue has been to get Jews out of the Soviet pesthole, regardless of where they want to settle." In the same article, Moshe Decter, by then no longer an agent of the Lishka, voiced contempt for his former Israel backers: "Why don't these officials run after the 250,000 Israeli citizens living in the U.S., instead of picking on a few wretched refugees trying to get a breath of fresh air in the West?"

The battle-scarred grass roots, familiar with the heavy-handed Lishka, were of course the least tempered in their response. Si Frumkin, a Union of Councils activist from Los Angeles, wrote in the September 1976 issue of the newsletter *Action-Central for Soviet Jews*: "No one, no one, has the right to tell people where to live and where to go, or not to go. Not the Russians. Not the Americans. Not the Israelis. . . . For years we have quoted the U.N. Declaration of Universal Human Rights at the Russians. I want to quote it at the 8 Jewish bureaucrats and at the Jewish bosses who sent them to stop the Exodus: EVERY

HUMAN BEING HAS THE RIGHT TO LEAVE THE COUNTRY OF HIS
RESIDENCE AND GO TO A DESTINATION OF HIS CHOICE. If we don't
believe this, then we have joined our enemies."

Many, though not all, of the refuseniks supported this position. In a
letter signed by Sasha Lunts, Alexander Voronel, and Vitaly Rubin, all
by then in Israel, they made their argument: "All of us are Zionists, not
only in word but by our actions, and we regard aliyah as enormously
important. At the same time we feel that emigration of Jews from the
USSR is necessary, even if they go to countries other than Israel—because of forced assimilation of Jews in the USSR, constantly increasing
mass and state anti-Semitism and—in the case of political instability
(such as war)—real danger of physical annihilation."

The reaction of American Jewish grass roots was not entirely unexpected. But the Israelis had not anticipated the forceful response of the
rest of the community. Not only did the proposal undermine freedom
of choice, a treasured American principle, it seemed to directly rebuke
American Jews who had chosen to remain in the Diaspora. Add to this
the perception—however exaggerated—that Soviet Jews would be
abandoned just like European Jews in the 1930s, and the policy change
was a very hard sell for the Israelis. When a special task force of Reform,
Conservative, and Orthodox rabbis made their recommendation on
the issue, these were the fears and resentments that guided their opinion. "The traditional Jewish concept of *Pidyon Shvuim* (redemption of
captives) imposes an overriding moral obligation to assist all Jews who
have managed to leave the Soviet Union," they wrote. "Moreover not to
assist may undermine the entire moral basis of our struggle on behalf
of Soviet Jews, which is based on the principle of reunion of families
and the right of free movement of population grounded in the United
Nations Declaration of Human Rights."

Even the Jewish federations revolted. The opinion of these local
umbrella groups—which brought together in each American city most
Jewish organizations and much of their fundraising—was not inconsequential. It was the money collected by these federations that went
to support the Jewish Agency; that organization was sustained largely
by Diaspora dollars. Leaders from the largest communities, such as
those in Chicago and Philadelphia, vowed never to support a policy
that would lock Jews into the Soviet Union. By the time the Israeli
plan was formally discussed at the General Assembly of the Council

of Jewish Federations and Welfare Funds, an annual gathering of local Jewish leaders, there wasn't much left to say. The session scheduled to discuss the dropouts attracted, according to the *New York Jewish Week,* an "overflow crowd of delegates, with many not able to get into the meeting room and others forced to stand throughout the long session." Both Nehemiah Levanon and Max Fisher made their case. The head of HIAS, Carl Glick, even more convinced that his organization needed to remain in Vienna, gave the opposing view. When it was time for audience comments, one man emotionally reminded everyone of the Holocaust. There was loud jeering at the suggestion of stopping aid. At the end, a dejected Max Fisher knew that if he brought the proposal to a vote, he would only embarrass himself and the Israelis. American Jewry was against it.

The plan to cut aid to dropouts was postponed indefinitely. A few days after the debate, the *Jewish Post and Opinion* dubbed this moment of vocal opposition to the Jewish State "the Magna Carta of the American Jewish community." It had been a long time since American Jews had taken such an independent stand. In effect, they were telling Israel that they had their own outlook and their own interests and would no longer hand over ultimate veto power, especially when it concerned an issue like freedom of choice, such a fundamental part of their communal identity. After the Yom Kippur War, Soviet Jews felt less drawn to Israel; similarly, American Jews felt less compelled to obey its every order. All this came at a moment when Israel was in the middle of peace negotiations with Egypt and badly needed a unified and supportive American Jewry to lean on the Carter administration if Egypt tried to impose a deal Israel could not accept. Unwilling to force the issue, the Israelis relented. And at that moment, the power of Nehemiah Levanon and the Lishka over the movement began to wane.

Meanwhile, Soviet Jews continued dropping out in ever greater numbers, topping 50 percent in 1977. And HIAS and the Joint continued helping them find their way to the United States. The sound of Russian could now be heard all over the Roman suburbs of Ostia and Ladispoli as these new refugees awaited their American visas.

———

The issue of human rights was beginning to dominate all coverage of the Soviet Union in the American press. In November of 1976, the

Washington Post had three stories that touched on the Soviets' human rights record; the *Los Angeles Times* ran five. In January of 1977, after Carter took office and the Helsinki Watch Group was repressed, this number jumped to thirteen and nine, respectively. In March, they were at twenty-eight and twenty-nine, almost one a day. But this did not come close to the *New York Times,* which in March had fifty-eight stories about the dissidents, constituting almost all its news from the Soviet Union that month. So prominent was this coverage that it caused a backlash. Writing in the *Columbia Journalism Review* in 1978, Peter Osnos, the Moscow correspondent for the *Washington Post,* wondered if Western journalists were blowing the dissident movement's importance out of proportion, whether their personal affinity for people like Shcharansky and Sakharov was influencing their coverage: "Are these dissidents really as important as our attention to them would indicate? What actually is their constituency among Russians? Are we encouraging dissent merely by writing about it? Indeed, do we sometimes act more as spokespersons for dissidents than as reporters?"

But doubts like these became irrelevant in the summer of 1977, when the Soviets finally announced the charges against Anatoly Shcharansky. He would be tried for treason, which carried a minimum of ten years in prison and could mean the death penalty. In the beginning of June, after Shcharansky had spent almost three months locked up and interrogated at Lefortovo Prison, his arrest made it onto the front pages of all the major American papers. Ida Milgrom, his mother, had received a letter from the state prosecutor informing her that Shcharansky would be charged under Article 64 of the criminal code, "rendering aid to a foreign state in carrying out hostile activity." Sanya Lipavsky's false accusation that Shcharansky was a CIA agent was going to be the basis of their case against him. As David Shipler put it in the *New York Times,* the move against Shcharansky had "few precedents since the days of Stalin."

The American government became involved as never before. Not only did the State Department immediately denounce the charge and praise Shcharansky as "well-known and respected," but a week later Carter himself called an unusual press conference. In front of a bank of television cameras, he said he had asked the State Department and the CIA if Shcharansky had ever been in their employ. "The answer is no," the president announced. "We've double-checked this and I have been hesitant to make that public announcement, but now I'm completely convinced that, contrary to the allegations that have been reported in the press, Mr. Shcharansky has never had any sort of relationship, to our knowledge, with the C.I.A."

The entire incident put Carter in a difficult situation. His two priorities—human rights and arms control—were coming into conflict. Throughout 1977, Carter held out the promise of passing SALT II, a treaty that would build on the nuclear arms reduction agreement that Nixon had signed in 1972. He wanted to show that he was continuing the de-escalating trend of détente. But to make progress, he needed to establish a good rapport with Brezhnev and his circle, as Kissinger had, and this became increasingly difficult every time the State Department pointed out a human rights violation. Shcharansky's arrest only added to this tension. It was a direct rebuke to Carter's outspoken human rights rhetoric. If the president took no position on the arrest, he would appear to be turning his back on the idealism of his inaugural address. So Carter made slight compromises. He gave the press conference denying Shcharansky's connection to the CIA but at the same time refused a symbolic photo op with Shcharansky's wife, who was then traveling the world trying to solicit support for her husband.

He walked the same fine line during a September 23 meeting at the White House with Andrei Gromyko, the Soviet foreign minister. Carter gingerly broached the topic. "We have different approaches to the question of human rights," he told Gromyko. "And I know that some of our statements on this question provoked L. I. Brezhnev's displeasure. However, adhering to our position on this question, we do not want to interfere in the domestic affairs of any state or to put you in an awkward position." But then Carter began to provide some examples of human rights violations, starting with the most celebrated case at the moment: Shcharansky. He explained that even before he took office, Congress had "linked the development of trade with the Soviet Union with the problem of the Jewish emigration from the USSR." His hands were tied. Unless Gromyko could do something to "ameliorate this source of tension and misunderstanding," he would not be able to overcome these "limitations established by Congress."

Gromyko responded with disdain: "If we would like to make a list of all violations of human rights in the USA or, say, in England, Italy, the Federal Republic of Germany, and in many other countries, it would be a long and impressive list. We are not doing it, however, because we do not want to interfere in other people's affairs." As far as Shcharansky, he told Carter, the case was of "infinitesimal significance." The president could harp on it all he wanted, but "such position of yours on this question can only harm the climate of our relations." Carter offered a weak rebuttal. Rather than claiming the cause of Shcharansky as his own, he pointed to his constituency. "We do not believe that the Shcharansky affair lacks significance," he answered Gromyko. "I did not blow it up. It concerns broad segments of the American public."

Carter was doing more than any past president had—and he really did believe that Shcharansky's case was one of the Soviets' most egregious human rights abuses. But he wasn't willing to allow it to completely destroy his relationship with the world's only other superpower. The ultimate test of Carter's commitment to a new kind of foreign policy had not yet presented itself. This would happen in the fall of 1977, with the opening of the first Helsinki monitoring conference. It was to take place in Belgrade, Yugoslavia, in October. If Carter genuinely wanted to hold the Soviets accountable for their human rights violations, that would be the place to do it.

The first indication that there might be a showdown in Belgrade was the September 1977 appointment of Arthur Goldberg to head the U.S. delegation. Goldberg, now nearing seventy, had suffered a number of disappointments in the previous decades. Lyndon Johnson had asked him to step down from the Supreme Court in 1965 to become ambassador to the United Nations (and to make room on the court for Johnson's ally Abe Fortas), and this had turned out to be an unfortunate move for him. He found himself in constant disagreement with the administration over its Vietnam policy and became disenchanted by his limited role at the United Nations. At the end of Johnson's tenure, Goldberg resigned in frustration. For a time in the late 1960s he was president of the American Jewish Committee, then he worked at a Washington, D.C., law firm, and in 1970 he ran, unsuccessfully, for governor of New York, losing badly to Nelson Rockefeller. His appointment to head the delegation to Belgrade happened almost by chance.

In the first few months of Carter's presidency, at Hubert Humphrey's suggestion, Goldberg was brought into the Oval Office to share his expertise on the Arab-Israeli conflict (he had helped compose the controversial UN resolution 242 following the Six-Day War). Carter was so impressed with Goldberg that he immediately offered him a position as chief Middle East negotiator. When Cyrus Vance, the new secretary of state, and Zbigniew Brzezinski, the national security adviser, heard about the spontaneous appointment, they complained that the outspoken Goldberg would undermine their efforts to make progress in the Middle East. In order to save face, another respectable position was found for Goldberg; the Belgrade conference was on the horizon, and he was named an ambassador at large and given the task of leading the American delegation.

Throughout his career, Goldberg had been a vocal defender of labor and human rights. He was one of the few public figures who'd been at the center of the Soviet Jewry movement since the early 1960s. He had spoken at the first American Jewish Conference on Soviet Jewry, in 1964, and had received at his Supreme Court office the small delegation of Jews from Cleveland who eventually formed the nucleus of the Union of Councils. Goldberg had tried to prod Kennedy to take action on Soviet Jewry early on. Over several decades, whether in the United Nations or in private practice, he had never ceased advocating for individual Soviet Jews and for the cause as a whole.

Carter's decision to appoint him—as blundering as it might have been—immediately raised the profile of the American delegation. It indicated a drastic departure from the past. In the negotiations leading up to the initial signing of the Helsinki Accords, in 1975, the Americans had tried to stay as low-key as possible, letting the Europeans take the lead. For the career officers in the State Department, the goal was to avoid confrontation and accusation, to work within the well-established boundaries of quiet diplomacy. Goldberg's appointment was a complete rejection of that approach. The man who'd been pushed aside to make room for Goldberg was Albert "Bud" Scherer, the State Department's chief negotiator at the initial Helsinki meetings and for years the point man for anything having to do with the Helsinki Accords. His name had already been sent to the Senate for confirmation. After he was replaced, Scherer had planned to quit the delegation completely, but some colleagues convinced him to stay on as Goldberg's deputy. This institutionalized the tension that already existed between Carter's bold public commitment to human rights and the quieter, nonconfrontational approach that was embedded in the culture of the State Department.

The appointment of Goldberg, with his owlish black glasses, thick white hair, stylish black suits, and fast-talking manner, was a public declaration that the game had changed. Goldberg considered the accords contractual, even though none of the signatories were bound by any form of law. The fact that the agreements were arrived at consensually made him even more convinced that no country should be spared criticism if it violated the act. Helsinki, as he saw it, had to be an ongoing series of meetings in which the countries' actions were judged against the principles to which they signed on. And he put the emphasis squarely on the human rights provisions, the third basket, the one the Soviets wanted to shove aside. When he started organizing his delegation, Goldberg stacked it with people who shared his approach, filling nine important spots with staffers from the Helsinki Commission. The State Department diplomats looked at these developments with dismay. They were threatened by the zealousness of these outsiders. Dorothy Goldberg, the ambassador's wife, recorded their reaction in her diary, writing that "some of our foreign service people" regard the commission as a "dubious element whose very outspoken commitment to the Helsinki process appears unduly enthusiastic, even a bit rash."

Goldberg arrived in Yugoslavia in early October. The presence of his delegation exploded the normally cordial, backroom, anticlimactic air that characterized these international gatherings among career diplomats. He brought with him citizens' representatives, including an Eskimo rights activist, a Roman Catholic monsignor, and a Polish American political science professor. No other country's delegation boasted such a colorful group. Goldberg promised to give a regular press conference after each session, especially those that were closed to the public. His notion of Helsinki as a process demanded that as many people as possible play a part. But he also believed that one of the purposes of the conference was to provide hope to dissidents in the Soviet Union and Eastern bloc countries, and this way they would hear him on the BBC or the Voice of America.

The first two weeks, modeled on the United Nations' General Assembly gatherings, were filled with long, showy speeches. Everyone watched Goldberg carefully. Mostly, the Soviets wondered if he would dare break one of the cardinal rules of international diplomacy: when speaking about human rights violations, a diplomat never condemned a country by name or referred to specific individuals or incidents. It was considered uncouth. UN ambassadors had learned the art of making veiled references that were still perfectly clear to the audience. And it wasn't just the Soviets who wanted to uphold the rules. The Western European countries in the NATO alliance, in closer proximity to a belligerent Soviet Union, also had an interest in keeping things civil. The State Department staffers in the American delegation warned Goldberg not to act too impetuously. They feared that if the Soviets were offended, they would leave the negotiating table.

In those first days, the fears about Goldberg seemed overblown. He did give a forceful opening speech, focusing almost entirely on human rights, but he named no names. He spoke generally of his inability to understand "restrictions on the rights of individuals to travel or emigrate." A few days later, in his final public speech, he went a small step further, asking, "Is it consistent with the humanitarian provisions of the Final Act to harass or imprison people for peaceful, nonviolent political dissent or religious belief?" But he didn't break the taboo. Observers at Belgrade thought this had to do with talks on SALT II then taking place at the White House between Carter and Gromyko. It seemed that quiet diplomacy was winning out after all.

Even without naming names, though, Goldberg was still ruffling feathers in Belgrade. A story in the *Washington Post*—based entirely on anonymous sources—was headlined "Goldberg and Aides Differ on Tactics at Belgrade Parley." While professional diplomats had a "natural inclination to work within narrowly defined limits," Goldberg's tactics "appear to have been to try to extend those boundaries by trying to shame the Soviets into a dialogue on human rights." The anonymous quotes in the story betrayed a slight anti-Semitic tone, portraying Goldberg as overly emotional and incapable of separating his personal feelings from the task at hand. "Most of us tend to leave our human instincts at the door when we walk in," one Western delegate was quoted as saying. Goldberg's "style" was described as "alternately hectoring, charming and whimsical." The only positive appraisal came from someone identified as a member of the Helsinki Commission who called him a "gutsy old man." In the halls of the Belgrade convention center, Goldberg was gaining a reputation for being self-righteous and sanctimonious. The Soviets nicknamed him, contemptuously, the Judge.

When the private meetings began, on October 17, it was unclear how confrontational Goldberg was actually going to be. At the first session of the Basket III Working Group, to discuss the human rights component, he wasn't even present, and one of his deputies spoke vaguely about "some signatory states" refusing to let their citizens reunite with family abroad. The following day, however, Goldberg unexpectedly took the microphone. And now, having gently tiptoed up to the forbidden door, he suddenly kicked it open. Reading from an article in *L'Humanité*, the French Communist newspaper, he described the trial in Czechoslovakia of four members of Charter 77, the group founded to monitor implementation of the Helsinki Accords. In that instant, he broke the taboo. The entire chamber began murmuring. The delegate from Czechoslovakia objected loudly. The Soviet representative couldn't contain his shock. "I am surprised," he said, by the actions of "this distinguished representative of the United States of America." It "is nothing other than an attempt to interfere in the internal affairs of a state represented here . . . This is not a forum for such statements."

Goldberg didn't stop there. He continued providing details of Helsinki violations in a manner that would have been unthinkable just two weeks earlier. He named names, though only in seven carefully considered instances. Shcharansky's case was described, as was Orlov's. And Goldberg made a specific point of talking about the problems of Soviet Jews. He mentioned Yosef Begun, one of the Hebrew teachers arrested for "parasitism" after he was fired from his job. As the *Washington Post* described it, "Whether the Russians like it or not, the happiness of the individual has become recognized as a legitimate subject for international negotiation." The Soviets did not like it. They shut down completely. As soon as the focus of the conference shifted to human rights—and specifically their violations—they did their best to bring Belgrade to a quick close.

Because consensus was necessary for any further amendments or revisions of the Helsinki Accords, it was clear that nothing concrete would be achieved. After a holiday recess, attention turned to formulating a concluding document. The Americans proposed more than one hundred additions to the accords—measures that would further protect individuals from persecution and promote emigration and reunification of families. None of them were approved by the Soviets. Goldberg wanted to include them anyway. But the Soviets insisted that the final document contain only those issues that had been agreed upon by all countries. There were only a few. And so the Soviet draft was simply a reaffirmation of the initial accords. After a few weeks of tug of war, this anodyne version was accepted. There was very little Goldberg could do to change their minds, especially since the Soviet delegation, deeply offended by the Judge and his allegations, was hardly speaking to him.

The only concrete piece of progress, as far as Goldberg was concerned, was the commitment to another follow-up conference, to take place in Madrid in 1980. The dissidents and activists would at least have this to look forward to, one more chance to publicly shame the regime.

In his closing remarks, Goldberg spoke out of frustration. He hoped that after the example he'd set, the Helsinki process might take a different path: "Efforts to squelch the truth at Belgrade or at home will not change the truth. And they will not deflect the United States from insisting that candor is as important to the healthy development of international confidence as is respect for sovereign equality and individuality." But not everyone thought his approach had been effective. And in the days following the end of the conference in March of 1978, many criticized his zealousness. Most notably the Communists, who couldn't believe that Goldberg had turned Belgrade into a trial. "The American tactics, or better said, the tactics of 'your judge' have poisoned the atmosphere," said the Polish ambassador. "Even if we want to do something we are reluctant to because it looks as though we are being forced." There was also criticism in the West from those who thought Goldberg too aggressive. In an analysis piece, the *Washington Post*'s Michael Getler wondered what the point of the Helsinki process was if it only led to stalemate: "Can it help the real life situation of dissidents in Eastern Europe or families who want to emigrate? Would a different American strategy—one that was quieter and didn't hammer away at the Soviets on human rights in front of 34 other countries—work better, or did the Soviets come here prepared not to give an inch on human rights no matter what anybody said or how they said it?"

For this, Goldberg had an answer: there was no other way. "We had to speak out honestly to maintain our credibility, because the Final Act of Helsinki provides for this," he told the press. He added, "Meanwhile, we have given hope to dissenters in Prague and the Soviet Union and others in Eastern Europe that they are not overlooked, that their right to organize into monitoring groups is not ignored because to do so would be a tremendous letdown. They're pretty realistic that we're not going to change the system, but it gives them heart."

For all his talk of having set a new precedent, Goldberg left Belgrade dejected that he hadn't done more, especially for Soviet Jews. But he kept insisting that a new era had arrived, that the time of ignoring human rights for the sake of diplomatic niceties was over. On the last day of the conference, Goldberg asked, "How long—after trying quiet diplomacy—could you sit here and not make a statement on a family reunification case in which the person loses his job because he asks for a visa and then is arrested as a parasite for not having a job?"

As Goldberg saw it, the dissonance in Belgrade, with the Soviets smarting at the open criticism, was a painful but necessary first step. Eventually, they would be shamed into change.

11

Trial and Exile

1977–1980

ACCORDING TO SOVIET LAW, nine months was the maximum period one could be detained without being formally charged with an offense. But on the nine-month anniversary of his arrest, Anatoly Shcharansky still sat in his cold concrete cell in Lefortovo Prison playing chess against himself. His closest friends and his young wife advocated for him in the world outside, but he spent those months in his own head. Shcharansky viewed the experience as an endurance test. Could he overcome fear? Could he outsmart the KGB agents who every day dragged him from the prison to their investigative wing for endless, numbing hours of interrogation? He approached each of these new challenges like a logic puzzle. Even in his first moments of captivity, standing naked in front of the prison officials and subjected to a full body search, his mouth and anus probed with gloved fingers, he came up with a mantra to preserve his dignity: *Nothing they do can humiliate me. I alone can humiliate myself.*

Once he overcame the shock of his new existence—the iron cot, the bright light bulb that remained illuminated at night, the talkative informer who shared his cell—his biggest problem became the interrogation. The KGB's tactics had changed in recent decades. They seldom resorted to outright violence. There were no midnight executions in the basement of Lefortovo as there had been under Stalin. Instead, the torture was talk. To elicit free-flowing confessions, they used a mixture of psychological games and emotional manipulation. His interrogators constantly tried to make him believe they knew everything, that his most steadfast friends—reliable people like Slepak and Lerner—had all confessed, that other refuseniks had exposed him as a spy. They told him once that his father had died (though they could simply have told him the truth, which was that he was gravely ill and had suffered a heart attack after his son's arrest). And when they got particularly frustrated at his unwillingness to cooperate, they resorted to harsher methods. In July, after three and a half months in Lefortovo and on the third anniversary of his marriage to Natasha, he was sent to the prison's punishment block for almost two weeks, ostensibly for the crime of sharpening the end of his toothbrush. There he lived in a damp cell where the plaster peeled off the walls and his bed was a wooden plank. He was given only underwear, a T-shirt, thin socks, and boots for clothing. He spent all his energy trying to keep warm, pacing the cell's two-meter length and, for the first time in his life, singing out loud in his tone-deaf voice. He sang Hebrew songs that he had learned from the refuseniks. One in particular gave him strength, a Hasidic saying put to music: *Kol ha-olam kulo gesher tzar m'od, V'haiker lo l'fachhed klal* (The whole world is a narrow bridge, and the important thing is not to be afraid at all).

Five years earlier, Shcharansky had completed his doctoral thesis, "Simulating the Decision-Making Process in Conflict Situations Based on the Chess Endgame," in which he examined ways that computers could solve the kind of strategic challenges that a chess player confronted when looking at a board. It was a perfect topic for him. He was the ultimate analytical thinker. Now he invented an almost mathematical equation for dealing with his interrogators. He established three basic rules. First, he would avoid any kind of cooperation with them. Second, he would try to understand as much as possible about what kind of case they were building. And third, he would find a way to expose them, either by establishing some kind of contact with the West or by pushing for an open trial. He then subdivided these goals. How, specifically, would he be uncooperative? He drew a diagram on a piece of toilet paper, and under this first goal, he wrote that he would not help them paint a picture of the movement as secretive or subversive, and he would never implicate any other refuseniks. In this way he developed a kind of logic tree, which he wrote out and threw away so many times it became ingrained in his head. The meetings with the interrogators—men whose general stupidity astounded Shcharansky—became a sort of game. It was not easy, however, to stick to his equation. Sometimes he became talkative or too weak to resist their ploys, and he compromised himself. But he was nonetheless grateful to have a formula to follow.

As he built up more confidence, he tried to gain the upper hand. At first, he was shocked and frightened by the severity of the charge—treason—which could easily lead to the firing squad. The only other Jewish activists who'd ever been accused under Article 64 of the criminal code were the Leningrad hijackers Kuznetsov and Dymshits, back in 1970. The interrogators used this mortal threat as a way of attaining information, dropping it crudely into conversation. In those first few months, he was plagued by a recurring daydream of his being led into a basement and then shot in the back of the head. But one day he decided to simply make light of the threat, grabbing this weapon from their arsenal. "What's the use of all these conversations when you're just going to shoot me anyway?" He laughed.

After almost three hundred interrogation sessions, he concluded that their case against him was very slight. It hung mostly on the testimony of Sanya Lipavsky and another young refusenik informer, Leonid Tsypin. The second denunciation, much like the first, painted innocuous activities as ominous. Tsypin wrote in *Viechernaya Moskva* that his mission, as dictated by forces abroad, was to "unite young people of Jewish nationality, that is what they wanted from us." For this goal he helped organize "so-called circles for the study of Hebrew." But, he confessed, "we did not teach Hebrew as much as we agitated for emigration to Israel and spoke about the 'life of paradise in the Promised Land' in accordance with what was written in the textbooks received illegally."

The most dangerous accusation against Shcharansky, that he was a CIA agent passing sensitive information to the West through foreign correspondents, was based on nothing. Their strongest piece of evidence, as far as he could tell, came in the form of a headline of an article in the *Los Angeles Times*. Written by Shcharansky's friend Robert Toth, the story told of refuseniks denied exit visas because of their work at Soviet institutions that demanded a high security clearance. Toth looked at the extensive lists of refuseniks, which included where they had been employed and why they were refused, and easily determined that many of the institutions they worked in were far from secret; in fact, some were even engaged in scientific or commercial exchange programs with the United States. But the headline Toth's editors decided to use had a much more nefarious tone: "Russia Indirectly Reveals 'State Secrets.'" It gave the impression that the refuseniks, who had simply shared with the reporter their well-circulated lists, were engaged in some subversive activity. Still, if this was all they had on him, it wasn't much.

When he wasn't playing his game with the KGB, he lived in his head. He used a relaxation technique Slepak had taught him to help conjure happy memories and avoid isolation. He would lie on his iron cot and relax each of the muscles in his body, one by one. Then he tried to remember every detail about his parents and Natasha, who had changed her name to Avital after arriving in Israel. He also practiced his Hebrew. Over a period of a few weeks, he attempted to write down every Hebrew word he knew, and it came to nearly two thousand. Then he started translating everything he heard and read into Hebrew using this basic lexicon. These types of exercises sustained him. He read the classics too. Lefortovo had an impressive library, mostly books confiscated from the Soviet elite during the purges of the 1930s. And Shcharansky had his prayer, the one routine under his control. He had made it up early on using his rudimentary Hebrew and said it twice before going into an interrogation, in his cell before he went to sleep, and out in the courtyard where he was allowed to exercise for an hour every day: "Blessed are you, Adonai, King of the Universe. Grant me the good fortune to live with my wife, my beloved Avital Sharon [the surname he imagined he would take], in the Land of Israel. Grant my parents, my wife, and my whole family the strength to endure all hardships until we meet. Grant me the strength, the power, the intelligence, the good fortune, and the patience to leave this jail and to reach the land of Israel in an honest and worthy way."

In December of 1977, on the nine-month anniversary of his arrest, his detention was extended beyond the legal limit, and he soon understood why. A few weeks after the new year, Shcharansky was told that his case was complete and he would now be given a chance to examine the evidence against him, a customary Soviet practice. He was escorted into a room and presented with his file, which consisted of fifty-one volumes, each containing nearly three hundred pages of typed text. The authorities had expended an incredible amount of energy to justify his arrest and build the narrative of espionage on which it hung. All his phone calls to the West were neatly cataloged, as was every newspaper article that contained a reference to him; there were transcripts of conversations that could only have been overheard by the KGB's bugging the apartments of his friends, hundreds of pages from the *Congressional Record* noting every utterance of his name by a senator or congressman. The first fifteen volumes contained the records of at least a hundred interrogations of refuseniks from cities and towns all over the Soviet Union.

Shcharansky dove into the material, eager to get some sense of the government's case. He spent the spring of 1978 going through the file piece by piece and copying out any relevant information, filling three thousand pages of notes. His interrogators sat in the room with him, all pretending to read the recently released second volume of Brezhnev's memoirs, which covered his years as a political commissar during the war. Shcharansky discovered very little hard evidence in all this material. All those months of isolation had made him fear that the movement had been destroyed or that his friends had crumbled under the pressure and started pointing fingers at one another. The witness statements were encouraging. To varying degrees, everyone had behaved well, and his closest friends had given the KGB little more than their names.

Shcharansky got a sense of how aggressively the refusenik activists and his friends in the West were responding to his case. He found a confiscated roll of film that an American tourist had tried to smuggle out of the Soviet Union. The KGB had developed the prints, and they turned out to be photos of reports written in Dina Beilin's neat hand detailing the interrogations of refuseniks. Then he made his most rewarding find. In the file was a copy of the British documentary *A Calculated Risk*, the film made two years earlier that featured Shcharansky and Slepak giving a tour of refusenik Moscow. Along with it was another film by the same production company, this one made after his arrest: *The Man Who Went Too Far.* He demanded to see both documentaries. He said he needed to familiarize himself with the evidence. Cornered by their own rules, the KGB investigators agreed. It felt like a thousand years had passed since the man he saw in the first film drove through the city streets. But it was the second, more recent documentary that contained the real surprise: footage of a rally in London in front of the Soviet embassy demanding his freedom. And his Avital was leading it. Michael Sherbourne was there, and Ludmilla Alexeyeva. It went by so fast that he asked to see it again. And again. Shcharansky was mesmerized by the image of the crowd and of his wife, who for so long had lived only in his imagination. The agents soon became frustrated and turned it off. "That's enough!" the lead investigator yelled. "What do you think, that your fate is in the hands of those people and not ours? They're nothing but students and housewives."

Throughout the long months of waiting in Lefortovo, Shcharansky wondered what was happening in the world outside his prison walls. Was the Belgrade conference successful? Had Carter's election changed anything for Sakharov? For Orlov? The files, though they were voluminous, gave him only an inkling. But the world *had* changed in that year, both for better and for worse. Partly owing to the publicity over Shcharansky's case, the Soviet Union's human rights record was getting more attention than ever before. It was now a major Cold War concern, close to the top of the American president's agenda at every meeting with Soviet leaders. For the refuseniks, this was an enormous achievement.

At the same time, the focus on human rights was slowly destroying détente, leading to an environment in which the Soviets had little incentive to tolerate dissent. This was the paradox of the new era. The response to the Belgrade conference was a perfect example. Though it shone a light on the dissidents and refuseniks, it also greatly humiliated the Soviets. They returned from Yugoslavia in March of 1978 even more intransigent than before, determined to crush any kind of opposition. Shcharansky's arrest marked the arrival of the darkest days yet for the refusenik community, darker than Shcharansky could have guessed from behind Lefortovo's high walls.

An atmosphere of terror swept through the refusenik community in the months following the Shcharansky arrest. Everyone was interrogated and treated like a potential suspect ("Today you are a witness, but soon you'll be a defendant," one was told). It seemed only a matter of time before the whole movement was dismantled—Slepak and Lerner, also mentioned in the Lipavsky denunciation, were sure their own arrests were imminent. In a collective appeal to the West, two hundred and fifty refuseniks warned that the accusation of espionage was "one of the most dramatic moments, perhaps one of the major turning-points in the history of Jews in Russia." They compared this new threat to the Dreyfus Affair, the Mendel Beilis trial, and the Doctors' Plot, all historic incidents when falsely accused Jews became scapegoats, an excuse for unleashing widespread anti-Semitism and even more persecution. "On the surface, only a small part of the erupting volcano can yet be seen. All the rest is inside, hidden, concealed from view. What is being cooked up down there in the depths is as yet unknown to us, but we shall no doubt very soon feel it, and experience the full effects of the depth of the anti-Jewish prejudice being stirred up to vomit forth from the mouth of the volcano."

Dina Beilin, Shcharansky's friend and the meticulous list keeper of the refuseniks, debriefed everyone who had been interrogated. She was trying to piece together a picture of the charges so she could refute them. It turned out that the questions all seemed to revolve around Shcharansky's role in an imagined organization the KGB had dubbed Aliyah. They weren't asking about connections to the CIA or spying techniques. They wanted to know about the most routine of their activities—how they contacted the West, why they supported the Jackson-Vanik amendment, how they reproduced samizdat. She was sure they were building a case against the Jewish movement as a whole. For Beilin, this was important information. It refuted what she was hearing from Nehemiah Levanon in Israel, that because of Shcharansky's dissident ties, he was a distraction, and his case should not be defended. A group of refuseniks wrote a letter to the West emphasizing that "interaction between the Jewish emigration and the general Human Rights movement has a versatile character," and "we cannot imagine the two movements to be absolutely separated."

The signs were not good for either refuseniks or democrats. In May of 1978, Yuri Orlov went on trial. After four days in which the actions of the Moscow Helsinki Watch were depicted as criminal, he received a seven-year prison sentence that was to be followed by five years of internal exile. The pressure was immense. And yet all the Moscow refuseniks could do was continue to try to bring attention to their cause. In fact, the logic of nonviolent demonstration demanded that they take advantage of this moment of great repression to further dramatize their situation.

It was this combination of dejection and determination that drove a group of refusenik women to involve their sons and daughters in a massive protest planned for June 1, the day the Soviet Union called International Children's Day. Originally the plan was to gather on five different balconies all over Moscow and at forty-five-minute intervals drape banners or hang signs protesting the government's emigration policies. But some of the women became frightened by the police cars surrounding their buildings the evening before and abandoned their protest. The rest decided to congregate in the apartment of Natasha Rosenshtein, where a year and a half earlier the remnants of the cultural symposium had taken place. There they spent the night on the floor in sleeping bags, preparing for the next day's battle.

In another apartment, alone that night, was Ida Nudel—chief advocate for the Jewish prisoners—a small, tough woman, now forty-seven and prematurely graying with a streak of silver shot through her long black hair. She had decided to join the protest, but alone, with a barricade of furniture pushed up against her apartment door. She wrote out her sign on a long piece of butcher paper: KGB—GIVE ME A VISA TO ISRAEL. On the morning of June 1, Nudel found a bulldozer parked in front of her building and four KGB agents sitting on the balcony next to her own. She prepared to defend herself against those whose job it would surely be to tear the banner out of her hands. She filled up a bucket of water to throw at them and lay pieces of nail-studded wood on the balcony floor. As evening approached and with it her appointed time to unfurl her sign, she became more anxious. A crowd of policemen was gathered below, all staring up at her apartment.

That same day, Masha Slepak was trying to decide whether to take part in the demonstration. The Slepaks had remained at the center of the Jewish movement. Volodya was now known all over the world—his apartment was still the first stop for Jewish tourists visiting Moscow. He never tired of telling his story, amusing them with his quirky appearance (the large beard and lumbering body) and good nature. The door to the apartment on Gorky Street, only a few yards from the Kremlin, was always open. But now, in the eighth year of refusal, the struggle had taken a toll on his family. For one thing, the Slepaks were technically divorced. They had always tried to keep their children from suffering for their stand, but their high profiles made this impossible. They divorced so that Masha might emigrate separately with their younger child. But this didn't work. OVIR was not fooled. The big worry had always been that their son Leonid would reach the age of conscription and be drafted into the army. And that's exactly what happened. Leonid responded to the draft notice in a letter that explained that he considered himself an Israeli citizen in absentia and so could not serve in the Soviet army. He then went underground. He traveled the country by train, first to Yerevan, Armenia, and then back to Leningrad and Moscow, where he hid in various apartments. Masha and Volodya constantly worried that he would be thrown into jail. Their elder boy, Sanya, had actually managed to get an exit visa in the fall of 1977, after years of being denied work or placement in any university. As the Belgrade conference was beginning, the KGB had offered to let him go if he would call foreign correspondents in Yugoslavia and announce that he had received permission. Sanya refused to help them in their publicity stunt, but they let him leave anyway, giving him a week to pack.

Deprived of her two children and far more fatalistic than her husband, Masha Slepak was increasingly despairing in her life of endless waiting. On the morning of the Children's Day protest, she tried to open the door to her apartment to walk their dog and found that it had been fastened shut, tied with rope to the stairway. Since Masha was part of the women's group, the KGB assumed the Slepaks had helped plan the protest. Masha had had it. She told Volodya that she couldn't stand to be humiliated anymore. She made up her mind to join the demonstration. Together they took a sheet and painted on it these words: LET US GO TO OUR SON IN ISRAEL. Volodya locked the door to their apartment and then the door to their bedroom. They stepped outside onto the balcony and draped the sheet over the balcony's edge so that all of Gorky Street, one of Moscow's busiest and grandest boulevards, could see the words hanging off the eighth floor.

After about half an hour a huge crowd began forming below, straining to see what was written. Traffic nearly stopped, and the passage of the trolleys that went up and down the street was blocked. A few people started screaming anti-Semitic slurs. Police officers on the adjacent upstairs balcony used a stick to try to knock the banner away. At one point Volodya got hold of the stick, snapped it in half, and threw it down to the street below. "They should use a pistol!" someone in the crowd shouted up at the police. It was a warm day and people were enjoying the cat-and-mouse spectacle. Soon almost a thousand people were clogging Gorky Street to get a look. The Slepaks gripped their sheet and, though astounded by the giant, jeering crowd, told each other they would not budge. Volodya suddenly felt a burning on his head and realized that boiling hot water was being poured on him from the ninth-floor balcony, the one above theirs. They stepped away from the edge, still clutching the sign, and then they heard the sound of their apartment door being hacked apart with axes. Masha didn't want to give the spectators the satisfaction of seeing them arrested. Just as KGB agents were destroying their locked bedroom door, the two reentered their apartment. The sheet was yanked from their hands and they were led downstairs and placed in a prison van.

This scene was repeated in the Rosenshtein apartment, where eleven women and their thirteen children had gathered. They tried to hold out, blocking their door with a sofa and desks, and chanting. But after twenty minutes, the KGB broke through and detained all of them.

At six in the evening Ida Nudel was ready to go out on her balcony, unaware of all the earlier arrests. Her apartment too had been sealed off. She attached her banner to the ends of two skis and carried it out to the balcony as the day's light was fading. Almost immediately, from the window of an adjoining apartment, the KGB reached in with hooked metal rods, caught the banner, and pulled it until it tore off the skis in two pieces and floated down to the street. Nudel was undeterred. She went back inside, wrote up another sign, returned, and fastened it to the skis again. This time when the agents tried to attack her banner, she threw water at them. They switched to a new strategy, going to the balcony above hers and swinging a wrench tied to the end of a rope until it eventually smashed her window. At the sound of breaking glass, the gathering crowd cheered as if at a football game. Frightened and assaulted from all sides, she moved back into her apartment, which was now covered in shards of glass. As day turned into night, the police stopped pounding on her barricaded doors, and Nudel lay down on her couch, fully dressed, and fell asleep.

She was seized on the street the next day, just after she'd met with foreign correspondents and recounted what had happened. Three uniformed policemen drove her back to her apartment; on her door, someone had pinned a drawing of three pigs under the words *Zionist swine*. Nudel sat in a chair and watched the KGB conduct a search. Her apartment was already a mess with the upturned furniture and shattered glass, and now they were dumping every piece of paper onto the living room floor. They charged her with malicious hooliganism and forbade her to leave the city.

The trials of Volodya Slepak and Ida Nudel took place three weeks later on the same day, June 21, and in the same courthouse. Both were accused of the same crime. Slepak chose to defend himself without the help of the court-appointed attorney. Nudel was surprised that her lawyer actually tried to defend her. But no witnesses were allowed to testify on behalf of either defendant. Both courtrooms were small and filled with unsympathetic audiences. Sakharov, Bonner, much of the refusenik community, and representatives from the American embassy were all kept out, as were reporters. They massed on the street instead. At one point the police turned a fire hose on the crowd when it got too close to the courthouse.

After a few hours of futile defense, Volodya Slepak was found guilty of public disorder and sentenced to five years of internal exile.

At Ida Nudel's trial, the evidence of her malicious hooliganism was laid out in front of the judge: a bottle of ink, a brush, a rolled-up piece of paper. The defense lawyer conceded that Nudel was a strange character (she "does not get along very well with our society") but still asked the court for an acquittal, an unusual move for a KGB-sanctioned attorney. This caught Nudel off-guard, and instead of remaining silent throughout the trial as she had planned, she decided to make a final statement before her sentencing. With her voice catching in her throat, she described her trial as an indictment of her activism:

I am being tried in fact for the last seven years, the most wonderful years of my life. If I should ever find myself obliged to deliver another final plea, I am absolutely convinced that I shall affirm once again that the seven years which are the cause of this trial were the most difficult but also the most wonderful of my life. During the seven years, I learned to walk with my head high, as a human being and as a Jew. The seven years have been full of daily struggle on behalf of myself and others. Every time that I was able to keep a victim alive, I experienced a rare and intense emotion comparable, perhaps, to the joy of a woman who has given birth. Even if the remainder of my life should turn out to be gray and uneventful, the memory of those seven years will warm my heart and reassure me that I have not lived my life in vain.

Ida Nudel received four years of internal exile.

Absent that day from Volodya Slepak's trial was his wife, Masha Slepak. She had eaten moldy black bread during her detention and was in the hospital suffering from extreme stomach ulcers. She heard the verdict on the radio. Just before her own trial, she went to visit Volodya in jail. Masha didn't know whether they would be exiled together or separately, since they were technically divorced. Looking at her husband through Plexiglas, she saw that his hair had grown even bushier than usual and she told him he needed a haircut. "No, it's all right; this way it's warmer," Volodya answered, smiling. They tried to strategize for her trial. They talked about their sons. And before they knew it, their time was up. On the next visit, the authorities informed her that Volodya was no longer there. He had been moved to a transit prison to begin his long journey east.

By the end of June 1978, the Jewish movement had had its heart ripped out. Volodya Slepak and Ida Nudel were preparing for their exile; Dina Beilin had suddenly been given an exit visa and rushed out of the country; and Anatoly Shcharansky's trial and possible execution was looming. Those who had worked the hardest to maintain political pressure on the Soviets, to publicize the situation of refuseniks and to remind the world of the prisoners then languishing in labor camps, were quickly disappearing. In the short history of the movement so far, new leaders had always taken the place of those who left. This fluidity and the lack of any rigid hierarchy meant that the movement could not readily be decapitated. Still, these now absent activists had spent almost a decade fighting. They had become widely known and trusted, both in the West and among other Soviet Jews. They could not easily be replaced. Their persecution also put the lie to one of the movement's central premises. Activist refuseniks had always argued that the more visible they made themselves in the West, the better chance they had of avoiding persecution. No one was more visible than Shcharansky, Slepak, and Nudel. But now, with the Soviets becoming ever more entrenched, no one was safe. What the Americans or anyone else thought didn't matter anymore.

The arrest and exile of Slepak and Nudel were challenging enough to Soviet-American relations, but Shcharansky's trial seemed to be the ultimate test of détente. Carter had gone out of his way to defend Shcharansky, still trying to meet the moral bar he had set for himself without damaging relations with the Soviets. It was a balancing act the Kremlin seemed to be trying to upset when it scheduled the trial for July 7, the same week that Secretary of State Vance was to meet Gromyko in Geneva to discuss SALT II. As David Shipler put it in the *New York Times:* "From Moscow's perspective, then, the trial's timing appears to be an effort to highlight the limits of détente, to dramatize what détente does and does not mean here: that its centerpiece is arms control, and that it does not imply acquiescence to American demands for internal social change."

The world waited to see the outcome of the trial, and Soviet leaders knew how they wanted to play their hand. In a meeting of the Politburo on June 22, 1978, the day after Slepak and Nudel were sentenced, Yuri Andropov announced to Brezhnev and the other members that the preparations for the Shcharansky trial had been completed: "The trial will take place in the same court as the Orlov case. This is a good place, a club, and the audience, properly prepared, will therefore be small . . . I consider that it is not in our interest to allow any correspondents at the trial." All agreed. There was just one question left to discuss. "What will be Shcharansky's sentence?" Andropov asked. "Everything will depend on how he behaves himself. For example, the intention was to give Orlov three years in accordance with the articles of the Criminal Code, but he behaved so indecently at the trial, that the court was obliged to sentence him to seven years with a subsequent exile for five years. Of course, Shcharansky will not receive the death penalty, but the court will give him a severe sentence, say, for example, fifteen years."

Two weeks later, Shcharansky, after sixteen months in detention, entered the courthouse—a small three-story building on a secluded, tree-lined street called Serebrennicheski Pereulok, about a mile from the Kremlin. He walked into the courtroom and quickly scanned the audience for his mother, for Sakharov, for a journalist friend. There wasn't a single familiar face. Anyone sympathetic to him, including foreign correspondents, had been barred from the trial. They all stood outside, next to Shcharansky's mother, a frail, white-haired seventy-year-old who clutched a handkerchief. "Not to be allowed into the courtroom is a mockery of a mother; it is sadistic torture," she told one journalist. Before her son was arrested, Ida Milgrom and Shcharansky's older brother, Leonid, had had no involvement with the refusenik movement; they lived comfortably in the town of Istra, on the outskirts of Moscow. But after the ordeal of the past year, they too had been turned into dissidents.

When he was finally given permission to speak, Shcharansky demanded that his mother and brother, not just government sympathizers, be allowed to observe the trial. The judge resisted at first, but after a ten-minute recess, Shcharansky returned to the courtroom to see his brother, Leonid, or Lenya, as he called him, sitting a few feet away. He smiled. "You've gotten fat," Shcharansky called out. He was told to remain quiet, and Leonid steeled himself for the difficult task of trying to memorize as much of the trial's proceedings as possible. Shcharansky asked if he could serve as his own defense attorney, and the judge agreed. Familiar now with Soviet law, Shcharansky understood what all this meant: he would not face a firing squad. Otherwise, the judge would never have agreed to either demand. Shcharansky relaxed. Then he pleaded not guilty to all the charges.

The next five days were a farce, both inside and outside the courtroom. The Soviet leadership faced a dilemma. They wanted the appearance of an open trial, but they didn't want too much scrutiny of the evidence. Though no journalists were allowed to record the proceedings, press conferences were given twice a day—unprecedented for the Soviets. But the seventy reporters who assembled at the courthouse every afternoon and evening learned nothing from the court spokesman that they couldn't have gotten from reading Pravda. Inside, the trial quickly turned into a broad indictment of the entire Jewish movement. The prosecutor blamed Shcharansky for supporting the Jackson-Vanik amendment and therefore adversely affecting the Soviet economy. He referred to meetings with journalists, meetings with congressmen. But as Shcharansky repeated again and again, all these activities were open; for fear of implicating his friends, he didn't mention that there were at least a few dozen refuseniks who had acted no differently than he. The prosecutor presented no concrete link to the CIA beyond insinuating that Robert Toth was a spy and that Shcharansky had helped him gather information.

More than half of the week was spent in closed sessions in which the prosecution's witnesses were questioned. The two informers, Leonid Tsypin and Sanya Lipavsky, spoke and repeated what they had written in their public denunciations. Shcharansky cross-examined them and easily tripped them up. They were confused about certain dates. Who met whom when? For example, Lipavsky described meetings in which American agents told Shcharansky how to help enforce the Helsinki Accords, but the dates of the meetings that Lipavsky reported were before the treaty had even been signed. In a normal courtroom, their credibility would have been thrown into question, but here their word was accepted as fact—their testimony was, after all, the linchpin of the State's case. A slew of character witnesses was introduced. One former neighbor of Shcharansky's said that he was "smart, intellectual, quiet"; pressured to provide some evidence of his "negative qualities," she offered that "he wasn't always neat."

The judge rejected almost all of Shcharansky's forty requests for documents and witnesses. When it was Shcharansky's turn to defend himself, four days into the proceedings, he told the court it was a "hopeless task." But he spoke anyway, figuring that at least Leonid could transmit his words to the outside world. Shcharansky explained the history of Zionism and Jewish persecution, from the Dreyfus Affair to the Doctors' Plot. He pointed out all the contradictions in his case, made some accusations of his own, and tried to express all the thoughts about the case's "absurdity," as he put it, that had been brewing in his mind for the past year. When he was returned to his cell in Lefortovo that night, he still felt he had more to say, and he began working on his final statement to the court. No one understood the opportunity of such a moment better than Shcharansky, who before his arrest had been Soviet Jewry's public relations man. He sat and wrote out the statement in one shot, trying to keep it short. This was his chance to help his advocates on the outside, especially Avital.

The next day, following his closing argument, the prosecutor said that although Shcharansky certainly deserved capital punishment, he would demand only fifteen years, the first three to be served in prison and the rest in a labor camp. Then it was Shcharansky's turn to speak. He got up and turned to Leonid, who was seated in the back of the room, and spoke slowly and deliberately, enunciating each word so his brother could capture it all. After another recess, Shcharansky was brought back into the courtroom, which was now full of television cameras and photographers. The judgment was read: thirteen years. The audience cried out, yelling that Shcharansky was a traitor and should be shot. He searched for Leonid in the crowd, and just before he was dragged away by the guards Shcharansky heard his brother call out, "Tolya! The whole world is with you!"

Outside on the street, journalists jostled one another to get closer to Leonid when he emerged from the courthouse. His voice choked with tears, he said only "Thirteen." Ida Milgrom started weeping and Sakharov put an arm around her. A light summer rain began falling and people opened up their umbrellas and huddled closer to the courthouse. The refuseniks in the crowd sang the "Hatikvah," the Israeli national anthem, as the police van carrying Shcharansky sped by. Then, in a strained voice, an exhausted Leonid shouted out his brother's closing statement as journalists and their translators jotted down the words in their notebooks:

In March and April, during interrogation, the chief investigator warned me that in the position I have taken during investigation and held to here in court, I would be threatened with execution by firing squad, or at least 15 years. If I would agree to cooperate with the investigation for the purpose of destroying the Jewish emigration movement, they promised me early freedom and a quick reunion with my wife.

Five years ago, I submitted my application for exit to Israel. Now I'm further than ever from my dream. It would seem to be cause for regret. But it is absolutely otherwise. I am happy. I am happy that I lived honestly, in peace with my conscience. I never compromised my soul, even under the threat of death.

I am happy that I helped people. I am proud that I knew and worked with such honest, brave and courageous people as Sakharov, Orlov, Ginzburg, who are carrying on the traditions of the Russian intelligentsia. I am fortunate to have been witness to the process of the liberation of Jews of the U.S.S.R.

I hope that the absurd accusation against me and the entire emigration movement will not hinder the liberation of my people. My near ones and friends know how I wanted to exchange activity in the emigration movement for a life with my wife, Avital, in Israel.

For more than 2,000 years the Jewish people, my people, have been dispersed. But wherever they are, wherever Jews are found, every year they have repeated, "Next year in Jerusalem." Now, when I am further than ever from my people, from Avital, facing many arduous years of imprisonment, I say, turning to my people, my Avital: Next year in Jerusalem.

Now I turn to you, the court, who were required to confirm a predetermined sentence: to you I have nothing to say.

The next day, these words were printed in newspapers all over the world. The Soviet Union had birthed another Jewish martyr.

Over the course of a week, as his trial made front-page news, Shcharansky was transformed from a particularly charismatic and connected but young and inexperienced refusenik into the face of both Soviet Jewry and the oppressed Soviet man.

Outside the Soviet Union, working tirelessly to keep this image alive, stoking it every day, was Avital Shcharansky. When her husband was arrested in March of 1977, she had already lived in Israel for three years. Her first months in her new country had felt like a revelation—the bright July sun that greeted her when she first stepped off the plane, the Galilee landscape of rolling green hills covered in orange trees, and the sight of Lake Kinneret in the distance, the vast blue water mirroring the vast blue sky. She imagined this was what a near-death experience felt like, catching a glimpse of paradise before being yanked back to reality—except that she was free of Moscow forever. She began learning Hebrew, picked up painting again, and let her brother, Mikhail, known as Misha, make many of the big decisions about her life. Misha Stieglitz was extremely handsome, well spoken, fluent in English, and commanding in his army uniform. He also possessed very right-wing political views. Since his arrival in Israel, in 1973, he had grown close to Gush Emunim, a new religious Zionist movement that had gained momentum since the Six-Day War and was inspiring settlers to challenge the government and build their homes in the occupied West Bank and Gaza. Supporters of this ideology congregated around Rabbi Zvi Yehuda Kook and his yeshiva, Mercaz Ha Rav, in the Jerusalem neighborhood of Kiryat Moshe. Kook was the son of Abraham Isaac Kook, the first Orthodox rabbi to blend Zionism with traditional prophetic Judaism, envisioning the settlement of all the biblical land of Israel as a way of bringing on the messianic era. In a new country and without her parents—who had basically disowned their children once they decided to emigrate—Avital now relied on her brother, embracing this new milieu of religiosity, warmth, and acceptance.

She gained many friends in those years. So many American Jews had made trips to Moscow and been affected by Shcharansky and his story of forced separation from his beloved; several of them searched out Avital in Israel, and soon a network was formed to pass along letters and verbal messages. Accompanied by Misha, Avital took her first trip to Canada and the United States, in the fall of 1975; it was hosted by Union of Councils activists, and they visited even far-flung cities, such as Des Moines and Baton Rouge. Everyone seemed to want to become her guardian. There was something about Avital's appearance, the doe eyes, the childlike face, that elicited pity from important people. A New York businessman and his wife, who'd been charmed by Shcharansky when they met him during a trip to Moscow, escorted Avital through the halls of Congress and introduced her to many legislators. Robert Drinan, the Jesuit priest turned Democratic congressman from Massachusetts (though he still wore his clerical collar) had seen Anatoly Shcharansky a few months earlier, and Avital listened raptly as he shared the details of Tolya's life.

She tried to maintain a normal existence in Israel—she attended art school in the southern town of Beersheba for a few months—but found herself thinking constantly of the moment they would reunite. At one point she even tried unsuccessfully to get a tourist visa to return to see him. A year after Avital's trip to the West, Enid Wurtman and Connie Smukler, the Philadelphia activists, traveled to Moscow, in part so they could see Shcharansky and bring out a message for Avital. They arrived in the middle of October 1976 and celebrated Simchat Torah with the refuseniks, singing and dancing with them in the streets. Shcharansky peppered Enid Wurtman with questions about his wife and her life in Israel, asking everything from what she was cooking to how her apartment looked. Wurtman gave him a tape recorder and he sat in the back room of Volodya Slepak's apartment, filling a cassette. "I would love to talk to you in a leisurely way for the whole tape, to sit and simply to talk, not about anything specific. It's nice to think that in a few days you'll be able to listen and to send me another tape. Only please as fast as possible ... Today is October nineteenth; in twenty-five days it will be our third anniversary. My God! How I would love to be with you, and perhaps I shall be with you yet. I think, if they'll let me go, they'll give me five days, and I won't ask for any more, it's enough. And three days—it's also enough. Only it should be soon ... Enid asks how to help us. Yes, many people love us." Wurtman and Smukler delivered this sweet, rambling audio message directly to the woman whom Shcharansky still called Natulenka.

Avital also learned during those years on whom she could *not* depend. Nehemiah Levanon had always believed that the Jewish emigration movement should keep its distance from the democrats and human rights activists in the Soviet Union. Shcharansky's very public participation in the Moscow Helsinki Watch group, even though it brought attention to the Jewish movement, seemed to him dangerous. Whenever the refuseniks engaged in these broader collaborations, it made it easier for the Soviets to portray them as subversive, anarchistic hooligans, and not simply Jews looking to be reunited with their families in their homeland. Levanon didn't exactly hide these strong opinions either. Once, at a meeting in Jerusalem, he told Avital that if anything were to happen to her husband, if he were to be brought down by the KGB, there was very little the Lishka would be able to do for him. It would be Shcharansky's own fault, a result of his own recklessness.

In March of 1977, news of Lipavsky's letter in *Izvestia* accusing Shcharansky of treason reached Israel, and it was only natural for Avital to turn to those people who had proved they would stand behind her: the religious Zionist followers of Rabbi Kook who had adopted her, and Shcharansky's American friends, the Union of

Councils activists whom he trusted most. A small apartment in Jerusalem became a command center of sorts. The octogenarian Rabbi Kook
sat up in his sickbed and gave the order to shut down the yeshiva so
everyone could do his part—"If your brother is in danger and you ask,
'How can I help?' you are like one who spills blood. Don't ask! Go and
do!" Rabbis and yeshiva students made phone calls to journalists all
over the world. Statements were drawn up and distributed by taxicab.
A press conference was called that involved Alexander Lunts, Vitaly
Rubin (both now in Israel), Masha Slepak's mother, and Alexander
Lerner's daughter. Avital slept and ate little in those days. She would
take breaks on the small balcony of their headquarters, breathe in the
fresh air, and cry. Otherwise it was a nonstop effort to tell whoever
would listen about Shcharansky.

Avital and Misha decided to go to Geneva, where an international
meeting of Jewish leaders was taking place. There in Switzerland, she
found out about the arrest. On March 15, a Reuters reporter called her
to the United Nations and pointed to a Teletype machine. A whirlwind
tour followed; Avital, barely given enough time to process the arrest,
was whisked from one city to the next, watched over by the activists
who had become her allies. A year later she remembered the surreal
quality of those first weeks:

> Now as I look back on those days, I see an endless movie reel:
> meetings, unfamiliar faces, halls where I speak. Now I am traveling
> in a huge bus to the square in front of Les Invalides.... Then
> it is London and damp snow. I sit by the entrance to the Soviet
> Embassy wrapped in some warm blankets. I have been fasting for
> three days. I am at the end of my strength; I feel I am about to lose
> consciousness. Meanwhile the passersby hurry along: someone
> smiles at me, someone signs a petition which is next to me on a
> small table. This table is heaped with flowers, the Londoners' way of
> expressing sympathy with me. San Francisco. A huge crowd is crying
> out: "Free Anatoly Shcharansky." I see everything as if in a dream;
> picture follows picture ...

In the middle of all this, she received Shcharansky's last letter to her,
written on March 13, 1977, two days before his arrest. He'd tried for his
usual cheerfulness but couldn't hide the premonition that he would

soon be locked up. He revealed his greatest regret, which he knew was hers as well: "How everything has changed over these past days. Thousands of things and words which used to fill my life have simply disappeared, ceased to exist. Only the most important and dearest thing to me remains—you and your love. A lucidity sets in, when you live not by the minute or the day, but your whole life at once.... Thinking about it all, I regretted only one thing—so much that I was ready to cry: I regretted that we didn't have any children."

Shcharansky's trial and conviction unleashed a wave of support. Dozens of petitions were signed. Committees were established on university campuses and in Congress. The thirty-five-thousand-member Association for Computer Machinery cut all ties with the Soviet Union. By the end of 1978, twenty-four hundred American scientists—including thirteen Nobel laureates as well as researchers representing the leading scientific institutions—had joined on to a "statement of conscience," pledging to avoid all cooperation with the Soviet Union until Orlov and Shcharansky were freed.

Avital's celebrity reached new heights. She found herself in the Rayburn House hearing room on Capitol Hill surrounded by lawmakers climbing over one another to issue the most indignant statements and the angriest proclamations about what should be done in retaliation. A bipartisan resolution had already been passed in protest. Senator Robert Dole wanted to put all arms negotiations on hold until the Soviets complied fully with Helsinki. The Helsinki Commission itself called a special hearing in which it debated whether America should completely withdraw from the accords. All kinds of economic sanctions were considered, and Jewish leaders issued a statement calling on the government to "seek an immediate freeze of the export of American technology to the USSR."

Avital had met with Cyrus Vance, the secretary of state, and UN ambassador Andrew Young the day after the verdict was announced, and on July 17, she was ushered into the White House for a half-hour meeting with Walter Mondale, the vice president. This was the highest American government official to grant her an audience. He praised her for her "courage, dignity and strength" and then referred to Shcharansky's final speech at the trial, saying that it would "go down in literature as a great statement by an oppressed person."

The meeting with Mondale was part of another American tour, one Avital made after the verdict. From Washington, she flew to California, where she met everyone from Joan Baez to Jane Fonda. Every detail of this trip was reported by the *Los Angeles Times*: "In the course of this L.A. visit—an 18½-hour stay from last Saturday to Sunday afternoon—Avital Shcharansky was cheered by thousands of supporters clogging the ABC Entertainment Center in Century City; she good-naturedly endured interviews, TV and radio appearances until she could no longer think in English and had to rely on a Hebrew translator; she shook the hands of everyone from Jerry Brown to Charlton Heston to Bobby Baker. It was clear the sole purpose of her life has become the media blitz she feels can swing public opinion and politicians to pressure the Soviet Union to release her husband." The trip ended with yet another rally, this time with Charlton Heston giving a dramatic reading of Shcharansky's statement in his stentorian voice.

In those few days, Avital established a place for herself in the popular culture. Her shy, downcast, and usually tear-filled eyes appeared on many television programs as she pleaded in her broken English for Tolya's release. Her undeniable beauty and the poignancy of her plea made her an irresistible guest on TV talk shows. So omnipresent was she that summer of 1978 that there was even a backlash. In an article in the *Washington Post*, Sally Quinn, a writer for the Style section and a grandee of Washington society, called Avital an "Israeli Audrey Hepburn" and did not mean it as a compliment. Quinn's piece was bitter and mistrusting of Avital, who, she declared, had become an "international media star," and it gazed skeptically at the amount of publicity she was getting: "The Avital Shcharansky story is more complicated than this spotlit morality play, more touching in some ways and, in others, more manipulative of public emotions. It is a case study in the politics of sorrow, the packaging of martyrdom." Quinn described the relative brevity of Avital's relationship with Shcharansky in Moscow ("only a little over six months") and how many years had passed since she had left ("a long time for a 27-year-old woman to carry an emotional burden like that"). She implied that Avital, "bewildered, unhappy and very shy," was being used for political gain by her brother, Misha, who was "involved in right-wing politics and is said to be grooming himself for public office." Quinn even intimated that Avital might be having an affair. In a paragraph filled with sordid innuendo and not much rooted in reality, she described Avital's relationship with Mordechai Gal, a young Israeli director who was part of her entourage and who was making a film about her: "With Avital he is protective and gentle. With him she is cheerful and gay. They tease each other and spar affectionately. He advises her, talks to her, kneels beside her chair as she testifies before Congress." The whole piece was catty and insensitive ("she carried a Gucci bag, strangely out of character"). It was further proof that Shcharansky had become a household name in America, and so quickly that it had confounded Sally Quinn, a person who generally could keep tabs on who was up and who down.

In the last week of July 1978, a drawing of Shcharansky's face made the cover of *Time* magazine. Above his bald head, the word *détente* was written in crumbling letters. The symbol had superseded the man. Shcharansky was now shorthand for all that was corrupt and repressive about the Soviet regime, a further indication that the "peaceful coexistence" envisioned by Henry Kissinger at the beginning of the decade was impossible. Americans—and more important, many of their elected officials—no longer seemed willing to accept the collateral damage to human rights that Kissingerian détente demanded. Not if it meant sacrificing someone like Shcharansky.

The Soviets were using their suppression of dissidents as a way to test Carter's resolve. And they were ready to declare victory. In a memo to Brezhnev and the Politburo written after the Shcharansky trial, Ambassador Anatoly Dobrynin was reassuring: "Our expression of firmness in relation to the prosecution of renegades like Shcharansky played its own role. The Carter Administration, despite all its rhetoric, was forced to retreat and announce its intention to continue the Soviet American negotiations on SALT aimed at the achievement of concrete results, and to declare that the agreement meets the interests not only of the Soviet Union, but also the national interests of the USA. 'The Russians won this mini-confrontation,' such is the conclusion of the local political observers."

The Soviets could dismiss Carter's human rights rhetoric partly because the USSR seemed to be gaining the upper hand in the Cold War. For one thing, more and more countries in the so-called Third World were turning Communist red. Soviet arms had bolstered Communist forces in Angola, Mozambique, and Ethiopia. Support for allies in the Middle East, such as Syria, Iraq, and—most detrimentally to American foreign policy—the PLO, was continuing unabated. In Southeast Asia, the Soviets' Vietnamese allies were conquering much of the region. And many of the pro-American regimes in Central America were beginning to look vulnerable. Then there was the Islamic revolution that had just broken out in Iran, the United States' most critical ally in the Persian Gulf region. In January 1979, the shah, who had helped secure American dominance, was forced to flee the country and replaced by the virulently anti-American Ayatollah Khomeini.

Meanwhile, Carter continued the post-Vietnam trend of military de-escalation that had been started by the Nixon and Ford administrations and that he saw as part of his political mandate. This gave him very little to leverage against his human rights demands.

The Soviets were motivated to continue with détente because they needed the grain sales (the 1979 wheat harvest was particularly poor) and the advanced technology that came with it. The extreme defense expenditures that had allowed them to outpace the United States by the end of the 1970s in almost every category of missile technology had also placed great strains on their economy. Their spending on arms rivaled or beat that of the United States, while their economy was half its size. Strategic arms limitations could only work to their advantage. On this circumscribed, overlapping ground, Carter and Brezhnev were able to move forward with détente, however slowly.

As talks over SALT II progressed and planning began for a summit, the Soviets had to confront what might be fierce opposition in the U.S. Congress to ratification of any agreement—and it was led by their familiar foe Jackson. But this did not turn them away. In fact, there were clear signs that the Jackson-Vanik amendment had taught the Soviets a lesson. They now seemed to understand how to buy themselves some goodwill from American senators and congresspeople: increase Jewish emigration. And so, in late 1978, even as the world was still reeling from the repressive measures taken against the dissidents and the widely publicized trial of Shcharansky, the number of exit visas started to rise.

Journalists first noticed the trend in late summer of that year when it became clear that the Soviets were letting out as many as 3,000 Jews a month. By the fall, it seemed that the total for the year would be somewhere around 30,000, matching the peak years of 1972 and 1973. The numbers had remained low since then, improving only slightly, from 13,222 in 1975 to 16,735 in 1977. It took a few months to detect the trend—the Soviets never announced when they were going to be more lenient—but with the arrival in Vienna of more and more Jews every day, it was obvious that something had changed. In the first months of 1979, with the Brezhnev-Carter summit slated for the summer, the numbers became even more dramatic. In March, a record was set when 4,418 Jews arrived in Vienna. This topped the previous highest month, October 1973, when 4,408 were let out. At this rate, with over 4,000 emigrating every month, it looked like an unprecedented 50,000 Jews were going to be granted visas in 1979.

These sudden high rates of emigration shocked everyone in the West. Most of those given visas were first-time applicants from the big urban centers like Kiev and Odessa, people who'd been motivated to apply by a widespread rumor that the Olympics, scheduled to take place in Moscow the following summer, was the reason for this sudden leniency. By this logic, the emigration would end when the games did. These were the thoroughly assimilated Jews, the group who'd been responsible for the increasing percentage of dropouts throughout the decade. Once news spread that people were not being rejected, OVIR offices all over the Soviet Union began seeing long lines, and Israel was inundated with more requests for invitations than they had seen since the Six-Day War—about fifteen thousand a month. The period of increased emigration did not, however, affect those long-term refuseniks, somewhere between ten and twenty thousand of them. A few were allowed to leave, but others—those who had protested their situation or made a little too much noise—quickly replaced them.

The burst of emigration—and subsequent increase in dropouts—had two immediate consequences. First, it made Israel frantic. Every month brought higher and higher rates of Jews arriving in Vienna with Israeli visas and then turning to the Joint and HIAS for help in getting to America. In January it was 60.6 percent, in February, 64.1 percent, and in March it jumped to 65.3 percent. There was very little the Israelis could do. American Jews had won the initial debate over whether to cut off funds for the dropouts. Even if Israel could convince

Carter to stop accepting so many Jews, the Israelis still had the problem of the Netherlands and Austria. The Dutch, whose embassy represented Israel in Moscow, refused to discriminate based on ultimate destination when it handed out exit visas. And the Austrian chancellor, Bruno Kreisky, remained vocal about his commitment to securing freedom of choice for Soviet Jews who arrived in his country. It seemed that even the Soviets preferred their Jews to go to America rather than Israel. As Bruno Kreisky explained to a journalist in a moment of candor, "The Russians are ambivalent about it all. They let the Jews go on Israeli visas, but we have the impression Moscow is glad that so many actually do not go to Israel. That saves trouble with the Arabs."

The other major consequence of the emigration, one that became more pressing in the spring of 1979 as the summit neared, was the question of whether to waive the Jackson-Vanik amendment. With forty-five hundred Jews leaving every month, it was not impossible for the Kremlin to meet the target figure of sixty thousand a year agreed upon by Henry Jackson and Henry Kissinger. According to the letters exchanged between the two men, this would technically permit the president to waive the trade restrictions. As the prospects for improving relations with the Soviets increased, a small contingent of congressmen began to consider the possibility of rewarding the emigration increase with a waiver. In a strange twist, the man who led this thrust was Charles Vanik, the Ohio representative who had cosponsored the initial amendment in the House. Vanik was encouraged by the numbers, and he worried that the current push in Congress to give most-favored-nation trading status to China would derail relations with the Soviets, who would be offended if they were overlooked. At the beginning of March, in an open letter to Carter, Vanik made his opinion public. A debate ensued inside the administration, with the president generally favorable toward the idea of granting a waiver.

Vanik's idea and Carter's consideration of it was immediately and passionately attacked. The refuseniks in Moscow, now led by an increasingly isolated Alexander Lerner—who had recently lost some of his closest allies to prison and exile—wrote a letter to Vanik arguing that emigration figures were no way to judge the Soviets. More people might be getting out, but not in proportion to the number applying to leave. "It amounts to evaluating a change in a worker's salary without taking into account any changes in prices or the purchasing power of that salary," Lerner wrote. In a sign of their increasing convergence on policy issues, both the Union of Councils and the National Conference came out against the idea. Eugene Gold, then chairman of the National Conference and Brooklyn's district attorney (and, famously, the prosecutor of David Berkowitz, the "Son of Sam" killer), wrote in a letter to the *New York Times* that "human rights is not a game of numbers. While one Soviet hand has partially opened the emigration tap, the other hand continues to squeeze Jews who live in the U.S.S.R."

But the real obstacle to a waiver was Henry Jackson, still a powerhouse in the Senate even after two failed presidential bids and the most outspoken critic of Carter's foreign and defense policies. He was violently opposed to any change in law that would give the Soviet Union an advantage, and especially one that undermined the strength of his legislation. Jackson was even disparaging of Carter's approach to human rights; he felt it failed on several points. It did not distinguish between a country in which the abuses were deeply embedded in the system and were justified by an ideology and a country ruled by a petty dictator in which abuses of power were understood to be aberrations and not endemic to that nation's policies. Jackson felt Carter did not adequately balance idealism and realism. His rhetoric on human rights was too moralizing and could lead to unintended consequences. In the case of Iran, for example, Jackson thought it was the president who had weakened the shah by not working harder to prop him up when the revolution began. The president had failed to realize that the shah was less dangerous than the revolutionary Islamic regime that would replace him.

When it came to SALT II, the most recent manifestation of détente, Jackson was especially harsh. In 1972, when the first SALT agreement passed 88 to 2, including Jackson's own reluctant vote for it, his was one of the few critical voices in Congress. But in 1979, following widespread disenchantment with détente and concern over Soviet defense spending, he was no longer alone. As Carter prepared to sign SALT II, it was far from clear that he would be able to get the two-thirds majority needed to ratify the treaty. Jackson fought on two fronts, Richard Perle still at his side. He opposed his former cosponsor Vanik, tamping down any talk of a waiver, and he warned that he would not support a new arms treaty that left America at a disadvantage or that didn't contain a mechanism for verifying Soviet adherence.

The summit was scheduled for early June. With a month remaining, the Soviets made one more attempt to win over a recalcitrant Congress. On the morning of April 25 at the Mordvinian Special Regime Labor Camp No. 1, three hundred miles south of Moscow, a KGB lieutenant colonel and a bevy of camp officials pushed open the door of Eduard Kuznetsov's cell. Nearly nine years had passed since Kuznetsov's commuted death sentence. He had spent them all in Mordvinia. Now he found himself put on a train to Moscow; after two days at Lefortovo Prison, he still didn't know whether he was being freed or put on trial again. His only hint was the glimpse he got as he left the labor camp of two other political prisoners who were also making the trip: Alexander Ginzburg, who had only recently joined him there, and Valentin Moroz, a Ukrainian nationalist who, like Kuznetsov, had been imprisoned since the early 1970s.

On the morning of the second day, Kuznetsov was brought into a room with a KGB captain and two Kremlin representatives and informed that he was being stripped of his Soviet citizenship and would be leaving the country that day. They gave him a suit that had been made in Czechoslovakia, and, guarded by two men, he was driven to the airport and placed on an Ilyushin jet. He saw other men put on the plane, and one of them was Mark Dymshits, the pilot of their failed hijacking plot. Only when they landed at John F. Kennedy Airport in New York did Kuznetsov figure out where he had been sent. Within minutes, two Russians, escorted by New York police officers, were hustled onto the plane, and Kuznetsov, Dymshits, and the others, all with shaved heads, gaunt faces, and cheap suits, descended onto the tarmac. A motorcade of seven bulletproof limousines was waiting for them. In the limo, a State Department official informed the former prisoners that they had just been exchanged for two Soviet spies.

The next few days were hallucinatory. Kuznetsov stood dumbfounded on the thirty-seventh floor of the United Nations Plaza Hotel staring out at the lights of Manhattan; he fell asleep in a room that seemed big enough to hold fifty people. Then Sylva was there, embracing him and unable to stop crying. Nehemiah Levanon showed up at the hotel and told him not to criticize the Soviets too harshly, but Kuznetsov just laughed in his face. There were press conferences and rallies. The arrival happened to coincide with Solidarity Sunday, the annual rally and march started in 1971 and organized by New York's Soviet Jewry umbrella organization. Eduard and Sylva, holding hands, smiled in front of a hundred thousand cheering people, and next to them stood a beaming Henry Jackson.

A year later, on the anniversary of his release, the normally cynical Kuznetsov described those days with wonder: "I have never rejected the idea of a miracle as such, but at the same time I also have not considered myself an important enough person (like a bon vivant or a cripple, for example) to have laid a claim on heaven's special blessing. But on April 27 I was tempted, if not to scream out, then at least to whisper that pretentious, comforting word: miracle. Out of darkness, I was cast into light; out of a stench into a garden; out of death into life."

With much less publicity, five other prisoners from the Leningrad trials were unexpectedly pardoned that same week. Anatoly Altman, Boris Penson, Areyeh Khnokh, and Sylva Zalmanson's older brother Vulf, all prospective passengers on the hijacked plane, were taken out of their prison camps in the Urals and put on trains bound for Riga. Hillel Butman, the last remaining prisoner from the Leningrad group, had been in Chistopol, a special camp set up the year before specifically to house political prisoners, five hundred miles east of Moscow in the Tatar province. He too was released. A few days later, they were all summoned to OVIR, given exit visas, and sent speeding through Vienna to Israel, where they were greeted like heroes. Only one person from the hijacking still remained in prison, in Chistopol, and that was Yosef Mendelevich.

News of the pardons broke just as Charles Vanik was visiting Moscow with a delegation of seventeen congresspeople. The releases were surely meant to shore up support for Vanik's campaign to waive his eponymous amendment and allow freer trade. A few other high-profile refuseniks were allowed to emigrate, including Volodya Slepak's son Leonid, who had been hiding from the authorities. Hearing all this good news, even Alexander Lerner, who had been visited by Vanik in his apartment in Moscow, was encouraged. The Soviets were on their way to fulfilling nearly all of the movement's demands.

The summit finally took place in June, in Vienna; the seventy-two-year-old Brezhnev was ailing and unable to make the trip to Washington.

The meeting amounted to little more than theater—and bad theater at that. Brezhnev was in worse shape than anybody had expected. His speech was slurred, he wore a large hearing aid in his left ear, and Carter had to steady him when he tripped on the stairs leading out of the Soviet embassy. The Austrian authorities were concerned enough that they ordered several hospitals in the city to keep beds and life-support systems ready. The major achievement was the signing of SALT II, which had already been negotiated. Everything else was stagecraft, visits to the opera and toasts over vodka. The only departure from the script was a ninety-minute private meeting on the last day between the two leaders at the American embassy. According to news reports, they discussed "Soviet emigration policy and U.S. restrictions on Soviet goods." If something substantive emerged from this meeting, neither Carter nor Brezhnev saw fit to tell the world. In the last moments, they signed the treaty. Tellingly, the Russian version of the seventy-eight-page document had been produced by a manual typewriter on paper as thick as cardboard and copied by a machine from the 1950s. The Americans used a high-speed word processor for theirs.

The Soviets' best chance for a waiver of Jackson-Vanik would be after the ratification of SALT II as part of what would be a general warming of relations. But in the months following the Vienna summit, Jackson and his growing number of allies made it clear that the treaty was going nowhere. The senator argued that it left the Soviets capable of developing more complex missile systems while compromising the American arsenal. Other senators just didn't trust that the Russians would adhere to the limitations. Events that summer and fall further reinforced the notion that America was losing influence in the world, which bolstered Jackson's hard-line position. In September, the State Department revealed that a combat unit of two to five thousand Soviet soldiers with about forty tanks was stationed in Cuba. Carter insisted they be removed, but Brezhnev simply ignored him, and the president backed off. Then in November, fifty-two people were taken hostage at the American embassy in Tehran, a crisis that consumed the American public and dragged on day after day.

Also that fall, there were signs that Soviet Jewish emigration rates, which had seemed so promising just a year before, were starting to decline again. The first reports of mass refusals came from the big Ukrainian cities of Kiev and Odessa, where hundreds of families were denied exit visas in August and September. Natalia Khassina, the woman who took over Dina Beilin's job as the keeper of the refusenik lists, told a Western reporter in October that "positive answers are now an exception." There was no immediate drop in the monthly *numbers* of Jews emigrating. In September, it was still 4,400. But with thousands more families now applying, the stable number meant that many were being denied.

The question of why emigration increased at certain times and decreased at others was a constant preoccupation of activists and Sovietologists alike. But the numbers of visas granted in 1979 seemed to provide fairly strong evidence that to a large extent, the temperature of the Cold War determined emigration. Inside the Politburo, Jews were clearly seen as pawns. When Soviet leaders had something to gain, the number of Jews leaving went up. But with SALT II blocked by Congress and Carter publicly acknowledging that he wouldn't consider trade benefits until the following year—while most-favored-nation status for China was steadily making its way toward congressional approval—the Soviets saw they had little to benefit from continued leniency.

Impervious to the fluctuation in emigration rates were Volodya and Masha Slepak and Ida Nudel, who by the fall of 1979 were feeling the effects of life in exile. All three were in the frozen steppes on the southeastern reaches of Siberia, thousands upon thousands of miles and at least five time zones away from Moscow. The Gulag memoirs of Stalin's era are filled with descriptions of the dreaded *etap,* the name given to the arduous train trip east toward captivity. Not much about its dreadfulness had changed over the years. Volodya Slepak spent weeks in transit, staying days at a time in prisons along the route. Most of the other prisoners traveling with him were on their way to a special camp for tuberculosis patients. He was forced to share drinking water with them, along with the daily ration of black bread, two lumps of sugar per person, and salted herring. It was a miserable journey. The conditions in the overcrowded, guarded train car and in each of the local prisons were horrendous. Often they were allowed to use the train's toilet only twice a day. By the time they arrived in Sverdlovsk, the first major stop, the whole group had dysentery. At one point, Volodya heard two female prisoners loaded onto a separate compartment and then repeatedly raped. Twice a day, water was delivered to the prisoners through a hose that was shoved through the chicken wire that covered the windows of each car.

Finally, after a little over a month, he arrived in the Siberian city of Chita. From there he was taken to the remote collective farm, or *kolkhoz*, of Tsokto-Khangil, not far from the Mongolian border and fifty kilometers from the birthplace of Genghis Khan. The village was inhabited entirely by Buryat farmers and shepherds. The land was parched and flat, devoid of trees, and the grass was green only one month a year, in June. His job was to unload harvested wheat from trucks and fill the collective's silos. Slepak, fifty-one and accustomed to urban life, was very far from home. In a few days, he received a phone call from Masha. She too had been convicted of hooliganism but was given a suspended sentence and was still in the capital, preparing to join him. She called to tell him that Solomon Slepak, Volodya's Communist father, had died of a heart attack upon hearing of his son's exile. Volodya was allowed to return for the funeral, and when he made his way back to Tsokto-Khangil, this time with Masha, the brutally cold winter had set in. He began his new job as a stoker. Working in shifts of twenty-four hours on, forty-eight hours off, Volodya, sweating and stripped to the waist, shoveled coal into a giant furnace in the boiler room of the *kolkhoz*'s garage to keep the jeeps and trucks from freezing.

The first year was an exercise in extreme patience. Especially for Masha. Unlike Volodya, she was free to come and go, but if they wanted to keep their *propiska*, their residence permit, for their apartment on Gorky Street, she could not stay away from Moscow for more than three or four months. So she made the five-thousand-mile trip many times. In Tsokto-Khangil, they found a small room that they slowly fixed up and made livable. They fought the extreme isolation by listening to a shortwave radio and watching a small television Masha had brought back from Moscow. Above his desk, Volodya pasted photos of friends: Tolya Shcharansky, Andrei Sakharov, and Ida Nudel. He got very ill that year, suffering from pneumonia during the endless winter when temperatures dropped to fifty below and only horses traversed the frozen plains. When spring came, Masha started a little garden on a plot given to her by local Buryat farmers, and there she grew carrots, squash, and potatoes. On her windowsill, in a cardboard box, she planted spices like dill, oregano, and garlic. Her one consolation was that now both her sons were in the West—Leonid had received an exit visa in April 1979. She marked off the days on a calendar and dreamed of her grandchildren. "Our life here resembles science fiction," Masha wrote in a letter to some Western friends in the last months of 1979. "We two are so alien to the environment here . . . Time slips away. Heat, dust, stuffy air, flies, foul smells . . ."

Ida Nudel had it even worse. She was a woman alone. After enduring her own difficult *etap,* she arrived at the Siberian village of Krivosheino, a small settlement of two thousand people built on drained swampland near the Ob River. Dressed in jeans and a denim jacket, her long gray hair held back and big glasses covering half her face, Nudel was not the typical political exile. Unable to find a job that didn't require physical labor in the village, she was sent to an even more rural area three miles away, the site of a land reclamation project where she could work as a draftsman. There she was forced to share a barrack with a group of former convicts who were draining swamps. "What kind of little birdie flew in here?" one of them said when he first saw her. Locked in her room behind a flimsy wooden door and terrified she would be attacked, Nudel was completely isolated, her only consolation being that she hadn't been sent to a psychiatric institution like some dissidents.

She lived for letters from her friends and supporters. But she had decided—as a matter of principle—that she would not write back. She would not be complicit in "normalizing" her situation. Occasionally, she broke her own pledge, like when she contacted a friend in Moscow and asked him to bring her a puppy on an upcoming visit. She wanted some company (he brought her a collie). When the Leningrad hijackers were freed, they called her. She had spent years advocating for these men, sending food packages, taking care of their families, visiting them when she was allowed. Still she stubbornly kept the promise she'd made in an open letter written when she first arrived in Siberia, in September 1978: "I become silent, confident that you will not be silent. Don't turn to me but to my tormentors for information about me and then my suffering will have meaning and their victory over me will be uneasy and their revenge bitter."

On December 27, 1979, a Soviet ground force of about eighty thousand troops invaded Afghanistan. Though the Soviets insisted that this was meant to stabilize a chaotic political environment in which a weak Communist regime was facing a radical Muslim faction, it was perceived by the West as a unilateral move to gain control over the region's oil supply. Americans were reminded of the Soviet invasion of Hungary in 1956 and of Czechoslovakia in 1968. Afghanistan was a game changer for the Carter administration. Eager to appear tough in the face of Soviet aggression, Carter retaliated. He immediately instructed the Senate to put a hold on SALT II ratification. He would have to "assess Soviet actions and intentions" before allowing the arms treaty to move forward. Then he gave a speech to the nation in which he withdrew his offer of an extra seventeen million metric tons of grain that the Russians badly needed. There would be a halt to sales of high-technology products, such as advanced computers and oil-drilling equipment. No more cultural or economic exchanges (which effectively meant that a waiver for Jackson-Vanik was off the table). And Carter warned that the United States would boycott the 1980 summer Olympic Games if the Soviets continued their "aggressive actions."

The invasion was seen as a trust betrayed. Henry Jackson had railed against détente since its inception and wasted no time declaring its demise: "The theory that has animated American policy towards the Soviet Union over the last decade and under three administrations—that the Soviets, lured by a series of cooperative agreements, would match our concessions and reward our restraint—is dangerously and demonstrably false. The Soviet invasion of Afghanistan has shown that détente for us was an illusion, and the Soviet 'restraint' merely the absence of opportunity. And the political, economic and military policies developed to fit the theory that we have moved from confrontation with the Soviets to cooperation now lies in ruins." Jackson's vindication was tinged with sadness and a sense of failure. "What must they think of us in the Kremlin?" he wondered aloud.

If the Soviets *did* care about American public opinion, they were doing less and less to help their cause. Returning from his weekly Tuesday-afternoon seminar at the Physical Institute of the Academy of Sciences on January 22, Andrei Sakharov found his car commandeered by police officers and he himself driven to the state prosecutor's office. There, the Nobel Prize winner was read a decree from the Presidium of the Supreme Soviet, signed by Brezhnev, informing him that he was being officially stripped of all state honors, from his Hero of Socialist Labor awards to his many Lenin Prizes. He was being banished from Moscow and confined to Gorky, two hundred and fifty miles away, a closed military city off-limits to foreigners and journalists. Elena Bonner could join him. He was told to call her and tell her to be prepared to leave in two hours.

Sakharov had been untouchable. His status as a world-renowned physicist combined with his recent Nobel Prize made him seem immune to harsh treatment. But he had become increasingly vocal in the days following the Afghanistan invasion, calling for a withdrawal—"What is essential now is for the United Nations to convene and put pressure on the Soviet Union to withdraw from Afghanistan, not in any humiliating way, but as part of some arrangement whereby the strategic equilibrium in the region would be restored." This was too much, and in a meeting of the Politburo the following day, Brezhnev approved the exile. The animosity was palpable. Gromyko perhaps put it best, fuming, "The question of Sakharov has ceased to be a purely domestic question. He finds an enormous number of responses abroad. All the anti-Soviet scum, all this rabble revolves around Sakharov. It is impossible to ignore this situation much longer."

Détente had collapsed, the lodestar of the dissident movement had been banished from Moscow, Jewish emigration was slowly coming to a halt, and the remaining refusenik activists were more embattled than ever. Meanwhile, hundreds of miles away in Chistopol prison, Anatoly Shcharansky and Yosef Mendelevich were trying to exchange a few words by speaking into their toilets.

In October of 1978, all the political prisoners had been moved to Chistopol prison at the edge of the Urals, and Shcharansky realized that Mendelevich and Hillel Butman were in the next cell over. He would bang with his tin cup against the wall, and then they would prepare the toilets for a few minutes of talk. They had found that by draining the bowls, a painstaking process that involved absorbing the water with a rag and then wringing it out into a bucket, the toilets could be converted into listening and speaking devices. Sometimes the three men were taken out to exercise at the same time in neighboring courtyards, and if the guards weren't looking they could throw a note over the barbed wire that separated them. Shcharansky got a few days of solitary confinement in the spring after he was discovered inserting a minuscule letter into a bar of soap that he left for his fellow Zionists in the washroom.

It was exhilarating to find that he was in jail with some of his heroes. He had made his first contact just two weeks after the end of his trial. The first prison he was taken to was the large complex in Vladimir, a structure built by the czars in the eighteenth century as a place to house insurrectionists. One day, as Shcharansky reached into the slot in his cell door to receive a bowl of soup, the prisoner tasked with delivering the food tucked a note into his sleeve. It was from Hillel Butman, offering welcome. Shcharansky was familiar with the story of the Leningrad hijacking. For years, he had written numerous petitions and attended many hunger strikes and demonstrations on their behalf. And now he was beginning a correspondence with Hillel Butman. They wrote in Hebrew so their words could not be understood if discovered, and the food servers, easily bribed with knickknacks sent from home, delivered the messages. In these long and detailed notes, Shcharansky explained what had happened in the eight years since Butman had been locked up. He told him about the movement that had flourished after his imprisonment, the great attention they had received from the West, the hundreds of tourists and the contacts with journalists, the organizations like the Union of Councils and the National Conference that had not even existed when Butman was arrested, the tens of thousands who had received permission to leave. Shcharansky told him about who was active in Moscow, who had been arrested, who was in exile (including Ida Nudel, whose constant correspondence with the hijackers had mysteriously stopped in June).

Not long after the move to Chistopol, Butman was released — in April of 1979. He called out "Shalom!" as he walked passed the row of cells, still unaware that he was on his way to freedom. Shcharansky still had Mendelevich. Over the past eight years, the fierce Zionist from Riga had remained stubbornly religious. The reason he was transferred out of a labor camp and sent to this higher security prison was that he insisted on observing the Sabbath and the Jewish holidays. Even here, in Chistopol, he sat in his cell every Friday night, lit a piece of string dipped in oil that he had purchased from the prison store, and recited the prayer for the beginning of the Sabbath. When Shcharansky once tried to pass him a note on a Saturday, Mendelevich reprimanded him for writing on the rest day, which only made Mendelevich's devotion more endearing. The authorities at Chistopol tried to prevent any physical contact between their political prisoners, so although they were able to secretly communicate, they had never seen each other. But one day in the winter of 1979, with the prison courtyard covered in thick snow, Shcharansky suddenly found himself facing another prisoner, a man in his thirties, who he sensed immediately was Mendelevich. The two men stood in the snow and silently embraced for a few seconds until the guards realized their mistake and pulled them away.

Knowing Mendelevich was in the cell next to his, praying, gave Shcharansky much strength. It had not been easy to adjust to life in the Soviet prison system. In the first year, he had lost more than twenty pounds. His daily food ration consisted of seventy grams of fish, twenty grams of sugar, and four hundred and fifty grams of bread. No fresh vegetables, eggs, or meat. He began having extreme pain in his eyes, and headaches from the constant artificial light in his cell. This made it hard to read for more than ten minutes or concentrate long enough to compose the one letter per month that he was allowed. After much lobbying, he was permitted to wear dark glasses. This at least allowed him to write to his family and Avital.

On January 21, 1980, the day after his thirty-second birthday and the day before Andrei Sakharov's arrest, Shcharansky received a telegram from his mother, Ida Milgrom. His father had died of a heart attack (Boris Shcharansky had been in Moscow and was on his way to a birthday party for his son at Alexander Lerner's apartment when he collapsed in a trolley car). Shcharansky lay down and wept out of helplessness and grief. When Mendelevich called out to him, he responded in Hebrew, *Avi met,* my father died. Mendelevich wanted to console his friend, and on a small piece of paper, he wrote the Kaddish, the Jewish prayer for mourning. For the next two days, he tried to toss the crumpled note over the barbed wire into Shcharansky's courtyard. On the third day he was successful, and Shcharansky went back to his cell slowly repeating the words and thinking of his father—and the recklessly brave young Jew in the next cell.

Over the following weeks, Shcharansky began painstakingly reading a small book of Psalms that had recently been returned to him. The next time he wrote to his mother, he described how cathartic the process of translating the Psalms from Hebrew had proven to be:

> The day after I received your telegram telling me of Papa's death I decided, in his memory, to read and study all hundred and fifty psalms of David. This is what I do morning till evening. I stop only to eat, take walks, do eye exercises, and glance at newspapers. What does this give me? First of all, it is quite tiring, it leaves me almost no energy for black thoughts and painful memories. Secondly, this study is very useful to me in several ways—learning the language is filling an enormous gap in my basic Jewish education. Thirdly—and this seems to be the main thing—as I read these verses, my thoughts return to Papa, to you, to Avital, to the past and the future, to the fate of our close and more distant family—but in a more general, more spiritual way. Gradually, my feeling of great loss and sorrow changes to one of bright hopes. I am denied the right to visit Papa's grave but when, in the future, I hear these wonderful verses, these lines that encompass the lives of all the Jews in Israel, and not only there, I shall remember Papa. It will be as if I had erected a memorial stone to him in my heart, and he will be with me all the days of my life.

Mendelevich and Shcharansky, the two martyrs, sat side by side but separated in their brightly lit cells, consoling themselves with Hebrew prayer—with the words of a tradition they had sacrificed almost everything to reclaim.

PART III

SLOUCHING TOWARDS GLASNOST

1981–1987

We feel like Lilliputians in the Swift novel.
The giants are playing with us.

ALEXANDER SLEPAK,
son of Vladimir Slepak,
October 13, 1986

12

Hopelessness
1981–1984

To survive the mental strain of constant waiting, of existing as pariahs in the only society they had ever known, refuseniks built an archipelago. Mostly these islands were the small, private spaces of their cramped, book-lined apartments—though often with the faucets turned on or the radios blaring so that the bugs could not pick up their conversations. But no island was more important than the one in Ovrazhki. It was in this clearing in the middle of a forest thick with birch trees just thirty kilometers outside of Moscow that they could be themselves, Jews in the company of other Jews. They could almost forget, at least for a Sunday afternoon, how far they were from the country of their dreams. There was a strong outdoor culture in the Soviet Union. The vastness of the empire, from the shores of the Black Sea to the rivers of the Baltics and the mountains of the Caucasus, attracted Russian city dwellers whenever they were able to escape work. In 1976, this is what led a group of Moscow refuseniks to seek out their own piece of wilderness.

To get there they took the regional train in the direction of Kazan, got out at Ovrazhki station, and walked three kilometers. For the next couple of years, it was to Ovrazhki, as they came to call it, that they went every other weekend from May to October. This was where they would celebrate the holidays, building a bonfire for Lag b'Omer and a thatched hut on Succoth. They would come with bulging picnic baskets, lay out reams of white printout paper on which to place the food and sit, and eat. Someone always had a guitar and would play emotional Russian folk songs as well as Yiddish and Israeli music. They set up a badminton court between the trees. Boris Gulko, the chess grand master who had won the 1977 USSR Chess Championship and shortly after became a refusenik, sometimes showed up and challenged people to friendly chess matches. Mostly they danced, gossiped, laughed. On Jerusalem Day, the children hung handmade maps of Israel on the trees or dangled postcards of Jerusalem from the branches. Sometimes the events were organized, like a festival of Jewish songs that became an annual happening around Succoth. It was so popular that in 1980 more than a thousand people came to the amateur singing competition. For the children of refuseniks, Ovrazhki was a world unlike the one they knew in the city. There their parents seemed more at ease. They could practice their Hebrew without having to whisper. In 1980, a Torah exam was held under the trees for the children who had been attending a makeshift Sunday school. The boys wore yarmulkes too big for their heads and eagerly raised their hands to show the adults all they had learned.

Aside from the policemen who sometimes lurked in the trees, often ostentatiously filming the get-togethers, Ovrazhki went largely unbothered. But in 1980, what had been regarded as innocent was now seen as malicious. On the day after the third song festival, Natan Shvartsman, the refusenik and itinerant hiker who had discovered Ovrazhki and who organized many of the gatherings, was called in to KGB offices and threatened with arrest if he didn't stop going to the forest. In May of 1981, as the refuseniks were preparing to begin a new season of summer socializing, the KGB flooded the Ovrazhki train station with police officers and sealed off the clearing. KGB chief Yuri Andropov himself wrote a memo to the Central Committee about the effective stanching of this nefarious activity: "Assuming the role of leaders of the nationalists, Abramovich, Shvartsman and Prestin have been attempting to unite individuals of Jewish nationality by drawing them into various spontaneous circles for the study of Hebrew, into religious and so-called 'scholarly' seminars and into groups for 'artistic' activity. In order to achieve these goals, they plan to organize on a regular basis, under the pretext of cultural recreation, mass gatherings of Jews in the forests outside Moscow, and carry out their pre-arranged religious-nationalistic program, setting each meeting to coincide with dates in the religious-nationalistic [Jewish] calendar."

Andropov then described what was to happen in the forest. "Abramovich, Shvartsman and other nationalists intended to organize one such gathering on May 3 in the forest near the village of Ovrazhki ... To conceal the anti-social character of the gathering they arranged it to coincide with the commemoration by nationalistically-minded Jews of so-called Holocaust and Heroism Remembrance Day (the killing of Jews in the Second World War). In accordance with a program developed well in advance, the gathering was planned to attract about 1500 people." But Andropov assured them that the "Committee for State Security, with the active participation of the Soviet public, carried out a series of prophylactic measures, as a result of which the anti-social action of the nationalists was thwarted."

Andropov and the KGB were effective. Ovrazhki was no longer safe. Emigration numbers were in a free fall—from the high of 51,000 in 1979, they had dipped to 21,471 in 1980, 9,447 in 1981, and 2,688 in 1982. And now it was clear that the tiny social sphere the refuseniks had worked so hard to create would also be sunk.

The hammer fell hard in the early 1980s, and it seemed to smash everything. Antagonism reigned. The old men in the Kremlin were waging a war in Afghanistan, completely deaf to the protests of the West. More than sixty countries had boycotted the Moscow Olympics in the summer of 1980, but it seemed to make no difference to Soviet leaders. Dissidents all over the empire were flushed out of their apartments and thrown into locked cells. In December of 1981, the Polish government imposed martial law, crushing the prodemocracy Solidarity movement and jailing thousands. The Soviet leaders looked on with approval. The hostility did not emanate from Moscow alone. In 1980, the United States elected Ronald Reagan as president, the aging actor turned unabashed Cold Warrior who had run on a promise of returning toughness to American foreign policy. As soon as he took office, in the beginning of 1981, a robust confrontational style not seen for at least two or three decades took hold. There would be no superpower summits. Anatoly Dobrynin, the longtime Soviet ambassador, was told that he would no longer enjoy the special privilege granted him by Kissinger of clandestinely entering the White House through the underground garage. He would now have to use the front door like everyone else. Reagan stated his intention clearly. He was not interested in managing the Cold War. He wanted to win it. And the first step was to tear down the Soviets' self-confidence. He started increasing defense spending, making Moscow compete just as the drop in oil prices was forcing them to confront a stagnating economy. And, in his most dramatic move, Reagan introduced the idea of a defensive missile shield based in outer space. The Strategic Defense Initiative—or Star Wars, as it was known—was effective more as a psychological weapon than as a program with any chance of success. But it scared the Soviets into considering that they might have to enter a whole new arms race, one they absolutely couldn't afford.

More than any specific policy, though, it was the way Reagan reframed the Cold War in his trembling, jocular voice that was so unsettling to the Soviets. He was not about to send American troops into Afghanistan to confront the USSR directly, but he did ratchet up the rhetoric. "The West will not contain Communism," he said in early 1981, "it will transcend Communism. We will not bother to renounce it, we'll dismiss it as a bizarre chapter in human history whose last pages are even now being written." In March of 1983, he made a speech to an association of Evangelicals in Orlando, Florida, that would become infamous for this sentence: "I urge you to beware the temptation of pride—the temptation of blithely declaring yourselves above it all and label both sides equally at fault, to ignore the facts of history and aggressive impulses of an evil empire, to simply call the arms race a giant misunderstanding and thereby remove yourself from the struggle between right and wrong and good and evil."

To sustain this vision of an "evil empire," to make sure Americans bought into it after a decade of détente, Reagan turned to human rights as a potent ideological weapon. He found his intellectual grounding in the ideas of the neoconservatives, former liberals turned Cold War hawks who came to see Communism as a debased and dehumanizing system that had to be fought as aggressively as Nazism had been. The main propagators of this doctrine were Jewish intellectuals like Norman Podhoretz, Irving Kristol, and Midge Decter (Podhoretz's wife and the ex-wife of Moshe Decter, the onetime Lishka agent), political critics who had been making their arguments with increasing influence in the pages of *Commentary,* a magazine produced by the American Jewish Committee and edited by Podhoretz. Their patron saint was Henry Jackson, and with him they had spent the past decade arguing for a robust American defense policy (even in the face of post-Vietnam retreat) and championing the human rights of those living under Communism.

Reagan not only rode many of Jackson's ideas into office, he also filled his administration with Scoop Jackson Democrats. Ten years after he got his start as a legislative aide in Jackson's office, Richard Perle became the assistant secretary of defense. Paul Wolfowitz, Perle's old friend, was made director of policy planning at the State Department. Jeanne Kirkpatrick was appointed American ambassador to the United Nations. A professor at Georgetown University, Kirkpatrick had gained Reagan's attention with an article in *Commentary* called "Dictatorships and Double Standards," which argued, as Jackson had, that a distinction had to be made between Communist regimes and right-wing authoritarian governments. While the former ignored personal liberty as part of its guiding principles, the latter were aberrations, usually instigated by strongmen or the result of democratic regimes that had temporarily lost their way. Human rights could not be championed equally everywhere, as Carter had tried to do. Strategic thinking had to play a part, and Communism was the greater evil. This became government policy.

Henry Jackson had faced an internal political crisis during the election campaign. He could not bring himself to endorse Carter, but he also could not leave the Democratic Party, his home for over four decades. And yet he was completely aligned with Reagan on almost every foreign policy issue. After Carter's nomination in the fall, Jackson offered the candidates a litmus test of sorts. He wanted their views on the Jackson-Vanik amendment. Reagan replied with a letter offering the most unequivocal support: "As President I would implement fully the letter and the spirit of the freedom of emigration provisions of the 1974 Trade Act. We would seek to make it clearly understood that we would uphold the law, and that we will make no effort to modify the Jackson-Vanik Amendment. Fine words about human rights are one thing; action is another.... I am proud indeed of the extraordinary bravery of those seeking to emigrate from the Soviet Union. The Soviet Jews in particular have shown the world what courage and determination to be free can mean even for men and women who could be imprisoned as a desire to emigrate." Jackson was eventually pressured by his party to offer Carter a lukewarm endorsement in the weeks before the election, but he secretly told many of his Jewish supporters, who looked to him for advice, that it was okay to back Reagan.

Soviet Jewry as a cause gained a huge boost with Reagan's presidency. The individual refuseniks struggling against a repressive Communist regime fit perfectly into Reagan's narrative. Only a few months after being sworn in, he invited Avital Shcharansky to visit him in the Oval Office. With her was Yosef Mendelevich. A year before his scheduled release date and after a hunger strike that lasted for weeks, Mendelevich was suddenly put on a train for Moscow and then sent out of the country. Now, living in Israel and finally allowed to grow a beard and practice his Orthodox Judaism, he became a fierce advocate for the refusenik activists that had been left behind. Like Avital, he found a home among the right-wing settlers and enrolled at Mercaz Ha Rav, the school at the center of their activity. He studied Torah, married, and finally let himself experience the openly religious life he had sought since his revelation in Riga more than fifteen years earlier. Avital and Mendelevich spent half an hour with the president and Vice President George Bush. Avital, now used to meeting with world leaders, told them of Tolya's worsening health. The photo that was taken at the visit captured the strange clash of worlds. Bookended by the tall and robust Reagan and Bush are the dour-looking Avital, her hair covered with a kerchief, and Yosef Mendelevich.

The Soviet Jewry movement could now count on the sympathies of those at the highest levels of the American government, but that seemed to have no effect on what was happening inside the Soviet Union. In a way, the refuseniks and activists in the West were suffering for their success. The major struggle of the 1970s, starting crudely with Kahane and culminating in the brilliant organization of Jackson-Vanik, was to make Soviet Jews a central issue in the Cold War, an unavoidable obstacle on the way to vaunted peace and prosperity. Helsinki then provided the Soviets with directions to remove the obstacle. The 1970s could be seen as a giant behavioral-conditioning project. There would be positive reinforcement for releasing Jews and negative reinforcement for treating them poorly. The Soviets had absorbed this—witness the burst of emigration in 1979 when Brezhnev wanted SALT II passed and the abrupt end to it when he realized he had failed. But this mechanism of reward and punishment only worked as long as the Soviets desired engagement with the West. When the superpowers chose to ignore or demonize each other—as they did once Reagan took office—the Soviet Jews became more like hostages than pawns.

For the Kremlin there was little left to lose by crushing any and all activity deemed anti-Soviet. Andrei Sakharov was confined to Gorky and watched constantly by KGB agents; his phone was disconnected and all communication with the outside world severed. He was sentenced to a de facto exile without even the fiction of a trial (a breach of the Soviets' own laws). The State had simply kidnapped its most forceful and influential critic and bundled him off to a place where he was deprived of his greatest source of strength: contact with the West. A few days after Sakharov's forced exile began, Elena Bonner, his wife, returned to Moscow and handed journalists Sakharov's statement demanding a trial. "I do not need a gilded cage," he wrote. "I need the right to fulfill my public duty."

The Helsinki Watch movement started by Yuri Orlov, who was still in a labor camp serving his seven-year sentence, had spawned a network of regional groups from Lithuania to the Ukraine. These had all been squashed. Thirty-three members of Helsinki Watch groups were imprisoned in 1980. The Moscow group was in tatters, all of its dwindling members increasingly susceptible to harassment or arrest. By the end of 1980, only Elena Bonner and two others, including Naum Meiman, a respected refusenik mathematician in his early seventies, were not in jail. Hobbled and depleted, they continued to put out reports in the group's name. But the destruction went beyond the Helsinki Watch groups. Between the fall of 1979 and the summer of 1980, a hundred and fifty dissidents of all sorts were put on trial. Any independent group with even the slightest civil or human rights bent—like the recently formed Working Commission Against the Use of Psychiatry for Political Purposes—became a target.

In Moscow, the refusenik activists tried to carry on. The ranks of the *politiki* had been decimated over the past few years. With the exception of the elderly Alexander Lerner, most of the main leaders of this group, people like Slepak, Shcharansky, and Dina Beilin, were in exile, jail, or Israel. Even Lerner had become demoralized and scared. He canceled the regular gatherings that took place in his apartment, one of the few safe spaces for refuseniks. The *kulturniki* suffered less, but many of their leaders had emigrated in the big wave of the late 1970s. Of the group of scientists that had helped establish the weekly scientific seminars and the samizdat journal *Jews in the USSR*, only one person remained, Victor Brailovsky, the goateed statistician and former lecturer on probability theory. He had been left in charge of both endeavors. Then, in November 1980, he too was arrested.

Brailovsky had stopped producing issues of *Jews in the USSR* in the summer of 1979. The logistics of underground publishing had become too difficult. But the journal had never caused problems for any of its editors, including Brailovsky, who had purposely stuck to scholarly content on Jewish culture and history. He had continued the Sunday seminars, which were a source of sustenance for the out-of-work refusenik physicists and mathematicians. Brailovsky had first felt a shift in KGB approach when they interrupted his planning of the Fourth International Conference on Collective Phenomena—a grand title for a gathering that was to take place in his modest two-room apartment over snacks prepared by his wife, Irina. Agents conducted a tumultuous search, overturning the furniture and grabbing many of the scientific papers for the conference. His arrest came a few months later. He was charged with "defaming the Soviet state and public order" based on his editorship of the now-defunct *Jews in the USSR*. The Sunday following his arrest, with her husband sitting in Butyrka Prison, Irina Brailovsky invited the scientists to continue the weekly seminar at their apartment. Looking out her window, she could see two policemen standing guard at the door to her building and turning away each of the twenty refuseniks who arrived to participate. When Irina finally descended the stairs to confront the policemen, they informed her that they had no idea why they had been instructed to prevent the seminar from taking place but that they would be there the following Sunday and every Sunday after that. The weekly meetings were over. "Today is the first time in eight years that we have missed a seminar," a distraught Irina Brailovsky told a Western journalist.

Brailovsky's arrest was the first shot in a new war on Jewish culture. Until that point, the less openly political refuseniks had mostly been left alone. Anything that might cause embarrassment was of course put down—like the 1976 Jewish cultural symposium or the international scientific conferences that sometimes drew the attention of Nobel Prize–winning foreign scientists. But the organizers were rarely if ever put on trial or detained for more than fifteen days. Hebrew teachers and activists like Brailovsky had largely been left untouched. Suddenly, no one was safe. Quiet, nonpolitical activity now elicited the same response as a self-immolation in the middle of Red Square. Both would be suppressed.

The new crackdown announced itself in Leningrad with another knock on the door on May 17, 1981—around the time that Ovrazhki was being broken up. The Seminar on Jewish History, Culture, and Traditions had been taking place for two years, single-handedly reviving a Jewish movement in the canal-lined city. When the 1970 hijacking plot was uncovered and most of the Zionist activists in the city arrested, a decade of reverberating fear ensued. Refuseniks were scattered and mostly isolated from one another. When they did converge, it was usually around charismatic characters like Aba Taratuta. He was Leningrad's answer to Volodya Slepak—a good-natured and generous man who connected various refuseniks with one another and was a main contact for the movement in the West. His balding head, thick black beard, and impish smile were well known to tourists. Denied an exit visa in 1973—making him second on the meticulous lists he kept of all the refuseniks in the city—Taratuta tried in his own way to duplicate what was happening in Moscow, though on a smaller and less conspicuous scale. He started a Jewish lending library with an eight-hundred-book collection that had been left behind by a departing refusenik. He organized in his apartment yearly Seders and Purim spiels, carnivalesque reenactments of Esther's story, which the kids loved. Later on, he and his wife, Ida, helped start a kindergarten for the children of the refuseniks. But nothing welded the community together quite like the seminars, which were begun in 1979 by a group of intellectuals looking to educate themselves about Jewish culture and history. What started as informal meetings with a handful of people and a self-proclaimed teacher evolved into a weekly event that drew anywhere from sixty to a hundred people.

The day the KGB came knocking, the subject of the seminar was the relevance of the Sabbath. All the furniture in the thirty-square-meter apartment had been placed in a storage space beneath the ceiling. In all, eighty-six people had shown up and were jammed into a single room; some sat on makeshift benches, but most stood. It was hot and the atmosphere was tense. Suddenly, eight plainclothes KGB agents led by a militia captain pushed open the door and, without saying a word, began snapping photographs of everyone in the room. The flashbulbs popped again and again. The large mass of people pushed together, and a few young students who had not yet applied for exit visas huddled close to the wall, pulling their shirts over their heads to hide their faces. In a few minutes, Evgeny Lein was taken into custody. Lein, a forty-two-year-old mathematician who had a long black goatee and dark rings around his eyes, had been a refusenik for three years. He demanded to see identification from the group of men who stormed the seminar. The last thing he heard outside before he was shoved onto one of the three waiting buses was an old woman yelling, "It's a pity Hitler didn't slaughter all of you!"

Lein was tried a few months later. Some eighty participants in the seminar pushed their way into the courtroom and were allowed to observe; several of them even wore yarmulkes. Representatives of the U.S. consulate in Leningrad were there as well. An American student present recorded the chaotic scene in a letter: "At last a door opened and a stampede ensued. I was pushed in the direction of the opening. I had no control over where I was being shoved ... Our body heat, combined with the cramped seating, made the courtroom extremely hot. I remember one very large man. His head rested against the wall, sweat poured down his face." Lein was accused of assaulting one of the policemen who had raided the seminar. In the end, he was given a relatively light punishment: instead of going to prison, he would spend two years in Siberia doing manual labor. As he stood up to hear his sentence, a few refuseniks outside the courtroom managed to take a photo through the window. With his eyes closed and his long goatee, flanked by uniformed guards more than twice his size, he had the beatific look of a Roman martyr on his way to the stake.

The Leningrad refuseniks, like those in Moscow, tried to go on. Keeping alive the seminar in some form became a cause in itself. One young refusenik insisted on finding a way. Misha Beizer, heavily bearded and with large square glasses, had always been interested in history. But in the Soviet Union, the humanities were dangerous for Jews. The direction of research and even an academic's findings could be affected by the whims of the state. So Jews tended to stay away from these subjects. Beizer, like so many other Jews, studied physics and mathematics instead. In college, when he first started to be curious about Israel, he made superficial contact with the early Leningrad Zionist circle. But it wasn't until the end of the 1970s, when people he knew, including his ex-wife and son, began emigrating, that he himself risked applying. He was refused in the summer of 1980 and soon joined the seminar, eventually becoming a regular lecturer. Beizer studied the few available history books so that he could teach others. His specialty was the Jewish history of Leningrad. And his new idea was to take the lectures outside and turn them into walking tours of the city.

Without access to archives or other reference material, Beizer conducted his own historical research, slowly building an encyclopedic knowledge of the Jewish presence in the city. He looked in old address books from the turn of the century, interviewed older people, rummaged through personal libraries. It was a desire for historical resuscitation that the Riga Jews who had excavated the mass graves at Rumbuli would have understood. And this is how Beizer built his tour. One stop, for example, was the home of the attorney who defended Mendel Beilis in the infamous blood libel case of 1913. Beizer looked up his name, Gruzenberg, in the address book and found his building intact. In this way, he found the homes of other famous Jews and the locations of old Jewish societies from before the revolution. The tours consisted of small groups of people who spent hours trudging around the city, often through thick snow, listening to Beizer as he pointed out the significant locations and slowly explained the history. The popularity of the tours grew week by week, and soon Beizer had as many as two dozen people at a time following him and his large fur hat. It wasn't long before KGB agents joined the tours also. They scared people off. And Beizer had no interest in creating an opportunity for mass arrest.

In mid-1982, he stopped acting as a guide, preferring instead to write up his notes in samizdat form so that anyone who wanted could take a self-guided tour (a version was smuggled out of the Soviet Union, translated by Michael Sherbourne in London, and published). Beizer continued his historical research, meeting clandestinely every two weeks with a few other academically minded refuseniks to share the material they were uncovering. Eventually this work produced a scholarly journal, the *Leningradsky Evreisky Almanakh* (Leningrad Jewish Almanac), similar in some ways to the defunct *Jews in the USSR*. The first issue, a collection of research articles, came out in September 1982; it was produced and distributed entirely underground.

One of the more active Leningrad refuseniks, Yakov Gorodezky, a witness at Lein's trial who had led an effort to collect evidence in his defense, tried to continue the seminars in some other form. He decided to legally register the group with the local Communist Party authorities as the "Leningrad Society for Study of Jewish Culture." More than fifty young participants, many of them students, signed a petition. One by one, they were asked to appear at the Communist Party offices of their respective jobs and universities and pressured to remove their names. Gorodezky himself was physically threatened at the Leningrad KGB headquarters, and he resigned from the head of the group. In 1983, the seminar ceased to exist. Even this harmless attempt at reviving cultural awareness among the smallest cross-section of Leningrad elite was perceived as a threat.

The war against Jewish culture blazed through every corner of the Soviet Union. Even in cities far from Moscow, where all that existed was a handful of active refuseniks and maybe a feeble attempt at Hebrew classes, the KGB hammered away with renewed ferocity. The Ukraine was particularly brutal. Nearly half a million Jews inhabited Odessa, Kharkov, and Kiev, places where anti-Semitism was deeply rooted. Jews there had always known that it was simply too dangerous to replicate the movements of Moscow and Leningrad. But even those few refuseniks who had attempted to organize some smaller-scale Jewish activities were harassed or imprisoned. In Kiev, the central figure of the small Jewish underground, a nuclear physicist, was put into a psychiatric ward and later arrested for allegedly being drunk in public and beating up an old woman. Another well-known refusenik was charged with parasitism.

The dramatic drop in emigration had the greatest effect on Jews living far from the capital. Thousands had applied in 1979 when emigration numbers were on the rise, and a majority of them had been refused, thrown out of their jobs, and ostracized. Now they were telling stories of being attacked in the street. "Most often the beatings are at night, when no one is around," an anonymous refusenik told an AP reporter. On the Jewish New Year in the fall of 1981, a group of five Jews on their way to lay a wreath at Babi Yar, the ravine where tens of thousands were killed during the war, was stopped at the Kiev train station and given fifteen-day detentions. In Kharkov in 1980, a resilient group of refuseniks tried to start an informal Jewish university, giving older refuseniks fired from their jobs a chance to help young refuseniks thrown out of school. Classes covered scientific subjects as well as Jewish tradition and Hebrew. An entire year passed without incident but just before the fall semester was to begin, one of the main organizers, Alexander Paritsky, was arrested. He was sentenced to three years in a prison camp for slandering the Soviet state. From Leningrad to Kiev, the KGB managed to extinguish any hope that Jewish life could find expression on Soviet soil.

Ida Nudel and her collie, Pizer, returned from Siberian exile in March of 1982. She found in Moscow a demoralized and depressed community of refuseniks. Everything was more dangerous now, more difficult. With fewer people receiving permission to leave, the number of refuseniks had climbed into the thousands, but they were mostly a scared and passive group. The sit-down protests and demonstrations of the 1970s were inconceivable.

Ida experienced this new more oppressive atmosphere when she tried to simply register for a *propiska,* a residence permit. Most ex-convicts were not allowed to live within a hundred kilometers of a major city. This restriction did not apply to exiles; still, Ida was told by the local police that there was an order forbidding her to live in Moscow. She tried everything, refusing to let herself be squeezed out by an unforgiving bureaucracy. She even resorted to calling a high Soviet official with whom she had struck up a strange relationship in the years before her exile. Albert Ivanov was the deputy director of the administrative department of the Central Committee of the Communist Party. Ida had gotten his number from Dina Beilin in 1973 and was told that he could sometimes be sympathetic. Ivanov, strangely, was willing to take her calls, to listen to her rant and complain about the conditions her adopted prisoners were forced to endure. She told him about what the KGB was doing and the reaction in the West. Something close to a friendship developed, teasing, often tense, but sometimes warm. In five years, they had never met, though Ivanov told Ida he had seen her in the protests he watched through his window. When the troubles with her *propiska* began, in 1982, she called him for help. His voice sounded twenty years older than when they had last spoken, defeated and tired. He could do nothing for her. What followed were months of wandering. No local authorities seemed willing to register her. She went to Riga, where the father of the Zalmansons tried to help her. She had people check with the local authorities in a town in Estonia, and then in Tbilisi. No one would take her. And without a *propiska* stamp in her internal passport she was vulnerable to arrest. Finally, a few refusenik families in a Moldovan town called Bendery helped her register and find a home. Half a year had passed. It was already the fall of 1982. The cold had set in. The move to Bendery ended her months as an internal refugee, but it also inaugurated a new hardship, a continuation of her life in exile—far away from her friends in Moscow.

The bleakness that Ida Nudel discovered in what remained of her old Moscow circle was partly due to the death of Alexander Lerner's wife, Judith, the previous year. The Lerner home had long been the center of refusenik activity, one of those relatively safe islands in that Moscow archipelago. Lerner, the now aging cyberneticist, had been in refusal for more than ten years, and Judith had played the role of nurturing matriarch for the younger activists. At the funeral, she was buried in a metal box inside a wooden coffin. This way, the body could be exhumed more easily if Lerner, hoping against all reason, got permission to leave. His wife could be reburied in Israel.

With the freeze on emigration and the silencing of all political and cultural expression, very few outlets remained for those refuseniks still willing to fight. Many of them simply returned to the quiet, basic building blocks of their activism. Ever since the earliest phases of the movement, Hebrew had been seen as the gateway to Jewish identity. Language provided access to culture. The Hebrew learner felt instantly connected to a long tradition, to the language of the Bible, and to the country where Hebrew was now spoken, Israel. The one constant activity that ran beneath the ups and downs of political engagement was the teaching of Hebrew, which went on in dozens of apartments throughout Moscow and Leningrad. Instructional books like *Elef Millim* (A Thousand Words) were the most reproduced materials in samizdat. A small group of respected teachers, mostly unharmed in the 1970s, organized summer retreats and instructed cells of four or five Hebrew students; those few people trained several new cadres of others, and these others went on to train many more, a pyramid-like system. In Moscow, Yuli Kosharovsky, a refusenik who had been waiting for a visa since 1971, was at the top of this pyramid. He taught the teachers.

Toward the end of the 1970s, with prominent refuseniks losing energy or simply not around anymore, Kosharovsky became one of the most important leaders of the movement. He moved to Moscow from the city of Sverdlovsk in the Ural Mountains, where he'd been relentlessly harassed, and he eventually began organizing Hebrew classes. Kosharovsky was one of the Lishka's main contacts in the Soviet Union. Israel trusted his judgment and increasingly chose to act through him. Communication with the Tel Aviv office was a convoluted and clandestine process. Well-briefed tourists would come with instructions and a secret sign to indicate that they represented Israel and should be given priority. They would bring the latest message or policy directive; Kosharovsky would load them down with requests—funds for the wife of a prisoner who needed financial help, a copy of a specific book he wanted to reproduce—and give them information and updated lists of refuseniks. It helped that Kosharovsky was a staunch Zionist and that his objectives lined up perfectly with Israel's—a tight focus on emigration and Jewish culture, and the avoidance of activity that might be perceived as anti-Soviet. Early on in his life as an activist, Kosharovsky had hit on the idea of using Hebrew teaching as a form of outreach. He was trying to widen the circle of aspiring emigrants. Hebrew classes provided a structure, a framework for bringing people together, a goal for them to work toward, and a relatively safe way to introduce Zionist concepts. He also saw the classes as a way to suss out people who were not committed or who could be informing for the KGB. Only those students who advanced to a certain level gained his trust and were allowed to deal with more sensitive operations, such as reproducing books or starting up new classes.

In 1979, Kosharovsky became even more ambitious. He began sending his teachers on missions to parts of the Soviet Union that contained Jewish populations but had almost no Jewish activity. These emissaries set up Hebrew classes in the hopes that new teachers would emerge to continue the lessons after the original instructors moved on to the next city. Everyone went to great lengths to make sure these activities went undetected. Kosharovsky himself would take his students high into the Caucasus Mountains in the summers to set up camp and study together. Other teachers went on hiking tours or lived together in unheated dachas. In a short time, a whole Hebrew teaching network had developed. Kosharovsky largely stepped back from the day-to-day planning, leaving three former students—the Kholmiansky brothers, Sasha and Mikhail, and Yuli Edelstein—to divide up the whole Soviet Union and focus on developing cells in all the cities where Jews lived. Meanwhile Kosharovsky built a kind of superstructure and invited all these new teachers to Moscow in the summer of 1979 for the first intercity seminar. The following year, he had fifty-six teachers from eight different cities come for a month of intensive Hebrew.

The growing network demanded a constant replenishing of materials, and this became Kosharovsky's preoccupation. He ran what was basically an underground publishing house, churning out copy after copy of mimeographed Hebrew-language books and cassette tapes that could then be sent out to Odessa or Tallinn. He had a bank of typewriters and a handful of secretaries to copy the books, but he couldn't invent new material. So Kosharovsky's contacts with the Lishka became critical. They backed his efforts completely and looked for any opportunity to sneak books into the country. The Soviets themselves inadvertently ended up providing one of the richest venues for smuggling books in: the hugely popular Moscow International Book Fair.

Beginning in 1977 and then continuing biennially, the trade fair was one of the very few remnants of détente and brought publishers from all over the world to the Soviet capital to display their wares.

The bibliophilic Russian intelligentsia was thrilled by the chance to see Western books otherwise forbidden to them. Predictably, though, the Soviets tried to control what was on offer. At the 1979 fair, forty-five books, including George Orwell's novels and anything with the word *Jewish* in the title, were seized, and Robert Bernstein, the head of Random House and the founder of a new human rights group in New York set up to monitor adherence to the Helsinki Accords, was not given an entry visa. In 1981, the previous bad press had caused a slight liberalization. Many more books were permitted, including an anthology of Russian literature that included verse by Andrei Amalrik and Joseph Brodsky, but a handful were still banned. Among the censored were the children's book version of *The History of the Jews,* by Abba Eban (though, strangely, the adult version was left alone); the *1981 Jewish Yearbook;* and Shmuel Ettinger's *History of the Jewish People.* The reason given by the authorities was that these were "works by renegades who have made a profession of slandering our life." Still, the stand of the American Association of Jewish Publishers and the Israeli pavilion had hundreds of books with Jewish themes. People waited in line for hours to get into the convention halls so they could grab these books, which the publishers fully intended to let them steal. The Soviet authorities saw this frenzy and stopped the distribution of ten thousand plastic records of Hebrew and Yiddish songs being handed out at one booth.

Kosharovsky coordinated with the Israelis to make sure he could take advantage of this opportunity to gather precious material. An intricate operation was set up in which his people repeatedly exited with book-filled bags that they then stockpiled in various locations. Arrangements were made to "steal" books at night as well. In this way, Kosharovsky was able to get as many as a thousand books out of the closely watched convention center. At the 1983 fair, although security had been tightened and nearly fifty books banned, the Israeli delegation still managed to leave hundreds of volumes in the Soviet Union.

Though teaching Hebrew was, by default, legal (there were no laws *against* it), the war on Jewish culture found its way to Kosharovsky and his rapidly expanding circle. By 1982, he was being followed everywhere. House searches and confiscations of material had become routine. A few times, he had been picked up and questioned. And the language of the KGB had shifted. The people Kosharovsky dealt with now seemed less restrained, more willing to threaten physical violence. One agent told Kosharovsky that if he didn't stop teaching, the KGB would break his arms and legs. When students of his—often just eighteen-year-olds from the university who had yet to apply for exit visas—began being questioned as well, he decided to go quiet for a while. By this point he could afford to stop teaching—the network would multiply without his help. And it was enough work just supporting the teachers he had trained. When they in turn started to be harassed, it was Kosharovsky who made sure they got some kind of legal aid, that their wives were cared for, that their cases got attention in the West. In this new, threatening environment, his role had changed from stimulating Hebrew culture to managing one crisis after another.

Leonid Brezhnev's infirmity had long plagued the Kremlin. When he finally died, in November of 1982, after years of falling asleep at summits and mumbling his way through speeches, the West was so eager for a reliable partner that the danger his successor posed was not initially perceived. Yuri Andropov had run the KGB since 1967 and had quit just six months earlier so that he could join the Politburo. Now, for the first time, a chief of the secret police would command the entire country. Still, there was hope in the West that he represented change. Despite the fact that he had overseen the recent crackdown on dissent, Western observers noted that he was "a witty conversationalist, a bibliophile, a connoisseur of modern art," and possibly even a "closet liberal." *Time* magazine quoted a KGB defector who had visited Andropov's five-bedroom apartment and seen an extensive record collection that included Chubby Checker, Frank Sinatra, and Peggy Lee.

The Jewish activists had no such illusions. They knew exactly what they were getting with this new leader. He had guided the institution that had harassed and interrogated and imprisoned them. It was at one of his first posts, as Soviet ambassador to Hungary in 1956, that Andropov had learned how quickly revolution could flower from even the most innocuous beginnings. He vowed from then on to squash even the smallest disturbance, the tiniest instance of what he called "anti-social behavior." This was the same man who in 1975 had told the Politburo that it was "impossible at this time to renounce the criminal prosecution of people who oppose the Soviet system ... since these would inevitably lead to further unacceptable demands on us." In a speech in late December of 1982, a month after taking power, he laid out an ominous-sounding vision for how to solve the nationalities problem in the Soviet Union: "Our end goal is clear. It, to quote Lenin, 'is not only to bring the nations closer together but to fuse them.'" This fusion would not be voluntary.

Andropov was responding to more than just ideological pressure. The failure to transition to a postindustrial economy was beginning to take its toll—there was a strange irony in a state that produced more steel and cement than any other country but made its citizens wait in long lines for food and toilet paper. He could not afford any brain drain, and Jews still constituted the most elite class of technocrats in the country, despite quotas at universities and research institutes. Andropov hoped that if he built the wall even higher, stopping even the low level of emigration that existed, Jews might just accept their fate and work hard for Soviet society. To do this, he needed to persuade the vast majority of Jews who weren't in the movement that Zionism was evil. And he had to convince those refuseniks intent on making noise that they would pay for it.

Almost immediately a high-profile arrest was made. It was Yosef Begun, a tenacious man who had become a sort of mascot for the Hebrew teachers of Moscow. Begun was short and stocky with a high forehead and bushy eyebrows. He had a perpetually mischievous smile and appeared to his refusenik friends to be absolutely fearless. In refusal since 1971, he was aligned with the *kulturniki* but also acted fairly independently, teaching Hebrew and duplicating and distributing material on his own. His personal crusade—the act that got him arrested the first time—was his insistence that Hebrew teaching should be legally recognized. Since being fired from the research institute where he had worked as a radio engineer and received a doctorate, Begun had been supporting himself with Hebrew. And, like all other refuseniks teachers, he had taken manual-labor jobs so that he couldn't be accused of parasitism. Over the years, he had worked as a stoker, a porter, and a fireman. But in the mid-1970s, he began sending letters to the authorities demanding that his status as a teacher be officially recognized. He even wrote to the Finance Ministry asking to pay income tax on his earnings from private Hebrew classes. He was making a hundred rubles a month, a respectable living wage. However, every request was rebuffed. Without labeling the teaching itself as illegal, the bureaucracy spun him in circles. First, he was told he didn't have the proper papers. Then they said that since Hebrew wasn't taught on any curriculum in the entire country, he couldn't possibly be a tutor. Begun eventually made a bold move. He simply stopped working at any other job. It didn't take long; he was charged with parasitism in March of 1977, two weeks before Shcharansky's arrest. Eventually he was tried and sentenced to two years of exile in far-off Kolyma, the site of Stalin's most feared Siberian labor camp. But that was not the end of it. When he returned to Moscow, he was once again arrested and put on trial, this time for violating the strict residence restrictions for ex-convicts. Again the harrowing weeks of transport in a tightly packed Stolypin car with only bread and salty herring for food, a visit to the toilet once a day, and a crew of hardened criminals as companions. For three more years he lived in exile.

Begun made his way back to Moscow in 1981. When he was refused a *propiska* for the capital, he didn't fight it; he registered to live in the town of Strunino, fifty kilometers away. But this didn't stop him from seeing his old students and making contact with the refuseniks. In the fall of 1982, the KGB struck again. After a five-hour search at his girlfriend's apartment (Begun, a notorious ladies' man, had already been married twice), more than a hundred books and audiotapes were collected: Hebrew dictionaries, copies of *Jews in the USSR*, pamphlets about Israel. Begun was arrested but released after hours of questioning. Three weeks later, on November 6, as he returned from a trip to Leningrad where he'd visited Aba Taratuta, Begun was stopped at the train station. His bags were searched, and a couple of Hebrew and Jewish history books were discovered. In a few days, he was taken to Vladimir Prison, the vast czarist-era complex, and charged with the much-feared Article 70. The authorities were building a case of anti-Soviet agitation or propaganda, a crime that carried a maximum sentence of seven years in prison, followed by five years in exile.

Arresting Begun was a quick way of terrorizing the refuseniks, but the members of Andropov's regime wanted more. They wanted to go on the offensive with a public campaign that would challenge Zionism on ideological grounds, branding it unappealing and dangerous. Usually the war was waged in interrogation rooms at KGB headquarters or, as with the Leningrad hijacking and Shcharansky, in closed show trials where the activities of the Zionists were linked to terrorism or espionage, not challenged on their face. That changed with the creation of the Soviet Anti-Zionist Committee in the spring of 1983.

The news of the group came on March 31, two weeks after the close of the Third International Conference on Soviet Jewry in Jerusalem. An article by the wire service TASS reported that eight prominent Soviet Jews were appealing for the formation of a group to expose the malevolent underpinnings of Zionism. This was an old trick. A small handful of "official" Jews were always kept on hand to speak in the name of Soviet Jewry. Some of them had been playing this role since Stalin's time. At the head of this group was David Dragunsky, one of the last high-ranking Jewish army officers, a seventy-three-year-old former tank corps officer who had fought in World War II and been decorated twice with the Hero of the Soviet Union medal. During the Doctors' Plot of 1953, just as rumors circulated about Stalin's plans for a mass Jewish expulsion to the east, a group of prominent Jews, including Ilya Ehrenburg, signed an obsequious letter reaffirming loyalty to the state and vowing to struggle against "Jewish millionaires and billionaires and their Zionist agents." Dragunsky's name was one of the first signatures. Now he was the author of an article appearing in *Pravda* the day after the TASS announcement. It was an attack on Zionism so vicious that it obliterated the line between anti-Zionism and anti-Semitism. Zionism, Dragunsky wrote, was "a concentration of extreme nationalism, chauvinism and racial intolerance, justification of territorial seizures and annexation, armed adventurism, a cult of political arbitrariness and impunity, demagogy and ideological sabotage, sordid maneuvers and perfidy."

The new committee's goals were clear: to attack Zionism in the most violent terms and to insist that most Jews were normal, well-adjusted Soviet citizens with no interest in emigrating. This also served the purpose of justifying the end of emigration (fewer than five hundred people had received permission to leave in the first half of 1983) and dissuading any refusenik from so much as humming an Israeli song. "The Zionist ringleaders try to persuade world opinion that a Jewish question allegedly exists in the U.S.S.R.," Dragunsky's letter proclaimed. "We vigorously protest against such concoctions.

The Jews, citizens of the U.S.S.R., are part and parcel of the Soviet people."

This was followed by a coordinated flurry of articles and television segments focused on the misery of Jews who had left for Israel and the contentedness of the Soviet Jewish population. A three-part series in *Pravda* highlighted the story of an elderly woman, Berta Moiseyevna, who had decided not to join her daughter in the West even though she too had received an exit visa. "For me, a mother, it's difficult to understand why all these emigrations have become possible," Moiseyevna was quoted as saying. "They say it's for the reunification of families. I don't understand why it's necessary to abandon parents to be reunified with some mythical uncles or aunts. This is not reunification, but separation." A polemic against the teaching of Hebrew, "Caution: Zionism!," ran in *Leningradskaya Pravda,* calling it a form of "extreme religious fanaticism, chauvinism, the striving to force on Jews the idea of exclusivity, their having been selected as the 'chosen people,' their superiority over other nations, and consequently, to force upon them racial intolerance toward 'inferior' nations."

The propaganda onslaught gained force through the spring and climaxed with the inaugural press conference of the committee on June 6, a day chosen to coincide with the first anniversary of Israel's invasion of Lebanon. Dragunsky was in uniform, his chest covered in medals. Next to him was the other major voice of the committee, also a longtime "official" Jew, Samuel Zivs, a sixty-one-year-old jurist at the Institute of State and Law and a Party ideologue. After explaining that the committee had been formed in order to aid "the political unmasking of Zionism," the eight founding members, all Jews with no connection to Jewish life, insisted that emigration had ended because Jews no longer wanted to go to Israel. The few Western reporters present kept hammering this point. The answer, given by Zivs, was based on a lie. He maintained the "basic motivation" for emigration was "family reunification" and that "those who want to leave have left the country." He completely absolved the government of any role in the fluctuation of emigration. Jews simply didn't want to leave anymore. That was it. Those who did had simply succumbed "to Zionist lures" and were "victims of Zionist propaganda," the very force the new committee would combat. Western activists immediately responded to this claim, citing the four hundred thousand invitations that had been sent from

Israel over the years and the list of more than ten thousand known refuseniks.

David Dragunsky used the conference to draw parallels between Zionism and Nazism, a longtime staple of Soviet anti-Semitism. Referring to the Lebanon war, he said, "The past year has made perfectly clear that Zionism is increasingly modeled on the ideas and methods of Hitler." No matter how preposterous this sounded to outside ears, the committee clearly thought it was a winning argument since it was soon amplified in a state-sanctioned book. Lev Korneyev's *The Class Essence of Zionism* made any earlier anti-Semitic Soviet book, such as *Judaism Without Embellishment,* seem mild by comparison. Zionists, in his telling, had actually collaborated with the Nazis in mass executions. Billing himself as an expert on Zionism, Korneyev argued that the Jewish people since ancient times had had "profit [as] their ideology" and could not be trusted. Jews in fact constituted "a fifth column in any country." Soviet citizens were told to beware. All sales of Levi's jeans on the black market went straight into the pocket of "Zionist militarists." The book was released in a press run of ten thousand copies and reviewed positively in *Izvestia* and *Sovetskaya Kultura.* Korneyev was given a platform: his articles appeared in literary journals and even in a newspaper for children, *Pionerskaya Pravda,* in which he warned young Communists to beware of Zionists who were trying to turn loyal citizens into "traitors."

The fact that Andropov was behind such a public attack on Jews demoralized the refuseniks tremendously. Even though they understood that some of this bluster was directed at the Soviets' Arab allies—propaganda red meat to assure them of continued Soviet support—the Soviet Anti-Zionist Committee was not a joke. It had a fourteen-person staff, thirty-seven members, and a smaller presidium, including Dragunsky and Zivs, who acted as chairman and first deputy, respectively. It also included some big players in Soviet media, like the deputy editor of the Novosti publishing house and the head of a section in the influential weekly *Literaturnaya Gazeta.* And the plans were ambitious. They wanted to open up municipal branches in each Soviet republic, starting with Moscow, Leningrad, Novosibirsk, and, of course, Birobidzhan. The committee would fund plays, films, and works of art, and even create a new state prize in the field of anti-Zionism.

This was the public face of the assault, and by no means just a pose.

It was at the center of a renewed attack on all Jewish activists. No longer were they simply "hooligans" or "anti-social elements." Now they were portrayed as a dangerous, subversive force that had to be eradicated. Just before Yosef Begun was finally brought to trial in the fall of 1983, after nearly a year spent in Vladimir Prison, the new head of the KGB, Viktor Chebrikov, prepared a brief for the Central Committee. In it, he explained the charges against Begun and what the long investigation had revealed. More than any other previous case, Begun's seemed to rest simply on his Hebrew teaching. Since this was not officially a crime, the teaching was presented as a front, a way to recruit innocent Soviet citizens into acting against the state. "In the course of the investigation, it was established that Begun, as a result of his hostile attitude toward the socialist order, adopted an active anti-Soviet line," the report began. "Under cover of distributing textbooks for the study of Hebrew (Ivrit) and 'bringing Jews into contact' with their 'national culture,' Begun illegally prepared anti-Soviet literature and other materials containing slanderous fabrications defaming the Soviet state and special order. He distributed these slanderous materials prepared by himself and by his accomplices in the Soviet USSR and transferred them abroad for use in subversive activity against the Soviet state, compromising the social order and political system of the USSR and deceiving and disorienting world opinion."

When the evidence was presented in the Vladimir courtroom, the "slanderous fabrications" consisted of nothing more than a few pages written by Begun about the need to support Hebrew teaching and Jewish culture. It seems the most accurate part of Chebrikov's memo was the bit about Begun "deceiving and disorienting world opinion." For this, and surely to send another message to the refusenik community, Begun was given the maximum sentence of seven years in a labor camp followed by five years of exile. Andropov might have had a thing for American music, but he was no closet liberal. His takeover of the leadership simply extended the power of the KGB and made an already harsh environment for the activists even worse.

Strangely, even during these black days, one subset of refuseniks had found a way to thrive: the small group of Jews who had discovered Orthodoxy.

For the most part, the intellectuals and scientists who became activists in the sixties and the seventies never embraced the religious life. Except for the enthusiastic celebration of a few holidays, like a Passover Seder or the swirling, dancing parties of Simchat Torah, the refuseniks saw their return to Jewish identity in mostly cultural terms. They were drawn to the secular Zionism of Israel, in which Judaism's highlights were plucked. Few engaged in the hard work of observing the Sabbath or wearing a yarmulke, let alone keeping kosher. This was much like the Judaism practiced by the overwhelming majority of American Jews. The refuseniks fought for an identity that allowed them full knowledge of their history, the freedom to learn their own ancient language and to practice whatever form of the religion they chose. Even *kulturniki* like Volodya Prestin and Pasha Abramovich, who had always argued vehemently for cultural and religious outreach to the greater Soviet Jewish population, didn't demand more than this. To reclaim some form of Jewish identity in the face of a Soviet society that denigrated any kind of spirituality was already a kind of achievement. To take the next step and abide by the strictures of Halakah, Jewish law, demanded an internal revolution that no one—or almost no one—was willing to undertake.

But then there was Ilya Essas. As a young graduate student in mathematics at Vilnius University, Essas got his first glimpse of positive Jewishness from old prerevolutionary books he discovered on library shelves, like Heinrich Graetz's encyclopedic nineteenth-century Jewish history. In Moscow in the early 1970s, Essas linked up with other refuseniks and began learning Hebrew. But unlike them, he discovered that his hunger for Jewish culture was not sated with a copy of *Exodus*. He wanted more. The only Jewish tradition he saw that could possibly rival the rich Russian one of Pushkin and Dostoyevsky was contained in the ancient books, the Torah and the tomes of commentary that had accumulated over the centuries. It was very clear to him that only this rich, religious culture could form the basis of a new identity. But where to even begin? In 1972, in preparation for Nixon's first visit to Moscow, the authorities allowed the city's Great Choral Synagogue to open a yeshiva in a show of religious tolerance. Essas signed up to be one of the first pupils but on day one realized that he was practically the only sentient person in the room. The rest of the students included a handful of senile old men and a mentally disabled teenager. But the teacher was authentic, an elder of the community who had studied Torah in his boyhood before the revolution. He put a *chumash*, a bound version of the Torah, into Essas's hands. It was a revelation. Even though he could hardly understand the ancient Hebrew, he knew that this would be his way. He quickly took to the study of the biblical text. When his teacher suffered a heart attack three months later, Essas began leading the weekly discussion of the Torah portion attended by five of the white-bearded men who frequented the synagogue.

Essas's time at the yeshiva, and the yeshiva itself, didn't last very long. In early 1974, he applied and was refused an exit visa on the grounds that his wife, an engineer who had three years earlier worked at a government construction office, had once held a high-level security clearance. He was soon banned from the synagogue by the nominal head of the Jewish community in Moscow, a man who, like the chief rabbi, took his orders from the KGB. But this did not stop Essas, now a full refusenik. Losing his place in Soviet society only intensified his pursuit of a spiritual life. The cultural parties at Ovrazhki and the intellectual camaraderie of other refuseniks were not enough. He wanted a new worldview, one that only religiosity could provide. What did it mean to be Jewish, he wondered, if he did not fully accept all the rules, follow God's tenets completely?

Essas's new piousness turned him into a singular figure among the refuseniks, a group whose taste and sensibility were not much different than the rest of the beleaguered Russian intelligentsia's. He grew a long beard and began wearing a black beret, a way of covering his head that, unlike a yarmulke, would not draw attention. He stopped working on the Sabbath and began keeping kosher as best he could. In a total vacuum, and without realizing it, he was becoming part of a small but vibrant worldwide movement: *baal teshuva* (meaning "one who has returned"). In the 1970s, completely secular Jews in the West were suddenly turning to Orthodoxy; many joined various Hasidic sects, especially the Lubavitchers, who had set up an ambitious international outreach arm known as Chabad. Essas's transformation, a man in his early thirties suddenly becoming a Torah-abiding Jew, would not have been unusual in New York or Tel Aviv. But in Moscow, he was largely on his own, and even the other refuseniks thought him extreme. They felt his new Orthodoxy was a judgment of their own secularism. But it was actually a sign of healthy diversification—something organically Jewish was growing in Moscow, even under worsening conditions. If Soviet Jews were going to be a normal community like any other in the world, why shouldn't there be at least one person representing the most devout end of the spectrum?

In 1977, Essas began teaching Torah classes in his apartment to groups no bigger than a dozen students. He was trying to single-handedly raise the spiritual level and biblical literacy of the community. As he told a *Baltimore Sun* reporter in the winter of 1979: "The spiritual life of Jews in the Soviet Union is non-existent. We have only one ideology. You can believe it or not. For a young Jew, it is natural for him to turn to his own background, to find out about his own religion. And a Jew cannot know his background without knowing Hebrew. It is the principal thing in Judaism. No translation can give you the knowledge. It can only give you the smell."

In early 1980, as the rest of the community was feeling the effects of the latest crackdown, Essas's enterprise really started taking off. He had managed to assemble a group of young men, most just out of their teens, who were eager to embrace a religious life. Together they studied, just as in the *cheders* (elementary schools) of Eastern European Jewish past, all crowded around a poorly duplicated page of Talmud. Essas, the eldest, was only in his early thirties but he tried to project confidence; he established a method that he thought might pull these atheists from darkness toward light. One of his idiosyncratic rules was that there would be no discussion of God's existence in the first few weeks of classes. "Right now, you are not equipped with the ideas or the terms to discuss this question with me. For the next two months, assume that there is an almighty guiding us. After two months of learning Torah, feel free to ask." The classes had a format. In the first half, Essas taught that week's Torah portion, and in the second half he instructed his students on some elementary aspect of Jewish practice—how to wrap phylacteries, the guidelines for keeping kosher, wedding rituals.

The network of young religious families grew, and Essas needed to set up an infrastructure that would enable them to live a Jewish life. Before this resurgence, the kosher needs of the handful of elderly men at the synagogue had been met with one piece of livestock a month that was slaughtered outside of Moscow and then carved up and distributed in the street behind the synagogue by one old *shochet,* the ritual slaughterer. But now there were more than a hundred people who needed meat. A network was set up to provide it. In Leningrad, a refusenik named Yitzchak Kogan had also become a *baal teshuva,* and he had made contacts with Chabad. He had taught himself how to be a *shochet* and was soon slaughtering animals at home, smoking the meat, and then sending it as sausages to Moscow. Since meat was difficult to attain, Essas had made contact with a local fish-packaging plant and instructed a few of the workers in how to pick out certain fish, like carp, that could be blessed as kosher. Eventually, the workers became familiar with the Jewish calendar and put aside hundreds of pounds of fish during the times of year, like Rosh Hashanah, that they knew Essas would come calling.

These families, no more than a few dozen, created their own devout world in hundreds of different ways. For circumcisions, a well-known Jewish heart surgeon was willing to make house calls on Sundays; he performed the *brit milah* on adults in living rooms all over Moscow. Not all the elements of Jewish tradition were possible to keep. In the entire Soviet Union, for example, there were only three working mikvahs, the ritual bath that religious women were obligated to take at least once a month following menstruation. Women would go to great lengths to visit these, sometimes traveling hundreds of miles. Essas wanted to create a kind of Jewish bubble around the children of these newly religious refuseniks, guarding them from Soviet society and passing on a new awareness. Classes for children began in apartments, taught by parents who had only recently become religious themselves. Essas eventually hit on the idea of summer camps, the standard solution for any activity that seemed too dangerous for the city. Starting in the summer of 1980, Essas brought his part of this burgeoning little community (fifteen children and ten adults that first year) to a two-story wooden house in the town of Bykovo, forty kilometers outside Moscow. They prayed in the morning, studied Torah during the day, and ran around the forest in the late afternoon. Back in Moscow, Essas started a weekly kindergarten for the younger children. After two summers in Bykovo, the camps were moved to the forest just outside Riga (the same forest where the Rumbuli memorial had been erected twenty years earlier). In 1982, forty people spent the summer together, eating kosher food, praying three times a day, and swimming in the Baltic. At the end of the summer, the children showed their parents what they had learned in a ceremony where each child recited a Torah commentary he or she had written.

What elevated Essas's work in the 1980s were the contacts he made with the Orthodox community outside the Soviet Union. He started receiving spiritual and, more important, material support from Ernie Hirsch, a redheaded English businessman who had first visited Moscow in 1980 and was shocked to discover Essas and his little, observant community. Hirsch immediately began raising money in England and America. He sent emissaries, or *shlichim,* as they were called in Hebrew, to provide classes and other training to Essas's flock. They were mostly American or English rabbis (or Israelis with foreign passports), and about once every two weeks, one of them would arrive in Moscow, call Essas on a public pay phone, and identify himself with a password (any one of the twelve tribes, from Asher to Zebulon). Then he would take the subway to the Sokol station, where Essas would be waiting for him to emerge from the first car. During the day, the *shaliach* (the singular form of *shlichim*) would train members of the community in ritual slaughter or in the calligraphic art of copying out holy texts like the Torah, and at night he would teach classes. The emissaries usually brought with them coveted consumer goods, like blank videocassettes and Japanese cameras, which were sold to provide funds for maintaining the supply of kosher food or to run the summer camps. Hirsch, who became known in the community as Gingy (a Hebrew diminutive for someone with red hair), got the Orthodox institutional world interested in these Soviet *baal teshuva.* After Agudath Israel, the international coordinating body for Orthodox Judaism, took on Essas as a project, he had a steady stream of books and funds to try to expand his circle.

Moscow wasn't the only city that saw religious revival in this otherwise oppressive period. Essas soon connected with Grisha Vasserman in Leningrad. Vasserman's apartment was the one raided in May of 1981, bringing the cultural seminar to an end. Like Essas, Vasserman had started out engaging in the same activities as the other refuseniks but soon discovered that he was drawn to the study and practice of Judaism. When the community acquired a library from a departing Jew, the religious books were funneled to him. For years before he could properly read Hebrew, Vasserman carried a prayer book in his pocket, taking it everywhere he went so he could practice sounding out the letters. Eventually, he found an older man at the Leningrad synagogue to instruct him, and he slowly began the process of becoming an observant Jew. He struggled to keep all the tenets at first—he relished the memory of the last film he ever saw, in 1976, a documentary about African elephants—but, like Essas, he immersed himself in a small community devoted to the same lifestyle. Vasserman's contribution to the religious movement, besides providing Torah classes in Leningrad, was figuring out a way to get more of the books of prayer and commentary needed for study. He cultivated a whole network of underground samizdat producers who either typed out his translations of Hebrew and English texts or photographed pages that could then be developed multiple times and collated. With tourists bringing in one or two books at a time, he was able to supply hundreds of texts to feed the hunger of this new community.

The KGB never tried to crush the community of *baal teshuva* refuseniks. With the exception of an occasional house search, the Torah lessons and recitations of Mishnah were never interrupted, even though Hebrew teachers were being arrested. Perhaps the agents in charge of monitoring Jewish activists simply weren't threatened by the sight of young men with wispy beards sitting around a table, poring over the multiple meanings of ancient words. The information supplied by the bugs placed in the apartments of people like Essas and Vasserman was probably boring and mystifying to the KGB. Raised to see religion as superstition, the Soviets likely considered the activities of the religious refuseniks as an eccentric throwback that could never take hold in the general population. There was an echo of the 1940s and early 1950s, when Stalin did everything to eradicate secular Jewish culture but seemed less focused on rooting out religion. Even though these devout Jews represented only a small subset of refuseniks, their existence was significant. They pushed the bounds of being Jewish to the ultimate extreme. Their survival was a kind of symbolic victory: even this most ill-suited and exotic flower could find a way to bloom in the Soviet Union. And ironically, at a time when much milder forms of Jewish expression were being brutally repressed, the authorities in their ignorance allowed this Orthodoxy to thrive.

The Soviet Union was not supposed to last until 1984. At least that's what the dissident Andrei Amalrik had predicted in the 1970s (it was his refusenik friend Vitaly Rubin who had given Amalrik the idea of using Orwell's year in his book title: *Will the Soviet Union Survive Until 1984?*). But now both Amalrik and Rubin were dead—killed in separate car crashes. The Sinologist refusenik Rubin had met his end in the Negev Desert, years after reaching Israel. Amalrik's accident had occurred on his way to Madrid, where another Helsinki follow-up conference was taking place. As one cruel guard reminded Tolya Shcharansky, then still at Chistopol in his seventh year of imprisonment, 1984 had arrived and while the Soviet Union had survived, his friends had not.

For Jews in the Soviet Union, and especially the activists and refuseniks, the government's determination to destroy their movement seemed to increase as the new year dawned. Emigration in 1983 had reached a record low of thirteen hundred. It might as well have been zero. The number of those arrested and exiled had grown. It was now impossible for certain Hebrew teachers to continue giving classes. The protests and petitions of the 1970s were a distant memory, remnants of a time when détente provided at least some protection. Now, in addition to the pounding meted out by the Soviet Anti-Zionist Committee, new provisions had been added to the Russian Criminal Code that were specifically aimed at Jewish activists. It was now illegal to receive gifts from foreigners, the primary source of sustenance for refuseniks. If "anti-Soviet agitation and propaganda" was carried out "with the use of money or valuables received from foreign organizations or from persons acting in the interests of these organizations," the punishment could be up to *fifteen years* of imprisonment and exile. That January, another decree was announced, this one mandating eight years of prison for anyone who passed "work-related secrets" to foreigners. The description of what fell into that category was broad but seemed to cover any talk of one's profession.

In February of 1984, after just fifteen months as general secretary, most of which he spent seriously ill with kidney problems, Andropov died. His replacement did not inspire any more confidence than he had. Konstantin Chernenko was another old-guard Communist, also in his seventies, who had climbed the ranks as one of Brezhnev's protégés. He was old and sickly, and his ascension only added to the impression of an unstable leadership out of touch and desperate to maintain control. At Andropov's funeral, Chernenko was too weak to descend the stairs of the Lenin mausoleum by himself (a newly installed elevator had taken him up).

Soon there were more anti-refusenik decrees. In May, a rule was announced forbidding foreigners to spend the night at a Soviet citizen's apartment without official permission. The penalty was a hundred rubles. It was now illegal for a Soviet to give a foreigner a ride in his car. The next decree seemed bureaucratic on the surface but struck at the heart of how "parasitic" refuseniks managed to support themselves without stable income: the receiver of any package entering the Soviet Union from abroad had to pay the customs duties himself. Prior to that, an activist in New York could send clothing or even electronics and prepay the huge custom tax him- or herself. No longer. This defeated the purpose of sending the goods to the refuseniks to sell; they simply couldn't afford to receive the packages. All lines of contact and support from the West, established over many years of trial and error, were being brutally cut.

In spite of this onslaught, the ambitious Hebrew outreach coordinated from Moscow by Yuli Kosharovsky continued apace. His project to create a sprawling network of Hebrew learning had set up teachers in the farthest corners of the empire. At the organization's height, at least two classes were running in each of thirty cities. But these too would soon go dark. The KGB was no longer interested in charging people with anti-Soviet activity. It took too much time to build a case in court, and the negative international publicity was irritating. They resorted to cruder means. One by one, each of Kosharovsky's main collaborators was arrested on all kinds of made-up charges, some so preposterous that even the KGB agents themselves could hardly contain a smirk when they came knocking.

Sasha Kholmiansky, one of four main leaders in the network, was arrested in the summer of 1984 in southern Estonia, where he was running a Hebrew camp. At first he was charged with petty hooliganism for allegedly stepping on flowers and destroying a mailbox. A few days later he was taken into an interrogation room where a high-ranking officer presented him with a pistol he said was found in a search of Kholmiansky's apartment, as was anti-Soviet literature. A quick trial ensued in a small Estonian town where all the phones had been disconnected. Kholmiansky was found guilty of possessing gun cartridges and sentenced to a year and a half. Weakened from a prolonged hunger strike and injured from forced feedings, he served out his term in a hospital in the Urals.

Yuli Edelstein, the youngest of the Hebrew leaders, had overseen instructors in the city of Kharkov and the region of Belarus. He was part of a new generation of refuseniks. In his late twenties, he had come to the movement not out of a strong Zionist desire but because he couldn't stand living in the Soviet Union anymore. He had begun teaching himself Hebrew at nineteen so that he could one day live in Israel. After becoming a refusenik, in 1979, he started instructing others and quickly gained a reputation as one of the more dynamic and engaging educators. His problems began after he joined forces with Kosharovsky and the other teachers. He was followed. His apartment was regularly searched. Then, one day in the fall of 1984, a few months after Kholmiansky's arrest and trial, a knock on the door turned Kafkaesque when a group of KGB agents searching his apartment dramatically presented him with a matchbox filled with hashish that they said was his. Within months he was in a labor camp on the Mongolian border.

Throughout the second half of 1984, Jewish activists and Hebrew teachers were arrested on all kinds of trumped-up charges—pushing someone, sexual assault, illegal drug possession. The KGB was replenishing their stock of Jewish prisoners as a way of paralyzing the movement. To the refuseniks, it was just one more sign that everything was getting worse. All the letters and phone calls to the West—when they could get through—were an unrelenting stream of bad news issued by exhausted, demoralized, and scared Jews. One letter in December, signed by nearly forty refuseniks in Leningrad, captured the despair. Addressed to the "Jews of the West," it was an accusatory rant that revealed the depth of their hopelessness. "We call on you, the Jews of the West, those who spend their efforts on the paperwork of endless conferences and 'races' and 'picnics in the grass' in defense of Soviet

Jewry, and those who are still full of illusions and see solidarity in philanthropy expressed in gifts of jeans—we call on you to show your
solidarity by your deeds," the letter lashed out. "Enough, brothers and
sisters, of chewing over our despair while lunching at Lindy's. Enough
of flaming cocktail party declarations and touching 'twin Bar-Mitzvah'
shows. There have been enough warning statements. The time has
come to sound the alarm . . . You, the sons and daughters of a nation
which has suffered the most terrible blows that human madness can
inflict, take the truth of the Messiah out of the sheaths of your souls
and beat it into the iron will of deeds. Who, if not you, can help us
remove the stone from the mouth of the well."

13

Pawns Again
1985–1986

FOR KREMLIN WATCHERS in the West, no public event was more revealing than a Red Square funeral. How were the members of the Politburo arranged? How big were the crowds? How much crying was permitted? As the goose-stepping honor guard made its way down the wide concrete expanse of the square, stopping to fire off a salute in front of Lenin's tomb, professors, think-tank analysts, and State Department workers pressed their faces close to their television screens so they could discern the slightest twitch in the monolithic Soviet face. The death of seventy-three-year-old Konstantin Chernenko, on March 10, 1985, the third Communist leader to expire in as many years, offered yet one more chance to dissect the ritual. Few signs, however, pointed to any deviation from the past. If one wanted to, one could make much of the fact that, unlike at the ceremony for Brezhnev or Andropov, the decorated generals of the Red Army were seated a rung below the civilian leaders. Otherwise, the same blank-faced delegations of farmers and factory workers marched past with the same kinds of placards, this time ones bearing Chernenko's equally impassive visage.

But the Kremlinologists' eyes were trained not on the rank and file but on the newly appointed general secretary of the Communist Party. Saving the day from farce was this new leader, a radical departure from the gerontocracy that had been ruling the empire. Mikhail Sergeyevich Gorbachev was the Soviet Union's trump card. At fifty-three, he appeared more modern and pragmatic—and certainly more educated—than any Soviet leader before him. The stout man in a tailored blue suit with a prominent wine red birthmark on his bald head represented a huge generational shift, the portent of which was still unclear as he stood atop Lenin's tomb.

The American delegation present that day consisted of Vice President George Bush and Secretary of State George Shultz. They stood for two hours watching the ceremony. Shultz had decided they should place themselves right behind the Pakistani prime minister in order to express their joint opposition to the Soviet occupation of Afghanistan. As for what he thought of the new Soviet leader, Shultz was reserving judgment. The rest of the world seemed to be swept up in a wave of premature hopefulness based on the very little that was known about Gorbachev. He had come of age after Stalin—joining the Communist Party only in 1952—and had grown up as an average Soviet citizen in the rural Stavropol region of southern Russia. His first job was driving a tractor. One of his grandfathers had spent nine years in the Gulag. He had risen through the Party ranks by gaining the confidence of influential mentors who pulled him up—the most important being Yuri Andropov, who had designated him his heir. By the time power was bestowed on Gorbachev by a Politburo eager for a fresh face to present to the world and its own citizens, he knew the system from the bottom up. The hope was that he might also be clear-eyed about its shortcomings.

So far, though, the impression of modernity had been bolstered more by style than substance. On a trip to England the previous December, his wife, Raisa, had worn a fashionable outfit one evening—a white satin dress and a pair of gold lamé sandals—which suggested to those who wanted to believe it that the Soviet Union was headed in a completely new direction. Unlike the dry, pedantic Gromyko, Gorbachev seemed to intuitively understand how to engage Western leaders. He showed he could be self-deprecating and pensive. More than anything he actually said, these surface qualities were what prompted Margaret Thatcher to stamp him "a man with whom we can do business." After the funeral of Chernenko, the attending world leaders took turns meeting privately with Gorbachev, and they all came away with a similar feeling. As German chancellor Helmut Kohl put it succinctly after his tête-à-tête, unlike the past Soviet leaders, Gorbachev did not give you "the impression that you are listening to a Tibetan prayer wheel."

It was nearly ten o'clock in the evening when Shultz and Bush were ushered into the Kremlin for their meeting. The secretary of state, though cautious, had much riding on Gorbachev. In the newly re-elected Reagan administration, his was the voice of pragmatism, and he was advising the president to look for opportunities for contact with the Soviets. The more neoconservative elements, such as Caspar Weinberger, the secretary of defense, and William Casey, director of the CIA, had started seeing Shultz as the enemy. For the neocons, the Soviets simply weren't to be trusted. As far as they were concerned, there was still only one way to fight the Cold War: by continuing the policies of Reagan's first term, increasing America's defense spending to such an extent that the Russians would be buried. As Shultz's conciliatory approach began resonating with Reagan—now secure in a second term and thinking about his legacy—the neocons became even more oppositional. The president had in fact recently sent Shultz to Geneva to begin arms reduction talks with Gromyko, a breakthrough after four years of unadulterated enmity. And though these discussions had commenced only in January, there seemed to be enough goodwill to move toward a new détente. A fresh leader like Gorbachev could add new energy, bolstering Shultz's position, or he could prove Weinberger and Casey right.

Because Bush was taking the lead in the meeting, Shultz could sit back and observe. The first thing he noticed was that Gorbachev talked extemporaneously, without notes. This was already a departure. Gorbachev's mind seemed agile, and his tone was friendly. He presented, in direct language, the most far-ranging analysis of foreign policy Shultz had ever heard from a Soviet leader. But Gorbachev was not saying anything strikingly new. Only the packaging was different. When it came time for Bush to speak, the conversation hit its first snag. The vice president brought up the issues of Soviet Jews and human rights. He spoke about specific cases. He asked about Sakharov and Shcharan-sky—and also about the imprisoned Hebrew teachers. He mentioned

Yosef Begun. "Understand," Bush told him, "this issue is extremely important to the president and the American people." For the first time, Gorbachev looked irritated. He mumbled something about maybe appointing rapporteurs to examine how the United States itself "brutally suppresses human rights." Then his defensiveness turned into the usual Soviet dismissal as he said that he "did not think this was an appropriate subject for discussion between our two states."

Shultz left the meeting impressed with the man but unsure about what it all might mean. As he told the press the following day, "Gorbachev is different from any Soviet leader I've met. But the U.S.-Soviet relationship is not just about personalities." Most observers agreed. The appointment of Yuri Andropov had raised similar hopes. Maybe his love of jazz would somehow translate into different policy? But he turned out to be just as obstinate as his predecessor. Writing in *Time* magazine days after the Chernenko funeral, Strobe Talbott, one of the more respected of the Kremlinologists, observed that Gorbachev might bring more "dynamism and pragmatism," but "he will put those qualities to work in the service primarily of competition, not conciliation." He might be someone with whom the West could do business. But, Talbott added, "it is the same tedious, difficult, sometimes dangerous business as before—the business of managing a rivalry with a country that is too powerful to fight but too inimical to appease and often too insecure to accommodate."

For the Soviet Jewry movement, there was nowhere to go but up. Over the past four years, emigration figures had plummeted to almost zero. In all of 1984, astonishingly, only 896 Jews had been given exit visas, the lowest number since 1969. Just five years earlier, in 1979, 51,000 Jews had left, a number that now seemed fantastical. It was generally agreed that there were about 10,000 to 20,000 long-term refuseniks and—according to the Lishka's figures—somewhere between 350,000 and 400,000 Jews who had requested invitations from Israel and either had never received them or were too scared to apply. Because of the successes in the 1970s, American activists had come to expect that every year would bring better news and higher numbers. This optimism had been totally sapped. Not only was no one getting out, but reports for the last few years had pointed to an atmosphere of unremitting oppression. Hebrew classes had been shut down. Yosef Begun was at a labor camp in Perm. And half a dozen Hebrew teachers had been arrested in the past year alone. As Martin Gilbert, the historian and Soviet Jewry activist, told an audience in Cape Town in April of 1984: "There is no doubt that the situation is grim today, that expectations so sharply aroused in the past decade are now derided and abused and that Soviet Jews are given the explicit signal, 'You will never be allowed out of the Soviet Union. You will be buried next to your parents, here in Russia.'"

The White House, for its part, was continuing to be supportive of the movement. But with the words *evil empire* still fresh from Reagan's lips, it was hard to see where an opening could be found, how it would be possible to edge the relationship out of pure antagonism. If anyone was trying to change the dynamic, it was George Shultz. His appointment as secretary of state in the summer of 1982 introduced a strong counterbalance to the neoconservative worldview, which perceived even a cocktail conversation with the Soviets as a form of appeasement. American Jews worried about Shultz at first. They looked at his background and his coolness and wondered if he would prove to be as committed to their cause as the president was. The son of a Wall Street banker, he was born into affluent Manhattan society, became a football star at Princeton (he was so devoted to the school that he had its mascot, a tiger, tattooed onto his backside), and as a Marine saw action in the Pacific during World War II. After the war, Shultz received a doctorate in industrial economics from MIT and eventually became dean of the University of Chicago's business school. Nixon brought him into public life, first appointing him secretary of labor, then director of the budget office, and eventually secretary of the treasury (he had traveled to Moscow to negotiate trade agreements in the middle of the Jackson-Vanik fight). When Reagan offered him the secretary of state position, he was working for Bechtel, the giant global construction company, and teaching part-time at Stanford. A physically large man, Shultz was known as self-confident and generally easygoing.

As it turned out, he was also a stronger supporter of human rights than the activists could have dreamed. But coming from a business background and being less ideological in outlook, Shultz approached the relationship with the Soviets very differently from his predecessors. Freedom was a rhetorical weapon for Reagan; for Shultz it was actually a goal to be achieved. He wanted to move beyond the public reprimands, which he thought did little other than humiliate the Soviets, and enter into more aggressive quiet diplomacy. Within a few months of taking office, he initiated the first meeting between Reagan and a Soviet official—an informal chat at the White House with Anatoly Dobrynin, the Soviet ambassador, in early 1983, the same month as the "evil empire" speech. Reagan talked for two hours, almost entirely about human rights, about the problems of refuseniks and prisoners of Zion. And the meeting had a tangible outcome. The president wanted to resolve the issue of the seven Pentecostal Christians (actually Russian Orthodox Old Believers) from Siberia who had been living in the basement of the American embassy in Moscow since 1978. The group had rushed past the guards, and the Americans felt compelled to give them asylum. Reagan asked that something be done for these families, and he promised in exchange not to take credit or brag if they were allowed to leave the Soviet Union. A few weeks after the impromptu meeting, all the Pentecostals left the embassy and their exit visas were approved.

This was the first sign for Shultz that Reagan wanted to move beyond rhetoric—to escape from the box his neoconservative staff had placed him in. Now, with a landslide reelection behind him, Reagan was intent on being remembered as a president who achieved peace. Having established during his first term of fierce words and little action that he would not easily abandon his bona fides as a Cold Warrior, he now wanted to find room to maneuver. He would engage from a position of strength if the right Soviet leader came around. Whether or not Gorbachev was that leader was still unclear.

Soviet Jewry activists were waiting as well. For them the questions were straightforward. Would Gorbachev play by the rules they had laid down in the 1970s and understand that the road to better relations went through emigration? The future of the movement, not to mention the fate of Soviet Jews, depended on the answer. And it couldn't come quick enough. The stagnation of the early 1980s had not served the movement well. For a cause to have momentum, success—even on a small scale—must seem attainable. The Soviets had cut off this oxygen. As a result, the fervor that had characterized the early years had dissipated.

At the same time, paradoxically, the plight of Soviet Jewry had finally become completely integrated into American Jewish life. The movement became an institution. Bracelets engraved with the names of "Prisoners of Zion" were popular accessories—even Reagan had one, with Begun's name, though he kept it on his desk instead of on his wrist. Solidarity Sunday was a regular fixture; every spring at least a hundred thousand people turned out to march in Manhattan. American politicians competed fiercely to be included on the list of speakers. No Passover Seder was complete without a "matzo of hope" and a special prayer for refuseniks. In 1985, an extremely successful national program paired up thousands of Jewish boys and girls approaching the bar or bat mitzvahs with a Soviet Jewish "twin" who was barred from participating in the rite of passage. Standing on the bema, the thirteen-year-old American Jew recited the name of the distant Russian teenager at every step in the ritual. The movement even found its way into pop culture. As early as 1976, it was the punch line of a joke on *Saturday Night Live.* Gilda Radner, in character as the elderly, hard-of-hearing Emily Litella, peered over her granny glasses and opined about issues she had misheard, such as the problems of "endangered feces" (species) and "violins on television" (violence). Litella began one rant, "What's all this fuss I hear about saving Soviet jewelry?" In order for the joke to work—and for the audience to laugh as hard as they did—people had to know the cause whose name she was mangling.

Soviet Jewry was ubiquitous, so much so that the National Conference on Soviet Jewry gave out awards in 1985 to both George Shultz and Jane Fonda. It's hard to imagine another cause that could celebrate in the same breath both Hanoi Jane and the Cold War cowboy's secretary of state.

The political power of American Jews was also on the rise. The legislative victories of the past decade, such as Jackson-Vanik, had greatly increased the community's confidence about its strength. American Jews were creating powerful lobbies and were responsible in large part for the tightening of the relationship between America and Israel. In 1974, after spending the previous two years fighting with Richard Perle for the Jackson-Vanik amendment, Morris Amitay, an aide to Senator Arthur Ribicoff, was made head of the American Israel Public Affairs Committee (AIPAC). Amitay took what was a small, passive outfit with a handful of staff members and over the next few years turned it into a lobbying powerhouse, expanding a meager list of contacts to eleven thousand names and increasing the budget to $1.2 million. Drawing on his neoconservative connections in the new Reagan administration and using money to lock in support from much of Congress, Amitay helped the group become a force in government. AIPAC's potency first became apparent in a fight they lost. In the early months of Reagan's presidency, they tried to stop the sale of five spy planes to Saudi Arabia, and they failed. But the administration's staff members were so impressed by the pressure AIPAC applied to Congress that they immediately invited AIPAC to help plan future government policy. Soon the group was working so closely with Reagan's people that they were even lobbying for issues unrelated to Israel, at the president's request, with the hope that it would garner goodwill for Israel's concerns. The first major payoff came in December 1981 at a low-key ceremony at the National Geographic Society in Washington when Israeli defense minister Ariel Sharon and his American counterpart, Caspar Weinberger, signed a memorandum of understanding. It bound the two countries as allies, each committed to "act cooperatively and in a timely manner" against any threat to the other. Billions of dollars in foreign aid followed, along with extremely close intelligence and technology sharing.

AIPAC helped make these new commitments profitable for American lawmakers. Israel needed the American Jewish community more than ever, especially after June of 1982, when Israel invaded Lebanon, bombed Beirut, and had to deal with the public relations catastrophe of its Lebanese Christian allies' massacre of eight hundred Palestinians at the Sabra and Shatila refugee camps. American Jews as a constituency were still extremely liberal (Reagan's capture of nearly 40 percent of the Jewish vote in 1980 was a surprising anomaly, not repeated in 1984). Still, the consistent backing of Israeli policy by an influential lobby made Israel much more beholden to American Jews as a whole.

This inevitably changed the dynamics in the fraught relationship between the grass roots in America and the Lishka. Already by the late 1970s, Nehemiah Levanon's grip on the movement had begun to loosen. He had lost the monopoly on information coming out of the Soviet Union, which had been his greatest form of leverage. Now, individuals, such as Michael Sherbourne, the London schoolteacher turned Russian-speaking activist, had just as much if not more contact with refuseniks and activists and were willing to disseminate their messages without any filter. The Union of Councils and other groups watched closely over all this information; they kept voluminous files on thousands of Soviet Jews, maintained lists of those in refusal, and regularly got updates on who was sick, who needed financial help, and who the KGB was harassing. Shcharansky was the ultimate example of this new dynamic. Levanon hadn't wanted to focus a campaign around his case, but once Avital, backed by members of the religious-right settler movement and the Union of Councils, began getting media attention, there was nothing the Israelis could do but jump onboard. They could no longer dictate the message. The Lishka still had the power to set the agenda of the National Conference, but there were still influential establishment groups, like the council of wealthy, local Jewish federations, that had their own opinions and interests. On the issue of dropouts, for example, a vast majority of the American Jewish community had turned on Israel, favoring freedom of choice for Soviet Jewish emigrants. In 1981, the Lishka and the Jewish Agency tried once again to cut off funding and support for those who wanted to go to the West—even going so far as to bypass HIAS and the Joint and sticking the dropouts in a detention camp in Naples until they changed their minds. American Jews were outraged, and the Israeli plan was abandoned after a couple of months. Now that their American cousins possessed the money and the power to influence foreign policy, Israel couldn't really put up much of a fight.

William Orbach, who wrote a book describing the first years of the movement, captured the soured mood of many American Soviet Jewry activists in the winter of 1980: "Israel's urge to dominate is quite natural, and perhaps beneficial in many areas, for a state can do things which individuals cannot—yet in the Soviet Jewry movement that urge is nothing less than catastrophic, for here individuals and groups possess certain inherent advantages over states—especially spontaneity. Israel should provide information and resources to the movement; its shading into guidance and control cripples the movement. Activist resources, instead of addressing Soviet oppression, must be squandered on squabbles with the Israeli government. If this continues, the Israeli 'Office Without a Name,' not the Soviet regime, may well destroy the Soviet Jewry campaign."

In December of 1980, Nehemiah Levanon resigned as head of the

Lishka. With him went the notion of an all-powerful, secretive office that aspired to be the central point of command for the Soviet Jewry movement. No longer would Israel devote as much energy to tearing down the vibrant American grass roots or hoarding information on refuseniks.

And yet even the complete integration of the Soviet Jewry cause into American Jewish life could not do anything to relieve the stagnancy of the Cold War. It minimized urgency. In the absence of real progress, the competition between the grass roots and establishment, which had once spurred both to greater success, devolved into petty and personal sniping. The two largest groups, the National Conference and the Union of Councils, spent their time arguing about how the other was undermining their work. With a membership of fifty thousand people all over the country and contacts with dozens of sympathetic lawmakers, the grassroots coalition presented more than just an annoyance to the establishment. In an op-ed in early 1985, Jerry Goodman, the longtime executive director of the National Conference, complained that since the two groups were "addressing the same issues and serving basically the same constituency," their "duplication of efforts," especially when it came to Washington lobbying, was seeding "confusion," which meant in the end that the Soviet Jews would "lose out." The activists, of course, would never concede that their efforts overlapped with those of the establishment. Everything was different, they claimed, from their tactics to their loyalties. And so the debilitating fighting and the feeling of impotence continued.

For a few Jewish leaders, however, even the slightest shift in relations between the superpowers was enough to convince them that American Jews needed to make some kind of gesture. Leading this charge was the unlikely figure of Edgar Bronfman, the liquor mogul. Tall, dapper, and with the air of entitlement that comes from being born into vast wealth, Bronfman had recently become an influential force in the world of Jewish politics. Heir to the multibillion-dollar Seagram Company—the world's biggest producer of distilled spirits and wines—Bronfman metamorphosed into a global Jewish diplomat as a way of eclipsing his father, an authoritarian who bought the Canadian-based distiller in the 1920s and built it into a powerhouse on the back of Prohibition. He had taken over the business upon his father's death, in 1971, but spent a few years playing the part of the prodigal son. He was a playboy, marrying and divorcing women every few years, dabbling in the movie business, and making headlines for the first time in 1975 in a bizarre kidnapping involving his son Sam. But after the recession of the mid-1970s, Bronfman woke up to the needs of the business and became involved as never before. The decision in 1980 to sell Seagram's oil and gas assets proved to be a brilliant move. Suddenly he was sitting on top of a two-billion-dollar war chest.

In 1981, he was named president of the World Jewish Congress, the independent organization that saw itself as representing the interests of global Jewry. The transformation of Bronfman was complete. His wealth bought him contacts all over the world. In his office on Park Avenue in the Mies van der Rohe–designed Seagram Building, he sat amid Rodin sculptures and Miró tapestries and talked on the phone to businesspeople and world leaders who knew he was a man with money to invest and causes he believed in. His first bit of publicity after taking over the presidency of the World Jewish Congress came when he used his connection to Anatoly Dobrynin in the Soviet embassy to secure the early release of Yosef Mendelevich.

Bronfman had a businessman's understanding of the Soviet Jewish issue. It was all a matter of negotiation, of coldly calculating what the Russians really wanted and leveraging that against emigration. This thinking put him in line with Nahum Goldmann, the equally headstrong founder of the World Jewish Congress and Bronfman's predecessor. For Soviet Jewry activists, Goldmann remained a totemic figure, symbolizing Old World Jewish cautiousness at its worst. As late as 1979 (he would die two years after) Goldmann was writing that public protest was "dangerous and immoral" because it might put Russian Jews at risk rather than help them. The best bet was secret diplomacy. "It is impossible to force the Russians to do something, and the most that can be done is to persuade them." Goldmann had been ridiculed since the 1960s for his consistent claim that the best way to solve the emigration problem was to get him alone in a room with Brezhnev. But Brezhnev, Goldmann never seemed to realize, had no interest in dealing with him. Bronfman was another matter.

Bronfman's secret contacts with the Soviets were always mysterious. What was he really talking to Dobrynin about? Was he mentioning his interest in distributing Stolichnaya vodka in America? Maybe dangling the possibility that he could invest in Russia's oil industry? Or was he talking about the refuseniks? Or all of the above? This mix of business and human rights made him someone Gorbachev or Gromyko would be interested in speaking with. In 1983, at one of the coldest moments in Soviet-American relations, Bronfman suggested on the op-ed page of the *New York Times* that American Jews should abandon their strongest weapon, the Jackson-Vanik amendment, "as a sign of goodwill that challenges the Soviets to respond in kind." Someone, he wrote, "had to take the first step." This idea, clouded not a little by his own potential business interests in reigniting trade, was met in both grassroots and establishment circles as absurd. There was nothing to indicate that the Soviets would respond in good faith. But now, with Gorbachev's ascension and the promise of a more liberal regime, there were signs that Bronfman's approach was resonating. Many people in the Jewish establishment thought that American Jews should have responded more positively in 1979 when the Soviets had increased emigration to an unprecedented fifty-one thousand in the hope of getting Jackson-Vanik repealed. If they had, the thinking went, maybe the doors wouldn't have slammed shut so firmly in 1980. Some in the establishment wanted to be careful not to miss another opportunity if it presented itself. A Soviet delegation visiting the United States in early March, days after Gorbachev's assumption of power, was met with an ad in the *Washington Post* placed by the National Conference that dangled, if not exactly a repeal of the amendment, then at least a willingness to bargain again: "Many people in this country would be responsive to positive changes, especially in your emigration policy. Why should emigration continue to be a barrier to improved trade and investment relations?"

In early 1985, Bronfman managed to secure the very thing Nahum Goldmann had always dreamed about: an invitation to the Kremlin. He announced in late January that he would be making an official trip to meet with Soviet leaders, probably in March, to talk about Jews. Chernenko's death postponed the visit, but Bronfman was convinced that his personal intervention would break the impasse over Soviet Jewry, heralding a new détente.

The grassroots activists were not impressed with Bronfman's invitation. They would hear of no compromise unless the Soviets acted first.

Gorbachev was just a newer, friendlier mask hiding the same monstrous face. The community was demoralized and lethargic. The wall seemed higher every day. No one felt this more profoundly than Avital Shcharansky. In March 1985, it had been eight years since Tolya's arrest, and she had spent that time in perpetual motion, living in hotel rooms as she traveled the world on a never-ending campaign to free her husband. Her message had not altered. There should be no negotiating, no compromising, not an inch of movement until her husband and all Soviet Jews were free. When expectant talk of a summit between Reagan and Gorbachev began circulating, Avital told Anthony Lewis, the *New York Times* columnist, that the United States should insist that four hundred thousand Soviet Jews be allowed to leave before any meeting took place.

Advocacy became Avital's life, despite the fact that she told her close friends that she detested the public spotlight and would happily retreat into a domesticity once Tolya was released. In the meantime she was extremely effective, one of the strongest voices for Soviet Jewry. She was independent, able to fundraise based on her own popularity; she didn't have to abide by the dictates of the Israelis. By the mid-1980s, she had made Shcharansky into a household name. For most young people coming of age at the time, the Soviet Jewry movement *was* Shcharansky. Every Jewish schoolchild could recognize his face. No camper managed to spend a summer in the Catskills without at least a few dozen times putting his arms around his friends' shoulders and swaying and singing along to the American Jewish band Safam's "Leaving Mother Russia":

> They call me Anatole.
> In prison I do lie,
> My little window looks out
> On a Russian sky.
> I've been arrested here for crimes they have not named
> But all my people know
> The charges will be a frame. . . .
>
> We are leaving Mother Russia,
> We have waited far too long.
> We are leaving Mother Russia,
> When they come for us we'll be gone.

There was no shortage of people who wanted to cradle Avital Shcharansky. But in America, she found a defender—and more important, a fundraiser—who had his own reasons for making Shcharansky the center of his activism. Avi Weiss was a bearish, bearded, sometimes combative man with a domineering presence. From the same Flatbush streets as Kahane and also the son of a rabbi but born a generation later, Weiss was a teacher at Stern College—Yeshiva University's women's school—and the leader of a successful modern Orthodox congregation in the Bronx community of Riverdale. He saw himself as not only a religious leader but also an activist for the Jewish people; he was devoted to the notion of turning his pulpit into a spearhead of social engagement. On his good days, he followed in the tradition of Abraham Joshua Heschel, practicing as few others did a life of spiritual witness. On his bad days, though, he could be just as self-promoting as Kahane (though Weiss lacked Kahane's violent streak) and with the same penchant for flashy public action that drew as much attention to himself as to his cause.

It was at one of these public displays, in the fall of 1982, that he first met Avital Shcharansky. In solidarity with Shcharansky, who was on a hunger strike because his correspondence privileges had been taken away, Weiss had decided to begin a fast in front of the Soviet mission in Manhattan. Weiss set himself up on a bench on the corner of Sixty-seventh Street and Third Avenue. Subsisting on mineral water alone, by the second day, the thirty-eight-year-old rabbi could hardly take the physical and mental strain. He hallucinated that KGB spies were peering out the mission's window and that FBI agents were snapping photos of him and the small group of friends that stood around him. To make matters worse, newspapers did not seem to care that one rabbi was publicly fasting in Midtown. He couldn't get a single journalist interested in the story. His sense of persecution was heightened when none of the establishment organizations endorsed his action, and the rabbi at the synagogue across the street—which had often been forcibly occupied by Kahane and his JDL boys in their New York heyday—denied him permission to take breaks inside the building. Even Weiss's wife begged him not to fast; it would exacerbate his heart problems. But he continued for a week, convinced that Shcharansky represented the heart and soul of the Soviet Jewry movement. If he could bring even a bit of attention to his plight, he would have succeeded. He lost seventeen pounds and got the chance to write an op-ed in the *New York Times,* in which he claimed he now had a spiritual kinship with Shcharansky, a glimpse into what his daily life must feel like, an "emptiness" full of "deep meaning." His conclusion, which he must have meant for himself as well: "The Shcharanskys, in fighting for human rights, lead full lives."

Avital visited Weiss on the fourth day of his weeklong hunger strike. It was the beginning of a close collaboration. He decided then that he needed to increase his Soviet Jewry activism even more and that an intense focus on Shcharansky's case would be the way to do it. He pledged to help Avital and her religious handlers fundraise so that she could continue her intrepid traveling and speaking—an expensive proposition, given the airfare and hotel stays, even with the amount of support she was receiving. Soon, Weiss became a kind of unofficial North American liaison for the international campaign out of Jerusalem. He arranged for small groups of people to have conversations with Avital in living rooms all over America and Canada. They had an effective script. Avital would quietly give the latest update on Tolya, talk about her despair, sometimes weep softly. And then Weiss would ask for contributions. In this way, he raised tens of thousands of dollars for the campaign. And he became particularly close to Avital. Weiss thought of them as having a pure love, like a brother and sister. But he was also aware that the more they traveled together, the more it looked like a romantic affair.

A few months after his fast, in early 1983, Weiss became the national chairman of Student Struggle for Soviet Jewry. The organization started by Yaakov Birnbaum in the early 1960s was floundering. Its protest style had been co-opted long ago by larger and more influential American Jewish organizations, and its activist philosophy was identical to that of the Union of Councils, a group that now had fifty thousand members in more than three dozen local councils, lobbyists in Washington, and an impressive budget. But besides its style and goals being overtaken by larger groups—a fact that deeply aggravated the aging and often sick Birnbaum—Student Struggle suffered the fate of many youth movements that had been powered in the 1960s and 1970s by a combination of youthful idealism and identity politics. These forces had dimmed. A rugged individualism had returned to American culture during the 1980s—fueled by an economic resurgence that began in 1983 and a president who romanticized and reinforced (through tax cuts) the lives of families and hard-working individuals while he demonized government and ignored the needs of minorities and the poor. The Jewish world was turning inward. Small groups of families disdained what they saw as the impersonal synagogue and gathered together in *chavurahs,* friendship circles, to pray, socialize, and create community on a small, human scale. Jewish power, for all its growing muscle, had largely left the streets of New York and was concentrated now in the corridors of Capitol Hill. Even Birnbaum, organizer of the first Soviet Jewry protest and many thereafter, had become far more occupied with the counterpart adult group he had set up, the Center for Russian Jewry, which focused on research and lobbying in Washington. But the fact that Student Struggle's mission had become mainstream did not discourage its die-hard activist core; it just made them hungrier for greater agitation. Weiss brought his charisma to the group and helped give it a second life. He worked with Glenn Richter, Birnbaum's quirky trench-coat-wearing lieutenant who had been at the center of the group's day-to-day activities for the past twenty years. Richter earned no more than a few thousand dollars a year to supplement his wife's teacher's salary, and yet amazingly he was just as indefatigable as the college kid he had been when he first started protesting.

In 1985, Avital Shcharansky and hard-liners like Weiss and the Student Struggle saw Gorbachev's rise as an opportunity to press their point. If engagement with the West was the Soviets' new tack, the activists' job would be to illustrate in clear terms what the nonnegotiable price of that engagement was. Avital intensified her public appearances and meetings with world leaders; Weiss initiated what he called Operation Redemption. He convinced groups of rabbis to let themselves be arrested in a series of civil disobedience actions. The first took place in early January to coincide with the opening of the Shultz-Gromyko arms limitation talks in Geneva. Together with five other rabbis, Weiss took over the Rockefeller Center offices of TASS, a regular target of the JDL fifteen years before. It had been a long time since TASS had been bothered like this. Weiss and the rabbis, all wearing fringed prayer shawls, demonstrated in the office in front of the dismayed Russian employees for an hour and a half before the police arrived. They chanted "Free Shcharansky" and "Am Yisrael Chai." One rabbi kept blowing a shofar.

Weiss saw the publicity potential of arrested rabbis and aimed for an even bigger protest. He and Lynn Singer—the intense Long Island housewife who had just ended her tenure as president of the Union of Councils—gathered rabbis for an unprecedented mass demonstration. So popular was his call that even the large New York umbrella organization responsible for the annual Solidarity Sunday rallies—the Greater New York Conference on Soviet Jewry, recently renamed the Coalition to Free Soviet Jewry—decided to help with recruiting. On the afternoon of March 5, more than a hundred rabbis sat down on Sixty-seventh Street in front of the Soviet mission, blocking traffic. The protesters included the most respected rabbis in the city from each of the major denominations. Weiss spoke to the group, hammering hard the idea of linkage: "To the Soviets, we proclaim: You seek trade; we dream freedom. You seek dollars; we search for human dignity. You seek technology; we demand Jewish emigration."

The day was a triumph for Weiss. He had tapped into a feeling of anxiousness that a coming détente might leave the Soviet Jews behind. Paradoxically, the possibility of change only pushed the activists further in the direction of extreme rhetoric and tactics. Weiss liked to tell a story about Avital. He had seen her at a rally at the end of 1982, shortly after Brezhnev's death. Usually much more understated, she'd fired up the crowd by saying, "Brezhnev did not free my husband, and that is why he died. I am warning Andropov that if doesn't free my husband, he too will die!" Weiss took her aside afterward and told her he thought the line didn't work, that it was over the top. But once Andropov died, she brought it up again. "I told Andropov that if he didn't free my Anatoly he would die, and now he is dead," she intoned. "Now, I'm giving the same warning to Chernenko; he too will die if he doesn't let Anatoly go." Weiss warned her once more that she might have gotten lucky with Andropov, but it was foolish to make such pronouncements. When Chernenko died, Weiss just stood by dumbfounded at another rally when she made the same remarks again, this time about the new Soviet leader Gorbachev.

The fourteenth iteration of Solidarity Sunday—in 1985—felt different. The form hadn't changed—the same march down Fifth Avenue, the same long queue of politicians standing behind loudmouthed Mayor Ed Koch, eager to follow him and wave their clenched fists at the Soviet Union. But this year, the Holocaust loomed larger than usual. That same day, Reagan was in West Germany commemorating the fortieth anniversary of V-E Day by laying a wreath at Bitburg military cemetery, where the bodies of forty-nine members of Hitler's Waffen-SS were buried. Reagan's insistence on visiting Bitburg had become an embarrassing fiasco and led, as one newspaper put it, to much "sorrow and dismay" on the part of the Jewish community. The president had accepted German chancellor Helmut Kohl's invitation before knowing about the SS remains. But to avoid looking like he was giving in to pressure—and to support Kohl, who histrionically claimed his government would collapse if Reagan didn't show up—Reagan decided not to renege. Coincidentally, on April 19, two weeks before the trip and at the emotional height of the crisis, Elie Wiesel was presented with the Congressional Gold Medal at a White House ceremony. With the president sitting a few feet away, the episode captured on television, Wiesel pleaded with Reagan not to go. "That place, Mr. President, is not your place," he told him, his voice breaking. "Your place is with the victims of the SS."

The reaction of the American Jewish community was revealing. Commemoration of the Holocaust now played a central role in American Jewish identity. A look at the budget priorities of any Jewish community would have told the story. No city was complete without a monument. Jimmy Carter had approved a Holocaust Commission that was now building a giant museum on the National Mall to memorialize the Jewish genocide. Elie Wiesel was the commission's chairman. This consciousness pervaded the general culture. Ever since the spring of 1978, when the blockbuster television miniseries *Holocaust* had aired, drawing an astounding 120 million viewers, new films and books had been appearing constantly. So the wreath laying was not just an affront to historical memory; it was a negation of what mattered most to American Jews. Bitburg also exposed the political power and moral authority that had been wrung from this history. Who else but Elie Wiesel could have publicly wagged a finger in Reagan's face? At the suggestion of his advisers and George Shultz—who seemed better attuned to the Jewish community than any one else in the administration—before going to Bitburg, the president made a visit to the Bergen-Belsen concentration camp. There he delivered an incredibly emotional speech that ended with these words: "And then, rising above all this cruelty, out of this tragic and nightmarish time, beyond the anguish, the pain and the suffering for all time, we can and must pledge: Never Again!" It is said that Martin Luther King Jr. shed a tear when he heard Lyndon Johnson, in a speech to Congress after the passage of the Voting Rights Act, say, "We shall overcome," appropriating words made famous by the civil rights movement. Meir Kahane, sitting in Jerusalem, must have at least smirked in satisfaction when he heard an American president uttering the expression he had made famous.

At Solidarity Sunday, also the day of the Bitburg visit, Elie Wiesel made explicit what had suddenly motivated an unprecedented 240,000 people to attend: "Is there a connection between Bitburg and this rally? Yes, there is. What was attempted at Bitburg—a denial of the past, a disregard of Jewish agony—the same but on a larger scale has been attempted in Russia." The memory of the Holocaust, which had always been an emotional engine of the movement, was invoked again and again in the service of freeing Soviet Jewry. One man had a sign with a swastika, a hammer and sickle, and the words INHUMANITY IS INHUMANITY. LET MY PEOPLE GO. The *New York Times* ran a large photograph of a Holocaust survivor crying and holding a sign that said LET SOVIET JEWS EMIGRATE. Fair or not, the analogy was real for many American Jews. The shame and rage that had driven a group of scientists in Cleveland and students at Yeshiva University to start a movement back in 1964 were now shared by an entire community.

As long as exit continued to be denied and refuseniks were being arrested, there was little to counteract the feeling that a genocide—even if it was only a spiritual one—loomed and had to be fought against. Certainly Gorbachev's youthfulness alone did not offer sufficient reassurance. In the spring and summer of 1985, one had to look hard for signs of change. But for those who cared to see them, it was possible to discern slight differences.

The greatest legacy of the Helsinki Accords, now ten years old, was its provision of venues to repeatedly humiliate the Soviet Union on the world stage. At the most recent follow-up conference, held in Madrid at the height of Cold War tension and lasting an interminable three years, from November 1980 to March 1983, the Helsinki process effectively turned into a cataloging of Communist human rights abuses. It was in Madrid that Arthur Goldberg's attempts in Belgrade to shame the Soviet Union became legitimized. Goldberg's mention of seven specific cases had been revolutionary at the time, a grave breach of diplomatic protocol; in Madrid, the head of the U.S. delegation referred to sixty-five individual refuseniks and prisoners in the first six weeks alone.

Leading the American assault in Madrid was Max Kampelman. A soft-spoken man with strong political instincts, Kampelman was a lawyer and an old-school Washington insider who had been born in the working-class, immigrant Bronx, the son of a Yiddish-speaking butcher. He was also one of those alienated Cold Warrior Democrats, like Henry Jackson, who along with a handful of neoconservative intellectuals created the Committee on the Present Danger, a policy shop meant to develop and promote a serious anti-détente alternative. Appointed by Carter to lead the delegation to Madrid, Kampelman was kept on when Reagan took office, the highest-profile Democrat to survive the transition. Reagan was a much better fit for him. The ideas that Reagan brought into office—about America's strength, about the evils of Communism, about the need for a strong defense and an offensive strategy to push back the Soviets—were an integral part of Kampelman's political identity.

He brought this ideological fight to the Palacio de Congresos, the concrete precipice of a building where the conference took place. From the first day, he was unrelenting, drawing sharp contrasts between an American system that he asserted was "rooted in the importance of the individual" and a Soviet system "whose collective values bring with them the suppression of the individual." Soviet Jewry was exhibit A in this indictment. Never before had so many speeches been devoted to the issue in such a public forum. And where Kampelman led, other Western countries followed. Unlike Belgrade, where America had been alone, in Madrid, every European delegation brought up Soviet Jewry. Little Belgium assaulted the Soviets on the issue of anti-Semitism before any other country did. Kampelman held this coalition together—drawing on the antipathy toward the Soviets then dominant in Western Europe. "The Soviet Union is a society that is large and powerful and has existed for more than sixty years," Kampelman declared in one of his typically gracious yet sharp speeches, this one on Soviet anti-Semitism. "There is no need for that society to crush human beings, small and insignificant as they may appear in the broader perspective of history. There should be no need to stimulate hatred among peoples. It is time for that society to develop a stronger faith in itself and in the inner strength of its people."

Madrid was in every way a departure from Belgrade. The city became a nonstop human rights circus. Every day brought news of another hunger strike or protest. On any random evening, one could attend an exhibition of Soviet samizdat or a choral concert in honor of Estonian independence. Madrid was a magnet for every conceivable organization concerned with minority or religious rights, from the Union of Russian Soldierists to the Congress of Free Ukrainians to the Anti-Bolshevik Bloc of Nations and the Gesellschaft für Menschenrechte.

Kampelman drew on these associations, turning often to a new human rights group, U.S. Helsinki Watch, that had been born in Belgrade's wake. A dejected Arthur Goldberg in 1978 had secured a grant of $400,000 from the Ford Foundation to start a watchdog group that would monitor and then provide to the Western public a steady stream of details on Soviet human rights transgressions. Led by Robert Bernstein, the publisher of Random House, U.S. Helsinki Watch had quickly become a reliable resource on human rights, supplying the media with meticulous reports on Helsinki Accords violations and keeping close contact with grassroots monitoring groups like those that had sprung up in the Soviet Union.

No movement, however, was better represented than Soviet Jewry. Both the National Conference and the Union of Councils understood that this was an opportunity to advocate publicly and lobby quietly for their cause—and at a time of deep freeze, when Soviet Jewry was not being discussed in any international venues. They both set up offices not far from the Palacio de Congresos and began issuing a steady stream of press releases. Kampelman was naturally sympathetic. When it became clear that the Madrid conference would not conclude as quickly as initially predicted, a more permanent presence was established. The Union of Councils set up the Robert F. Drinan Human

Rights Center, named after the Massachusetts congressman, a full-time office that became a clearinghouse for information on various refuse-niks and prisoners of Zion. Kampelman became a regular visitor. On the second night of Hanukkah in December of 1980, he was invited to light the first candle in the Union activists' Hanukkah Freedom Light Ceremony. While he was there, a phone call came from Moscow. Kampelman got on the line with Alexander Lerner, who told him about his various friends in exile or in jail. To the amazement and satisfaction of the gathered activists, Kampelman's voice began to break, and tears formed in his eyes.

In the end, though, Madrid was a stalemate. The Soviets had come with the intent of focusing the conference—and moving the Helsinki process—away from human rights and toward a discussion of how to increase trade and tamp down the arms race. "The USSR is not pre-pared to be a bull in the corrida of Madrid," said Andrei Gromyko at the conference's outset. But Kampelman and his NATO allies had stayed on message. At the end of three years of the superpowers' talking past each other, only a leveraging of their two interests would allow Madrid to end with any kind of concluding document. With another follow-up conference already scheduled for 1986 in Vienna, the bargaining took place over a series of smaller, interim meetings. Specifically, the Soviets were angry about NATO's decision to counterbalance the me-dium-range, SS-20 nuclear-tipped missiles then aimed at Europe with U.S.-made Pershing II and cruise missiles to be placed in Germany. They wanted a forum to denounce what they saw as Reagan's escala-tion of the Cold War. Kampelman let the Soviets have their meeting, which opened the following year in Stockholm (too late to stop the controversial deployment). In exchange, after much wrangling and re-sistance, Kampelman and his allies gained Soviet participation in two more interim meetings. One would be a gathering of human rights experts in Ottawa in 1985 and the other a six-week conference dealing exclusively with the issue of "reunion of families" (read: Soviet Jewry) in Bern in 1986. Apart from a few fairly anodyne new human rights resolutions added to the accords, this was the sum total of Madrid's success. If Helsinki had finally provided human rights with a powerful megaphone, it was one the Soviets were still ignoring.

But this seemed to change in a small and subtle way at the Ottawa conference in May 1985, three months after Gorbachev's ascendance.

Once again, the U.S. representative was someone whose background and philosophy aligned with not only the neoconservatives' view but also the American Jewish community's. Richard Schifter was born in Austria, the child of Polish Jews. At the age of fifteen, he was permitted to immigrate to America following the Anschluss but was forced to leave his parents—the Austrian Jewish quota was much larger than the Polish one. Schifter's parents died in Majdanek while he was studying at an American high school. After a thirty-year career as a lawyer, he was convinced by Jeanne Kirkpatrick to join the Reagan administration as a delegate to the UN Human Rights Commission. He would often tell people—particularly Soviet Jewry activists—that his attachment to the issue was highly personal; it came out of his inability to help his parents escape from Europe in 1939.

Just before the Ottawa meeting opened, Schifter took the Russian delegation out to lunch. He was hoping that Gorbachev's rise would make the human rights conversation easier. The Soviets quickly disabused him of this notion, informing Schifter that no more than three hundred Jews even wanted to leave and that all he had heard about religious or cultural persecution was simply Zionist propaganda. The proceedings, which lasted six weeks, were no more productive. Schifter continued to name names, speaking daily about Shcharansky and Begun. He used hard language, calling the Soviet treatment of Jews "schizophrenic." His job, as he explained to the press in Ottawa, was to use this relentless pointing out of violations as a way of "drawing a map for the Soviet Union and its allies . . . [as to] what they have to do."

This time, the Soviets answered the charges somewhat differently. At the shaming sessions in Belgrade and then Madrid, the Russian delegates had merely complained that the West was interfering in their internal affairs. Now they fought back. Tentatively at first and then with great defensiveness, they started pointing out Western human rights violations. Their examples were mostly economic and social—the rights valued by Communists—such as the right to free health care and job security, education and maternity benefits. They even tried to attack on the issue of minority rights, using the Anti-Defamation League's statistics to argue that it was in fact the United States that had the real problem with anti-Semitism.

Schifter recognized that this was a shift in tactics that would work in the Americans' favor. The Soviets were tacitly acknowledging the legitimacy of debating another country's human rights record. This was a kind of progress. "We talk about human rights and they talk about unemployment and racism," he said at the time. "Rather than making them think we are running away from these issues, we need to respond clearly to them." Schifter had his staff compile information to equip him for this new field of play. He pointed out that the Soviet Union had a living standard one-third that of the United States', that at the current rate, it would take a hundred and fifty years before the Soviets got the quality of their housing to Western levels, and that the only economic statistic in which the Soviets led the world was in per capita consumption of hard liquor. The average Soviet citizen, Schifter told the gathered delegates, "lived less well than someone living at the official US poverty line."

To the outside this looked very much like two children fighting in a sandbox. At the ten-year anniversary of the signing of the Helsinki Accords, two months later, many commentators would perceive the process as a failure. To the hard-core Cold Warriors, it looked like a gain for the Russians, who just by sitting at the table had achieved some kind of moral legitimacy. But to those closer to the process, like Schifter, this slight change was very significant. Once the Soviets opened themselves to being criticized, the process could start to have an effect. The Ottawa meeting was a failure in that the Western countries and the Soviets could not agree on any concluding document—even Madrid had achieved that. But as the British delegate put it in his closing remarks: "Even if few satisfactory answers were secured, we at least established in practice that it is possible to discuss each other's records."

That summer of 1985, American and Soviet Jews watched to see what Gorbachev might do differently; the changes were subtle and anticlimactic. A shift in debating tactics from a stance of nonengagement to one of abrasiveness, as had occurred at Ottawa, did not feel like progress. The one place where light did begin to peek through the tiny cracks was Israeli-Soviet relations.

Israel's part in the movement had always been covert, managed mostly by the secretive Lishka. Soviet Jewry was hardly ever debated as a foreign policy issue in the Knesset. Even the sensitive and fateful issue of the dropouts played out behind closed doors, with sympathetic American Jewish leaders arguing Israel's position in public. The reasons remained the same. The Cold War was too precarious to enter directly. Israel would never risk going up against American priorities or giving the Russians an excuse to retaliate by arming their Arab allies. Even a prime minister like Menachem Begin, the great hope of militant activists, had disappointed by keeping a low profile on the issue.

But forces were starting to alter this status quo. When emigration ceased in the early 1980s, a debate began in Israel about the effectiveness of a behind-the-scenes strategy. Right-wing parliament members like Geula Cohen—Kahane's clandestine financial backer during his New York days—attacked what she called the Lishka's "hush hush" policy. When Shimon Peres became prime minister in September of 1984, bringing the more dovish Labor Party back to power, he instituted a more openly conciliatory approach to the Soviet Union that, if not what Geula Cohen had in mind, at least gave Israel a position. In small ways, Gorbachev seemed to reciprocate. In May of 1985, on the fortieth anniversary of the end of World War II, *Izvestia* printed a greeting from Israeli president Chaim Herzog expressing the gratitude of Jews for the role the Soviets had played in "the final rout of the Nazi scum in Europe." Considering how often *Izvestia* had characterized Israel itself as "Nazi scum," this was an interesting development.

Beyond the occasional grand gesture, there were many geopolitical factors at work. The United States seemed to be reigniting a peace process. By spring, there was a new joint Palestinian-Jordanian negotiating team, backed by Egypt and even Iraq. The Kremlin's influence in the Middle East was diminishing, and it found itself caught. It wanted a seat at the table at any future peace conference, but it risked angering its only remaining ally in the region, Syria, if it engaged in the process without first demanding that Israel end its occupation of the Golan Heights, the Syrian territory captured in 1967. Israel held both the admission to the peace process and the Golan Heights firmly in its hands. It now had something the Soviet Union wanted.

Indication of Soviet willingness to make a quick deal came in July, when a confidential report sent from Paris to Jerusalem was leaked to Israeli radio. It contained notes from a secret meeting between the Israeli and Soviet ambassadors to France held at the Paris apartment of the pianist-conductor Daniel Barenboim. The Soviets had taken the initiative, and it appeared they were ready to make what the Soviet ambassador Yuli Vorontsov called a "package deal." He was willing to offer diplomatic relations and unfettered emigration of Soviet Jews on three conditions. First, Israel would have to retreat from part of the Golan Heights—a concession to the Soviets' Syrian allies. Second, all the emigrants would need to go to Israel and not, as most of them had in the past, to the West. Third and most remarkable: the Soviets were demanding that Israel get American Jews to shut up about Soviet Jewry.

The leak was met with astonishment. Not only were the two countries engaging for the first time since 1967, but the conversation was a serious give-and-take about the core issues. The promise of some kind of linkage resulting in an exodus seemed almost too good to be true. Yitzhak Rabin, then defense minister, was interviewed on Israeli radio the day after the news broke. He was ecstatic—not an everyday emotion for Rabin—and admitted that the talks contained "several amazing things." Obliquely referring to the agitating work of the Lishka, he offered that those activities could easily be stopped if the Soviets were serious: "I am convinced that if the Soviet Union were to open its gates to an exit of Soviet Jews—a mass exit to Israel—that activity which was designed to bring this about would no longer be necessary."

The Paris meeting led to nothing. As soon as news of it leaked, the Soviets announced that the supposed top-secret negotiations were nothing but a figment of the Israeli imagination. They wouldn't even admit the two ambassadors had met. But the idea of some kind of linkage that would serve both Israel and the Soviet Union did not die. Throughout that spring, rumors of secret meetings between diplomats continued. And there were some signs that the countries were moving closer to each other. Shimon Peres sent a friendly note to Gorbachev—Israel "is not an enemy of the Soviet Union," he wrote—and had an amicable conversation at the United Nations with the new Soviet foreign minister Eduard Shevardnadze (a refreshing replacement for the long-serving Comrade Nyet, Andrei Gromyko). In October, Poland unexpectedly announced that it would be restoring some diplomatic relations with Israel. Given the tight control Moscow held over its Warsaw Pact countries—following 1967, only Romania had maintained ties with Israel—this was another sign that Gorbachev was opening up to the Israelis, or at least using his relationship with Israel (and world Jewry) to impress the West.

Edgar Bronfman was at the center of much of this activity. In early September, he landed in his private jet at Moscow's Sheremetyevo airport—a rare privilege accorded the billionaire philanthropist. He had been trumpeting his planned meeting with Soviet leaders for a year. But since he was accountable to no one, at first it was hard to tell what had come of his quiet diplomacy. All anyone knew was that he had carried a note from Shimon Peres, a man Bronfman counted as a close personal friend. In the weeks following the trip, the rumors multiplied: Peres's note contained an offer of a seat at the peace conference in exchange for normalization of relations and free emigration to Israel; if Gorbachev could deliver Syria to the negotiating table, Israel would withdraw from the Golan Heights.

The most bizarre but promising development by far was the beginning of a plan for a Soviet Jewish airlift. About twenty thousand Jews would be moved to Poland, and French planes would collect them there and deliver them to Israel. At first written off as an exaggeration by Bronfman, the plan, or at least its substance, was confirmed when Peres visited France a month later, at the end of October. After a lunch meeting with François Mitterrand, he told reporters that there was indeed an airlift in the works and that France had offered planes and pilots.

After a few months, it became clear that the airlift idea was dead. The Soviets lost interest. The only concrete result of Bronfman's freelance diplomacy was the eventual emigration of Ilya Essas. Bronfman made a special plea for Essas, who had been leading the small movement of Orthodox Soviet Jews. In a profile for the *Washington Post* a few months after Bronfman's trip, in response to another Jewish leader's jokingly—and anonymously—saying Bronfman thought of himself as "king of the Jews," he laid out what he thought had been accomplished. He had spoken mostly with Anatoly Dobrynin, who had been moved back to Moscow to run the Kremlin's international department after spending decades as the Soviet ambassador to the United States. "I think my friend Anatoly's going to invite a lot of people over there to talk. There's going to be a buildup of pressure through the business community. The Russians know the Soviet Jewry issue is tied to trade . . . My guess is that over a period of time, five to 10 years, some of our goals will be achieved."

The talk of a Jewish airlift, the courting of Bronfman, and the overtures to Israel were all read as signs of Soviet softening in the run-up to the first summit between Reagan and Gorbachev. The meeting was to take place in Geneva on November 19, and it was a chance to test the theory that Gorbachev represented a new direction. It would be not only the first encounter in six years between the superpowers but also the first time that Reagan, the ultimate Cold Warrior, would meet face to face with a Communist leader. Just as they had in the 1970s in the months before the Nixon summits, the Soviets believed that a few token human rights gestures would ensure a more cordial atmosphere. As a result, Elena Bonner, Sakharov's wife, was finally given permission to leave their isolation in the sealed-off city of Gorky to get medical treatment in the West for her heart condition. But there were few other signs that the cause would be advanced. Asked publicly about the is- sue for the first time—during his October trip to France—Gorbachev answered that the issue of human rights was "artificially played up by Western propaganda and exploited to poison relations among peoples and countries." As for Jews: "I would be glad to hear of Jews enjoying anywhere such political and other rights as they have in our country."

Gorbachev, like his predecessors, may have been trying to change the subject, but the activist forces that had been waiting years for such an opportunity were just gearing up. The lead-in to the summit was full of articles presenting human rights as a giant obstacle for both men. "Summit Parley Overshadowed by Rights Issue" read one head- line. "Soviets Trying to Ignore Question That Won't Go Away: Human Rights" read another. The Soviet Jewry organizations came to life, planning dozens of local protests, letter-writing campaigns, and ad- vertisements exhorting the president to make an issue of Soviet Jewry. The Soviets were doing their part to keep the focus on human rights by continuing the tactic first used at the Ottawa conference: trying to turn the tables on the United States. One typical article by TASS gave this assessment of Reagan's America: "Rampant racism in many states, a policy of genocide against the native peoples, Indians, and harass- ment of dissidents, up to and including their being gunned down and bombed as in Philadelphia, are facts of life in the U.S. today." The news agency Novosti even carried a petition asking for an end to the "wave of anti-Semitism sweeping the U.S."

George Shultz, sensitive to human rights and now well known as a defender of refuseniks, had constructed a new argument for liberalized emigration that he thought might resonate with Gorbachev. In Shultz's first meetings with Shevardnadze, the new foreign minister let Shultz know that he would have to find a way to make the case for human rights in more Soviet-centered terms. The Soviet Union would not open up simply in response to the moral indignation of the West. Shultz's response came in early November when he flew to Moscow to meet with Gorbachev in preparation for the upcoming summit. Carefully sidestepping an argument about competing ideologies, Shultz painted a picture of a world headed quickly toward a new "information age" that would replace the "industrial age." This new world, he explained to Gorbachev, would be smaller. Information and innovation would be the ultimate commodity and could be passed in seconds from one side of the globe to the other. "Closed and compartmented societies cannot take advantage of the information age," Shultz explained. "People must be free to express themselves, move around, emigrate and travel if they want to, challenge accepted ways without fear." Rather than blow up at what was clearly a lecture—Shultz's advisers had warned that he would be seen as condescending—Gorbachev lit up. "You should take up the planning office here in Moscow," he told him. "You have more ideas than they have." Once again, Shultz had the impression that he was dealing with a man who wanted to embrace change.

During this meeting, Shultz asked Gorbachev point-blank if he could take Shcharansky and Ida Nudel back with him on his plane. This received cold stares. But the connection was clear. Dealing with the Soviet Jewry problem would be a good first step toward reform. This idea had already been floated in Gorbachev's circle. In a diary entry around this time, one of the Soviet leader's closest advisers, Anatoly Chernyaev, wrote that he hoped Gorbachev's efforts to change the West's "perception" of the Soviet Union would be matched by an effort to shift the policies away from what he called "ideological intolerance." In order to achieve that, he wrote, "we have to resolve the Jewish question, the most burning among human-rights problems."

An unprecedented three thousand journalists showed up in Geneva for the summit. Soviet Jewry activists hoped to steal some of this spotlight, and none was more determined than Avi Weiss. He arrived in Switzerland with a handful of activists intent on engaging in some kind of civil disobedience. Among them was Yosef Mendelevich, gaunt and with a long, wispy beard, still soft-spoken and looking even more like a prophet than he had in his days as a serious young man in Riga, before the Gulag. Weiss announced his presence the first day during a press conference organized by American Jewish leaders. Edgar Bronfman was there, the incarnation of Nahum Goldmann as he made the point that any protests should remain free of anti-Soviet rhetoric. Weiss, posing as a journalist for the *Jewish Press*—Kahane's old paper—asked Bronfman if he had money invested in the Soviet Union and, if so, how he could credibly claim to represent the Jews. Bronfman tried to defuse the question with humor, claiming he didn't "make enough money in the Soviet Union to pay for gas from here to the airport." Soon, Weiss and Mendelevich found their protest target. On the opening day of the summit, together with three other activists, they staged a sit-in at the offices of Aeroflot, the Soviet airline. Weiss walked up to the ticket counter and asked to book a flight for Anatoly Shcharansky, and then all the activists sat down, unfurled banners, tacked photos of refuseniks to the walls, and began to study Torah loudly. When Russian security men weren't able to dislodge the protesters, the Swiss police were called in and arrested the group. The activists spent the next two days in jail, enduring conditions that Weiss would describe two weeks later in a *New York Times* op-ed: "We were held in a maximum security prison, stripped and body searched, placed in isolation in small cubicles for extended periods of time, denied kosher food, and locked in cells with thieves, murderers and drug dealers." If Weiss and Mendelevich's objective was to focus attention on the refuseniks and prisoners, they got their wish.

Avital Shcharansky was also in Geneva. Even though her protest was much less flamboyant, she too was briefly detained by the Swiss police for blocking the entrance to the Soviet mission. Media savvy now after years of campaigning, she said her only goal at the summit was to deliver a letter to Raisa Gorbachev pleading for her husband's release and saying that "if your love for the General Secretary means sharing with him the joys of children and grandchildren, of planning and living a life together, then you must know, Mrs. Gorbachev, that these joys are all denied to me." She was a forlorn presence at the summit as she stood for hours in the snow outside the barbed-wire barricade that blocked off the Soviet mission, her head covered by a shawl. To the many journalists who swarmed around her knowing she was a reliable producer of dramatic quotes, she handed out copies of her letter.

The issue of Soviet Jewry was everywhere present at the summit, a kind of shorthand that came to represent all that was repressive and evil about Soviet society. Without even referring to the actual individual refuseniks and prisoners at the heart of the movement, the words *Soviet Jewry* were the quickest—maybe even trendiest—way to level an argument about human rights at the Soviets. The strangest example of this came with the highest-profile public invocation of Soviet Jewry during the summit: an impromptu exchange between Gorbachev and Jesse Jackson. The civil rights leader and former Democratic presidential candidate along with a group of antinuclear peace activists had invited the Soviet leader to a meeting in the lobby of the Soviet mission. To their surprise, not only did Gorbachev show up but Dobrynin and Shevardnadze came as well, all of them fresh from their first session with the Americans. For forty-five minutes, three feet apart and surrounded by Russian security and a tight ring of activists, Gorbachev and Jackson engaged each other in a debate while television cameras broadcast the exchange live. Jackson, who the previous year had become a controversial figure for American Jews when he described New York as "Hymietown," almost immediately brought up "the plight of Soviet Jews." Gorbachev was smiling and unfazed. "Jews are a part of the Soviet people," he said through his translator. "They are a fine people. They contribute a lot to disarmament. They are a very talented people and they are very valued in the Soviet Union." When Jackson pushed him on the question again, Gorbachev fell back on the standard Soviet response: "The problem—the so-called problem—in the Soviet Union does not exist. Perhaps this problem only exists with those who would like to mar the relations with us, who cast doubts and aspersions." Jackson later announced that Gorbachev's answer had been "not adequate." He had "recognized no problem."

More airtime was given to Soviet Jewry outside the closed doors of the summit than within. Reagan did devote an entire session to the issue on the second day, and he specifically mentioned Shcharansky. But there was no concrete progress on this or any other substantive issues, such as arms control. The conversation went in circles. The main point of contention was Reagan's Star Wars project, which Gorbachev feared was not just a defensive shield, as it was described, but a sophisticated space-based weapon that would trigger a new arms race. As long as Star Wars existed, Gorbachev refused to discuss the dismantling of intermediate-range nuclear warheads in Europe. The only tangible result at the end of the three days was an anodyne joint statement reaffirming that a nuclear war could never be won and should not be fought. There was also a commitment to two further summits, one in Washington and one in Moscow.

But the real success of Geneva, as was immediately clear to all observers, was the personal connection forged between Reagan and Gorbachev. The two spent nearly five of the fifteen official hours of the summit alone in conversation with only their translators. Somehow, through Reagan's corny anecdotes and jokes and Gorbachev's slightly sardonic wit, the two began to feel comfortable, even to think they could trust each other. The bigger move was on Reagan's part. He had spent his first term demonizing the Soviet Union, as he had his entire political life. But Reagan was a man led by intuition more than anything else, and something told him that Gorbachev signified a real change. He was willing to bet on this feeling, even if it meant upsetting the right flank of his party and the neocons in his administration — not to mention activists like Avi Weiss — who saw confrontation as the only way to deal with the USSR.

Soviet Jewry had something to gain from Reagan's approach. Nixon and Kissinger had refused to deal with an issue that seemed too moralistic, and Carter had dealt with it too dogmatically and without any real weight behind his words. For Reagan, Soviet Jewry was both ideological and tactical. He was going to give Gorbachev the space he needed to reform. His intuition told him that much. But the relationship would have to be based on trust. And Reagan had made it exceedingly clear that the proof of that trust would be in human rights. Morris Abram, the head of the National Conference and a confidant of Reagan, reported in a memo that the president had told him after Geneva that "if the Soviet Union cannot be trusted to keep its word with respect to existing international obligations on emigration and other Jewish rights, it cannot be trusted to keep its word with respect to arms." The issue of Soviet Jewry, he was saying, was now the barometer.

Two months after her frozen vigil in Geneva, Avital Shcharansky received a phone call from George Shultz. A deal had been reached. Her husband was going to be freed. Shultz told her to make her way to Europe to meet him. Even though she knew about the negotiations, she had been trying not to get her hopes up. After all, it wasn't the first time they had seemed close to reunion—rumors of an imminent release had surfaced at least half a dozen times before. But now Shultz gave her a date, a time, and a place: sometime before noon on Tuesday, February 11, 1986, Shcharansky would cross the Glienicke Bridge, which spanned the Havel River and linked West Berlin with Potsdam, the East German town where generations of Prussian kings once resided. The small, unassuming iron bridge had become one of the most notorious border crossings between East and West. Francis Gary Powers, the U-2 pilot downed over the Soviet Union, was returned to his countrymen across this bridge, as were numerous other prisoners and spies who'd been caught on the wrong sides of the iron curtain. Avital heard the words but couldn't digest their meaning at first. For nearly nine years she had spent almost every waking hour in pursuit of this moment, but the flesh-and-blood man she was fighting for, whom she had not seen since the morning after their wedding night, in 1974, had long since become an abstraction. He was a memory she labored hard to keep fresh as she pursued an exhausting task that she'd never thought she was particularly well suited for. A few times she had confided to Avi Weiss that imagining the reunion with her husband filled her with fear and anxiety. I think I'll die when I see him, she once told Weiss.

The Geneva summit and the general warming of relations had provided the latest prod for an early Shcharansky release. In the late spring of 1985, Wolfgang Vogel, a wealthy East German lawyer with deep connections to the Stasi, had reported to his West German contact that he had a mandate from Moscow to negotiate for Shcharansky's release. Vogel had made a lucrative career out of arranging thousands of prisoner exchanges and spy swaps over the past three decades, starting with the 1962 exchange of Francis Gary Powers for the KGB agent Rudolf Abel. The West German government paid him two hundred thousand dollars a year for his services. Shcharansky was a sensitive case; while he was charged as a spy in the Soviet Union, the Americans did not consider him as such and would not agree to a normal tit-for-tat spy-exchange deal. Throughout that year, Vogel had met secretly with West German officials and Richard Burt, the new American ambassador to Bonn, to try to work out an arrangement. The latitude Vogel was given from Moscow increased following the Geneva summit, as did the rumors that something was in the works. One persistent story, partly true, was that Shcharansky's release was linked to the freeing of Nelson Mandela, whose political party, the African National Congress, had been receiving financial backing from the Soviet Union since the 1950s. P. W. Botha, the South African president, let it be known that he was interested in such an exchange. During his visit to Moscow in September, Edgar Bronfman had conveyed Botha's willingness and tried to convince his Soviet contacts to take the deal. In January, Botha fed the rumor mill by speaking publicly about the high-profile East-West swap.

But the deal that Vogel ended up putting together did not involve Mandela. He arranged instead an ordinary spy swap—Shcharansky, two East Germans who were serving life sentences for spying, and one Czechoslovakian imprisoned for helping Eastern bloc citizens flee to the West were exchanged for four people who had been caught spying for the Soviet Union in the United States and West Germany. At the Americans' insistence, Shcharansky would cross the Glienicke Bridge alone and twenty minutes before the others. This way, the United States could view his release as simply a sweetener unrelated to the spies, and the Soviets could maintain their fiction that Shcharansky had been a CIA agent. This elaborate choreography was finalized by Vogel and his American and West German counterparts at the end of January after a full day of nonstop negotiations at an Austrian ski resort. The Soviets, eager to get full publicity for the release, leaked the news first. On February 2, it made the cover of *Bild*, the popular Hamburg tabloid.

Shcharansky, isolated thousands of miles away in Perm 35, a labor camp deep in the Ural Mountains, had no idea what was happening. He did not know that the American president had mentioned him to the new Soviet general secretary during their first meeting; he knew nothing about the fevered negotiations or the nervous anticipation of his wife. He did know, however, that his captors were trying to fatten him up. Starting at the end of December, he was given daily intravenous infusions of vitamins. A doctor began treating him for a heart condition he had developed in the camp. In seven weeks, he gained more than twenty pounds. But he figured this was in anticipation of a visit from his mother and brother. The last time he had seen them, in 1984, not long after arriving in Perm, the meeting was preceded by two months of hospital care and better food. But after a recent hunger strike—to protest the confiscation of his letters to Avital and his mother—all visitation rights had been taken away until 1987 as punishment.

His answer came on January 22, the same day the deal was concluded in Austria. Without warning, guards brought Shcharansky to the gate that led to the camp, opened the large iron door, ushered him out, and shut it behind him. Four men in civilian clothes—obviously KGB agents—stood there waiting for him. The rest of the day was surreal, as evidence mounted that he might just be heading for freedom. A convoy of Volgas and police cars escorted him on the four-hour ride from Perm. Then he was loaded onto an airplane, which took off with him as the only passenger. As the plane lifted and Shcharansky saw the severe landscape growing smaller and smaller, then receding under the clouds, he finally began to believe what was happening. His first reaction, however, was not excitement. It was anxiety. Just like Avital in Israel, he was leaving the life he knew for a life stripped of the black-and-white morality that had guided him in the Gulag. He described the moment a year later:

> When I probed my feelings, I found to my astonishment that my dominant emotion was sorrow. Below me was a world I knew so well, where I was familiar with every detail, every sound, where they couldn't pull any dirty tricks on me, where I knew how to help a friend and deal with an enemy. Down there was a stern world that accepted and acknowledged me, and where I was secure, the master of my own fate. Now, lost in speculation and apprehension, driving away the hope that was now becoming impossible to dismiss, I lost my self-confidence. Suddenly I no longer felt in control.

Shcharansky was brought to Lefortovo, his first prison, which he had left nine years before. There he stayed for the next two weeks, still unclear why he had been transferred to Moscow. He spent his time rediscovering the prison's vast library of books confiscated during the Great Terror of the 1930s and immersed himself in a translation of Schiller. On the morning of February 10 the guards came for him. They gave him a suit, socks and shoes, a long blue coat, a scarf, and a large black Russian fur hat. The pants were too big and kept falling down. When Shcharansky complained, he was given a piece of twine because a belt, he was told, was forbidden.

He was driven to Bykovo airport. Before he could board the plane, Shcharansky asked about the miniature book of Psalms that had become a talisman for him throughout his years in prison. Along with his letters and books, it had been taken away when he arrived at Lefortovo. The guards could not be bothered, and Shcharansky threatened not to move until it was given back to him. A cameraman and photographers were recording the scene on the tarmac. Shcharansky lay down on the snow-covered ground yelling that he would not leave without the Psalms. After a consultation and a check of the book, it was handed to him, and he boarded the plane, clutching it tightly. All this time, he was reciting the prayer he had composed in the desperation of his initial stay at Lefortovo and that had been reverberating through his head in the decade since. "Blessed are you, Adonai, King of the Universe. Grant me the good fortune to live with my wife, my beloved ... Grant me the strength, the power, the intelligence, the good fortune, and the patience to leave this jail and to reach the land of Israel in an honest and worthy way." The plane was headed west. He could see by the direction of the sun. Finally, the Soviet officials with him informed Shcharansky that he was being deprived of his Soviet citizenship and expelled from the Soviet Union for being an American spy. He had imagined this moment in his head for years. Shcharansky wanted them to take down a statement. He was denied. So, with a smile on his face, he said in an official voice that he was happy that the very thing he had asked for thirteen years ago was finally being granted. And he reasserted that he had had nothing to do with espionage or treason. Then he sat down with his Psalm book and started quietly reading to himself.

After the plane landed in East Germany, Shcharansky's KGB escorts ordered him to walk in a straight line to a waiting black limousine. He found this final order grating. So, instead, he zigzagged his way to the car, confusing the watching agents. In Berlin, Shcharansky was taken first to Wolfgang Vogel's house, where Vogel explained what would happen the following day, and then to a villa in the forests of Wannsee, southwest of Berlin. He adjusted surprisingly well for someone who had woken up that morning in a Soviet prison. He could not get enough of the earthy smell and bitter taste of freshly ground coffee, forbidden him during his imprisonment. That night he couldn't sleep; all the black coffee he drank through the evening probably didn't help, but the bed he was given was entirely too soft for him to sleep in. His back had become accustomed to the wooden board in his cell. He paced all night, sleepless, and meditated some more with his Psalms, nervous about what it would be like to see Avital again.

Around eleven the next morning, he stood on one end of the snowy Glienicke Bridge, the enormous black fur hat on his head, a too-large coat draped around him, and his pants held up with a piece of twine. Above his head was the flag of the German Democratic Republic. The Havel River was covered in a layer of frost. Shcharansky began walking with Richard Burt, the American ambassador, who towered over him. He asked where the border was, and Burt pointed out a thin, painted line halfway across the bridge. Shcharansky, with the impish smile he hadn't lost, gleefully jumped across the line, holding up his pants to keep them from falling down. The next moments passed in a blur. A large crowd of journalists, diplomats, and sightseers were cheering on the other end of the bridge. He was rushed into a waiting car. The ambassador pressed his own cuff links, which had been given to him by the secretary of state, into Shcharansky's palm as a gift. There was a call to Washington, small talk aboard a plane, food, and more coffee. And all he wanted was Avital. He was told that she would be waiting for him in Frankfurt, his first stop on the way to Israel.

At the American air base in Frankfurt, Shcharansky was led down a long corridor to a room. He opened the door and looked around. There, sitting in the corner, was a woman dressed in a long wool skirt and dark sweater, her head covered with a kerchief. It was Natasha, now Avital, the girl he had last seen in 1974, transformed into a devout middle-aged woman. The emotional impact of the moment was too much for both of them. He took a few steps toward her and she stood up. They embraced strongly and through tears he said, in a laughing voice and in Hebrew, "Sorry I'm a little late."

Anatoly Shcharansky's reception upon his arriving in Israel would have overwhelmed anyone, never mind someone who had just emerged from nine years of prison. It was a self-consciously historic moment, an international media event. After the Shcharanskys landed at Ben-Gurion Airport, Avital's brother, Mikhail Stieglitz, ran to the plane with a change of clothes—and a belt. Shcharansky soon emerged from the plane; he looked pale, his eyes were rubbed a raw red, and his hand clutched Avital's, but he seemed ready to face the massive audience that began changing "Tolya! Tolya!" The entire Israeli government was waiting on the tarmac to receive him. Shimon Peres, the prime minister, grabbed Shcharansky in a bear hug. Next came the open arms of Yitzhak Shamir, the right-wing vice premier, who was then in a power-sharing government with Peres. The rest of the cabinet waited patiently to shake his hand. The interior minister, a rabbi, lifted his hands over Shcharansky's head and started praying: "Blessed be thou, O Lord, who resurrects the dead."

After a phone call with Reagan, during which he thanked the president for his and the American people's commitment to his case and insisted, emphatically, that he had not been a spy, he was pulled along to the absorption hall of the airport. Hundreds of journalists and former refuseniks were in the crowd, and Shcharansky kept squinting into the bright lights and spotting people he knew. Robert Toth and David Shipler, two of his important Moscow journalist contacts, were there, beaming at him. So were Yosef Mendelevich and Hillel Butman, who had shared the cell adjoining his in the Chistopol prison. After the absorption minister handed him his Israeli ID card, and after Peres spoke—calling Avital a "lioness"—it was Shcharansky's turn. The entire world seemed to be watching to see if this longtime symbol—a touchstone for anti-Communism, for human rights, for Jewish pride—could live up to all the hopes that people had invested in him. Amazingly, Shcharansky had not lost any of the charisma or poise that had made him such an effective spokesman for the refuseniks before his arrest. When he got up to speak, he immediately commanded the room. He apologized for his stumbling Hebrew—which was nonetheless impressive given his years of isolation—and admitted that "there are some events in a person's life which are impossible to describe in any language."

Shcharansky talked of the shock of the past day. As he spoke, he held on to Avital's hand, and she laughed and wiped tears away. He tried to touch on the Jewish element of his fight, telling the enraptured room: "The very fact that this day has come is a strong indication of the justness of our cause. This successful struggle was possible because Jews everywhere in the world understood that the fate of Jews in any country is their fate, too." But he also emphasized that "compliments must go to those who struggle for human rights . . ." He searched for words, wiping his forehead with a handkerchief. "You know, I dreamed many times while in prison of arriving in our land and there my Avital would be waiting for me. But in my dreams, whenever we began to embrace . . . I would wake up in my cell. But I must add that in my dream I never saw as many people as I saw when it finally came true." He closed with words that Soviet Jewry and human rights activists were waiting to hear: "On this happiest day of our lives, I am not going to forget those whom I left in the camps, in the prisons, who are still in exile or who still continue their struggle for their right to emigrate, their human rights."

Even before Tolya and Avital arrived in Israel, the speculation about what would happen to them began. Her outward religiosity and now long affiliation with the hard-line greater Israel movement Gush Emunim seemed like a poor fit for a man who prided himself on being an intellectual and a defender of human rights, a follower of Sakharov. People wondered about their future as a couple. Shcharansky himself joked over the next days that "everyone is waiting either for me to put on a skullcap or her to take off her head-scarf." One of the people worried about them was the Leningrad hijacker Sylva Zalmanson, now living with her six-year-old daughter, Anat, and working as an engineer in Ashdod, an industrial town south of Tel Aviv. She listened to the news of Shcharansky's arrival on the radio and had flashbacks of her own reunion with Eduard Kuznetsov in 1979. She knew firsthand how hard it could be to rebuild a relationship after years of separation. She and Eduard had stayed together only long enough for her to become pregnant. Then he left. The years of prison had hardened the man she had met in Riga so long before, and he could not handle Sylva's love or her desire to settle down. In 1986 Kuznetsov was no longer living in Israel but working at the Munich station of Radio Liberty. She worried that Avital and Tolya might suffer the same fate. Watching them moments after they arrived, some observers focused on the way Avital pulled away from Tolya's public shows of affection.

It seemed everyone had a stake in Shcharansky's political and religious decisions. The anxiety underlined the singular position that
Shcharansky—and the Soviet Jewry movement—had come to occupy
in a Jewish world that was becoming increasingly fragmented ideologically. He was an important mascot for human rights advocates on the
left who focused on his commitment to the Helsinki process. And he
was a Jewish hero, the latest symbol of Jewish suffering, husband to a
pious woman, herself redeemed, and possibly a recruit to the cause
of messianic Zionism. He contained both. And until he opened his
mouth he could represent everything to everyone. Yehuda Amichai,
Israel's most beloved poet, watched the ecstasy of Shcharansky's arrival
and worried. "I hope they don't ruin him," he said. "He's the last man
who belongs to all of us."

This tension was evident from his first hours in Israel. After his address to journalists and friends, he walked outside to face a large public rally set up in front of the airport. The audience was made up of
thousands of boisterous young yarmulke-clad men and long-skirted
women from the West Bank settlements who were singing folk songs,
like Shlomo Carlebach's "Am Yisrael Chai," and dancing a vigorous
hora. In his speech to the crowd, Yosef Mendelevich, who had long
ago joined this milieu, said that "only one community, the religious
nationalist community," had come to greet Shcharansky. Swept up
by the immense fervor, Shcharansky led them in the singing of a famous version of Psalm 133, "How good it is to be together, as brothers"
(*Heene ma tov u ma'naim, shevet achim gam yachad*). They went wild,
and Shcharansky could barely continue his speech. But the biggest applause came for Avital. She didn't hide her political alignment: "Just
as Natan [his new Israeli name] has arrived, so will all Jews, from the
Soviet Union, from America, from Europe, from everywhere. I call on
the government to protect our entire country, not to give up one bit of
it, so that all these Jews can build the country." The most climactic moment of the rally came at the end of Avital's speech when she slapped
a large blue and white yarmulke on Shcharansky's head. A roar went
up from the crowd. She and the screaming religious nationalists before
her were staking their claim.

The big question for the Soviet Jewry movement as a whole—and
those many refuseniks back in the Soviet Union—was whether this

dramatic release augured a new era or was, as had happened in the past, just a small token meant to grease the wheels of diplomacy. This was impossible to tell. But whatever the Soviet Union intended and however complicated the path ahead for Shcharansky personally, the moment felt like a massive catharsis. People wept openly. Longtime activists who had become hardened by the immensity of what they were attempting and the dismal state of affairs were suddenly hopeful in spite of themselves. So much energy had been poured into the Shcharansky case, both in Moscow and among the American activists. His release came as one of the few moments of payback the movement had been afforded of late. Out of this small triumph it seemed possible that American Jews might just feel inspired again. They could see that their efforts — long years of pasting Shcharansky's face on posters, pacing in front of the Soviet mission, sending letters, and listening to synagogue lectures — could achieve a concrete, unequivocal victory. He was out.

Shcharansky seemed to understand, even in the daze of those first hours, that his freedom meant more than his just being able to hold Avital again. Once he left the airport, he and Avital were driven through the darkening Judean Hills to Jerusalem. They stopped on Mount Scopus, and he looked down at the lights of the Old City coming through the night mist. Little more than the golden Dome of the Rock was visible. He was taken down to the Western Wall. A large crowd was waiting for him, mostly yeshiva boys singing and dancing. He waded in and started to feel claustrophobic from the bodies massed around him. He resisted their outstretched arms until finally, unable to push them back, he gave in. Soon his body was hoisted up and he was being held aloft by what seemed like hundreds of hands. An ocean of Jews kept him afloat, moving him slowly closer and closer to the wall he had dreamed about so often and for so long.

14

"Mr. Gorbachev, Let These People Go!"
1986–1987

IDA NUDEL LIVED in the small Moldovan village of Bendery, almost six hundred miles south of the nuclear reactor in Chernobyl. But she swore she could feel the effects of the radiation in the weeks after the catastrophic accident, which blasted fallout in such a wide radius it was found in Western Europe. One morning in early May of 1986, she woke up with a painful ache in her bones and difficulty breathing. Nausea and an unquenchable thirst followed. She soon learned what had happened on April 26 at the atomic reactor—only sixty miles outside Kiev. The Soviet media avoided reporting the full extent of the Chernobyl disaster for eighteen days, a period in which the panicked authorities sought mainly to minimize and obfuscate. That whole spring, Nudel, a pessimist at heart, saw contamination everywhere. The physical landscape of her exile seemed an expression of the despair and loneliness she felt. The leaves on the trees turned brown and fell off. Her collie, Pizer, was listless. The cherries that looked so temptingly red and bursting that year were a menacing sign of sickness and death.

The refuseniks didn't need to observe the handling of the Chernobyl incident to convince them that they were living under a deceitful regime. But for those who existed within the normal boundaries of Soviet society, the delay on reporting Chernobyl was shocking, the sign of a world in collapse. The big lie of this totalitarian system, which Soviet citizens had become so adept at living with, was slowly peeling away. And if Chernobyl was any guide, Gorbachev, for all his talk of openness, was turning out to be no different from the decrepit leaders before him. But this too was not surprising to the refuseniks.

In the spring of 1986, Volodya and Masha Slepak entered their sixteenth year of refusal. In March they had moved out of the rough-and-tumble Gorky Street apartment that had become so familiar to many Western visitors. Now they lived in a two-bedroom apartment on Vesnina Street, about a twenty-minute walk from the Kremlin. Volodya was working as an elevator operator in a large hospital. Alexander Lerner, now in his seventies, saw few visitors anymore. And sitting in the Chistopol prison in the Urals—where Shcharansky and Mendelevich were once inmates—was Yosef Begun, the Hebrew teacher, still serving the seven years of his third sentence. The other Hebrew teachers arrested on trumped-up charges in 1984, including Yuli Edelstein and Alexander Kholmiansky, were still in prison as well. The emigration numbers told an equally dismal story: in March 1986, a year after Gorbachev's ascension, only forty-seven Jews emigrated.

The refuseniks in Moscow and Leningrad continued to function as a community of internal exiles, but leaving no longer felt like a realizable goal. Instead, they focused increasingly on sustaining their own alternative world. They struggled to hold on to menial jobs as doormen and elevator operators. More than their activist supporters in the West, they were highly dubious that Gorbachev would bring change. They viewed his slick, friendly exterior as nothing more than a dangerous deception that would lull American Jews into forgetting about them.

The malaise of the refuseniks—not to mention the many Soviet Jews who wanted to apply but now saw no way out—was mirrored to some degree in Soviet society at large. The economy had been stagnating since Khrushchev's reign, the oil boom of the 1970s being the only exception. But the price of oil—on which nearly the entire economy hinged—was now in decline. From a one-time $40 dollars a barrel, the price had dropped to $15. The most basic consumer goods were in short supply. Standing for hours in long lines became a staple of Soviet life. When it came to the new computer technology rapidly advancing in the West, the Russians simply could not keep up. These economic difficulties, combined with the bungled handling of Chernobyl, helped dissipate the aura of Soviet authority and control that had for so long made the Kremlin seem invincible. You didn't need to be a member of the Politburo—in fact, it probably helped if you weren't—to understand that the vitality and dynamism that had characterized the Soviet world in the immediate post–World War II years was long gone.

Gorbachev had come into office believing that the key to resuscitating his dying empire was to ratchet down confrontation with the West. It was no longer affordable. Resources had to move to the domestic front. He began withdrawing from Afghanistan, and his push for a mutual reduction in arms—especially the elimination of Reagan's spooky Star Wars program—took on an increasingly desperate tone. In January of 1986, he announced his willingness to get rid of the SS-20 intermediate-range nuclear missiles that had pushed Reagan to place dueling American Pershing missiles in Europe. Even more dramatic, Gorbachev wondered aloud about whether it was possible to eliminate all nuclear weapons by the year 2000. Behind these gestures—bold though they were—was a pervasive anxiety. The refuseniks and Jewish activists might have seen Gorbachev as another Soviet leader, but they couldn't hear his pleas to his Politburo comrades. He knew that something had to give. "If we don't back down on some specific, maybe even important issues, if we don't budge from the positions we've held for a long time, we will lose in the end," Gorbachev said at one meeting in 1986. "We will be drawn into an arms race that we cannot manage. We will lose because right now we are at the end of our tether."

The change began with rhetoric. At the Twenty-seventh Congress of the Communist Party, Gorbachev formally presented his ideas for how to revitalize the Soviet Union. During his major policy address on February 25, he introduced concepts that indicated not only a radical departure from the past but a serious challenge to Soviet dogma. He wanted perestroika, a restructuring that would bring some democracy and transparency to government and allow for a more versatile and enterprising economic system. He wanted glasnost, openness. To become prosperous and competitive, Soviet society would have to be more self-critical, would have to look honestly at itself and not lie about the things that were happening right under its nose. The very words he used were shocking in their newness: he mentioned "restraint," "tactical flexibility," and "a readiness for mutually acceptable compromises ... the aim not being confrontation, but dialogue and mutual understanding." And most dramatic of all for Soviet Jews, he spoke positively about the human rights goals of Helsinki, even using the language of the third basket to define his objectives. He understood that "an all-embracing system of international security" would necessitate "the resolution ... of questions related to the reunion of families, marriage, and promotion of contacts between people and between organizations." This was unprecedented. No Soviet leader had ever mentioned the human rights provisions of Helsinki, let alone referred specifically to "family reunification," which everyone knew was code for Jewish emigration.

In the following months, there were more symbolic gestures. On a visit to France in July, he uttered the words *human rights*—a piece of progress in itself—and spoke of a civilization no longer willing to "tolerate arbitrariness and lawlessness." That same month, the Soviet Ministry of Foreign Affairs announced the establishment of a new office: a bureau of humanitarian and cultural affairs, to be headed by Yuri Kashlev, a knowledgeable and cultured diplomat who shared the approachable and genial character of his boss, Eduard Shevardnadze.

Though these moves led to little real difference in the lives of Soviet Jews, they showed that Gorbachev understood that he had to present an entirely new face to the West. This meant being receptive to what seemed like an incessant harping on human rights. But, equally important, the Soviet Jewry movement had effectively closed the door to détente until this issue was dealt with. The Jackson-Vanik amendment made any economic cooperation impossible. And now George Shultz was using every opportunity to drive home the point that arms negotiations, though not legislatively linked to human rights, could not go forward in good faith if concessions weren't made to the demands of American Jews and human rights activists. This was the price of admission. Gorbachev certainly had self-interested reasons for trying to open up his society. He saw it as the only way forward. But he was also cornered. If he wanted to avoid another arms race, he would have to solve his Jewish problem.

While Soviet Jews waited to see if this new tone might affect their reality, the gradual liberalization of Soviet society was having actual effects elsewhere. As happened under Khrushchev's thaw, once the ice began to melt, historical memory began to resurface. The particularly Jewish character of the Holocaust had always been obscured by Soviet propaganda that spoke generally of the victims as "Soviet citizens." When Yevgeny Yevtushenko's poem "Babi Yar" had appeared, twenty-five years before, it lifted the veil and spoke with emotion about a Jewish tragedy that had occurred on Soviet soil. During the Brezhnev years and since, there had been a return to the "Great War" rhetoric. But in July of 1986, in a government-sanctioned youth magazine called *Yunost,* there was an article, part prose and part poetry, by the Russian poet Andrei Voznesensky, a cohort of Yevtushenko, that picked up the earlier themes. Titled "The Ditch: A Spiritual Trial," Voznesensky's article examined the mass killing of twelve thousand Jews in the Crimea during World War II and the subsequent robbing of their graves by Soviet citizens. He described discovering the site and finding a "squalid monument" that "suggested oblivion much more than remembrance." Also, he pointed out, "there was no mention that most of the victims were Jews." Voznesensky was interviewed by Western journalists about his piece, and he said he saw it as a protest against anti-Semitism. "A year ago, it would have been impossible to publish this work," he admitted.

History—the undistorted, sometimes ugly past—made its appearance in other ways. A 1984 film by the Georgian director Tengiz Abuladze, *Repentance,* a powerful allegory about Stalin's crimes that had been previously suppressed, was screened in Moscow and Tbilisi. In the fall, the seventy-five-year-old Soviet Jewish writer Anatoli Rybakov announced that his magnum opus, *Children of the Arbat,* would finally be published the following spring in the literary monthly *Druzhba Norodov.* Circulating for years in samizdat, the novel told the unabashed story of a group of friends coming of age in 1934, just before the start of Stalin's purge—Communist believers who then suffered under the regime's arbitrary terror. Rybakov, whose previous work, the 1978 novel *Heavy Sand,* told the story of one Soviet Jewish family's fate during the Nazi invasion, had written a book that was mostly autobiographical and seemed a perfect test of the limits of glasnost. Not only did it describe in great human detail what Stalin had wrought, but Rybakov had managed to leap into the dictator's mind and provide a picture of his machinations and psychosis. *Children of the Arbat*, which became the *Doctor Zhivago* of the 1980s, had been rejected for publication by the Soviet government twice before. Now, both *Repentance* and *Children of the Arbat* were personally approved by Gorbachev.

By the end of the year, the government's powerful censorship agency had been instructed not to concern itself anymore with literary material, with the policing of fiction. Its sole mandate would be to safeguard military secrets.

Elie Wiesel arrived to test the openness. In October, on the twenty-first anniversary of the trip that resulted in *The Jews of Silence* and a week after being awarded that year's Nobel Peace Prize, he arrived in Moscow. From his new platform of world prominence, he declared that one of his goals was to insist that the Soviet Union "recognize the specific character of the Jewish tragedy, which has not been recognized officially yet in the Soviet Union." Confirmation of the regime's new willingness to engage this history arrived the moment Wiesel stepped off his plane at Sheremetyevo airport. He was greeted by a retired Red Army officer with a chest full of ancient medals. Vasily Petrenko, who as a colonel in January 1945 helped liberate Auschwitz, wrapped his arms around Wiesel in a large bear hug. The painfully thin, sallow-faced, wild-haired new Nobel laureate elaborately proclaimed his thanks to Petrenko, whose arrival in Auschwitz, he said, was anticipated "like religious people await the messiah."

The rest of Wiesel's trip was a whirlwind of refusenik meetings that culminated at the synagogue on Arkhipova Street on Simchat Torah, where Wiesel witnessed the same ecstatic dancing that had greeted him in 1965. The narrow cobblestoned street in front of the synagogue—another of Moscow's minuscule Jewish islands—was filled with four thousand people. He stood in front of the congregation, the white-bearded Vladimir Slepak at his side. "Not a day passes when I don't talk of you, dream of you, sing of you, pray for you. You give us so much hope throughout the world, all of you," Wiesel told the masses crowding into the dilapidated yellow synagogue. "We owe you a thousand times more than you owe us."

Another indicator, however symbolic, that the Kremlin was becoming more flexible was the continued courting of Israel. Whether because he wanted to play a role in the perpetually postponed peace talks or because he was still trying to earn American trust, Gorbachev persisted in pursuing a conversation with the Israelis into 1986, even at the risk of angering his Arab allies. On August 20, for the first time since the breaking of diplomatic relations nearly twenty years earlier, a small group of Israeli and Soviet consular officials met in a tightly guarded Finnish government compound in downtown Helsinki. The highly anticipated meeting, which was scheduled to last for more than two days, was broken off by the Soviets after ninety minutes. They insisted on sticking to a discussion of the status of Russian Orthodox Church property in Jerusalem. The Israelis had no choice but to bring up emigration and the Jewish prisoners. There was simply too much pressure from the vociferous and increasingly powerful lobby of Soviet Jewish immigrants in Israel. Each side walked away claiming the other was at fault for the breakdown. What got lost in the commentary was the very fact of the meeting. Israel and the Soviet Union were moving toward a normalization of relations. Only a month later, in New York, Shimon Peres, the prime minister, and Shevardnadze met at the United Nations for more than an hour, the highest-level official meeting since 1967. A photograph of them emerging from the office of the president of the UN Security Council shows two men enjoying each other's company, Peres laughing as he listens to Shevardnadze, who looks like he's in the middle of telling some particularly funny anecdote.

In late September of 1986, a surprise meeting between Gorbachev and Reagan was announced. It would not be a proper summit but rather a "pre-summit" tête-à-tête to prepare the way for a proposed Washington visit. The glacial North Atlantic island of Iceland, a cold, hard place, particularly in the winter months, was selected as the unadorned location where the two leaders could conduct business without pomp or media. It was scheduled for early October. In the short time they had to prepare, Soviet Jewry groups gathered their forces. A plane chartered by the National Conference flew to Reykjavik; the group was led by Morris Abram, the former civil rights lawyer. Abram was a Southern Democrat who had voted for Reagan in 1980, was friends with many members of the administration, including George Shultz, and had briefly served the president on the U.S. Civil Rights Commission. In 1986, chairman of both the Presidents Conference, the influential umbrella group, and the National Conference, Abram was by far the most powerful voice on the issue of Soviet Jewry, at least in the United States. He had already personally handed Shultz a two-foot-high package containing detailed information on eleven thousand refuseniks.

Yosef Mendelevich was also in the Icelandic capital, pelted with freezing rain as he led a Torah service outside the Soviet delegation's hotel, his head covered only by a prayer shawl. Ida Nudel's sister was there, as was Vladimir Slepak's son. Their expectations were high. Shultz had repeatedly said that human rights would have equal billing with arms negotiations. In an emotional speech to the National Conference in the days before he left for Iceland, Shultz talked about the importance of emphasizing Soviet Jewry "over and over and over again." He told the establishment leaders, "The Soviets need to know that we cannot continue to improve relations with them unless we see significant, sustained progress on human rights, including the right to emigrate." A few days before their delegation set out for Reykjavik, the Soviets had released Yuri Orlov, the Moscow Helsinki Watch founder and Shcharansky's one-time collaborator. As Orlov was leaving his Siberian labor camp, a KGB official told him confidentially, "Know that changes are being prepared in our country such as you yourself once dreamed of."

Over the course of the two-day meeting, Gorbachev made stunning concessions, agreeing to eliminate all intermediate-range nuclear missiles from Europe; halving both countries' strategic weapons, including heavy intercontinental ballistic missiles; and even considering a wholesale destruction of all nuclear weapons. The fine print was hammered out in feverish, all-night sessions by a group that included Richard Perle, then undersecretary of defense, and Max Kampelman. Another group was working, also through the night, on various human rights issues—in itself a major concession on the part of the Soviets.

But the resulting agreement on arms control, for all the excitement it inspired, fell apart in the last hours. It turned out that Gorbachev had one major condition: the abandonment of Reagan's beloved Star Wars program. Reagan refused to confine the defensive shield to laboratory testing, and the meeting ended with both sides walking out tired and frustrated. As a result, no concluding statement was ever produced. Lost in the mix, as George Shultz later told the press, was the agreement reached during the human rights negotiations, which was as remarkable as Gorbachev's radical new position on arms reductions. The Soviets had conceded that human rights should remain a regular, open, and legitimate part of any bilateral negotiations. As Morris Abram and Jerry Goodman put it in a letter to the editor the following week as criticism of Reykjavik's failures mounted: "There can never be another summit at which human rights, including Jewish emigration, are not central."

If the human rights advances at Reykjavik were only theoretical and made behind closed doors, another international meeting only a few weeks later provided an opportunity for the Soviets to continue what was beginning to look like a full-scale public relations campaign to improve their image. The third Helsinki review conference would take place in Vienna, and for the first time since Madrid, all thirty-five signatory countries would be present. All three baskets would also be up for discussion. Disarmament talks would resume in Vienna but clearly would be even more dependent on resolving human rights issues. Shultz used a speech in Los Angeles before the conference to make the point: "Until there is substantial Soviet progress in the vital area of human rights, advances in other areas of the relationship are bound to be constrained."

From the beginning, the behavior of the Soviet delegates in Vienna differed starkly from earlier conferences. "There will be no forbidden themes, no taboos," announced a senior member of the delegation, Yuri Kashlev, to a group of journalists in Moscow a week before the opening. In Vienna, a younger, more educated team of Soviet diplomats went out of their way to respond courteously to the families of refuseniks and political prisoners, engaging directly rather than resorting to the usual dismissals. At one press conference on human rights called by the Soviets, a high-ranking official, Vladimir Lorneiko, spoke in a combination of English, German, and Russian about how the Soviet Union was "concerned with both the fate of humanity as well as the fate of a single individual." His country, he said proudly, had started "the increasing and broadening of human rights." In the audience was Alexander Slepak, one of Volodya and Masha's sons. Then a medical student in Philadelphia, he had managed to get into the conference as an accredited reporter for the *Jewish Exponent.* "I would like to know why the rights of my father have been violated for 17 years," he said. Lorneiko thanked him politely for his inquiry. He apologized for the situation and told a story about a friend of his, a young Soviet Jew, denied permission to leave because his parents had refused to sign the requisite forms demanded by OVIR that released their son from any financial obligation to them. Sadly, he said, "there are hundreds of cases like this."

Two days after the conference opened on November 4, Eduard Shevardnadze dropped a bombshell. In an incredibly bold move intended to complete the image overhaul, he gave a speech presenting the Soviet Union as one of the world's leading defenders of human rights. It was Moscow that attached "paramount significance" to Helsinki's human rights provisions. Furthermore, Shevardnadze said, the world community needed to revisit the "unjustly forgotten" Universal Declaration on Human Rights, which should be regarded as the touchstone, a "fundamental document," to guide them as they tried to build a more peaceful world. Then he delivered the coup de grâce. He proposed an international human rights conference to take place in Moscow. All the Helsinki signatories would be invited to the Soviet capital. There they would be free to discuss and scrutinize one another's records. Shevardnadze kept the details vague, but there was no doubt he intended this proposal to completely change the conversation. At a press conference following Shevardnadze's speech, Anatoly Kovalev, a first deputy foreign minister, pleaded, "I want to convince this audience, I want you to believe, that great efforts are being made on humanitarian contacts."

But this was still the realm of rhetoric, and newly emboldened critics of the Soviet Union were relentless in pointing out the disconnect between the regime's words and its deeds. These critics were not just Soviet Jewry activists. As the conference opened, Helsinki Watch in New York issued a condemning three-hundred-fifty-page report concluding that Gorbachev had made a number of recent "gestures . . . that may have obscured the government's continued and systematic violation of international human rights." As if to drive the point home, in the beginning of December—on the eve of Human Rights Day, no less—Anatoly Marchenko died at the Chistopol prison after a five-month hunger strike. Marchenko was the barely literate son of railroad workers who had become one of the most well-known dissidents in the Soviet Union. He was the author of *My Testimony,* a damning samizdat memoir about his time in the Gulag that was later published in the West. Mostly as a result of his stubborn activism, he had spent much of his adult life in and out of prison or exile. When he began his hunger strike, he was in the fifth year of a fifteen-year term for anti-Soviet propaganda and was demanding a visit with his wife as well as the arrest of the prison guards who had beaten him to bloody unconsciousness in 1983. His death resonated around the world, threatening to make a mockery of the Soviets' sudden embrace of human rights. It was one more prod to Gorbachev to move beyond empty gestures.

On the evening of December 15, two engineers showed up at Andrei Sakharov's apartment in Gorky and told him they had come to install a phone line. As they were leaving, they said he should expect a call the following day at ten in the morning. The life of exile that Sakharov and his wife, Elena Bonner, had been living for the past six years had prepared them for anything. The indignities large and small that they had suffered, compounded by health problems and the constant psychological terror of the ever-present KGB, had worn them down. Not only had they not had a phone for years, but the public phones in their vicinity had been disconnected. Radio-jamming devices had been placed on their front door. When Bonner was finally given permission to travel to the United States to treat her heart condition, they received an anonymous letter in the mail with photographs of mutilated faces. The eminent physicist was forced to carry a thirty-pound shoulder bag with him at all times that contained drafts of his memoir and his shortwave radio. KGB agents followed him constantly trying to steal it. Twice they succeeded, and he was forced to begin again. To protest his wife's deteriorating health, he went on a hunger strike and was painfully force-fed through a tube. And all this time, he had not stopped writing letters and sending articles and missives to the West. Bonner carried them with her on trips to Moscow until she was charged with anti-Soviet activity in 1984 and confined to Gorky as well.

When the new phone rang—at three in the afternoon, not ten in the morning—Sakharov found Mikhail Gorbachev on the end of the line. The general secretary informed Sakharov that his exile was over. He could return to Moscow. Elena Bonner's sentence was also overturned. Gorbachev listened with annoyance as Sakharov, not missing a beat, began listing *his* demands. The Soviet leader might have expected gratitude, but instead Sakharov referred to a letter he had sent Gorbachev in February calling for a general amnesty for "prisoners of conscience," all of whom were locked up or in exile because of their political or religious beliefs. The unusual call lasted only a few minutes, and Gorbachev did little more than listen. But it indicated, for the first time, concrete change. The Soviet leader was inviting the country's most celebrated and respected critic back to the heart of the capital, letting him know that he would now be free to say whatever he pleased.

Sakharov wasted no time. As soon as he stepped off train number 37 at Yaroslavl station in Moscow the following week, he launched into a tirade against the regime. Dressed in a gray parka and a large brown fur hat, and not a little overwhelmed by the crowd of more than two hundred journalists and friends who had massed there to welcome him after his eight-hour train ride, Sakharov got his bearings and then began criticizing the continued Soviet presence in Afghanistan, which he called "the most painful point in our foreign policy"—this was the same issue that had gotten him exiled in the first place. In the following days, he settled back into his old apartment and his office at the Academy of Sciences, and although protesting that he was too old and sickly to lead the dwindling army of dissidents, Sakharov managed to express himself on a wide range of topics. He had respect for Gorbachev and what he was attempting, he said. But he didn't think the Soviets should let arms negotiations hinge on the dismantling of the American Star Wars program. As a physicist who knew something about defense technology, he didn't think it would work anyway.

But what was most remarkable about Sakharov's return was how much Moscow had changed in the years he had been gone. In many ways, the argument for convergence between East and West that was at the center of his famous 1968 samizdat essay could be found in the language Gorbachev was now using. Sakharov understood immediately. "I think that the word 'dissident' may be losing some of its resonance," he told one reporter during his first days of freedom. "People are now expressing their opinion more freely and this brings benefit to our society. The sort of articles that are now appearing read like some of the declarations from dissidents that were issued in the 1970's and for which many of my friends were jailed."

The refuseniks and activists of Moscow had always regarded Sakharov as a kind of godfather to their cause, a protector. The authorities, ironically, had fantasized that it was the other way around — that what they called international Zionism was controlling Sakharov through his Jewish wife. There was a lot at stake in Sakharov's release, for the Soviet Jews especially. Almost immediately, they wanted to test whether this dramatic sign of change was indicative of a greater force at work. Before Sakharov's train arrived in Moscow, a small group of activist refuseniks gathered for a demonstration outside the main Moscow post office. They told the press that they shouldn't be taken in by what was just a "gesture of good will" and nothing more. But to the demonstrators' surprise, they weren't dispersed after a few seconds as usually happened. Instead, the plainclothes policemen kindly asked them to keep their demonstration on the sidewalk.

For months, Ida Nudel had been trying to contact Sakharov and Bonner, her old friends. But the call never went through. Then suddenly, once Sakharov's exile ended, she was allowed to speak with them both on the phone for ten minutes without interruption. Sakharov asked if she would come to Moscow to greet them on their return. Nudel wanted to, but she fully expected to be stopped and sent back to her village. Before she left, she sent telegrams to the interior ministers and prosecutors of the Soviet Union and Moldova reminding them of the Soviet constitution's assurance of the right of free movement. Once on her way, she couldn't believe there was no one following her or ordering her back. At the bus station, she looked around and was shocked to see not a single policeman. When she arrived at the airport, she went through her regular precautions, informing her friends in Moscow that she was about to board a plane and that if they didn't hear from her by three, that meant she was being detained. But soon she was sitting in her seat and the plane was on its way, cutting through the clouds. She realized how complicated the simplest of tasks had become, how easy it should be to just buy a ticket, board a plane, and fly somewhere. For so long now, each of these steps had been a small nightmare. At the Sakharovs' apartment, she drank tea with them and they talked about all their mutual friends, about her exile and theirs. But she couldn't get over how Sakharov had been transformed in such a brief time into a very old man. The lines on his face, the crooked back and large glasses, his voice just above a whisper. If change was indeed coming—and Nudel was beginning to believe it might be—she cursed all those shortsighted, ignorant leaders for waiting so long, for the wasted years that this decent man had been made to suffer for simply being honest.

Soviet Jews and their American supporters, from George Shultz to the Student Struggle activists, wanted more than just Sakharov's release. They questioned whether Gorbachev would make the systemic changes that would almost certainly anger the hard-liners who dominated the elite ranks of the Communist Party, the KGB, and the military. How much was he willing to risk? Would he make the real concessions that the Soviet Jewry movement had been demanding for so long?

An initial answer came with the announcement that for the first time in its history, the Soviet Union was going to issue a legal code for emigration in the form of a decree from the Supreme Soviet. There would now be a formal process codified by Soviet law, which would go into effect January 1, 1987. This was, at the very least, a major ideological concession, a tacit admission that there were people who would choose *not* to live in the Communist paradise. But it also did away with a powerful psychological weapon of intimidation, used effectively for decades against Soviet Jews: arbitrariness. For this reason, the announcement, which came on the same day that Shevardnadze unveiled his country's surprising new commitment to human rights in Vienna, could not be seen as an empty gesture. It made the Soviet authorities accountable.

Nonetheless, the new rules did not exactly portend an exodus. The Soviet Council of Ministers, who formulated and adopted the decree in August, had basically codified the practices of OVIR, which refuseniks already knew well, and they'd even added a few more barriers. Emigration could be granted for the purpose of "reunification with members of one's family." But *family* was defined explicitly as direct relatives only—husband, wife, son, daughter, father, mother, brother, sister. Decisions on emigration would be made within a month, and no longer than six months for extenuating circumstances. Applicants would be informed why they were rejected. The decree listed nine possible reasons. But these were very broad. They ranged from the commonly used "state secrets" excuse to this vague explanation: "in the interest of insuring the protection of social order, health or the morals of the population." The new law was equivocal in many respects. Could someone be denied emigration indefinitely? Was there any way to challenge a rejection? How long could secrecy be used as a reason? The Soviet state still had ultimate power over the lives of its citizens. And though the new rules made Soviet practice explicit, they didn't change the central problem: a person did not have a right to emigrate simply because he wanted to leave. The only indication that the Soviets might be more flexible came in a small-print provision at the bottom of the decree allowing that emigration "may also be regulated by bilateral agreements between the USSR and other states."

To those who wanted to see Gorbachev as a different kind of Soviet leader, a real reformer, the emigration law offered a significant piece of evidence that this was the case. The man was willing to do more than change just the aesthetics of the Soviet Union. But to the increasingly vocal group of activists who would never trust any Soviet leader, it provided more reason to panic. The most vocal elements of this highly skeptical opposition were the recent Soviet Jewish emigrants to Israel. Yosef Mendelevich had already effectively organized a group of former refuseniks and prisoners into a powerful Jerusalem lobby that was pushing the Israeli government to take an uncompromising position in any dealings with the Soviets. But this hard-nosed approach got its strongest boost from Natan Shcharansky (his first name had been officially Hebraized). If Mendelevich had become the long-bearded holy prophet, willing to do or say anything to bear witness, Shcharansky had emerged as a much more politic and pragmatic figure, still the chess player, measuring his moves and angling for the most dramatic impact.

From the moment of his release, Shcharansky confidently established himself as the ultimate voice of authority on Soviet Jewry, a man with a large store of moral capital. His transition from political symbol to political activist was seamless. He was very conscious of remaining as independent as possible, refusing to be co-opted by one or another side of the movement. Israeli political parties and American Jewish groups wanted to sponsor his every move. But he did not want to be beholden to anyone. "Sometimes I have nightmares," he laughingly told a reporter. "Some of them are about the Soviet guards outside the punishment cell, but nowadays, I chuckle because some of them are about the heads of those Jewish organizations." If he had a proclivity it was for the grass roots, the Union of Councils and Student Struggle activists. He still remembered that during his activist days in Moscow, it was these American Jews who seemed to care most. Avital insisted that they were his true base.

At the beginning of May 1986, three months after his release, he embarked on a ten-day visit to the United States. All major media covered the event. Shcharansky had recuperated and was looking pudgy again. And Avital, to the great joy of their many supporters, had just announced that she was two months pregnant and would not be traveling. Every aspect of his high-profile trip turned into a tug of war between the grass roots and the establishment as old resentments bubbled to the surface. Mostly, Shcharansky settled the arguments in favor of the grass roots, though he always remained respectful of the American Jewish leaders. On his first Sabbath in New York, Avi Weiss, the activist rabbi who was also chairman of Student Struggle, invited Shcharansky to speak at his synagogue in Riverdale; it would be his first public appearance. Weiss knew that Shcharansky had already been invited to spend the same evening at Kehilath Jeshurun, the wealthy modern Orthodox congregation on the Upper East Side of Manhattan led by Haskel Lookstein, then chairman of the large New York Soviet Jewry umbrella organization. Weiss wanted Shcharansky by his side to boost his own ego but also to make the point that, as Weiss saw it, it was the activists who had truly supported Shcharansky and not the rich suits of the Jewish establishment. Through Avital's intercession, Weiss got his wish. Shcharansky walked into the synagogue to wild applause and took his place on the dais in a chair that had been kept unoccupied for the past nine years and over which hung a sign: RESERVED FOR ANATOLY SHCHARANSKY, PRISONER OF ZION. The moment was as dramatic as Weiss had hoped, and the leaders of the National Conference were denied their own symbolic coup. They were soon denied again. Morris Abram, as close to an overall American Jewish leader as existed, insisted on joining Shcharansky for his visit to the White House. Shcharansky, not wanting to alienate any one part of the movement, suggested that in addition to Abram, Morey Schapira, the president of the Union of Councils, and Weiss should be invited. Abram wanted to avoid bringing the volatile Avi Weiss to meet the president and told Shcharansky he should just go alone.

Over the next few days, Shcharansky reiterated again and again a consistent and simple message, one that was slightly more nuanced than that of activist supporters like Weiss. Shcharansky thought that both quiet diplomacy *and* public diplomacy had a place in the struggle. In an appearance before a congressional committee, he explained how this interplay worked, using himself as an example: "Exactly as it was in my case, the final exchange, my final release was reached in quiet diplomacy in exchanging of spies, but as you all understand it, it would never take place if there wasn't such a strong campaign . . ." First of all, he was saying, there had to be noise. But this noise was not an end in itself. It was a way to push negotiations along. Of course, this had characterized the physics of the movement from the beginning. But those who made the noise and those who negotiated behind closed doors were so invested in their own roles that they tended to ignore the importance of the other. It took a unifying figure like Shcharansky to state the obvious. He presented the threat that Jewish emigration posed to the Soviet system in very cold terms. "It's simply dangerous for this system," he told a group of editors and reporters at the *New York Times*. "It threatens the very principles on which this system is based."

His visit coincided with the annual Solidarity Sunday, which saw the biggest turnout of its fifteen-year history. Three hundred thousand people crowded into Dag Hammarskjold Plaza to see Shcharansky, dressed in a white button-down shirt and white cap, standing on a red-carpeted platform. Here he made a point of talking about not just Jewish support, but also the support of human rights activists. "As a Zionist and a Jew, I support universal justice, the call from Sinai," he said. "We must never forget Sakharov and Orlov, who raised their voices for Soviet Jewry."

Speaking to a group of a hundred American Jewish leaders, he emphasized the public protest part of his approach. And he got specific. That spring, there was talk of a Washington summit that might take place the following winter. Shcharansky wanted Gorbachev to be greeted by a massive demonstration. "While President Reagan can use quiet diplomacy, American Jews should not take this approach," he scolded the leaders. "When Mikhail Gorbachev arrives in Washington for talks, at least 400,000 Americans should come to Washington to remind the Kremlin that 400,000 Soviet Jews who have applied to leave the Soviet Union have been denied exit visas. The solidarity of American Jewry with Soviet Jewry is the brightest example that we Jews all over the world are one people." On the face of it, this seemed like a crazy proposition—and many of the leaders that day snickered under their breath or worried about Shcharansky raising expectations they could never possibly meet. The biggest rally in Washington for Soviet Jewry had been twelve thousand people—for Brezhnev's 1973 visit—and it was bound to embarrass the Jewish establishment if Shcharansky, still glorified as a hero, set an unreasonably high bar. But it was also unclear just what the objectives of such a massive protest would be. No one wanted to condemn the Reagan administration. The president and his staff were pushing Soviet Jewry harder than any of his predecessors had. Maybe they would march against Gorbachev? But he too seemed to be moving in the right direction, even challenging hard-line Communist forces in order to continue with his liberalization project. Protesting him directly might be counterproductive. Would it be a celebration of what had been accomplished? Or would a party be premature? Shcharansky's suggestion was intriguing. But these leaders would first have to understand what the point of rallying so many American Jews was.

The visit to America solidified Shcharansky's position as the leader of the Soviet Jewry movement. He made a ceremonial trip to Washington—looking itchy and uncomfortable in a suit and tie, his first in more than twenty years. He picked up a Congressional Gold Medal at a ceremony in the Capitol, where hundreds of congresspeople—his "accomplices," he flatteringly called them—gave him a ten-minute standing ovation. He spent forty minutes at the White House with Reagan, presenting his views on the Soviet Union and the need for an interplay between public and quiet diplomacy. It was a major triumph for the Soviet Jewry movement, and an unthinkable leap for him personally. Just a decade earlier, he had been an unknown computer scientist in Moscow. Now he was lecturing the American president on how to handle the Soviets. The lecturing continued after the visit, and Shcharansky's views became sought after. Throughout 1986, he set the agenda for the movement, telling the Helsinki Commission what its minimum conditions should be before it signed a concluding document at the Vienna monitoring conference: "The reunion of families by means of Jewish emigration must take place," he told Congress. In addition, "all prisoners of conscience must be released." This became the lowest bar the Soviet Union would have to overcome in order to get what it wanted out of Vienna, including the symbolic victory of a human rights conference in Moscow.

The new emigration law did not impress Shcharansky. Speaking to the neoconservative Heritage Foundation in December 1986, a few days before the freeing of Sakharov, he called it "the most dangerous anti-emigration step of the Soviet Union since 1972, when they tried to stop emigration by taxes on education." He pushed hard, but it seemed like a calculated push, a matter of strategy more than fanaticism. By the beginning of 1987, it was impossible to ignore what was happening in the Soviet Union.

The clearest sign yet that emigration might pick up again was the panic emanating from Israel. The contentious issue of Jews dropping out once they left the Soviet Union had lain dormant since 1980 — though even in those lean years, over 80 percent were still making their way to America. In the meantime, the Israeli government — now with a bit of leverage over Gorbachev — had become increasingly confident, speaking about Soviet Jewry at full volume instead of limiting itself to the subterranean whispers of the Lishka. The unsubstantiated but still strong feeling that Jews would start leaving the Soviet Union in big numbers inspired as much fear as excitement in Israeli leaders. Would any of these emigrants come to Israel? Shimon Peres, speaking in West Berlin early in 1986, ended his appeal for free emigration with this flourish: "Let those who survived move to their destiny. Let our people go — and come!" That *come* was a telling sign of Israeli anxiety.

A year later, in February 1987, new prime minister Yitzhak Shamir made this anxiety manifest. During his first visit to Washington, he stated publicly that he was going to ask Reagan to stop giving refugee status to emigrating Soviet Jews, the policy that had made the drop-out phenomenon possible. Before he could bring this complaint to the Oval Office, Shultz told Shamir what he surely already knew. His hard-line position had no support among American Jews—it was even criticized by groups like the Zionist Organization of America, which reflexively backed every Israeli policy. Not to mention the Soviet Jewry organizations, which across the board reiterated that they favored free choice. Natan Shcharansky spoke for many refuseniks and activists when he said, "I have no doubt that the best place for a Jew to live is in Israel. But I don't want anyone brought here against his will." Still, Shamir, not known as a particularly couth operator on the world stage, was unrelenting. He took his argument to American Jewish audiences, telling them that he saw the American policy as an "insult." These Soviet Jews were not refugees. They had a home. He won no converts with his Zionist argument, which he must have realized denigrated American Jews as well: "Our struggle is not to change for our brethren one place of dispersion for another." Shamir left empty-handed but he was not bothered. To him this was just a start. He wanted to trigger a debate. Shamir and, presumably, his unity government of left and right were willing to risk alienating Reagan and American Jewish donors to make his point—even with just 904 Jews emigrating that year. Clearly, he believed that Soviet Jews were standing on one side of a dam that was about the break.

Yosef Begun, the Hebrew teacher then entering the fourth of his seven-year prison term, noticed something unusual in the first weeks of 1987. For more than a year, he had been imprisoned at Chistopol, officially a punishment jail for the hardest political prisoner cases (Anatoly Marchenko had recently died there, succumbing to his hunger strike), after he'd spent time at the Perm labor camp. At the beginning of February, each of these political prisoners had been brought one by one into the office of the camp director, asked to renounce any future "anti-social" behavior, and then told they were going to be freed as part of Gorbachev's new reforms. Begun saw the prison begin to empty out. At first he refused to sign the statement committing him to a quiet life once he was released. But after negotiations that dragged on for a month, he too was put on a train and sent back to Moscow. When he left, he was the last person in Chistopol who'd been imprisoned for "anti-Soviet activity."

Begun arrived at Kazan station still wearing his prison outfit, a padded blue cotton jacket over a brown jumpsuit that had his name sewn onto the chest. His wife, Inna, and son, Boris, who had traveled the five hundred miles to collect him from the prison, helped him down. Begun smiled widely. Most of his teeth were missing. Enormous square glasses sat on his face, and he had a thick beard. Even though he was fifty-five, he looked at least a decade older. Begun could hardly believe how different this Moscow was from the one he had left. Formerly a place of desolation with no way out, the signs of liberalization were everywhere, especially that winter.

Begun's release, and that of 140 other political prisoners including almost all of the Hebrew teachers and other Jewish activists locked up in the recent crackdown, was part of a wide range of initiatives announced by Gorbachev at the beginning of the year to boost glasnost and perestroika. The large-scale amnesty was the biggest prisoner release since Khrushchev came into office and emptied Stalin's Gulag. Unknown to anyone outside the Politburo, the Kremlin had also decided to stop prosecuting citizens under Articles 70 and 190, the infamous criminal codes used against dissidents and religious activists. Gorbachev hosted a glittering three-day event at the Kremlin, the International Forum for a Non-Nuclear World and the Survival of Humanity, for which he flew in and put up hundreds of Western celebrities (including Yoko Ono, Gore Vidal, and Gregory Peck). Andrei Sakharov was given a front-row seat. Gorbachev announced that the jamming of the BBC and other major Western stations would end (though stations like Radio Liberty and Radio Free Europe that had purposely been established to play a propaganda role in the Cold War were still blocked). His plans for democratization made headway, and at the Communist Central Committee plenum, he won support for a proposal to have multiple candidates and secret ballots in local party elections. Even non-Party members could run. Disarmament was making progress as well. Gorbachev had decided to untie the contentious knot that had led to stalemate at Reykjavik. He said he was willing to make a separate arms deal that didn't include ending the Star Wars program, opening the way for a major arms agreement. The historical reawakening that had begun in 1986 continued apace, with newspaper and journal sales exploding. Every week brought some new revelation, slowly filling in the vast gaps of the past seventy years. "There should be no forgotten names or blank spaces, either in history or literature," Gorbachev declared.

For the refuseniks, hardened by so many years of fruitless waiting, a restrained, cautious optimism took over. In the flush of new proposals and sweeping pronouncements, a few different Soviet officials had said publicly in early March that the Kremlin envisioned anywhere from ten thousand to twelve thousand Jews emigrating that year. They wanted to resolve the longest refusenik cases. The ultimate indicator was the monthly emigration figures, which had been in the double digits since 1980. Now they were suddenly, dramatically rising. Ninety-eight left in January and 146 the next month. Then in March, nearly five hundred Soviet Jews emigrated. This was by far the highest monthly figure in more than five years. These were mostly long-standing refuseniks from the list of eleven thousand handed to the Soviets at Reykjavik. They would get calls from OVIR inviting them to come in and resubmit their applications. And then they would get permission.

In the refusenik community that spring, not a week passed without a farewell party, frenzied get-togethers with lots of vodka and cheek kissing and the passing of notes and information for relatives abroad. Many did begin to feel hopeful. But others became frantic that they would somehow be left out, that Gorbachev was tricking them, just offering a small carrot to the West that would soon be chewed up. Hunger strikes proliferated in March, a form of protest but also an expression of this anxiety. Some of the refuseniks were afraid that they were in a fleeting period of warmth, just like 1979, and that if they didn't do something dramatic, it might just pass them by. A well-organized group of seventy-five Jewish women in nine cities across the Soviet Union, from Riga to Baku, collectively abstained from food for three days. One young refusenik fasted for more than forty days. Another demonstrated by sitting cross-legged in the middle of Pushkin Square until his sign demanding an exit visa was torn up by a group of young men.

The rate of emigration—still modest by 1970s standards—was not the only indicator of change. The oppressive atmosphere suddenly seemed to lift. In February, activists in Moscow thought that Yosef Begun was not going to be included in the general prisoner amnesty, and about twenty people held a series of protests led by Begun's son Boris on the Arbat shopping promenade. For two days, they were left alone. They arrived with their signs, marched up and down Moscow's most fashionable outdoor mall, elicited some catcalls and shouts about what Hitler should have done, and then packed up. This in itself felt like an achievement of glasnost. Some bystanders were even supportive. But then, on the third day, a group of a hundred plainclothes KGB agents tried to break up the protest, aggressively striking out at both the refuseniks and reporters covering them, cutting the wire to the ABC television crew's camera. A journalist for the London *Times* was present and described how the violent scene escalated: "After being punched, jostled, and abused by burly men in plain clothes—many wearing identical tartan scarves—I was present as they repeatedly kicked a female refusenik in the breasts and kidney as she screamed in agony and pleaded for help from a uniformed policeman, who looked on with studied indifference." Boris Begun and two other men were detained and charged with hooliganism but never forced to serve the fifteen-day detention. The brutal response was reminiscent of Brezhnev's darkest days, except that immediately after the incident was over, the foreign ministry tried to distance itself, claiming that the attack was simply the "arbitrary action of local residents." A month later, gathering at a spot on Moscow's busy Garden Ring Road, a group of thirty refuseniks protested with placards around their necks day after day. Nobody bothered them. For the first time, a protest—in the past no more than thirty seconds of banner waving before arrest—was allowed to proceed uninterrupted. Policemen simply smiled at them.

In Leningrad that March, a few of the more active refuseniks decided they too would test the limits of glasnost. Misha Beizer, who had been leading the dissident Soviet Jewish history tours through Leningrad and publishing his samizdat *Leningrad Jewish Almanac,* decided to hold a demonstration. He sensed that something was changing and thought this was the time to fight. He wanted to organize a big protest, something that would force the local authorities to act. But almost everyone in the activist community was too scared to take part. In the end he managed to gather only seven people, including Aba and Ida Taratuta, the godfather and godmother of Leningrad's refusenik community, to stand with him in the cold near the bronze bust of Marx at the entrance to the Smolny Institute, Leningrad headquarters of the Communist Party. Beizer was sure they would be arrested; changes in Leningrad were occurring much more slowly than in Moscow. He wore used clothes to the protest and didn't cut his hair or trim his beard—he knew that in prison they would give him a uniform and shave him. As soon as they took their places, carrying placards above their heads, the local police surrounded them. But rather than arrest them, they shielded them from the growing crowd so that passersby couldn't see them. Then the protesters were informed that an official would speak with them. They agreed, but on condition that they be allowed to stand for two hours in protest. After freezing in the snow, they were brought in and introduced to the third secretary of the Leningrad district Party committee, the head of the local OVIR office. The protesters made their case, all the while sure that any moment they would be taken away. But they weren't. The next day the tiny demonstration was even covered in one of the Leningrad newspapers, with a photo. The Soviets were now openly promoting the fact that they allowed dissent. A couple of days after the protest, Beizer received a phone call from OVIR. They were inviting him to renew his application. A month later he was in Israel. The Leningrad protest led to two more that spring, each with a larger crowd.

At the beginning of April, during Passover, the American embassy hosted a Seder. It had been doing so for a few years as a small, symbolic gesture, serving matzo ball soup in the enormous czarist-era ballroom of the neoclassically grand Spaso house. This year, all the well-known refuseniks were present. Vladimir and Masha Slepak had just completed a seventeen-day hunger strike to mark their seventeenth year of refusal. Yosef Begun, slowly gaining weight and strength, was there. Alexander Lerner and Naum Meiman, both in their seventies, were given places of honor. Victor Brailovsky, his exile in Kazakhstan over, sat at one of the dozen tables. Ida Nudel had flown in from Bendery. The Seder began with the reading of the Haggadah. Then, about halfway through, George Shultz walked through the door, a yarmulke on his head.

The secretary of state was in Moscow for discussions with Shevardnadze and Gorbachev and had made much of the fact that he would be attending the Seder. When he arrived, he began to walk slowly around the room. He seemed to know the names of every refusenik. Shultz knelt down by the Slepaks and gave them a photograph of their grandchildren, whom they had never met. He appeared sincerely moved and inspired by what he saw as the great courage of these activists. When he addressed the refuseniks, it was with rare emotion in his voice. "You are on our minds; you are in our hearts," he told them. Then he channeled Winston Churchill's famous speech: "We never give up, we never stop trying, and in the end some good things do happen. But never give up, never give up. And please note that there are people all over the world, not just in the United States, who think about you and wish you well and are on your side." Once the Seder was over and Shultz and most of the refuseniks had left, the Slepaks and Alexander Lerner stayed up late into the night at the embassy discussing the problems of Soviet Jews with Richard Schifter, the assistant secretary of state for human rights, who was now regarded by the refuseniks as a good friend.

Shultz's visit was well publicized—Western journalists and television cameras covered the event—and Gorbachev was annoyed. At a meeting the following day, the general secretary asked Shultz why he dealt "only with a certain group of Jews, people who do not like it here and have complaints, and show no interest in the millions of other Soviet Jews, who are out of your field of vision." Shultz answered, as he had in the past, that he would be glad to take those unhappy Jews back home with him. "I've got a deal for you. I've got a great big airplane. If you don't want them, there isn't a person in my party, including the reporters, that wouldn't give up his seat for those people. And you can just put them all on and get rid of them if you don't want them. We'll take them."

Gorbachev ignored this comment, but it demonstrated just how serious the United States was about dealing with this problem before anything else. Shultz used his visit to try to continue an intellectual conversation about liberalization with Gorbachev and, even more so, with Shevardnadze, which he had begun before Geneva. Shultz had become personally close to the congenial Georgian-born foreign minister and even sang a version of "Georgia on My Mind" to him during an informal lunch, a joking gift that was followed by a quartet singing a Russian rendition. The argument that Shultz continued to make to him was that the freedom of individuals was in the Soviet Union's own interest, a necessary evolution for any country hoping to keep up in a changing world. "The degree of constraint that you now exercise over information flows, economic opportunities, and consumer choices will not permit sufficient development of the human potential needed to keep pace with more open societies," he told Shevardnadze the evening after the Seder. "There is no way to get there from here without lifting many of the restraints you place on your people." Shultz told him that though he didn't see a change on human rights as a "concession to the United States," it would "build support among the American people for further improvements in our relations." Shevardnadze and Gorbachev were listening.

The rapid changes in the Soviet Union seemed to arrive overnight. It was disorienting, especially to those who for so long had thought of the Communist empire as fundamentally malevolent. Although faced with the reality that political prisoners were being freed, human rights championed, protests permitted, and emigration rates rising —reaching 717 for the month of April and 871 in May—the skeptics continued to insist that the West was being duped. There could be no other explanation. Gorbachev was simply more artful than his predecessors. Still, it was hard not to see the signs of genuine progress that were staring American Jews in the face in the late spring and summer of 1987.

This encouraged those who saw quiet diplomacy as the answer. The billionaire diplomat with the Soviets' ear, Edgar Bronfman, decided to take another trip to Moscow to see his contacts in the Kremlin. And this time he brought Morris Abram with him. The two were an unlikely pair—the former civil rights lawyer from Georgia and the privileged son of a Canadian bootlegger. Abram, who wielded more power than any other American Jewish leader—and was more connected to the Reagan administration—had resented Bronfman's attempts over the past few years to act in the name of the Jewish people while not actually being accountable to anyone. As chairman of the National Conference, Abram had to be more responsive to the community, and this often forced him to vacillate between an aggressive approach and a conciliatory one. Bronfman, on the other hand, was more business-minded and quick to compromise with the Soviets. The two had frequently sparred on the letters pages of the *New York Times* over the issue of repealing Jackson-Vanik, with Bronfman encouraging American Jews to make the first move, eliminating the trade restrictions as a goodwill gesture, and Abram demanding the Soviets act first if they wanted to be rewarded. But in spite of this rivalry, each had something to gain from the other. The Soviets listened to Bronfman because of his wealth. And Abram, as the respected head of the official Soviet Jewry organization, had a legitimacy that Bronfman could not buy. Traveling together served both their interests.

They arrived in Moscow in late March, carrying in their plane an electrocardiograph for the refuseniks as well as two knives for the kosher slaughter of animals. Anatoly Dobrynin, now back in Moscow leading the government's international department, was initially reluctant to include Abram in the discussions—understanding the symbolic significance of meeting the head of an organization called the National Conference on Soviet Jewry—but he eventually relented. The talks involved Dobrynin and Alexander Yakovlev, one of the more reform-minded advisers in Gorbachev's inner circle, and were genial (at one point Dobrynin told Abram not to worry about the new emigration laws, which, he said, were meant "to expand emigration, not to restrict it"). After their negotiations, the Americans gathered a group of thirty refuseniks in a hotel room, including the recently released Yosef Begun, and told them what they had managed to extract: all the long-term refusenik cases would be resolved within the year, with the exception of real national security threats; as many as twelve thousand Soviet Jews would emigrate in the short term by direct flights to Israel that would go through Romania; and more Jewish cultural expression would be allowed, including the unhindered study of Hebrew, the addition of a kosher restaurant near the Moscow synagogue, facilitation of rabbinical training outside the Soviet Union, and accommodations for kashrut. The agreement on direct flights through Romania was particularly noteworthy, as it effectively eliminated the dropout problem by bypassing Western Europe altogether and removing an escape route to the United States. In exchange for these promises, Abram and Bronfman had pledged that they would recommend a repeal of both the Jackson-Vanik and Stevenson amendments so that the Soviets could freely get credit and trade at a lower tariff.

The refuseniks and grassroots activists immediately attacked the Bronfman-Abram trip as an act of hubris and naiveté. Alexander Ler-

ner, sitting in the two men's hotel room as they described their dealings, could not believe that they hadn't first consulted the people
they were supposedly representing. Lerner was sure the two had been
fooled by wily Soviet leaders. A few of the most prominent refuseniks,
including Lerner, Kosharovsky, and Slepak, wrote a letter addressed to
"the leadership of the state of Israel and Jewish organizations of the
Diaspora." Even though recent developments "show that now real possibilities have appeared to lead out of the cul-de-sac the entire complex
of Jewish national problems," they were disturbed by the lack of any
consultation with them before the meeting, which, they wrote, could
have prevented "many possible side effects." In America, the reaction
was equally fierce. Pamela Cohen, a Chicago housewife who had gotten involved locally and then risen to the top of the Union of Councils, was indignant on behalf of the thousands of Soviet Jewry activists
she represented. They believed deeply in the principle of freedom of
choice. And in addition to not involving the Union of Councils in their
negotiations, Bronfman and Abram had cut a deal that would funnel
Jews to Israel without giving them the opportunity to decide if that's
where they wanted to go. It seemed a paternalistic move — American
Jewish leaders telling these Soviet Jews what was good for them — one
that went against the founding principle of the Union of Councils: to
simply represent the interests of the refuseniks in America, to do whatever they wanted.

All through the spring, anger grew, compounded by the general
anxiety of the moment. Would Soviet Jews really be allowed out? And
if so, which ones? And when? The JDL struck again after years of lying dormant. A tear-gas bomb was set off during a performance of
the Bolshoi Ballet at Carnegie Hall. That year's Solidarity Sunday rally
did not match the previous year's numbers, when Shcharansky's first
visit to America drew three hundred thousand people, but it still drew
tens of thousands. Sitting on the stage was Yosef Mendelevich, seething
with resentment at the American Jewish leaders around him. When
Shcharansky, who was again attending the rally, finished his speech,
Mendelevich unexpectedly jumped up and grabbed the microphone.
He began a long rant — most of which was unintelligible in his thick accent — while stabbing his finger in the air and staring at Morris Abram,
who was a few feet away. "I know you have your leaders," Mendelevich shouted. "You elected them. You like them? Have them. But don't

send them anymore to Moscow. They don't know how to deal with the Russians." The interruption caused an embarrassing commotion, shattering the appearance of "solidarity" as Mendelevich, a hero of the movement, stormed off the stage.

It seems that Abram himself came to regret the March trip. In July, worried that Gorbachev might resolve only the long-term refusenik cases and then shut the door again, he made a damning assessment of Soviet Jews' prospects that put him more in line with the activists' view. "I must conclude that glasnost, as far as the Jewish population is concerned, at best doesn't exist and at worst is a fraud," he said after a meeting with George Shultz. Gorbachev was deceiving the American people and Jews with "blandishments and soft soap."

Even so, by the time Abram uttered these comments, many of the promises that had been made to him had been realized. Six Jews were given permission to travel to the United States to study for the rabbinate and then return, presumably to open more synagogues. A few months later, for the first time since 1929, kosher food was available in Moscow, imported from Hungary and served at a modest canteen near the Arkhipova Street synagogue. The synagogue was allowed to receive a shipment from abroad of five thousand works of scripture in Hebrew and Russian. A retired Red Army officer, Yuri Sokol, opened up a small Jewish library in a room of his home. He invited local Communist Party officials to a tour, showed them the books on the shelves and the posters with the Hebrew alphabet on the wall. All they did was give him their blessing. In July, a Soviet consular delegation visited Israel for the first time in twenty years to continue discussing the normalization of relations. On the same plane arriving in Tel Aviv was Yuli Edelstein, the young Hebrew teacher who had been arrested on trumped-up charges of illegal drug possession. His release meant there was only one more Prisoner of Zion left in a labor camp, Alexei Magarik, also imprisoned on drug charges. The pale, thin cellist and Hebrew teacher finally returned to Moscow from his Siberian prison in early September, and after that there were no longer any Jews serving prison sentences for being Jews.

As the situation of Soviet Jews improved, the other spheres of conflict between the superpowers also began easing. Once Gorbachev agreed to remove Star Wars from the arms reduction talks—effectively conceding that the program would continue—the path was open to negotiating a pact that would eliminate all the intermediate-range nuclear missiles from Europe. In September, on another trip to Moscow, George Shultz finalized the details of what would be a major de-escalation of the arms race. Reagan and Gorbachev could finally have their first official summit. The Soviet Jewry movement in all its varied manifestations had been waiting for this moment. Shcharansky had continued to call for four hundred thousand American Jews to greet Gorbachev in Washington, which unnerved Jewish leaders. Though there was no clear date yet, a coordinator was chosen. David Harris was emotionally formed by the Soviet Jewry movement and seemed to embody its myriad strains, fusing them together in a single whole. He was one of the few people who could hope to come close to Shcharansky's grand vision.

Harris was tall and gangly, a bespectacled Jimmy Stewart; a Jewish professional in his thirties, he had already acquired a reputation for extreme competence. But it was his recent past that made him interesting and in many ways more in touch with the Jewish grass roots than his colleagues. When he was chosen to coordinate the rally, he was running the American Jewish Committee's Washington office. Harris had grown up in the liberal, cosmopolitan enclave of the Upper West Side, surrounded by a very self-assured Jewish community. This allowed him to take his Jewishness for granted—identity was a combination of bagels, synagogue twice a year, and, especially, the foreign languages that his parents spoke. He was the first of his family to be born in America, and as a child he learned Russian and French—his grandparents had fled the Soviet Union for Paris after the revolution. This superficial Jewish identity changed, however, on a trip to Israel, where he gazed jealously at the soldiers, boys the same age as he was who could serve in an army and, it seemed, actively engage in making history. He had the quintessential conversion moment—one shared by a group of NASA scientists in Cleveland—when as a graduate student at the London School of Economics, he discovered Arthur Morse's sensational *While Six Million Died*. He was shocked at the passivity of American Jews and began learning as much as he could about the wartime period and what he came to see as the community's shameful behavior.

This new sense of responsibility to his people was galvanized when he got a rare chance to live in the Soviet Union in 1974 on an exchange program for teachers. He never intended for it to happen, but the time spent with refuseniks ended up being the most meaningful part of this experience. In Moscow, he spent his Saturdays at the synagogue on Arkhipova. He spoke Russian, and this allowed him a rare entrée into the lives of Soviet Jews, who seemed to pull him in. One day he was walking down the hall of a school in Leningrad where he taught when a young girl passed by and slipped a note into his hand. He went to the bathroom, locked himself in an empty stall, and read: "David Harris, I think you are a Jew. I feel it. If I'm right, please know that my parents are refuseniks. Would you come to our house one day after school?" After three months in the Soviet Union fraternizing with refuseniks, Harris was detained near the Moscow synagogue and then kicked out of the country.

He could not abandon what now felt like a mission. From Moscow he made his way to Rome, where Soviet Jews waited to receive visas to the United States. There he began working for HIAS, processing new arrivals and quickly seeing the flaws in the system. He worried that these refugees were not getting any kind of introduction to the world that was about to engulf them. So Harris composed a manual in Russian, *Entering a New Culture*, that gave information about America, and then he worked on a second book, *The Jewish World*, which tried to expose them to all the elements of Jewish civilization that had been closed to them for so long. In the process of researching and putting the book together, he realized that he needed to learn more himself. He was not the first American Jew to be struck with this epiphany: how could he ask these new immigrants to embrace a Jewish identity if his own knowledge was so cursory?

After several years in Rome and then a stint at the main reception center in Vienna—meeting thousands of Soviet Jews—Harris came back to America and took a job with the American Jewish Committee. Although he loved working on the ground, directly with people, the Jewish organizational world offered the chance to make an even greater impact. He was the perfect choice to lead the rally. Soviet Jewry had played a big role in his intellectual evolution—in the mid-1980s he had even compiled a book of Soviet Jewish humor, *The Jokes of Op-*

pression—he had legitimacy with the grassroots activists of the Union of Councils, and he was recognized by the Park Avenue Jewish leaders as one of their own.

On October 30, Shevardnadze arrived in Washington for talks with Reagan. At the end of the day, the president, flanked by Shultz and Shevardnadze, announced that the summit would take place on December 7 in Washington and would last for three days. To Reagan's disappointment, the Soviets wouldn't go for his original plan of taking Gorbachev on a countrywide tour that ended at his California ranch. But he could take pleasure in finally signing the intermediate-range nuclear forces treaty, which would diffuse the tense nuclear standoff in Europe. A few hours later, Harris announced that American Jews would hold a giant rally on Sunday, December 6, the day before the start of the summit. This gave him thirty-seven days to make concrete what until then had only been an abstract vision. He had to quickly find an answer to the question of what exactly the rally would be about. What point were American Jews trying to make at this moment when progress was clearly visible?

Everyone was leaving. At least that's how it felt to the tight community of refuseniks. Every day seemed to bring another phone call from OVIR. It started in early September when Yosef Begun was given an exit visa, along with other long-term refuseniks like Victor Brailovsky. And then it did not stop. Some refuseniks were so anxious and excited that they literally sat by the phone all day. Naum Meiman, seventy-six and now a widower (his wife had succumbed to cancer three weeks after she'd finally arrived in the United States for special medical treatment), stared at the receiver with anticipation. His only child and most of his friends had recently left. Now he had nothing to do but wait. All through the fall, exit visas cascaded out of OVIR. And soon it wasn't only long-term refuseniks who were part of the nearly nine hundred people a month leaving. Richard Schifter had received reports from Vienna that some of the newer applicants had lied to OVIR about having close relatives in Israel, but no one had tried to verify their claims. Accompanying George Shultz on a trip to Moscow that October, Schifter asked his counterpart if this meant that the Soviets had altered their new emigration policy, which contained strict guidelines about who could be counted as family. "We are now being flexible," the Russian said with a smile. Schifter left Moscow feeling for the first time that the Soviets—at least those in the foreign ministry—had turned from adversaries to allies. They were now working together to help convince the other government agencies that more people should be let out more quickly.

In early October, Ida Nudel went to Moscow to see if she could get a residence permit to move back there. As soon as she arrived, she received a call from her village back in Moldavia. The police there were looking for her. They had a summons from OVIR: her exit visa was waiting. Nudel didn't believe it. She couldn't believe it. Surely, they were trying to fool her. She called the central OVIR and to her astonishment was patched through to Rudolf Kuznetsov, the head of the whole agency. He told her it was true, she was really leaving. In Nudel's excitement, she began thanking him profusely. Only afterward did she curse herself for the kind words. How could she have forgotten that they had made her wait for sixteen years for this moment? She was in a frenzy, overwhelmed and excited. The next few days whirled by. The agents of OVIR seemed intent on getting her out of the country within two weeks, helping her gather all the necessary documents. As her departure got closer, she was presented with a strange request. Would she be willing to fly to Israel aboard the private plane of Armand Hammer, the eighty-nine-year-old billionaire head of Occidental Petroleum who had close ties to the Communists (going back to Lenin)? He had asked the Soviet leaders for this favor. Nudel agreed, and she and her collie, Pizer, began preparing for the trip.

The Slepaks' phone rang on the afternoon of October 13. Masha picked up and a representative of OVIR asked to speak to Volodya. When she said he wasn't home, the man on the line asked if she was Maria Isakovna. "Yes," she told him. He introduced himself and then said the words she had been waiting since 1971 to hear: "You are granted permission to leave the USSR." She was to go tomorrow to the OVIR office to get the card listing the documents she needed in order to obtain her visa. She too was in disbelief. How could something they had all struggled for, anguished over, dreamed about for so long be resolved in a phone call? It was the same feeling the next day when Volodya held in his hands the small slip of paper—just a piece of paper—that promised him an exit visa. How could this be? They had endured exile, seen their children leave, missed the births of their grandchildren—all for this slip of paper? After they left OVIR, jubilant and a little disoriented, they went to a goodbye party for Ida Nudel at a restaurant called the Vilnius. Volodya walked in waving the paper from OVIR. Everyone knew what it meant. The room filled with cheering and crying. A close friend rushed to embrace him, and Volodya could feel the man's tears against his cheek.

The arrival in Israel of Ida Nudel and then the Slepaks sparked emotional media events. The very names of these activists had become touchstones for Jews all over the world. Like Shcharansky, they were symbols, living embodiments of the struggle. And now they were free. There was no more visceral proof than this that some deep change was taking place—despite the hard-liners' continued claims that the wool was being pulled over everyone's eyes. American Jews and Israelis watched on television as Nudel, her gray hair held back, her dog in her arms, walked down the stairs of Armand Hammer's Boeing 707 and was embraced by the sister she hadn't seen in fifteen years. Even Jane Fonda was standing there to receive her. "For me it is the moment," Nudel told the cameras, big tears streaming down her cheeks. "It is the moment of my life. I am at home. I am on the soil of my people. Now I am an absolutely free person among my own people." Soon after landing she was connected by phone to George Shultz, who had recently met her at the Seder in Moscow. "This is Ida Nudel. I'm in Jerusalem," she told him, then paused. "I'm home." Shultz couldn't explain the rush of emotion he suddenly felt. Later he described this as one of the most meaningful moments of his tenure.

On their flight from Vienna, the Slepaks opened a bottle of champagne when they saw Tel Aviv in the distance. Masha would not let go of her son Sanya, whom she had not seen in ten years. Volodya looked out the window at the blue of the Mediterranean Sea as it lapped up against the Israeli coastline. He could still not believe his struggle had ended. Two weeks later they flew to the United States, where at John F. Kennedy Airport they met their five grandchildren for the first time.

Scenes of reunion, images of redemption, proliferated that fall, most of them much less public. One by one, the people who had given the last decade or two of their lives to open the doors were getting out. Ironically, these activists were the last people willing to accept that their departures held a deeper meaning about the direction of the Soviet Union. "If they do something, it is a concession made under the pressure of the West," Volodya Slepak said during a press conference in Vienna, his first words after leaving the Soviet Union. "If there were no pressure or if the Soviet Union was strong enough, they would do nothing. . . . They are tyrants." And for all the prominent people leaving, there were many who were still stuck. It took another two months before Alexander Lerner, the grandfatherly doyen of the refuseniks, received his exit visa. At the end of 1987, the few activists who were left, like Yuli Kosharovsky, felt that their struggle had gotten much lonelier.

At the same time, the space for unhindered protest continued to expand. In November, a group of a hundred refuseniks gathered in the apartment of Vladimir Kislik for a conference to discuss the problem of state secrecy, the most common excuse for denying exit visas. The symposium met for three days without interruption. Kislik, who twenty-one years before had worked at a plutonium production plant and was first refused an exit visa in 1973, bore into the issue with legalistic acuity and led an attempt to devise a more rational policy. Also in November, a former refusenik, Alexander Goldfarb, paid a return visit to Moscow. Goldfarb had left in 1975—his job as unofficial spokesman of the refuseniks was the one Shcharansky took over—and he eventually became a professor of microbiology at Columbia University. The fact that he was allowed to come back as a tourist after twelve years was shocking to the Moscow activists and dissidents. Goldfarb himself saw his visit as a "test case," as he later put it in a long essay in the *New York Times Magazine.* Though he thought the forces of glasnost and perestroika were moving too slowly and headed for a terrible confrontation with a vast Communist bureaucracy unwilling to part with its centralized power, he had to admit that "the socio-ideological atmosphere in Moscow" had been completely transformed. In anecdote after anecdote, he showed how people were vastly freer to express themselves and were doing so, voicing frustration that their material lives had not improved as promised.

As part of glasnost, Gorbachev had permitted the founding of nongovernmental organizations. By the fall of 1987, over thirty thousand had been created, reflecting the full range of Soviet society. On one end was Memorial, a group of young dissidents who initially came together to try to build a memorial to the victims of Stalin and ended up supporting the clear-eyed examination of Soviet history. And then there was Pamyat (Russian for "memory"). Started in May as a "historical and patriotic association," the group was almost uniquely and virulently focused on the "Zionist (that is Jewish) Masonic conspiracy" against the Russian people. At increasingly loud demonstrations with hundreds of Muscovites, Pamyat leaders blamed Jews for every ill of Soviet society, promoting the oldest of anti-Semitic conspiracy theories. The most disturbing aspect of the group was that it seemed to have the support of some conservative elements in the government who were angry at the fast pace of Gorbachev's reforms.

It was beginning to look like this new freedom might contain as many dangers as the old authoritarian system had. Soviet Jews glanced around at the end of 1987. They saw the sudden opening up of emigration and heard the stories of friends and family who had started new lives. Set against the uncertainty of a society whose foundation was shifting beneath their feet, leaving became a viable option even for those who had never considered it before. They began to reassess—just as refuseniks had for the last twenty years—whether Russia could ever really be their home or if they had to look elsewhere.

While he was planning for the Washington rally, David Harris had the thought, ironic though it was, that his job would be much easier if things were worse for Soviet Jews. He still faced the challenge of fashioning an appropriate theme for the rally. A consensus, however, soon emerged, almost universally accepted even by the activists, that the gathering should not be a protest but rather a way of offering encouragement to Reagan and reminding Gorbachev that they were still there, watching. The rally would be positive, celebratory, a show of unity bringing together the entire community and the many elements that made up the movement. For this reason, it would take place the day before the start of the summit so as not to distract or impede what they saw as a good process. With the first nuclear disarmament agreement in the history of the Cold War on the table, they didn't want to be seen as spoilers.

As November progressed and Harris and his many collaborators spread the word, the event began to take on a life of its own. Maybe it was because Shcharansky himself traveled from city to city for weeks trying to drum up participation, and his presence was persuasive. But thousands of rabbis pleaded with their congregations to go. Little girls saved up their babysitting money. Jewish groups from as far away as Anchorage, Alaska, chartered planes. It was as if the community's collective identity depended on making sure there was a respectable number of Jews present when Gorbachev arrived. All the elements that had animated the movement from the beginning, from Holocaust guilt and anti-Communism to tribal identity and humanist principles, all coalesced and hurtled toward Washington.

This momentum did not facilitate Harris's task. Working with a budget of half a million dollars collected from local Jewish federations all over the country, he still had to find a way to make the rally represent the wide coalition of people it was bringing together. The National Conference and the Union of Councils were cooperating with each other, which was a big achievement in itself. The organizers had unanimously agreed to avoid criticizing the administration, especially for its rejection of any kind of formal linkage between arms deals and human rights. The speakers needed to be on the same page about this. And most were. The only problem was the refuseniks. Harris let them decide for themselves who would speak, amused that there were as many divisions among them as among the American groups. Mendelevich, still considered a brave early leader, was chosen as one of the few who would address the rally, and there was no question that he would speak his mind in aggressive terms, as he had at Solidarity Sunday. Avi Weiss and Student Struggle were even planning to engage with him in some act of civil disobedience, convinced that the gathering would be too docile.

Harris also had to deal with the question of political representation. He had initially invited Jane Fonda and Mary Travers of Peter, Paul, and Mary. But both women had histories of being perceived as supporting Communist forces (Fonda in Hanoi, Travers in Managua) and their presence would alienate the right. There was talk of disinviting them, but then Fonda canceled and Harris came up with another solution. One of his fellow organizers called Pearl Bailey, the black singer who also happened to be Republican. She would provide some balance. This triggered another problem. It was against Orthodox Jewish law for a woman to sing in public. Would Bailey alienate the Orthodox members of the audience? These complexities went on and on. In addition to all this, the rally was going to take place on a freezing December day. Would the weather keep people away? Even though all reports indicated a big turnout, Harris was kept up at night by the thought that a pathetically small group of Jews would show up and the Soviets would be able to laugh them off. So insecure were the organizers that they were only willing to predict that it would be the biggest rally ever in the capital for a Jewish cause, which wasn't saying much.

As it turned out, tens of thousands arrived, by the busload and planeload and trainload, and then tens of thousands more. In New York City alone, eleven hundred buses were chartered, nearly the entire fleet of available buses in the city. Three jumbo jets full of Jews from Chicago arrived. Every place with a sizable Jewish population was represented, from Houston to Palm Beach to Orange County. And these were not all activists—in fact, the majority weren't. They were just ordinary American Jews, most of whom had never marched for anything as Jews. They simply felt compelled, swept up by the feeling that they could make some collective statement just by being there. Parents wanted to bring their children. Lenore Weinstein from Minneapolis captured the mood of many of those making the trek. Walking with her two children and husband, she said, "We came here for the weekend to give our children an education. I feel much more strongly about this than I did during the war in Vietnam. Then I felt very American, but now I feel very American and very Jewish."

They came pouring down Constitution Avenue and onto the National Mall, dressed warmly in parkas and jackets, scarves and hats. There were older women in full-length furs, and babies swaddled in their strollers. A strong sun burned off some of the cold. People carried banners that included the names of the cities they represented, such as "Houston Stands Tall for Soviet Jewry." Children had the names of their Soviet bar or bat mitzvah twins taped to their shirts. It was hard to believe that the vast ocean of people stretching out in all directions was here for a Jewish cause. A quarter of a million people had shown up, far exceeding David Harris's most hopeful expectation.

The program was perfectly choreographed and projected onto large screens. First, Morris Abram read a supportive letter from the president. Then Pearl Bailey stretched out her arms and sang the spiritual "Let

My People Go." A roster of speakers followed. Harris tried to keep everyone's comments short, setting up stage lights that would flash when
time was up, but it was useless. Even the rabbi giving the invocation,
which he'd promised would take up no more than ninety seconds, decided to make his own remarks, speaking for four minutes. Most of the
main political contenders for the following year's presidential election
were there. Vice President George Bush, the early but widely acknowledged front-runner, gave a forceful speech that echoed Reagan's recent
exhortation to Gorbachev to tear down the Berlin Wall: "Let's see not
five or six or 10 or 20 refuseniks released at a time, but thousands, tens
of thousands. Mr. Gorbachev, let these people go!" Ed Koch went un-
scripted and as usual made a gaffe by saying that Gorbachev was acting like "Joe Stalin." John Lewis represented the civil rights movement.
Elie Wiesel reminded everyone who wasn't already thinking about it
that this type of mass gathering had not happened during the Holocaust—or ever. "Too many of us were silent then. We are not silent
today." Then a group of refuseniks spoke. All the prominent activists,
people who had only been known as names and depressed faces on
posters, were there, and it was stirring to see them all, some with large
fur hats on their heads, standing on a stage together: Shcharansky, Nudel, Begun, Slepak. Mendelevich, of course, broke away from the day's
otherwise upbeat tone and yelled, "Linkage, linkage, linkage!" into the
microphone during his turn, demanding that the United States not
give an inch until all Jews were freed.

Many questions hung in the freezing air that day. Would the Soviet
Union ever really allow free emigration? That year, eight thousand had
gotten out, a vast improvement over the past decade but nowhere near
the fifty-one thousand that had left in 1979. Would it open the doors
completely? Would Gorbachev be allowed to continue his project of
humanizing the Communist system, or would something stop him?
And if the Soviets did allow the Jews to leave, how many would actually
go? The activists had always assumed that if emigration was unfettered,
hundreds of thousands would choose to make their lives somewhere
else. The number four hundred thousand had been thrown around
for a long time. Would this many leave? And if they did, where would
they go? More than 80 percent of emigrants were now dropping out,
heading to the United States or Western Europe. Was this sustainable?

Would the Israelis succeed, by argument or by force, in making any exodus out of the Soviet Union a Zionist exodus? And if the Israelis didn't, would these Soviet Jews headed to the West remain Jews, or would they assimilate and become Americans or Germans? Would the movement to rescue a Jewish identity succeed or would it prove to be just a dream shared by a few thousand brave activists and not by the vast majority of Soviet Jews?

All these unknowns. And yet, in the closing moments of the rally, with all the people who had given years of their lives to a struggle that felt historic to them — biblical almost — there seemed to be a strong feeling of victory. Yaakov Birnbaum, now in his sixties, sat in a chair in the back, bitter that he had not been given a bigger role. He thought he should get more credit for being the father of this movement. But as he looked at the American Jews stretched out on the Mall as far as he could see, he nevertheless had a sense of fulfillment. This is what he had been struggling for, after all, the idea that Jews would not be afraid to defend other Jews, publicly, loudly, that they should be invested in the survival of their people. And the most stunning aspect of that moment was the feeling of collective strength, the unabashed reveling in their ability, as a community, to turn the attention of the world's two superpowers to their concerns. It simply would have been impossible twenty-five years before.

Yosef Mendelevich was also on the stage, and although he had wanted a greater show of anger at the rally, in the final moments he linked arms with Shcharansky and Ida Nudel, the Slepaks, Yuli Edelstein, and Morris Abram. They sang the "Hatikvah," the Israeli national anthem, and swayed together. Looking out at those thousands upon thousands of freezing people, Mendelevich must have remembered himself as a boy coming across the forest at Rumbuli and seeing for the first time a group of Jews working together, toiling over the ground, smoothing the earth down to make it respectable for the massacred bodies lying beneath it. Back then, he had never seen so many Jews together in one place. And now here he was, looking at all these faces. That same jolt of unfamiliar power he'd felt as a boy, that was here too. They had come to do something together, and they had done it.

Afterword:
Hundreds of Thousands
1988–1991

THAT FALL DAY when the Berlin Wall crumbled under the force of thousands of pickax-wielding Germans was a historic moment that occurred at astonishing speed. The known world flipped on its head in a few hours. By nightfall on November 9, 1989, the Cold War was effectively over. The end of the Soviet Jewry movement, however, was not as swift and unambiguous. Victory accreted slowly with every planeload of Soviet Jews. But from 1988 and into the early 1990s—a relatively short period of time compared with the decades of struggle—the mass of people who left the Soviet Union exceeded even the most optimistic expectations. In 1988, 18,919 Jews left, a modest figure but still more than double the previous year. Then the numbers exploded: 71,196 in 1989; 181,802 in 1990; 178,566 in 1991; 108,292 in 1992; 102,134 in 1993. By the end of the 1990s, more than one million Soviet Jews had emigrated to Israel. Another half a million had gone to the United States, and a couple hundred thousand to other countries in the West, such as Germany. During the years of the protest movement, the activists and refuseniks, sustained mostly by faith, had believed that hundreds of thousands would leave if given the chance. Now came a surge of humanity that fulfilled those dreams: an exodus.

The incredible numbers hid a bumpier denouement. The unity and triumph of the rally in Washington was, in retrospect, a rare moment of grace. The actual arrival in the West of the hundreds of thousands was filled with the intrigue and tension that had characterized the years of struggle. All the familiar conflicts—grass roots versus establishment, American Jews versus Israel, freedom of choice versus Zionism—intensified just as success was finally within reach.

Lost sometimes in these heated ideological debates were the emigrants themselves. They had left their lives and everything they had ever known. The vast majority were not the brave fighters cheered on by the Western world, the Shcharanskys and the Slepaks. They were ordinary people who had seen no future for themselves inside the Soviet Union, who had feared what would follow the collapse of the empire. Most were not Zionists. They were engineers and doctors, physicists and musicians, looking for a better life. They had children and elderly parents. They looked at the Soviet Union in its death throes and saw a place of great political and economic instability. Freedom had unleashed certain demons. Anti-Semitic groups like Pamyat blamed the Jews for the disintegration of their society. They were calling for blood. For the vast—and, until then, silent—majority of Soviet Jews, this was enough to convince them to walk through the doors that had been unbolted.

American Jews were disoriented by this victory. They didn't know quite how to accept that they had succeeded. The movement began folding up after the triumphant rally in December 1987. The following year, for the first time since 1971, there was no Solidarity Sunday. No one saw any point. The National Conference on Soviet Jewry (though it still exists today) began scaling back its activities and focused on pushing the American government to reward Gorbachev more quickly for the changes he had made. The Union of Councils and the other grassroots activist groups did not quiet down so easily. Those who saw the movement as a freedom struggle were still waiting for something huge to happen, for the heavens to open up and declare that they had won. Even when presented with the incredible emigration numbers, they refused to believe that they could pack up their signs and banners and go home. For them, the sheer ordinariness of the emigrants—not heroes, just regular Sashas and Borises and Mashas looking to make a living—was depressing and demoralizing. Most of these activists were never able to take the next step and embrace the much more prosaic and perhaps less gratifying work of absorbing these new citizens.

The mass emigration itself—how it was carried out and what happened to the emigrants—is a subject worthy of another book. But our story ends at the moment when the two communities that generated the Soviet Jewry movement finally found the redemption they had been seeking. American Jews, now liberated from the fear of agitating for their own, had discovered a political voice and a sense of common purpose. Soviet Jews were on the verge of getting out and would be free to stay or leave, embrace their Jewishness or assimilate. The choice was theirs to make.

But this feeling of redemption soon dissipated. Nothing since has united American Jewry in quite the same way, drawing together both right and left. In fact, at the very moment that American Jews were finding common cause in Washington, an intifada was beginning in the streets of Gaza. After a series of violent episodes that began a day before the 1987 rally, mass rioting broke out that would engulf Israel and force it to confront its occupation of the West Bank and Gaza. The Lebanon war in the early 1980s had divided American Jews, and the conflict with the Palestinians only widened the chasm. It seems inconceivable today that there was ever a moment in the recent past when liberal Jews professing universal principles of human rights could join, however tenuously, with die-hard Jabotinskyite believers of Jewish power. But there was such a time. And for those who took part in the movement, there is great sadness that a community that gained so much from the struggle seems too fractured to ever rally together again.

For Soviet Jews, of course, the redemption was physical. The act of leaving was a fulfillment of the movement. But what awaited them in their new countries was less than ideal. Both the United States and Israel were ill equipped to handle the mass immigration. As soon as the gates opened wider, the dropout problem escalated. In 1988, an incredible 88.5 percent of Soviet emigrants dropped out in Vienna. In 1989, it was 82.9 percent. Israel, and the agents of the Lishka, watched these percentages with horror. This was supposed to be the culmination of all their efforts—their secret demographic weapon to secure Israel's future as Jewish and democratic—and the Soviet Jews were overwhelmingly choosing to go elsewhere. The situation caused chaos and heartache for American Jews. Some activists tried to hold a firm line, demanding freedom of choice for the emigrants. Others in the community empathized with the Israelis' anguish and pushed for direct flights from Moscow to Tel Aviv—something the Soviets had promised to do but hadn't yet.

The situation finally began to change in the summer of 1988, when the American embassy in Moscow stopped processing visa applications. Overwhelmed, underfinanced, and understaffed, the embassy simply could not handle the thousands of Armenians and Pentecostal Soviet citizens bursting to get out. Soviet Jews were still leaving with Israeli visas that they abandoned in Vienna. But soon they too began to feel the lack of resources. That same summer, the State Department decided to redefine refugee status; now Soviet Jews had to prove a "well-founded fear of persecution" to get immediate American citizenship, a task that became more and more difficult for them in light of Gorbachev's liberalizations. Then, in the early months of 1989, the United States simply stopped giving visas to many of the dropouts in Vienna. The number of those rejected for American visas after they'd already reached Rome rose from 11 percent in January to 36 percent in March. The American option was quickly closing for Soviet emigrants. By July, sixteen thousand Jews were in limbo in the suburbs of the Italian capital, anxiously waiting for news of their applications. Almost fifty thousand waited in Moscow for the American embassy to begin issuing applications again.

The new Bush administration declared a refugee emergency. Not as ideologically attached to the movement as the previous administration, these politicians were less inclined to accept the budgetary strain that would accompany an unending flow of immigrants—and they were skeptical that Soviet Jews should be counted as a threatened people who didn't have a natural home. After long negotiations between Jewish organizations and the administration, a deal was finally worked out. Starting October 1, 1989, Soviet Jews would no longer be processed in Vienna or Rome. The United States set a quota: forty thousand Soviet Jews would be admitted every year, and of those, only thirty-two thousand would be financially supported by the government as refugees; American Jews would have to pick up the tab for the remaining eight thousand. Their visas would be issued in the Soviet capital, and preference would be given to people who had close family members already in the United States. The tens of thousands stuck in the pipeline—either waiting in Rome or backlogged in Moscow—would get out first. Israel, gleeful at this resolution, became the main destination for Soviet Jews who wanted to get out. The dropout problem, which the Israelis had worked so hard to combat, was over. Hundreds of thousands of Soviet Jews were flown via Bucharest or Warsaw (countries that would not let them drop out) to Tel Aviv to become new Israelis.

Many Soviet Jews perceived this as a betrayal by the United States. Their plight had served as good ideological ammunition when the Cold War raged, but now that they were no longer needed, America would not make the necessary sacrifices to take them in. The life many Soviet Jews found in Israel also gave them cause to complain. The challenge of absorbing a million people into a state that had only five million to begin with proved huge, and the Israelis did not approach it with either resourcefulness or humility. In truth, the task was enormous. More than 70 percent of the new immigrants had advanced degrees, including a hundred thousand engineers and twenty-three thousand doctors. Today, Israel can look at its transformation into a science and high-tech capital of the world and be thankful for this infusion of intellectual power, but in the early years it was overwhelming to find a professional home for these people—hardly any of whom spoke Hebrew.

Now Soviet Jews make up the largest single immigrant bloc, and their presence has changed the face of Israel. There are a hundred and thirty Israeli Russian periodicals, including four daily newspapers and dozens of weeklies; two hundred Russian bookstores; a Russian television station; and hundreds of Israeli Russian Internet sites. The symphony orchestras of Israel are bursting with Soviet Jewish pianists and violinists. The Russian emigrant community has gained a political voice as a substantial conservative bloc—perhaps a reaction to living in a leftist totalitarian state. In the early 1990s they were happy to give political power to Natan Sharansky—he rose to the position of deputy prime minister—but now they vote for deeply conservative figures, such as Avigdor Lieberman, appointed foreign minister after the 2009 elections and a staunch advocate of forced population exchange to deal with the Palestinian conflict. Absorption still remains a challenge. Along with the Soviet Jews who arrived in Israel came tens of thousands of non-Jewish spouses and relatives, as well as people whose Jewish roots were tenuous at best. They have added another layer of complexity to the Israeli story. As for the old refusenik leaders, they often feel ignored or disrespected, their role in Jewish history forgotten. Volodya Slepak, now in his eighties—stooped, his beard completely white, but his face still bright and open—struggled with economic hardship for years while the Israeli government refused to pay sufficient pensions for those refuseniks who'd given up careers to fight for their right to go to Israel. Other former activists have become destitute in Israel, subsisting on grants from individual donors and foundations, like the one set up by Enid Wurtman, the Soviet Jewry activist from Philadelphia who herself made aliyah.

But for all these difficulties and disappointments, on any given day in any street in Israel, one can still see and hear an Israeli soldier in an olive uniform chatting away on a cell phone in Russian—a boy or girl who would have grown up ignorant of his or her Jewish identity if not for the Soviet Jewry movement. The difficulties of resettlement don't take away from the successes of a campaign that injected itself into the middle of the Cold War and demanded a place next to discussions of nuclear weapons and billion-dollar trade deals. If the first half of the twentieth century gave us the ultimate example of Jews as victims of history, then the second half gave us—in addition to the establishment of Israel—this triumphant story, one in which Jews grabbed history and changed its course.

The Soviet Union's dismal economic conditions certainly precipitated its swift collapse. By the second half of the 1980s, the failures of a centrally planned system were manifest. The line for toilet paper was simply too long. The economies of the Eastern bloc countries, modeled on the Soviet system, were basically large Ponzi schemes; they borrowed money from the West and then borrowed even more money to pay off those debts. It was untenable.

But although the Soviet Union's economic system was doomed, was its totalitarian structure destined to fail as well? China had managed to compete with the capitalists while still crushing dissent and ignoring human rights. The tanks of Tiananmen Square in 1989 could have reassured the Soviet Communist Party and the military establishment that it was possible to open up their economy without relinquishing total power. But that option was not available to them. Soviet Jewry—and the dissident movement—had worked very hard to ensure that their freedom was the price of reengagement with the West, a necessary element of glasnost and perestroika. And once that thread was pulled, it wasn't long before everything unraveled. Just a quick look at the demands placed on Gorbachev and Shevardnadze when the Helsinki conference in Vienna concluded in January 1989 shows how thoroughly the Soviet government had to dismantle the all-seeing, all-powerful apparatus that had controlled the USSR for six decades. The Soviet leaders had made extraordinary promises, exceeding even the commitments of the initial accords. A country's citizens had the right to leave; religious rights; ethnic rights; the right to information. The Soviets were even *rewarded;* they were given the chance to hold a human rights conference in Moscow. Once these changes were made, they could not be reversed easily, and they only fed people's hunger for more freedom.

The Soviet Jews were among the first to demand these rights, but they had been on the frontlines of the other major attack against the integrity of the Soviet empire. Through the coldest years of the Cold War, they had insisted that their own national, tribal interests be respected. The swift domino collapse of the Eastern bloc and then the Soviet empire that occurred in the late 1980s and early 1990s had as much to do with a hunger for democracy as it did with this purely nationalist desire. Everyone wanted an "exodus" from the Soviet Union. In the end, even the state of Russia opted out of the empire. The refuseniks had demanded these national rights persistently and loudly for decades before the final moment. Gorbachev understood that allowing the Soviet Jews their freedom was one of the concessions he had to make—and once he'd made it, there was no end to the concessions until the Soviet Union was no longer.

The Soviet Jewry movement cannot claim responsibility for finally shoving the Soviet state off the cliff—there were too many other factors responsible for that—but the existential challenge it posed in many ways presaged the end. It's the reason the Soviets always felt threatened by the movement. They knew that once they allowed Jews to leave, they would have a crisis on their hands. Every other ethnic group that wanted a separate identity would follow. The right to leave gave one the chance to vote with his or her feet—that's why Andrei Sakharov so valued and supported the movement. He knew that if Soviet leaders capitulated on this right, they would quickly find a cascade of other rights crashing down on their heads. And this is what happened.

Perhaps it was an unintended consequence. Certainly the Soviet Jews who wanted out and the American Jews who helped them weren't thinking about bringing down the Soviet Union—though they probably fantasized about it. For them, a second exodus meant a second chance. In many ways, it was a final chapter to the chaos wrought by World War II. By devoting themselves to saving their brethren, American Jews felt they could stand tall as a community, that they had not squandered their freedom and prosperity but had used it to defend both the universal and the particular: the human principles they believed in and their tribal instinct to rescue their own. Soviet Jews, whose grandparents had dreamed—and in many cases fought—for an egalitarian vision, had saved themselves from the nightmare that dream had become. Living in a totalitarian state, these were people who decided, almost out of nowhere, to assert an ancient identity, turn themselves into pariahs, risk everything, and become living proof of man's capacity for bravery—all so they could simply be Jews.

Acknowledgments

What I feel most grateful for—after finishing a project that was nearly five years in the making—is the patience of others. From the many people I interviewed for this book to my indulgent publishing house to friends and family and, most recently, to my newborn daughter, everyone in my life has been incredibly understanding about a process that has been, frustratingly but necessarily, very long.

Since so much of this book is based on oral testimony, I have to offer my thanks first to the many former activists in Israel, America, and Russia who opened their homes to me. Their names are listed in the notes, but each one represents hours over cups of tea—or sometimes vodka and pickled mushrooms—that provided a living picture of the movement, one I simply could not have gotten from archives alone. I only hope this book does justice to the struggle that many of them devoted their lives to. My only regret is that a few of my most helpful and warmest sources aren't around anymore to read this—I'm thinking specifically of Si Frumkin, Lynn Singer, Yuri Shtern, and that indispensable chronicler of the movement William Korey.

My key navigator through the world of the refuseniks was Enid Wurtman; she provided me with most of my initial contacts and continued to be an endless source of help. Laura Bialis, who directed *Re-*

fusenik, a powerful documentary about the movement, was extremely generous, allowing me access to the transcripts of interviews she conducted.

Enid offered to look over the manuscript early, and she, Joshua Rubenstein, Steven Bayme, Michael Beizer, Glenn Richter, and Yaakov Birnbaum played the critical part of first readers, saving me from myself in more than a few instances.

Long, long before there were readers, there were people who believed in the book, even when it was just half a chapter written by a twenty-seven-year-old. Andrew Blauner, who became my agent, was the first who showed that faith. Jane Rosenman, who acquired the book and believed in the project, provided much moral support in the early years of research.

For the past two years, I have been extraordinarily lucky to have this book in the hands of Amanda Cook. Until I started working with Amanda, I had stopped believing that there were editors who did what she does so expertly—respect a writer's vision while not shirking from the details, looking over every line with intelligence and patience and care. This book is inestimably better because of her.

A few folks at Houghton proved particularly helpful. Shuchi Saraswat went above and beyond to help me with the grueling task of gaining permissions. Megan Wilson has been excellent on the publicity front. And Tracy Roe did a masterly job copyediting the book.

Along the way, I have been buoyed up by a variety of people. First is my mentor Sam Freedman. It was in his seminar at the Columbia Journalism School and under his guidance that this book was born. I am thankful for his wise counsel and for the tough love he has doled out over the years.

The *Columbia Journalism Review* was an important home for me during the first years of this project. I am thankful to Mike Hoyt and Brent Cunningham for their support and friendship. I also benefited from editors, such as Alana Newhouse, who were willing to take risks on me again and again. My most recent home has been the *Forward,* where Jane Eisner hired me sight unseen and has allowed me to continue earning a living as a writer, something one can't take for granted these days.

From May 2008 to September 2009, I spent a glorious year in Berlin,

thanks to a German Chancellor Fellowship from the Alexander von
Humboldt Foundation. I am grateful to the foundation for giving me
the time I needed to finish the book and to Berlin for the serene quiet
of the Staatsbibliothek. During the months I was in Bonn, a very generous professor, Herbert Dreiner, provided me with keys to the university's physics institute so that I could have a quiet place to work.

On a reporting trip to Moscow, I was well taken care of by Carl
Shakhnis; he made sure that I and my courageous companion, my father, had everything we needed, from bodyguard to *banya*.

And my friends. Once upon a time there was a dark side. The group
that was there at the beginning has continued to prod me along with
love and good humor and the occasional drink: Kavitha Rajagopalan,
Shoshana Guy, Allan Jalon, Mara Hvistendahl, and David Biello. Along
the way, other good friends propped me up at various dark moments
and were more responsible than they probably realize for helping
me to push through: Helen Frazier, Maha Ziadeh, Agata Lisiak, Paul
McLeary, and my dear cousin Boaz Barkan.

I gained a new family over these past couple of years—Alex and
Nancy Kolben, Kevin Kolben, and Michal Lando (my friend turned
sister). They are a constant source of sustenance on all fronts—particularly the emotional and culinary.

The greatest fortune in my life is to have a family that is the epitome
of warmth and unconditional affection: my grandparents Shoshana
and Elkana, who gave me a home for months when I was in Israel on
a reporting trip and who have built a family that would be the envy of
anyone; my other grandparents, Cesia and Bubi, who won't see this
book but whose spirits infuse it in more than a few places; and all the
many uncles and aunts and cousins.

I thank my sisters, Natalie and Maya, for the love and indulgence
they offer a brother who, sadly, is often far away. And most important,
I thank my parents, to whom this book is dedicated. There are many
ways they could have viewed the zigzag path their *luftmensch* took in
life. But even when they didn't understand it, they trusted and supported me; I always knew that if and when everything else fell away,
they would still be there.

Finally, I started this project as a lonely bachelor and end it now
with a family of my own. Responsible for this happy occurrence is the

love of my life, Deborah Kolben, who has never known me as anyone but the long-suffering author of this book. She has sustained countless (and I mean countless) kvetching sessions, lifted me back on my feet, talked me off the ledge, and never tired of reminding me that I could do this. My gratitude to her for all she has given me—especially our beautiful Mika—is boundless. My only hope is that this book is worthy of the undying faith she has always had in me and which, more than anything else, enabled me to get up every morning and face it all anew.

Notes

1. Beneath the Earth

page

13 *Mendelevich was a shy:* Biographical information on Mendelevich from interview with author and from Mendelevich, *Operation "Wedding,"* 9–53.

16 *It was strange:* History of Riga's Jews from Steimanis, *Latvian Jews,* 57–123.

18 *Betar had sprung from the mind:* Jabotinsky, *Political and Social Philosophy.*

19 *"[Betar], as we think of it":* Quoted in Kaplan, *Jewish Radical Right,* 26.

20 *Their end came quickly:* Ezergailis, *Holocaust,* 240–50.

21 *for 2,267,814 Soviet citizens:* Number comes from the 1959 Soviet population census, cited in Altshuler, *Soviet Jewry,* 21. Jews made up 1.1 percent of the total Soviet population; in Riga, the number of Jewish citizens was 30,267, 5 percent of the city's population (ibid., 88). Out of that number, 14,526 designated Yiddish as their mother tongue.

23 *Even more important than:* Biographical information on Mendel Gordin from Schroeter, *Last Exodus,* 74–75.
Hardly anything worthy: The history of the early Riga Zionist movement is recounted in Ro'i, *The Struggle,* 292–93; Schroeter, *Last Exodus,* 61–83; and author interviews with Boris and Leah (Lydia) Slovin, Eli Volk, and Yosef Mendelevich.

25 *In this way, Riga became:* Author interviews with the Slovins, Volk, and Mendelevich.
In Riga, Yosef Schneider: Biographical information on Schneider from Ro'i, *The Struggle,* 78–79.

26 *From then on, one of the embassy's:* The role of the Israelis covertly working in the Soviet Union is described in Levanon, *Code Name,* 15–134; Eliav, *Hammer and Sickle;* Ro'i, *The Struggle.*

27 *As early as 1964:* Author interview with the Slovins.

28 *Ezra Rusinek, the bare-chested:* Biographical information on Rusinek from Schroeter, *Last Exodus,* 76.

30 *"And I myself/am one":* Yevtushenko, *Yevtushenko's Reader,* 135–38.

31 *Here were silenced:* The number in the memorial was inaccurate. At the time, it was thought that 38,000 Jews had been killed in Rumbuli; the more accurate figure is probably 25,000 (cited in Ezergailis, *Holocaust*).

32 *Rumbuli was the first group:* Mark Blum, who changed his name to Mordecai Lapid, wrote an extensive account of the events at Rumbuli in "Memorial at Rumbuli."

36 *Every city where Gill performed:* Accounts of the Gill concerts in Schroeter, *Last Exodus,* 72–73; Ro'i, *The Struggle,* 323–24.

37 *Within minutes, a riot:* Account of Gill riot in Lapid, "Memorial at Rumbuli"; Ro'i, *The Struggle,* 323–24; Mendelevich, *Operation "Wedding,"* 27–28.

2. "Failure May Have Become Our Habit"

39 *"I believe with perfect":* Nizkor Project, session 68, June 7, 1961.
    Lou Rosenblum was a scientist: Biographical details on Lou Rosenblum come from his interviews with the author and a detailed series of interviews he conducted with his son Daniel from 1996 to 1999.

40 *"epidemic inability":* Greenberg's "Bankrupt," dated February 12, 1943, was reprinted in *Midstream* in March of 1964.

41 *Multiple studies by local:* Statistics from Sachar, *History of the Jews,* 646–47.

42 *In 1923, only:* Ibid., 666.
    The American Jewish Committee conducted: Study is quoted in Novick, *Holocaust in American Life,* 113.

43 *Both the play and the film:* Ibid., 117–20.
    "had had remarkably slight effects": Glazer, *American Judaism,* 114–15.

44 *"You know, I was elected":* Sachar, *History of the Jews,* 731.

45 *"From our Jewish historic":* Prinz's speech is reprinted in Staub, ed., *Jewish 1960s,* 90.
    Milton Himmelfarb, a leading: Milton Himmelfarb, "In the Community," *Commentary* 30 (August 1960): 160.

46 *"The Jew cannot settle down":* Arthur Hertzberg, "America Is Galut," *Jewish Frontier* 31 (July 1964): 7–8.

47 *But the loss of a Jewish community:* History of Beth Israel from author interviews with Lou Rosenblum, Herb Caron.

48 *In an address given:* Jabotinsky, *The War,* 289.

50 *"American Jews suffer these days":* Irving Howe, "Tevye on Broadway," *Commentary* 38 (November 1964): 73–75.

51 *Avigur was typical:* Raviv and Melman, *Every Spy,* 103–04.

Avigur was soon called back: Early history of Nativ detailed in Levanon, *Code Name*; Peretz, "Nativ's Emissaries"; AJC Oral Interviews with Nehemiah Levanon, Moshe Decter, Meir Rosenne; author interview with Meir Rosenne.

53 *Decter had grown up:* Biographical information on Decter and his involvement in the Lishka from AJC Oral Interview, February 22, 1990; Peretz, "Nativ's Emissaries," 118–19; and Levanon, *Code Name,* 192–93.

"Make it specific with facts": Levanon, *Code Name,* 193.

54 *In order to avoid:* Peretz, "Nativ's Emissaries," 119.

55 *"Soviet policy as a whole":* Decter, "Status of Jews."

57 *"In selling wheat":* CCSA Archives, container 1, folder 3.

59 *Caron recorded the:* Answers to survey from Herb Caron's personal files.

60 *"a few statistics about us":* CCSA Archives, container 1, folder 2.

In the fall of 1963: Details of appeal to Kennedy in Lawrence, *Three Million,* 169–75; Ro'i, *The Struggle,* 186–89.

61 *Behind the scenes:* Richard H. Davis to W. Averell Harriman, August 30, 1963, quoted in Frey dissertation, "Challenging the World's Conscience."

62 *"We are proud of our":* Lawrence, *Three Million,* 173.

The Conference of Presidents: History of the Presidents Conference's founding in Sachar, *History of the Jews,* 726; J. J. Goldberg, *Jewish Power,* 152–53.

64 *"It is wrong to generate":* Quoted in Orbach, *American Movement,* 34.

65 *"Intellectual evasion":* Heschel, *Insecurity,* 217–18.

66 *"A Jew is asked":* Ibid., 137–38.

The year 1963: Branch, 30–32.

"This does not mean": *Day-Morning Journal,* September 13, 1963.

67 *"If we are ready":* Heschel, *Insecurity,* 273.

69 *"The question is not":* CCSA Archives, container 1, folder 2.

"Knowing how responsible": Goldmann to Weinstein, February 20, 1964, included as an addendum to Weinstein, "Soviet Jewry," 616.

71 *"What's next?":* Rosenblum interview with his son.

"'Immediately upon'": Quoted in Orbach, *American Movement,* 25.

72 *In early 1964:* Information on Yaakov Birnbaum and early years of SSSJ comes from Birnbaum interviews with the author, as well as material provided by Birnbaum.

76 *And he could see:* Additional background on the early days of SSSJ from interviews with Glenn Richter, Sandy Frucher, Irving "Yitz" Greenberg, and Yossi Klein Halevi.

77 *"If Soviet authorities":* *Jewish Exponent,* April 10, 1964.

78 *"The time has come":* SSSJ Archives, box 1, folder 1.

79 *One of these:* Author interview with Glenn Richter.

81 *"Our great demonstration":* SSSJ Archives, box 1, folder 1.

82 *"to make possible":* AJCSJ Declaration of Purpose, NCSJ Archives, box 1, folder 1.

"our action": Statement to Secretary of State Dean Rusk, April 7, 1963, NCSJ Archives, box 1, folder 1.

"You have lost": Sachar, *History of the Jews,* 731.

83 *In a closed meeting:* NCSJ Archives, box 1, folder 1.

Maislen later described: Maislen report to AJC meeting, October 19, 1964, NCSJ Archives, box 1, folder 1.

84 *"Who is leading":* Birnbaum to Javits, July 19, 1964, SSSJ Archives, box 1, folder 2.

3. A Circumcision at the Dacha

86 *The six men:* Information on Leningrad organization and biographies of activists from interviews with Hillel Butman, Shmuel (Syoma) Dreizner, Aron Shpilberg, David Chernoglaz, Lev Yagman, Lassal Kaminsky, and Anatoly Goldfeld; *Refusenik* transcripts with some of the same men; Schroeter, *Last Exodus,* 50–60; Butman, *From Leningrad,* 13–74.

89 *Starting in the mid-1950s:* Ro'i, *Struggle,* 318.

90 *They managed:* Details of Tsirulnikov case in ibid., 279–80; Schroeter, *Last Exodus,* 55.

93 *"So what if I've":* Gitelman, *Century of Ambivalence,* 80.

During the war: History of the Jewish Anti-Fascist Committee and its demise from the introduction to Rubenstein and Naumov, eds., *Stalin's Secret Pogrom.*

94 *And though it has:* Most recent discussion of the Doctors' Plot and alleged mass deportation in Brent and Naumov, *Stalin's Last Crime.*

98 *As their work:* Story of suitcase from interviews with Butman, Shpilberg, Boris Slovin; Butman, *From Leningrad,* 66–72.

100 *On one of the war's:* Kochubievsky story from the author's interview with Boris Ashi (formerly Kochubievsky) and from Decter, ed., *A Hero.*

"invaders are killing prisoners": Quoted in Korey, *Soviet Cage,* 126.

"want to copy": Ibid.

101 *"We are convinced":* Decter, ed., *A Hero,* 34.

103 *"I am a Jew":* Ibid., 12.

104 *"The Soviet government":* From *Izvestia,* June 11, 1967, quoted in Morozov, ed., *Documents,* 66.

"We, on our side": Quoted in Ro'i, *The Struggle,* 246.

105 *"The autumn Jewish religious":* Memorandum from Andropov to the CPSU Central Committee in Morozov, ed., *Documents,* 63–64.

107 *But it was Yasha:* Kazakov story from author's interview with Yasha Kazakov (later Kedmi); Schroeter, *Last Exodus,* 88–90; *Refusenik* transcripts.

108 *"I, Yakov Iosifovich":* Schroeter, *Last Exodus,* 89.

"I am a Jew": Decter, ed., *Redemption!,* 16.

109 *"systematically disseminating":* Decter, ed., *A Hero,* 19.

110 *The judge cut him:* Ibid., 22.

112 *"In the highest bureaucratic":* Quoted in Schroeter, *Last Exodus,* 384.

113 *Andropov extended this:* Memorandum from Andropov and Gromyko to the CPSU Central Committee in Morozov, ed., *Documents,* 65–66.

114 *The Slovins were:* Author interview with Boris and Leah (Lydia) Slovin.

116 *Yosef Mendelevich:* His process of applying and aftermath comes from his interview with the author; Mendelevich, *Operation "Wedding,"* 32–36.

119 *"We are not wanted":* Cohen, *Let My People,* 33.
"I categorically declare": Schroeter, *Last Exodus,* 75.

121 *"Showered with insults":* Ibid., 123–24.

122 *Even though such:* Story of VKK from author interviews with Shlomo (Soyma) Dreizner, Aron Shpilberg, David Khavkin; Schroeter, *Last Exodus,* 91.

123 *They decided to:* Details of Riga group evolution and work on *Iton* in Mendelevich, *Operation "Wedding,"* 37–42.

124 *A major initiative:* Schroeter, *Last Exodus,* 95–96.

4. The Overall Orchestra

125 *The Reb Shlomo:* Story of Prague trip and origins of "Am Yisrael Chai" from undated interview with Shlomo Carlebach conducted by Yossi Klein Halevi; author interview with Yaakov Birnbaum.
Already a recognizable: Biographical information on Carlebach from Mandelbaum, *Holy Brother,* xxix–xxxv.

128 *"Ever since the days":* SSSJ Archives, box 1, folder 2.

130 *"The sound of":* SSSJ Archives audio file, tape 317, NBC News report on SSSJ Jericho March (April 4, 1965).
"A group that uses": Ibid., ABC News report on Menorah March (December 19, 1965).
Yossi Klein was only: Halevi, *Memoirs,* 47–48.

131 *Later that night:* Ibid., 51.
"The Soviet Jewry protest": "Student Struggle for Soviet Jewry," *Hadassah* magazine, December 1965.
Yeshiva students were not: According to a study conducted in 1973 by Jim Schwartz, 65 percent of the members considered themselves Orthodox.

132 *"There's a fire burning":* Lyrics provided by Birnbaum and in *Hadassah* magazine, December 1965.

133 *When Moshe Decter:* SSSJ Archives audio file, tape 318, Moshe Decter at Westside Jewish Center, November 1, 1964.

134 *"We don't have":* CCSA Archives, container 1, folder 3.
"From its inception": CCSA Archives, Louis Rosenblum, *Spotlight,* November 1965.

135 *"operating under the premise":* Rosenblum to Nemzer, May 17, 1965, quoted by Rosenblum in interview with son.
He decided to focus: Information on development of CCSA from interviews with Lou Rosenblum and Herb Caron.

137 *"We, the representatives":* Declaration of Rights for Soviet Jewry, NCSJ Archives, box 1, folder 4.

"event was merely": CCSA Archives, Louis Rosenblum, *Spotlight,* May 1966.

138 *"In a spirit":* Description of Madison Square Garden event and Johnson's quote in Friedman and Chernin, eds., *Second Exodus,* 41; Ro'i, *The Struggle,* 198.

"the sincere and genuine": SSSJ Archives audio file, tape 324, address by Martin Luther King Jr., December 11, 1966.

139 *"the current Vietnam":* Memorandum of conversation, Department of State, August 4, 1966, files of W. W. Rostow, box 17, folder: Visitors 1966 (WWR), Lyndon B. Johnson Library, quoted in Frey, "Changing the World's Conscience."

"it is not the purpose": Madison Square Garden material, NCSJ Archives, box 1, folder 4.

"To compare in any way": Statement by Dr. Nahum Goldmann, June 10, 1965, Horace Kallen Papers, box 10, folder 21, quoted in Frey, "Changing the World's Conscience."

140 *"wait-and-see ostrich":* Moshe Decter to Sidney L. Regner, Central Conference of American Rabbis Records, box 19, folder 7, quoted in ibid.

Starting in 1965: Biographical information on Levanon from Peretz, "Nativ's Emissaries," 116–17; AJC Oral Interview with Levanon, December 3, 1989; Levanon, *Code Name,* 15–183.

141 *"Let me again":* Moshe Decter to Louis Rosenblum, November 15, 1965, CCSA Archives, container 1, folder 4.

142 *"nearly Byzantine":* Ibid.

"As you well know": Moshe Decter to Herb Caron, December 16, 1965, Herb Caron personal files.

143 *"it is time":* Moshe Decter to Rabbi Shimon Paskow, April 17, 1966, in ibid.

Since the publication: Wiesel biographical information from Wiesel, *All Rivers;* Stern, *Elie Wiesel.*

The jovial Rosenne: Wiesel, *All Rivers,* 366.

144 *"I refused to believe":* Wiesel, *Jews of Silence,* 13–14.

145 *"Do you know":* Ibid., 19–20.

"Time after time": Ibid., 23–24.

"Where did they": Ibid., 58–85.

147 *"One may question":* Ibid., 126–27.

148 *"American Jews, so frequently":* Lucy Dawidowicz, *American Jewish Yearbook* (1968): 204.

In New York: Description of Six-Day War's effect on American Jews is from special section in *American Jewish Yearbook* (1968).

"Many Jews would never have": Arthur Hertzberg, "Israel and American Jewry," *Commentary* (August 1967): 69–73.

149 *"I think it must":* Quoted in *American Jewish Yearbook* (1968): 211.

The answers show: Results of survey discussed in ibid., 214–16.

150 *On the streets of Borough Park:* Halevi, *Memoirs,* 55–57.

152 *"the liberal Jew"*: Fackenheim, "Liberal Judaism," 301.

"the authentic Jew": Staub, *Torn at the Roots*, 132.

The neighborhood of: History of Ocean Hill–Brownsville conflict from newspaper reports and Podair, *The Strike*.

155 *The schism was:* Harris and Swanson, *Black-Jewish Relations*, 106.

"The age we live": Kahane, *On Jews*, 34.

156 *On June 18, 1968:* Biographical information on Meir Kahane and the history of the JDL come from Friedman, *False Prophet*; Kahane, *Jewish Defense League*; Russ, "'Zionist Hooligan'"; Goodman, "I'd Love to See"; Kaufman, "Complex Past"; author interviews with Yossi Klein Halevi, Eli Birnbaum.

"founder of a group": Quoted in Friedman, *False Prophet*, 89.

158 *"Most Jews came"*: Kahane, *Jewish Defense League*, 101.

"The Jewish Defense": Ibid., 98.

159 *"Jews, carrying baseball"*: "Defense League Scored by Rabbi," *New York Times*, May 18, 1969.

160 *"maybe destiny sent"*: Friedman, *False Prophet*, 19.

162 *In June of 1966:* The Estelle Donna Evans story was uncovered in Kaufman, "Complex Past"; it's discussed further in Friedman, *False Prophet*, 71–75.

165 *The disenchantment had begun:* Author interview with Lou Rosenblum.

166 *"should they not"*: Hillel Levine to Lou Rosenblum, March 1968, quoted in interview of Hillel Levine by Lou Rosenblum, December 27, 1987, from Rosenblum personal files.

Rosenblum wanted: Author interview with Lou Rosenblum; Rosenblum's interview with son.

168 *"Why are you"*: Kahane connection to Geula Cohen, Yitzhak Shamir, and the Herut Party detailed in Friedman, *False Prophet*, 105–07.

169 *In the city:* Ibid., 94–96.

On Halloween: Halevi, *Memoirs*, 79.

Nothing, however, prepared: December 1969 JDL Soviet Jewry actions and riot from news reports and Kahane, *Jewish Defense League*, 1–4.

171 *"Our attacks upon"*: Friedman, *False Prophet*, 109.

5. "Escape, Daughter of Zion Dwelling in Babylon"

172 *Kuznetsov's decision to:* Biographical information on Kuznetsov from author interview with him; Rubenstein, *Soviet Dissidents*, 169–71; Schroeter, *Last Exodus*, 145–47.

175 *By chance, the first:* Author interview with Mendelevich.

Sylva Zalmanson: Sylva Zalmanson biographical information from author interview with her.

177 *Like Kuznetsov had been:* Mark Dymshits biographical information from author interview with him; Butman, *From Leningrad*, 77–78.

179 *"You don't have to fantasize"*: Butman, *From Leningrad*, 78.

Dymshits laid out: Story of Operation Wedding from author interviews with Hillel Butman, Shlomo (Soyma) Dreizner, Lev Yagman, David Chernoglaz, Lassal Kaminsky, and Anatoly Goldfeld; Butman, *From Leningrad*, 78–143.

184 *"Just you listen":* Kuznetsov, *Prison Diaries*, 95–96.

185 *"Would you be willing":* Mendelevich, *Operation "Wedding,"* 43.

187 *"Our organization now":* Butman, *From Leningrad*, 120.

188 *"If Butman doesn't":* Ibid.

190 *The mini-cell of:* Story of hijacking drawn from author interviews with Eduard Kuznetsov, Mark Dymshits, Sylva Zalmanson, Israel Zalmanson, Zev (Vulf) Zalmanson, Yosef Mendelevich, Anatoly Altman, Boris Penson, and Aryeh Khnokh; Mendelevich, *Operation "Wedding,"* 43–53; Kuznetsov, *Prison Diaries*, 92–99; Schroeter, *Last Exodus*, 141–212.

191 *"This is our driver":* Mendelevich, *Operation "Wedding,"* 46.
"Jewish ears should": Butman, *From Leningrad*, 139.

192 *"Unconfirmed sources report":* Memorandum from Andropov to the CPSU Central Committee in Morozov, *Documents*, 84–85.

194 *He began working:* Details of last testament from interview with Mendelevich; Mendelevich, *Operation "Wedding,"* 51; Schroeter, *Last Exodus*, 182–83.

195 *"Flee from the Northern":* Text of testament reprinted in Schroeter, *Last Exodus*, 182–83.

197 *"The leaders stayed":* Author interview with Aryeh Khnokh.

200 *Plan for Basic:* Memorandum from V. Stepakov to the CPSU Central Committee, in Morozov, *Documents*, 71–73.
"'Every day brings'": Ibid., 72–73.

201 *"I have had Leonid":* Bernard Gwertzman, "Soviet Jews, at a News Parley, Back Moscow's Mideast Policy," *New York Times*, March 5, 1970.

202 *To obscure what he:* Author interview with Eduard Kuznetsov.
"It's kept unoccupied": Kuznetsov, *Prison Diaries*, 20–21.
"with the intimate": Ibid., 108.

203 *"Why ever did I":* Ibid., 105.
The trial finally: Details of the trial from author interviews with Eduard Kuznetsov, Mark Dymshits, Sylva Zalmanson, Israel Zalmanson, Zev (Vulf) Zalmanson, Yosef Mendelevich, Anatoly Altman, Boris Penson, and Aryeh Khnokh; Mendelevich, *Operation "Wedding,"* 88–94; Kuznetsov, *Prison Diaries*, 74–92; Schroeter, *Last Exodus*, 157–212; Korey, *Soviet Cage*, 201–28.

204 *"Permit me to decide":* Schroeter, *Last Exodus*, 161.

205 *"Did you commit":* Korey, *Soviet Cage*, 215.
"We have been speaking": Transcripts of the trial were informal; people who were present in the courtroom went home and wrote down what they remembered (as was common practice for all dissident cases). These documents were then reproduced in the samizdat journal *Chronicle of Current Events*, issue number 17, and subsequently translated and published in the United States by Amnesty International as *Chronicle of Current Events*, issues number 16 to 27.

206 *"Does it really"*: Kuznetsov, *Prison Diaries*, 112.

"We shall never": Statements at the Leningrad Hijacking Trial, *Chronicle of Current Events* (1971): 57–65.

207 *"Today on the day"*: Ibid.

"indiscriminate in the": Ibid.

"Haven't these Bolsheviks": Mendelevich, Operation "Wedding," 93.

They should sing: Ibid., 94.

6. Outrageous Things

211 *As the sixties curdled*: Description of Meir Kahane and the JDL taken from Friedman, *False Prophet*; Kahane, *Jewish Defense League*; Russ, "'Zionist Hooligans'"; Goodman, "I'd Love to See"; Kaufman, "Complex Past"; Rosenthal, *Rookie Cop*; author interviews with Yossi Klein Halevi, Eli Birnbaum.

One officer from: Rosenthal, *Rookie Cop*, 83–86.

213 *"The most important"*: Goodman, "I'd Love to See."

"I know Meir": Halevi, *Memoirs*, 86.

214 *"Listen, Brezhnev, and listen well"*: Kahane, *Jewish Defense League*, 24–25; Halevi, *Memoirs*, 94–95.

215 *"We meet this afternoon"*: Irving Spiegel, "Lindsay Urges U.S. Stand," *New York Times*, December 29, 1970.

216 *At ten in the evening*: Description of commutation in Kuznetsov, *Prison Diaries*, 132–35.

"I cannot remember": Ibid., 134.

217 *This time, the trial*: Details of second Leningrad trial, Riga trial, and Kishinev trial from author interviews with Butman, Dreizner, Shpilberg, Chernoglaz, Goldfeld, Yagman, Kaminsky, and Shepshalovich; Schroeter, *Last Exodus*, 195–238; Korey, *Soviet Cage*, 229–75.

219 *"We shall avoid"*: Memo from Rosenblum, Louis Rosenblum papers, box 1, folder 1.

Rosenblum had a list: Author interview with Lou Rosenblum; Rosenblum interview with son.

221 *In synagogue after*: Ozick, "24 Years."

"All my life": Cynthia Ozick to Rosenblum, December 18, 1970, CCSA Archives, container 2, folder 44.

222 *"The Six-Day War"*: Ozick, "24 Years."

Rather than gently: In an AJC Oral Interview, November 28, 1989, Yoram Dinstein said, "I told my superiors, we have, in my opinion, to declare war on them. To declare war on them."

223 *Lou Rosenblum had never*: Conversation from interview with Lou Rosenblum and his interview with his son.

"He went on to inform": Yaroslavsky to Rosenblum, April 25, 1970, CCSA Archives, container 4, folder 120.

"the first martyr": Rosenblum to Union of Councils members, April 27, 1970, CCSA Archives, container 5, folder 134.

In his note: Rosenblum to Ambassador Y. Rabin, May 4, 1970, CCSA Archives, container 4, folder 120.

224 *Feeling like he had:* Description of meeting and Rosenblum's demands from handwritten personal recollection by Rosenblum in CCSA Archives, container 4, folder 120, as well as author interview with Rosenblum.

225 Pravda *warned that:* Bernard Gwertzman, "Jews in Soviet Are Warned Against Espousing Zionism," *New York Times,* February 20, 1971.

226 *"If I could speak":* Kahane, *Jewish Defense League,* 50.

"I have listened": Henry Ginger, "World Jews Make a Plea to Moscow," *New York Times,* February 26, 1971.

227 *"lost opportunity":* Dr. Herbert S. Caron, "Point of View," *Cleveland Jewish News,* March 12, 1971.

Menachem Begin, encountering: Levanon, *Code Name,* 381.

228 *"I went to Brussels":* Kahane, *Jewish Defense League,* 56.

When a black limousine: Halevi, *Memoirs,* 98.

229 *Most of the daily reports:* Material from Meir Kahane FBI file #105-207795.

"Kahane has seriously": Ibid.

230 *"take over the entire":* Ibid.

232 *In fact, it felt:* Halevi, *Memoirs,* 103–05.

"What marked March 21": Kahane, *Jewish Defense League,* 145.

233 *After news of:* Kahane's reaction reported in Rosenthal, *Rookie Cop,* 166.

He needed a good: Kahane's connection to Colombo detailed in Friedman, *False Prophet,* 121–26.

234 *"It's a human brotherhood":* Morris Kaplan, "Kahane and Colombo Join Forces to Fight Reported U.S. Harassment," *New York Times,* May 14, 1971.

A few months: Kaufman, "Complex Past."

235 *"In this country":* Morris Kaplan, "Kahane Gets Suspended Five-Year Sentence in Bomb Plot," *New York Times,* July 24, 1971.

237 *A friend of Yossi:* Halevi, *Memoirs,* 110.

"It was the Soviet": Tad Szulc, "Shots at Soviet Mission Stir Bitter Debate in the U.N.," *New York Times,* October 22, 1971.

He called Kahane: "Kahane Is Rebuffed by Bush at Meeting," *New York Times,* October 26, 1971.

238 *"whose appetite for profits":* Kahane, *Jewish Defense League,* 9.

239 *"We were scared":* Les Ledbetter, "Firebomb Kills Woman, Hurts 13 in Hurok Office," *New York Times,* January 27, 1972.

240 *"I think the people":* Walter Goodman, "A Firebomb for an Impresario," *New York Times,* January 30, 1972.

As if this publicity: "Yevtushenko Composing Poem on Hurok Fire," *New York Times,* January 28, 1972.

241 *"Poor Iris":* "Bombs for Balalaikas," *Yevtushenko's Reader,* 147–50.

Before dropping out: Halevi, *Memoirs,* 122–54.

7. Birth of the Refusenik

243 *Vladimir Slepak was home:* Biographical information on Slepak from author interview with him; *Refusenik* transcript of interview with Vladimir and Masha Slepak; Potok, *Gates of November.*

244 *"sent a letter":* Memorandum from Andropov to the CPSU Central Committee in ibid., 103–04.

"nationalist convictions": Memorandum from Andropov to the CPSU Central Committee, in Morozov, *Documents,* 102.

248 *"Whenever you cut":* Potok, *Gates of November,* 103.

250 *Among their friends:* Author interview with David Drabkin.

252 *"to isolate the applicant":* Azbel, *Refusenik,* 247.

253 *Christopher Wren:* Author interview with David Shipler.

254 *"Who am I":* Quoted in Rubenstein, *Soviet Dissidents,* 154.

255 *"As a result of enemy":* Andropov to Central Committee in Rubenstein and Gribanov, eds., *KGB File,* 120–21.

256 *It survived its:* Rubenstein, *Soviet Dissidents,* 131.

"Any mass restrictions": Chalidze, *To Defend,* 101.

"We sign this": Schroeter, *Last Exodus,* 118.

257 *"The right of Jews":* Quoted in the *Near East Report,* "Soviet Jews Seek Right to Emigrate," vol. 15–17 (1971): 32.

Iskhod was a documentary: Story of *Iskhod* in Schroeter, *Last Exodus,* 98–102.

258 *"The movement continues":* Ibid., 102.

That they were: Description of sit-ins from press reports; Schroeter, *Last Exodus,* 328–35; Azbel, *Refusenik,* 242–45.

259 *"changed the face":* Azbel, *Refusenik,* 243.

"Zionism is Fascism!": Ibid., 245.

"The people from Riga": Ibid.

260 *That night for the first:* Author interview with Vladimir Slepak; Potok, *Gates of November,* 162–64.

261 *"because of your noncompliance":* Potok, *Gates of November,* 162.

262 *"We demand that":* Quoted in Cohen, ed., *Let My People,* 232.

At the beginning: Statistics from Altshuler, *Soviet Jewry,* 234–35.

Mark Azbel, the physicist: Azbel, *Refusenik,* 91.

263 *"a privileged caste":* Ibid., 132.

Alexander Lerner was: Biographical information on Lerner is drawn from his memoir *Change of Heart.*

266 *"Anyone who took":* Ibid., 17.

"When we had made": Ibid., 12.

"Stop to think": Ibid., 20.

267 *"I tried to identify":* Theodore Shabad, "Representative Scheuer Is Held Briefly by the Police in Moscow," *New York Times,* January 13, 1972.

270 *"In order to facilitate":* Schroeter, *Last Exodus,* 337.

"We would be very": NCSJ Archives, box 30, folder 2.

271 *To his surprise:* Lerner, *Change of Heart,* 191–92.

8. Linkage

273 *Senator Henry Jackson:* Biographical information on Jackson from Kaufman, *Henry M. Jackson;* Ognibene, *Scoop.*

274 *"This society is":* Kaufman, *Henry M. Jackson,* 230.

276 *"holding these people":* "McGovern Criticizes Soviet," *New York Times,* August 17, 1972.

Kahane, predictably: "Warning by Kahane," *New York Times,* August 22, 1972.

An editorial cartoon: The cartoon, by Paul Conrad, appeared in the *Los Angeles Times* on September 24, 1972.

Perle, a thirty-year-old: Biographical information on Perle from his interview with the author; Winik, *On the Brink,* 47–49.

277 *Running the shop:* Fosdick bio in Kaufman, *Henry M. Jackson,* 83–85.

279 *"You will understand":* Martin J. Hillenbrand, Assistant Secretary for European Affairs, State Department, to Herschel Schacter, November 7, 1970, NCSJ Archives, box 30, folder 2.

"Since the president's trip": Richard Maass to Max Fisher, July 27, 1972, in ibid.

Perle decided: Story of Jackson-Vanik amendment from author interviews with Perle, Amitay, Korey; *Refusenik* transcript of interview with Mark Talisman; Stern, *Water's Edge;* Korey, "Jackson-Vanik Amendment," "Struggle Over Jackson-Mills-Vanik," "Jackson Amendment"; Albright, "The Pact."

280 *"The time has come":* Quoted in Stern, *Water's Edge,* 32.

"I am mindful": Richard Maass to Jerry Goodman, April 17, 1972, NCSJ Archives, box 5, folder 3.

281 *"does not intend":* "Nixon 'Won't Politicize' on Soviet Jewry," *Los Angeles Times,* September 27, 1972.

"unnecessarily irritating": Javits is quoted in Korey, "Struggle Over Jackson-Mills-Vanik."

282 *"they expressed the opinion":* The memo was composed for the administration by Leonard Schroeter, the Seattle lawyer who wrote *The Last Exodus.* Its contents were revealed in "Private Note Says Nixon Visit Worsened Jews' Problem," *Los Angeles Times,* September 24, 1972.

283 *"Just imagine":* Rabin, *Rabin Memoirs,* 231.

"Mr. Secretary, two-thirds": From *Washington Post,* October 18, 1972, in NCSJ Archives, box 30, folder 7.

284 *"There are now a lot":* Isaacs, *Jews and American Politics,* 255; in an interview with the author, Amitay revealed that he'd thought he was speaking off the record when Isaacs recorded him.

285 *"Hello, Professor Einbinder":* Congressman Albert Quie of Minnesota talking to Boris Einbinder, November 20, 1972, NCSJ Archives, box 5, folder 8.

286 *"If we get":* Isaacs, *Jews and American Politics,* 256.

288 *"The problem is":* Rabin, *Rabin Memoirs,* 230.

"You must understand": Ibid.

289 *In a Politburo meeting:* Excerpts from minutes of the Politburo meeting in Morozov, *Documents*, 170–76.

290 *"Now, I have heard":* Quoted in Stern, *Water's Edge*, 68.

291 *"a brash, opinionated":* Memo from Bert Gold to Hyman Bookbinder, Jerry Goodman, and Richard Maass, NCSJ Archives, box 6, folder 1.

292 *"Mr. President, if you":* Description of meeting with Nixon and quote is from Albright, "The Pact," 34.

"I am standing": Quoted in Stern, *Water's Edge*, 70.

"a storm will hit": Nixon quoted in Dallek, *Nixon and Kissinger*, 477.

A retired multimillionaire: Fisher biographical material from Golden, *Quiet Diplomat*.

293 *It was a historic:* Description of event from author interview with Jerry Goodman.

"You're now back": Albright, "The Pact," 25–26.

"You gentlemen have": Golden, *Quiet Diplomat*, 279.

294 *"This may be":* Safire, *Before the Fall*, 575.

295 *"They had their own":* Recording of conversation between Kyrill Henkin and Lou Rosenblum, April 21, 1973, CCSA Archives, cassette A-41.

"Remember—the history": Recording of message from Kyrill Henkin, April 23, 1973, CCSA Archives, cassette A-42.

"effort to alleviate": Quoted in Korey, "Struggle Over Jackson-Mills-Vanik," 219.

296 *"Look, you go":* Quoted in Stern, *Water's Edge*, 81.

"Of all the human": Henry Jackson commencement address to Yeshiva University, June 4, 1973, from NCSJ Archives, box 31, folder 6.

"Now, the White House": Ibid.

297 *"We do not have":* Hedrick Smith, "Brezhnev Praises Nixon for 'Realistic' Approach," *New York Times,* June 15, 1973.

On Monday night: Description of Fisher and Stein at Brezhnev reception in Golden, *Quiet Diplomat*, 282–83.

298 *"Mr. President":* Ibid., 279–80.

"I do not know": Ibid., 284–85.

299 *"The administration is always":* Albright, "The Pact," 28.

"will result in": Transcript of remarks by Hertzberg at the network conference, Paramount Hotel, December 25, 1973, in CCSA Archives, container 8, folder 244.

On December 4: Korey, "Struggle Over Jackson-Mills-Vanik," 233.

"a defense of international": Sakharov's letter reprinted in Schroeter, *Last Exodus*, 387–88.

301 *"Would you agree":* Transcript of press conference on June 29, 1974, in NCSJ Archives, box 30, folder 8.

302 *"Eloquent appeals":* Philip Shabecoff, "President Warns Policy of Détente Bars Interfering," *New York Times,* June 6, 1974.

303 *"Experience shows":* "Excerpts from Speeches by Brezhnev and Nixon During a Dinner in Moscow," *New York Times,* June 28, 1974.

"he expressed": Jerry Goodman memo of meeting with Vice President Ford, May 3, 1974, in NCSJ Archives, box 6, folder 2.

304 *"the President's direct"*: "Accord Expected on Jews in Soviet," *New York Times*, August 16, 1974.

305 *"We have reached"*: Stern, *Water's Edge*, 163–64.

306 *"I doubt whether"*: Haskel Lookstein to Jerry Goodman, October 21, 1974, in NCSJ Archives, box 6, folder 2.

"The Soviets felt": Bernard Gwertzman, "Kissinger Leaves Moscow Hopeful on Arms Accord," *New York Times*, October 28, 1974.

"create[d] a distorted": Stern, *Water's Edge*, 168.

307 *"among the shabbiest"*: Quoted in Buwalda, *They Did Not*, 243.

Jackson told: Bernard Gwertzman, "Bill Advances Despite Russian Disavowal," *New York Times*, December 19, 1975.

"advocates of tension": Soviet commentary from Korey, "Jackson Amendment," 169.

308 *As Kissinger would:* Ibid., 166.

"When the Soviet": Henry Kissinger to Stanley Lowell, April 14, 1975, in NCSJ Archives, box 30, folder 8.

"I will, of course": Korey, "Jackson Amendment," 170.

"The 1972 Trade": "Text of Kissinger Statement on Accord Cancellation," *New York Times*, January 15, 1975.

309 *"shock and consternation"*: Stanley Lowell to Gerald Ford, December 19, 1974, in NCSJ Archives, box 30, folder 3.

"For the rest": Albright, "The Pact."

9. *Politiki* and *Kulturniki*

312 *A serious divide:* Story of rift from author interviews with Lunts, Prestin, Abramovich, Voronel, Fain, and Beilin; Azbel, *Refusenik*, 412–14; Sharansky, *Fear No Evil*, 99–101; Toth, "Split Among."

313 *Shcharansky had grown:* Biographical information on Shcharansky (who later changed the spelling of his last name to Sharansky) from author interview; *Refusenik* transcript with Natan and Avital Sharansky; Sharansky, *Fear No Evil*; Gilbert, *Shcharansky; Jerusalem Post* staff, *Anatoly and Avital*.

314 *"Does anyone have"*: Sharansky, *Fear No Evil*, xv.

Lunts was a: Author interview with Lunts.

Starting in 1972: Description of seminar origins and *Jews in the USSR* from author interviews with Voronel and Lunts.

315 *"a form of getting"*: From "Jewish Samizdat," essay by Alexander Voronel in Ro'i and Beker, eds., *Jewish Culture*, 257.

"those who are critical": *Jews in the USSR* was translated into English and published as a pamphlet.

They jokingly called: Information on the Hong Wei Bing from author interviews with Einbinder, Lunts, and Sharansky.

318 *"I'm writing to you":* Quoted in Gilbert, *Shcharansky,* 64.

319 *Dina Beilin had:* Biographical information on Beilin (sometimes referred to as Beilina) and details of refusenik lists from author interview with Dina Beilin.

320 *"in 1973–74":* Memorandum from Andropov to CPSU Central Committee in Morozov, *Documents,* 214–15.

Typically, a check: Details of money transfer from the West from author interviews with Beilin and Slepak.

321 *A tiny, bespectacled:* Biographical information on Nudel from author interview with her; Nudel, *A Hand in the Darkness.*

322 *This is just what:* Details of Lunts's KGB experiment from author interviews with Lunts, Slepak, Voronel, Prestin, and Abramovich.

In early 1975: Author interview with Abramovich.

323 *"For us, the central":* Toth, "Split Among."

324 *And they did:* The Western visitor was Joseph Smukler, whose efforts to mediate are detailed in Potok, *Gates of November,* 188.

325 *This new agreement:* Details of Helsinki process from Korey, *Promises We Keep;* Goldberg, *Final Act.*

326 *"No one should":* Christopher Wren, "Brezhnev, at Parley, Sees Bar to Dictating to Others," *New York Times,* August 1, 1975.

"divisiveness, disorganization": Quoted in Hans J. Morgenthau, "A Russian Tells Us How to Treat Russia," *New York Times,* November 9, 1975.

327 *Just a few weeks after:* Izvestia, September 3, 1975.

"In a convincing": "Sakharov Named Winner of '75 Nobel Peace Prize," *New York Times,* October 19, 1975.

Sakharov was cursed: David K. Shipler, "Soviet Calls Sakharov a Judas, Nobel Prize '30 Pieces of Silver,'" *New York Times,* October 29, 1975.

328 *"Every time the Soviet":* Quoted in Gilbert, *Shcharansky,* 93.

Then, in March of 1976: Origins of Moscow Helsinki Watch described in Goldberg, *Final Act,* 33–41; Orlov, *Dangerous Thoughts,* 188–92; Rubenstein, *Soviet Dissidents,* 217–35.

Orlov was a small: Biographical material on Orlov from Orlov, *Dangerous Thoughts;* Rubenstein, *Soviet Dissidents,* 215–17.

329 *"We should stop":* Sharansky and Dermer, *Case for Democracy,* 128.

The group, Orlov: Orlov, *Dangerous Thoughts,* 191.

330 *"The Group's information":* Goldberg, *Final Act,* 90.

331 *The task of reproducing:* Author interview with Ludmilla Alexeyeva.

Shcharansky's celebrity: A Calculated Risk was part of a series called World in Action; it was produced by Granada and aired on ITV.

333 *He denied any:* Shindler, *Exit Visa,* 196.

334 *"I have read with great":* Ibid., 197.

Dina Beilin, the keeper: Description of Chernobilsky and Ash defense from author interview with Dina Beilin.

"It's unprecedented": David K. Shipler, "2 Moscow Jews Who Faced Prison Up to Five Years for Protests Are Released as First Offenders and Family Men," *New York Times,* November 16, 1976.

336   *A lanky, athletic man:* Biographical information on Prestin from author interview with him.

"When people who": Azbel, *Refusenik,* 420.

337   *In 1975, Prestin:* Biographical information on Fain from author interview with him; Fain, *Yesh Me-Ayin.*

Together, Prestin and Fain: Details of *kulturniki* activity, including planning of the symposium, from author interviews with Prestin, Abramovich, and Fain; Fain, *Yesh Me-Ayin.*

338   *Lerner conceded the:* Lerner's lecture in Drachman, *Challenging the Kremlin,* 292–303.

340   *When the camera zoomed: Traders of Souls* is described in Gilbert, *Shcharansky,* 163.

"These people are": Ibid.

341   *"There is always":* Robert C. Toth, "Soviet Jews in 9 Cities Claim Official Drive Is Fostering 'Pogrom Atmosphere,'" *Los Angeles Times,* February 3, 1977.

Shcharansky filed: Gilbert, *Shcharansky,* 164.

It was hard: Demise of the Moscow Helsinki Watch described in Goldberg, *Final Act,* 210–34; Orlov, *Dangerous Thoughts,* 205–24; Rubenstein, *Soviet Dissidents,* 233–35.

"I would like to be": Recounted in author's interview with Ludmilla Alexeyeva and in Alexeyeva and Goldberg, *Thaw Generation,* 292.

342   *A kindly, soft-spoken:* Biographical information on Sanya Lipavsky from Gilbert, *Shcharansky,* 174–80.

Only after his betrayal: Author interview with Dina Beilin.

Lipavsky's story was: The origins of Lipavsky's connections to the KGB remained a mystery until 1979, when David Shipler encountered a man in Israel, a former prosecutor from Uzbekistan, who told him the story; Shipler wrote it up in an article called "Shcharansky Case: An Émigré's Version," *New York Times,* December 17, 1979.

343   *"It was not easy":* Goldberg, *Final Act,* 236.

Shcharansky was fingered: Gilbert, *Shcharansky,* 171.

"Today I talked": Vitaly Rubin's diary was made available to me by his wife, Inna. This passage was in Goldberg, *Final Act,* 242.

344   *"They're nervous":* Sharansky, *Fear No Evil,* 6.

10. The Shaming

345   *Martin Garbus, an American:* Visit by Garbus is described in Sakharov, *Memoirs,* 686.

346 *"I received your letter"*: Christopher S. Wren, "Sakharov Receives Carter Letter Affirming Commitment on Rights," *New York Times*, February 18, 1977.

"I said in a congratulatory": Ibid.

As Carter put it: Charles Mohr, "Carter Suggests That U.S. Foster Rights Overseas," *New York Times*, September 9, 1976.

347 *As one anonymous*: Bernard Gwertzman, "U.S. Asserts Prague Violates Covenants About Human Rights; Helsinki Agreement Is Cited," *New York Times*, January 27, 1977.

"Any attempt by the Soviet": "U.S. Cautions Soviet on Sakharov Curbs," *New York Times*, January 27, 1977.

348 *Millicent Fenwick had*: Biographical information on Fenwick from Schapiro, *Millicent Fenwick*.

One night a group: Ibid., 170–72.

349 *"To know the pain"*: Christopher S. Wren, "House Delegation Sees Soviet Jews," *New York Times*, August 11, 1975.

It was Wren: Visit to Orlov described in Schapiro, *Millicent Fenwick*, 168–70.

Within a month: Creation of the Helsinki Commission in Korey, *Promises We Keep*, 21–43; Goldberg, *Final Act*, 59–64.

350 *As Case put it*: Korey, *Promises We Keep*, 24.

"They and we": Goldberg, *Final Act*, 60.

351 *The administration had no*: Scowcroft memo quoted in Schapiro, *Millicent Fenwick*, 175.

"The President signed": Quoted in ibid.

Dante Fascell exchanged: Goldberg, *Final Act*, 64.

So extreme was: The rumor of Kissinger's intervention was fueled by the timing of a meeting he had with Dobrynin just before the Warsaw Pact countries rejected the commission's request; see Korey, *Promises We Keep*, 33–34.

352 *"THE PROMISES MADE"*: Quoted in Goldberg, *Final Act*, 186.

354 *A fiery self-admitted*: Biographical information on Lynn Singer from author interview with her.

Two young couples: Philadelphia activism from author interview with Enid Wurtman; Harrison, *Passover Revisited*.

355 *Another couple from*: Report by Shirley and Alan Molod on their visit with refuseniks in the Soviet Union, May 8–16, 1977, quoted in Harrison, *Passover Revisited*, 121–22.

In the early 1970s: Biographical information on Michael Sherbourne from *Refusenik* transcript.

356 *In March of 1976*: All dropout figures supplied by the Jewish Agency for Israel and reprinted in Lazin, *Struggle for Soviet Jewry*, 310.

357 *Throughout the 1970s*: The figure comes from William Korey, "Soviet Jews' Rights," *New York Times*, November 14, 1985. He cited a 1982 volume on higher education in Moscow that has the percentage of Jews enrolled in universities in 1970–71 as 3.16 percent of the total (or 19,509 people) and compares it to the numbers for 1980–81, with Jews making up just 1.5 percent of enrollment (or 9,911).

358 *In 1973 there:* For dropout figures from Jewish Agency see Lazin, *Struggle for Soviet Jewry*, 310.

359 *"The Israelis admit":* American Jewish Yearbook 77 (1977): 162.

360 *"We succeeded in":* "Notes of secret meeting on *Noshrim*, July 23, 1976," from JDC files, quoted in Lazin, *Struggle for Soviet Jewry*, 98.
     Others were even harsher: Ibid.

361 *As soon as it became:* Ibid., 101.
     "We didn't campaign": "Immigrants: Israel Wants Them All," *Time*, November 22, 1976.
     "Why don't these": Ibid.
     "No one, no one": Frumkin commentary, September 1976, in CCSA Archives, container 3, folder 98.

362 *"All of us are Zionists":* "Open Letter to the 'Committee of 8' concerning the cessation of support to Soviet Jewish aliyah drop-outs," Jerusalem, August 18, 1976, in ibid.
     "The traditional Jewish": Quoted in Lazin, *Struggle for Soviet Jewry*, 103.

363 *In November of 1976:* Statistics on the number of stories from Peter Osnos, "Soviet Dissidents and the American Press," *Columbia Journalism Review* 16 (November/December 1977): 32.

364 *"Are these dissidents":* Ibid.

365 *"We've double-checked":* Bernard Gwertzman, "Carter Denies C.I.A. Engaged Soviet Jew," *New York Times*, June 14, 1977.
     Carter gingerly broached: "Record of Conversation between Soviet Foreign Minister Gromyko and President Carter," September 23, 1977, in virtual archive of Woodrow Wilson International Center for Scholars.

366 *His appointment to head:* Goldberg's appointment described in Kampelman, *Entering New Worlds*, 220–22.

368 *The appointment of Goldberg:* Significance of Goldberg's appointment explained in Korey, *Promises We Keep*, 69–75.
     Dorothy Goldberg, the ambassador's: The unpublished memoirs of Dorothy Goldberg, who was included as a member of the delegation, are quoted in Korey, *Promises We Keep*. This observation is on page 75.

369 *The first two weeks:* Belgrade conference is detailed in ibid., 77–100.
     A few days later: Shindler, *Exit Visa*, 240.

370 *"I am surprised":* Korey, *Promises We Keep*, 82–83.

371 *"Efforts to squelch":* "The Belgrade Follow-up Meeting to the Conference on Security and Cooperation in Europe, United States," transcript published by the U.S. Congress, 79.
     "The American tactics": Michael Getler, "Belgrade Meeting: Lost Hopes and Stalled Effort at Détente," *Washington Post*, February 23, 1978.
     "Can it help": Ibid.

372 *"We had to speak":* Ibid.
     On the last day: Ibid.

11. Trial and Exile

373 *But on the nine-month anniversary:* Account of Shcharansky prison time from author interview with him; *Refusenik* transcript; Sharansky, *Fear No Evil.*

375 *"What's the use":* Sharansky, *Fear No Evil,* 40.

Tsypin wrote in: Tsypin's denunciation letter in Gilbert, *Shcharansky,* 197.

376 *But the headline:* Robert C. Toth, "Russia Indirectly Reveals 'State Secrets,'" *Los Angeles Times,* November 22, 1976.

"Blessed are you": Sharansky, *Fear No Evil,* 50.

378 *"What do you think":* Ibid., 170.

Everyone was interrogated: Details on the interrogations from author interview with Dina Beilin.

379 *"On the surface":* "Appeal by 250 Soviet Jewish Activists to the Knesset and All Jewish Communities Throughout the World," March 1977, reprinted in Drachman, *Challenging the Kremlin,* 261–62.

A group of refuseniks: Quoted in Gilbert, *Shcharansky,* 198.

380 *It was this combination:* Description of June 1, 1978, protest from author interviews with Ida Nudel and Vladimir and Masha Slepak; *Refusenik* transcript of Masha Slepak interview; Potok, *Gates of November,* 191–97; Nudel, *Hand in the Darkness,* 145–58.

383 *At Ida Nudel's trial:* Trial described in Nudel, *Hand in the Darkness,* 160–64.

"I am being tried": "Nudel's Final Plea" in *Chronicle of Human Rights in the USSR* 30 (April–June 1978): 26, reprinted in Drachman, *Challenging the Kremlin,* 291–92.

384 *"No, it's all right":* Potok, *Gates of November,* 195.

385 *In a meeting:* Excerpt from the minutes of a Politburo session in Moscow, June 22, 1978, in Morozov, *Documents,* 228–29.

Two weeks later: Trial described in Sharansky, *Fear No Evil,* 184–226; *Jerusalem Post* staff, *Anatoly and Avital,* 129–42; Gilbert, *Shcharansky,* 231–76.

386 *"Not to be allowed":* "The Shcharansky Trial," *Time,* July 24, 1978.

388 *"In March and April":* "Next Year in Jerusalem," *New York Times,* July 15, 1978.

390 *She gained many friends:* Description of Avital's campaign in *Refusenik* transcript of interview with Avital Sharansky; *Jerusalem Post* staff, *Anatoly and Avital,* 71–75, 101–02; Avital Shcharansky, *Next Year.*

391 *"I would love to talk":* Gilbert, *Shcharansky,* 140.

Whenever the refuseniks: Levanon laid out his negative views on Anatoly and Avital Shcharansky in Levanon, *Code Name,* 474–79.

Once, at a meeting: Ibid.

392 *The octogenarian:* *Refusenik* transcript of interview with Avital Sharansky.

"Now as I look back": Avital Shcharansky, *Next Year,* 121–22.

393 *"How everything has":* Gilbert, *Shcharansky,* 182–83.

He praised her: *American Jewish Yearbook* 80 (1980): 127.

394 *In an article:* Sally Quinn, "Avital Shcharansky and the Politics of Sorrow," *Washington Post,* July 20, 1978.

395 *In the last week:* "The Shcharansky Trial," *Time,* July 24, 1978.

"Our expression": "Political Letter of Soviet Ambassador to the United States Anatoly F. Dobrynin," July 11, 1978, in virtual archive of Woodrow Wilson International Center for Scholars.

398 *"The Russians are"*: Paul Hofmann, "Many Russian Jews 'Drop Out' in Vienna," *New York Times,* August 12, 1979.

"It amounts to evaluating": "An Open Letter to United States Representative Vanik, by Prof. Alexander Lerner, Moscow, March 26, 1979, dictated to Michael Sherbourne, London" in Drachman, *Challenging the Kremlin,* 450–52.

399 *"human rights is not"*: Eugene Gold, "Letter: On Soviet Trade Credits; Why Alter Jackson-Vanik Amendment?," *New York Times,* April 26, 1979.

400 *On the morning of:* Description of release from prison from author interviews with Kuznetsov and Dymshits.

Nehemiah Levanon showed: Author interview with Eduard Kuznetsov.

401 *"I have never rejected"*: Eduard Kuznetsov, "Flight from the Gulag," *New York Times Magazine,* April 27, 1980.

403 *Natalia Khassina, the woman:* Dan Fisher, "Soviets Now Barring Many from Emigrating, Jews Say," *Los Angeles Times,* October 9, 1979.

Volodya Slepak spent: Description of Slepak's exile from author interview; *Refusenik* transcript; Potok, *Gates of November,* 199–227.

405 *"Our life here"*: Potok, *Gates of November,* 222.

Ida Nudel had it: Description of Nudel's exile from author interview with her; Nudel, *Hand in the Darkness,* 185–238.

"I become silent": Nudel, *Hand in the Darkness,* 191.

406 *"The theory that has"*: Kaufman, *Henry M. Jackson,* 390.

407 *"What is essential now"*: Anthony Austin, "Sakharov Proposes Soviet Withdrawal," *New York Times,* January 3, 1980.

"The question of Sakharov": Politburo Meeting of January 3, 1980, in Rubenstein and Gribanov, eds., *KGB File,* 247.

In October of 1978: Description of meeting in prison from author interviews with Natan Sharansky, Hillel Butman, Yosef Mendelevich; described in Sharansky, *Fear No Evil,* 240–41, 252–54.

409 *Shcharansky lay down:* Sharansky, *Fear No Evil,* 270–71.

410 *"The day after I received"*: Gilbert, *Shcharansky,* 332.

12. Hopelessness

413 *But no island was:* Story of Ovrazhki from author interviews with Kosharovsky, Begun, Volvovsky, Prestin, Abramovich, and Vladimir Slepak.

414 *"Assuming the role"*: Memorandum from Andropov to the CPSU Central Committee in Morozov, *Documents,* 238–39.

415 *Emigration numbers:* All figures from Action for Post-Soviet Jewry, reprinted in Lazin, *Struggle for Soviet Jewry,* 309.

417 *"As President I would"*: Ronald Reagan to Henry Jackson, October 24, 1980, quoted in Kaufman, *Henry M. Jackson,* 401–02.

418 *Jackson was eventually:* 1980 presidential campaign in ibid., 392–408.

419 *"I do not need":* Kevin Klose, "Sakharov Defies Soviets," *Washington Post,* January 29, 1980.

420 *Brailovsky had stopped:* Biographical information on Brailovsky and state of *kulturniki* activities from author interview with him; interview with Brailovsky by Aba Taratuta at the Remember and Save website; Gilbert, *Jews of Hope,* 139–47.

421 *"Today is the first":* "Soviet Jews Prevented from Meeting," *New York Times,* November 24, 1980.

When they did: Biographical information on Aba Taratuta from author interview with him.

But nothing welded: Origin of the seminar from author interview with Taratuta, Gorodezky, Beizer, and Vasserman.

422 *The day the KGB:* Leningrad seminar crackdown described in Gilbert, *Jews of Hope,* 7–12; Lein, *Lest We Forget,* 5–9.

The last thing: Lein, *Lest We Forget,* 9.

"At last a door": Quoted in ibid., 37.

423 *Misha Beizer:* Biographical information on Beizer and details about his tours and the Leningrad Jewish Almanac from author interview with him; *Refusenik* transcript of his interview; Gilbert, *Jews of Hope,* 32–42.

424 *One of the more:* Biographical information on Gorodezky and details of his activities from author interview with him.

425 *Ida experienced this:* Nudel's problems after exile from author interview with her; Nudel, *Hand in the Darkness,* 240–73.

426 *Ivanov, strangely:* Relationship with Ivanov detailed in ibid., 110–12, 241–43.

427 *Toward the end:* Biographical information on Kosharovsky and details of his activity from author interview with him; *Refusenik* transcript of interview with Kosharovsky.

428 *These emissaries set up:* Details of Hebrew teaching network from author interviews with Kosharovsky and Kholmiansky; *Refusenik* transcript of interview with Yuli Edelstein.

429 *The reason given:* Serge Schmemann, "U.S.-Shunned Moscow Book Fair Opens," *New York Times,* September 3, 1981.

430 *Despite the fact:* "A Top Cop Takes the Helm," *Time,* November 22, 1982.

This was the same: Andropov to Central Committee, December 29, 1975, in Rubenstein and Gribanov, eds., *KGB File,* 207–12.

431 *In a speech:* "Report by Andropov at 21st December Kremlin Session," BBC World Broadcast, Sixtieth Anniversary of the USSR, SU/7215/C/1.

It was Yosef: Biographical information on Yosef Begun and details of his arrests from author interview with him; *Refusenik* transcript of interview with Yosef Begun; English summary of unpublished memoir provided to author by Begun.

433 *The news of the group:* The formation and development of the committee is detailed in Freedman, *Soviet Jewry,* 26–50.

During the Doctors': The letter, including Dragunsky's name, is reproduced in Brent and Naumov, *Stalin's Last Crime,* 300–05.

Zionism, Dragunsky wrote: Pravda, April 1, 1983, quoted in Freedman, *Soviet Jewry,* 28.

"The Zionist ringleaders": Ibid.

434 *"For me, a mother":* Serge Schmemann, "8 Soviet Jews Seek to Combat Zionism," *New York Times,* April 2, 1983.

The propaganda onslaught: June 6, 1983, press conference detailed in Freedman, *Soviet Jewry,* 31–35.

435 *Referring to the Lebanon:* Serge Schmemann, "Soviet Says the Jews Who Asked to Leave Have Largely Gone," *New York Times,* June 7, 1983.

Billing himself as an expert: Quotes from Korneyev in Dusko Duder, "Soviet Book Assails Jews," *Washington Post,* June 30, 1983.

436 *In it, he explained:* Memorandum from V. Chebrikov to the CPSU Central Committee in Morozov, *Documents,* 244–45.

437 *But then there was:* Biographical information on Essas and the details of his religious revival from author interview with him; Zakon, *Silent Revolution.*

439 *"Right now, you are not":* Zakon, *Silent Revolution,* 46.

441 *Essas soon connected:* Biographical information on Grisha Vasserman and details of his activities from author interview with him.

443 *It was now illegal:* Description of the additions to the criminal code in Korey, *Promises We Keep,* 164–65.

444 *Sasha Kholmiansky:* Details of his arrest from author interview with him.

445 *Yuli Edelstein, the youngest:* Details of his arrest from *Refusenik* transcript.

"We call on you": "Appeal for Urgent Action by Distraught Refuseniks," December 23, 1984, printed in the *Jewish Advocate,* January 17, 1985, and reprinted in Drachman, *Challenging the Kremlin,* 322–24.

13. Pawns Again

449 *As German chancellor:* "Ending an Era of Drift," *Time,* March 15, 1985.

Because Bush was taking: First encounter with Gorbachev described in Shultz, *Turmoil and Triumph,* 528–33.

450 *"Understand," Bush told:* Ibid., 531.

As he told: Ibid., 332–33.

Writing in Time: Strobe Talbott, "Both Continuity and Vitality," *Time,* March 25, 1985.

451 *"There is no doubt":* Gilbert, *Jewry in Crisis,* 8.

They looked at: Biographical information on Shultz from his memoir *Turmoil and Triumph.*

452 *Reagan talked for:* Ibid., 164–65.

453 *"What's all this fuss":* *Saturday Night Live,* season one; episode originally aired on January 24, 1976.

455 *"Israel's urge to dominate":* William Orbach, "Israel vs. Soviet Jewry," in *Response: A Contemporary Jewish Review* 38 (Winter 1979–1980).

456 *In an op-ed:* Jerry Goodman, quoted in Altshuler, *Exodus to Freedom,* 68.

Leading this charge: Biographical information on Bronfman from David Remnick, "Bronfman and the Search for the Past," *Washington Post,* April 2, 1986.

457 *"It is impossible":* Nahum Goldmann, "The Hammer-and-Sickle and Star of David," *New York Times,* January 8, 1979.

458 *In 1983, at one:* Edgar Bronfman, "To Help Soviet Jews," *New York Times,* July 1, 1983.

"Many people in this": Quoted in Anthony Lewis, "Opening for Gorbachev," *New York Times,* March 14, 1985.

459 *When expectant talk:* Anthony Lewis, "Cat and Mouse," *New York Times,* May 23, 1985.

460 *Avi Weiss was a:* Biographical information on Weiss from author interview with him and from his unpublished memoir.

Weiss set himself up: From unpublished memoir of Avi Weiss, provided to author. Weiss's memoir is in various draft forms. The hunger-strike section is from chapter 6, "The Struggle for Soviet Jewry," 1–13.

461 *His conclusion:* Avraham Weiss, "With Shcharansky," *New York Times,* December 11, 1982.

Weiss thought of: From Avi Weiss's unpublished memoir, the fragment titled "With Avital and Anatoly," 6: "In those years we developed almost a brother-sister relationship; a pure love that was absolutely above board and on the highest spiritual level. I am aware there was malicious gossip during those years about my relationship with Avital from some who may have envied the rapport we had developed. Such gossip was, of course, the incarnation of *lashon hara* [evil tongue], and absolute nonsense to boot."

462 *Weiss initiated what:* Operation Redemption described in Weiss memoir, ibid., 14–20.

463 *"To the Soviets":* Ibid., 17–18.

Usually much more: Ibid., 7–8.

464 *Reagan's insistence on:* Robert F. McFadden, "Americans Voice Anger on Bitburg," *New York Times,* May 6, 1985.

"That place, Mr. President": Bernard Weinraub, "Wiesel Confronts Reagan on Trip," *New York Times,* April 20, 1985.

465 *"And then, rising above":* "Speech by Reagan at Bergen-Belsen," *New York Times,* May 6, 1985.

"Is there a connection": William R. Greer, "Demonstration for Soviet Jews Jams Fifth Ave.," *New York Times,* May 6, 1985.

466 *A soft-spoken:* Biographical information on Kampelman from Kampelman, *Entering New Worlds.*

From the first day: Kampelman, *East-West Divide,* 9.

"The Soviet Union is": Ibid., 65.

467 *Madrid was in every:* Detailed description of the Madrid conference in Korey, *Promises We Keep,* 123–62.

468 *"The USSR is not":* "Stonewalling Human Rights," *Time,* November 24, 1980.

469 *Richard Schifter was:* Biographical information on Schifter from *Refusenik* transcript of interview with him.

   He would often tell: Schifter makes this point in the opening of an essay in Friedman and Chernin, eds., *Second Exodus,* 136: "I wanted to make sure I would not fail as I had failed in 1939 and 1940, when I tried to extricate my parents from Europe."

   Just before the Ottawa: Ibid., 137.

   His job, as he explained: Quoted in Korey, *Promises We Keep,* 179.

470 *"We talk about":* Christopher S. Wren, "Reporter's Notebook: A Rights Parley in Ottawa," *New York Times,* May 25, 1985.

   He pointed out: Korey, *Promises We Keep,* 174.

   But as the British: Quoted in ibid., 172.

471 *Right-wing parliament:* Cohen comment quoted in Freedman, ed., *Jewry in the 1980s,* 61–96.

   Indication of Soviet: Details of the exchange in ibid., 82.

472 *"I am convinced":* "Israel-Soviet Contacts Held in Paris," July 20, 1985, BBC World Service, Middle East, ME/8008/A/1.

473 *At first written off:* Judith Miller, "Peres Reports French Offer to Fly Soviet Jews to Israel," *New York Times,* October 26, 1985.

   "I think my friend": David Remnick, "Bronfman and the Search for the Past," *Washington Post,* April 2, 1986.

474 *Asked publicly about:* Serge Schmemann, "Summit Parley Overshadowed by Rights Issue," *New York Times,* November 13, 1985.

   "Rampant racism in many": Celestine Bohlen, "Kremlin Says U.S. Violates Rights," *Washington Post,* November 17, 1985.

475 *"Closed and compartmented":* Shultz, *Turmoil and Triumph,* 591.

   "You should take up": Ibid.

   During this meeting: Ibid., 588–89.

   In order to achieve: Chernyaev, *Six Years,* 41.

476 *Bronfman tried to:* Episode is described in Weiss memoir, "With Avital and Anatoly," 23.

   The activists spent: Avraham Weiss, "The Dark Side to the Summit," *New York Times,* December 7, 1985.

   Media savvy now: Avital Shcharansky's letter to Raisa Gorbachev reprinted in Gilbert, *Shcharansky,* 409–10.

477 *"Jews are a part":* Joseph Lelyveld, "Jackson, in Impromptu Session, Presses Gorbachev on Soviet Jews," *New York Times,* November 20, 1985.

478 *Morris Abram, the head of:* Bernard Gwertzman, "U.S. Jewish Group Cautions on Arms," *New York Times,* January 7, 1986.

479 *I think I'll die:* Weiss memoir, "With Avital and Anatoly," 30–31.

   Throughout that year: Story of the negotiations for Shcharansky's release in *Jerusalem Post* staff, *Anatoly and Avital,* 220–25.

480 *Shcharansky, isolated:* Account of release in Sharansky, *Fear No Evil*, 399–416.

481 *"When I probed my":* Ibid., 399.

483 *They embraced strongly:* Ibid., 415.

484 *He apologized for:* Shcharansky's airport speech in *Jerusalem Post* staff, *Anatoly and Avital*, 249.

485 *People wondered about:* Dan Fisher, "I'm the One to Decide," *Los Angeles Times*, May 2, 1986.

   One of the people: Author interview with Sylva Zalmanson; *Jerusalem Post* staff, *Anatoly and Avital*, 239–43.

486 *"He's the last man":* David K. Shipler, "The Question in Israel: Whither Shcharansky?" *New York Times*, February 15, 1986.

   In his speech: Shcharansky's appearance in front of the airport terminal in *Jerusalem Post* staff, *Anatoly and Avital*, 252–54.

487 *A large crowd:* Scene at the Western Wall described in Sharansky, *Fear No Evil*, 416; *Jerusalem Post* staff, *Anatoly and Avital*, 256–57.

14. "Mr. Gorbachev, Let These People Go!"

488 *But she swore:* Nudel, *Hand in the Darkness*, 290–93.

490 *"If we don't back":* Chernyaev, *Six Years*, 84.

491 *The very words:* *Pravda*, February 26, 1986, quoted in Korey, *Promises We Keep*, 189.

492 *He described discovering:* Philip Taubman, "Soviet Poet Looks Hard at Suffering of the Jews," *New York Times*, October 20, 1986.

493 *From his new platform:* "Elie Wiesel, in Moscow, Meets Good Friends," *New York Times*, October 24, 1986.

   "Not a day passes": Christine Bohlen, "Moscow Jews Celebrate; Thousands Applaud Nobel Winner Wiesel," *Washington Post*, October 25, 1986.

495 *He told the:* William Johnson, "Arms Deal Possible, Shultz Says Reagan Leaves for Iceland with Tough Talk on Rights," *Globe and Mail*, October 9, 1986.

   As Orlov was leaving: Orlov, *Dangerous Thoughts*, 296.

496 *As Morris Abram:* Abram and Goodman, "Reykjavik Talks Hold Out Hope on Emigration of Soviet Jews," *New York Times*, October 19, 1986.

   Shultz used a speech: "The Right Priority for Human Rights," *New York Times*, November 13, 1986.

   "There will be no": Paul Quinn-Judge, "Measuring the Mood in Vienna," *Christian Science Monitor*, November 4, 1986.

   In Vienna, a younger: Details of the Vienna monitoring conference in Korey, *Promises We Keep*, 213–76.

   At one press conference: James M. Markham, "Soviet Spokesmen Joust with Critics," *New York Times*, November 4, 1986.

497 *"I would like":* Ibid.

   Two days after: Shevardnadze's announcement in Korey, *Promises We Keep*, 228.

At a press conference: Philip Taubman, "Soviet Offers East-West Rights Talks in Moscow," *New York Times,* November 6, 1986.

As the conference opened: "Group: Soviet Jails Are Getting Worse," *Philadelphia Inquirer,* November 4, 1986.

498 *When the new phone:* Account of Sakharov-Gorbachev phone call in Sakharov, *Memoirs,* 614–17.

499 *Dressed in a gray:* Philip Taubman, "Sakharov and Wife Back in Moscow," *New York Times,* December 23, 1986.

"I think that the word": Bill Keller, "Physicist Sees Major Changes For Soviet," *New York Times,* December 25, 1986.

500 *They told the press:* Moscow demonstration described in Philip Taubman, "The Release of Sakharov: Its Broader Implications," *New York Times,* December 21, 1986.

For months, Ida: Nudel's visit to Sakharov in Nudel, *Hand in the Darkness,* 294–95.

501 *Emigration could be:* USSR Council of Ministers Resolution, "On addenda to the Regulations of Entering or Leaving the USSR," BBC World Service Broadcast, SU/8424/C/1.

503 *"Sometimes I have":* David Remnick, "Émigré as Eminence: Shcharansky Facing the Burdens of Celebrity," *Washington Post,* May 13, 1986.

Weiss wanted Shcharansky: Shcharansky visit and Weiss motivation described in *Jerusalem Post* staff, *Anatoly and Avital,* 277–80; Weiss's unpublished memoir "With Avital and Anatoly," 36–39: "I was undoubtedly motivated by a variety of motives, of which ego gratification may have been one. Still, I was convinced then and remain so today that my principal motivation was that Natan make a gesture that would set clear for the historical record what part of the Soviet Jewry movement had been his staunchest supporters during the years when he lay near death at the mercy of the KGB."

504 *"Exactly as it was":* Helsinki Commission, *Hearings,* May 14, 1986, quoted in Korey, *Promises We Keep,* 215–19.

"As a Zionist": *Jerusalem Post* staff, *Anatoly and Avital,* 280.

505 *"When Mikhail Gorbachev":* Yitzhak Rabi, "Sharansky Calls on American Jewry to Continue Its Public Campaign on Behalf of Soviet Jewry," *Jewish Telegraphic Agency,* September 4, 1986, quoted in Altshuler, *From Exodus,* 81.

506 *"The reunion of families":* Helsinki Commission, *Hearings,* May 14, 1986, quoted in Korey, *Promises We Keep,* 215–19.

Speaking to the neoconservative: "The Limits of Glasnost," speech delivered by Natan Sharansky to the Heritage Foundation, December 12, 1986.

Shimon Peres, speaking: James M. Markham, "Israel's Premier, in West Berlin, Appeals to Soviets to Let Jews Go," *New York Times,* January 30, 1986.

507 *Natan Shcharansky spoke:* "Sharansky Proposes That the West Offer the USSR Quid Pro Quo," *Jewish Telegraphic Agency,* March 27, 1987, quoted in Feingold, *"Silent No More,"* 256.

He won no converts: Ari L. Goldman, "Israel Asking U.S. to Bar Soviet Jews," *New York Times,* March 1, 1987.

Yosef Begun, the Hebrew: Account of Begun's release from author interview with him; *Refusenik* transcript of interview with Yosef Begun.

509 *"There should be no":* Celestine Bohlen, "Soviet Urges New Look at History; Gorbachev Says It Is 'Immoral to Forget,'" *Washington Post,* February 13, 1987.

510 *"After being punched":* Christopher Walker, "Brutal Attack on Protesting Moscow Jews," *Times* (London), February 14, 1987.

In Leningrad that: Details of the Leningrad protests from author interviews with Beizer and Taratuta; *Refusenik* transcripts of interviews with them.

511 *When he arrived:* Seder is described in Shultz, *Turmoil and Triumph,* 886–87.

512 *At a meeting the following:* Ibid., 894–95.

513 *"The degree of constraint":* Ibid., 888.

514 *They arrived in Moscow:* Details of the meetings, including Dobrynin's comments to Abram, in confidential memorandum from Jerry Goodman, in NCSJ Archives, box 41, folder 1.

Alexander Lerner, sitting: Lerner, *Change of Heart,* 210–11.

515 *A few of the most:* Letter from refuseniks to "the leadership of the state of Israel and Jewish organizations of the Diaspora in Conjunction with the Visit of Morris Abram and Edgar Bronfman," April 9, 1987, in NCSJ Archives, box 41, folder 1.

"I know you have": Washington Jewish Week, May 7, 1987.

516 *"I must conclude":* "Soviets Said Failing to Ease Jews' Emigration," *Washington Post,* July 10, 1987.

517 *Harris was tall:* Biographical information on Harris from author interview with him; Harris, *In the Trenches,* 3–22.

520 *"We are now being":* Friedman and Chernin, eds., *Second Exodus,* 144.

In early October: Nudel departure from author interview with her; Nudel, *Hand in the Darkness,* 297–305.

The Slepaks' phone rang: Slepaks departure from author interview with them; Potok, *Gates of November,* 230–34.

521 *"For me it is":* Thomas L. Friedman, "Soviet Émigré Starts Life as an Israeli," *New York Times,* October 16, 1987.

Later he described: Shultz, *Turmoil and Triumph,* 990: "This was one of the most moving moments of my years as secretary of state."

522 *In November, a group:* Author interview with Vladimir Kislik.

Goldfarb himself saw: Alexander Goldfarb, "Testing Glasnost," *New York Times Magazine,* December 6, 1987.

523 *Started in May:* Origins of Pamyat in Freedman, ed., *Soviet Jewry in the 1980s,* 51–60.

524 *This momentum did not:* Process of planning for rally from author interview with Harris; AJC Oral Interview, October 7, 1991.

525 *Walking with her:* "March by 200,000 in Capital Presses Soviet on Rights," *New York Times,* December 7, 1987.

526 *Vice President George Bush:* "Free Jews, Thousands Demand," *Washington Post,* December 7, 1987.

Sources and Further Reading

This book is primarily based on oral histories and backed by archival and secondary material. I was able to draw on three different sources for the interviews. The testimonies I conducted and recorded myself—mostly between the fall of 2004 and the winter of 2006—are listed below. Early in my research, I drew heavily on the oral interviews that are part of the American Jewish Committee Oral History Collection, which is now housed at the New York Public Library's Dorot Jewish Division. Hundreds of oral histories with the principal actors in the Soviet Jewry movement were recorded as part of this project, most of them between 1989 and 1992. I was fortunate to gain a third source of first-person testimony when Laura Bialis, the director of *Refusenik* (2007), a documentary film about the Soviet Jewry movement, gave me access to transcripts of the many interviews she had filmed. These two collections offered an added wealth of narrative detail to the interviews I conducted, and I was able to use them to triangulate, checking the facts in one person's story against another's and reviewing the same person's testimony in two or three different places. In the endnotes, I refer to the interviews from the film as *Refusenik* transcripts; the American Jewish Committee testimonies are referred to as AJC Oral Interviews.

I also drew on newspaper articles from both the national papers and the local Jewish press. For purposes of brevity, when the details of the newspaper items are given in the body of the text, the article is not cited in the endnotes. However, if quotations or details are taken from a newspaper article whose source is not mentioned in the text, that article is duly cited in the endnotes.

Archives

Student Struggle for Soviet Jewry Archives at Yeshiva University

Cleveland Council on Soviet Anti-Semitism Archives at Western Reserve Historical Society

Union of Councils for Soviet Jews Archives at the American Jewish Historical Society (I-410)

National Conference on Soviet Jewry Archives at the American Jewish Historical Society (I-181, I-181A)

Abraham Joshua Heschel Papers at Jewish Theological Seminary

Louis Rosenblum Papers at Western Reserve Historical Society

Herb Caron personal papers

Yaakov Birnbaum personal papers

Nizkor Project, "The Trial of Adolf Eichmann," http://www.nizkor.org/hweb/people/e/eichmann-adolf/transcripts/

Author Interviews

Abeshaus, Evgeny—July 3, 2005

Abramovich, Pavel—June 21, 2005

Alexandrovich, Ruth—May 25, 2005

Alexeyeva, Ludmilla—May 5, 2006

Altman, Anatoly—May 19, 2005

Amitay, Morris—November 22, 2006

Begun, Yosef—July 11, 2005

Beilin, Dina—July 6, 2005

Beizer, Michael—June 24, 2005

Birnbaum, Eli—July 17, 2005

Birnbaum, Yaakov—March 16 and March 23, 2003; April 12, 2005

Boguslavsky, Irina—May 26, 2005

Brailovsky, Victor—June 28, 2005

Butman, Hillel—May 9, 2005

Caron, Herb—January 28, 2005

Chernoglaz, David—June 9, 2005

Chlenov, Mikhail—May 5, 2006

Cohen, Pamela—December 7, 2006

Dashevsky, Zev—May 23, 2006

Drabkin, David—June 19, 2005

Dreizner, Shmuel—May 23, 2005

Dymshits, Mark—July 17, 2005

Einbinder, Boris—July 10, 2005

Essas, Ilya—July 5, 2005

Fain, Benjamin—June 29, 2005

Frauenglas, Robert—February 24, 2005

Frucher, Sandy—January 7, 2005

Frumkin, Si—October 13, 2005

Goffin, Sherwood—February 14, 2005

Goldfeld, Anatoly—June 2, 2005

Goodman, Jerry—October 9, October 17, and December 2, 2004

Gorodezky, Yakov—March 28, 2005

Green, Susan—February 2, 2005

Greenberg, Irving—February 17, 2005

Gulko, Bella—July 1, 2005

Halevi, Yossi Klein—May 5, 2005

Harris, David—February 23, 2005

Kaminsky, Lassal—May 24, 2005

Kazakov (Kedmi), Yasha—May 17, 2005

Khassina, Natalia—July 21, 2005

Khavkin, David—June 1, 2005

Khnokh, Aryeh—June 22, 2005

Kholmiansky, Alexander—May 22, 2006

Kislik, Vladimir—July 1, 2005

Kochubievsky, Boris (later Barach
    Ashi)—May 18, 2005

Korey, William—March 22, 2005

Kosharovsky, Yuli—May 9, 2005

Kuznetsov, Eduard—June 29, 2005

Lookstein, Haskel—February 1, 2005

Lunts, Alexander—May 11, 2005

Lvov, Leonid—May 6, 2006

Mendelevich, Yosef—May 16, 2005

Nudel, Ida—July 21, 2005

Penson, Boris—May 15, 2005

Perle, Richard—November 21, 2006

Prestin, Vladimir—June 27 and 28, 2005

Richter, Glenn—February 27 and
    October 3, 2005

Rosenblum, Louis—January 27 and
    January 28, 2005

Rosenne, Meir—May 18, 2005

Rubin, Inna—June 24, 2005

Schapira, Morey—January 23, 2008

Sharansky, Natan—July 24, 2005

Sheer, Charles—January 13, 2005

Shepshalovich, Misha—June 6, 2005

Shipler, David—March 3, 2008

Shpilberg, Aron—May 26, 2005

Shtern, Yuri—May 19, 2006

Shtilbans, Victor—February 7, 2005

Singer, Lynn—December 6, 2004;
    January 31, 2005

Slepak, Vladimir—April 1, 2007

Slovin, Boris and Leah (Lydia)—June 9
    and June 16, 2005

Sprayregen, Joel—September 12, 2005

Stein, Mel—January 12, 2005

Stonov, Leonid—December 8, 2006

Taratuta, Aba—June 22, 2005

Uspensky, Igor and Inna—May 18, 2006

Vasserman, Grigory—June 30, 2005

Volk, Eli—June 1, 2005

Volvovsky, Leonid—June 28, 2005

Voronel, Alexander—May 17, 2006

Weiss, Avi—January 4, 2005

Wurtman, Enid—July 24, 2005

Yagman, Lev—May 19, 2005

Yakir, Evgeny—June 21, 2005

Zalmanson, Israel—March 26, 2005

Zalmanson, Sylva—May 22, 2005

Zalmanson, Vulf—May 27, 2005

Zelichonok, Roald—July 8, 2005

Books

Abram, Morris B. *The Day Is Short: An Autobiography.* New York: Harcourt Brace
    Jovanovich, 1982.

Alexeyeva, Ludmilla. *Soviet Dissent.* Middletown, CT: Wesleyan University Press, 1985.

Alexeyeva, Ludmilla, and Paul Goldberg. *The Thaw Generation: Coming of Age in the
    Post-Stalin Era.* Pittsburgh: University of Pittsburgh Press, 1990.

Alpert, Yakov. *Making Waves.* New Haven, CT: Yale University Press, 2000.

Altshuler, Mordechai. *Soviet Jewry Since the Second World War.* New York: Greenwood
    Press, 1987.

Altshuler, Stuart. *From Exodus to Freedom: A History of the Soviet Jewry Movement.*
    Lanham, MD: Rowman and Littlefield, 2005.

Amalrik, Andrei. *Will the Soviet Union Survive Until 1984?* New York: Harper and Row, 1970.

Andrew, Christopher, and Vasili Mitrokhin. *The Sword and the Shield: The Mitrokhin Archive and the Secret History of the KGB.* New York: Basic Books, 1999.

———. *The World Was Going Our Way: The KGB and the Battle for the Third World.* New York: Basic Books, 2005.

Axelbank, Albert. *Soviet Dissent: Intellectuals, Jews and Détente.* New York: F. Watts, 1975.

Azbel, Mark Ya. *Refusenik: Trapped in the Soviet Union.* Boston: Houghton Mifflin, 1981.

Bloed, Arie, ed. *The Conference on Security and Cooperation in Europe: Analysis and Basic Documents, 1972–1993.* Dordrecht, Netherlands: Kluwer Academic Publishers, 1993.

Bonner, Elena. *Alone Together.* New York: Alfred A. Knopf, 1986.

Boukovsky, Vladimir. *Et le vent reprend ses tours: ma vie de dissident.* Paris: Robert Laffont, 1978.

———. *To Build a Castle: My Life as a Dissenter.* New York: Viking, 1978.

Brent, Jonathan, and Vladimir P. Naumov. *Stalin's Last Crime.* New York: HarperCollins, 2003.

Butman, Hillel. *From Leningrad to Jerusalem.* Berkeley, CA: Benmir Books, 1990.

Buwalda, Petrus. *They Did Not Dwell Alone: Jewish Emigration from the Soviet Union, 1967–1990.* Baltimore: Johns Hopkins University Press, 1997.

Carter, Jimmy. *Keeping Faith: Memoirs of a President.* New York: Bantam, 1982.

Chalidze, Valery. *To Defend These Rights.* New York: Random House, 1974.

Chernyaev, Anatoly. *My Six Years with Gorbachev.* University Park: Pennsylvania State University Press, 2000.

Cohen, Richard, ed. *Let My People Go.* New York: Popular Library, 1971.

Collins, Robert B. *Transforming America: Politics and Culture During the Reagan Years.* New York: Columbia University Press, 2007.

Dallek, Robert. *Nixon and Kissinger: Partners in Power.* New York: HarperCollins, 2007.

Decter, Moshe, ed. *A Hero for Our Time: The Trial and Fate of Boris Kochubievsky.* New York: Conference on Status of Soviet Jewry and the Academic Committee on Soviet Jews, 1970.

———. *Israel and the Jews in the Soviet Mirror.* New York: Conference on the Status of Soviet Jews, 1967.

———. *Redemption: Jewish Freedom Letters from Russia.* New York: American Conference on Soviet Jewry, 1969.

Dershowitz, Alan M. *The Best Defense.* New York: Random House, 1982.

Dobrynin, Anatoly. *In Confidence: Moscow's Ambassador to America's Six Cold War Presidents.* New York: Times Books, 1995.

Drachman, Edward. *Challenging the Kremlin: The Soviet Jewish Movement for Freedom.* New York: Paragon House, 1991.

Eliav, Arie L. *Between Hammer and Sickle*. New York: Signet Books, 1967.

Ezergailis, Andrew. *The Holocaust in Latvia, 1941–1944*. Riga: Historical Institute of Latvia, 1996.

Fain, Benjamin. *Yesh Me-Ayin* [Hebrew]. Jerusalem: Rubin Mass, Ltd., 2004.

Fain, Benjamin, and Mervin F. Verbit. *Jewishness in the Soviet Union*. Jerusalem: Jerusalem Center for Public Affairs, 1984.

Feingold, Henry L. *"Silent No More": Saving the Jews of Russia, the American-Jewish Effort, 1967–1989*. Syracuse, NY: Syracuse University Press, 2007.

Ford, Gerald. *A Time to Heal: The Autobiography of Gerald Ford*. New York: Harper, 1979.

Fosdick, Dorothy, ed. *Henry Jackson and World Affairs: Selected Speeches, 1953–1983*. Seattle: University of Washington Press, 1990.

——. *Staying the Course: Henry M. Jackson and National Security*. Seattle: University of Washington Press, 1987.

Freedman, Robert O., ed. *Soviet Jewry in the Decisive Decade, 1971–1980*. Durham, NC: Duke University Press, 1984.

——. *Soviet Jewry in the 1980s*. Durham, NC: Duke University Press, 1989.

Freedman, Samuel G. *Jew vs. Jew*. New York: Simon and Schuster, 2000.

Friedman, Murray. *What Went Wrong?: The Creation and Collapse of the Black-Jewish Alliance*. New York: Free Press, 1995.

Friedman, Murray, and Albert D. Chernin, eds. *A Second Exodus: The American Movement to Free Soviet Jews*. Lebanon, NH: Brandeis University Press, 1999.

Friedman, Robert I. *The False Prophet: Rabbi Meir Kahane—From FBI Informant to Knesset Member*. Brooklyn: Lawrence Hill Books, 1990.

Gaddis, John Lewis. *The Cold War: A New History*. New York: Penguin Press, 2005.

Gilbert, Martin. *The Jews of Hope*. New York: Penguin, 1985.

——. *Shcharansky: Hero of Our Time*. New York: Viking, 1986.

——. *Soviet Jewry in Crisis*. Rondebosch, South Africa: Kaplan Centre, University of Cape Town, 1984.

Gilboa, Yehoshua. *The Black Years of Soviet Jewry, 1939–1953*. Boston: Little, Brown, 1971.

Gitelman, Zvi. *A Century of Ambivalence: The Jews of Russia and the Soviet Union, 1881 to the Present*. Bloomington: Indiana University Press, 1988.

Glazer, Nathan. *American Judaism*. Chicago: University of Chicago Press, 1957.

Goldberg, J. J. *Jewish Power: Inside the American Jewish Establishment*. Reading, MA: Addison-Wesley, 1996.

Goldberg, Paul. *The Final Act: The Dramatic, Revealing Story of the Moscow Helsinki Watch Group*. New York: Morrow, 1988.

Golden, Peter. *Quiet Diplomat: A Biography of Max M. Fisher*. New York: Cornwall Books, 1992.

Gorbanevskaya, Natalia. *Red Square at Noon*. New York: Holt, Rinehart and Winston, 1972.

Govrin, Yosef. *Israeli-Soviet Relations, 1953–1967*. London: Frank Cass Publishers, 1998.

Gromyko, Andrei. *Memoirs from Stalin to Gorbachev*. London: Arrow Books, 1989.

Halevi, Yossi Klein. *Memoirs of a Jewish Extremist: An American Story*. Boston: Little, Brown, 1995.

Harris, David A. *In the Trenches: Selected Speeches and Writing of an American Jewish Activist, 1979–1999*. Hoboken, NJ: Ktav Publishing House, 2000.

Harris, Louis, and Bert E. Swanson. *Black-Jewish Relations in New York City*. New York: Praeger, 1970.

Harrison, Andrew. *Passover Revisited: Philadelphia's Efforts to Aid Soviet Jews, 1963–1998*. Madison, NJ: Fairleigh Dickinson University Press, 2001.

Hertzberg, Arthur. *The Jews in America: Four Centuries of an Uneasy Encounter*. New York: Simon and Schuster, 1989.

Heschel, Abraham Joshua. *The Insecurity of Freedom*. New York: Farrar, Straus and Giroux, 1966.

Isaacs, Stephen. *Jews and American Politics*. New York: Doubleday, 1974.

Isaacson, Walter. *Kissinger*. New York: Simon and Schuster, 1992.

Jabotinsky, Ze'ev. *The Political and Social Philosophy of Ze'ev Jabotinsky*. Edited by Mordechai Sarig. London: Vallentine Mitchell, 1999.

——. *The War and the Jew*. 1942. Reprint, New York: Altalena Press, 1987.

Javits, Jacob. *The Autobiography of a Public Man*. Boston: Houghton Mifflin, 1981.

Jerusalem Post staff. *Anatoly and Avital Shcharansky: The Journey Home*. New York: Harcourt Brace Jovanovich, 1986.

Jones, C. B. *The Cold War*. Chicago: Contemporary Books, 2004.

Kahane, Meir. *On Jews and Judaism: Selected Articles, 1961–1990*. Jerusalem: Institute for Publications of the Writings of Meir Kahane, 1993.

——. *The Story of the Jewish Defense League*. Radnor, PA: Chilton Book Company, 1975.

Kampelman, Max. *Entering New Worlds: The Memoirs of a Private Man in Public Life*. New York: HarperCollins, 1991.

——. *Three Years at the East-West Divide*. New York: Freedom House, 1983.

Kandel, Felix. *Shaare Yitziat Russiya* [Hebrew]. Tel Aviv: Hakibbutz Hameuchad, 1982.

Kaplan, Eran. *The Jewish Radical Right: Revisionism and Its Ideological Legacy*. Madison: University of Wisconsin Press, 2005.

Kaufman, Jonathan. *Broken Alliance: The Turbulent Times Between Blacks and Jews in America*. New York: Scribner, 1988.

Kaufman, Robert G. *Henry M. Jackson: A Life in Politics*. Seattle: University of Washington Press, 2000.

Kissinger, Henry. *Diplomacy*. New York: Simon and Schuster, 1994.

——. *White House Years*. Boston: Little, Brown, 1979.

——. *Years of Upheaval*. Boston: Little, Brown, 1982.

Korey, William. *Human Rights and the Helsinki Accord*. New York: Foreign Policy Association, 1983.

———. *The Promises We Keep: Human Rights, the Helsinki Process and American Foreign Policy.* New York: Institute of East-West Studies, 1993.

———. *The Soviet Cage.* New York: Viking, 1971.

Kotler, Yair. *Heil Kahane.* New York: Adama Books, 1986.

Kuznetsov, Eduard. *Lettres de Mordovie.* Paris: Editions Gallimard, 1979.

———. *Prison Diaries.* New York: Stein and Day, 1975.

Lawrence, Gunther. *Three Million More?* Garden City, NY: Doubleday, 1970.

Lazin, Fred. *The Struggle for Soviet Jewry in American Politics: Israel versus the American Jewish Establishment.* Lanham, MD: Lexington Books, 2005.

Lein, Evgeny. *Lest We Forget: The Refuseniks' Struggle and World Jewish Solidarity.* Jerusalem: Jerusalem Publishing Centre, 1997.

Lerner, Alexander. *Change of Heart.* Minneapolis, MN: Lerner Publications, 1992.

Levanon, Nehemiah. *"Nativ" Was the Code Name* [Hebrew]. Tel Aviv: Am Oved Publishers, 1996.

Levin, Dov. *Encyclopedia of the Holocaust.* New York: Macmillan, 1990.

Levin, Nora. *The Jews in the Soviet Union since 1917.* New York: New York University Press, 1988.

Mandelbaum, Yitta Halberstam. *Holy Brother: Inspiring Stories and Enchanted Tales about Rabbi Shlomo Carlebach.* Northvale, NJ: Jason Aronson, 2002.

Mann, James. *The Rebellion of Ronald Reagan: A History of the End of the Cold War.* New York: Viking, 2009.

Maranz, Paul, and David Goldberg, eds. *The Decline of the Soviet Union and the Middle East.* Boulder, CO: Westview Press, 1994.

Mastny, Vojtech. *Helsinki, Human Rights and European Security: Analysis and Documentation.* Durham, NC: Duke University Press, 1986.

Matlock, Jack F. *Autopsy of an Empire.* New York: Random House, 1995.

Mendelevich, Yosef. *Operation "Wedding": The Struggle, the Arrest, and the Release of a Prisoner of Zion* [Hebrew]. Jerusalem: Keter Publishing House, 1985.

Moniquet, Claude. *Histoire des juifs sovietiques, 1948–1988.* Paris: Olivier Orban, 1989.

Morozov, Boris, ed. *Documents on Soviet Jewish Emigration.* London: Frank Cass Publishers, 1999.

Morrison, Donald. *Gorbachev: An Intimate Biography.* New York: Time, Inc., 1988.

Nixon, Richard M. *RN: The Memoirs of Richard Nixon.* New York: Grosset and Dunlap, 1978.

Novick, Peter. *The Holocaust in American Life.* Boston: Houghton Mifflin, 2000.

Nudel, Ida. *A Hand in the Darkness.* New York: Warner Books, 1990.

Ognibene, Peter J. *Scoop: The Life and Politics of Henry M. Jackson.* New York: Stein and Day, 1975.

Orbach, William W. *The American Movement to Aid Soviet Jews.* Amherst: University of Massachusetts Press, 1979.

Orlov, Yuri. *Dangerous Thoughts: Memoirs of a Russian Life.* Translated by Thomas Whitney. New York: William Morrow, 1991.

Pinkus, Benjamin. *The Jews of the Soviet Union: The History of a National Minority.* Cambridge: Cambridge University Press, 1988.

——. *National Rebirth and Reestablishment: Zionism and the Zionist Movement in the Soviet Union, 1947–1987.* Sede Boker: Ben-Gurion University of the Negev Press, 1993.

——. *The Soviet Government and the Jews, 1948–1967.* Cambridge: Cambridge University Press, 1984.

Podair, Jerald E. *The Strike That Changed New York: Blacks, Whites, and the Ocean Hill–Brownsville Crisis.* New Haven, CT: Yale University Press, 2004.

Podhoretz, Norman. *The Present Danger.* New York: Simon and Schuster, 1980.

Potok, Chaim. *The Gates of November.* New York: Fawcett Columbine, 1996.

Prital, David, ed. *In Search of Self: The Soviet Jewish Intelligentsia and the Exodus.* Jerusalem: Mount Scopus Publications, 1982.

Rabin, Yitzhak. *The Rabin Memoirs.* Berkeley: University of California Press, 1996.

Raviv, Dan, and Yossi Melman. *Every Spy a Prince.* Boston: Houghton Mifflin, 1990.

Ro'i, Yaacov. *The Struggle for Soviet-Jewish Emigration, 1948–1967.* Cambridge: Cambridge University Press, 1991.

Ro'i, Yaacov, and Avi Beker, eds. *Jewish Culture and Identity in the Soviet Union.* New York: New York University Press, 1991.

Rorty, James, and Moshe Decter. *McCarthy and the Communists.* Boston: Beacon Press, 1954.

Rosenfeld, Nancy. *Unfinished Journey.* New York: University Press of America, 1993.

Rosenthal, Richard. *Rookie Cop: Deep Undercover in the Jewish Defense League.* Wellfleet, MA: Leapfrog Press, 2000.

Roth, Stephen J. *The Helsinki Final Act and Soviet Jewry.* London: Institute of Jewish Affairs, 1976.

——. *Human Contacts: Reunion of Families and Soviet Jewry.* London: Institute of Jewish Affairs, 1986.

Rubenstein, Joshua. *Soviet Dissidents: Their Struggle for Human Rights.* Boston: Beacon Press, 1985.

Rubenstein, Joshua, and Alexander Gribanov, eds. *The KGB File of Andrei Sakharov.* New Haven, CT: Yale University Press, 2005.

Rubenstein, Joshua, and Vladimir P. Naumov, eds. *Stalin's Secret Pogrom.* New Haven, CT: Yale University Press, 2001.

Rubin, Ronald, ed. *The Unredeemed: Anti-Semitism in the Soviet Union.* Chicago: Quadrangle, 1968.

Sachar, Howard M. *A History of the Jews in America.* New York: Alfred A. Knopf, 1992.

Safire, William. *Before the Fall: An Inside View of the Pre-Watergate White House.* New York: Belmont Tower Books, 1975.

Sakharov, Andrei. *Memoirs.* Translated by Richard Lourie. New York: Knopf, 1990.

Salitan, Laurie P. *Politics and Nationality in Contemporary Soviet-Jewish Emigration, 1968–89.* New York: St. Martin's Press, 1992.

Sarna, Jonathan D. *American Judaism: A History.* New Haven, CT: Yale University Press, 2004.

Schapiro, Amy. *Millicent Fenwick: Her Way.* New Brunswick, NJ: Rutgers University Press, 2003.

Schechtman, Joseph B. *History of the Revisionist Movement.* Tel Aviv: Hadar Publishing House, Ltd., 1970.

——. *The Vladimir Jabotinsky Story: Fighter and Prophet: The Last Years.* New York: Thomas Yoseloff, 1961.

Schroeter, Leonard. *The Last Exodus.* New York: Universe Books, 1974.

Shapiro, Edward S. *A Time for Healing: American Jewry Since World War II.* Baltimore: Johns Hopkins University Press, 1992.

Sharansky, Natan. *Fear No Evil.* New York: Random House, 1988.

Sharansky, Natan, and Ron Dermer. *The Case for Democracy.* New York: PublicAffairs, 2004.

Shcharansky, Avital, and Ilana Ben-Josef. *Next Year in Jerusalem.* New York: William Morrow, 1979.

Shevardnadze, Eduard A. *The Future Belongs to Freedom.* New York: Free Press, 1991.

Shindler, Colin. *Exit Visa: Détente, Human Rights, and the Jewish Emigration Movement in the USSR.* London: Bachman and Turner, 1978.

Shrayer, Maxim D., ed. *An Anthology of Jewish Russian Literature, Volume 2: 1953–2001.* Armonk, NY: M. E. Sharpe, 2007.

Shultz, George P. *Turmoil and Triumph: My Years as Secretary of State.* New York: Scribner, 1993.

Slezkine, Yuri. *The Jewish Century.* Princeton, NJ: Princeton University Press, 2004.

Smith, Hedrick. *The Russians.* New York: Crown, 1976.

Spiegel, Philip. *Triumph Over Tyranny: The Heroic Campaign That Saved 2,000,000 Soviet Jews.* New York: Devora Publishing, 2008.

Staub, Michael E. *Torn at the Roots: The Crisis of Jewish Liberalism in Postwar America.* New York: Columbia University Press, 2002.

Staub, Michael E., ed. *The Jewish 1960s: An American Sourcebook.* Lebanon, NH: Brandeis University Press, 2004.

Steimanis, Josifs. *History of Latvian Jews.* New York: Columbia University Press, 2002.

Stern, August, ed. *The USSR vs. Dr. Mikhail Stern.* New York: Urizen Books, 1977.

Stern, Ellen Norman. *Elie Wiesel: Witness for Life.* New York: Ktav Publishing House, 1982.

Stern, Paula. *Water's Edge: Domestic Politics and the Making of American Foreign Policy.* Westport, CT: Greenwood Press, 1981.

Svirsky, Grigory. *Hostages: The Personal Testimony of a Soviet Jew.* New York: Alfred Knopf, 1976.

Tarnopolsky, Yuri. *Memoirs of 1984.* New York: University Press of America, 1993.

Uris, Leon. *Exodus.* New York: Doubleday, 1958.

Vaissié, Cécile. *Pour votre liberté et le notre.* Paris: Editions Robert Laffont, 1999.

Voronel, Alexander, and Viktor Yakhot. *I Am a Jew: Essays on Jewish Identity in the Soviet Union.* New York: Academic Committee on Soviet Jewry and the Anti-Defamation League of B'nai B'rith, 1973.

Wald, Alan M. *The New York Intellectuals: The Rise and Decline of the Anti-Stalinist Left from the 1930s to the 1980s.* Chapel Hill: University of North Carolina Press, 1987.

Walker, Martin. *The Cold War.* New York: Henry Holt, 1993.

Walzer, Michael. *Exodus and Revolution.* New York: Basic Books, 1984.

Weisbord, Robert G., and Arthur Stein. *Bittersweet Encounter: The Afro-American and the American Jew.* Westport, CT: Negro Universities Press, 1970.

Weiss, Avi. *Principles of Spiritual Activism.* Hoboken, NJ: Ktav Publishing, 2002.

Werth, Nicolas. *Histoire de l'Union sovietique de Khrouchtchev a Gorbatchev, 1953–1985.* Paris: Presses Universitaires de France, 1995.

Wiesel, Elie. *All Rivers Run to the Sea.* New York: Knopf, 1995.

———. *The Jews of Silence.* New York: Henry Holt, 1966.

Winik, Jay. *On the Brink: The Dramatic, Behind-the-Scenes Saga of the Reagan Era and the Men and Women Who Won the Cold War.* New York: Simon and Schuster, 1996.

Yantovsky, Shimon. *To Where We Belong.* Jerusalem: Yantovsky, 2000.

Yevtushenko, Yevgeny. *Yevtushenko's Reader.* New York: E. P. Dutton, 1972.

Yurchak, Alexei. *Everything Was Forever, Until It Was No More.* Princeton, NJ: Princeton University Press, 2006.

Zakon, Miriam Stark. *Silent Revolution: A Torah Network in the Soviet Union.* Brooklyn: Mesorah Publications, 1992.

Zaslovsky, Victor, and Robert Brym. *Soviet-Jewish Emigration and Soviet Nationality Policy.* New York: St. Martin's Press, 1983.

Periodicals

Albright, Joseph. "The Pact of the Two Henrys." *New York Times Magazine,* January 5, 1970.

Brym, Robert T. "Soviet-Jewish Emigration: A Statistical Test of Two Theories." *Soviet Jewish Affairs* 18 (1988): 104.

Cullen, Robert. "Soviet Jewry." *Foreign Affairs* 65 (Winter 1986–87): 252–65.

Decter, Moshe. "The Status of the Jews in the Soviet Union." *Foreign Affairs* 41 (January 1963): 420–30.

Fackenheim, Emil. "The Dilemma of Liberal Judaism." *Commentary* 30 (1960): 301.

Feldbrugge, F.J.M. "The New Soviet Law on Emigration." *Soviet Jewish Affairs* 17 (1987): 11–24.

Friedman, Robert I. "The Kahane Connection: How Shamir Used JDL Terrorism." *Nation,* October 31, 1988.

Goodman, Walter. "I'd Love to See the JDL Fold Up. But—." *New York Times Magazine,* November 21, 1972.

Halevi, Yossi Klein. "Jacob Birnbaum and the Struggle for Soviet Jewry." *Azure* 17 (Spring 2004): 1–21.

Heitman, Sidney. "Jews in the 1989 U.S.S.R. Census." *Soviet Jewish Affairs* 20 (1990): 28.

Kagedan, Allan. "Gorbachev and the Jews." *Commentary* (May 1986): 47–50.

Kahane, Meir. "Playboy Interview: Meir Kahane." *Playboy* (October 1972): 69.

Kaufman, Michael T. "The Complex Past of Meir Kahane." *New York Times,* January 24, 1971.

Korey, William. "Andrey Sakharov—The Soviet Jewish Perspective." *Soviet Jewish Affairs* 16 (1986): 17–28.

———. "The Future of Soviet Jewry: Emigration and Assimilation." *Foreign Affairs* 58 (Fall 1979): 72–73.

———. "The Story of the Jackson Amendment, 1973–1975." *Midstream* (March 1975).

———. "The Struggle Over Jackson-Mills-Vanik." *American Jewish Yearbook 1974–75.* Philadelphia: American Jewish Committee and Jewish Publication Society of America, 1975.

———. "The Struggle Over the Jackson Amendment." *American Jewish Yearbook 1976.* Philadelphia: American Jewish Committee and Jewish Publication Society of America, 1976.

Krosney, Herbert. "Russia's Jews Come 'Home.'" *Nation,* April 3, 1972.

Lapid, Mordecai. "The Memorial at Rumbuli: A First-Hand Account." *Jewish Frontier* (June 1971): 10–19.

Lazaris, Vladimir. "The Saga of Jewish Samizdat." *Soviet Jewish Affairs* 9 (1979): 4–19.

Ozick, Cynthia (under pseudonym Trudie Vocse). "24 Years in the Life of Lyuba Bershadskaya." *New York Times Magazine,* March 14, 1971.

Peretz, Pauline. "The Action of Nativ's Emissaries in the United States." *Bulletin du Centre de recherche français de Jerusalem* (Spring 2004): 112–28.

Reddaway, Peter. "Dissent in the Soviet Union." *Dissent* (Spring 1976): 136–54.

Redlich, Shimon. "Jewish Appeals in the USSR: An Expression of National Revival." *Soviet Jewish Affairs* 4 (1974): 24–37.

Roth, Stephen J. "Facing the Belgrade Meeting: Helsinki—Two Years After." *Soviet Jewish Affairs* 7 (1977): 3–18.

Stevenson, Adlai, and Alton Frye. "Trading with Communists." *Foreign Affairs* 68 (1989): 53–71.

Toth, Robert C. "Split Among Activist Soviet Jews Breaks into Open Over Talks with U.S. Senators." *Los Angeles Times,* July 1, 1975.

Weinstein, Lewis H. "Soviet Jewry and the American Jewish Community." *American Jewish History* 77 (1988): 600–17.

Wieseltier, Leon. "The Demon of the Jews." *New Republic,* November 11, 1985.

Dissertations

Frey, Mark. "Challenging the World's Conscience: The Soviet Jewry Movement, American Political Culture, and U.S. Foreign Policy, 1952–1967." PhD diss., Temple University, 2002.

Russ, Shlomo Mordechai. "The 'Zionist Hooligans': The Jewish Defense League." PhD diss., City University of New York, 1981.

Index